Advances
in COMPUTERS
VOLUME 46

Advances in
COMPUTERS

The Engineering of Large Systems

EDITED BY

MARVIN V. ZELKOWITZ

Department of Computer Science
and Institute for Advanced Computer Studies
University of Maryland
College Park, Maryland

VOLUME 46

ACADEMIC PRESS
San Diego   London   Boston
New York   Sydney   Tokyo   Toronto

This book is printed on acid-free paper.

Copyright © 1998 by ACADEMIC PRESS

All Rights Reserved.
No part of this publication may be reproduced or transmitted in any form or by any means electronic or mechanical, including photocopy, recording, or any information storage and retrieval system, without permission in writing from the publisher.

Academic Press
525 B Street, Suite 1900, San Diego, California 92101-4495, USA
http://www.apnet.com

Academic Press
24-28 Oval Road, London NW1 7DX, UK
http://www.hbuk.co.uk/ap/

ISBN 0-12-012146-8

A catalogue record for this book is available from the British Library

Typeset by Mathematical Composition Setters Ltd, Salisbury, UK
Printed in the United States by Maple-Vail Book Manufacturing Group, Binghamton, New York

98 99 00 01 02 03 MV 9 8 7 6 5 4 3 2 1

Contents

CONTRIBUTORS ix
PREFACE xv

Software Process Appraisal and Improvement: Models and Standards

Mark C. Paulk

1. Introduction 2
2. ISO 9000—Quality Management Systems 4
3. The Capability Maturity Model for Software 9
4. ISO 15504—An International Standard for Software Process Assessment 17
5. Other Models and Standards 27
6. Conclusions 29
   References 30

A Software Process Engineering Framework

Jyrki Kontio

1. Introduction 36
2. Background 38
3. Process Management 52
4. Process Reference Architecture and its Components 71
5. Process Management Process 84
6. Conclusions 100
   References 101

Gaining Business Value from IT Investments

Pamela Simmons

1. Introduction 110
2. The Evaluation Problem 113
3. Measuring IT Value 117
4. Evaluation Methods 126

5. Evaluation Frameworks 138
6. The Investment Decision 141
7. Managing the Benefits. 146
8. Conclusion 152
   References 154

Reliability Measurement, Analysis, and Improvement for Large Software Systems

Jeff Tian

1. Overview and Organization 160
2. Techniques and Models for Analyzing Software Reliability 162
3. Analyzing Reliability for Large Software Systems 174
4. Usage Measurement and Reliability Analysis with SRGMs 181
5. Tree-based Reliability Models 198
6. SRGM Based on Data Clusters 210
7. Integration, Implementation and Tool Support 219
8. Conclusions and Perspectives 230
   References 231

Role-based Access Control

Ravi S. Sandhu

1. Introduction 238
2. The RBAC96 Models 243
3. The ARBAC97 Administrative Models 257
4. Roles and Lattices 270
5. Three-tier Architecture 278
6. Conclusion 284
   References 285

Multithreaded Systems

Krishna M. Kavi, Ben Lee and Ali R. Hurson

1. Introduction 288
2. Programming Models 290
3. Execution Models 302
4. Architectural Support for Multithreading 307
5. Example Multithreaded Systems 308

6. Performance Models 319
7. Conclusions and Prognostication 323
   Glossary 324
   References 325

Coordination Models and Languages

George A. Papadopoulos and Farhad Arbab

1. Introduction 330
2. From Multilingual and Heterogeneous Systems to Coordination Models 331
3. Coordination Models and Languages 334
4. Comparison 391
5. Conclusions 394
   References 396

Multidisciplinary Problem-solving Environments for Computational Science

Elias N. Houstis, John R. Rice, Naren Ramakrishnan, Tzvetan Drashansky, Sanjiva Weerawarana, Anupam Joshi and C. E. Houstis

1. Introduction 402
2. Domain-specific PSEs 404
3. MPSEs for Prototyping of Physical Systems 405
4. Agent-based Computing Paradigm for MPSEs 408
5. The Resource Selection Paradigm for MPSEs 409
6. SciAgents System 412
7. PYTHIA System 418
8. Case Studies 421
9. Conclusions 435
   References 435

AUTHOR INDEX 439

SUBJECT INDEX 449

CONTENTS OF VOLUMES IN THIS SERIES 457

Contributors

Farhad Arbab received his Ph.D. in Computer Science from the University of California, Los Angeles, in 1982. In 1983 he was a visiting professor at UCLA, and joined the faculty of the Computer Science Department at the University of Southern California in January 1984. He left USC to join the CWI (Centre for Mathematics and Computer Science) in Amsterdam, the Netherlands, in January 1990, as a senior researcher. His current fields of interest include Coordination Models and Languages, Parallel and Distributed Computing, Visual Programming Environments, Constraints, Logic and Object-Oriented Programming. He is currently leading a group working on the design, implementation, and application of Manifold: a coordination language for managing the interactions among cooperating autonomous concurrent processes in heterogeneous distributed computing environments.

Tzvetan Drashansky is a member of the technical staff at Juno Online Services, L.P., in New York City. He received his Ph.D. in Computer Science from Purdue University in 1996. He also has a B.S. (1987) in Mathematics and M.S. (1988) in Mathematics/Computer Science from the University of Sofia, Bulgaria, and an M.S. in Computer Science from Purdue University (1995). He has done research in the areas of multidisciplinary and ubiquitous problem-solving environments for scientific computing, agent-based computing, multiagent systems, and mobile and wireless computing. His current work is in the areas of internetworking, scalable distributed systems, and network computing. He is a member of the ACM, UPE, Phi Kappa Phi.

Catherine E. Houstis is an associate professor of Computer Science at the University of Crete in Heraklion, Greece. She received her Ph.D. in 1977 from Purdue University, West Lafayette, Indiana. She is also a research associate at the Institute of Computer Science of the Foundation for Research and Technology of Crete, in Heraklion Crete. She currently leads a project on information systems for the coastal zone management of the Mediterranean Sea funded by the Telematics program of the European Union. Her research interests include performance evaluation of distributed systems, digital libraries, and distance learning. She is on the editorial board of the *Mediterranean* magazine.

Elias N. Houstis is a Professor of Computer Sciences at Purdue University, where he received his Ph.D. in 1974. He is currently the director of the computational science and engineering program at Purdue and leads the

Purdue-On-Line project in distributed education. His research interests include problem-solving environments, computational finance, parallel/neural/mobile computing, performance evaluation and modeling, expert systems for scientific computing, numerical analysis, and distributed learning. He is the co-editor of several proceedings in the areas of "super-computing" and "expert systems for scientific computing", a member of IFIP working group 2.5 in numerical software and on the editorial board of Neural, Parallel and Scientific Computations and HPC Users Journal.

A. R. Hurson is on the Computer Science and Engineering Faculty at The Pennsylvania State University. His research for the past 15 years has been directed toward the design and analysis of general as well as special purpose computer architectures. Dr. Hurson served as the Guest Co-Editor of special issues of the *IEEE Proceedings on Supercomputing Technology*, the *Journal of Parallel and Distributed Computing* on Load Balancing and Scheduling, and the *Journal of Integrated Computer-Aided Engineering* on Multidatabase and Interoperable Systems. He is the co-founder of the IEEE Symposium on Parallel and Distributed Processing. He served as a member of the IEEE Computer Society Press Editorial Board and an IEEE Distinguished speaker. Currently, he is serving in the IEEE/ACM Computer Sciences Accreditation Board, an editor of IEEE transactions on computers and an ACM lecturer.

Anupam Joshi received the B.Tech. degree in electrical engineering from the Indian Institute of Technology, Delhi, in 1989, and the Ph.D. degree in computer science from Purdue University in 1993. From August 1993 to August 1996, he was a member of the Research Faculty at the Department of Computer Sciences at Purdue University. He is currently an Assistant Professor of Computer Engineering and Computer Science at the University of Missouri, Columbia. His research interests include artificial and computational intelligence, concentrating on neuro-fuzzy techniques, multiagent systems, scientific computing, mobile and networked computing, and computer vision. He is a member of the IEEE Computer Society, the ACM, and Upsilon Pi Epsilon.

Krishna Kavi is currently an Eminent Scholar in the Electrical and Computer Engineering Department at the University of Alabama in Huntsville. From 1982 to 1997 he was on the faculty of Computer Science and Engineering at the University of Texas at Arlington. His personal research deals with multithreaded computer systems, customization of microkernels, and compiler optimizations for multithreaded systems. He has been an editor of the *IEEE Transactions on Computers* and a senior member of the IEEE. He was a Distinguished Visitor of the Computer Society and an editor of the IEEE Computer Society.

Jyrki Kontio is a process development manager at Nokia Telecommunications IP Networking division. He also holds a position as a professor at the Helsinki University of Technology in the area of software engineering. His research interests include risk management, software process improvement, process modeling, software reuse, and technology management. Prior to his current positions he was a researcher at the Experimental Software Engineering Group (ESEG) at the University of Maryland. Between 1986 and 1994 he managed knowledge-based systems and software engineering research groups at the Nokia Research Center.

Ben Lee received his B.E. degree in Electrical Engineering in 1984 from the Department of Electrical Engineering at State University of New York at Stony Brook, and his Ph.D. degree in Computer Engineering in 1991 from the Department of Electrical and Computer Engineering, The Pennsylvania State University. He is currently an Associate Professor in the ECE department at Oregon State University. His research has been directed toward the design and analysis of computer architecture and parallel processors. He has published numerous technical papers in areas including parallel processing, computer architecture, program partitioning and scheduling, and software support for multithreaded systems.

George A. Papadopoulos is currently an Associate Professor at the Department of Computer Science of the University of Cyprus in Nicosia, Cyprus. Before that he was an Assistant Professor at the same university and a Research Associate at the University of East Anglia in Norwich, UK, and the University of Athens in Greece. He holds a B.Sc. and an M.Sc. in Computer Science from Aston University in the UK and a Ph.D. in Computer Science from the University of East Anglia. He is also a 1995 recipient of the ERCIM-HCM scholarship. His research interests include logic programming, graph rewriting, coordination models, and multimedia systems.

Mark C. Paulk is a Senior Member of the Technical Staff at the Software Engineering Institute in Pittsburgh, Pennsylvania. He has been with the SEI since 1987, initially working with the Software Capability Evaluation project. He has worked with the Capability Maturity Model project since its inception and was the project leader during the development of Version 1.1 of the Software CMM. He is the product manager for version 2 of the Software CMM and a contributor to ISO 15504 (also known as SPICE), a suite of international standards for process assessment. Mark received his Master's degree in computer science from Vanderbilt University and a Bachelor's degree in mathematics and computer science from the University of Alabama in Huntsville, Alabama.

Naren Ramakrishnan is a Visiting Assistant Professor of Computer Sciences at Purdue University, where he obtained his Ph.D. in 1997. His research interests include recommender systems, computational science, problem-solving environments, and data mining. He is also active in computational models for pattern recognition and other problems that lie at the intersection of artificial intelligence and computational science. He is a member of the IEEE, the IEEE Computer Society, ACM, ACM SIGART, and Upsilon Pi Epsilon.

John R. Rice is W. Brooks Fortune Professor of Computer Sciences at Purdue University. After receiving a Ph.D. in mathematics from the California Institute of Technology in 1959, he worked at the National Bureau of Standards and General Motors Research Labs. In 1964 he joined the Purdue faculty and headed the Computer Sciences Department from 1983 to 1996. Rice founded the *ACM Transactions on Mathematical Software* in 1975 and was editor-in-chief until 1993. He is a member of the National Academy of Engineering, the IEEE Computer Society, ACM, IMACS and SIAM, and serves as one of IEEE CS&E's area editors for software.

Ravi Sandhu is Director of the Laboratory for Information Security Technology, and Professor of Information and Software Engineering at George Mason University. He holds Ph.D. and M.S. in Computer Science from Rutgers University, New Jersey, and Bachelor's and Master's degrees from the Indian Institutes of Technology in Bombay and New Delhi respectively. He is founding editor-in-chief of the *ACM Transactions on Information and System Security*, and founding Steering Committee Chair of the ACM Conference on Computer and Communications Security and of the ACM Workshop on Role-Based Access Control. Since 1995 he has been Chairman of ACM's Special Interest Group on Security Audit and Control (SIGSAC). He has been a security consultant to several organizations, currently including the National Institute of Standards and Technology and SETA Corporation. His current research interests are focused on role- and task-based access control, and on enterprise and cross-enterprise information security.

Pamela Simmons is a senior lecturer at the School of Information Systems, Swinburne University of Technology, Melbourne, Australia, where she is manager of postgraduate courses in information systems. Her research interests include the evaluation of IT investments and the application of quality concepts and measurement to IT management. Before joining the academic world ten years ago, she worked in industry—in the earlier years in the field of statistics and operations research, and more recently in the IT industry, managing one of the first information centres in Australia. She received a B.Sc. with honours in mathematics and statistics from the University of

Sheffield, UK, and a Master of Business from the Royal Melbourne Institute of Technology, Australia. She is a member of the Australian Computer Society.

Jeff (Jianhui) Tian received a B.S. degree in electrical engineering from Xi'an Jiaotong University, Xi'an, China, an M.S. degree in engineering science from Harvard University, and a Ph.D. degree in computer science from the University of Maryland. He is currently an assistant professor in the Department of Computer Science and Engineering, Southern Methodist University. He worked for the IBM Software Solutions Toronto Laboratory as a software process and quality analyst from 1992 to 1995, working on software testing and reliability, metrics application and analysis, process measurement and improvement, and related technology transfer. His current research interests include testing techniques and tools, and the measurement, modeling, management and improvement of software process, quality, reliability, safety, and complexity. He is a member of IEEE and ACM.

Sanjiva Weerawarana is a Research Staff Member at IBM TJ Watson Research Center, where he has been since 1997. His research is centered around application frameworks for building network computing applications in Java. He was previously a Visiting Assistant Professor of Computer Sciences at Purdue University where he worked on designing and building problem-solving environments for scientific computing with concentration on partial differential equation-based applications. Weerawarana received his B.S. (1988) and M.S. (1989) in Applied Mathematics/Computer Science from Kent State University and his Ph.D. (1994) in Computer Science from Purdue University. He is a member of the ACM and UPE.

Preface

Since 1960, *Advances in Computers* has been publishing articles chronicling the evolution of the computer industry. From the early days of "number crunching" ballistics calculations to today's "information technology" industries on the World Wide Web, these pages have provided in-depth coverage of those changes. This present volume continues in that tradition. However, continuing with a change that began with Volume 45, approximately half of the volumes will have a theme. This present volume is organized around the theme of the engineering of large-scale software systems. What technologies are useful for building such systems, what technologies are useful to incorporate in such systems, and what technologies are useful to evaluate such systems? The eight chapters in this volume all address parts of these questions.

The first chapter, "Software Process Appraisal and Improvement: Models and Standards", by Mark C. Paulk, presents an overview of the software Capability Maturity Model (CMM) and the international ISO 9000 software quality standard. Companies are rightly concerned about the quality of the products that they produce. Many are too expensive to build and contain too many flaws, even after completion. The CMM and ISO 9000 are both attempts at organizing the production process better so that companies have a better understanding of their own development practices and thus are better able to understand and improve them over time.

In the second chapter, "A Software Process Engineering Framework", by Jyrki Kontio, Mr. Kontio continues the process engineering developments presented by Mr. Paulk from the first chapter. The CMM and ISO 9000 both require the software development process and its evolution to be managed, but they do not provide detailed guidance on how to do it. This chapter presents one view of that development process. The chapter presents a taxonomy and an architectural model for presenting process information for modeling the development process. The chapter also gives guidelines on how this process can be used to improve development practices over time.

The third chapter, "Gaining Business Value from IT Investments", by Pamela Simmons, addresses the important question of what benefits accrue from using information technology. Serious discussions have been raised concerning the true benefits of the massive proliferation of computers throughout our society. There is no question that computers have greatly changed the way industry works. But how does one measure the benefits, in increased productivity, profits, employee satisfaction, or other tangible or intangible attributes resulting from increased computer use? This chapter surveys many of these performance measures.

In "Reliability Measurement, Analysis, and Improvement for Large Software Systems", Dr. Jeff Tian looks at the technical issues of software reliability engineering. How does one identify the high risk areas that would require increased attention from management while a product is under development? The chapter surveys some recent advances in this area and provides in-depth coverage of some industrial experience in using this technology in practice.

The last four chapters in this volume address specific technologies useful in the development of specific computer applications. In "Role-Based Access Control", by Ravi Sandhu, security aspects of system design are discussed. Rather than giving users certain permissions to access sensitive files in a computer system, the information in a system can be organized around roles, so that only individuals with those roles may access that information. By assigning users into and out of these roles, a flexible system is maintained that provides for effective system security.

In "Multithreaded Systems", by Krishna Kavi, Ben Lee and Ali Hurson, the authors address the design of software that allows multiple processors to execute different parts of a program simultaneously. The chapter illustrates how multithreaded programs can be written in various programming languages and describes how multithreaded architectures can be implemented.

In "Coordination Models and Languages", by George Papadopoulos and Farhad Arbab, the authors take a different approach to concurrent execution. They describe linguistic constructs that permit the integration of independent components in such a way that the collective set forms a single application in order to take advantage of parallel distributed systems. They classify such methods as data-driven or control- (or process- or task-) driven and then compare these various models.

In the final chapter, "Multidisciplinary Problem Solving Environments for Computational Science", by Elias Houstis, John Rice, Naren Ramakrishnan, Tzvetan Drashansky, Sanjiva Weerawarena, Anupam Joshi and C. Houstis, the authors address the design of a specific environment useful for the solving of computational problems, particularly those involving partial differential equations. As in the previous two chapters, the underlying computational model is a system consisting of a set of distributed processor working in concert to solve a single problem. They are looking at the design of a Multidisciplinary Problem Solving Environment (MPSE) that can be used in a variety of disciplines.

I would like to thank all of the contributors for their time and effort in preparing their chapters for publication. Each chapter represents a significant investment from the authors, and I hope that you, the reader, find these chapters to be useful. If I have missed some important topic that you would like to see included in this series, please let me know at mvz@cs.umd.edu. I hope you find this volume of use in your work.

MARVIN V. ZELKOWITZ

Software Process Appraisal and Improvement: Models and Standards

MARK C. PAULK

Software Engineering Institute
Carnegie Mellon University
Pittsburgh, PA 15213-3890
USA

Abstract

The "software crisis" has inspired a number of efforts by software suppliers and customers to improve the state-of-the-practice in building software. This chapter provides an overview of models and standards underlying the three best-known approaches to software process improvement: the ISO 9001 standard for quality management systems, the Software Engineering Institute's Capability Maturity Model[1] for Software, and the proposed ISO 15504 standard for software process assessment. Other approaches are also briefly discussed.

1.	Introduction	2
2.	ISO 9000—Quality Management Systems	4
	2.1 An Overview of ISO 9001	4
	2.2 Placing ISO 9001 in Context	7
	2.3 ISO 9000 Certification	7
	2.4 Strengths and Weaknesses of ISO 9000	7
	2.5 The Future of ISO 9000	8
3.	The Capability Maturity Model for Software	9
	3.1 An Overview of the Software CMM®	9
	3.2 Placing the Software CMM in Context	12
	3.3 CMM-based Appraisals	13
	3.4 Strengths and Weaknesses of the Software CMM	14
	3.5 The Future of the Software CMM	16
4.	ISO 15504—An International Standard for Software Process Assessment	17
	4.1 An Overview of ISO 15504	18
	4.2 An Overview of the ISO 15504-2 Reference Model	20
	4.3 Strengths and Weaknesses of ISO 15504	23
	4.4 The Future of ISO 15504	27

[1] Capability Maturity Model, and IDEAL are service marks of Carnegie Mellon University.
®CMM is registered with the U.S. Patent and Trademark Office.

5.	Other Models and Standards	27
6.	Conclusions	29
References	. . . .	30

1. Introduction

The size, complexity, and power of software-intensive systems have exploded since the beginning of the Information Age, and software has become a core competency that is critical to high-technology companies. Computers are now an integral part of our day-to-day lives. We use them, even if we don't realize it, when we drive a car, withdraw money from an automated teller machine, or telephone a friend.

At the same time, anyone familiar with computers is also familiar, frequently painfully so, with the "software crisis" (Gibbs, 1994). Our ability to build software-intensive systems is orders of magnitude greater today than it was five decades ago, but our appetite for software has grown even faster, and the software industry is still evolving from a craft to an engineering discipline (Shaw, 1990). Historically, the result has been the chronic software crisis: software is (almost) always later than expected, more expensive than planned, and with less functionality than hoped. There is hope, however, that we have turned the corner on the software crisis.

Why do we have a chronic software crisis? Partially it is because the software discipline is still maturing, but some of the pain is caused by human nature. In response to the question "Why does software cost so much?," Weinberg replies "Compared to what?," and DeMarco points out that the question is based on the assertion that software is too pricey (DeMarco, 1995). DeMarco suggests that this assertion is a negotiating position; people complain because they know we work harder when they complain. In one survey, most of the responding professional software managers reported that their estimates were dismal, but they weren't on the whole dissatisfied with the estimating process (Lederer, 1992)!

All too many software professionals would agree with DeMarco, but many software managers and customers are vitally interested in understanding how to manage software projects more effectively. Can we plan and manage software projects effectively? While some have argued not, the evidence is that we can—within the bounds of the business paradigm that is chosen.

The business paradigm is crucial, because for significant software projects we rarely understand all the requirements at the beginning of the software project. The waterfall software life cycle model, which assumes that the requirements are frozen at the beginning of the software project, has largely been superseded by evolutionary or incremental life cycles. Software project management thus emphasizes managing risks and controlling change.

Customers and managers who use schedule pressure and overtime as motivational tools have to deal with the resulting quality tradeoff. Customers and managers who are interested in truly managing software projects—and facing up to a sometimes unpleasant reality—have available a number of approaches for systematically improving the process for developing and maintaining software. The results of successfully applying these approaches give us hope that the software crisis is finally coming to an end. A growing number of software organizations credit their increasing ability to achieve functionality, quality, schedule, and budget goals to systematic improvement of their software processes.

Perhaps the best-known approaches to software process improvement are the International Organization for Standardization's ISO 9001 standard for quality management systems, the Software Engineering Institute's Capability Maturity Model for Software (CMM or SW-CMM), and the proposed ISO 15504 standard for software process assessment. These approaches, among others, apply Total Quality Management (TQM) principles to the software process.

ISO 9000 is a suite of standards dealing with quality management systems that can be used for external quality assurance purposes. ISO 9001, which addresses quality assurance in design, development, production, installation, and servicing (ISO 9001, 1994), is the standard of specific interest to the software community, but it is much broader in scope than just software; software-specific guidance is provided in ISO 9000-3 (1991). Although the scope of ISO 9001 is broader than software, its application can be of value to software organizations (Stelzer *et al.*, 1996), and ISO 9001 certification is required to do business in many markets.

The Capability Maturity Model for Software (Paulk *et al.*, 1995a) describes the process capability of software organizations and provides a road map for software process improvement. Developed at the request of the US Department of Defense to help identify the capability of software contractors (Humphrey and Sweet, 1987; Byrnes and Phillips, 1996; Besselman *et al.*, 1993), its use for improving the software process has spread far beyond the DoD community. The Software CMM is arguably the best known and most widely used model for software process appraisal and improvement today. The author of this chapter is the product manager for the Software CMM, so there may be some bias in this discussion.

Many models and standards for software process improvement have been developed. This proliferation led to the development of ISO 15504, a suite of standards for software process assessment (Dorling, 1993). Popularly known as SPICE (Software Process Improvement and Capability dEtermination), ISO 15504 is currently under development and may change significantly before its final release. ISO 15504 will provide a framework for harmonizing different approaches to assessing and improving the software process.

The importance of high-quality software products cannot be overemphasized. Recent UK court decisions and proposed changes to the US Uniform Commercial Code foreshadow a potential for legal action by dissatisfied customers: "UK Court of Appeal judges have ruled for the first time that software should be sold free of major bugs and should work as intended, like other commercial goods ... attempts by software vendors to exclude or limit liability for product performance will be judged in terms of the Unfair Contract Terms Act (1977)" (*IEEE Computer*, 1996). Fortunately, the increasing maturity of the software field encourages us to think this goal may now be within our grasp.

2. ISO 9000—Quality Management Systems

The ISO 9000 series of standards is a set of documents dealing with quality management systems that can be used for external quality assurance purposes. They specify quality system requirements for use where a contract between two parties requires the demonstration of a supplier's capability to design and supply a product. The two parties could be an external client and a supplier, or both could be internal, e.g. marketing and engineering groups in a company.

There are several standards and guidelines in the ISO 9000 series. ISO 9001 is the standard that is pertinent to software development and maintenance. It is for use when conformance to specified requirements is to be assured by the supplier during several stages, which may include design, development, production, installation, and servicing. ISO 9001 addresses the minimum criteria for an acceptable quality system[2] within a broad scope: hardware, software, processed materials, and services.

ISO 9000-3 provides guidelines for the application of ISO 9001 to the development, supply, and maintenance of software. A British program called TickIT (DTI and BCS, 1992; Lloyd's Register, 1994) provides additional information and training for using ISO 9001 and ISO 9000-3 in the software arena.

2.1 An Overview of ISO 9001

The fundamental premise of ISO 9001 is that every important process should be documented and every deliverable should have its quality checked through a quality control activity. This is sometimes expressed as "Say what

---

[2] This statement is somewhat controversial. Some members of the standards community maintain that if you read ISO 9001 with insight, it does address continuous process improvement.

TABLE 1
THE CLAUSES IN ISO 9001

ISO 9001 Clause		ISO 9001 requires that
4.1.	Management responsibility	The quality policy is defined, documented, understood, implemented, and maintained; responsibilities and authorities for all personnel specifying, achieving, and monitoring quality are defined; and in-house verification resources are defined, trained, and funded. A designated manager ensures that the quality program is implemented and maintained.
4.2.	Quality system	A documented quality system, including procedures and instructions, is established. ISO 9000-3 characterizes this quality system as an integrated process throughout the entire life-cycle.
4.3.	Contract review	Contracts are reviewed to determine whether the requirements are adequately defined, agree with the bid, and can be implemented.
4.4.	Design control	Procedures to control and verify the design are established. This includes planning design and development activities; defining organizational and technical interfaces; identifying inputs and outputs; reviewing, verifying, and validating the design; and controlling design changes. ISO 9000-3 elaborates this clause with clauses on the purchaser's requirements specification (5.3), development planning (5.4), quality planning (5.5), design and implementation (5.6), testing and validation (5.7), and configuration management (6.1).
4.5.	Document and data control	Distribution and modification of documents and data are controlled.
4.6.	Purchasing	Purchased products conform to their specified requirements. This includes the evaluation of potential subcontractors and verification of purchased products.
4.7.	Control of customer-supplied product	Any customer-supplied material is verified, controlled, and maintained. ISO 9000-3 discusses this clause in the context of included software product (6.8), including commercial-off-the-shelf software.
4.8.	Product identification and traceability	The product is identified and traceable during all stages of production, delivery, and installation.
4.9.	Process control	Production processes are defined and planned. This includes carrying out production under controlled conditions, according to documented instructions. When the results of a process cannot be fully verified after the fact, the process is continuously monitored and controlled. ISO 9000-3 clauses include design and implementation (5.6); rules, practices, and conventions (6.5); and tools and techniques (6.6).

continued

TABLE 1
(*CONTINUED*)

ISO 9001 Clause	ISO 9001 requires that
4.10. Inspection and testing	Incoming materials are inspected or verified before use and in-process inspection and testing is performed. Final inspection and testing are performed prior to release of finished product. Records of inspection and test are kept.
4.11. Control of inspection, measuring, and test equipment	Equipment used to demonstrate conformance are controlled, calibrated, and maintained. Test hardware or software are checked to prove they are capable of verifying the acceptability of a product before use and rechecked at prescribed intervals. ISO 9000-3 clarifies this clause with clauses on testing and validation (5.7); rules, practices, and conventions (6.5); and tools and techniques (6.6).
4.12. Inspection and test status	The status of inspections and tests is maintained for items as they progress through various processing steps.
4.13. Control of nonconforming product	Nonconforming product is controlled to prevent inadvertent use or installation. ISO 9000-3 maps this concept to clauses on design and implementation (5.6); testing and validation (5.7); replication, delivery, and installation (5.9); and configuration management (6.1).
4.14. Corrective and preventive action	The causes of nonconforming product are identified. Corrective action is directed toward eliminating the causes of actual nonconformities. Preventive action is directed toward eliminating the causes of potential nonconformities. ISO 9000-3 quotes this clause verbatim, with no elaboration, from the 1987 release of ISO 9001.
4.15. Handling, storage, packaging, preservation, and delivery	Procedures for handling, storage, packaging, preservation, and delivery are established and maintained. ISO 9000-3 maps this to clauses on acceptance (5.8) and replication, delivery, and installation (5.9).
4.16. Control of quality records	Quality records are collected, maintained, and dispositioned.
4.17. Internal quality audits	Audits are planned and performed. The results of audits are communicated to management, and any deficiencies found are corrected.
4.18 Training	Training needs are identified and training is provided, since selected tasks may require qualified personnel. Records of training are maintained.
4.19. Servicing	Servicing activities are performed as specified. ISO 9000-3 addresses this clause as maintenance (5.10).
4.20. Statistical techniques	Statistical techniques are identified and used to verify the acceptability of process capability and product characteristics. ISO 9000-3 simply characterizes this clause as measurement (6.4).

you do; do what you say." ISO 9001 requires documentation that contains instructions or guidance on what should be done or how it should be done.

ISO 9001 has only 20 clauses, expressed in less than five pages, which are discussed in Table 1.

2.2 Placing ISO 9001 in Context

ISO 9001 may be the minimal criteria for a quality management system, but it also provides a foundation that other parts of the ISO 9000 series elaborate. In particular, ISO 9004-1 describes a basic set of elements by which quality management systems can be developed and implemented (ISO 9004, 1987).

Shaughnessy (1994) points out three themes that run through the ISO 9000 series: quality, capability, and evidence. Quality means satisfying both stated and implied needs. Capability is based on statistical understanding. Evidence is required that quality is being managed and outcomes are reliable and predictable. If these three are addressed, then an organization is well on its way to continual process improvement.

2.3 ISO 9000 Certification

Although originally intended for two-party contractual purposes, the most common use of ISO 9001 today is for third-party certification. The precise meaning of the terms "certification," "registration," and "accreditation" vary in different countries (Sanders and Curran, 1994), and technically the term "certification" should be reserved for the verification of conformance of products to standards. In the USA "registrars" assess organizations against ISO 9001 (or one of the other ISO 9000 standards) and "register" that the organization has passed the audit — that it has an acceptable quality management system according to the requirements of the standard—and a "certificate of registration" is issued. "Accreditation" refers to the process for ensuring that the registrar is reputable and objective.

There is currently no international "certification," "registration," or "accreditation" body, although ISO has published criteria for the accreditation of registration bodies. National bodies around the world have established accreditation bodies with their own certification or registration schemes. Many of these accreditation bodies have agreed to mutual recognition of their ISO 9000 certificates, but mutual recognition is currently established by pairwise agreements.

2.4 Strengths and Weaknesses of ISO 9000

Many companies share a belief that ISO 9000 is an inadequate standard in today's highly competitive world. Motorola, for example, has criticized ISO

9000 as being expensive and of limited value (Buetow, 1994):

> Motorola will make its purchases based on excellence in product and service, not on compliance to a system of standards... ISO 9000 certification has no direct connection to a product or service... ISO 9000 represents the old paradigm of an internal, overlay, quality program implying that quality costs money.

The piece-wise nature of certification and the mutual recognition needed between national bodies has led to criticism that ISO 9001 certification is being used by some countries for restraint of trade. Requirements for ISO 9001 certification according to restrictive criteria, e.g. by a local registrar, can be an effective market barrier.

In addition to these general complaints, ISO 9001 has been criticized by the software industry for being written from a manufacturing perspective and not providing adequate guidance in the software world. ISO 9000-3, which provides the official guidance for applying ISO 9001 to software, is considered inadequate by many (Matsubara, 1994; Harauz, 1994). Even the architecture of ISO 9000-3 does not reflect that of ISO 9001; there are many-to-many relationships between the clauses in the standard and those in the guide.

The British TickIT program was established to ensure that ISO 9001 auditors are knowledgeable about software engineering and management and have been trained in how to interpret ISO 9001 for the software domain. Sector-specific schemes such as TickIT have their detractors, however. A similar effort to TickIT was proposed for the USA called Software Quality System Registration (SQSR). After much debate, SQSR was killed, as was a similar effort in Japan. There are at least two opposition camps to sector-specific guides. The first argues that "if you can audit, you can audit anything." The second argues that the added cost of sector-specific certification far outweighs the benefits, especially if the value of the baseline standard is considered questionable.

Studies have shown that ISO 9001 can be used in successfully improving the software process (Stelzer et al., 1996). One surprising result, however, was the observation that only two of the ten critical success factors were explicit requirements of ISO 9001. Success depends on whether the spirit or the letter of the standard is followed.

2.5 The Future of ISO 9000

ISO 9001 was released in 1987 and revised in 1994, and further revisions are currently under review (Marquardt et al., 1991; Tsiakals and Cionfrani, 1996). Major changes planned include:

- removing the manufacturing bias
- restructuring the standard logically as linked processes

- simplifying the expression and increase user friendliness
- emphasizing effectiveness of the quality management system
- expanding customer interface requirements
- linking to ISO 9004-1

ISO 9000-3 was released in 1991, and a new version is currently under development. The next release of ISO 9000-3 will reflect the architecture of ISO 9001, and early reviews suggest that the revision is a much more satisfactory guide. Some have argued against another release of ISO 9000-3, however, as part of a general campaign against sector-specific guides.

For further information on ISO, see the World Wide Web page

http://www.iso.ch/

3. The Capability Maturity Model for Software

The Capability Maturity Model for Software (Paulk *et al.*, 1995a) describes the principles and practices underlying software process maturity and is intended to help software organizations improve the maturity of their software processes in terms of an evolutionary path from *ad hoc*, chaotic processes to mature, disciplined software processes. The current release is Version 1.1.

The success of the SW-CMM has led to the development of other capability maturity models that deal with systems engineering (Bate *et al.*, 1995), people issues (Curtis *et al.*, 1995), and software acquisition (Ferguson *et al.*, 1996).

3.1 An Overview of the Software CMM

The SW-CMM is organized into the five maturity levels, described in Table 2. Except for Level 1, each maturity level is decomposed into several key process areas that indicate the areas an organization should focus on to improve its software process.

The key process areas at Level 2 focus on the software project's concerns related to establishing basic project management controls.

- *Requirements management*: establish a common understanding between the customer and the software project of the customer's requirements that will be addressed by the software project. This agreement with the customer is the basis for planning and managing the software project.
- *Software project planning*: establish reasonable plans for performing the software engineering and for managing the software project. These plans are the necessary foundation for managing the software project.

TABLE 2
THE MATURITY LEVELS IN THE SOFTWARE CMM

SW-CMM maturity level	Description of SW-CMM maturity levels
1. Initial	The software process is characterized as *ad hoc*, and occasionally even chaotic. Few processes are defined, and success depends on individual effort and heroics.
2. Repeatable	Basic project management processes are established to track cost, schedule, and functionality. The necessary process discipline is in place to repeat earlier successes on projects with similar applications.
3. Defined	The software process for both management and engineering activities is documented, standardized, and integrated into a set of standard software processes for the organization. Projects use a defined software process that is tailored from the organization's standard software processes.
4. Managed	Detailed measures of the software process and product quality are collected. Both the software process and products are quantitatively understood and controlled.
5. Optimizing	Continuous process improvement is enabled by quantitative feedback from the process and from piloting innovative ideas and technologies.

- *Software project tracking & oversight*: establish adequate visibility into actual progress so that management can take effective actions when the software project's performance deviates significantly from the software plans.
- *Software subcontract management*: select qualified software subcontractors and manage them effectively.
- *Software quality assurance*: provide management with appropriate visibility into the process being used by the software project and of the products being built.
- *Software configuration management*: establish and maintain the integrity of the products of the software project throughout the project's software life cycle.

The key process areas at Level 3 address both project and organizational issues, as the organization establishes an infrastructure that institutionalizes effective software engineering and management processes across all projects.

- *Organization process focus*: establish the organizational responsibility for software process activities that improve the organization's overall software process capability.
- *Organization process definition*: develop and maintain a usable set of software process assets that improve process performance across the

projects and provide a basis for defining meaningful data for quantitative process management. These assets provide a stable foundation that can be institutionalized via mechanisms such as training.
- *Training program*: develop the skills and knowledge of individuals so they can perform their roles effectively and efficiently. Training is an organizational responsibility, but the software projects should identify their needed skills and provide the necessary training when the project's needs are unique.
- *Integrated software management*: integrate the software engineering and management activities into a coherent, defined software process that is tailored from the organization's standard software process and related process assets. This tailoring is based on the business environment and technical needs of the project.
- *Software product engineering*: consistently perform a well-defined engineering process that integrates all the software engineering activities to produce correct, consistent software products effectively and efficiently. Software product engineering describes the technical activities of the project; for instance requirements analysis, design, code, and test.
- *Intergroup coordination*: establish a means for the software engineering group to participate actively with the other engineering groups so that the project is better able to satisfy the customer's needs effectively and efficiently.
- *Peer reviews*: remove defects from the software work products early and efficiently. An important corollary effect is to develop a better understanding of the software work products and of the defects that can be prevented. The peer review is an important and effective engineering method that can be implemented via inspections, structured walk-throughs, or a number of other collegial review methods.

The key process areas at Level 4 focus on establishing a quantitative understanding of both the software process and the software work products being built.

- *Quantitative process management*: control process performance of the software project quantitatively. Software process performance represents the actual results achieved from following a software process. The focus is on identifying special causes of variation within a measurably stable process and correcting, as appropriate, the circumstances that drove the transient variation to occur.
- *Software quality management*: develop a quantitative understanding of the quality of the project's software products and achieve specific quality goals.

The key process areas at Level 5 cover the issues that both the organization and the projects must address to implement continuous and measurable software process improvement.

- *Defect prevention*: identify the causes of defects and prevent them from recurring. The software project analyzes defects, identifies their causes, and changes its defined software process.
- *Technology change management*: identify beneficial new technologies (such as tools, methods, and processes) and transfer them into the organization in an orderly manner. The focus of technology change management is on performing innovation efficiently in an ever-changing world.
- *Process change management*: continually improve the software processes used in the organization with the intent of improving software quality, increasing productivity, and decreasing the cycle time for product development.

Each key process area is described in terms of the key practices that contribute to satisfying its goals and that are allocated to the common features. The key practices describe the specific infrastructure and activities that contribute most to the effective implementation and institutionalization of the key process area.

The Software CMM is approximately 500 pages long and is now available as a book: *The Capability Maturity Model: Guidelines for Improving the Software Process* (Paulk et al., 1995a).

3.2 Placing the Software CMM in Context

Although most discussions of the SEI's software process improvement work focus on the SW-CMM, the model is part of a comprehensive approach—the IDEAL approach—to software process improvement (McFeeley, 1996). IDEAL consists of five phases:

I   *Initiating*. Laying the groundwork for a successful improvement effort.
D   *Diagnosing*. Determining where you are relative to where you want to be.
E   *Establishing*. Planning the specifics of how you will reach your destination.
A   *Acting*. Doing the work according to the plan.
L   *Learning*. Learning from the experience and improving your ability to adopt new technologies in the future.

The *Initiating* phase is perhaps the most significant difference between IDEAL and most other improvement models. Giving explicit and thorough attention to the activities of this phase is critical to the success of an improvement effort. While attending to the issues of the Initiating phase will not guarantee success by itself, skipping or neglecting this phase will almost certainly lead to reduced effectiveness or failure. The business reasons for undertaking the effort are clearly articulated. The effort's contributions to business goals and objectives are identified, as are its relationships with the organization's other work. The support of critical managers is secured, and resources are allocated on an order-of-magnitude basis. Finally, an infrastructure for managing implementation details is put in place.

The *Diagnosing* phase builds upon the Initiating phase to develop a more complete understanding of the improvement work that needs to be done. During the Diagnosing phase two characterizations of the organization are developed: one as it is at present and the second as it is intended to be after implementing the improvement. These organizational states are used to develop an approach to achieving improved business practice.

The purpose of the *Establishing* phase is to develop a detailed plan for doing the work. Priorities are set that reflect not only the recommendations made during the Diagnosing phase, but also the organization's broader operations and the constraints of its operating environment. An approach is then developed that honors and factors in the priorities. Finally, specific actions, milestones, deliverables, and responsibilities are incorporated into an action plan.

The activities of the *Acting* phase help an organization implement the work that has been so carefully conceptualized and planned in the previous three phases. These activities will typically consume much more calendar time and many more resources than all of the other phases combined. If the work of the first three phases has been done conscientiously, the likelihood of success during the Acting phase is greatly improved.

The *Learning* phase completes the improvement cycle. One of the concerns of the IDEAL approach is continuously improving the ability to implement change. In the Learning phase, the entire IDEAL experience is reviewed to determine what was accomplished, whether the effort accomplished the intended goals, and how the organization can implement change more effectively and/or efficiently in the future.

3.3 CMM-based Appraisals

CMM-based appraisals come in two major classes: assessments performed for internal process improvement and evaluations performed by a customer. All CMM-based appraisal methods should satisfy requirements documented in the CMM Appraisal Framework (Masters and Bothwell, 1995).

A *software process assessment* is an appraisal by a trained team of software professionals to determine the state of an organization's current software process, to determine the high-priority software process-related issues facing an organization, and to obtain the organizational support for software process improvement. There are various degrees of formality in the assessment method chosen; the most rigorous is the CMM-Based Appraisal for Internal Process Improvement (CBA IPI) (Dunaway and Masters, 1996).

In contrast, a *software capability evaluation* (SCE) is an appraisal by a trained team of professionals to identify contractors who are qualified to perform the software work or to monitor the state of the software process used on an existing software effort (Byrnes and Phillips, 1996; Besselman *et al.*, 1993). The use of the CMM in evaluations has inspired government contractors, particularly for the Department of Defense, to establish software process improvement programs based on the CMM to remain competitive.

In a similar vein, a number of companies have chosen to use the SW-CMM to encourage software process improvement and build stronger customer–supplier relationships with their suppliers of software-intensive systems. Perhaps the best known of these is Boeing's Advanced Quality System for Software: D1-9001 (Boeing, 1994). Boeing is increasingly reliant on the integrity of supplier software quality systems; D1-9001 requires that Boeing suppliers commit to process and product improvement. Boeing visualizes its suppliers reaching a level of capability in which reliable processes and world-class product quality goals are institutionalized. Boeing's policy is to work with suppliers to measure and continuously improve software processes and products. Suppliers are expected to commit to improvement and go through several stages, beginning with establishing a process improvement commitment.

3.4 Strengths and Weaknesses of the Software CMM

Several papers have been published criticizing the CMM (Bach, 1994; Jones, 1995), particularly its application in SCEs (Bollinger and McGowan, 1991; Saiedian and Kuzara, 1995). Criticisms of the SW-CMM include:

- The SW-CMM does not address all of the critical factors for successful software projects, including non-software disciplines such as systems engineering and marketing; hiring, developing, and retaining a competent software staff; strategic business planning; and so forth.
- The SW-CMM is a large and complex document that is difficult to understand.
- The SW-CMM is primarily addressed at large organizations performing contractual work.
- Maturity levels are gross measures of process capability, oversimplifying a complex set of issues.

- Key process areas are static and do not provide an evolutionary view of processes, which would be of value to the individuals responsible for implementing, controlling, and improving a specific process.
- It may be difficult for the non-expert to tailor or extend the SW-CMM.
- Appraisals, especially software capability evaluations, are frequently performed by untrained and unqualified appraisers, leading to inconsistency and unreliability in appraisal results.
- Appraisals frequently do not result in action to address the problems identified, thus failing to achieve the objective of software process improvement.

There are counter-arguments to these criticisms (Curtis, 1994; Humphrey and Curtis, 1991):

- The SW-CMM is deliberately focused on the software process, and other factors should be addressed as part of a larger program, such as a TQM initiative. Other CMMs can aid organizations dealing with these issues (Konrad et al., 1996; Bate et al., 1995; Curtis et al., 1995; Ferguson et al., 1996).
- The SW-CMM is structured hierarchically. The normative component is fairly short: 18 key process areas and 52 goals. The practices are informative components that help CMM users interpret what is intended. The guidance in the key practices and subpractices is a significant help in understanding what a key practice or goal means.
- The SW-CMM explicitly describes organizational capability in terms of the maturity levels.
- The SW-CMM focuses organizations on the vital few issues in process improvement. It identifies improvement priorities that are generally true for any (software) organization.
- Training is available for assessors and evaluators from both the SEI and authorized distribution partners.
- The SEI recommends that software process maturity be a consideration in choosing software suppliers rather than a maturity level being a requirement for competing.
- Use of the SW-CMM by the government and companies in selecting and monitoring software suppliers has inspired many suppliers to tackle software process improvement.
- The SW-CMM has been reviewed by thousands of software professionals as it has evolved (Paulk, 1995a).
- There is a large body of CMM users who interact through local software process improvement networks and annual Software Engineering Process Group conferences in both the USA and Europe.

- The SW-CMM has become the *de facto* standard for software process improvement around the world and spanning application domains.

Using the SW-CMM correctly requires professional judgment (Paulk, 1996, 1997). The software process may be repeatable, but it is not a deterministic, repetitive process. Software engineering is a human-centered, design-intensive process that requires both discipline and creativity. Although the SW-CMM provides a significant amount of guidance for making judgments on the software process, it is not a rigid set of objective requirements.

3.5 The Future of the Software CMM

Version 2.0 of the Software CMM is currently under development. The drivers for Version 2 include:

- addressing change requests for Version 1.1
- reflecting a better understanding of "best practices," particularly at levels 4 and 5
- making it easier to use other models and standards in conjunction with the Software CMM (Konrad, *et al.*, 1996; Paulk, *et al.*, 1995b, Paulk, 1995b)

Many of the changes for Version 2 are intended to make it easier to understand what is intended. For example:

- the key practices are being rewritten in active voice
- templates are being systematically used to express common constructs, particularly for the institutionalization practices
- concepts that were implicit are being made explicit

Major changes include:

- expanding *Software subcontract management* at level 2 to include off-the-shelf and customer-supplied software
- focusing *Training program* at level 3 on organizational training issues
- rewriting *Integrated software management* at level 3 to emphasize the differences with *Software project planning* and *Software project tracking & oversight* at level 2
- expanding *Software product engineering* at level 3 to cover the software life cycle processes from requirements elicitation to operation and maintenance

Version 2.0 will be in many ways a beta release because many of the supporting products and services will be either bootstrapping or in pilot test.

Version 1.1 and Version 2.0 will be supported in parallel until Version 2.1 is released as part of an integrated product suite.

For further information on the SEI's process work, see the World Wide Web page

    http://www.sei.cmu.edu/technology/process.html

Announcements of SW-CMM events, including the release of drafts of SW-CMM Version 2 for review, may be found on the World Wide Web page

    http://www.sei.cmu.edu/technology/cmm/

4. ISO 15504—An International Standard for Software Process Assessment

The International Organization for Standardization (ISO) is developing a suite of standards on software process assessment: ISO 15504. This work, frequently referred to as SPICE—Software Process Improvement and Capability dEtermination, was inspired by the numerous efforts on software process around the world (ImproveIT: Dorling *et al.*, 1991).

ISO 15504 focuses on software process issues but will also be concerned with people, technology, management practices, customer support, and quality, as well as software development and maintenance practices. Organizations will be able to use this standard in many ways:

- in capability determination mode, to help a purchasing organization determine the capability of a potential software supplier against a recognized international standard;
- in process improvement mode, to help a software organization improve its own software development and maintenance processes; and
- in self-assessment mode, to help an organization determine its ability to implement a new software project.

The initial draft of the SPICE documents was released for review in July 1995 and then entered the ISO balloting process for type 2 technical reports, which are intended to become international standards after a period of trial use by the community. A proposed draft technical report (PDTR) baseline was released in October 1996, and a draft technical report (DTR) baseline was released in July 1997.

The requirements for ISO 15504 (ISO, 1992) are that the process assessment standard shall:

    A. encourage predictable quality products
    B. encourage optimum productivity

C. promote a repeatable software process
D. provide guidance for improving software processes aligned to business goals, including starting point and target
E. support process capability determination for risk identification and analysis within an organization
F. support process capability determination for risk identification and analysis within a two-party contractual situation
G. be capable of being employed reliably and consistently
H. be simple to use and understand
I. be culturally independent
J. not presume specific organizational structures, management philosophies, software life cycle models, software technologies, or software development methods
K. recognize different application domains, business needs, and sizes of organizations
L. for each process, define baseline practices which are appropriate across all application domains, business needs, and sizes of organization. The baseline practices should be extensible to allow for industry or business variants.
M. define standard requirements for the development of industry or business variants of the baseline practices
N. be applicable at the project and organizational levels with connectivity between the two
O. focus on process, but also address people and application of technology
P. be objective
Q. be quantitative wherever possible
R. support output as process profiles which allow views at different levels of detail. The profiling method should support comparisons against other similar entities or industry "norms."
S. require that agreement is reached over ownership and confidentiality of assessment results prior to assessment
T. define the initial and ongoing qualification of assessors
U. be supportive of and consistent with other ISO JTC1/SC7 standards and projects
V. be supportive of, and consistent with, the ISO 9000 series of standards.
W. be subject to continuous improvement through periodic reviews to maintain consistency with current good practice

4.1 An Overview of ISO 15504

ISO 15504 provides a framework for the assessment of software processes. This framework can be used by organizations involved in planning, managing, monitoring, controlling, and improving the acquisition, supply, development, operation, evolution and support of software. The DTR draft of ISO 15504 consists of nine parts, described in Table 3, under the general title *Software process assessment*.

The approach to process assessment defined in ISO 15504 is designed to provide a basis for a common approach to describing the results of process

TABLE 3
THE COMPONENTS OF ISO 15504 DTR

ISO 15504 DTR Part	ISO 15504 DTR Part Description
Part 1: Concepts and introductory guide	Describes how the parts of the suite fit together, and provides guidance for their selection and use.
Part 2: A reference model for processes and process capability	Defines a two-dimensional reference model for describing the outcomes of process assessment. The reference model defines a set of processes, defined in terms of their purpose, and a framework for evaluating the capability of the processes through assessment of process attributes structured into capability levels.
Part 3: Performing an assessment	Defines the requirements for performing an assessment in such a way that the outcomes will be repeatable, reliable and consistent.
Part 4: Guide to performing assessments	Provides guidance on performing software process assessments and interpreting the requirements of Part 3 for different assessment contexts.
Part 5: An assessment model and indicator guidance	Provides an exemplar model for performing process assessments that is based upon and directly compatible with the reference model in Part 2.
Part 6: Guide to qualification of assessors	Describes the competence, education, training and experience of assessors that are relevant to conducting process assessments.
Part 7: Guide for use in process improvement	Describes how to define the inputs to and use the results of an assessment for the purposes of process improvement.
Part 8: Guide for use in determining supplier process capability	Describes how to define the inputs to and use the results of an assessment for the purpose of process capability determination. The guidance is applicable either for use within an organization to determine its own capability, or by an acquirer to determine the capability of a (potential) supplier.
Part 9: Vocabulary	A consolidated vocabulary of all terms specifically defined for the purposes of ISO 15504.

assessment, allowing for some degree of comparison of assessments based upon different but compatible models and methods.

Process assessment has two principal contexts for its use, as shown in Figure 1. Within a process improvement context, process assessment provides the means of characterizing the current practice within an organizational unit in terms of the capability of the selected processes. Analysis of the results in the light of the organization's business needs identifies strengths, weaknesses, and risks inherent in the processes. This, in turn, leads to the ability to determine whether the processes are effective in achieving their goals, and to identify significant causes of poor quality, or overruns in time or cost. These provide the drivers for prioritizing improvements to processes.

Process capability determination is concerned with analyzing the proposed capability of selected processes against a target process capability profile in order to identify the risks involved in undertaking a project using the selected processes. The proposed capability may be based on the results of relevant previous process assessments, or may be based on an assessment carried out for the purpose of establishing the proposed capability.

4.2 An Overview of the ISO 15504-2 Reference Model

Part 2 of ISO 15504 defines a reference model of processes and process capability which forms the basis for any model to be used for the purposes of process assessment (ISO, 1997). The reference model architecture is made up of two dimensions. The process dimension is characterized by process purposes, which are the essential measurable objectives of a process. The

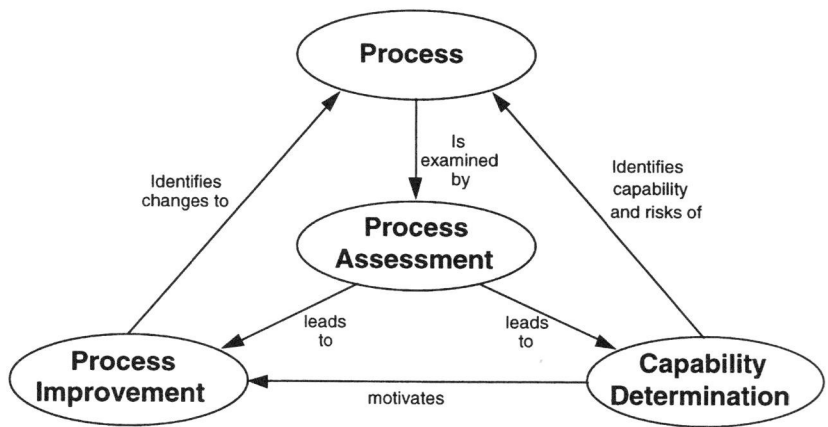

FIG. 1. The context for software process assessment.

process capability dimension is characterized by a series of process attributes, applicable to any process, which represent measurable characteristics necessary to manage a process and improve its capability to perform.

The Part 2 processes are shown in Figure 2. They are related, but not identical (at least in the DTR draft), to the processes described in ISO 12207, which is the ISO standard for software life cycle processes (ISO, 1995a).

Evolving process capability is expressed in terms of process attributes grouped into capability levels that establish an ordinal measurement scale. Each level provides a major enhancement of capability in the performance of a process. The levels constitute a rational way of progressing through improvement of the capability of any process. The six capability levels in the reference model are described in Table 4.

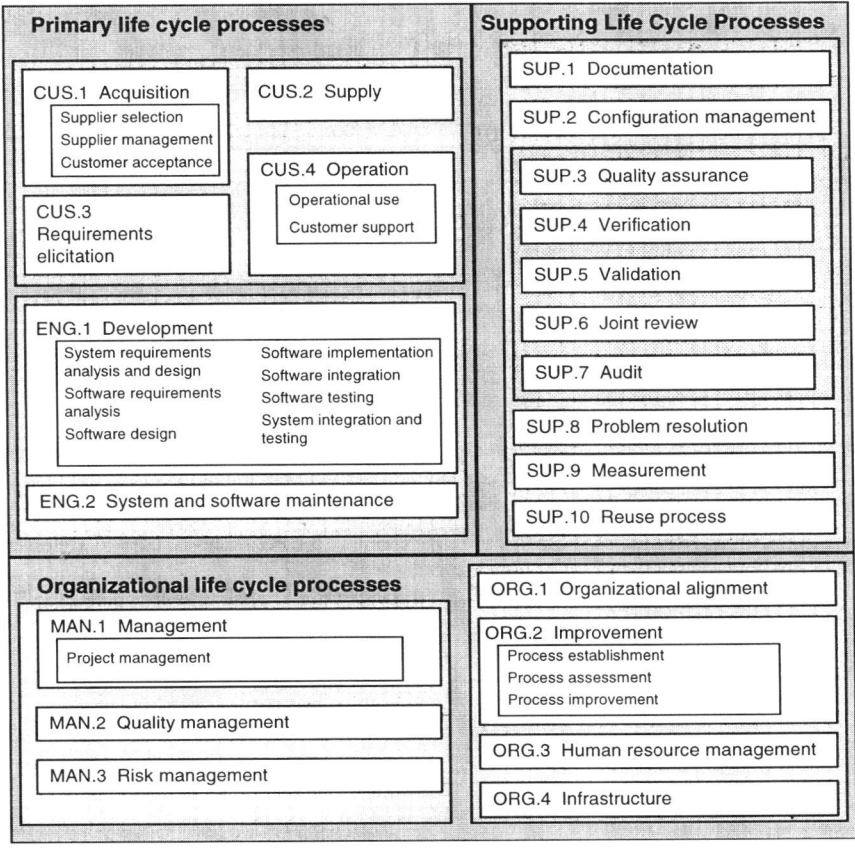

FIG. 2. ISO 15504-2 DTR processes.

TABLE 4
THE CAPABILITY LEVELS IN THE 1997 ISO 15504-2 DTR

ISO 15504-2 DTR capability level	ISO 15504-2 DTR capability level description
Level 0: Incomplete	There is general failure to attain the purpose of the process. There are little or no easily identifiable work products or outputs of the process.
Level 1: Performed	The purpose of the process is generally achieved. The achievement may not be rigorously planned and tracked. Individuals within the organization recognize that an action should be performed, and there is general agreement that this action is performed as and when required. There are identifiable work products for the process, and these testify to the achievement of the purpose.
Level 2: Managed	The process delivers work products according to specified procedures and is planned and tracked. Work products conform to specified standards and requirements. The primary distinction from the Performed Level is that the performance of the process now delivers work products that fulfill expressed quality requirements within defined time scales and resource needs.
Level 3: Established	The process is performed and managed using a defined process based upon good software engineering principles. Individual implementations of the process use approved, tailored versions of standard, documented processes to achieve the defined process outcomes. The resources necessary to establish the process definition are also in place. The primary distinction from the Managed Level is that the process of the Established Level is using a defined process that is capable of achieving its defined process outcomes.
Level 4: Predictable	The defined process is performed consistently in practice within defined control limits, to achieve its defined process goals. Detailed measures of performance are collected and analyzed. This leads to a quantitative understanding of process capability and an improved ability to predict performance. Performance is objectively managed. The quality of work products is quantitatively known. The primary distinction from the Established Level is that the defined process is now performed consistently within defined limits to achieve its defined process outcomes.
Level 5: Optimizing	Performance of the process is optimized to meet current and future business needs, and the process achieves repeatability in meeting its defined business goals. Quantitative process effectiveness and efficiency goals (targets) for performance are established, based on the business goals of the organization. Continuous process monitoring against these goals is enabled by obtaining quantitative feedback and improvement is achieved by analysis of the results. Optimizing a process involves piloting innovative ideas and technologies and changing non-effective processes to meet defined goals or objectives. The primary distinction from the Predictable Level is that the defined and standard processes now dynamically change and adapt to effectively meet current and future business goals.

TABLE 5
ISO 15504-2 DTR CAPABILITY LEVELS AND PROCESS ATTRIBUTES

ISO 15504-2 DTR capability level	ISO 15504-2 DTR process attributes
Level 0: Incomplete process	
Level 1: Performed process	PA 1.1 Process performance
Level 2: Managed process	PA 2.1 Performance management PA 2.2 Work product management
Level 3: Established process	PA 3.1 Process definition PA 3.2 Process resource
Level 4: Predictable process	PA 4.1 Process measurement PA 4.2 Process control
Level 5: Optimizing process	PA 5.1 Process change PA 5.2 Continuous improvement

A capability level is further characterized by a set of attribute(s) that work together to provide a major enhancement in the capability to perform a process. Process attributes are features of a process that can be evaluated on a scale of achievement, providing a measure of the capability of the process. They are rating components of ISO 15504-2 DTR. They are applicable to all processes.

Each process attribute describes a facet of the overall capability of managing and improving the effectiveness of a process in achieving its purpose and contributing to the business goals of the organization. Capability levels and process attributes are summarized in Table 5.

4.3 Strengths and Weaknesses of ISO 15504

It is intended that the international standard on software process assessment will:

- provide a public, shared model for process assessment;
- lead to a common understanding of the use of process assessment for process improvement and capability evaluation;
- facilitate capability determination in procurement;
- be controlled and regularly reviewed in the light of experience of use;
- be changed only by international consensus; and
- encourage harmonization of existing schemes.

In particular, the reference model fully describes the evolution of processes from *ad hoc* to continuously improving, and adding processes and integrating with other models is relatively simple. Its weaknesses, however, include

TABLE 6
MAPPING BETWEEN THE 1995 SPICE REFERENCE MODEL AND THE 1996 ISO 15504-5 PDTR

1995 SPICE reference model		1996 ISO 15504-5 PDTR	
Level 1: Performed-Informally		**Level 1: Performed process**	
1.1:	*Performing Base Practices*	PA 1.1	*Process performance attribute*
1.1.1	Perform the process	1.1.1	Ensure that base practices are performed
Level 2: Planned-and-Tracked		**Level 2: Managed process**	
		PA 2.1	*Performance management attribute*
2.1	*Planning Performance*		
2.1.1	Allocate resources	2.1.1	Identify resource requirements
2.1.2	Assign responsibilities		
2.1.6	Plan the process	2.1.2	Plan the performance of the process
2.2	*Disciplined Performance*		
2.2.1	Use plans, standards, and procedures	2.1.3	Implement the defined activities
2.3	*Verifying Performance*		
2.3.1	Verify process compliance		
2.4	*Tracking Performance*		
2.4.1	Track with measurement		
2.4.2	Take corrective action	2.1.4	Manage the execution of the activities
		PA 2.2	*Work product management attribute*
		2.2.1	Identify requirements
2.1.3	Document the process	2.2.2	Identify the activities
2.2.2	Do configuration management	2.2.3	Manage the configuration of work products
2.3.2	Audit work products	2.2.4	Manage the quality of work products
2.1.4	Provide tools		
2.1.5	Ensure training		
Level 3: Well-Defined		**Level 3: Established process**	
3.1	*Defining a Standard Process*	PA 3.1	*Process definition attribute*
3.1.1	Standardize the process		
		3.1.1	Identify the standard process definition
3.1.2	Tailor the standard process	3.1.2	Tailor the standard process
3.2	*Performing the Defined Process*		
3.2.1	Use a well-defined process	3.1.3	Implement the defined process
		3.1.4	Provide feedback
		PA 3.2	*Process resource attribute*
		3.2.1	Define the human resource competencies
		3.2.2	Define process infrastructure requirements
	See 2.1.5 on training	3.2.3	Provide adequate skilled human resources
	See 2.1.4 on tools	3.2.4	Provide adequate process infrastructure
3.2.2	Perform peer reviews		*See PA 2.2 on work product management*
3.2.3	Use well-defined data		*See PA 4.2 on process control*

TABLE 6
(*CONTINUED*)

1995 SPICE reference model		1996 ISO 15504-5 PDTR	
	Level 4: Quantitatively Controlled		**Level 4: Predictable process**
4.1	*Establishing Measurable Quality Goals*	PA 4.1	*Process measurement attribute*
4.1.1	Establish quality goals	4.1.1	Define process goals and associated measures
		4.1.2	Provide adequate resources and infrastructure for data collection
		4.1.3	Collect the specified measurement data
		4.1.4	Evaluate achievement of process goals
4.2.1	Determine process capability		
4.2	*Objectively Managing Performance*	PA 4.2	*Process control attribute*
		4.2.1	Identify analysis and control techniques
		4.2.2	Provide adequate resources and infrastructure
		4.2.3	Analyze available measures
4.2.2	Use process capability	4.2.4	Identify deviations and take required control actions
	Level 5: Continuously Improving		**Level 5: Optimizing process**
		PA 5.1	*Process change attribute*
5.1.2	Continuously improve the standard process	5.1.1	Identify and approve changes to the standard process definition
		5.1.2	Provide adequate resources
5.2.3	Continuously improve the defined process	5.1.3	Implement the approved changes to the affected tailored processes
		5.1.4	Validate the effectiveness of process change
		PA 5.2	*Continuous improvement attribute*
		5.2.1	Identify improvement opportunities
		5.2.2	Establish an implementation strategy
		5.2.3	Implement changes to selected areas of the tailored process
		5.2.4	Validate the effectiveness of process change
5.1	*Improving Organizational Capability*		
5.1.1	Establish process effectiveness goals		
5.2	*Improving Process Effectiveness*		
5.2.1	Perform causal analysis		
5.2.2	Eliminate defect causes		

difficulty in interpretation and the possibility that less critical process issues can drown out the "vital few" when there are clashes over improvement priorities.

The author of this chapter is the product manager of the Software CMM and was an active participant in the development of the 1995 SPICE baseline of

ISO 15504 (Paulk and Konrad, 1994). In particular, I was co-product manager for the SPICE reference model (Konrad *et al.*, 1995). The ISO 15504 reference model has continued to evolve since I stopped being an active participant in ISO and in ways that diverge in some significant aspects from what was originally intended. The reader should be aware of this bias and factor it in when considering the following comments.

The processes in Part 2 and how they are rated have changed significantly (ISO, 1995b, 1996, 1997). In the 1995 SPICE baseline, processes were rated according to 26 generic practices. The generic practices were based on the SW-CMM concepts, but as applied to processes rather than organizations. The nine process attributes were developed to provide a more abstract rating mechanism, and the generic practices that elaborate the process attributes were moved to Part 5.

The new generic practices are significantly different from what was originally intended, as is illustrated in Table 6. Part 5 has not been released in DTR form at this writing, but the definitions in the DTR release of Part 2 remain consistent with these generic practices. Table 6 provides a snapshot at this point in time, but it cannot be considered definitive since the issues identified by ISO reviewers, including the SEI, may be addressed in future versions of ISO 15504.

Whether the changing definition of the capability levels is an improvement over the earlier proposals is arguable. From a standpoint of compatibility with existing work, specifically the Software CMM, these changes are problematic. As noted earlier, the Software CMM is also evolving, but its evolution is more in line with the 1995 SPICE baseline of the generic practices. This is admittedly a biased view, but it is unclear that these changes add significant value, and they could have a significant impact on the sizable number of Software CMM users.

Another concern is incompatibility with the flagship software engineering standard on "Software Life Cycle Processes," ISO 12207. It establishes a common framework for software life cycle processes. It contains processes, activities, and tasks that are to be applied during the acquisition of a system that contains software, a standalone software product, and software service and during the supply, development, operation, and maintenance of software products. Although each baseline of ISO 15504-2 has converged toward ISO 12207, significant differences—for arguably good reasons—remain. It is likely that feedback from the ISO 15504 developers may result in changes to ISO 12207 in its next revision that support convergence from both directions.

Based on the Phase 1 trials, the length of time to rate processes completely and rigorously is of the order of 10 hours per process instance, which implies a process assessment lasting over 300 hours (Woodman and Hunter, 1996). An assessment of each process in ISO 15504-2 against each generic practice or each process attribute provides a thorough, but perhaps overly detailed, process profile. Some appraisal methods focus on the "vital few" issues for the improvement effort, but the criteria for identifying the vital few may vary in different assessment approaches. One of the strengths of the SPICE effort, however, is the trials program and the emphasis on gaining empirical evidence to base decisions on how the standard should evolve (Emam and Goldenson, 1996; Marshall *et al.*, 1996).

Although it is agreed that ISO 15504 should not be used in any scheme for certification or registration of process capability, there is a danger that the standard will be used for certification. The topic comes up repeatedly, and there are differences within the international community regarding whether certification should be encouraged or discouraged. Most members of the SPICE project oppose certification, but ISO cannot prevent certification mechanisms being established by the user community, as occurred for ISO 9001.

There is also a concern that ISO 15504 will inappropriately replace existing assessment approaches, although the SPICE goal is to harmonize existing approaches rather than replace them. If any ISO 15504-conformant model and method can generate comparable process profiles, then a useful framework will have been developed for navigating the quagmire of process assessment models and standards. If, on the other hand, ISO 15504 becomes a competing model and method for software process assessment and improvement, perhaps required by some customers and markets, it will further confuse an already turbulent environment. In such a case, ISO 15504 will have the advantage of being an international standard, but it will be competing with a number of already well-established approaches.

4.4 The Future of ISO 15504

ISO 15504 cannot be considered a stable set of documents at this time, but its potential is significant. Further major changes may be expected as concerns are addressed (Kitson, 1997; Paulk, 1995c).

ISO 15504 is still evolving rapidly. Current plans are that the Type 2 technical reports will be published in 1998. After approximately two years of use and feedback, the reports will be revised and begin the international standardization process.

For further information on ISO 15504, see the World Wide Web page

    http://www-sqi.cit.gu.edu.au/spice/

5. Other Models and Standards

While the three approaches to software process appraisal and improvement described in this chapter may be the best known, there are many others that the reader should be aware of, such as Bootstrap, SDCE, SPR, and Trillium.

Bootstrap was developed by an ESPRIT project (Kuvaja *et al.*, 1994; Haase *et al.*, 1994). It extended the SEI's work with features based on guidelines from ISO 9000 and European Space Agency process model standards. The extensions were made to fit the methodology into the European context, and to attain more detailed capability profiles in addition to maturity levels, separately for both organizations and projects. Although the Bootstrap approach was formed by extending the SW-CMM with new and reshaped features, it is still possible to distinguish maturity levels that are equivalent to the SEI model. For further information on Bootstrap, see the World Wide Web page

http://www.etnoteam.it/bootstrap/institut.html

Software Development Capability Evaluation (SDCE) is a method to evaluate the capability and capacity of organizations proposing to develop software-intensive defense systems (Babel, 1997; US Air Force, 1994), developed for the US Air Force. SDCE not only addresses software engineering capability, but also the systems engineering and related development disciplines integral to the successful development of a software-intensive defense system. It is based on the Software Development Capability/Capacity Review (SDCCR) method (US Air Force, 1987), developed by the US Air Force Aeronautical Systems Center, and the SEI's SCE method. The SDCE method's primary objective is to reduce development risk by selecting contractors who are capable of successfully developing embedded software to meet program life cycle requirements. For further information on SDCE, see the World Wide Web page

http://www.afmc.wpafb.af.mil/pdl/afmc/63afmc.htm

Trillium is a telecommunications product development and support capability model developed by Bell Canada, Northern Telecom and Bell-Northern Research (Bell Canada, 1994). It is used to assess the product development and support capability of prospective and existing suppliers of telecommunications or information technology-based products. Trillium can also be used as a reference benchmark in an internal capability improvement program. Trillium is based on the SW-CMM, but it also addresses ISO 9001, Bellcore standards, and the relevant parts of the Malcolm Baldrige National Quality Award criteria. For further information on Trillium, see the World Wide Web page

http://ricis.cl.uh.edu/process_maturity/trillium/

Capers Jones's SPR (Software Productivity Research) method includes software quality and productivity research data on productivity, quality, schedules, costs, and other quantifiable factors. SPR assessments rate organizations on a five-level scale against industry norms using this data (Jones, 1996; 1997). For further information on SPR, see the World Wide Web page

> http://www.spr.com/homepage.htm

Many other models and standards for process appraisal and improvement are available, but this chapter provides an overview of the most prominent ones.

6. Conclusions

The three approaches to software process appraisal and improvement discussed in this chapter provide useful information from somewhat different perspectives. To survive, much less thrive, modern organizations must continually improve all aspects of their business. Improvement in software-intensive products and services is crucial—and difficult.

There are many sources for best practices in the software industry (Brown, 1996; Maguire, 1994; McConnell, 1996). The challenge is to implement good software engineering and management practices in the high-pressure environment that software organizations face. A disciplined and systematic approach to software process and quality improvement, such as these models and standards support, is necessary to survive and thrive.

The relative merits of these three approaches depend to large degree on the business environment of the organization. Companies doing business with customers or in markets where ISO 9001 certification is required will naturally use ISO 9001. Companies doing business with the US government, in particular the Department of Defense, will be motivated to use the Software CMM. Multinational companies or companies that have to deal with multiple approaches are likely to be interested in ISO 15504, but since it is still under development, it is difficult to make definitive statements about its intrinsic merits or problems at this time.

The ISO 9000 series has the intrinsic advantage of being a well-recognized and widely used international standard. It is a short document, so interpretation of the standard can be an issue. This is much less of a problem with the Software CMM, which provides detailed guidance and is widely used in the software world. An extensive infrastructure has developed to support both ISO 9000 and the Software CMM. For organizations that must deal with both ISO 9000 and the Software CMM, a frequent recommendation is to begin with ISO 9001 certification and continue the process improvement journey using the Software CMM.

Regardless of the approach selected, building competitive advantage should be focused on improvement, not on achieving a score, whether the score is a maturity level, a certificate, or a process profile.

ACKNOWLEDGMENTS

I would like to express my appreciation to my reviewers: Mike Konrad, Mike Nicol, Terry Rout, Joc Sanders, Helen Thomson and Marvin Zelkowitz. Their comments significantly improved this chapter.

REFERENCES

Babel, P. (1997) Software development capability evaluation: an integrated systems and software approach. *Crosstalk, The Journal of Defense Software Engineering* **10**(4), 3–7.

Bach, J. (1994) The immaturity of the CMM. *American Programmer* **7**(9), 13–18.

Bate, R. *et al.* (1995) *A Systems Engineering Capability Maturity Model, Version 1.1*. Software Engineering Institute, CMU/SEI-95-MM-003.

Bell Canada (1994) *Trillium: Model for Telecom Product Development and Support Process Capability, Release 3.0*. Bell Canada.

Besselman, J. J., Byrnes, P., Lin, C. J., Paulk, M. C., and Puranik, R. (1993) Software capability evaluations: experiences from the field. *SEI Technical Review '93*.

Boeing (1994) *Advanced Quality System for Software Development and Maintenance: D1-9001*. The Boeing Company, Seattle WA.

Bollinger, T., and McGowan, C. (1991) A critical look at software capability evaluations. *IEEE Software* **8**(4), 25–41.

Brown, N. (1996) Industrial-strength management strategies. *IEEE Software* **13**(4), 94–103.

Buetow, R. C. (1994) A statement from Motorola regarding ISO 9000. *American Programmer* **7**(2), 7–8.

Byrnes, P., and Phillips, M. (1996) *Software Capability Evaluation Version 3.0 Method Description*. Software Engineering Institute, Carnegie Mellon University, CMU/SEI-96-TR-002, DTIC Number ADA309160.

Curtis, W. (1994) A mature view of the CMM. *American Programmer* **7**(9), 19–28.

Curtis, W., Hefley, W. E., and Miller, S. (1995) *People Capability Maturity Model*. Software Engineering Institute, CMU/SEI-95-MM-02.

DeMarco, T. (1995) *Why Does Software Cost So Much?* Dorset House, New York NY.

Dorling, A. (1993) Software Process, Improvement and Capability dEtermination. *Software Quality Journal* **2**(4), 209–224.

Dorling, A., Simms, P., and Barker, H. (1991) *ImproveIT*. UK Ministry of Defence.

DTI and BCS (1992) *TickIT: A Guide to Software Quality Management System Construction and Certification Using EN29001, Issue 2.0*. UK Department of Trade and Industry and the British Computer Society.

Dunaway, D. K., and Masters, S. M. (1996) *CMM-Based Appraisal for Internal Process Improvement (CBA IPI): Method Description*. Software Engineering Institute, Carnegie Mellon University, CMU/SEI-96-TR-007, DTIC Number ADA307934.

Emam, K. E., and Goldenson, D. R. (1996) Some initial results from the international SPICE trials. *Software Process Newsletter*, IEEE Computer Society Technical Council on Software Engineering, No. 6, 1–5.

Ferguson, J., Cooper, J., *et al.* (1996) *Software Acquisition Capability Maturity Model*

(*SA-CMM*) *Version 1.01*. Software Engineering Institute, Carnegie Mellon University, CMU/SEI-96-TR-020.

Gibbs, W. W. (1994) Software's chronic crisis. *Scientific American*, September, 86–95.

Haase, V., Koch, G., Kugler, H. J., and Decrinis, P. (1994) Bootstrap: fine-tuning process assessment. *IEEE Software* **11**(4), 25–35.

Harauz, J. (1994) ISO standards for software engineering. *Standards Engineering*, July/August, 4–6.

Humphrey, W. S., and Curtis, W. (1991) Comments on 'A Critical Look'. *IEEE Software* **8**(4), 42–46.

Humphrey, W. S., and Sweet, W. L. (1987) *A Method for Assessing the Software Engineering Capability of Contractors*. Software Engineering Institute, Carnegie Mellon University, CMU/SEI-87-TR-23, DTIC Number ADA187320.

IEEE Computer (1996) UK judges: software must be sold bug-free. *IEEE Computer* **29**(10), 16.

ISO (1987) ISO 9004, *Quality Management and Quality System Elements—Guidelines*. International Organization for Standardization, Geneva.

ISO (1991) ISO 9000-3, *Guidelines for the Application of ISO 9001 to the Development, Supply, and Maintenance of Software*. International Organization for Standardization.

ISO (1992) *Study Report: The Need and Requirements for a Software Process Assessment Standard*. ISO/IEC JTC1/SC7, Document N944R, Issue 2.0.

ISO (1994) ISO 9001, Quality Systems—*Model for Quality Assurance in Design, Development, Production, Installation, and Servicing*. International Organization for Standardization, Geneva.

ISO (1995a) ISO/IEC 12207, *Information Technology—Software Life Cycle Processes*. International Organization for Standardization, Geneva.

ISO (1995b) *Software Process Assessment Part 2: A Model for Process Management*. International Organization for Standardization, ISO/IEC JTC1/SC7/WG10 Working Draft.

ISO (1996) ISO/IEC PDTR 15504-5, Software process assessment—Part 5: an assessment model and indicator guidance. *Proposed Draft Technical Report*. International Organization for Standardization, Geneva.

ISO (1997) ISO/IEC DTR 15504-2, Software process assessment—Part 2: a reference model for processes and process capability. *Proposed Draft Technical Report*, International Organization for Standardization, Geneva, Switzerland.

Jones, C. (1995) The SEI's CMM—flawed? *Software Development* **3**(3), 41–48.

Jones, C. (1996) *Patterns of Software System Failure and Success*. International Thomson Computer Press, New York.

Jones, C. (1997) *Software Quality: Analysis and Guidelines for Success*, International Thomson Computer Press, New York.

Kitson, D. H. (1997) An emerging international standard for software process assessment. *Proceedings of the Third IEEE International Software Engineering Standards Symposium and Forum*. Walnut Creek CA, 1–6 June, pp. 83–90.

Konrad, M. D., Paulk, M. C., and Graydon, A. W. (1995) An overview of SPICE's model for process management. *Proceedings of the Fifth International Conference on Software Quality*. Austin TX, 23–26 October, pp. 291–301.

Konrad, M., Chrissis, M. B., Ferguson, J., Garcia, S., Hefley, B., Kitson, D., and Paulk, M. Capability Maturity Modeling at the SEI. *Software Process: Improvement and Practice* **2**(1), 21–34.

Kuvaja, P., Simila, J. et al. (1994) *Software Process Assessment & Improvement: The BOOTSTRAP Approach*. Blackwell Business, Oxford.

Lederer, A. L., and Prasad, J. (1992) Nine management guidelines for better cost estimating. *Communications of the ACM* **35**(2), 51–59.

Lloyd's Register (1994) *Lloyd's Register TickIT Auditors' Course, Issue 1.4.* Lloyd's Register.

Mackie, C. A., and Rigby, P. G. (1993) Practical experience in assessing the health of the software process. *Software Quality Journal* **2**(4), 265–276.

Maguire, S. (1994) *Debugging the Development Process.* Microsoft Press, Redmond WA.

Marquardt, D., *et al.* (1991) Vision 2000: the strategy for the ISO 9000 series standards in the '90s. *ASQC Quality Progress* **24**(5), 25–31.

Marshall, P., Maclennan, F., and Tobin, M. (1996) Analysis of observation and problem reports from phase one of the SPICE trials. *Software Process Newsletter, IEEE Computer Society Technical Council on Software Engineering*, No. 6, Spring, 10–12.

Masters, S., and Bothwell, C. (1995) *CMM Appraisal Framework, Version 1.0.* Software Engineering Institute, Carnegie Mellon University, CMU/SEI 95-TR-001.

Matsubara, T. (1994) Does ISO 9000 really help improve software quality? *American Programmer* **7**(2), 38–45.

McConnell, S. (1996) *Rapid Development: Taming Wild Software Schedules.* Microsoft Press, Redmond WA.

McFeeley, R. (1996) *IDEAL: A User's Guide for Software Process Improvement.* Software Engineering Institute, CMU/SEI-96-HB-001.

Paulk, M. C. (1995a) The evolution of the SEI's capability maturity model for software. *Software Process: Improvement and Practice* **1**, 3–15.

Paulk, M. C. (1995b) How ISO 9001 compares with the CMM. *IEEE Software* **12**(1), 74–83.

Paulk, M. C. (1995c) A perspective on the issues facing SPICE. *Proceedings of the Fifth International Conference on Software Quality.* Austin TX, 23–26 October, pp. 415–424.

Paulk, M. C. (1996) Effective CMM-based process improvement. *Proceedings of the 6th International Conference on Software Quality.* Ottawa, Canada, 28–31 October, pp. 226–237.

Paulk, M. C. (1997) Software process proverbs. *Crosstalk: The Journal of Defense Software Engineering* **10**(1), 4–7.

Paulk, M. C., and Konrad, M. D. (1994) An overview of ISO's SPICE project. *American Programmer* **7**(2), 16–20.

Paulk, M. C., Weber, C. V., Curtis, W., and Chrissis, M. B. (eds) (1995a), *The Capability Maturity Model: Guidelines for Improving the Software Process.* Addison-Wesley, Reading MA.

Paulk, M. C., Konrad, M. D., and Garcia, S. M. (1995b) CMM versus SPICE architectures. *IEEE Computer Society Technical Council on Software Engineering, Software Process Newsletter* No. 3, 7–11.

Saiedian, S., and Kuzara, R. (1995) SEI capability Maturity Model's impact on contractors. *IEEE Computer* **28**(1), 16–26.

Sanders, J., and Curran, E. (1994) *Software Quality: A Framework for Success in Software Development and Support.* Addison-Wesley, Reading MA.

Shaughnessy, R. N. (1994) ISO 9000 current status & future challenges. *Straight Talk About ISO 9000 Conference.* ASQC and ANSI, Los Angeles CA, 27–28 October.

Shaw, M. (1990) Prospects for an engineering discipline of software. *IEEE Software* **7**(6), 15–24.

Stelzer, D., Mellis, W., and Herzwurm, G. (1996) Software process improvement via ISO 9000? Results of two surveys among European software houses. *Software Process: Improvement and Practice* **2**(3) 197–210.

Tsiakals, J., and Cianfrani, C. (1996) ISO 9001 in the next millennium: the future revision of ISO 9001, ISO 9002, and ISO 9003. *Proceedings of the ASQC's 50th Annual Quality Congress and Exposition.* Chicago IL, 13–15 May, pp. 356–363.

US Air Force (1987) *Software Development Capability/Capacity Review.* ASD Pamphlet 800–5.

US Air Force (1994) *Acquisition—Software Development Capability Evaluation.* AFMC Pamphlet 63–103, Volumes 1 and 2.

Woodman, I., and Hunter, R. (1996) Analysis of assessment data from phase one of the SPICE trials. *IEEE Computer Society Technical Council on Software Engineering, Software Process Newsletter*, No. 6, 5–9.

A Software Process Engineering Framework

JYRKI KONTIO

Helsinki University of Technology
Department of Computer Science and Engineering
Laboratory of Information Processing Sciences
P.O. Box 1100
FIN-02015 HUT, Finland
and
Nokia Telecommunications
IP Networking
P.O. Box 315
FIN-00045 NOKIA GROUP, Finland
http://www.cs.hut.fi/users/jyrki.kontio

Abstract

This paper presents a framework for software process engineering. The main contributions of the framework are a taxonomy and dependency model of process modeling objectives, an architectural model for representing process information and a generic definition of a process modeling process. In addition, this paper proposes a consistent set of terminology and several techniques to be used to support process modeling.

1. Introduction 36
2. Background 38
   2.1 Approaches to Process Modeling 38
   2.2 Business Process Re-engineering 44
   2.3 Terminology 46
3. Process Management 52
   3.1 Process Improvement Objectives 52
   3.2 Process Modeling Objectives 55
   3.3 Process Modeling Objectives and Process Improvement Goals 67
4. Process Reference Architecture and its Components 71
   4.1 Reference Architecture for Process Models 71
   4.2 Process Model Information Entities 77
   4.3 Process Modeling Objectives and Information Content 80
   4.4 Process Perspectives Revisited 82
5. Process Management Process 84
   5.1 Process Modeling in Process Improvement 85
   5.2 Process Modeling Process 86

        5.3   Practical Experiences   98
6.   Conclusions   100
References   101

1. Introduction

Software is everywhere in modern society. Practically all products and services are dependent on software in one form or another. Modern cars are controlled by on-board computers, all electronic consumer products are packed with functionality provided through software, and most office workers interface with software on a daily basis. Most services are also produced with the help of software: video rental companies and libraries use databases to track their customers, banks carry out and store their transactions electronically, and even the neighborhood bakery may depend on computers to handle accounting. Even products that do not contain embedded software, such as tires, paper and food products, are often produced by a computerized production process. Software is a fundamental tool in the modern society to keep it running.

The role of software in all facets of the society is likely to continue to increase. Organizations will continue to use software to improve their performance and to maintain their competitiveness, individuals will buy products whose added value has been produced by software, and the new opportunities offered by the rapidly improving telecommunications networks, such as Internet, World Wide Web, and mobile communications, open up new opportunities to obtain and provide services and products through software.

Given that software is everywhere in society and we are very dependent on it, the availability, cost, reliability, and features of software become important aspects for all people that need to deal with software. This is where the software development process steps in. The software development process is a major factor in determining the characteristics of software that is produced. If we are concerned with the characteristics of software, we also need to be concerned with the characteristics of the software development process.

This chapter presents a framework for understanding and engineering the software development process so that it can be controlled and improved according to the business goals of the organization.

The chapter is organized as follows. Section 2 presents the background and related work in software process modeling, summarizing the most relevant recent results from academia and industry. Section 2 also introduces the terminology that will be used in the remainder of the paper. Section 3 presents a classification of process improvement objectives as well as a taxonomy and a dependency model of process modeling objectives. Section 4 presents a conceptual reference architecture for representing process information (Section 4.1) and classifies the types of information that can be represented in a process model (Section 4.2). Section 5 presents our process modeling process, which utilizes the concepts and models introduced in earlier sections.

The relationships of the main contributions in these sections are described in Fig. 1. The process improvement objectives introduced in Section 3.1 help identify the business motives for process improvement. The process modeling objectives' taxonomy and their dependencies, introduced in Section 3.2, are used to help define the scope, granularity and goals of the focus in the process modeling process. Section 3.3 proposes a model of how effectively different process modeling objectives support process improvement objectives, allowing the linking of process modeling work to the business objectives of an organization.

The process reference architecture described in Section 4.1 provides the conceptual and representational framework for process models. The reference architecture was developed to provide a notation-independent abstraction mechanism to improve communication and understanding of the process, as well as to improve the reuse of processes. The process information entities presented in Section 4.2 further support process elicitation and representation by providing guidelines for identifying the critical information entities that need to be modeled in a process, depending on process modeling objectives.

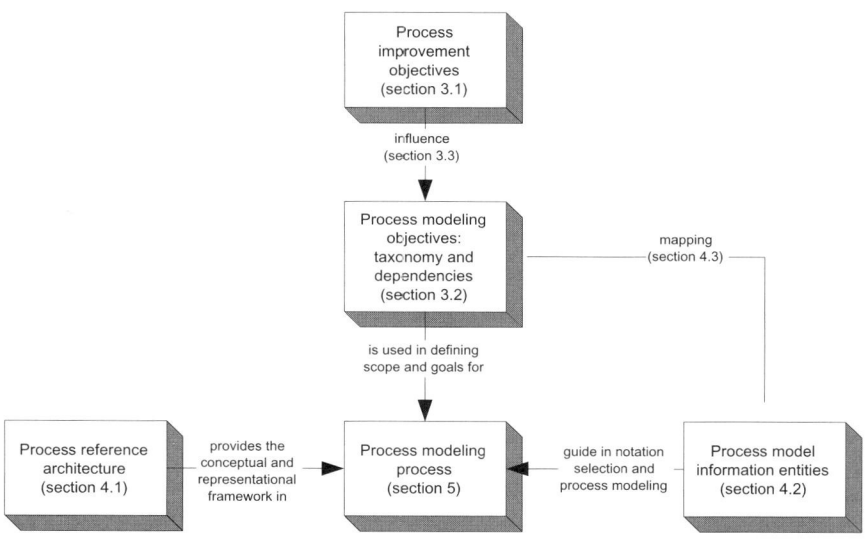

FIG. 1. Structure of the chapter.

2. Background

In this section we present highlights from the software process engineering field and introduce a consistent process terminology to be used in the remainder of the paper.

2.1 Approaches to Process Modeling

Work on the software process dates back almost as far as software has been developed. While the software development process may not have been a central concern for the very first programmers, the software development process has been explicitly discussed since the 1950s (Benington, 1956). At that time the prevalent term was *software life cycle model*. This early work tried to define what is the "right" overall process in developing software. However, as McCracken pointed out (McCracken and Jackson, 1982), the trend to define the ideal life cycle turned out to be an unrealistic goal. The universally acceptable life cycle model would be so abstract that it would be practically useless.

Benington proposed the first phase-based model for software development (Benington, 1956). The software development, as he argued, consists of logical steps that should follow one another in sequence, as they build on each other. Benington defined the main characteristics of these phases and the dependencies between these phases, including the use of specifications for testing. The term *waterfall life cycle* was popularized by Royce in 1970 (Royce, 1970). He presented a life cycle model similar to Benington's model. However, Royce's model was more detailed and it added an important new principle: the first version of the software will need to be revised based on user feedback.[1]

Both of these approaches emphasized the idea of developing software in phases and providing descriptions and output standards for each phase. The waterfall development life cycle is, even today, a major development approach for most organizations. However, most organizations do realize that the reality, i.e. the real dependencies, interactions, and flow of information are much more complex and dynamic than the waterfall model conveys.

The waterfall model also included feedback loops to earlier stages to allow more flexibility in development. Important additional work on life cycle models was done by Boehm (Boehm, 1981) and McCracken (McCracken and Jackson, 1982).

The strictly waterfall-oriented view was questioned in several papers from the late 1970s onwards. For instance, Basili and Turner proposed an

---

[1] Note that although Benington did not mention it in his original paper, the SAGE project first developed a prototype of their system before full implementation (Boehm, 1987).

interactive enhancement development model (Basili and Turner, 1975), in which the development is based on a skeletal kernel implementation and each additional development cycle aims at perfecting and extending this "first guess" to the desired final product. Boehm's spiral model has had a strong influence on many organizations, allowing more flexibility and focusing on risk management in planning and managing software development (Boehm, 1988; Boehm and Bels, 1989).

A contributing line of research on the software process was initiated in the late 1980s. This "process programming" community was to a large degree established on the principles expressed by Leon Osterweil (Osterweil, 1987): the software processes could be, and should be, "programmed", i.e. formalized, represented, and executed like software. Osterweil argued that these process programs can be used for communication and to increase process reuse, and that processes could be analyzed for errors and could be automated. Osterweil's original approach was very much geared towards describing processes by an appropriate language and executing that language.

Much of the subsequent research has focused on process execution, i.e. enactment by a computer and finding the right process programming language for enacting the process. Since the 1980s, a substantial amount of research has been devoted to the development of different formalisms for process modeling (Kellner and Rombach, 1991; Curtis *et al.*, 1992). However, the principles of process programming have also been criticized for being only feasible for well-understood parts of software development, leaving the poorly defined, most critical aspects without support (Lehman, 1987). Formalizing processes may also make them less flexible. As situations and projects vary, it may be difficult to modify the process definition to support different processes (Curtis *et al.*, 1987). It has also been argued that we do not have enough experience and data about the software development process to develop stable enough models for effective process automation (Notkin, 1989).

The suitability of different process modeling formalisms may also pose problems for process automation. It has been argued that the effectiveness of the language depends on the "context in which it is used, the objectives it is used for and the degree to which its features are understood and used" (Rombach, 1991). Organizations would need to use more than one formalism if they want to obtain optimal representation for each purpose or accept that the formalism selected will not support some usage types.

The "process programming" research resulted in a number of process-centered environments that were developed to support process automation. Over the past years, several process-centered environments have been developed and some are now commercial products (Fuggetta, 1993).

While the process programming community approached the software development process from the automation and modeling language perspectives, a complementary line of research also raised the software process on the center stage. The software process improvement field (Humphrey, 1990; Dorling, 1993; Koch, 1993; Thomas and McGarry, 1994) has further increased the importance of the software process and, in particular, the importance of process models as essential tools in (Curtis et al., 1992; Heineman et al., 1994):

- facilitating human understanding and communication
- supporting process improvement
- automating process guidance
- automating process execution
- supporting process management

As many organizations have initiated process improvement projects, they are actively developing detailed and comprehensive process models to support these objectives. However, our experience indicates that process modeling is often initiated without a clear statement of what the objectives for the effort are and how the process models should be used. This can result in lack of direction and focus in process modeling and difficulties in actual work.

The process modeling task can be divided into two distinct, yet closely related tasks: *process capture* and *process representation*. Process capture refers to the acquisition of process knowledge, including techniques for eliciting knowledge from process experts and structuring process knowledge (Dowson, 1993), whereas process representation refers to documenting this knowledge explicitly, including the selection and use of formalisms. As mentioned earlier, the representation formalisms and automation have been addressed exhaustively by the process programming community (Curtis et al., 1987; Lehman, 1987; Osterweil, 1987; Kellner, 1989; Lehman, 1991; Rombach, 1991; Armenise et al., 1993; Fernström, 1993; Finkelstein et al., 1994; Garg and Jazayeri, 1994).

Although the process models have had a central role in the software process domain since the 1980s, process capture has not been addressed explicitly until recently. Even the software process workshops have made only brief references to the topic (Huseth and Vines, 1987; Ochimizu and Yamaguchi, 1987). However, in recent years process capture has received increasing attention by researchers as well as practitioners.

In 1989 Kellner and Hansen published a case study that reported experiences from a large process modeling project carried out with the US Air Force (Kellner and Hansen, 1989). They presented practical experiences from their case study and also presented a list of requirements for a process modeling approach. Their requirements can be considered as guidelines for the issues that should be considered in process modeling. Kellner was also involved in the development of "entity process modeling" approach, which also provided initial guidelines on how to capture process models (Humphrey and Kellner, 1989).

A couple of years later Madhavji and Schäfer presented the principles of the PRISM environment, which included the capabilities to include the process engineering process explicitly in the process model (Madhavji and Schäfer, 1991). As a part of the PRISM framework, they included a "process-building methodology," a set of steps included in developing a process model. However, the steps were not very detailed and they did not include any empirical validation of the approach in their paper.

In 1993 several papers made explicit references to a "process modeling methodology," although none of them went into much detail. Culver-Lozo presented an approach on how to combine different views during the modeling process (Culver-Lozo and Gelman, 1993). Dutton presented results of a study to define a process modeling approach, suggesting a notation and some high-level steps for the process (Dutton, 1993). Gelman described a modeling approach used successfully at AT&T (Gelman, 1994), providing some details of the practical aspects of their approach.

During the same time, several papers discussing process evolution in process-centered environments also addressed the importance of systematic methods for process capture, but none of them provided any details of such methods (Penedo and Shu, 1991; Conradi *et al.*, 1993; Bandinelli *et al.*, 1993a,b, 1994; Jaccheri and Conradi, 1993). Only more recently has more research taken place to support process capture (Humphrey and Kellner, 1989; Madhavji, 1991; Madhavji and Schäfer, 1991; Curtis *et al.*, 1992; Culver-Lozo and Gelman, 1993; Dutton, 1993; Heineman *et al.*, 1994; Madhavji *et al.*, 1994; Gelman, 1994; Armitage *et al.*, 1995; Cook and Wolf, 1995; Kontio, 1995, 1996).

Recently, two major approaches in process capture have been presented: the Elicit method developed at the McGill University (Madhavji *et al.*, 1994) and the approach developed by the Software Engineering Institute (SEI) (Armitage *et al.*, 1995). As both of these approaches represent more comprehensive methods than the ones published earlier, they will be discussed in more detail in the following.

The Elicit method is based on the following main steps (Höltje *et al.*, 1994):

1. Understand the organizational environment in order to set realistic objectives for the project.
2. Define objectives for the elicitation task.

3. Plan the elicitation strategy, i.e. produce a plan, select techniques and allocate resources.
4. Develop process models, which includes three substeps:
   - elicit process information
   - translate the process information into a more formal representation
   - review models
5. Validate process models to confirm their accuracy with the documented process information or the way process is enacted.
6. Analyze process models to suggest improvements.
7. Post analysis: analysis of the process model elicitation process in order to find areas for improvement.
8. Packaging of process information elicitation experiences.

The Elicit process is similar to the steps in the Quality Improvement Paradigm (Basili *et al.*, 1994b). The steps that mainly focus on process capture are steps four and five. The Elicit method contains a relatively detailed description of the Elicit process model: the activities and their information flows are explicitly documented. The Elicit method has been presented in a process improvement context (Heineman *et al.*, 1994; Madhavji, 1991).

Höltje *et al.* describe two tools that can be used to support the Elicit method. The Elicit tool is a structuring tool that allows the display and manipulation of the information ("attributes") collected during process knowledge capture (Höltje *et al.*, 1994). The Statemate tool is used to document the process model in its final form (Harel *et al.*, 1988; Humphrey and Kellner, 1989; Kellner and Hansen, 1989).

An important contribution of the Elicit method is the way Elicit structures process information. The Elicit method supports the representation of five process perspectives:[2] process steps, artifacts, roles, resources, and constraints (Höltje *et al.*, 1994). Each of these perspectives is characterized by descriptive, static and dynamic properties. This structuring is used as a template in capturing process knowledge.

The Elicit method has been applied in one pilot study and two industrial projects (Höltje *et al.*, 1994; Madhavji *et al.*, 1994) and the method has been found usable. However, there have not been any comparative studies between Elicit and other process capture methods, perhaps because comparable methods have not been published.

SEI's process modeling team has made many valuable contributions to the software process modeling field over the past years (Curtis *et al.*, 1988;

---

[2] Note that Höltje's "perspectives" are different from the ones used by Curtis *et al.* (1992).

Humphrey and Kellner, 1989; Kellner and Hansen, 1989; Kellner, 1991; Curtis *et al.*, 1992; Heineman *et al.*, 1994). Their most recent contribution is the software *process development process* (PDP) (Kellner, 1996). The PDP is also supported by extensive definitions for process model information (Armitage *et al.*, 1994, 1995).

The PDP divides process development into three main activities: process requirements and planning, process definition, and evaluate process capability (Kellner, 1996). These are, in turn, divided further into more detailed steps. The PDP itself is a well-defined process model. It contains definitions for the roles and responsibilities for the participants in process development, explicit activity definitions (inputs, outputs as well as entry and exit criteria), definition of main artifacts, and guidelines for enactment.

The conceptual schema for process information can be seen as a mechanism to support process representation (Armitage *et al.*, 1995). The purpose of the conceptual schema is to provide a basis for transformations between process modeling formalisms, provide the representational basis for storing process knowledge, act as a basis for collecting process knowledge, assist in improving process models, provide a reference point for comparing process modeling formalisms and contribute to the development of process-centered environments (Armitage *et al.*, 1995).

The PDP conceptual schema is based on three main entity classes—activities, agents and artifacts—and "aspects" that characterize their relationships and their behavior (Armitage *et al.*, 1995). The PDP includes detailed templates for collecting process information so that it can be mapped to the PDP conceptual schema. The PDP also has several checklists that can be used to support the review of process models (Armitage *et al.*, 1995). The PDP has been designed to be independent of any process modeling formalism.

The SEI has used the four process perspectives (Table 1) to structure information in process models. Process perspectives are a partial view of the process information; they represent "separate yet interrelated" views to the process (Curtis *et al.*, 1992).

The motivation for using more than one perspective is that process information is complex and cannot be conveniently expressed, for instance, in a single graph. By using different perspectives it is possible to provide views that emphasize the relevant aspects of the process without overloading the presentation with unnecessary information. They claim that process perspectives provide an important way of structuring process information and thus getting a conceptual grip on it. Process perspectives have been used in several SEI projects (Humphrey and Kellner, 1989; Kellner, 1991). However, their use outside the SEI context has been limited, judging from the lack of reports on them. It may be that the definition of the perspectives may not be appropriate for all situations.

TABLE 1
DESCRIPTION OF KELLNER'S PROCESS PERSPECTIVES

The *functional perspective* looks at what activities are carried out, what products (artifacts) are produced in the process and how information flows in the process. It is a static view of the process. The functional perspective is useful for getting an overview of the process and it acts as a "road map" for other perspectives. Control information and feedback loops are typically not represented in the functional perspective. This makes the diagrams simpler but often too abstract to act as a basis for day to day work.

The *behavioral perspective* is concerned with how the tasks in the process are executed: when they are started, what their sequence is, how they are controlled, where the feedback loops occur, where iteration is, how decisions are made, how conditional processes relate to the overall process, what the entry and exit criteria for processes are. A "pure" behavioral perspective differs from the functional perspective in three main respects: artifacts are not represented, control information is added, and process sequence is represented explicitly.

The *organizational perspective* covers two main aspects of the process. On the one hand, it describes who will participate in the process and what their responsibilities are. On the other hand, the organizational perspective also describes the infrastructure used in the process: how information is stored, communication mechanisms, what tools and methods are used.

The *informational perspective* presents what information is handled in the process. These "informational entities" include artifacts that are produced, information that flows in the process and other data that is used or manipulated. Informational perspective includes also descriptions of the structure and relationship of such entities. Examples of such descriptions are artifact dependency diagrams and product structure descriptions.

SEI's Software Process Framework can also be a useful guide in identifying and managing processes (Olson *et al.*, 1994). It contains process descriptions that support the SEI Capability Maturity Model and its key process areas (Paulk *et al.*, 1993b).

The method engineering field has also contributed to the process modeling field, as reported by Rossi and Silander (Rossi and Sillander, 1997). Method engineering refers to the design and implementation of software engineering methods (Kumar and Welke, 1992). Compared with the field of process modeling, method engineering focuses on technical tasks of software production, whereas process modeling field often takes other aspects, such as project management and testing, into account as well (Kumar and Welke, 1992; Rossi and Sillander, 1997).

2.2 Business Process Re-engineering

Independently of the developments in the software process engineering field, the business management community has had a recent trend in emphasizing the need to manage and re-engineer business processes (Hammer, 1990; Pralahad and Hamel, 1990; Kaplan and Murdock, 1991; Hammer and

Champy, 1993; Champy, 1995). Business process re-engineering attempts to "use the power of modern information technology to radically redesign our business processes in order to achieve dramatic improvements in their performance" (Hammer, 1990). The main assumption of business process re-engineering is that organizations have developed ways of working that have not changed much over the years. However, at the same time there have been significant technological advances. It has been argued that most organizations have not recognized the new opportunities for streamlining their operations that the new technology has made possible (Hammer and Champy, 1993).

The business process re-engineering field is based on an assumption that radical changes in processes are not only possible but vital for survival. Furthermore, it is assumed that these radical changes cannot be "carried out in small and cautious steps" (Hammer and Champy, 1993). However, there is little empirical evidence of the validity of these assumptions in general. Some of the key authors in the field have admitted that re-engineering hype promised more than was able to deliver for most companies (Champy, 1995). There have also been reports of companies running into difficulties when they have taken too radical steps in their re-engineering projects (Pearlstein, 1995; Mathews, 1995).

The feasibility of radical changes can be questioned especially in areas where the process and the product itself are complex or involve complex technology, as in software engineering. Jacobson *et al.*, have presented a view where the radical change approach, the BPR, is an alternative to process improvement, a gradual, evolutionary change in the process (Jacobson *et al.*, 1995). While the original motivations for BPR may still be valid, in software engineering it may be more appropriate to plan gradual evolution. Although the feasibility of radical change may not apply to software development, it clearly has had a strong influence in the current management culture. If nothing else, this has increased the process awareness of general management. It is therefore important for software engineering management to be aware of this influence. The main implications of the business process re-engineering for software engineering management can be summarized as follows:

- General management is likely to require more information about the software development process, be that process documentation or process measurement.
- General management may expect to see radical changes in the software development process, regardless of whether this is realistic or not. The software development management should be ready to discuss the risks and implications of such changes with the top management.
- Tighter integration to other processes in organization may be required.

- Changes in other processes may influence the software development process.
- General management may question the efficiency and appropriateness of the current technology used in software development.

Because of these reasons, it is important that the software development management is actively involved in the organization's other process management activities.

2.3 Terminology

The previous sections outlined recent developments in the software process engineering field. In this section we will introduce a general process terminology to be used in the remainder of the paper.

Starting with the term "life cycle," it refers to a "progression through a series of differing stages of development" (Anonymous, 1992). Thus, it merely refers to the development process as a whole. In the context of software development, the software life cycle model is a description of the software process that identifies the main activities in the development, their main products, and the relationships between them, and defines the principles of dealing with feedback, concurrency and iteration in the process. Examples of life cycle models are the original waterfall life cycle model, the spiral life cycle model (Boehm, 1988), and the iterative enhancement model (Basili and Turner, 1975). The term "software process" began to replace the term "software life cycle" in the 1980s (Radice et al., 1985; Osterweil, 1987; Lehman, 1987; Curtis et al., 1987). Broadly speaking, the terms can be considered synonyms, but implying a slightly different emphasis on key issues.

There are significant variations in the way the term "software process" is used, despite recent terminology unification efforts (Conradi et al., 1992, 1993; Dowson, 1993; Feiler and Humphrey, 1993; Longchamp, 1993). However, some of these recent definitions are inconsistent with each other. For example, Feiler and Humphrey only include activities ("partially ordered steps") in the definition of the software process: "process is a set of partially ordered steps intended to reach a goal" (Feiler and Humphrey, 1993). However, Longchamp, in addition to activities ("process steps"), explicitly includes artifacts, resources, organizational structures, and constraints in the concept of "software process" (Longchamp, 1993). The obvious confusion in the terms is highlighted by the fact that while most authors use definitions similar to Feiler and Humphrey, many process models published include the elements mentioned by Longchamp (Curtis et al., 1992; Lai, 1991; Kellner, 1991; Krasner et al., 1992; Singh and Rein, 1992).

Clearly, there is variance in what is meant by the word "process." If the term "software process" were interpreted strictly, it might be tempting to define it as only referring to activities. However, this is impractical for two reasons: (i) it is against the common usage of the term and (ii) activities alone provide a limited view of what goes on during software development: what artifacts are produced, by whom, when, what tools and methods are used, etc. Therefore, we have opted for a broad definition of the concept:

> The software development process refers to the activities that are taken to produce software. These activities have information flows and dependencies with each other; they utilize resources, tools, and methods; they produce and utilize artifacts; and they take place in an organization that has a certain infrastructure. The concept of the software development process covers any of these aspects.

The term "software process" is often used as a short form for "software development process" in the remainder of this chapter. Note that the definition above is not limited to software process; if the software-specific terms are left out, the definition can be used as a general definition of the word "process."

When dealing with the software process it is often important to differentiate between the instance of that process, i.e. a real project that is enacted, and class of projects that the concept of the process represents. While this separation has been rather obvious for a long time (Osterweil, 1987), confusing references are often made, e.g., Thomas claims that a large number of organizations have "nothing that can be recognized as a *software process*" (Thomas and McGarry, 1994). The statement by Thomas, strictly speaking, is incorrect. However, given the fuzzy nature of the term process, most people understand that he is actually referring to a *defined process* or a *process definition*. Another example is by Longchamp where he defines "meta-process" directly as a process model ("a process describing the engineering of software process") (Longchamp, 1993, p. 48), not differentiating between the process and its representation. Such terminological confusion is primarily due to the fact that an important concept, the *process class*, has been largely implicit in the process management field and people inadvertently associate a process model with this concept. In order to avoid this kind of confusion we use the concept of process class to refer to a group of projects with similar characteristics:

> "Process class" refers to a set of processes that have similar characteristics so that similar approaches can be used and shared between individual process instances.

Similarly, a process instance is defined as follows:

> "Process instance" refers to an actual—past, present, or future—set of activities that actually take place.

We have tried to clarify the relationship between projects, process classes and process models in Fig. 2. The main point of Fig. 2 is that process class is a conceptual entity that typically captures relevant characteristics of more than one process instance (i.e. project). It is often the case that this conceptual entity is documented; if so, the documented process class is referred to as a model. Normally, process models are first conceptualized and then documented. However, it is also possible to document, i.e. model, a single project, as is normally done in a project plan. This is visualized by a horizontal arrow from the "real world" contour to the "representational level" contour in Fig. 2.

We have used the term "model" to refer to any representation of a process class or instance. We are using the term process definition to imply a formally approved, accepted process model in an organization.

Process enactment means carrying out activities that result in the production of the required output. When enactment is done by humans, we refer to process performance, and when by a computer, the term process execution is used. Note that some authors use the term "enactment" to refer to process execution by a computer.

The terminology introduced here is similar to the one used in object-oriented modeling. A process class is an abstract entity that captures the relevant aspects of several similar real entities, i.e. instances. When a process class has been identified, it is often documented in a process model. An

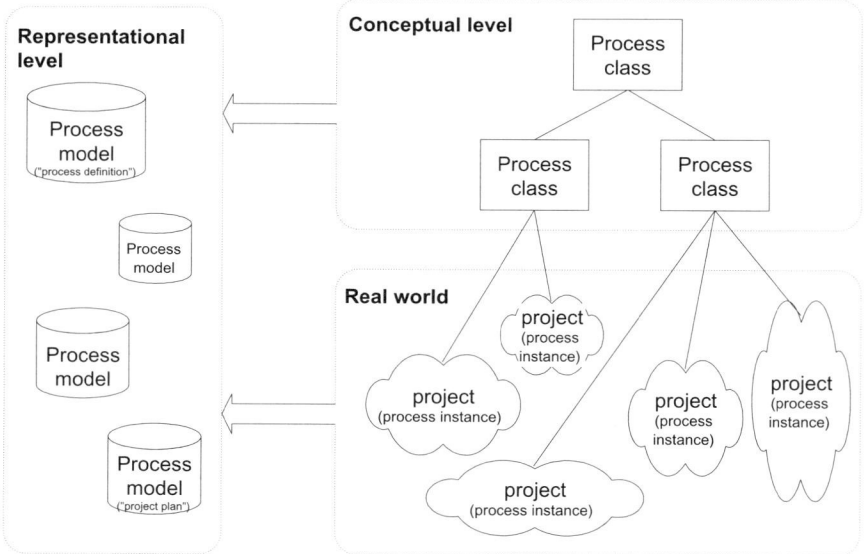

FIG. 2. Conceptual relationships between projects, process classes, and process models.

important principle in developing process definitions is that the goal is to identify main process classes and document them in the process definition.

Now that we have established the definitions for the main concepts associated with the software process, we will define software process management:

> Software process management is a continuous process that monitors the status of the software process, plans and implements improvements in it, and maintains and develops the infrastructure for its management. Process management can be divided into four main activities: project management, process and technology monitoring, process engineering, and process asset management.

The term process improvement is a natural part of process management. It refers to all changes in process management that are done to improve process performance, product quality or process asset management.

Figure 3 presents these main aspects of process management visually. Although all of the activities in process management can be continuous, the flow of information between them can be seen as a cycle. Project management produces data on how a process is performing, process and technology monitoring produce a profile of the current process and what changes are plausible, process asset management determines what changes should be implemented, and process engineering implements these changes. New projects will be based on the "engineered" process and produce updated status information.

Each of the terms in Fig. 3 will be defined in the following.

> Project management refers to the planning, organizing, staffing, directing and controlling of individual projects.

This definition has been derived from existing definitions (Mackenzie, 1969; Thayer, 1988). Project management differs from process management in its focus on finer level of detail, in its need to find local solutions to problems, in its shorter, project-specific time horizon, and in its need to address the operational issues that real instances of projects bring about, such as task assignments to personnel, making day-to-day management decisions and reviewing project progress. Project management determines how the process definition is applied in practice.

FIG. 3. Main aspects of software process management.

Process and technology monitoring represents activities that are carried out to accumulate internal experience and to analyze externally available technologies.

The accumulation of internal experience can be based on data collection (Basili *et al.*, 1994a) and other forms of experience available from projects or specific experiments (Basili *et al.*, 1992b, 1994b). Technology monitoring can be based on internal R&D, monitoring of technical developments in relevant fields, benchmarking (Bean and Gros, 1992), competitor analysis, or use of technology assessment models (Saiedian and Kuzara, 1995). This information should result in the understanding of the current characteristics of the process as well as what changes are possible to it.

Software process asset management is an activity that determines what changes would be made to the process, and develops and maintains the infrastructure for managing and utilizing the process.

Software process asset management determines what changes in the process are most effective for the organization to support its business goals. At the same time, process asset management also develops and maintains the infrastructure required for effective process management: process and means for process documentation, process monitoring practices; and the utilization of process models in process and project management.

Software process engineering refers to the act of systematically evolving the software development process, i.e. making changes to the development process itself.

Process engineering implements the changes that have been determined appropriate in the process. This includes planning of how changes will be made and implementing and institutionalizing the changes. Note that this definition of software process engineering is slightly different from the ones presented earlier in the field. We do not use it to refer to a discipline, as Longchamp does (Longchamp, 1993). Madhavji also includes the development methods, tools, and techniques for process engineering in his definition (Madhavji, 1991). These activities are considered as belonging to the discipline of software process management. Out definition of the term is similar to the one used by (Jacobson *et al.*, 1995).

The responsibility of process engineering and improvement belongs to a process owner:

The process owner is a person who has been allocated the ownership of the process class, i.e. the responsibility to improve the process performance of ongoing and future projects.

The process owner evaluates process performance and should also be an expert on the process (Conradi *et al.*, 1994). An alternative definition of the

A SOFTWARE PROCESS ENGINEERING FRAMEWORK

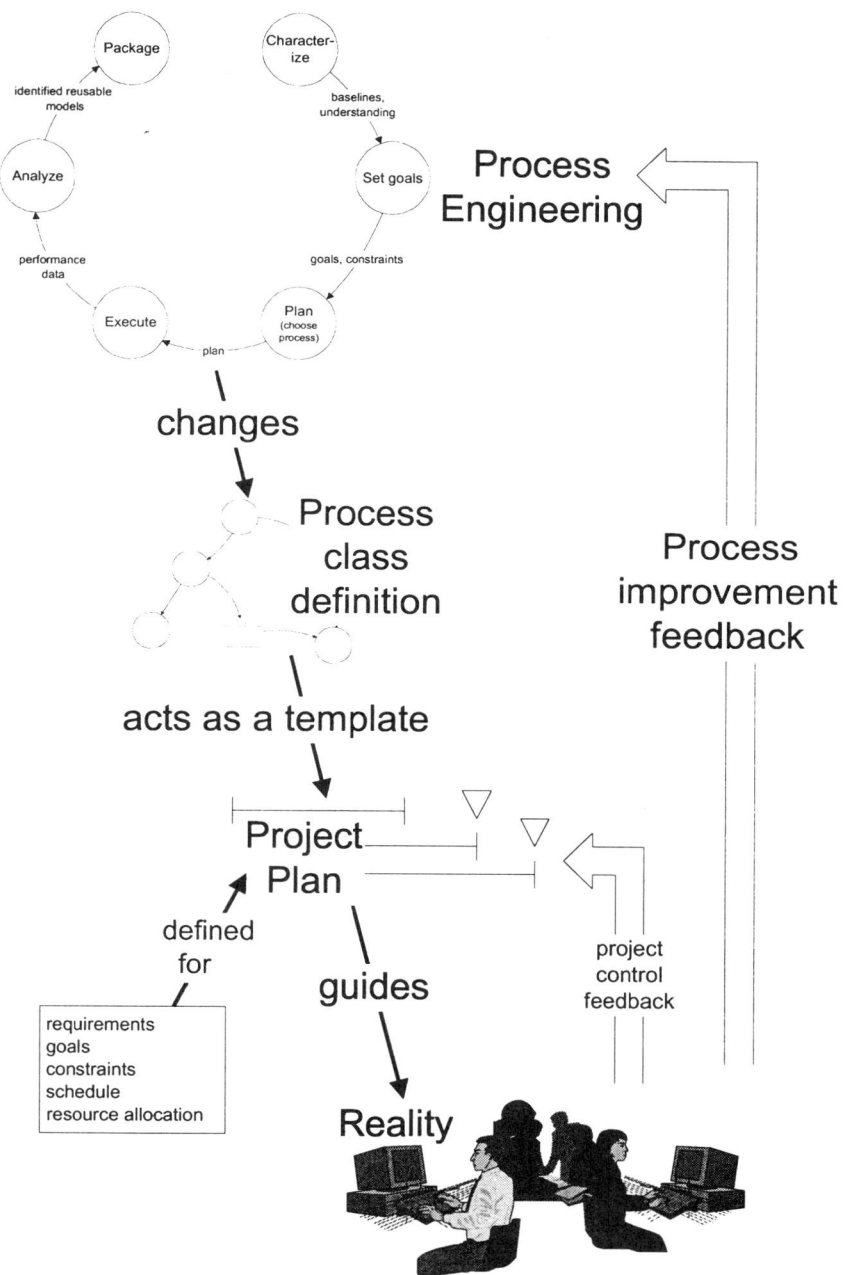

FIG. 4. Relationships between the process definition project plan and enactment.

process owner's responsibilities is to limit the ownership responsibility to initiation and implementation of process change (Harrington, 1991). In this case, the process class ownership may not imply ownership of individual projects; they may have separate owners, e.g. project managers or line managers. In such a case, the role of *process manager* can be identified as a person responsible for the effective enactment of a process and for compliance to process class definition.

In an organization that has identified its process classes and documented them in a process definition, the process class and its definition have a central role, as presented in Fig. 4. First, the right process class is selected to act as a basis for development. Second, this process class—and its model—is used to customize a project plan. This involves making some modifications to the process class and fixing some "parameters" that make the project plan enactable. Such parameters include initial requirements, goals and constraints, schedule, and resource allocations. The project plan, i.e. an instantiated process model for a single project, acts as a guide for agents enacting the process. Experiences from the enacted projects are used to initiate changes in the process class through the process engineering process.

3. Process Management

3.1 Process Improvement Objectives

It is important to analyze the possible objectives for process engineering in order to understand how process models can be used to support them. The process engineering objectives can be derived from product, process, business context, and process asset characteristics. In principle, any combination of the above can act as a set of goals for process engineering.

The improvement in product characteristics is based on the assumption that product quality is dependent on the quality of the development process (Humphrey, 1990; ISO, 1987). *Improving product quality* means making such changes in the process that result in improvements in the quality characteristics of the software product. In addition to functionality, these characteristics may include items like reliability, maintainability, usability, performance, and portability (ISO, 1991a). Improving the product quality clearly is one of the primary goals in process engineering and many approaches claim to support this goal.

The second group of process engineering objectives can be derived from process characteristics. There are three main aspects of the process that can be targeted by process engineering: process productivity, cycle time, and consistency and predictability.

Improving process productivity aims at changes that result in a more efficient process—the same functionality and quality of the product can be produced with lower costs. Cost includes several items, such as labor costs, capital costs (hardware and software for development), and other infrastructure costs. Improving process productivity can also include changes in the means of production, e.g. using more advanced or automated tools to reduce human effort. Many new technologies promoted by their vendors claim high productivity improvements (e.g. CASE tools), although the real improvement benefits are often difficult to verify.

"Time to market" is a critical competitive characteristic in many industries (Stalk, 1988; Anonymous, 1989). *Reducing the process cycle time*, therefore, may be a high priority for companies in such markets. The microcomputer software market and cellular phone markets are good examples of such markets: in the PC software market the market shares are largely fought through making new, advanced versions of software packages available sooner than competitors' products; in the cellular phone market the prices decline rapidly on newer models: the earlier your product enters the market, the higher margins you can charge. The two main techniques for reducing cycle time are more effective development techniques and increasing concurrency in development. Increasing concurrency in the development, however, may result in higher communication overhead and increased rework, which may increase costs.

Improving the process consistency and predictability is important for successful and profitable software development in the long run. A process that is consistent and predictable allows better cost and timing estimates. These, in turn, translate into lower development risks, better fulfillment of customer commitment and better long-term profitability. The challenge in improving process consistency and predictability, however, is in being able to satisfy the customer when the project and requirements evolve.

Processes may be engineered in order to improve the business prospects of an organization. Two distinct types of process engineering goals can be identified. First, process certification, such as ISO 9001 (ISO, 1987, 1991b), or going through a software capability evaluation (SCE) to obtain proof of a given maturity level in software development (Paulk *et al.*, 1993a), can improve the *perceived business value*. Regardless of the possible impact in the software process itself, obtaining a "process quality certificate" can have two kinds of business implication: it may act as an entry pass to access some markets or customers that require such a certificate from their vendors, and it can increase the perceived value of the vendor, resulting in a better competitive position. A better competitive position may result in the ability to attract more customers or to charge higher profit margins.

The academic community has largely ignored the above aspects of process engineering. Yet, in practice a considerable amount of process engineering is based on this objective. This may be the case even when the real improvements resulting from such efforts are questioned by the organization: quality certificates are obtained if customers value them, although the organization may perceive them as having no or even negative impact on quality (Buetow, 1994). Based on our experience, this process engineering goal represents an important and real motivation for many organizations to initiate process engineering projects. Consequently, it should not be ignored when process engineering objectives are discussed.

The second business-driven process engineering goal is *acquiring new capabilities*. This refers to situation where new skills or technologies are acquired in order to improve competitiveness—either in the current market or to enter new markets. For instance, a software consulting house traditionally specializing in management information system (MIS) will need to acquire real-time and embedded systems knowledge and capabilities if it wants to become a viable vendor for telecommunications companies.

Finally, process engineering may be motivated also by the need to *improve process management*. Processes may be changed, for instance, to improve their reusability, measurability, or compatibility with other processes. This is done both from the perspective of project management and process management, representing the short-term and long-term improvement perspectives. The management cannot control the development process without having recognizable phases, activities, or milestones, without feedback on process performance, and without knowing how changes in the process can be made and what their effect will be. Although the goal of improving process management may initially appear as a secondary goal, in the long run the process management characteristics determine how well other improvements can be recognized, how their impact can be estimated, and how their implementation can be carried out effectively. Examples of process changes for process improvement include defining milestones and entry/exit criteria for processes, collecting measurements about the process, and enforcing certain procedures or processes to maintain the consistency of comparisons between projects.

In summary, the following is a list of possible aspects with which process engineering objectives can be associated:

- Improve product quality
- Improve process productivity
- Reduce process cycle time
- Improve process consistency and predictability
- Acquire new capabilities

- Improve perceived business value
- Improve process management

When making changes to the process it is important to evaluate each change's potential impact on all of these characteristics. Sometimes changes in the process result in improvements in more than one area; sometimes there can be significant tradeoffs between these process characteristics. For instance, improvements in product quality typically have a negative impact on process productivity, and reducing the process cycle time may result in lower productivity and predictability. However, the long-term business benefits of these changes may still be positive.

In the following, we will use the process engineering objectives taxonomy and discuss the relationship between them and process modeling objectives.

3.2 Process Modeling Objectives

Our experience with actual process definition activities in the industry indicates that process modeling is often initiated without a clear statement of what the objectives for the effort are and how the process models should be used. This results in a lack of direction and focus in process modeling and in difficulties in actual work. In this section we will introduce a taxonomy of these objectives as well as a model describing their dependencies.

3.2.1 Taxonomy of Process Modeling Objectives

Possible uses of process models have been discussed in the literature in some detail (Radice *et al.*, 1985; Curtis *et al.*, 1987; Osterweil, 1987; Boehm and Bels, 1989; Humphrey and Kellner, 1989; Riddle, 1989; Kaiser *et al.*, 1990; Basili and Rombach, 1991; Madhavji, 1991; Rombach, 1991; Curtis *et al.*, 1992; Brandl and Worley, 1993; Christie, 1993; Dowson, 1993; Dutton, 1993; Heineman *et al.*, 1994; Kontio, 1994b, 1995). We have synthesized a comprehensive list of process modeling objectives from these sources. This list is reproduced in Table 2.

Although process modeling objectives have been listed extensively in the literature, they have rarely been analyzed in detail, especially with respect to their relationships to each other. To our knowledge, Heineman *et al.*, (1994) have been the only ones pointing out the possible relationship between the process modeling objectives, but they did not describe these relationships in detail.

This taxonomy has been created by first compiling a comprehensive list of process modeling objectives from the literature and from our experience. The list was refined into a form that represented independent, reasonable scenarios

TABLE 2

A COMPREHENSIVE LIST OF PROCESS MODELING OBJECTIVES

1. Support communication about the process
2. Support training and education
3. Provide enough details for people to work according to the process model
4. Document responsibilities of individuals, roles and organizational units
5. Formalize the interactions and responsibilities in the process so that people can cooperate more effectively
6. Provide accessible documentation about the process
7. Provide integrated, context-sensitive help in a SEE
8. Support the instantiation of project plans from the process model
9. Use the process model to generate cost and timing estimates
10. Identify and predict problems and risks in projects
11. Estimate impacts of project management decisions
12. Standardize processes across the organization
13. Enforce process conformance
14. Define alternative process fragments that can act as contingency plans
15. Identify and define changes to the process
16. Support systematic management of process evolution over time
17. Assist in technology evaluation and introduction
18. Identify and prioritize improvement areas
19. Use process models for benchmarking between units
20. Plan process changes
21. Monitor the status and evolution of process elements
22. Provide a basis for defining process measurements
23. Automate collection of process measurements
24. Analyze current process performance
25. Check process definitions for consistency, correctness, and completeness
26. Evaluate (simulate) changes to the process before implementing them
27. Accumulate experience/support organizational learning
28. Reuse processes: encourage the use of existing process fragments
29. Support the changes in the process during enactment
30. Define an effective software development environment
31. Support storing and manipulation of process models
32. Automate parts of the process
33. Support and automate cooperative work between humans
34. Support process certification

for process modeling objectives, i.e. all duplicate entries were removed and irrelevant or too generic ones removed. This resulted in a list that was presented in Table 2. Some of the objectives were generalized and renamed to represent a group of objectives, based on whether they represented a potential, distinct category. This grouping process was repeated and revised until it was possible to map all the initial objectives into one objective group. The results of this process are presented in Table 3 and each objective group will be discussed separately in the following. Note that the items in Table 3 are not in any particular order.

TABLE 3
PROCESS MODELING OBJECTIVES TAXONOMY

Support process certification
- Support process certification

Support understanding and communication
- Support communication about the process
- Support training and education
- Document responsibilities of individuals, roles, and organizational units
- Provide accessible documentation about the process
- Provide integrated context-sensitive help in an SEE

Support harmonization and standardization
- Provide enough details for people to work according to the process model
- Document responsibilities of individuals, roles, and organizational units
- Formalize the interactions and responsibilities in the process so that people can cooperate more effectively
- Standardize processes across the organization
- Enforce process conformance

Support planning and control of projects
- Support the instantiation of project plans from the process model
- Use the process model to generate cost and timing estimates
- Identify and predict problems and risks in projects
- Estimate impacts of project management decisions
- Define alternative process fragments that can act as contingency plans
- Support the changes in the process during enactment

Facilitate process execution
- Automate parts of the process
- Support and automate cooperative work between humans
- Define an effective software development environment

Support process monitoring
- Provide a basis for defining process measurements
- Analyze current process performance
- Use process models for benchmarking between units
- Automate collection of process measurements

Facilitate process reuse
- Accumulate experience/support organizational learning
- Reuse processes: encourage the use of existing process fragments

Facilitate process simulation and analysis
- Check process definitions for consistency, correctness and completeness
- Evaluate (simulate) changes to the process before implementing them

Support process management and improvement
- Identify and define changes to the process
- Identify and prioritize improvement areas
- Plan process changes
- Monitor the status and evolution of process elements
- Support storing and manipulation of process models
- Support systematic management of process evolution over time
- Assist in technology evaluation and introduction

Process certification means obtaining some kind of certification about the characteristics of the process. Such certificates can include official ones, such as an ISO 9001 certificate and SCE (ISO, 1991b; Paulk *et al.*, 1993a; Paulk, 1998), or informal "assessment results," such as Bootstrap (Haase *et al.*, 1994) or the SEI capability assessment (Curtis and Paulk, 1993). As we have pointed out earlier, the motivations for achieving a certificate can be independent of other process improvement goals. Both the ISO 9001 certificate and a high CMM maturity level can be seen as valuable marketing tools. Regardless of whether the certification is done solely for business reasons or whether it is part of a "genuine" process improvement effort, it sets its own specific requirements for process modeling. The nature of these requirements is specific to the type of certification sought and the nature of the certification process, i.e. what the requirements of the person or organization conducting the certification audit are. Because of this difference in goals and motivation, the supporting of process is considered to be one of the general process modeling goals in this document.

The goal of *supporting understanding and communication* is essential not only for day-to-day management of project but also for any other activity about the process. Process models are important in making the communication possible and helping people understand the nature and characteristics of the process. The process models used for understanding and communication can be informal and they do not have to be detailed. In fact, lack of detail and avoiding complex formalisms may initially help communication and understanding. Process may include intuitive graphical representations (such as data flow diagrams, block diagrams, or flowcharts) and textual descriptions. As the process awareness in the organization increases and participants become more familiar with the process and formalisms used to document it, more details and more precise formalisms may be used to formalize the organization's process knowledge.

Supporting harmonization and standardization aims at reducing unnecessary process variance—projects that are similar should have a similar process. This improves the predictability of process performance, makes it easier for people to transfer between projects, makes it easier to compare projects and learn from them, and, in the long run, reduces the amount of inefficient practices.

Process models aimed at supporting harmonization and standardization will need to be more detailed than the ones developed for communications and understanding. Especially the interactions and responsibilities of agents need to be documented well and unambiguously. This may call for a more formal representation scheme as well.

The goal *support planning and control of projects* has two main modes of action. On the one hand it is a question of supporting the planning process:

estimating effort and schedule, selecting the life cycle model, selecting methods and tools, etc. A simple form of project planning support is to provide existing process definitions to the project manager and let her use them as a starting point in planning. This requires that the organization has institutionalized its process: process definition should correspond to the real practices of the organization, otherwise the process definition is not a useful template for project planning. A more advanced model is to provide her with process specific cost and timing models that have been calibrated with information about the data from past projects.

The second aspect of support planning and control of projects is concerned with comparing project progress with the plan, identifying problems early and taking corrective actions as necessary. As process definitions and project plans contain a large amount of information about the standard and stable parts of the process, they release the project manager's attention for the issues that are specific to each project. Process definitions may also include some process fragments or procedures that can be used as predefined plans to carry out some activities in the project. However, process models are perhaps even more valuable in monitoring project progress. Information about the normal performance of the process, together with the process definitions, provides a baseline that can be used to compare the current process progress and estimate its outcome.

The goal *facilitate process execution*[3] deals with automation of some parts of the process with the help of a process engine. A process engine is an interpreter that can read the process definition and perform actions defined in it. Examples of process fragments that can be automated are activation of tools in a given sequence (e.g. versioning, compile and link), activation of tools based on product type or process state and forwarding software product components between human agents. There are a few process automation tools available but they have not reached a large usage base yet.

Process modeling formalisms used for process automation must be formal enough for machine interpretation and detailed enough to provide the necessary level of support for human agents. The commercial process automation tools seem to have adopted primarily Petri net-based representation schemes, emphasizing the process flow and states in the process (Murata, 1989; Fernström, 1993; Fuggetta, 1993).

The goal *support process monitoring* includes process measurement and other forms of information collection about the process. Process measurement is the central element in process monitoring. While it is possible to collect some general measures—such as total effort, total duration, and total KLOCs[4]

---

[3] In this context the term "process execution" refers to process enactment by a computer, as defined in Section 2.3.
[4] KLOC stands for thousand lines of code (K stands for "kilo").

produced—about the process without a well-defined process model, these measures give only a black-box view of the process. They would not help understanding the internals of the process. Furthermore, internal process measures are only as good as the corresponding definitions in the process. For instance, if the definitions for beginning and starting of the phase are vague or these definitions are not enforced, the corresponding phase measures have a high margin of error due to variance between projects. Even with similar types of work involved, one project manager may transfer a large amount of requirements analysis to the design phase, whereas another one insists on a more complete requirements analysis before officially initiating the design phase. Without a precise process definition the nature of the process is fuzzy and this results in fuzzy measures.

Process models are also important in benchmarking between development organizations. It is necessary to understand both the development context and the nature of the development process to be able to draw valid conclusions of such comparisons.

Process models can help in automating the data collection in two ways. First, process models help in identifying and defining the appropriate and meaningful measurement points in the process. Some of these measurements can be automated if the appropriate tools are consistently used. Second, if executable process definitions exist and they are used, a wider set of measurements can be collected as more process events are recorded by the process engine.

Process monitoring requires that the elements that are measured in the process are clearly defined. They should have operational definitions i.e. definitions that are unambiguous and detailed enough so that they have similar interpretations regardless of who applies them (Deming, 1986). If the automation of process measurement is integrated with process automation this, of course, requires an executable process representation formalism.

Process reuse is the mechanism for using the accumulated knowledge in an organization. This requires, of course, that there are some mechanisms to validate the experiences so that only beneficial processes are reused. Process reuse can be best utilized when the organization's processes have been standardized. This makes it possible to define generic process fragments that can be "plugged in" to other processes. Standardization of process modeling formalisms also makes it easier for people to understand each process definition across the organization.

Process reuse can take place in several forms. Process fragments can be used to support human communication, and be general and informal, or they can be used for process automation, i.e. be executable by a process engine, in which case they would need to be formal and detailed.

Facilitate process simulation and analysis refers to the use of advanced tools to predict process behavior. Process simulation is not common in the industry, although some commercial tools (Chichakly, 1993) and application examples (Abdel-Hamid and Madnick, 1991; Kellner, 1991) exist. Perhaps part of the reason is that for process simulation to be realistic, i.e. for it to reflect the real process truthfully and in adequate detail, the process definitions must be detailed, process model and enactment conformance must be high, and there must have been adequate process measurement information to calibrate the simulation and analysis models for the specific process. Clearly, most organizations have not reached a point where they could claim to satisfy these requirements, and this severely limits the practical value of process simulation and analysis. However, as many of the requirements listed will be met as the maturity of organizations improves, process simulation and analysis may become a technology that can be used effectively with marginal costs. Process simulation and analysis requires a high degree of formality of the notations used.

Process management and improvement is a very comprehensive category of goals. As the above list shows, it can be divided into two main categories: (i) process improvement, including identification, definition, prioritization, and planning of process changes, and (ii) managing the process knowledge. Process models help process improvement, e.g. by enabling communications, allowing analysis of the process model and allowing simulation of the proposed new process before implementing the changes. As process knowledge is an important organizational competitive asset, process models act as a repository of this knowledge.

As process management and improvement consolidates all process-related activities, its requirements for the process modeling formalisms range from very general and easy to understand (e.g. using informal graphs in discussions) to very specific, executable formalisms (e.g. simulating the proposed process behavior).

The process modeling objectives taxonomy presented in Table 3 can be used in the definition and refinement of process modeling objectives. It is a useful checklist for any process modeling project to verify why the process is being documented. Our experience indicates that it is important to make the process modeling objectives clear whenever process modeling activity is started. Without such clarification the process modeling effort will proceed without a proper sense of direction.

3.2.2 Dependencies of Process Modeling Objectives

We have studied and evaluated the relationships between process modeling objectives on several occasions during the past few years (Kontio, 1994b, 1995). We have identified and revised these relationships based on the use of the model and the feedback we have received. The resulting model of the

TABLE 4
CRITERIA FOR PROCESS ASSET MANAGEMENT GOALS

Process asset utilization goals	Criteria
Support process certification	• Process definition and process conformance are approved by the certification process
Support understanding and communication	• Process definition covers the whole process in an abstract level • Process definition is used in personnel training • Process definition is used in communicating plans and procedures within projects • All project personnel have easy access to process documentation • Process definition corresponds to the way the process is enacted
Support harmonization and standardization	• Consistent process definitions exist between interacting processes • Operational definitions for all relevant process entities exist • Interfaces between interacting processes have been defined in process definitions • Process conformance is formally enforced to projects • Variance in process definitions of process enactment is only allowed when a clear rationale for it exists
Support planning and control of projects	• There is a defined process for initiating projects and it explicitly includes the use of existing process definitions • Process definitions include characterization of their applicability to different projects • Process definitions are used in planning of new projects • Project planning tools (e.g. cost and time estimation tools) are calibrated for the type of process in question and are based on data collected on similar projects • Projects are based on an approved set of process classes and corresponding definitions • Process baselines are available and based on the same process class definition
Facilitate process execution	• The necessary process definitions are implemented in an executable formalism • Process automation tools have been implemented and are used by projects
Support process monitoring	• Detailed operational definitions for all process entities that are measured exist • Operational definitions of measured process entities are communicated to process participants and they are easily available • Process measurements and benchmarking data are collected and analyzed in the context of process definitions

TABLE 4
(*CONTINUED*)

Process asset utilization goals	Criteria
Facilitate process reuse	• There is an established procedure to review and validate good processes • There are resources available for packaging and disseminating reusable processes
Facilitate process simulation and analysis	• Executable or analyzable process definition exists • Process analysis or simulation tools have been taken into use • If simulation tools are used, the simulation models have been calibrated based on project data from projects of the same process class
Support process management and improvement	• There is an established procedure for monitoring process performance to identify potential changes • There are established practices and procedures for maintaining and developing process definitions • Process changes are defined in advance and their impacts estimated before implementing them • Process and process definition evolution are explicitly controlled and managed, i.e. there is a process for initiating, reviewing, and making changes; changes, their objectives, and their rationale are documented; changes are versioned; and the experiences from making changes are collected and analyzed

dependencies can be used to assess the status of process asset utilization in an organization, to prioritize process modeling objectives, to plan improvements in the level of utilization of process models, and to select appropriate process modeling formalisms.

Analysis of process modeling objectives is essential also because all of the objectives cannot be reached at the same time: organizations will need to prioritize their objectives and consider how different objectives support each other. Reaching some of the objectives will, at the same time, develop capabilities that will support reaching other objectives that build upon these new capabilities. The idea is that one should first focus on process modeling objectives that develop capabilities that can be utilized by later process modeling efforts. Furthermore, the modeling of these relationships will support the planning of long-term objectives for process modeling and provide a systematic and comprehensive view of process modeling objectives. In the long run, such an approach would minimize the overall cost of process modeling. We have not been able to identify any published work on this aspect of process modeling objectives.

For each of the process modeling objectives introduced in the previous section, we have defined a set of criteria that determine whether the goal has been reached. Reaching a goal can be seen as reaching a process management state that is part of the process asset management profile. The criteria have been presented in Table 4.

We have used the goals defined in Table 4 to analyze how different goals depend on each other in building the foundations for reaching these goals. The results of this analysis have been presented in Fig. 5. The relationships between the process asset utilization goals are marked with named arrows. The word "facilitates" means that the goal where the arrow originates is necessary for fully reaching the criteria of the goal the arrow points to. The word "supports" means that the originating goal is necessary for improving the efficiency of the process model utilization in the other goal.

The relationships in Fig. 5 are, for the most part, based on what is required by each goal and how the requirements of each goal are linked to each other.

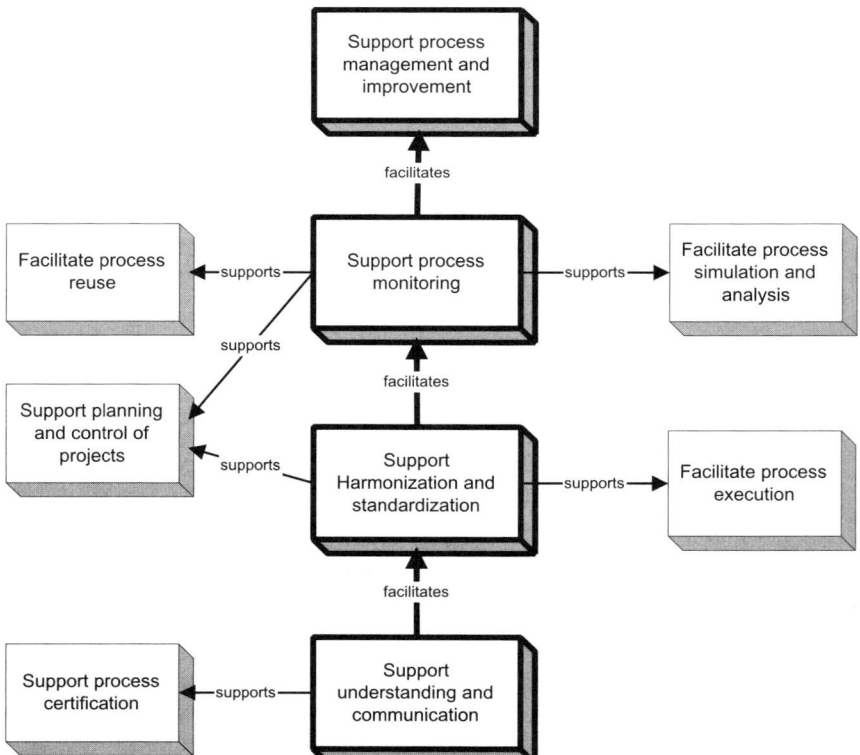

FIG. 5. Dependency model between process modeling goals.

Table 4 and the discussion on the process modeling goal taxonomy alluded to most of these relationships. The most important relationships (marked by arrows named "facilitates" in Fig. 5) form a kernel of this model. These dependencies are most critical and present a logical order of goals to pursue in utilizing process models.

The dependency between *support understanding and communication* and *support harmonization and standardization* is required because harmonization and standardization can only take place if all participants have reached an adequate understanding about the process, are motivated to comply with the standard, and have access to the process definitions. Without understanding people would not know what to do, and without communication they would not be able to get their understandings across to other people. As processes are complex entities, it is unreasonable to assume that harmonization and standardization could effectively take place without the use of process definitions.

The dependency between *support harmonization and standardization* and *support process monitoring* is based on a fact mentioned earlier: operational definitions are necessary for the measurements to be reliable. Measurements have very limited value if they are not based on a well-defined standard process that is followed (Daskalantonakis, 1992; Lott and Rombach, 1993; Pfleeger, 1993).

Systematic *process management and improvement* requires that process improvement is based on systematic and continued *process monitoring* (Basili et al., 1994b; Thomas and McGarry, 1994). This will allow accumulation of understanding of the characteristics of the organization's own process.

These primary goals are presented in the center column of Fig. 5 and they have been marked with boxes drawn in bold. The additional relationships between goals have been marked by arrows named "supports" and they are discussed in the following.

The goal *support planning and control of projects* requires *support harmonization and standardization* because a documented process model acts as a benchmark for supporting project management. Similarly, the link from *process monitoring* is necessary because process measurements can be utilized in assessing project progress.

The goal *support process execution* also requires *support harmonization and standardization*. If an organization's processes do not converge, i.e. they do not follow any consistent pattern, there are big differences in the processes that projects follow. Consequently, it is difficult to find areas where repeatable and predictable process steps exist to justify automated *process execution*. In fact, it may even be that projects end up spending time and effort in circumventing the automated procedures if they do not serve their purposes.

Process reuse requires *process monitoring* because effective processes and their fragments can be best recognized when there is some evidence of their goodness. Process monitoring is the way to recognize and validate their value.

Finally, *process simulation and analysis* requires *process monitoring* largely for the same reasons as the use of estimation models: historical data on past process class performance allows the calibration of simulation models, which leads to more reliable simulation results.

There are some interesting general conclusions that can be made. First, although we believe that the process modeling objectives dependency model is a sound basis for most organizations to plan their process definition activities, it does not mean that it provides the best answer for all situations. In the short run, a company may find opportunities in reaching later objectives for some reason. For instance, it may be cost-effective to automate some small parts of the process (i.e. "facilitate process execution") and this may give a good pay-off in some situations. However, we believe that this is rarely the case. In most situations organizations can rely on the dependency model presented in this chapter.

Second, the process modeling objectives taxonomy and dependency model point out the current discrepancy between the priorities in software process improvement and what the primary focus of the research community has been. Based on the dependency model of process modeling objectives, process execution becomes feasible only after an organization has standardized and harmonized its processes. In the CMM this would happen at level three (defined). As it seems that about 90% of organizations assessed (Kitson and Masters, 1993; Koch, 1993) are on levels lower than that, we have reason to believe that process automation should not be the first priority for most organizations. Most organizations will need to focus on harmonization and standardization first.

It is useful to study the differences between the CMM and process modeling objectives dependency model in more detail, especially how the process modeling objectives relate to the CMM levels (Paulk *et al.*, 1993a). If an organization follows a strategy of reaching maturity levels as indicated by the CMM, a fundamental question for them is how process models can help in reaching each level. The CMM does acknowledge the importance of process models (Paulk *et al.*, 1993b, Section 4.3) but does not give any detailed guidance on how to use process models in the process improvement effort. From the perspective of the dependency model presented in Fig. 5 the CMM implies a different motivation and order for developing process models: it results in development process models for project planning without emphasizing the need for understanding and standardization prior to that (Kontio, 1995). This does not mean that the CMM and our dependency model are in conflict. Instead, they emphasize different aspects, and it can be argued that the CMM assumes that the objectives of *support understanding and communication* and *support harmonization and standardization* have been taken care of as life cycle models for project planning are defined. However, the CMM itself does not provide any guidance or support to recognize this.

The dependency model presented in Fig. 4 should not be interpreted as indicating "levels" that determine the "maturity" of an organization's process asset management. Such an interpretation would not be meaningful. As we have argued in this chapter, each organization's goals and situation may influence the appropriate way of utilizing its process asset. The different aspects and goals cannot be condensed into a single, meaningful metric or "level." Instead, the dependency model should be seen as a profile that characterizes the process asset utilization.

In summary, the main benefits of using the process modeling objectives dependency model are the following:

- It helps in selecting and refining process modeling objectives for an organization. This will also help in defining a better focus for the process modeling project.
- It helps in prioritizing the process modeling objectives in a given situation.
- The process modeling dependency model will support the definition of a longer term plan of what kind of process models are developed, when they are developed, and how they are used.

We believe that the process modeling objectives dependency model does indicate what the cost-effective routes in process asset utilization are. However, this does not prevent organizations from pursuing more than one goal at a time in order to speed up the reaching of goals. Also, some goals may have such a high pay-off that they should be targeted even though our dependency model would indicate that the goal needs support from other goals. However, we argue that the full benefits of a process modeling goal cannot be reached until the preceding goals have been reached.

3.3 Process Modeling Objectives and Process Improvement Goals

Given the process modeling objectives taxonomy and the classification of the process engineering objectives, we have analyzed the relationships between the two. In other words, we have constructed a proposed model of how process modeling objectives support different process improvement goals.

Our analysis is based on estimating the potential impact of reaching each of the process modeling goals on the process engineering objectives presented

TABLE 5
Relationship Between Process Modeling Objectives and Process Improvement Objectives

Modeling objectives \ Engineering objectives	Improve product quality	Improve process productivity	Reduce process cycle time	Improve process consistency and predictability	Acquire new capabilities	Improve perceived business value	Improve process management
Support process certification	none	none	none	none	medium — preparation for certification may indirectly result in actual new capabilities	high — possibility to charge more from customers	high — gives more information about the process and increase process awareness
Support understanding and communication	medium — only indirect impact on the product	medium — reduces unintended deviations from the process	medium — reduces unintended deviations from the process	medium — reduces unintended deviations from the process	high — critical for introducing new processes and tools	none	high — makes process explicit to analysis and discussion
Support harmonization and standardization	low — only corrects problems resulting from deviations from process	medium — only corrects problems resulting from deviations from process	high — allows higher levels of concurrency	high — same process repeated, previous experience more applicable	high — may limit process deviations caused by new processes	low — may be valued by some customers, if supported by evidence	high — makes process repeatable and allows comparison of processes
Support planning and control of projects	high — allows early corrective action	high — corrects rework caused by inappropriate plans, allows early corrective action	high — allows higher concurrency	high — good planning yields reliable plans, allows early corrective action	medium — enforces process conformance, but the relevance of past experience is limited	high — correct and reliable estimates reduce the risk premium of projects	low — aimed at project management
Facilitate process execution	low — difficult to automate activities that produce most errors	low — difficult to automate cost intensive activities	high — reduces wait times in the process	medium — enforces process conformance, but full automation not realistic	low — can rarely be utilized, unless stable processes can be acquired	none	medium — allows higher visibility of process and process conformance
Support process monitoring	high — allows early corrective action	high — allows early corrective action	high — allows early corrective action	high — allows early corrective action	medium — gives indication of the effectiveness of new capabilities	low — may be perceived valuable by some customer	high — allows collection of detailed data about the process
Facilitate process reuse	low — only corrects problems that can be solved by reusing processes	low — only corrects problems that can be solved by reusing processes	low — only corrects problems that can be solved by reusing processes	high — allows use of appropriate, validated processes	medium — potentially high if reusable processes available, otherwise low	none	high — successful experiences can be replicated
Facilitate process simulation and analysis	none — process models are rarely accurate enough to provide product quality impact estimates	low — influences only the selection of the right process class	medium — supports the analysis of concurrency problems, but current tools have limited capabilities	low — alternative processes can be evaluated and the most suitable selected, subject to reliability of simulation	low — process simulation technology immature	low — correct and reliable simulations may reduce the risk premium of projects	high — changes to the process can be simulated before implementation
Support process management and improvement	high — product quality is dependent on the process	high — effective productivity improvements can be implemented	high — effective cycle time improvements can be implemented	high — process conformance can be enforced and variance reduced	high — critical for evaluating and implementing new processes	low — not necessarily visible to the customer	high — aimed at process management

earlier in this section. The estimates themselves are our own interpretations of these impacts, based on our knowledge of the technologies involved and on our experience and knowledge of process improvement projects in the industry.

We have not validated these relationships empirically and they should be interpreted as initial indications of possible impacts. However, we believe that the model presented in Table 5 is a useful analysis tool even in its current form to indicate possible relationships between process modeling objectives and process improvement objectives. While our impact estimates are subjective, they are based on a consensus opinion of several researchers and practitioners and they have been defined using a pair-wise ranking approach.

The relationships in Table 5 have been presented in four categories and they have been defined by each column, i.e. each statement about the impact

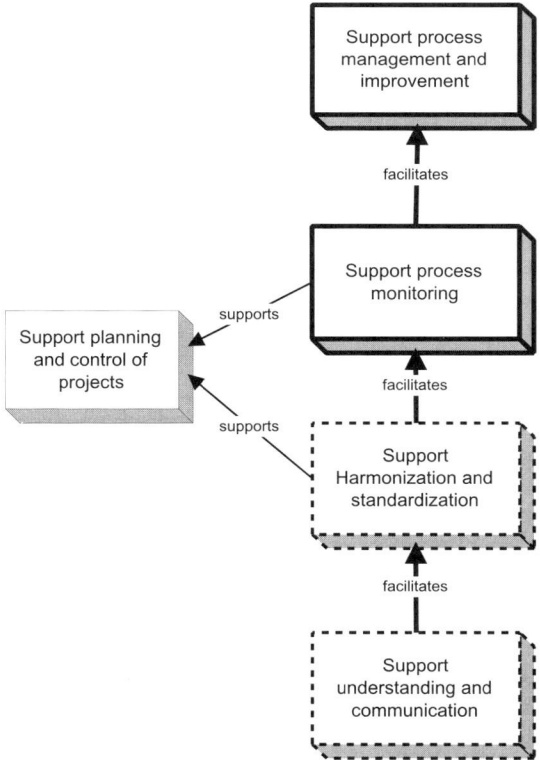

FIG. 6. Process development scenario for objective of "improve product quality".

of a process modeling goal is relative to other goals *in that same column*. For instance, Table 5 indicates that the goal "Support understanding and communication" has a "medium" potential impact on "Improve process productivity." The categories used are explained below:

none	There is no meaningful impact even if the goal is successfully reached
low	If the goal is successfully reached, there is a potential impact but it is not significant
medium	If the goal is successfully reached, there is a potential impact but some other objectives have greater impact potential
high	If the goal is successfully reached there is a high potential impact

Note that the rationale for each impact estimate has been documented in each cell.

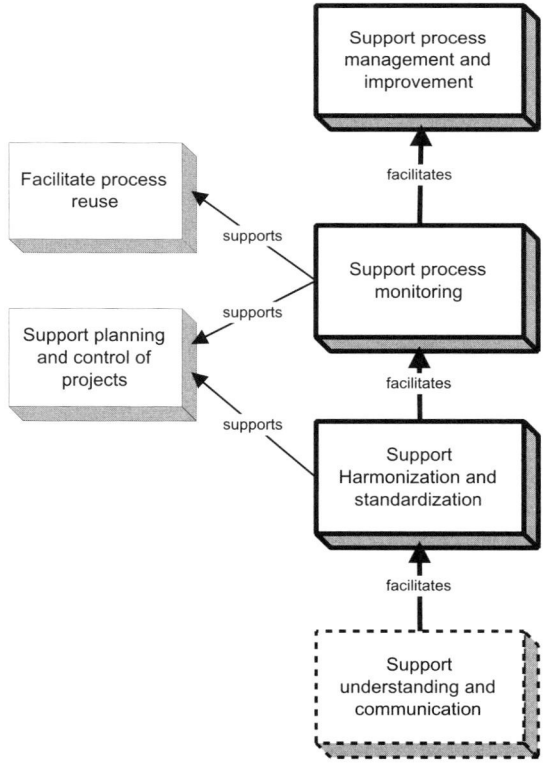

FIG. 7. Process development scenario for objective of "improve predictability and consistency".

We have created a set of scenarios based on the process engineering objectives and process modeling goals. These scenarios represent situations where one of the process engineering objective classes has been selected as the only objective for a hypothetical organization and the high impact process modeling goals are selected as goals for the organization. Using the process modeling objective dependency model we have presented a "high impact route" in process asset utilization for those organizations.

Figure 6 gives an example of such scenario, using the process improvement objective of "improve product quality" as an example. The dashed boxes represent the process modeling goals which need to be reached to reach the targeted goals but do not yield a high pay-off. The distance from the bottom to all solid goals is an indication of the time or cost until there is a higher return on the investments in process asset utilization. Figure 7 gives another example of a scenario.

The scenarios presented in Figs 6 and 7 are simplified views of the real situations in organizations. In practice, there are always several process improvement objectives that need to be considered, both short-term and long-term. The purpose of our dependency model is not to act as a normative model to prioritize process model goals. Instead, it can be used as a guide in discussing and analyzing the situation and considering different process modeling objectives and their tradeoffs with respect to different process improvement objectives.

4. Process Reference Architecture and its Components

In this section we will introduce two main concepts. First, we will present the architectural framework for representing process models. This framework is later used when we present our process modeling process. Second, we present a comprehensive model of process model information entities that can be included in a process model. These information entities and their combinations will also be referred to in our process modeling process.

4.1 Reference Architecture for Process Models

The purpose of process reference architecture is to provide a clear, conceptual model for different types of information contained in a process model. Such an architecture will make it easier to understand different aspects of the process and allow gradual definition of the process. In this section we present a process reference architecture that has been synthesized from past work in this area as well as from our own experiences in process modeling.

Process reference architecture was initially addressed by the general process modeling researchers. This line of research initially discussed how processes in an organization should be modeled and represented (Armitage and Kellner, 1994; Armitage *et al.*, 1995; Curtis *et al.*, 1992; Frailey *et al.*, 1991; Humphrey and Kellner, 1989; Katayama, 1989; Kellner, 1989). While no single model has surfaced as the only modeling approach, there seems to be a consensus on the four types of element that need to be represented in an enactable process definition: activities, artifacts, agents, and the relationships between them. However, merely identifying process model elements does not yet constitute a conceptual framework that would allow more abstract discussion and analysis of the process.

The process perspectives proposed by Curtis *et al.* also can be seen as a contribution towards defining a process reference architecture (Table 1) (Curtis *et al.*, 1992). The value of process perspectives is that they contain the idea of having different viewpoints on the same underlying model, much like there can be several blueprints representing views of a house from the front, top, and side. However, merely having different perspectives, again, is a partial solution towards representing and discussing an architecture.

More recently Feiler and Humphrey proposed a conceptual framework for process definition (Feiler and Humphrey, 1993). They derived their framework from software development analogy. Their framework is divided into three main levels: *process architecture* is a conceptual framework that describes the structure and relationships between process elements; *process design* defines the functions and relationships of process elements; and *process definition* is an enactable process description. They also include additional levels for concepts that correspond to project plan and enacting process (Feiler and Humphrey, 1993). The conceptual framework proposed by Feiler and Humphrey explicitly contained the process architecture as a distinct component in process modeling. However, the contents of the architecture have not been discussed in detail.

Independently of the work done by Feiler and Humphrey, Basili *et al.* have proposed and used a conceptual framework for representing the component factory (Basili and Caldiera, 1991; Basili *et al.*, 1991, 1992a), a specialization of the Experience Factory (Basili, 1989; Basili *et al.*, 1992b; McGarry *et al.*, 1994). While their contribution was primarily aimed at discussing the component factory, the reference architecture proposed is a valuable contribution on its own right towards identifying conceptual elements in the process architecture. According to Basili *et al.*, the reference architecture can be expressed in three levels: *reference level*, representing the active elements performing tasks; *conceptual level*, representing the interfaces and organizational relationships between these elements; and *implementation level*, representing an actual implementation in a given organization (Basili *et al.*, 1991, 1992a).

Although some of the terminology in the Basili *et al.* reference architecture is potentially debatable and slightly ambiguous, their model was one of the first attempts to conceptually structure the information required to document organizations' processes.

We have refined the model proposed by Basili *et al.* and defined a conceptual process reference architecture that, we hope, is clearly defined and more appropriately identifies different conceptual elements for the purposes of general process modeling. The main revisions from the Basili *et al.* model are:

- Principles and rules of operation have been expressed separately in what we call "paradigm definition." The paradigm definition is separate because it can be used to support definition and operation of processes in all levels.

- The process purpose and goals statement is presented separately to allow an implementation-neutral statement of what the process is supposed to do.

- Generic process definition represents a high-level view of the process without assigning actors or responsibilities.

- Organization-specific localization of the process is a distinct element in the architecture.

- Enactable process definition and its actual enactment, or instance, are conceptually two separate entities in the architecture.

Our conceptual reference model is presented in Fig. 8 and is discussed in the following.

The *paradigm definition* contains the main assumptions, theories, methods, guidelines and research methods that define the paradigm[5] under which the process is enacted. In our architectural framework, the paradigm definition allows the documentation of the main principles and interpretation rules for the process. The paradigm definition does not have to be comprehensive. It is adequate to document the main principles that correctly characterize the

---

[5] Note that the contemporary meaning of the term is somewhat different from its original meaning. Originally the word paradigm meant an "example that serves as pattern or model," originating from Greek words "para," alongside, and "deikunai," to show (Anonymous, 1992). In 1962 Thomas S. Kuhn defined the word paradigm as a set of accepted principles of scientific practice that are common to a group of researchers (Kuhn, 1970). Since then, the definition of paradigm has evolved (Burrel and Morgan, 1979; Hirschheim and Klein, 1989) and we are defining paradigm as "a point of view in which some principles, assumptions, approaches, concepts, and theories have been stated uniformly" (Kontio, 1995).

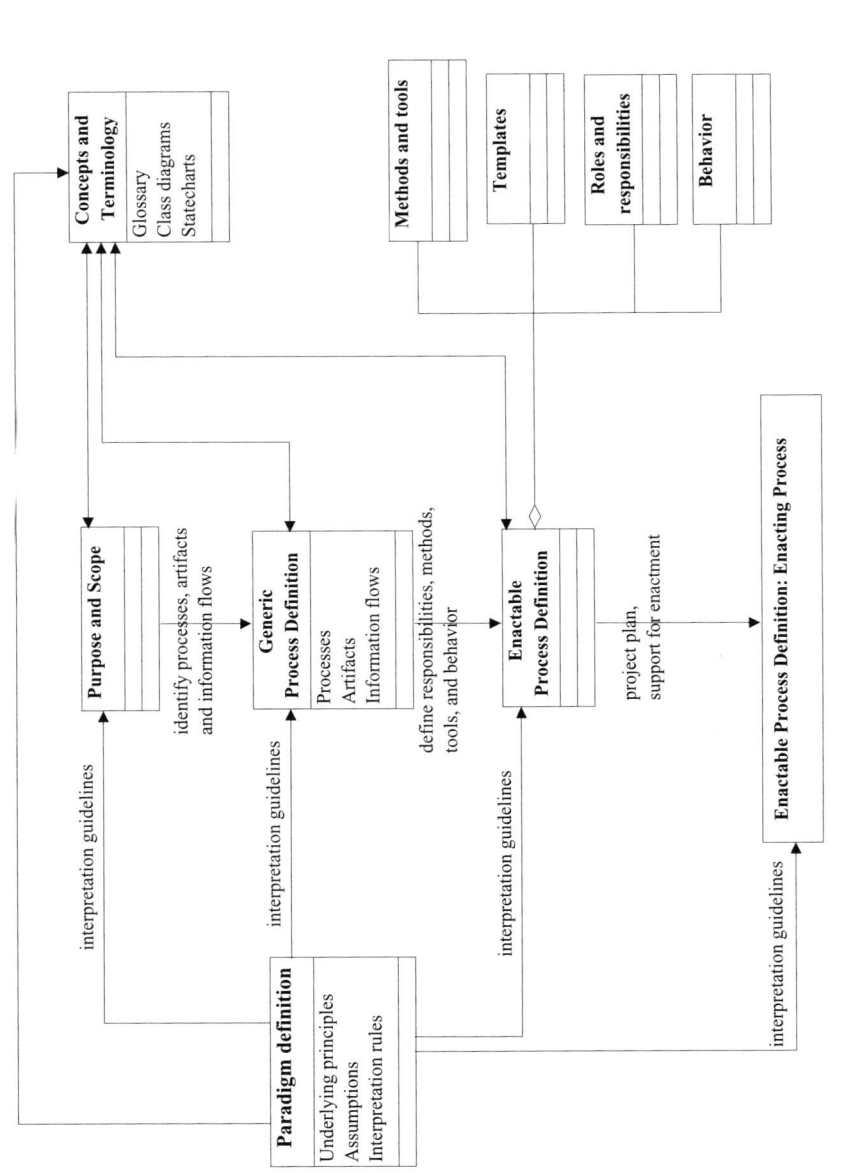

FIG. 8. Process modeling architectural framework.

paradigm. For instance, the following is a partial list of statements characterizing the Quality Improvement Paradigm (Basili, 1989, 1993):

1. Continuous learning is essential for all evolutionary fields, such as software development.
2. Continuous, sustained improvement is not possible without understanding of the current situation and environment.
3. Measurement and modeling are essential for understanding and learning (the best way to learn is to observe).
4. All knowledge is potentially reusable and, therefore, should be explicitly represented.
5. Improvement and organizational goals must be explicitly stated and measured.
6. All software development knowledge must be localized. We do not yet have universal models for software quality or productivity but if and when such universal models are identified they will need to be localized as well.

The paradigm definition affects all layers of the process reference architecture. It determines some of the goals and functions for the process to be defined, as well as acting as a guideline at the enactment level.

Another main element in Fig. 8 is called *concepts and terminology*. This represents the definition of key concepts that are to be used in the process. Such concepts can be represented in a glossary or dictionary, but it is often beneficial to model key concepts more thoroughly using entity relationship diagrams, class diagrams (Awad *et al.*, 1996; Rumbaugh *et al.*, 1991), or other suitable formalism, such as state transition diagrams, to represent artifacts or process states (Harel, 1987).

The *purpose and scope definition* states the objectives, main output, and scope of the process. The goals can be relatively abstract statements of purpose, such as "improve product quality" or "improve development cycle time." These high-level goals are broken down to objectives (subgoals) or functions. Objectives are more concrete statements of what is required to reach the high level goals, and functions state how these objectives can be met.

Definition of the main output determines what the value-adding product of the process is, be that a concrete, physical product, a service, or a piece of information. These define the process goals on a concrete level. The process scope is the third important element in the goal and scope definition. It states where the process starts and where it ends.

The *generic process definition* defines, on an abstract level, what the main activities and artifacts are and their information flows in the process. There can be several potential alternative generic process definitions that might satisfy the purpose and scope definition, and representing them in an organization-independent fashion allows comparison and evaluation between them. The generic process definition essentially corresponds to the functional perspective defined by Curtis *et al.*, (1992).

The *enactable process definition* refines and localizes the generic process definition and describes how the process behaves. A process definition is enactable when adequate information on methods and tools, roles and responsibilities, templates, and behavior is available for process agents. What is "adequate" depends on the types of agents involved. A process engine requires detailed and formal specifications for all of these aspects, whereas people can perform a process with less formal specification. However, the skills, background and experience of personnel also influence how much detail and formality are required to make a process model enactable.

Methods, tools, and templates define how things are done in a process. A generic process definition might state that a "high-level design document" is produced in an "initial design" process. The method definition would indicate what approach, method, and techniques are used in the process, the templates would indicate what format and style the output should be in, and the tool definition would determine what tools are used and how.

When roles and responsibilities are defined, they clarify, for example, who enacts the process, what their responsibilities are, and how they interact. Again, the level of detail in clarifying roles depends on the types of agent involved, but it also depends on the repeatability and level of control required from the process.

The behavioral specification can refer to several aspects of the process. It can include the definitions of:

- entry and exit criteria of activities
- loops and iterations in the process
- alternative process paths
- decision points in the process
- dependencies of activities
- concurrency rules of activities.

Whether all of these items are defined and how precisely they are defined depends on the process modeling objectives and on how much freedom is given to process agents in enacting the process. Experienced developers are able to enact a process with minimal or no behavioral specification, whereas a process engine requires detailed and unambiguous behavioral specification.

Finally, when actual work is done, the processes defined in the previous level are enacted in practice, as represented by the level *enacting processes*.

Note that the architectural elements in the center column of Fig. 8 contain the notion of gradual refinement and localization. Part of this localization is also reflected in the concept and terminology definition, as the arrows in Fig. 8 show.

The interesting aspect of the architectural view presented in Fig. 8 is that it allows explicit and clear representation of the main elements of a process in a manner that allows incremental definition and customization of the process. The generic aspects of the process are documented explicitly and separately from how they might be implemented in different situations. Such a structure enhances the reusability of processes as well as it making it easier to localize the processes. Our experience also indicates that the development of process models becomes more systematic using the architecture presented here.

4.2 Process Model Information Entities

A process model information entity is a concept that is relevant in understanding and documenting the process. Based on a survey of existing classifications of process model information (Armenise *et al.*, 1993; Bandinelli *et al.*, 1993a,b; Basili *et al.*, 1992a; Brandl, 1991; Conradi *et al.*, 1993; Crowley and Silverthorn, 1991; Curtis *et al.*, 1992; Dowson *et al.* 1991; Feiler and Humphrey, 1993; Frailey *et al.*, 1991; Huseth and Vines, 1987; Kellner, 1989; Kellner and Rombach, 1991; Rombach, 1991), we have synthesized seven different classes of process model information entities and they will be presented in the following paragraphs. The entity classes are also listed in Table 6.

The *process activities* refer to the activities involved in the process. The concept of activities also includes the aggregate relationships between them, i.e. hierarchical decomposition of activities into sub-activities.

The *process behavior* refers to how activities are performed in the process, how they are sequenced, how they overlap, when and how they are started and finished, and re-enacting of activities. Depending on the situation, process behavior can be seen as representing the flow of events that actually happened or the principles that are used to control the enactment.

The *process artifacts* are identifiable pieces of information, or physical objects, that are produced or modified during the process. They can be parts of the *software product* or they can be *project management artifacts*. The project management artifacts are pieces of information produced or modified during the process for the purpose of managing the development process. Examples include items like project plan, meeting minutes, or management decisions. Note that process artifacts do not necessarily have to be identifiable documents. They can also be informal communications (such as a decision

TABLE 6
PROCESS MODEL INFORMATION ENTITIES

Process model information entities	Examples

Process activities	• Processes that are identified
	• Examples:
	  – life cycle phases
	  – hierarchical composition of processes and subprocesses

Process behavior	• Initiation and control rules in the process
	• Examples:
	  – process sequence
	  – initiation condition for processes
	  – decision points in process activation
	  – process concurrency
	  – reactivation of processes

Process artifacts	• Items that are used or produced in the process
	• Examples:
	  – product structure, e.g. document structure, executable code structure
	  – relationships between artifacts, e.g. dependencies, groupings ("part of the same release")

Process agents	• People or software that enact the process • Roles can be defined for agents, e.g. project manager, tester, programmer
Process resources	• Resources that are used in the process, e.g. hardware, software, methods and tools, communications media
Process infrastructure	• Organizational infrastructure that affects the process, e.g. organization structure, data collection and reporting procedures, administration
Process information flow	• Flow of information between entities

that is made but never documented) or electronic messages or files (such as email messages).

Note that we have considered as artifacts only such items that *directly influence the substance produced* or which are *produced or modified* during the process. This definition includes key input information, such as requirement specifications, in a process, but excludes, for example, method descriptions and tool manuals. Our definition is similar to that of Longchamp (Longchamp, 1993). However, it may be tempting to include any document under the category of artifact, such as project plan templates, method guidelines, and tool documentation. Although many of these examples may be physically similar to process artifacts, they have distinctly different roles in the process. Either they are used as if they were resources (e.g. a project management template) or they are used as process definitions (e.g. a method description). If they are used as resources, they should be considered as resources by the process model. If they are modified, their modified version becomes an artifact, however. In the case of method description the decision to classify them either as resources or process activities is a judgment call. However, they should not be classified as artifacts, because of their different role from other artifacts, according to our definition of the term.

Process agents are human or computer resources that have an active role in the process; an "entity that enacts the process" (Feiler and Humphrey, 1993). Agents perform activities. While humans as agents are, of course, common and established practice in all software development organizations, some activities can be performed by a computer, i.e. software, if the necessary tools and process definitions have been made available. An agent is often given one or more roles in the process. A *role* refers to a set of responsibilities and permissions given to an agent in a process (Feiler and Humphrey, 1993; Longchamp, 1993).

Process resources are any documents, equipment, software, or guidelines that are used to support the process. Process resources differ from process artifacts in that they are not modified or changed by the process. If they are changed, they become process artifacts. Process resources also differ from process agents in the sense that process agents have active roles and responsibilities in the process. Note that our definition of the term "resource" excludes "human resources" when they are active participants in the process.

Note that our use of the term "resource" is slightly different from its general usage. In management literature personnel and software are generally considered to be resources. However, since process models can give explicit responsibilities and roles to these entities and these are explicitly modeled in process models, it would be misleading to consider them similar to the resources, e.g. office space or a telephone. The differentiating factor is whether a resource has an active role in the process or not. If software does not perform any activities, it is considered to be a resource; if it does enact parts of the process, that particular piece of software is an agent.

Process infrastructure consists of the basic facilities and services needed in software development. The main infrastructure components include organizational structure, computer hardware used in the project, physical office equipment, communications media, data collection and reporting procedures, administration and support staff, and software development process support. All of these elements influence the development process. However, it may be impractical to try to model all of them.

The *process information flow* refers to the flow of information between process model information entities. Entities involved in this information flow can include activities, agents, artifacts, or elements in the process infrastructure. The information flow is an essential component in most process definitions.

Process model information entities can be used to make an accurate reference to a process or to a pocess model. With the help of process model information entities it is possible to communicate clearly which entities are included in a process model. For instance, one can state that a particular process model documents process activities, process artifacts, process agents, and process information flow. Of course, an indication of the detail of each will further clarify the contents and coverage of the process model.

4.3 Process Modeling Objectives and Information Content

Process modeling objectives influence what type of information should be stored in the process model. The implications of the process modeling objectives should be considered before finalizing the process modeling approach. The information content also influences the suitability of process modeling formalisms.

We have analyzed the main information requirements for each of the process modeling objective groups. Our analysis was based on identifying the types of information required for reaching each of the process modeling objective groups. The results of this analysis are presented in Table 7. Blank cells in Table 7 indicate that the process model information entity class is not necessary for reaching the process modeling objective, "optional" means that the information is useful but not essential.

The information in Table 7 can be used to determine what kind of process information is most important in the process modeling effort. This should result in more productive and focused process modeling project and more usable process models. For instance, if an organization is interested developing process definitions to support communication, e.g. for training purposes, the process models do not necessarily need to cover process infrastructure, process behavior or process resources.

The above information can also be used to consider what process modeling formalisms are most appropriate for a given process modeling task. Formalisms differ in their coverage of process model information entities and how well they represent each of them. One should select a formalism that supports the types of information required by the process modeling objective. There have been several studies comparing different process modeling formalisms using different criteria (Kellner, 1989; Kellner and Rombach,

TABLE 7
PROCESS MODELING OBJECTIVES AND PROCESS INFORMATION ENTITIES

Process model information entity class / Objectives	Process activities	Process behavior	Process artifacts	Process agents	Process resources	Process infrastructure	Process information flow
Support process certification	required		required	optional			
Support understanding and communication	required	optional	required	required	optional		required
Support harmonization and standardization	required	required	required	required	optional		required
Support planning and control of projects	required	optional	required	optional			required
Facilitate process execution	required	required	required	required	optional		required
Support process monitoring	required	required	required	optional		required	
Facilitate process reuse	required	required	required	optional	optional	optional	required
Facilitate process simulation and analysis	required	required	required	optional			optional
Support process management and improvement	required	required	required	required	required	required	required

1991; Armenise *et al.*, 1993; Rombach and Verlage, 1993; Kontio, 1994b). Although a detailed analysis of those results is beyond the scope of this paper it can be noted that there are considerable differences in how well different formalisms support each of the process model information entities. There are particularly strong differences between formalisms that have been developed solely to support process automation (Fernström, 1993; Murata, 1989) and formalisms that are aimed at supporting human communications, such as SADT (Marca and McGowan, 1988) and dataflow diagrams (DFD). Some formalisms have been developed to support both, i.e. they are formal enough for execution yet they have been defined for easy understanding (Harel, 1987; Harel *et al.*, 1988; Ould and Roberts, 1987; Ould, 1992; Singh, 1992; Singh and Rein, 1992; Christie, 1993).

The definition of required information content and the choice of a process modeling formalism should not only be based on a short-term process modeling objective. The process modeling objectives dependency model can be used to define a long-term strategy for process modeling. If the direction of the process modeling plans calls for inclusion of some process model information entity classes later and they can be conveniently documented in the current process modeling effort, they may well be included. Similarly, the selection of process modeling formalism should consider long-term process model utilization plan. For instance, if the current process modeling objective is to support communication but it is expected that process execution will be needed shortly, it is reasonable to select a process modeling formalism that allows easy transition to an executable process definition. Examples of such formalisms include ProNet (Christie, 1993) and RIN (Singh and Rein, 1992).

4.4 Process Perspectives Revisited

Curtis *et al.* pointed out that it is impractical to try to represent all process information in a single graph, or view (Curtis *et al.*, 1992). They proposed that several perspectives to the process are required and proposed four of them, as discussed earlier in this document. However, our experience with process modeling indicates that these four perspectives do not necessarily cover all process model information entities, and sometimes it may be beneficial to present process information in combinations different from the four perspectives suggested. In fact, it can be argued that the four perspectives proposed by Curtis *et al.* are just examples of possible perspectives. Also, although the process perspectives are useful for emphasizing the different aspects of process, there is a considerable amount of overlap in the perspectives and separation rules for the overlapping areas are not very clear. For instance, both functional and behavioral perspectives inevitably present activities. While the functional and behavioral perspectives seem natural, the organizational perspective seems to contain

TABLE 8
PROCESS PERSPECTIVES AND PROCESS MODEL INFORMATION ENTITIES CROSS-REFERENCE

Process model information entities / Perspectives	Process activities	Process behavior	Process artifacts	Process agents	Process resources	Process infrastructure	Process information flow
Functional perspective	included		partially included				included
Behavioral perspective	included	included					
Organizational perspective				included	included	partially included	
Informational perspective			included				

two quite different perspectives to the process, one related to the agents and one to the organizational infrastructure. Furthermore, given the process model information entities introduced earlier (Table 6), it seems that there are more than just four possible and useful perspectives. In Table 8 we have listed the process model information entities in columns and process perspectives in rows. Each cell represents whether the process model information entity in that row is covered by the perspective in that column.

Based on the analysis of Table 8, we suggest some modifications to the concept of using process perspectives. First of all, the number and content of possible perspectives is not constant. It may be necessary to "configure" specific perspectives for some process models. For example, one perspective could contain process activities, process behavior, and process agents. Also, one possible perspective could be dedicated to process activities, describing the activity hierarchies and their relationships. However, the organizational perspective could be perhaps better handled by dividing it further. The definition of perspectives should be based on the process model information entities we have defined. Theoretically, there are 127 possible perspectives[6]. However, not all combinations of process model information entities are meaningful, so the number of useful process perspectives is significantly smaller. In our earlier work we have proposed a set 25 perspectives that we believe to be most relevant in practice (Kontio, 1995). However, our intention is not to argue which perspectives are the right ones for all situations. We do, though, recommend that the number and content of possible perspectives for presenting process information is carefully considered. This will help in the modeling of process information as well as in presenting this information.

5. Process Management Process

In this section we present the process modeling process we have defined and used during the past few years (Kontio, 1994a, 1995, 1996). We will present the process using the architectural framework described in Section 4.1. However, as we are defining a generic process—not organization-specific nor an enactable one—we are not "filling in" all aspects of the architectural framework presented in Fig. 8. Such localization will be done by organizations adopting this framework and process for their process modeling tasks.

---

[6] Given by the sum of binomial coefficients:

$$\sum_{j=1}^{7} \binom{7}{j} = 127$$

5.1 Process Modeling in Process Improvement

Given our aim of producing a generic model of the process modeling process, our process modeling paradigm definition is also rather generic. Instead of presenting a set of interpretation rules, as would normally be done, we are representing the paradigm definition by depicting the process modeling process in the context of process management.

Process improvement programs often provide the initial thrust to launch a process modeling effort. Although we will discuss the specific objectives of developing process modeling in detail later in this document, it is useful to discuss how process models relate to process improvement in general. According to the principles presented by Basili (1989), process improvement should be based on organization's own experience. Thus, process improvement can be seen as consisting of the following main activities:

- *Establish improvement infrastructure:* obtain management commitment, motivate and train personnel, institutionalize the improvement process, define process modeling formalisms and conventions.
- *Identify improvement needs:* understand current environment and process, recognize strengths and weaknesses, identify potential areas for improvement.
- *Plan improvements:* prioritize improvement areas, identify possible improvement action, prioritize improvement actions, define objectives, detail plans, allocate resources.
- *Implement improvements:* perform the process improvement plan, make the changes necessary.
- *Validate success:* check whether objectives were met.

Process models play a central role in the above steps, as Table 9 shows. Step 1 uses process models to document the process improvement and modeling process itself. In step 2 (identify improvement needs) process models are needed to understand what the current process is like. Process models are also used to interpret process measurements. In step 3 (plan improvements) process models are used to speculate about the impact of process improvement actions and plan how to implement them. In step 4 (implement improvements) process models are used for communicating the new process definition and to standardize process enactment. In step 5 (validate success) the process models are used to check how well the process improvement objectives were met.

In summary, process models are essential in making process improvement happen. They help in understanding the current process, they support planning of process changes, and they facilitate the change process by enabling communication and process conformance.

TABLE 9
PROCESS IMPROVEMENT STEPS AND PROCESS MODEL SUPPORT

Process improvement step	Process model support
Establish improvement infrastructure	• Definition of the improvement process
Identify improvement needs	• Description of current practices • Process measurement
Plan improvements	• Use alternative process models for planning support • (process simulation)
Implement improvements	• Understand and communicate the new process • Harmonize and standardize the new process
Validate success	• Process measurement • Process conformance

5.2 Process Modeling Process

Our process modeling process assumes that the relevant process improvement objectives and actions have been identified and planned correspondingly. There are two basic scenarios under which process modeling can take place: to support specific process improvement plans and actions or to improve process model utilization. The former was alluded to in the previous section; the latter refers to better utilization of the process asset (which itself can be considered as a subset of process improvement).

We have adopted Basili's Quality Improvement Paradigm (Basili, 1989, 1992) as a starting point in defining the process modeling method. The main steps in our process modeling method can be summarized as follows:[7]

(1) *Characterize*. Understand the current process and environment based on the available data, models, experience, and insights.
(2) *Set goals*. Based on the characterization of the environment, set quantifiable goals for the process modeling project.
(3) *Plan process modeling*. Based on the characterization and goals, choose the methods, formalisms tools and techniques appropriate for the process modeling project, making sure that they are consistent with the goals and constraints set for the project.
(4) *Process elicitation and representation*. Perform the process modeling activity.
(5) *Experience capture*. At the end of the process modeling project, analyze the experiences and the information gathered to evaluate the current

---

[7] We have changed the names of the QIP steps to refer to process modeling explicitly.

practices, determine problems, record findings, and make recommendations for future process modeling projects. Consolidate the experience gained in the form of new or updated models, documents, and other forms of knowledge and store this knowledge in the experience base.

The last step is aimed at organizational learning and accumulating process modeling knowledge. Strictly speaking, it is not part of our method, but as they are important steps in improving the process modeling process itself they have been included in this presentation.

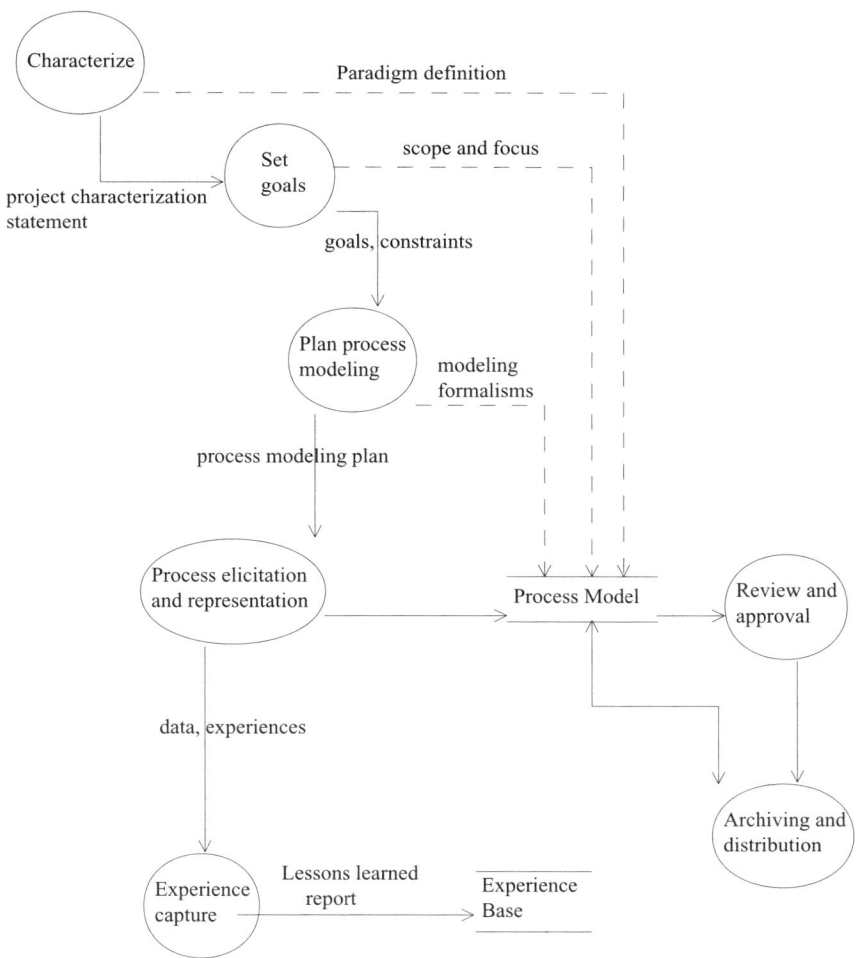

FIG. 9. The process modeling process.

We have presented our process modeling process in Fig. 9. Each process will be presented in more detail in the following sections. However, the review and approval activity, as well as the archiving and distribution activity, are presented in Fig. 9 only, as they are specific to each organization.

5.2.1 Characterize

The purpose of the characterization step is to understand the current status of process documentation and utilization in the organization. "Understanding" does not necessarily produce a concrete deliverable; it can result in participants' intuitive, undocumented knowledge of the situation. However, we recommend that the results of the characterization activity are explicitly documented, as this will reduce possible misinterpretations. Furthermore, the techniques we recommend easily allow partial documentation of the results.

The characterization activity should produce the artifact *project characterization statement*. The main contents of this document are outlined below:

- Description of the main characteristics of the process to be modeled and requirements set for the project.
- Description of processes, methods, tools, and experiences from previous process modeling projects and assessment of the applicability of these experiences to this project.
- Description of any links or constraints to past or existing process models or process modeling efforts, e.g. need to maintain compatibility with current process modeling formalisms used, need to coordinate work with other process modeling efforts or organizational units.
- Assessment of the process model utilization profile.
- Definition of the focus and scope for process modeling.
- Statement of the expected performance baseline for the project, based on the analysis of the above factors, i.e. initial schedule and effort estimate.

The project characterization statement is a document, possibly a short one. Two of the above bullets can be supported by the specific methods adapted to our method: assessing process model utilization and definition of the focus and scope for process modeling.

The model utilization profile assessment can be done by using the process modeling objectives taxonomy and dependency model. They can be used to assess the state of process model utilization by using the criteria presented in Table 4. Each process modeling objective has some criteria that help determine whether the organization currently meets the objective. The characterization results in a profile that describes how process models are currently utilized in the organization.

The scope and focus of the current process definitions can be defined with the help of process model focus grid. The process model focus grid is a graphical technique for representing the level of granularity and scope and level of reuse for a process definition. The current version of the focus grid is based on the feedback and experiences obtained from its earlier versions (Kontio, 1994a, 1995, 1996). The Process Model Focus Grid consists of a two-dimensional grid that is used to describe the organizational scope and level of detail in the process model. The two dimensions are organizational scope and level of granularity. The *organizational scope* is defined as the number of organizational units and personnel roles the model covers. In the example in Fig. 10 we have divided the organizational scope into six levels: inter-company, company-wide, division, functional unit, team, and individual[8] (Kontio, 1995). The number and definition of these classes must be defined for each organization.

The other dimension in the Process Model Focus Grid is the *level of granularity* of a process model. This refers to the level of detail included in the model. Detail can be characterized by the size of the smallest process step included in the process definition ("an atomic action of a process" as defined in Feiler and Humphrey (1993)). The size of the process step can be quantified, e.g. by the typical duration of the process step or effort typically expended on a process step. We have found it meaningful to divide the level of granularity into five classes: phases, activities, tasks, assignments, and transactions.[9] Again, the number of classes, their names, and their interpretation should be customized for each organization.

The level of granularity in a process definition is expressed by a rectangle in the Process Model Focus Grid (see Fig. 10). The left edge of the rectangle is determined by the size of the smallest process elements in the process model and the right-hand side by the largest process elements. For instance, a detailed inspection process may describe some activities in a meeting at a detailed level, e.g. record-keeping process, and thus the left edge of the inspection process definition would be in the transactions column. The largest process elements in an inspection process may be in the assignment level, e.g. the reading of the code to be reviewed, being an "assignment" in our example in Fig. 10. The normal size of the process can also be expressed, if desired. This is expressed by a horizontal line from the right edge of the process rectangle, ending with a small square, as shown in the inspection process in

---

[8] The taxonomy is applicable to large organizations: a small company of 20 people may not have the company-wide and functional unit scopes in their operations, given the definitions we have used. Their team scope would actually cover the whole company.

[9] Note that these terms have a specific meaning in this chapter and in this context. Readers' organizations may use some of these terms differently in their organization in their process descriptions.

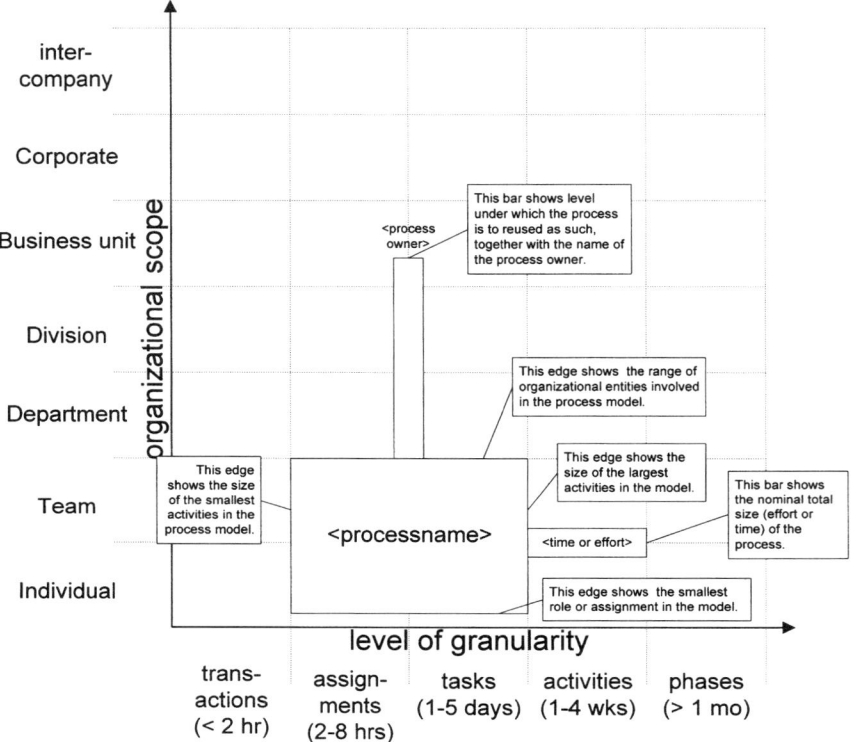

FIG. 10. Example of the Process Model Focus Grid in project characterization.

Fig. 10. Thus the granularity dimension represents two aspects of the process definition: range of granularity in process elements in the process model and the normal size of the process when it is enacted.

The organizational scope dimension of a process model is expressed by the vertical axis in the Process Model Focus Grid. The lower and upper edges of the process rectangle are determined by the range of roles and responsibilities documented in the process model. The lower edge is determined by the smallest role or agent assignments in the process. For instance, in an inspection process there may be references to the author and moderator, whereas a functional perspective of a more general review process might only make references to teams that are responsible for activities.

The upper edge of the process rectangle is determined by the range of organizational entities included in the process model. If the process involves only a single team, the upper edge is set on the top of the "team" row. If several teams are involved within a functional unit, the upper edge is extended to the functional unit line. The upper edge can also be used to represent degree of involvement. For instance, if the process model calls for participation of same, but not all, team members, the upper edge can be placed partially in the "team" row to represent the approximate share of team members to be involved.

Finally, the level of intended reuse of the process is represented by an ellipse drawn for the upper edge of the process rectangle. The ellipse contains the name of the process owner and it is drawn at a level under which all sub-units will use the same process definition.

The Process Model Focus Grid can be beneficial if it is used with appropriate flexibility. It is not intended to be a formal definition of organizational scope and granularity. Instead, it should be seen as a visualization tool that allows graphical approximations that encourage discussion and analysis. It is also quite possible to use the grid and its notations partially, e.g. by omitting the process reuse and overall length aspects initially.

5.2.2 Set Goals

The purpose of the set goals step is to define the goals and constraints for the process modeling effort. Goals and constraints should be set based on the project authorization information given by the management and on the knowledge gained in the characterization step, documented in the project characterization statement. The project authorization typically presents general goals for process modeling. However, the general goals given by the management often will need to be made more concrete and detailed. A part of this process also involves a critical review of the feasibility and appropriateness of the proposed goals. Should the more careful analysis of goals show that the initial goals were inappropriate, the new set of goals will need to be agreed on with the management.

The model of process model objective dependencies can be used to verify whether the process modeling objectives are appropriate and realistic for the organization, given the existing resources and constraints. The model presented in Fig. 5, together with the profile obtained in the characterize step (Table 4) will help in this process. By comparing the current process asset management profile against the stated objective one can evaluate the feasibility of the goals proposed. For instance, if the management has stated that the goal is to support process simulation but there is no measurement system in place, it will be necessary to make sure that the goals "support understanding and communication," "support harmonization and standardization," and "support process monitoring" are reached as well. In fact, the objective of this example may be unrealistic if the above objectives are not currently met.

Note that the set goals activity can also verify how well the process modeling objectives support process improvement and business objectives (Table 5).

One important task in the set goals activity is to make the process modeling goals measurable or testable. This may involve defining appropriate metrics for the goals, e.g. by using the Goal/Question/Metric approach (Basili, 1992; Basili *et al.*, 1994a), or providing concrete, operational definitions for determining whether the goals have been reached.

5.2.3 Plan Process Modeling

The purpose of the plan project activity is to complete the project plan for the project and select appropriate methods and tools. The project planning activity is analogous to any project planning activity: it involves effort estimation, staffing plans, and making sure that the necessary organizational issues are resolved. This process may involve several revisions to objectives and constraints. The unique aspect of the project planning activity in our method is the selection of the process modeling formalism. We recommend that the formalism is selected early in order to allow the project to get up to speed quickly.

The selection of the formalism should be done in accordance with the organization's policies. If formalisms are not currently supported, the project plan should include resources for providing the necessary infrastructure for the use of the process modeling formalisms selected.

The selection of the process modeling formalism is important as it can have a strong impact on the results of the project. We have observed that process modeling formalisms influence the process modeling process itself, as well as the information content of the process models. A formalism provides some conceptual tools for modeling the reality, and process model developers easily follow the formalism's view. This is beneficial when the formalism selected supports the purpose of the project but counterproductive when this is not the case. For instance, if the modeling of artifacts is important, it may be unwise to select a formalism that does not support the concept of artifacts well. Examples of such formalisms are SADT (Marca and McGowan, 1988) and Petri Nets (Murata, 1989).

Some support for determining the right process modeling formalism can be found in papers that compare different formalisms (Armenise *et al.*, 1993; Kellner, 1989; Kontio, 1994b; Rombach, 1991). Note that formalism comparisons done by other organizations rarely give clear answers directly. We recommend that each organization defines the selection criteria for formalism evaluation separately with respect to the goals of the project and selects a formalism that is best suited for its situation. It may also be necessary to customize the notation(s) used for the organization and modeling task (Rossi and Sillander, 1997).

Additional support for formalism selection can be obtained by comparing how well the formalisms support the critical software process information entities. Again, the model of process modeling objective dependencies can be used to support this task. In Table 5 we presented which process model information entities are critical for each process modeling objective.

5.2.4 Process Elicitation and Representation

The purpose of the process elicitation and representation activity is to develop the process models defined in the project plan. The process elicitation and representation activity has five sub-activities, as shown in Fig. 11. The conceptual analysis identifies defines the process paradigm, models the main concepts and terms in the process and, if necessary, revises the purpose and scope definition of the process. The generic process definition activity produces the generic process definition. The remaining three processes produce the enactable process definition by defining the methods, tools, roles, responsibilities, and behavior in the process. The resulting process definition is fully compatible with the architectural framework we presented earlier in this chapter.

Figure 11 presents the activities, artifacts. and information flow in the process elicitation and representation process. The following sections provide more details on the three activities presented in Fig. 11. A common activity for all processes in Fig. 11 is the elicitation of process information from various sources. This can be done through interviews, reviewing existing documents, and observing current process performance. As Rossi and Sillander have pointed out (Rossi and Sillander, 1997), triangulation, i.e. the use of multiple sources of data is important to ensure that objective and balanced information about the process is obtained.

5.2.4.1 Conceptual Analysis The purpose of the conceptual analysis activity is to define the process paradigm and identify and define the main conceptual information entities in the process. It provides the conceptual framework for the process definition. In addition, the purpose and scope definition may be revised if needed. The conceptual analysis produces two deliverables: the paradigm definition and the process concepts definition.

The paradigm definition can be a collection of statements, e.g. a set of policies or operating principles. It can be extended by references to other documents that describe the philosophy and motivation of the approaches in the process. For instance, a process modeling process of an organization

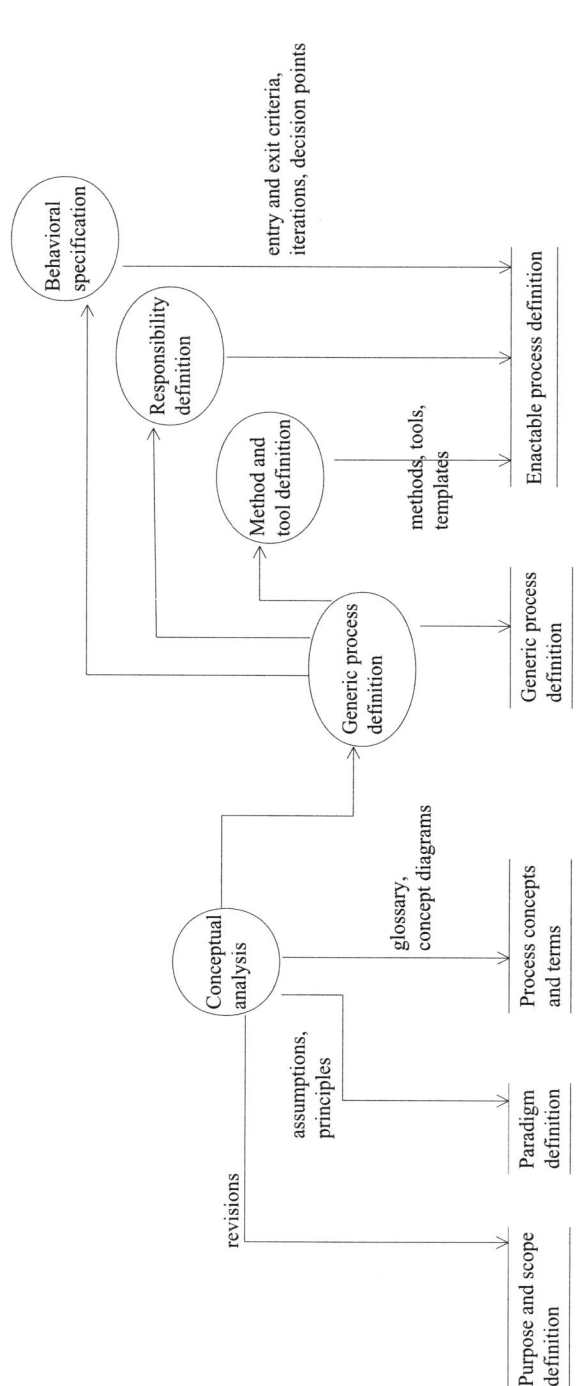

FIG. 11. The process elicitation and representation process.

might have this chapter as such an external reference to a paradigm and the following statements as concrete items in the paradigm definition:

"This process definition is meant to act as guidance; there are no requirements for process conformance. However, the process definition itself must be presented in the form and syntax included in this process definition, i.e. the process definition must be implemented on TDE using the framework presented here.

"Quality of the product is dependent on the quality of the process that produces it. Process management is one of the primary means for improving product quality.

"Process models are a key mechanism to define how an organization should work. Processes that are—or should be—repeatable must be documented so that they can be improved.

"As we are setting up our organization and processes, process definitions need to be flexible, not too formal and not too detailed. Once we have gained more experience we can refine and formalize process definitions further".

The process concept definition can take various forms. A simple form of it is a process concept dictionary, or a glossary. A process glossary is a collection of terminology definitions that can be used both during process model development and process enactment. The glossary should identify and define all main terms so that process participants can communicate effectively about the process. The main classes of concepts to be identified can be based on the entities identified in Table 6, the most important ones being activities, artifacts, and agents. For each such concept we have defined a sample template to be used in the glossary; see Table 10.

Often a mere glossary provides too narrow a perspective on the main concepts in the process. It is therefore recommended that the glossary is augmented by diagrams that can visually and more formally model the relationships between key concepts. To identify and model relationships between concepts a traditional entity relationship diagram may be used (Hull and King, 1987), but the class diagrams used in object-oriented analysis and design may provide added representational power and flexibility (Rumbaugh *et al.*, 1991; Jacobson *et al.*, 1992; Awad *et al.*, 1996). Also, modeling of artifact states may be necessary, e.g. when dealing with states of artifacts (draft → reviewed → approved). State machines (Ward and Mellor, 1985) or Statecharts (Harel, 1987) can be used for this purpose.

The process can be considered completed when the purpose and scope definition has been reviewed, and the paradigm definition as well as the process concepts and terms have been completed.

TABLE 10
EXAMPLE TEMPLATE FOR PROCESS GLOSSARY ENTRIES

Name of concept:	The name of the concept in a clear and unambiguous form
Acronym:	Optional item, defined if the acronym is likely to be needed
Description:	Clear and unambiguous description of the concept
Parent concept:	List of "parent" concepts that this concept is a refinement of
Replaced terms:	List of terms that are replaced by this concept. The use of replaced terms is not recommended any longer
Synonyms:	List of terms that are synonyms of the concept
Related terms:	List of terms that are closely related to the concept

5.2.4.2 Generic Process Definition The purpose of the generic process definition is to produce a high-level description of the main activities, artifacts, and information flows in a process. The generic process definition is used as a general process guide. It is not meant to be an enactable process definition; instead, it is high-level description of the main activities, artifacts, and information flows in the process. The lack of enactment detail make it easier to generalize and reuse the process, if required.

A number of possible process representation formalisms can be used to represent the generic process definition. For instance, dataflow diagrams (Yourdon, 1992) explicitly represent the three types of process elements and SADT (Marca and McGowan, 1988) does approximately the same.

The generic process definition can be hierarchical and a main decision issue in this task is to define the right level of granularity. The Process Model Focus Grid can be used to guide this decision. As a general rule, we recommend that the generic process definition should have processes in two to three levels, each graph containing fewer than ten process items.

5.2.4.3 Method and Tool Definition The purpose of the method and tool definition activity is to identify and define the methods, techniques, tools, and templates that can be used to support enactment of the process. Methods and techniques themselves may be defined as processes and thus reused by various other processes. They can also be more general and abstract definitions, such as references to books and internal training material. Tool definitions specify what hardware or software tools can or must be used in a task.

Templates are predefined examples and "shells" for artifacts. They can be word processor documents or design drawings in a CASE tool. They can guide and structure the process significantly by focusing activities towards "filling in the missing sections" in the template. We have found that templates are very effective tools in supporting process conformance.

5.2.4.4 Responsibility Definition
The purpose of the responsibility definition activity is to define responsibilities and interactions between process agents. It defines who participates in and who "drives" the process. Normally these are defined using organizational units or a set of roles in an organization, such as programmer, tester, or project manager.

Responsibilities can be defined textually in process descriptions, as part of process modeling notations, such as SADT resource arrows (Yourdon, 1992), or role interaction-based notations can be used to represent responsibilities and interactions explicitly (Ould and Roberts, 1987; Singh and Rein, 1992b).

5.2.4.5 Behavioral Specification
The purpose of behavioral specification is to provide an adequate definition of the dynamic behavior of the process, i.e. determine the "rules of enactment." The behavior of the process can refer to (i) *expression of control* in the process, such as transfer of state in the process or artifacts, representation of constraints that are placed on the process, synchronization points between concurrent activities, and representation of entities or relationships that control state transfers in the process; (ii) *timing of activities* in the process, such as a time-based sequence of activities, duration of activities, delays between activities, and fixed points in time in the process; (iii) *concurrency* in the process, such as overlapping phases and simultaneously enacted activities; and (iv) *conditional paths* in the process, such as iteration cycles and alternative actions.

The required level of detail in the behavioral specification depends primarily on two factors: the interpretation capabilities of the enactors and the control and synchronization requirements for the process. If the process model is interpreted by humans, its behavior can be left relatively unspecified, as humans are capable of using common sense to determine the appropriate behavioral aspect in many cases. Only such behavioral rules that are determined to be essential need to be explicitly defined. Examples of such rules include review procedures, authorization and commitment procedures, and completion rules.

If the process model is enacted by a computer or is a part of a computer-supported process environment, the level of detail required for the behavioral specification is much finer. Process engines[10] are not capable of inventing behavior, all relevant behavioral rules will need to be explicitly defined.

The other factor that determines the level of detail in the behavioral specification is the need for control and synchronization in the process. If the management requires a tight, formal control of the process, more behavioral rules will need to be expressed explicitly. The need to synchronize processes

---

[10] That is, the software interpreting the process model.

may also increase the need for behavioral detail, e.g. when there is a lot of concurrency in the process in order to reduce cycle time.

5.2.5 Experience Capture

The purpose of the experience capture process is to learn from the process modeling project to improve the modeling process for future use. The experience capture process has three main steps: collection of raw experience, analysis of this experience, and packaging of reusable experience. The collection of experience can be based on metrics collected during the process (such as effort and time), lessons learned reports, interviews, and data from pre-planned case studies or experiments (Basili *et al.*, 1996).

The analysis of the experience should involve not only the process modeling process owner but also the people who performed the actual work. The analysis methods to be used depend on the type of data available and can include anything from statistical analyses to qualitative research methods (Judd *et al.*, 1991; Simon, 1969; Yin, 1994) and to straightforward subjective discussions and brainstorming.

An important final stage in the experience capture process is the packaging and distribution of the new knowledge that was identified and evaluated. This can mean updating any guidelines or documents so that new experiences and knowledge can be reused in future projects. Packaging involves proper documentation of knowledge, training of personnel, distribution of information (either as physical documents or electronically) and institutionalization of the knowledge. In other words, the packaging activity is responsible for the *use* of the new information.

5.3 Practical Experiences

We have used the framework presented here in the past couple of years in several small process modeling tasks. However, more recently we have used the whole framework in documenting the key processes of a business division of the Nokia Corporation. The conceptual framework presented here was implemented on a cooperative design repository that allowed linking of process model information on various levels (Taivalsaari and Vaaraniemi, 1997).

The design repository used, the Telecom Design Environment (TDE), supports specific diagramming notations that were selected as the process modeling formalisms. Furthermore, the TDE environment allows multidimensional linking of this information between any element in the framework, making the utilization of such links even more powerful than available in HTML code (Taivalsaari, 1997). The TDE environment also allows

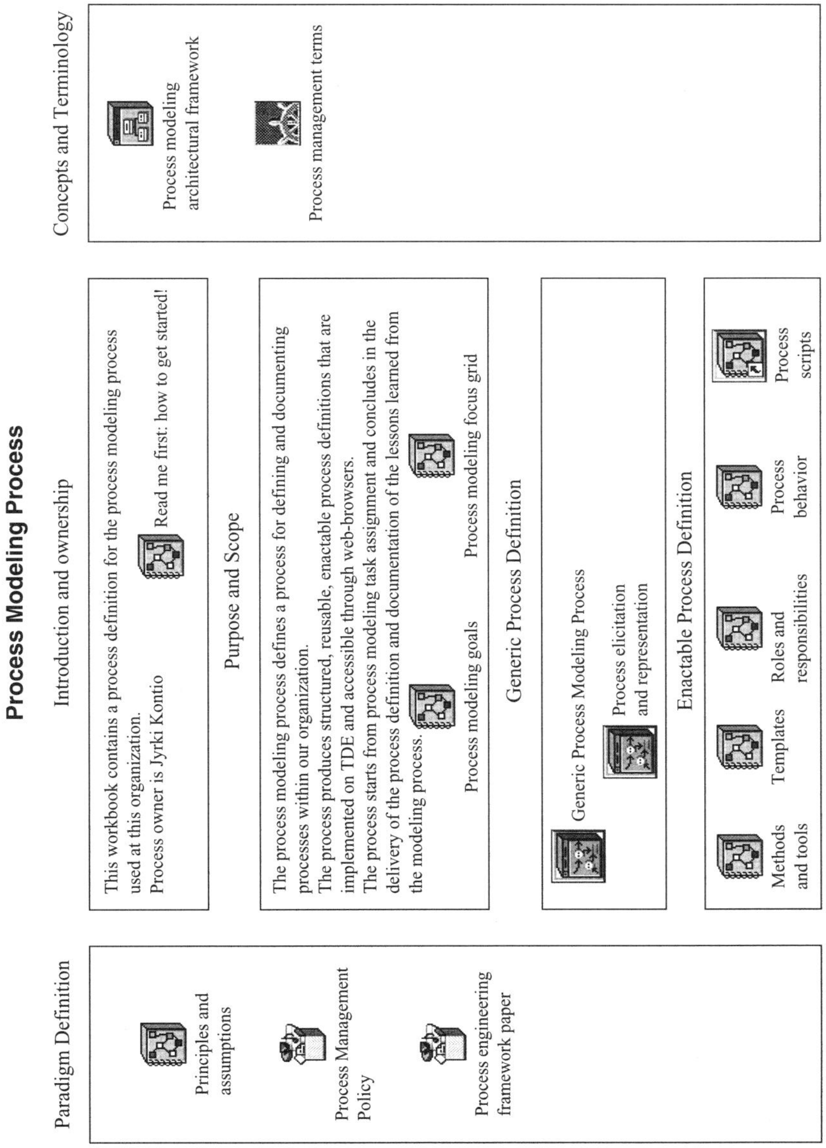

A SOFTWARE PROCESS ENGINEERING FRAMEWORK

Process Modeling Process

Concepts and Terminology
- Process modeling architectural framework
- Process management terms

Introduction and ownership
This workbook contains a process definition for the process modeling process used at this organization.
Process owner is Jyrki Kontio
Read me first: how to get started!

Purpose and Scope
The process modeling process defines a process for defining and documenting processes within our organization.
The process produces structured, reusable, enactable process definitions that are implemented on TDE and accessible through web-browsers.
The process starts from process modeling task assignment and concludes in the delivery of the process definition and documentation of the lessons learned from the modeling process.

- Process modeling goals
- Process modeling focus grid

Generic Process Definition
- Generic Process Modeling Process
- Process elicitation and representation

Enactable Process Definition
- Methods and tools
- Templates
- Roles and responsibilities
- Process behavior
- Process scripts

Paradigm Definition
- Principles and assumptions
- Process Management Policy
- Process engineering framework paper

FIG. 12. Front page of the process modeling process in the TDE environment.

process owners to edit process definitions interactively and concurrently, if necessary, regardless of their geographical location. For users that only need to browse—not edit—the process definitions, the TDE environment has a World Wide Web interface that allows the browsing of the process definition using a Web browser.

We implemented the whole process engineering framework in the TDE environment and used the multidimensional linking possibilities extensively. Figure 12 presents the front page of our TDE implementation of the framework. Any item on the framework can be used to browse further and links to relevant information are extensively included at all levels. For instance, a data-flow based process in the "generic process definition" includes links to specific method and tools definitions that are relevant to that process, as well as links to roles and responsibilities and entry and exit criteria for the process.

We have documented practically all the main processes of a division at Nokia Telecommunications using the framework described here. The process owners and process engineers have found the framework useful and consider it a structured and maintainable way to document and model the process asset within the organization. Although we lack appropriate comparison data, it seems that the framework enables process owners to focus their modeling efforts and structure otherwise fuzzy and "hard-to-grab" process information. It also seems that our framework and process may take less time and effort compared with earlier process modeling experiences.

The general user acceptance of our process engineering framework has been good. However, less frequent users have perceived the framework to be complex and theoretical, complaining that they easily get lost in the framework. For processes that think their agents may not want to use the framework we have defined a traditional paper document that contains the same information as in the framework in Fig. 12. Such a document is easier to read for many people but, of course, lacks the ability to link process information as extensively as in the TDE implementation.

6. Conclusions

We have presented a comprehensive framework for process engineering and a process modeling process in this chapter. It is clear that when dealing with such a broad topic as process management there is no single model or approach that would fit the needs of all organizations and situations. Therefore, while the initial experiences from the use of the framework are positive, the framework presented here should be considered as a first step towards one of the models that can be used to model and manage processes more effectively.

We believe that our framework is a useful tool for process management, for the following reasons. First, it provides a useful and understandable framework for documenting different information about the process. The meaning and relationships of process information can be discussed and explicitly viewed from different perspectives.

Second, abstraction of the information in a process is notation independent. Process engineers can focus on the substance and semantics of the process information that is being modeled, instead of being constrained by the syntax of a single notation. Traditionally a process modeling formalism easily dictates the information content in a process model.

Third, the framework provides a standard frame of reference between the people using it, making it easy to communicate about and understand the different process. People do not have to learn process modeling notations and syntax to be able to discuss their process.

Fourth, the modular structure of the framework supports more effective reuse of the process. As process model information is conceptually separated into components, especially in the enactable process definition level, it is easier to identify what parts of a process can be reused as such and which require localization. For instance, in reusing a review process, an organization could re-assign the roles and responsibilities but use other parts of the process as such.

Finally, the definition of the process modeling process itself allows more effective process modeling to take place and, as we are using a consistent and standard approach, it allows accumulation of experience that will lead to continuous improvement of the process.

We believe that the above benefits are particularly relevant for large software development organizations, where process management and reuse play an important role. On the other hand, for smaller organizations the model may be less useful; informal ways of communication may allow the process management to take place implicitly, yet quite effectively.

The way we develop software influences the characteristics of the software we produce. However, our understanding of the exact role and influence of different process characteristics to the product characteristics is far from clear. This is the challenge for the software process management community—to reach a better understanding of the factors that influence product and process quality. The field of software process management attempts to do exactly that: identify better ways of producing software and making them work in practice. The framework presented here will hopefully help in making the software development process more visible and manageable.

Acknowledgments

I would like to thank professor Victor R. Basili for his inspiration and support during the time most of this work was done. I am grateful to my colleagues Kari Alho from Helsinki University of Technology and Simo Rossi and Timo Kaltio from Nokia Telecommunication and Nokia

Research Center, respectively. They provided several important corrections and new insights that greatly helped improve this work.

REFERENCES

Anonymous (1989) Response time is the next competitive weapon. *Chief Executive* 72–73.

Anonymous (1992) *The American Heritage Dictionary of the English Language*, 3rd edn. Microsoft Bookshelf/Houghton Mifflin Company.

Abdel-Hamid, T. K., and Madnick, S. E. (1991) *Software Project Dynamics, An Integrated Approach.* Prentice-Hall, Englewood Cliffs NJ.

Armenise, P., Ghezzi, C., and Morzenti, A. (1993) A survey and assessment of software process representation formalisms. *Int. J. Softw. Eng. Knowl. Eng.* **3**, 401–426.

Armitage, J. W., and Kellner, M. I. (1994) A conceptual schema for process definitions and models. *Proceedings of the Third International Conference on the Software Process.* Washington, IEEE Computer Society. pp. 153–165.

Armitage, J. W., Briand, L., Kellner, M. I., Over, J., and Phillips, R. W. (1994) *Software Process Definition Guide: Content of Enactable Software Process Representations.*

Armitage, J. W., Briand, L., Kellner, M. I., Over, J. W., and Phillips, R. W. (1995) *Software Process Definition Guide: Content of Enactable Software Process Representations.* Unpublished draft report.

Awad, M., Kuusela, J., and Ziegler, J. (1996) *Object-Oriented Technology for Real-Time Systems.* Prentice Hall, Upper Saddle River.

Bandinelli, S. C., Baresi, L., Fuggetta, A., and Lavazza, L. (1993a) Requirements and early experiences in the implementation of the SPADE repository. *Proceedings of the 8th International Software Process Workshop*, (ed. W. Schäfer). Wadern, Germany. IEEE Computer Society Press, Los Alamitos. pp. 30–32.

Bandinelli, S. C., Fuggetta, A., and Ghezzi, C. (1993b) Software process model evolution in the SPADE environment. *IEEE Transactions on Software Engineering* **19**, 1128–1144.

Bandinelli, S. C., Di Nitto, E., and Fuggetta, A. (1994) *Policies and Mechanisms to Support Process Evolution in PSEEs.* IEEE Computer Society Press, Washington DC. pp. 9–20.

Basili, V. R. (1989) Software development: A paradigm for the future. *Proceedings of the 13th Annual Computer Software and Applications Conference (COMPSAC).* IEEE Computer Society Press, Washington, DC. pp. 471–485.

Basili, V. R. (1992) *Software Modeling and Measurement: The Goal/Question/Metric Paradigm.* CS-TR-2956. University of Maryland, College Park MD.

Basili, V. R. (1993) The experience factory and its relationship to other improvement paradigms. *Proceedings of the 4th European Software Engineering Conference.* Springer-Verlag, Berlin.

Basili, V. R., and Caldiera, G. (1991) *Methodological and Architectural Issues in the Experience Factory.* NASA, Greenbelt MD. pp. 17–28.

Basili, V. R., and Rombach, H. D. (1991) Support for comprehensive reuse. *Software Engineering Journal* **6**, 303–316.

Basili, V. R., and Turner, A. (1975) Iterative enhancement: a practical technique for software engineering. *IEEE Transactions on Software Engineering* **1**, 390–396.

Basili, V. R., Caldiera, G., and Cantone, G. (1991) *A Reference Architecture for the Component Factory.* UMIACS-TR-91–24. University of Maryland, College Park MD.

Basili, V. R., Caldiera, G., and Cantone, G. (1992a) A reference architecture for the component factory. *ACM Transactions on Software Engineering and Methodology* **1**, 53–80.

Basili, V. R., Caldiera, G., McGarry, F., Pajerski, R., Page, G., and Waligora, S. (1992b) The software engineering laboratory—an operational software experience factory. *Proceedings of* the *International Conference on Software Engineering*, May 1992. IEEE Computer Society Press, Washington DC. pp. 370–381.

Basili, V. R., Caldiera, G., and Rombach, H. D. (1994a) Goal question metric paradigm. *Encyclopedia of Software Engineering* (ed. J. J. Marciniak). John Wiley & Sons, New York. pp. 528–532.

Basili, V. R., Caldiera, G., and Rombach, H. D. (1994b) The experience factory. *Encyclopedia of Software Engineering* (ed. J. J. Marciniak). John Wiley & Sons, New York. pp. 470–476.

Basili, V. R., Green, S., Laitenberger, O., Lanubile, F., Shull, F., Sørumgård, S., and Zelkowitz, M. V. (1996) The empirical investigation of perspective-based reading. *Empirical Software Engineering* **1**, 133–164.

Bean, T.J., and Gros, J. G. (1992) R&D benchmarking at AT&T. *Research & Technology Management* **35**, 32–37.

Benington, H. D. (1956) Production of Large Computer Programs. *Proceedings of ONR Symp. Advanced Programming Methods for Digital Computers*, June, pp. 15–27.

Boehm, B. W. (1981) *Software Engineering Economics*. Prentice Hall, Englewood Cliffs.

Boehm, B. W. (1987) Software Process Management: Lessons Learned from History. *Proceedings of the 9th International Conference on Software Engineering*, Monterey, California. IEEE Computer Society Press, Washington DC. pp. 296–298.

Boehm, B. W., (1988) A spiral model of software development and enhancement. *IEEE Computer* **21**, 61–72.

Boehm, B. W., and Bels, F. (1989) Applying process programming to the spiral model. *ACM SIGSOFT Software Engineering Notes* **14**, 46–56.

Brandl, D. (1991) Modeling and describing really complex processes. *Texas Instruments Technical Journal* May–June, 21–27.

Brandl, D., and Worley, J. H. (1993) An implemented object model of the software engineering process. *Journal of Systems and Software* **23**, 171–181.

Buetow, R. C. (1994) A statement from Motorola regarding ISO 9000. *American Programmer* **7**, 7–8.

Burrel, G., and Morgan, G. (1979) *Sociological Paradigms and Organizational Analysis*. Heineman, London.

Champy, J. (1995) *Reengineering Management: The Mandate for New Leadership*, HarperBusiness, New York.

Chichakly, K. J. (1993) The bifocal vantage point: managing software projects from a systems thinking perspective. *American Programmer* **6**, 18–25.

Christie, A. M. (1993) A graphical process definition language and its application to a maintenance project. *Information and Software Technology* **35**, 364–374.

Conradi, R., Fernström, C., and Fuggetta, A. (1993) A conceptual framework for evolving software process. *ACM SIGSOFT Software Engineering Notes* **18**, 26–35.

Conradi, R., Fernström, C., and Fuggetta, A. (1994) Concepts for evolving software process. *Software Process Modelling and Technology* (eds A. Finkelstein, J. Kramer, and B. Nuseibeh) Research Studies Press, Somerset. pp. 9–31.

Conradi, R., Fernström, C., Fuggetta, A., and Snowdon, R. (1992) Towards a reference framework for process concepts. *Proceedings of the Second European Workshop on Software Process Technology*, Trondheim. Lecture Notes in Computer Science, 635. Springer-Verlag, Berlin. pp. 2–17.

Cook, J. E., and Wolf, A. L. (1995) Automating Process Discovery through Event-Data Analysis. *Proceedings of the 17th International Conference on Software Engineering*, Seattle WA. ACM, New York. pp. 73–82.

Crowley, J., and Silverthorn, M. (1991) Software artifacts: recorded information in STEP. *Texas Instruments Technical Journal*, May–June, pp. 38–47.

Culver-Lozo, K., and Gelman, S. (1993) A process definition methodology for software development organizations. *Proceedings of the seventh International Software Process Workshop*, Yountville, California. IEEE Computer Society Press, Los Alamitos. pp. 54–56.

Curtis, B., and Paulk, M. C. (1993) Creating a software process improvement program. *Information and Software Technology* **35**, 381–386.

Curtis, B., Krasner, H., Shen, V., and Iscoe, N. (1987) On building software process models under the lamppost. *Proceedings of the 9th international conference on software engineering*, Monterey, California. IEEE Computer Society Press, Los Alamitos. pp. 96–103.

Curtis, B., Krasner, H., and Iscoe, N. (1988) A field study of the software design process for large systems. *Communications of the ACM* **31**, 1268–1287.

Curtis, B., Kellner, M. I., and Over, J. (1992) Process Modeling. *Communications of the ACM* **35**, 75–90.

Daskalantonakis, M. K. (1992) A practical view of software measurement and implementation experiences within Motorola. *IEEE Transactions on Software Engineering* **18**, 998–1010.

Deming, W. E. (1986) *Out of the Crisis*. Massachusetts Institute of Technology, Cambridge.

Dorling, A. (1993) SPICE: Software Process Improvement and Capability dEtermination. *Information and Software Technology* **35**, 404–406.

Dowson, M. (1993) Software process themes and issues. *Proceedings of the 2nd International Conference on the Software Process*, Berlin. IEEE Computer Society Press, Los Alamitos. pp. 54–62.

Dowson, M., Nejmeh, B. A., and Riddle, W. E. (1991) Concepts for Process Definition and Support. *Proceedings of the 6th International Software Process Workshop*. IEEE, Washington DC. pp. 87–90.

Dutton, J. E. (1993) Commonsense approach to process modeling. *IEEE Software* **10**, 56–64.

Feiler, P. H., and Humphrey, W. S. (1993) *Software Process Development and Enactment: Concepts and Definitions*. IEEE Computer Society Press, Los Alamitos. pp. 28–40.

Fernström, C. (1993) PROCESS WEAVER: adding process support to UNIX. *Proceedings of the 2nd International Conference on the Software Process*, Berlin. IEEE Computer Society Press, Los Alamitos. pp. 12–26.

Finkelstein, A., Kramer, J., and Nuseibeh, B. (1994) *Software Process Modeling and Technology*, John Wiley & Sons, New York.

Frailey, D. J., Bate, R. R., Crowley, J., and Hills, S. (1991) Modeling information in a software process. *Proceedings of the First International Conference on the Software Process*, Redondo Beach, California. IEEE Computer Society Press, Los Alamitos. pp. 60–67.

Fuggetta, A. (1993) A classification of CASE technology. *IEEE Computer* **26**, 25–38.

Garg, P. K., and Jazayeri, M. (1994) Selected, annotated bibliography on process-centered software engineering environments. *ACM SIGSOFT Software Engineering Notes* **19**, 18–21.

Gelman, S. (1994) Silver bullet: an iterative model for process definition and improvement. *AT&T Technical Journal* **73**, 35–45.

Haase, V., Messnarz, R., Koch, G. R., Kugler, H. J., and Decrinis, P. (1994) Bootstrap: fine-tuning process assessment. *IEEE Software* **11**, 25–35.

Hammer, M. (1990) Reengineering work: don't automate, obliterate. *Harvard Business Review*, July–August, pp. 104–112.

Hammer, M., and Champy, J. (1993) *Reengineering the Corporation—A Manifesto for Business Revolution*. HarperBusiness, New York.

Harel, D. (1987) Statecharts: a visual formalism for complex systems. *Science of Computer Programming* **8**, 231–274.

Harel, D., Lachover, H., Naamad, A., Pnueli, A., Politi, M., Sherman, R., and Shtul-Trauring, A. (1988) *STATEMATE: A Working Environment for the Development of Complex Reactive Systems*. IEEE Computer Society, Los Alamitos. pp. 396–406.

Harrington, H. J. (1991) *Business Process Improvement. The Breakthrough Strategy or Total Quality, Productivity and Competitiveness.* McGraw-Hill, New York.

Heineman, G. T., Botsdorf, J. E., Caldiera, G., Kaiser, G. E., Kellner, M. I., and Madhavji, N. H. (1994) Emerging technologies that support a software process life cycle. *IBM Systems Journal* **33**, 501–529.

Hirschheim, R., and Klein, H. K. (1989) Four paradigms of information systems development. *Communications of the ACM* **32**, 1199–1216.

Hull, R., and King, R. (1987) Semantic database modeling: survey, applications and research issues. *ACM Computing Surveys* **19**(3), 201–260.

Humphrey, W. S. (1990) *Managing the Software Process.* Addison-Wesley, Reading MA.

Humphrey, W. S., and Kellner, M. I. (1989) Software process modeling: principles of entity process models. *Proceedings of the 11th International Conference on Software Engineering.* ACM, New York. pp. 331–342.

Huseth, S., and Vines, D. (1987) Describing the Software Process. *Proceedings of the 3rd International Software Process Workshop*, Breckenridge CO. IEEE Computer Society Press, Washington DC. pp. 33–35.

Höltje, D., Madhavji, N. H., Bruckhaus, T. F., and Hong, W. (1994) *Eliciting Formal Models of Software Engineering Processes.* IBM Canada.

ISO (1987) *ISO 9001, Quality systems—Model for quality assurance in design/development, production, installation and servicing.* International Organization for Standardization, Geneva.

ISO (1991a) *Information technology—Software product evaluation—Quality characteristics and guidelines for their use, ISO/IEC 9126:1991(E).* 1st edn. International Organization for Standardization, Geneva.

ISO (1991b) *ISO 9000-3, Guidelines for the application of ISO 9001 to the development, supply and maintenance of software, ISO 9000-3:1991(E).* International Organization for Standardization, Geneva.

Jaccheri, M. L., and Conradi, R. (1993) Techniques for process model evolution in EPOS. *IEEE Transactions on Software Engineering* **19**, 1145–1156.

Jacobson, I., Christerson, M., Jonsson, P., and Overgaard, G. (1992) *Object-Oriented Software Engineering: A Use Case Driven Approach.* Addison-Wesley, Reading MA.

Jacobson, I., Ericsson, M., and Jacobson, A. (1995) *The Object Advantage: Business Process Re-engineering with Object Technology.* Addison-Wesley, Reading MA.

Judd, C. M., Smith, E. R., and Kidder, L. H. (1991) *Research Methods in Social Relations*, 6th edn. Harcourt Brace Jovanovich College Publishers, Fort Worth TX.

Kaiser, G. E., Barghouti, N. S., and Sokolsky, M. (1990) Preliminary experience with process modeling in the Marvel SDE kernel. *Proceedings IEEE 23rd Hawaii International Conference on System Sciences.* IEEE Computer Society Press, Los Alamitos, CA. pp. 131–140.

Kaplan, R. B., and Murdock, L. (1991) Core Process Redesign. *The McKinsey Quarterly* No. 2, pp. 27–43.

Katayama, T. A. (1989) A Hierarchical and Functional Software Process Description and its Enaction. *Proceedings of the 11th International Conference on Software Engineering.* ACM, New York. pp. 343–352.

Kellner, M. I. (1989) Representation formalisms for software process modeling. *ACM SIGSOFT Software Engineering Notes* **14**, 93–96.

Kellner, M. I. (1991) Software Process Modeling Support for Management Planning and Control. *Proceedings of the 1st International Conference on the Software Process*, Redondo Beach, California. (ed. M. Dowson). IEEE Computer Society, Los Alamitos. pp. 8–28.

Kellner, M. I. (1996) A Method for Designing, Defining and Evolving Software Processes. *Proceedings of the 1996 SEPG Conference*, Atlantic City NJ. SEI, Pittsburgh PA.

Kellner, M. I., and Hansen, G. A. (1989) Software Process Modeling: A Case Study. *Proceedings of the 22nd Annual Hawaii International Conference on System Sciences* **2**. IEEE Computer Society, Washington DC. pp. 175–188.

Kellner, M. I., and Rombach, H. D. (1991) Session summary: comparison of software process descriptions. *Proceedings of the 6th International Software Process Workshop*, Hakodate, Japan. IEEE Computer Society, Los Alamitos. pp. 7–18.

Kitson, D. H., and Masters, S. M. (1993) An Analysis of SEI Software Process Assessment Results: 1987–1991. *Proceedings of the 15th International Conference on Software Engineering*, Baltimore, Maryland. IEEE Computer Society Press, Los Alamitos. pp. 68–77.

Koch, G. R. (1993) Process assessment: the "BOOTSTRAP" Approach. *Information and Software Technology* **35**, 387–403.

Kontio, J. (1994a) *Nokia's Software Process Modeling Guidelines*. Internal deliverable PI_1.2 of the Process Improvement Project.

Kontio, J. (1994b) *Software Process Modeling: A Technology Review and Notation Analysis*. Nokia Research Center Report, Process Improvement Project deliverable PI_1.6.

Kontio, J. (1995) *Promises: A Framework for Utilizing Process Models in Process Asset Management*. Licentiate thesis at Helsinki University of Technology.

Kontio, J. (1996) *Process Modeling Guide*. Nokia Research Center, Helsinki.

Krasner, H., Terrel, J., Linehan, A., Arnold, P., and Ett, W. H. (1992) Lessons learned from a software process modeling system. *Communications of the ACM* **35**, 91–100.

Kuhn, T. S. (1970) *The Structure of Scientific Revolutions*, 2nd edn. University of Chicago Press, Chicago.

Kumar, K., and Welke, R. J. (1992) Methodology engineering: a proposal for situation-specific methodology construction. *Challenges and Strategies for Research in Systems Development* (eds W. W. Cotterman and J. A. Senn). John Wiley & Sons, New York. pp. 257–269.

Lai, R. C. T. (1991) *Process Definition and Process Modeling Methods*. Research Report SPC-91084-N, Software Productivity Consortium.

Lehman, M. M. (1987) Process models, process programs, programming support. *Proceedings of the 9th international conference on software engineering*, Monterey, California. IEEE Computer Society Press, Los Alamitos. pp. 14–16.

Lehman, M. M. (1991) Software engineering, the software process and their support. *Software Engineering Journal*, pp. 243–258.

Longchamp, J. (1993) A structured conceptual and terminological framework for software process engineering. *Proceedings of the 2nd International Conference on the Software Process*, Berlin. IEEE Computer Society Press, Los Alamitos. pp. 41–53.

Lott, C. M. and Rombach, H. D. (1993) Measurement-based guidance of software projects using explicit project plans. *Information and Software Technology* **35**, 407–419.

Mackenzie, R. A. (1969) The management process in 3-D. *Harvard Business Review* 80–87.

Madhavji, N. H. (1991) The process cycle. *Software Engineering Journal* 234–242.

Madhavji, N. H., and Schäfer, W. (1991) Prism—methodology and process-oriented environment. *IEEE Transactions on Software Engineering* **17**(12), 1270–1283.

Madhavji, N. H., Höltje, D., Hong, W., and Bruckhaus, T. F. (1994) *Elicit: A Method for Eliciting Process Models*. IEEE Computer Society Press, Washington DC. pp. 111–122.

Marca, D. A., and McGowan, C. L. (1988) *SADT Structured Analysis and Design Technique*. McGraw-Hill, New York.

Mathews, J. (1995) The little reengine that can't always. *The Washington Post*, March 9, B10–B12.

McCracken, D. D., and Jackson, M. A. (1982) Life-cycle concept considered harmful. *ACM SIGSOFT Software Engineering Notes* **7**, 29–32.

McGarry, F., Pajerski, R., Page, G., Waligora, S., Basili, V. R., and Zelkowitz, M. V. (1994)

Software Process Improvement in the NASA Software Engineering Laboratory. CMU/SEI-94-TR-22. Software Engineering Institute, Pittsburgh PA.

Murata, T. (1989) Petri nets: properties, analysis and applications. *Proceedings of the IEEE* **77**, 541–580.

Notkin, D. (1989) Applying software process models to the full life cycle is premature. *ACM SIGSOFT Software Engineering Notes* **14**, 116–117.

Ochimizu, K., and Yamaguchi, T. (1987) A process-oriented architecture with knowledge acquisition and refinement mechanisms on software processes. *Proceedings of the 6th International Software Process Workshop*, Hakodate, Japan. IEEE Computer Society Press, Washington DC.

Olson, T., Reizer, N., and Over, J. W. (1994) *A software process framework for the SEI Capability Maturity Model.* CMU/SEI-94-HB-001. Software Engineering Institute, Pittsburgh PA.

Osterweil, L. J. (1987) Software processes are software too. *Proceedings of the Ninth International Conference on Software Engineering.* IEEE Computer Society, Washington DC. pp. 2–13.

Ould, M. A. (1992) *Process Modeling with RADS.* Praxis Technology/TRMC.

Ould, M. A., and Roberts, C. (1987) Modeling iteration in the software process. *Proceedings of the Third International Software Process Workshop.* IEEE Computer Society, Washington DC. pp. 101–104.

Paulk, M. C. (1998) Software process appraisal and improvement: models and standards. *This volume.* pp. 1–33.

Paulk, M. C., Curtis, B., Chrissis, M. B., and Weber, C. V. (1993a) *Capability Maturity Model for Software*, Version 1.1. SEI-93-TR-024. Software Engineering Institute, Carnegie Mellon University, Pittsburgh PA.

Paulk, M. C., Weber, C. V., Garcia, S. M., Chrissis, M. B., and Bush, M. (1993b) *Key Practices of the Capability Maturity Model.* SEI-93-TR-025. Software Engineering Institute, Pittsburgh. PA.

Pearlstein, S. (1995) "Reengineering management": a sequel of musings and mush. *The Washington Post*, 29, January, H7.

Penedo, M. H., and Shu, C. (1991) Acquiring experiences with the modelling and implementation of the project life-cycle process: the PMDB work. *Software Engineering Journal* pp. 259–274.

Pfleeger, S. L. (1993) Lessons learned in building a corporate metrics program. *IEEE Software* **10**, 67–74.

Pralahad, C. K., and Hamel, G. (1990) The core competencies of the corporation. *Harvard Business Review* 79–91.

Radice, R. A., Roth, N. K., O'Hara, A. C., and Ciarfella, W. A. (1985) A programming process architecture. *IBM Systems Journal* **24**, 79–90.

Riddle, W. E. (1989) Session summary, opening session. *Proceedings of the 4th International Software Process Workshop*, Moretonhampstead, Devon, UK *ACM SIGSOFT Software Engineering Notes* **14**, 5–10.

Rombach, H. D. (1991) A framework for assessing process representations. *Proceedings of the 6th International Software Process Workshop.* IEEE Computer Society, Los Alamitos. pp. 175–183.

Rombach, H. D., and Verlage, M. (1993) How to Assess a Software Process Modeling Formalism from a Project Member's Point of View. *Proceedings of the 2nd International Conference on the Software Process*, Berlin, Germany. IEEE Computer Society, Washington DC.

Rossi, S., and Sillander, T. (1997) *Four Fundamental Software Process Modeling Principles.* M.Sc. Thesis, University of Jyväskylä.

Royce, W. W. (1970) Managing the Development of Large Software Systems. *Proceedings of the IEEE WESCON*. IEEE, New York. pp. 1–9.

Rumbaugh, J., Blaha, M., Premerlani, W., and Lorensen, W. (1991) *Object-Oriented Modeling and Design*. Prentice Hall, Englewood Cliffs NJ.

Saiedian, H., and Kuzara, R. (1995) SEI Capability Maturity Model's impact on contractors. *IEEE Computer* **28**, 16–26.

Simon, J. L. (1969) *Basic Research Methods in Social Science*. Random House, New York.

Singh, B. (1992) *Interconnected Roles (IR): A Coordination Model*. CT-084-92 MCC, Austin TX.

Singh, B., and Rein, G. L. (1992) *Role Interaction Nets (RINs): A Process Description Formalism*. CT-083-92 MCC, Austria TX.

Stalk, G. Jr (1988) Time—The next source of competitive advantage. *Harvard Business Review* 41–51.

Taivalsaari, A. (1997) *Multidimensional Browsing*. IEEE Computer Society Press, Washington DC. pp. 11–22.

Taivalsaari, A., and Vaaraniemi, S. (1997) *TDE:* Supporting Geographically Distributed Software Design with Shared, Collaborative Workspaces. *Proceedings of the CAiSE'97 Conference*, Barcelona, Spain. Springer-Verlag, Berlin. pp. 389–408.

Thayer, R. H. (1988) Introduction to tutorial. *Tutorial: Software Engineering Project Management* (ed. R. H. Theyer). IEEE Computer Society, Washington DC.

Thomas, M., and McGarry, F. (1994) Top-down vs. bottom-up process improvement. *IEEE Software* **11**, 12–13.

Ward, P., and Mellor, S. (1985) *Structured Development for Real-time Systems*. Prentice Hall, Englewood Cliffs NJ.

Yin, R. K. (1994) *Case Study Research: Design and Methods*, 2nd edn. Sage Publications, Thousand Oaks CA.

Yourdon, E. (1992) *Decline and Fall of the American Programmer*. Prentice Hall, Upper Saddle River NJ.

Gaining Business Value from IT Investments

PAMELA SIMMONS

*Senior lecturer and
manager of post-graduate courses at the
School of Information Technology
Swinburne University of Technology
Melbourne, Australia*

Abstract

The evaluation of information technology (IT) investments has been of concern to researchers and industrial management for many years. Much of the discussion has been concerned with techniques: the difficulty in measuring the less tangible benefits, the problems surrounding the application of the most commonly used method, cost–benefit analysis and the search for a better approach. This chapter reviews the progress made in these areas. The need for a flexible evaluation method that includes not only the financial but also the more strategic benefits, and that can be applied to the diversity of IT investment decisions is highlighted.

The impact of the context in which IT evaluation takes place—the business context, organizational culture, and management style—on an organization's criteria for effectiveness and its attitude towards evaluation is examined. It is also recognized that benefits will not accrue automatically; the IT system provides the opportunity for changing business methods and processes, but it is these changes that will lead to the benefits, not the system itself. Thus the business changes and the delivery of the benefits need to be proactively managed; a model for managing this process is proposed.

If investments in IT are to result in enhanced business value, the focus of IT evaluation must change—from a "once-off" exercise, undertaken as a means of gaining approval for the investment, to seeing IT evaluation as part of a process which identifies the benefits, assigns responsibility for delivering them, plans for the organizational change which will be required, and regularly monitors the achievement. In this chapter, we consider the entire process of managing the IT investment: the initial justification, including specifying and measuring the benefits, making the investment decision and, continuing after implementation, managing the realization of the expected benefits.

1. Introduction 110
2. The Evaluation Problem 113
   2.1 Changing Role of IT 113

2.2	Relationship Between IT and Business Performance	114
2.3	Evaluation of IT Investments	116
3.	Measuring IT Value	117
3.1	Value	117
3.2	Benefits	119
3.3	Classifying and Measuring Benefits	123
4.	Evaluation Methods	126
4.1	Cost–Benefit Analysis	127
4.2	Alternative Methods	129
4.3	Current Practices	138
5.	Evaluation Frameworks	138
6.	The Investment Decision	141
6.1	Content	142
6.2	Context	144
6.3	Process	145
7.	Managing the Benefits	146
8.	Conclusion	152
References		154

1. Introduction

Since the early 1970s, senior management and researchers have been concerned with the problem of determining the contribution of information technology (IT) to organizations' business performance. Over this time, organizations have become increasingly dependent on IT and in turn, IT has demanded an increasing proportion of available resources. Expenditure on information processing and communications rose 14.6% annually from 1975 to 1985 and annual investment in IT represents half of total corporate capital spending (Keen, 1991). Willcocks and Lester (1996) reported that by 1996 UK company expenditure on IT was estimated as exceeding £33 billion per year, equivalent to an average of 2% of annual turnover.

In the early days of corporate computing, the assumption was held, largely unquestioned, that this investment would lead to more efficient operations which would in turn be reflected in the standard measures of business performance. But studies of IT expenditure and business performance have not generally been able to substantiate the assumption that increased investment in IT can be linked to improved business performance (Roach, 1988; Loveman, 1988; Kauffman and Weill, 1989). It is therefore not surprising that senior executives are questioning the wisdom of continuing to invest in IT at such high levels. The respondents to a Datamation survey (1991) expressed doubts concerning the real benefits of IT investment. A study of Australian and New Zealand organizations revealed that information systems managers in these countries have similar concerns; the problem of determining the return on IT investments was considered important by 65% of the managers questioned (Broadbent *et al.*, 1992). In a survey reported by Hochstrasser and Griffiths (1991), only 24% of managers were positive that their IT investments showed a higher than average return on capital when compared with other investments.

The problem of justifying investments in IT has existed since computers were introduced to the business world (as evidenced by a conference on the Economics of Informatics held by the International Federation for Information Processing (IFIP) in 1961), but the changing role of IT in organizations means that the nature of the problem has evolved. The early applications of IT were directed towards improving efficiency, usually through staffing reductions, but by the late 1970s the concept of IT enabling competitive advantage emerged, with the much reported experience of American Airlines and their computer reservation system, Sabre. Although it is now questioned whether IT provides sustainable competitive advantage (Earl, 1989), in a 1980 report to its board of directors American Airlines concluded that 1980 profits would have been $78.5 million lower if American had not had Sabre (Rotemberg and Saloner, 1991).

Since the mid-1980s, it has been recognized that the role of IT is being influenced by two important trends. First, there have been rapid advances in the capabilities of IT (such as increased power and improved communications), together with dramatic reductions in cost. Concurrently, organizations in both public and private sectors have been exposed to severe competitive pressures and turbulence in their spheres of operation. If they are to survive, organizations must react to these external forces associated with environmental turbulence. IT offers the opportunity for organizations to react constructively (Scott Moreton, 1991). As a result of research conducted during the MIT 1990s program, Scott Moreton suggested that the three findings—new ways of doing work, electronic integration, and the shifting competitive climate—present organizations with an opportunity, if not a pressing need, to step back and rethink their mission and the way they are going to conduct their operations. Thus IT does more than automate support functional processes. It is increasingly being applied to the core of businesses; more than just automating, it is transforming industries, organizations, business processes and management methods (Farbey *et al.*, 1993).

The term "transformation" indicates the extent of the organizational change that is required if the benefits of these newer IT investments are to be realized. IT does not on its own deliver benefits, but it provides opportunities for delivering benefit (Ward *et al.*, 1996). To take advantage of these opportunities, changes must be made to the way business activities are performed or the way in which information is used. The pursuit of organizational enhancement through the use of IT demands organizational change (Eason, 1988). The benefit will only result from these changes. This implies that if the desired benefit is to achieved, the necessary organizational changes must be actively managed. This concept of *benefits management* is comparatively new; it has long been recognized that costs must be continually monitored and controlled, but not generally accepted that benefits will not accrue automatically but need to be monitored and managed.

Moreton (1995) suggested that we have yet to achieve the full potential of IT, and in order to succeed in the environment of the 1990s, organizations and their information systems must be flexible and able to respond rapidly to change. His statement that "The ability of any organization to exploit IT is determined by the pace at which change can be absorbed" (Moreton, 1995, p. 159) highlights the importance of managing the change resulting from IT. Information systems analysts tend to place more importance on systems matters than organizational and people issues, but Moreton suggested that they should continue to work with the business users after implementation and help them exploit, master, and extend the information system and the use of information.

Both the literature and practice of IT evaluation have until comparatively recently been focused on the initial project justification, with little attention being paid to evaluating whether the expected benefits were actually achieved. Although project methodologies usually include some form of post-implementation review, surveys have shown that few organizations regularly conduct these reviews, and when performed, they tend to focus on the development process (Kumar, 1990; Simmons, 1993). But the leading organizations have recognized that regular reviews can be part of a program which encourages business management to manage the organizational change and resulting benefits actively (Simmons, 1993).

> In the 1990s, IT is perceived not as a technical issue but as a management issue. As the technology becomes more mature and reliable, the management focus has shifted from controlling the technology to controlling the business, and the implications of the human and organizational impact of large-scale IT deployment (Hochstrasser and Griffiths, 1991).

Thus a new view of IT evaluation is emerging. Framel (1993) described the traditional "expense management" approach, which focused on cost containment, as adopting a narrow and short-term view of value with little business management direction. This traditional approach was a once-off exercise undertaken in order to obtain project approval and with little expectation that the achievement of the proposed benefits would be monitored; Ward *et al.* (1996, p. 218) reported that in their survey, "many respondents openly admitted that their current project justification processes overstated the benefits in order to get approval, hence benefits are claimed which are unlikely to be achieved in practice." However, an alternative view considers the entire life approach to managing IT investments in order to gain the maximum value from the investment. Framel (1993) suggested that a value management approach, which is management driven, focusing on business need and opportunity with a broader and longer term view of value is required. This view recognizes that the benefits will not be achieved without active management, and throughout the whole project life the focus should be on obtaining the maximum business value from the investment.

In this chapter, we will consider the entire process of managing the IT investment: the initial justification, including specifying and measuring the benefits, making the investment decision and, continuing after implementation, managing the realization of the expected benefits.

2. The Evaluation Problem

The difficulties with justifying investment in IT go back to the early days of corporate computing; in the early 1970s authors raised the issue of achieving effective rather than merely efficient use and began to question the application of cost–benefit analysis to such decisions. Knutsen and Nolan (1974) were probably the first to suggest that cost savings or return on investment should not be the only consideration. Keen (1975) also identified that it was increasingly difficult to apply cost–benefit analysis to systems concerned with aiding management decisions and that the problem of qualitative benefits must be addressed.

2.1 Changing Role of IT

Since these particular problems with justifying IT investments were identified, over 25 years ago, the changing role of IT has exacerbated the difficulties while forcing senior management to pay greater attention to IT decisions.

The trend towards the application of IT to mainstream or core business processes means that the benefits resulting from IT are much wider than cost and staffing reductions. For example, interorganizational systems, such as electronic document interchange (EDI), significantly change how organizations conduct business with their suppliers and customers. Mukhopadhyay *et al.* (1995) described how the introduction of EDI at Chrysler improved communication between Chrysler and its suppliers, facilitating the implementation of frequent, accurate delivery schedules and reducing buffer inventories.

The increased dependency of organizations on IT has been accompanied by a continued increase in IT spending. For example, a survey by Morgan and Banks revealed that the Australian financial services sector spends an average

13.5% of revenues on IT (*Australian Financial Review*, 18 July 1996). But in many industries, it is necessary to spend vast amounts on information systems just to stay in business. In banking, for example, an enormous IT infrastructure is required and few banks expect to derive significant competitive advantage from their large investments in IT. But failing to spend, or spending inappropriately, can lead to competitive disadvantage.

IT can no longer be managed solely within functional or even organizational boundaries; the broad reach and interrelatedness of information systems mean that the strategic issues must be addressed at senior management levels.

This evolution in the role of IT in organizations has necessitated a similar modification to the nature of IT investment evaluation. Hogbin and Thomas (1994) describe investment in IT as changing from affecting a single business area, with the risks being mainly technical, to cross-functional systems with a high degree of organizational risk. As a result, evaluation needs to take a holistic perspective rather than a mainly financial one, and to focus on strategic opportunities rather than on cost savings and shorter term tactical benefits.

So, as the amount being spent on IT increases, senior management is increasingly concerned that IT should provide value for money. At the same time, the techniques that have traditionally been used to evaluate capital investments such as return on investment (ROI) and cost–benefit analysis (CBA) are not able to capture the strategic benefits that result from the organizational transformation enabled by IT. Moreton (1995) emphasized the importance of organizations needing to respond to the fundamental changes in the global market-place by effecting organizational transformations which balance short-term financial benefits against the best possible basis for long-term survival and growth. The criteria inherent in IT evaluation techniques should be derived from these multidimensional objectives. Farbey *et al.* (1993) argued that better evaluation processes are required, as evaluation provides the driving forces for the implementation of successful strategic IT.

2.2 Relationship Between IT and Business Performance

The widespread concern of senior management regarding the value obtained from their IT investments is partly a reflection of the difficulty in demonstrating a relationship between IT and business performance on a broader scale.

Studies investigating the relationship between IT expenditure and various measures of business performance at all levels of analysis have generally not been able to demonstrate that increased IT investment was related to improved business performance (Kauffman and Weill, 1989). Hitt and

Brynjolfsson (1996) suggested that this confusion concerning the payoff of IT and the seemingly contradictory results were due to the issue of IT value not being a single question, but composed of several related but distinct issues:

(1) Have investments in IT increased productivity?
(2) Have investments in IT improved business profitability?
(3) Have investments in IT created value for consumers?

Analyzing data on 370 firms over a five-year period revealed:

(1) IT investment had a significant impact on firm output.
(2) No evidence of link between IT investment and profitability.
(3) But total benefit to consumers was substantial.

This indicates that it is possible for firms to realize productivity benefits from the effective management of IT, without seeing those benefits translate into higher profitability. The results suggested that, on average, "firms are making the IT investments necessary to maintain competitive parity but are not able to gain competitive advantage." (Hitt and Brynjolfsson, 1996, p. 139). They reported other researchers whose work supports the argument that while IT creates enormous value, in many cases it is the consumers who benefit, for example in banking and computerized share trading.

A study by Barua et al. (1995) took a similar direction; they identified separately the intermediate and final output variables for measuring IT contribution in the manufacturing sector. The study revealed a significant impact of IT on intermediate variables (e.g. capacity utilization, inventory turnover, product quality), but little impact on return on assets or market share.

Moreton (1995) suggested that the model adopted by most organizations limits their ability to realize the potential gains offered by IT. He proposed that as a consequence of adopting an organizational model based on Taylor's concept of "scientific management," organizations have suffered a loss of business flexibility, both in terms of productive capability and in terms of culture and employee relations. IT has generally been introduced using Taylor's organizational model (with a focus on internal efficiency and inflexible work processes) which, Moreton suggested, is not appropriate in times of change nor when the business objective relies on organizational change. He proposed that an "organic" model, that values and fosters learning, understanding, and responsiveness, and which is flexible and delegates authority to meet and exploit new opportunities, would be more suited to harnessing the potential offered by IT.

2.3 Evaluation of IT Investments

Evaluation supports decision-making both at the justification stage (*ex ante*) and after implementation (*ex post*). Good evaluation techniques will assist the organization to identify those investments that will make the greatest contribution to meeting organizational goals and will then allow the organization to determine whether the project's objectives have been achieved. Although there is great scope in seeking innovative ways to serve customers better through the use of IT, yielding benefits that can be individual to each company, there is little evidence that this opportunity is being significantly exploited. Hochstrasser and Griffiths (1991) suggested that the comparatively small proportion of IT investments directed towards the external effectiveness of a company has resulted from the difficulty in measuring, in immediate financial terms, the payback from these longer-term investments.

Hogbin and Thomas (1994) emphasized the importance of the evaluation process, suggesting that the process itself is as important as the result it generates. The processes which are used to evaluate the system may not reveal the softer benefits and the impact that the system may have in human and organizational terms. They may even positively obscure them (Farbey *et al.*, 1993).

Although there are some difficulties in determining the cost of IT projects (the allocation of fixed costs can be arbitrary, and estimating development and lifetime costs is still difficult and unreliable), the greater challenge results from the identification and measurement of the benefits. Again the preceding discussions point to a number of major problems.

- Many applications are targeted at achieving indirect benefits. There is broad agreement in the literature that the difficulties involved in the evaluation of IT investment stem from the indirect or supporting role that IT usually plays in the organizational business processes (Whiting *et al.*, 1996). It is difficult to predict the extent to which improved information will lead to better decision-making and even if this is so, placing a value on the better decision presents a new set of problems (Farbey *et al.*, 1993).

- Frequently, the IT investment is an integral part of a business initiative which involves major organizational changes. In these cases, the organizational change needs to be actively managed and it is more appropriate to evaluate the entire business initiative, not the IT component in isolation (Simmons, 1993; Willcocks, 1996). Research indicates that the quality of management is an important factor in adding value to the organization (Weill, 1989).

- Many investments are directed towards improving customer service or quality. The immediate beneficiary of such changes is the consumer; the

benefits to the organization are likely to be longer term through retaining market share or repeat business (Hitt and Brynjolfsson, 1996).
- Investments in the IT infrastructure are usually intended to provide flexibility and enable later investments, rather than lead to a direct economic benefit (Weill and Broadbent, 1994). Keen (1991) suggested that such investments should be justified by the requirements of corporate policy.
- Despite high levels of spending, there is a widespread lack of understanding that IT is a major capital asset, bought by the high annual expenditure (Willcocks, 1996). Investment in IT increases the asset base of the organization, but the investment perhaps allows an increased volume of business to be handled by fewer staff. Thus return on assets as a measure of performance does not favour a strategy based on reducing current expenditure and building a capital base (Keen, 1991).
- Even when the investment targets cost savings—e.g. a reduction in headcount—the actual savings realized by reducing the work of the office staff by, say, 15% are unlikely to reduce the headcount by the same percentage (Farbey *et al.*, 1993).

Thus the evaluation of IT investments continues to present many challenges. Willcocks (1996) summarized the current dilemma for organizations attempting to manage IT investments—for competitive reasons they cannot afford not to invest in IT, but economically cannot find sufficient justification, and evaluation practice does not provide sufficient underpinning, for making the investment decision.

3. Measuring IT Value

The general concern about whether IT provides value for money stems from one of two situations: it may be either that "value" is not delivered or value is not recognized (Remenyi *et al.*, 1995). There needs to be agreement on what constitutes value and appropriate measures of performance derived.

3.1 Value

Analyzing the definitions of value provided by the *Shorter Oxford English Dictionary*:
- that amount of a commodity, medium of exchange etc., considered to be an equivalent for something else;
- a fair or satisfactory equivalent or return;

- relative status or merit according to the estimated desirability or utility of a thing,

Orna (1996) identified the key terms to be "considered," "estimated," and "relative." He concluded that establishing a value is always an indirect process that involves finding appropriate equivalents and standards, not necessarily in money terms, and the subjective nature of value is clearly acknowledged. Value is dependent on context and perception. Or, as Strassman (1988, p. 18) expressed it, "questions of IT's value are settled when one decides how to measure it." Information Economics, the evaluation technique developed by Parker and Benson (1988), extended the traditional purely economic view of value to encompass the broader objectives of the organization, including such dimensions as strategic direction and exposure to technological risk.

Marchand and Horton (1986, p. 21) asserted that "information and knowledge are factors of production as authentic and as critical as capital and labour" and the value of an information system is inextricably linked with the value of information produced by that system (Ahituv, 1989). Thus the problem of placing a value on an information system may be largely due to the difficulty of placing a value on the output of that system, information. In fact, Moody and Walsh (1996) asserted that information is the underlying business asset; the hardware and software are merely mechanisms used to create and maintain information. They considered alternative approaches for evaluating assets and suggested that different valuation paradigms are appropriate for different types of information.

Although this framework assists in identifying how different types of information held by an organization may be valued, other researchers argue that the value of information cannot be isolated from the medium that encapsulates and processes it. Van Wegan and De Hoog (1996, p. 248) argued that focusing on information alone ignores the "furnishing" aspect of information; the need to send the information to the right person, at the right time and location and in the right form. "[A]lthough information of course acquires its value from its role in decision making, the information product as a whole also adds (furnishes) value to the other activities in information processing." They therefore affirmed that the object of valuation should be the information system as a special type of information commodity.

This consideration of the valuation of information has highlighted some of the reasons for the difficulty in ascribing value to an information system, but has not yielded a solution. Cronk and Fitzgerald (1996, p. 130) suggested that "IT business value represents a rich complex reality that cannot be distilled or collapsed into a few simple measurements." Before progress can be made on the measurement of IT business value, a better understanding of the construct itself is required. They proffered the following definition:

> IT business value is the sustainable value added to the business by IT, either collectively or by individual systems, considered from an organizational perspective, relative to the resource expenditure required.

They identified three sources of value:

- System-dependent characteristics—value attributed as a result of the type and characteristics of the system.
- Organization-dependent characteristics—value attributed as a result of alignment with business strategy.
- Organizational impact—value attributed to the role the system plays in the organization, and recognized also the influence of the context surrounding the system and the evaluation process.

This multidimensional view of IT business value is based on the *source* of the value; an alternative multidimensional perspective that considers the *impact* of the system will be discussed in the next sections, which explore the range of benefits offered by investments in IT, differing approaches to classifying the benefits, and how they might be measured.

3.2 Benefits

A number of authors have made a contribution to the classification of IT benefits, recognizing that IT can add value in different ways (e.g. Eason, 1988; Berger, 1988; Carlson and McNurlin, 1989). The earliest information systems focused on improving organizational efficiency by automating routine clerical functions, reducing costs, and improving productivity, but it was soon recognized that the application of IT to the mainstream business processes could yield greater benefits (Knutson and Nolan, 1974). McDowell (in Carlson and McNurlin, 1989) identified three levels of benefit.

- Efficiency—these benefits impact an organization's operating efficiency by allowing it to do more with existing resources, do the same with fewer resources, or grow using fewer resources than otherwise would be required.
- Effectiveness—these benefits come from improving the organization's effectiveness, such as improving the timeliness and accuracy of information or the quality of presentation.
- Value added—all benefits at this level directly support the critical success factors of the organization and usually require organizational change.

The changing role of IT has resulted in a wider range of benefits, with the emphasis shifting from internal efficiency to external relationships and markets. Farbey *et al.* (1993) provided some examples of the newer types of application:

- Competitive advantage—e.g. increasing bargaining power in the competitive arena, creating barriers to entry, tying in customers.
- Cooperative advantage—strategic alliances based on IT.
- Diversification—widening business scope, offering new products.
- Marketing—improving customer service, targeting markets, adding value to products.
- Effective management—improving delivery information, getting new products to market faster, providing a just-in-time service.

Hochstrasser and Griffiths (1991) described how the Kobler Unit find it useful to distinguish between how well a company succeeds in optimizing its internal organization, and how well it succeeds in operating within its external market environment. The opportunities offered by IT are then assessed by how IT can contribute to improving a company's efficiency in getting the job done with the minimum of waste, improving a company's effectiveness in selling its products, and building up a loyal and expanding customer base. Figure 1 illustrates some examples of IT applications that support organizations" aims in these three areas of improving internal efficiency, enhancing external effectiveness and developing new markets.

It is sometimes suggested that this type of categorization of benefits represents a development of IT maturity and that organizations should progress through such stages or levels of benefit, learning how the organization can best utilize IT by first implementing systems that focus on internal efficiencies. However, the study conducted by Hochstrasser and Griffiths found that the more successful companies were able to address these different business aims simultaneously through a well-balanced strategy of appropriate IT deployment. The less successful practice was found to be a strategy that concentrates on developing IT investments in a single area to the exclusion of others. Hochstrasser and Griffiths suggested that the IT application strategy of progressing from efficiency to external effectiveness and then looking at new markets seriously restricts the true business potential of IT.

Their study also demonstrated that, in general, the emphasis for future investments is still strongly slanted towards gaining internal efficiency and that developing the external effectiveness is regarded as a lower priority activity (see Fig. 2).

Peters (1996) placed benefit categories on a continuum, recognizing that categorization is, to some extent, artificial. At one end of the continuum

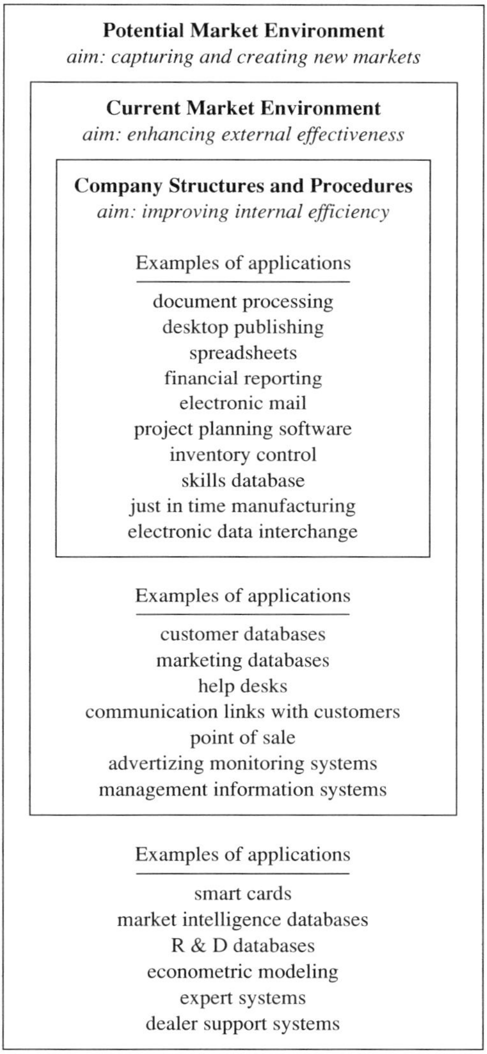

Potential Market Environment
aim: capturing and creating new markets

Current Market Environment
aim: enhancing external effectiveness

Company Structures and Procedures
aim: improving internal efficiency

Examples of applications
―――――――――――――
document processing
desktop publishing
spreadsheets
financial reporting
electronic mail
project planning software
inventory control
skills database
just in time manufacturing
electronic data interchange

Examples of applications
―――――――――――――
customer databases
marketing databases
help desks
communication links with customers
point of sale
advertizing monitoring systems
management information systems

Examples of applications
―――――――――――――
smart cards
market intelligence databases
R & D databases
econometric modeling
expert systems
dealer support systems

FIG. 1. IT applications that can help to improve internal efficiency, enhance external effectiveness and develop new markets.

he placed benefits associated with enhancing productivity, and at the other benefits associated with business expansion. Between these two extremes, he placed the category of risk minimization—examples include benefits that occur through improvements in quality, minimizing accounting losses, and reducing the risk of failure, shutdown, or the loss of market share.

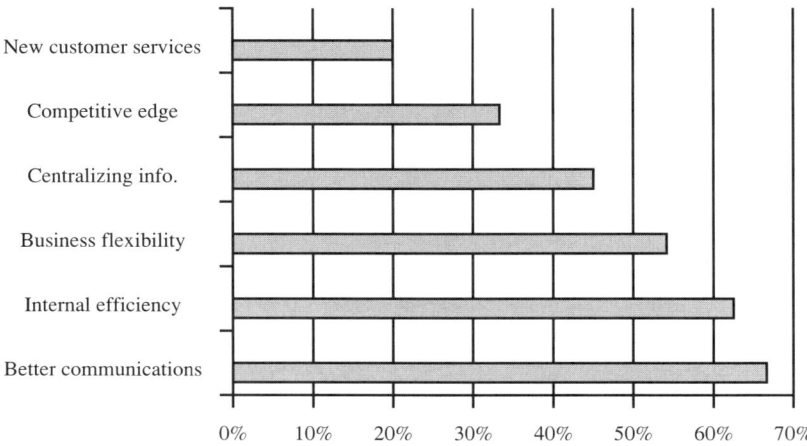

FIG. 2. Priorities for future IT investments.

The nature of the continuum enables benefits to span more than one category and allows the relative positioning of different benefits to be compared.

Kaplan and Norton (1992) have developed a simple but powerful measurement framework that integrates the different perspectives that are important to management. This Balanced Scorecard encourages management to look beyond the financial performance and to consider a more complete set of perspectives that reflect the longer term prospects of the organization. It incorporates four views:

- Customer—How do our customers see us?
- Financial—How do we look to our shareholders?
- Internal—What must we excel at?
- Innovation and learning—How can we continue to improve and create value?

The organization's goals in each of these areas are determined and appropriate performance measures derived. Assessing IT on the extent to which it contributes to each of these multidimensional goals and measures will assist management to apply IT across the full spectrum of business objectives.

Much of the difficulty associated with demonstrating the impact of IT stems from the intangible nature of many of the benefits. Efficiency gains are comparatively easy to measure, but the impact of applications which are directed towards enhancing external effectiveness and developing new markets is more difficult to quantify. Most authors equate the terms tangible/intangible with quantified/unquantified (e.g. Hogbin and Thomas, 1994) but Remenyi *et al.* (1995) distinguished between them. They defined a tangible benefit as one that directly influences the business and a quantifiable benefit as one that can be objectively measured.

An alternative view perceives tangible–intangible as a scale or spectrum, relating tangibility to the degree of agreement about the attribute (Farbey *et al.*, 1993). However, Hogbin and Thomas (1994, p. 181) suggested that the limiting factor is the lack of a direct connection between the function provided and the effect on the performance parameter. They provided a practical definition of an intangible benefit: "[it] cannot be confidently quantified or directly and solely related to the implementation of the IT application," suggesting that the real problem is the associated degree of certainty, as it does not give an absolute measure of the impact of the change brought about by the new investment.

Although measuring these intangible benefits remains a problem, it has not prevented organizations from investing in systems which are directed towards organizational enhancement. An analysis of the benefits expected from 50 large projects revealed that the "top ten" benefits (ranked in order of importance to top management) included changing the way in which the organization does business (number 1), access to information, enhancing competitive advantage, and enabling the organization to respond more quickly to change (Mirani and Lederer, 1993). Thus it is essential that the evaluation criteria and techniques allow the consideration of these less tangible benefits.

3.3 Classifying and Measuring Benefits

A number of approaches to classifying the benefits have been presented in the literature, but how do such classifications assist evaluation? They certainly provide some structure to the list of benefits, and having a framework or set of categories can serve as a prompt, suggesting potential opportunities for benefit that had not been considered (Farbey *et al.*, 1993). Categorizing the benefits also assists in measuring them; some of the benefits classifications include recommendations as to how each type of benefit may be measured. By mapping benefit types against the orientation of their IT investments, Peters (1994) also showed how organizations could compare their overall IT investment strategy with their business objectives.

We have already described the approach taken by the Kobler Unit, which classified benefits according to whether they increased internal efficiency, enhanced external effectiveness, or developed new markets (Hochstrasser and Griffiths, 1991). A similar set of benefits was developed by the author, but in addition to the categories of increased efficiency, increased effectiveness, and added value, categories covering marketable products and the IT infrastructure were included (Simmons, 1996).

Farbey *et al.* (1993) developed their framework by analogy with Mintzberg's model of organizational structure, leading to benefits associated with strategy, management, operational efficiency and effectiveness, functionality, and support. They also considered that an information systems perspective was required, and so added categories associated with informing, communications, and learning. A similar but more simply structured classification can be derived from the four perspectives (customer, financial, internal effectiveness, organizational learning) of Kaplan and Norton's Balanced Scorecard (1992).

The selection of appropriate performance measures is important, as the measures adopted largely reflect the amount of value that is uncovered (Strassman, 1988); in addition they can influence the behavior of an organization and where it places its emphasis (Carlson and McNurlin, 1989). A model of IS success, developed by DeLone and McLean (1992) and based on a very comprehensive analysis of the literature, shows the different levels of the impact of an information systems (system quality, information quality, use, user satisfaction, individual impact, and organizational impact) and thus the different levels at which benefits may result. The benefits that are directly attributable to the functionality of an IT system may be several steps removed from the actual achievements of profits, making it difficult to quantify the value of the investment in financial terms (Whiting *et al.*, 1996).

Benefits that result from increased efficiency are the most easily quantified, with the impact measured in terms of cost avoidance or cost reduction. Although it is more difficult to measure enhanced effectiveness in financial terms, case studies provided examples of organizations identifying how better information can lead to direct economic savings (Simmons, 1994). For example:

- The information produced by a human resources system would allow sick leave to be better controlled and therefore reduced.
- More accurate raw materials inventory would reduce the inventory cost.
- Increased time available for negotiation would lead to better contract prices.

Benefits that enhance the strategic position of the organization are generally directed outside the organization, towards its customers and trading partners, and measuring the impact of such initiatives presents great difficulty. The chain of causation from system functionality to the factor which is of value to the company, for example competitive advantage, may be complex and uncertain (Whiting *et al.*, 1996). Even though the perception of the customer towards a new banking service can be measured by survey, the translation into increased market share cannot be assumed. Conversely, an improved market share is not necessarily the result of the new service; many other factors (other changes within the bank, actions by competitors or the general economic and political environment) can confound the effect.

Although it is generally difficult to measure the more strategic benefits in financial terms, it is often possible to measure them if a broader concept of measurement is adopted. We are not limited to the standard accounting measures; the process of measurement involves "the definition and calibration of a metric, determination of a reference, standard and goal, monitored observations, comparison of observations against a standard and a record of the result" (Kauffman and Kriebel, 1988). The Balanced Scorecard technique complements financial measures with operational measures on customer satisfaction, internal processes, and the organization's innovation and improvement activities (Kaplan and Norton, 1992). These operational measures, derived from the organization's key objectives, are the drivers of future financial performance and provide very sound performance targets against which the contribution of an IT investment may be measured.

Quantifying the expected benefits is important at the initial justification stage, as it facilitates an objective rational decision-making process, but it is also important that the expected benefits are specified in a way that can be monitored after implementation. It is now recognized that the potential of an IT investment will only be fully realized if the outcomes are actively managed. The expected benefits must therefore be expressed in operational terms that can be monitored so that business managers are able to determine whether further organizational change is required.

Utilizing such operational indicators to measure the business impact of an IT investment is of course facilitated if the organization's activities are already being guided and controlled by using such performance measures. As Remenyi *et al.* (1995) pointed out, for target levels of future performance to be meaningful they should be based on an existing known level of performance, and ideally a history of data is required so that an understanding of random and periodic variations can be gained.

An alternative way of presenting the link between operational performance parameters and their potential financial impact is shown in Fig. 3. This emphasizes two concepts: the migration from numerical to financial performance criteria, and the integration of many small savings and of cross-functional linkages (Hogbin and Thomas, 1994).

This section has presented a number of alternative ways of categorizing benefits. Although the approaches described were quite similar, there is no agreed "best" framework, each author presenting a slightly different view. But there was consensus that the evaluation method adopted should recognize the broad range of benefits that can result from an investment in IT and that measurement should not be restricted to financial performance. Increasingly, organizations are measuring IT business value by its impact on operational indicators that are derived from the organization's key objectives.

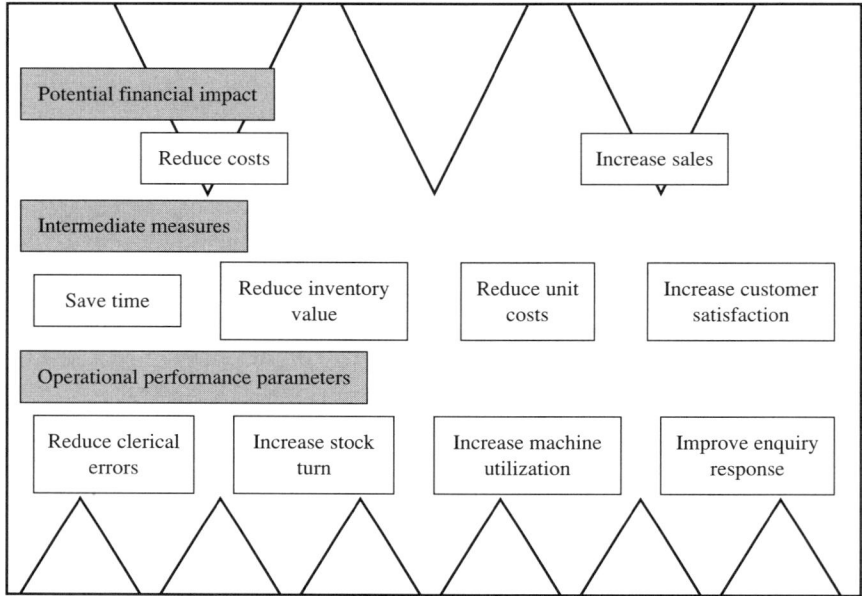

FIG. 3. The potential financial impact of operational performance parameters.

4. Evaluation Methods

A wide range of methods for evaluating IT have been proposed and reviewed in the literature, covering many aspects of evaluation and examining the impact of IT at all levels, from the effect on an individual to the impact of IT on the national economy, but this review of evaluation methods will be confined to those that are suggested for application at the level of the IT project. This discussion will also be restricted to those methods that aim to assess the value resulting from an IT investment, either at the justification stage (*ex ante*) or after implementation (*ex post*), rather than methods which provide formative feedback on the development process. Blackler and Brown (1988) suggested that a considerable gap exists between the work being done by researchers and evaluation as it is practiced in industry; we therefore need to consider characteristics such as complexity, ease of communication, degree of precision and quantification, the facilities provided by the method, congruency with established IT methodologies, and the extent of senior management involvement if the methods are to be of use to industry practitioners (Farbey *et al.*, 1993).

Hirschheim and Smithson (1988) based their classification of evaluation approaches on the underlying assumptions about the whole process of evaluation. The nature of these assumptions can be thought of as a continuum ranging from the highly objective and rational at one end to the subjective or political at the other. At the objective end of the scale, the field of economics suggested methods, such as Frontier Analysis and Data Envelope Analysis, which measure the relative efficiency of a production process, and work done in operations research has led to the work measurement approaches. Cost–benefit analysis originated as an accounting tool in the justification of capital expenditure, but enhancements have been proposed to overcome some of the problems that arise from applying CBA to IT projects. These enhancements broaden the concept of benefit and include in the analysis some of the intangible and subjective benefits which are not encapsulated in the traditional application of the method, and this approach has therefore progressed a little towards the subjective end of the continuum. Other approaches do not even attempt to measure objectively the benefits of a system, but accept that there will be a number of benefits, often described in terms of the organization's objectives, and subjective assessments of the system's contribution to these goals are made. These methods are more suited to a comparison of projects, rather than assessing the absolute value of a single project. Finally, entirely subjective methods have been suggested, for example, the surrogate measure of user satisfaction.

Within the range of objective techniques, Remenyi *et al.* (1995) distinguished between a deterministic evaluation approach which uses single point estimates for input values (e.g. costs, benefits), thus generating a single estimate of the result (e.g. internal rate of return), and stochastic methods that recognize that input values are estimates rather than known values. The latter approach accommodates, rather than ignores, the inherent variability in the input estimates and produces a result that reflects the level of uncertainty experienced in the real world. Costs and benefits are specified as ranges, and simulation techniques are used to generate a distribution of the possible outcomes. This graphical representation used in Fig. 4 clearly shows the uncertainty associated with the outcome.

First, however, this examination of evaluation methods will begin with a discussion of the method which is most frequently used by organizations, cost–benefit analysis.

4.1 Cost–Benefit Analysis

As Parker and Benson pointed out, the management practice of justifying information systems projects is well established. "The logic is clear: the anticipated benefits from investments in IT should be greater than the costs" (Parker and Benson, 1988, p. 62). This consensus led to the utilization of the technique known as cost–benefit analysis (CBA).

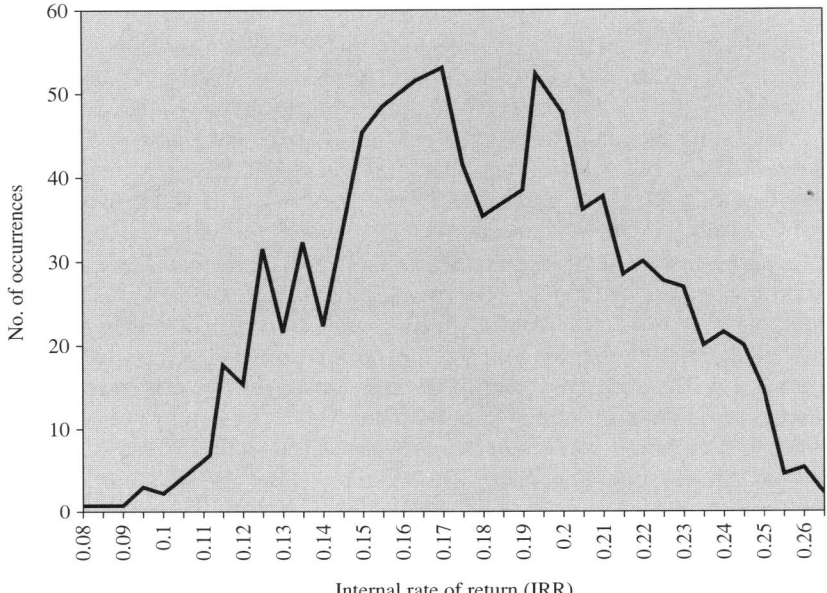

FIG. 4. Graphical representation of risk analysis of results for IRR.
Source: Remenyi *et al.* (1995).

Sassone and Schaffer (1978) defined CBA as "an estimation and evaluation of net benefits associated with alternatives for achieving defined public goals." Copp (1985) described CBA as a family of techniques and approaches, as it is applied in widely differing ways which depend on the particular application and the theoretical perspective held by the experimenter. He defined CBA as (p. 129):

> a means of evaluating and ranking proposed social policies and projects; and it uses economic techniques to assign quantitative values (usually monetary values) to the different costs and benefits of various options for social choice, and to aggregate these values into a quantitative measure of each of the options.

All of the costs and benefits to all of the individual members of the relevant society are supposed to be taken into account, discounting future costs and benefits. He suggested that the standard procedures of CBA lacked adequate rationale, particularly when applied to the evaluation of social programmes and "when issues other than efficiency are involved, it is arguable that CBA should recede into the background" (Copp, 1985, p. 133).

As early as 1974, Knutsen and Nolan identified that the real issue is that computer-based systems are agents of change, and they questioned the applicability of CBA to investments in IT. A number of authors have expressed concern over the deterministic nature of CBA, which tends to mask the uncertainty concerning the outcomes of the project. "A general weakness of the cost benefits approach is that it requires knowledge, accuracy and confidence about issues which for innovations are unknown, ill-defined and uncertain" (Keen, 1981, p. 12). A further problem identified by Keen in the same paper was that CBA is highly sensitive to assumptions, such as discount rates, and needs "artificial and often arbitrary modifications" to handle qualitative factors such as the value of improved communications or improved job satisfaction. This concern over the *meaning* of some of the data used in CBA was echoed by Chismar and Kriebel who, from their experiences in working with organizations, found that such an exercise required "as much creativity and art as it does precision" (Chismar and Kriebel, 1985, p. 46). In order to present a more realistic picture of the uncertainty of the outcome, Ward *et al.* (1996) suggested that use of these techniques should be accompanied by a clear statement of the confidence attached to each piece of information.

Although there is general agreement in the literature on the problems arising from the use of CBA in assessing IT projects, it remains a popular method (Simmons, 1993; Ward *et al.*, 1996). Lay (1985) suggested that the popularity of the technique stems from a desire by management to base decisions on quantifiable costs and benefits, and they are either unaware, or choose to ignore, the inaccuracy and uncertainty surrounding these figures. The CBA process is usually portrayed as a rigorous, scientific procedure, but it masks the highly subjective nature of many of the assumptions made.

Despite the very substantial effort devoted by researchers to the problem of evaluating IT, it would seem that little real progress has been made since the difficulties of applying CBA to the evaluation of IT were first identified over twenty years ago. The contribution of some of the alternative evaluation methods proposed in the literature, classified according to their theory base and their place on the rational/objective continuum, will now be discussed.

4.2   Alternative Methods

4.2.1   Methods Derived from Economics

4.2.1.1   Production Frontier Analysis Chismar and Kriebel (1985) viewed an organization or strategic business unit as "an economic artifact engaged in production processes." The business unit utilizes input resources to produce its desired output and the efficiency of the production process may be determined by comparing the levels of input utilized with the levels of output produced. In comparing production across firms, microeconomics provides the concept of a frontier which defines industry's "best practice" and provides a reference from which to judge the efficiency of firms. A more recent application of the production frontier approach to the problem of measuring the efficiency with which IT has been utilized has used the term

Data Envelopment Analysis (DEA) to describe essentially the same process. Kauffman and Kriebel (1988) applied this method to a network of 30 automatic teller machines (ATM). DEA was used to measure and compare the technical efficiency of the ATMs as production units.

This method can provide some insights into the comparative efficiency of different units and in particular the extent to which IT is being efficiently used to displace other costs. However, external influences on productivity are not part of this type of analysis and Kauffman and Kriebel suggested that DEA is better suited to input reduction. The comparisons of efficiency may also be misleading as time lags between investment and the resulting performance are often ignored. This approach requires actual input and output data from existing production systems and so cannot be used to justify a new investment, although it may contribute to the review of the performance of existing systems. However, it does not provide an absolute measure of the value obtained from an investment in IT.

4.2.1.2 Business Value Linkage Impact Analysis Banker and Kauffman (1988a) proposed this method which considers the inputs to the local production process (labour, materials, capital, energy, and IT), the intermediate processes influenced by IT, and the set of outputs attributable to or modified by the IT investment. This method recognizes the different types of impact and addresses their measurement in different ways. Banker and Kauffman proposed that econometric models be developed to explain variations in labour usage and operating efficiency, sales forecasting models be used to estimate future direct revenues, and econometric models be developed to represent the competitive environment. They demonstrated how this method (or suite of methods) could be applied to an ATM network (Banker and Kauffman, 1988b).

Although Banker and Kauffman stressed the need for "simple and intuitive" methods to determine the relationship between business value and information technology (Banker and Kauffman, 1988a), the econometric models they developed were far from simple. However, the variables that were used were meaningful in business terms and management was able to relate the results to the business environment. In many cases, the link between the information system and corporate profitability is not well understood, making the development of a structural model of the relationship exceedingly difficult. The models also tend to be unique, each being developed to represent a particular business situation, leading to substantial costs (Sassone, 1988).

4.2.2 Methods Derived from Operations Research

4.2.2.1 Work Value Model The practice of measuring work patterns, which is a technique frequently applied in the field of operations research, has been enhanced by Sassone and Schwartz (1986) and applied to the measurement of the benefits resulting from the implementation of office automation systems. They recognized that one of the major benefits of information systems is the capacity to restructure work patterns and enable office workers to spend more time on higher value work.

The Work Value Model addresses the fact that information systems lead to increased effectiveness in addition to increased efficiency, and certainly has the objective of ascertaining the business value obtained from investing in an office automation system. In fact, the process measures work inputs rather than outputs, and an assumption that the allocation of labour resources reflects rational optimizing behavior must be made if an inference about the business value of the system is to be drawn (Strassman, 1990). This method facilitates an audit of the projected benefits through the pre- and post-implementation work profile matrices. However, obtaining the extensive and detailed information about the organization's work patterns can be time-consuming and expensive. Sassone (1988) also found that the relative complexity of the approach made it difficult to explain quickly in management briefings, confirming the concerns expressed by Blackler and Brown (1988).

4.2.2.2 Return on Management Strassman (1985, 1988, 1990) argued that the primary payoff from computers comes from improving the ways in which organizations are managed, and proposed that the productivity of management must be determined if the benefits of computers are to be measured. He defined the output of management as management's "value-added," which cannot be computed directly but "is simply everything left after subtracting from labour value-added all the direct operating costs" (Strassman, 1988). In turn, labour value-added is that which is left when the contribution of capital is removed from the total value-added of an organization (the difference between net revenues and payments to all suppliers). Using this elimination process leads to an estimate of the net management value-added, and, when divided by the costs of management, an indicator of the total performance, return on management, is obtained.

This is a top-down approach and it may well be difficult to isolate the organizational costs and the value-added components attributable to an individual project. Also the residue assigned as the value added by management cannot be directly attributed to the management process; the observed change in the value added by management may be the consequence of any number of other factors. Farbey *et al.*, (1993) suggested that, although the technique provides interesting insights, in practice it is not a serious contender as an evaluation technique.

4.2.3 Methods Derived from Accounting Practices

Cost–benefit analysis is an approach which was developed in order to assess the economic viability of capital investment projects. It has been further developed since its early applications to include the time-discounted present values of costs and benefits. Considerable effort has been devoted to enhancing the basic approach and deriving a method which overcomes the major problems described earlier.

4.2.3.1 SESAME The SESAME program was started by IBM in the mid-1970s with the objective of demonstrating the economic benefits of investment in information technology. The basis of the SESAME method (which is also known as the EPDP method–Executive Planning for Data Processing) is a comparison of an existing computer system against a hypothetical manual alternative. A SESAME study seeks to identify the full costs associated with the system, including development, user involvement, operations, and all related overheads. The benefits are identified by asking users how they would meet their current objectives without the system under review. A number of financial measures are then calculated, usually the breakeven point, the mean benefit/cost ratio over the life of the system and the internal rate of return. Lincoln (1988) described some results of SESAME studies which indicated very favorable returns on investments in information systems, with many cases showing internal rates of return of over 100% p.a. and two-thirds of all applications reviewed reached a breakeven point in less than one year after implementation.

This opportunity cost approach is appropriate for applications intended to increase efficiency but not for those which are directed to producing new (information-intensive) products or services; it would not be feasible to produce these products or services manually. The approach is designed for retrospectively appraising an existing system, and so is not suited to evaluating a proposed investment.

4.2.3.2 Excess Tangible Cost Method Litecky (1981) recognized the difficulty in analyzing the costs and benefits associated with decision support systems and proposed this method, which caused management to focus on the value of the additional intangible benefits. The tangible costs and benefits are identified and estimated and the dollar value of the tangible benefits is subtracted from the dollar value of the tangible costs to give the net figure of excess tangible costs. This is an important figure to management, as it is this amount that must be overcome by the intangible benefits, e.g. improved decision-making or customer satisfaction. Management then consider the intangible benefits and can systematically judge the probabilities of the possible outcomes and their associated economic values. Some methods described in more recent references have taken exactly the same approach as Litecky (for example Weill (1990) described an approach which he called DCF Value Analysis), and others, which will be discussed, have built on Litecky's work.

This method addresses the problem of the intangible benefits and clearly separates them from other costs and benefits which can be estimated with relative accuracy. Management is caused to focus on the uncertainties and make a conscious judgment, rather than these figures being incorporated into the CBA, where the rather shaky foundations of the "guesstimates" are obscured by the seemingly scientific and rigorous nature of the approach. Litecky suggested that the main disadvantage of the method is that more intensive management involvement may be required, but this could just as easily be considered a major strength. The excess tangible cost method is used to assess an individual project (rather than comparing or ranking projects) and can be applied at both the justification and review stages of a project. Although the tangible costs and benefits are measured, the method also allows other benefits to be considered. Thus the values of different stakeholders may be included and the value that each of them would place on the intangible benefits can be compared with the excess tangible cost. The concepts underlying the approach are straightforward and readily acceptable to management.

4.2.3.3 Information Economics (also known as Business Value Analysis) Parker and Benson (1988) have extended the basic cost–benefit analysis method and have included dimensions that are usually ignored in the traditional processes. Its structure encompasses three categories of factors: economic impact quantifications, business domain assessments and technology domain assessments. First, a thorough analysis of all the factors that provide an economic benefit is considered, including the ripple effect of the changes due to the new system throughout the organization (Value Linking), the time-dependent benefits (Value Acceleration) and the productivity benefits resulting from work restructuring (Value Restructuring). A return on investment is calculated from this detailed cost–benefit analysis. The concept of value is then extended to include factors such as strategic match, competitive advantage, management information, competitive response, and strategic IS architecture. The consideration of costs is also extended to an assessment of the risks and uncertainties associated with the proposed system. Detailed guidance is provided to assist management to ascribe scores to each aspect of value and risk, from both the business and technical viewpoints, and the result is a "score card" for each project. These individual scores for the various dimensions of value and risk may be aggregated using a weighting process to produce a single score for each project which allows competing projects to be compared and ranked. It is possible to examine the impact on the relative positions of projects as weights ascribed to the dimensions are varied. For example, the weighting of the purely economic factors compared with the weights given to other aspects of value, such as competitive position, can significantly affect the relative positions of projects.

Information economics provides both a collection of tools for quantifying benefits and costs, and a process of decision-making (Hogbin and Thomas, 1994). The approach is broadly similar to processes described by some others who have addressed the problem of evaluating investments which have multiple objectives (e.g. Canada and White, 1980). Buss (1983) proposed a very similar method, ranking projects on the basis of economic contribution, intangible benefits, technical importance, and fit with business objectives. Buss considered that it was more useful to display the results as a series of grids so that management could easily see the relative positions of different projects in each dimension. The very detailed guidance provided by Parker and Benson is most valuable in ensuring that all relevant factors are included in the decision process. It even addresses the question of whether the organization is capable of carrying out the business changes required by the project. But a large part of the process is based on subjective assessments by management of organizational opportunities and capabilities, which are then coded and incorporated into the fairly complex model. It is all too easy to overlook the uncertainty and the possible over-optimism associated with these scores. This process would make even greater demands on management time than Litecky's excess tangible cost method (although the approaches are basically similar), but the strong involvement of management throughout the decision process should lead to a better appreciation of the issues and therefore result in better investment decisions. The process is more suited to the comparison of projects than an evaluation of an individual project, as it does not generate an absolute dollar value of an information system. Although the method was designed to evaluate potential IS investments, with slight modification it could be applied to the evaluation of existing systems.

4.2.4 Subjective Assessments

Most of the previously described methods incorporated subjective assessment as a means of handling the intangible benefits resulting from an investment in information technology. The following approaches do not attempt to measure the economic benefits, but base the evaluation process entirely on the subjective assessments of the managers and users of the system.

4.2.4.1 Analytic Hierarchy Process
This process addresses the determination of the relative importance of a set of activities in a multi-criteria

setting and allows competing projects or solutions to be ranked. Hierarchical decomposition is used to break down a complex problem into a series of more manageable sub-problems, and the use of pair-wise comparisons assists the decision makers to focus on one issue at a time. Muralidhar *et al.* (1990) described the application of the technique to the problem of IS project selection.

This method handles very well two of the main criticisms that are made of the cost–benefit approach, namely the existence of a number of criteria for selection and the difficulty of including the intangible benefits in the process. In addition, Muralidhar *et al.* described how the views of different stakeholders may be incorporated into the decision-making process. The method is easy to use, conceptually appealing (if the detailed mathematics is ignored!), and could be used to compare IT projects with other investments. However, the process rests on comparisons and does not lead to an absolute value of the project. It does not present the outcome in business terms nor employ the financial terms that managers have grown to expect from project submissions.

4.2.4.2 User Information Satisfaction The problem of measuring the impact of an information system on an organization is tackled differently by Ives *et al.* (1983), who proposed that the surrogate measure User Information Satisfaction be used as a substitute for objective determinants of the impact of an information system on organizational effectiveness. A number of other researchers had developed measures of user satisfaction that were appropriate for specific applications, but Ives *et al.* sought to develop a more standard form which could be applied to different types of systems.

The concept of user satisfaction is most important, as the users' perception of a system can determine the extent to which a system will be used (if use is voluntary), and it provides one dimension of system success. However, to extend this idea to the proposition that User Information Satisfaction can be used as a surrogate measure of the impact of an information system on an organization's effectiveness is challenged in the literature. The user of the system is an agent rather than a principal of the organization, and his or her objectives may differ from those of the organization (Marsden and Pingrey, 1988). Chismar and Kriebel (1985) considered the logic defending "user satisfaction" as a measure of system effectiveness to be specious, and referred to the extensive literature on research that disproved the causality relationship between "job satisfaction" and "job performance."

4.2.5 Summary

Eleven methods which have been proposed in the literature as being suitable for evaluating the benefits that organizations will derive, or have derived, have been discussed. They have been drawn from the fields of economics, operational research, and accounting, and additional subjective approaches have also been included.

The methods which have origins in the field of economics take an objective view which focuses strictly on the inputs and outputs that can be measured, either directly or indirectly, in dollar terms. They analyze existing systems, and therefore the methods cannot be applied to the justification of a project at its proposal stage. Production Frontier Analysis is for use when different projects or situations are to be compared, and Business Value Linkage Impact Analysis can be used to measure the economic value of a system in absolute terms.

The methods which have derived from operations research take a similarly objective view and again focus on variables that can be measured: observation of work patterns, comparison of costs with a control group who do not use the system, and analysis of the financial statements of the organization to isolate the costs and value derived from a particular system. All three methods in this group provide an absolute estimate of the value of the system. Again they are more generally suited to the review of an existing system rather than for justifying a proposed investment, with the exception of Sassone's Work Value Model, which is used to estimate the impact of a proposed office automation system.

A number of methods have been proposed which are enhancements to the traditional cost–benefit analysis approach. The basic technique again focuses on benefits that can be measured in economic terms, but, as was discussed earlier, the objectives of many IS investments are not to provide a quick economic return but to have a longer term strategic impact on an organization's competitive position. The approaches taken by Litecky and Parker and Benson are similar, in that both methods started with a conventional analysis of the economic costs and benefits. Litecky posed the question of whether the intangible benefits outweigh the net costs, but Parker and Benson went further and used a system of scores and weights to produce a final score for each project. Thus both these techniques enhance the basic CBA approach through the addition of subjective assessments of factors which cannot be measured. Both methods are applied at the proposal stage of a project, but Parker and Benson's approach compared competing projects and Litecky's approach examined projects singly. The SESAME method however, reviewed projects 12 months after implementation and therefore by definition the method is not applicable to project proposals.

Finally, two methods which are based entirely on subjective assessments have been described. The Analytic Hierarchy Process uses complex mathematical manipulation to derive single measures for comparing a number of projects with diverse objectives competing for limited investment resources. The other method employs a measure of user satisfaction as a surrogate

TABLE 1
IT PROJECT EVALUATION METHODS

Discipline	Method	Reference	Process	Objective/ subjective	Relative/ absolute	Justification review	Benefits included	Comments on implementation
Economics	Production Frontier Analysis (inc. DEA)	Chismar and Kriebel (1985)	Compares efficiency of production units	O	R	R	Economic	Difficult to identify appropriate measures
	Business Values Linkage Impact Analysis	Banker and Kauffman (1988a)	Structural modeling of relationships between inputs and outputs	O	A	R	All that can be quantified and modeled	Relationships poorly understood Complex models, unique to application
Operations Research	Work Value Model	Sassone (1988)	Estimates value of changed work practices	O	A	J	Efficiency effectiveness	Data collection expensive
	Cost Avoidance	Edelman (1981)	Compares operational costs with and without system	O	A	R	Efficiency	Control groups required
	Return on Management	Strassman (1988)	Estimates contribution of value added by management	O	A	R	All that show up in financial statement of organization	Isolation of appropriate costs is difficult
Accounting	Cost–benefit analysis	various	Analysis of economic costs and benefits only	O	A	J + R	Economic	No major difficulties
	SESAME (i.e. EPDP)	Lincoln (1988)	Comparison with manual hypothetical system	O + S	A	R	Economic	Subjective estimates of equivalent costs
	Excess Tangible Cost	Litecky (1981)	Compares net cost with intangible benefits	O + S	A	J	Economic intangible	No major difficulties
	Information Economics	Parker and Benson (1988)	CBA enhanced to include other dimensions of value	O + S	R	J	Economic intangible (risk)	No major difficulties
Subjective Assessment	Analytic Hierarchy Process	Muralidhar, Santhanam and Wilson (1990)	Comparison of projects on multiple criteria	S	R	J	All	No major difficulties
	User Information Satisfaction	Ives, Olson and Baroudi (1983)	Surrogate measure of value of system	S	A	R	To user only	No major difficulties

measure of the value of the system, an extrapolation which is of concern to some researchers.

Table 1 summarizes some characteristics of the methods which have been reviewed. It is interesting to note that none of the techniques described above presents the benefits in terms that may be readily assessed both before and after implementation. The techniques appear to have been developed for the purpose of either *ex ante* or *ex post* evaluation, but not both. In these instances evaluation has been perceived as a single event, rather than part of a process in which the specified benefits which provide the basis of the initial justification are reviewed after implementation to evaluate whether the predicted benefits have been achieved.

4.3 Current Practices

Although the literature provides a number of alternatives to cost–benefit analysis, there is no evidence that they have been adopted to any significant extent. In a recent survey, the most commonly reported appraisal techniques were still CBA and return on investment (Ward *et al.*, 1996). Coleman and Jamieson (1994) suggested "this supports the view that these [alternative] methods lack something in practical application." In an attempt to address the weaknesses inherent in CBA, it seems that many organizations use more than one method, supplementing the economic considerations encapsulated within CBA with other criteria such as competitive advantage or service to the public (Willcocks and Lester, 1996). Although Information Economics stands out as offering a structured approach to incorporating a number of dimensions in the evaluation, there is no evidence that the technique has been adopted to any great extent by practitioners. However, a series of case studies revealed one organization which was using a variation of the technique; they used the same categories of value, but did not attempt to aggregate these into a single score, deciding instead to present the economic, strategic, and risk dimensions separately (Simmons, 1993).

5. Evaluation Frameworks

Evidence therefore suggests that a single evaluation method does not exist that meets the evaluation needs of organizations. Organizations generally use more than one criterion in assessing their IT investments, and they also recognize that different types of project require different approaches to evaluation. "Doctrines which claim that a single approach suffices are increasingly being recognized as inadequate and restrictive in evaluating most of today's sophisticated IT installations." (Hochstrasser and Griffiths, 1991, p. 9)

The business strategy of the organization will have a strong part to play in determining appropriate evaluation methods. For example, an organization with a strategy of product differentiation will use different criteria to assess its IT investments from those used by an organization with a strategy of cost leadership (Remenyi et al., 1995). Many organizations classify their projects in some way, and this classification can also influence the way in which they are evaluated. A simple classification according to whether the project is viewed as mandatory, necessary, or desirable is used by some organizations to rank the priority of projects, but it does not provide an assessment of their standalone value.

One approach to developing an evaluation framework is presented by Willcocks and Lester (1996). They proposed that an IT investment be classified according to the nature of the costs and benefits—for example a system with efficiency objectives would have clearly definable costs and benefits, whereas a system seeking to gain a competitive edge for the organization would be more likely to have much softer costs and benefits. They then recommended possible evaluation approaches, depending on the tangibility of the costs and benefits.

Weill (1990) proposed a framework of approaches to evaluation in which he classified systems as transactional, informational, and strategic, but the terms "transactional" and "informational" present an IT-centred view of systems and are not immediately relevant to a business manager. Although many organizations do categorize their IT investments, they view them as providing different types of support to the business, and use terms such as "legislative" or "mandatory," "operational," "product related," and "strategy support" (Simmons, 1993).

Farbey et al. (1993) postulated a model which takes a similar business view; applications are categorized according to the type of change desired and the categories perceived as rungs of a ladder. The applications typical for each higher rung represent increasing potential benefits, but also increasing uncertainty on outcomes, increasing risk of failure and increasing difficulty of communicating the case for change to the stakeholders.

Rung 8	Business transformation
Rung 7	Strategic systems
Rung 6	Interorganizational systems
Rung 5	Infrastructure
Rung 4	MIS and DSS systems
Rung 3	Direct value added
Rung 2	Automation
Rung 1	Mandatory changes

The focus of evaluation and the appropriate evaluation techniques are different for each rung of the ladder. Whereas precise quantification of costs and benefits is possible near the bottom of the ladder, the higher rungs rely more on experimental and judgmental processes. Risk assessment becomes an important component of evaluation near the top of the ladder. At the top of the ladder decisions require not merely the consent of the top management team but also their continuous involvement. Farbey *et al.* suggested that they represent some of the most difficult activities faced by senior management.

Although this concept of an evaluation ladder is most useful, Hochstrasser and Griffiths (1991) cautioned against the expectation that organizations would progress through the stages of such a ladder, emphasizing that successful organizations maintain a portfolio of different types of system that serve their spectrum of business objectives, and thus would use a range of evaluation techniques. A single system will frequently have more than one objective —a study by the author found that almost half the projects examined had more than one major objective (Simmons, 1993). Farbey *et al.* recognized that a system may have components on a number of rungs, and suggested that each component be evaluated accordingly.

Peters (1994) presented another IT evaluation framework, but with the objective of evaluating an organization's spread of IT investments, rather than a single investment. As a result of a survey of over 50 IT projects, he discovered that both the benefits to the organization and the orientation of the investment were important in evaluation. He described the benefits as falling into three categories on a continuum, ranging from *enhancing productivity* at one end, through *risk minimization*, to *business expansion* at the other. The orientation of the investment to the business was also an important criterion and again he perceived these as three broad categories forming a continuum. At one extreme, investments were targeted specifically at *market-influencing* initiatives, while at the other extreme the focus was aimed at supporting the technical *infrastructure*. Between these two extremes, applications were designed to process the normal *business operations* of the organization. The fact that most IT systems cover a range of benefit and investment orientation categories, and recognizing the interrelationship of each investment attribute, led Peters to map these systems on a grid composed of the two parameters. Different levels of shading are used to identify levels of expenditure. The investment map so developed provides an organization with a clear assessment as to the extent to which their current IT investment supports the business direction. Peters also used the investment maps to compare the IT investment strategies of two companies operating in similar markets. The first company, with a price-led strategy, concentrated on IT investments which cut costs and improved efficiency. The other company focused on product differentiation, and its IT investment was concentrated in the area of innovation and business expansion. Peters found that this process assisted non-IT managers to evaluate existing and proposed projects in the context of the overall business strategy and reduced the relative importance of financial indicators, such as internal rate of return as a means of investment appraisal.

Thus researchers have responded to the need of organizations for evaluation frameworks which recognize the diversity of IT investment decisions. There are no simple solutions but the frameworks presented in this section offer approaches which are well-grounded in practice and should provide organizations with guidelines that take into account the business strategy of the organization and the potential benefits of the particular applications.

6. The Investment Decision

Although much of the emphasis in this chapter so far has been on techniques and methods for measuring benefits and evaluating IT systems, the issue of the organizational context has been an important thread throughout the discussion. Appraising new investment is always a political process as it touches on the diverse interests of many people and groups. Hogbin and Thomas (1994, p. 193) emphasized the influence of the human factor on the seemingly rational process of decision-making: "Decision-making is a blend of rational thinking and intuition working within the framework of an organization's culture and politics." If a socio-technical perspective is accepted, technology is seen as as an integral part, not merely a contextual variable, of organized social systems. It is founded on the notion that "technology does not determine specific forms of work organization, but that on the contrary, social norms and organizational strategies influence the introduction and utilization of technology." (Mayntz, 1984, p. 178). Thus IT investment decisions are as much concerned with the organizational context and the human participation in the process as with the mechanics of evaluation techniques.

Symons (1990) provided a useful model, distinguishing between the content of the evaluation, i.e. what is measured, the context in which the evaluation takes place and the process of evaluation, which is seen as a social process.

- The *content* perspective perceives evaluation as concerned with identifying costs and benefits and balancing the two. In *ex ante* evaluation, the concern is with estimation, and in *ex post* evaluation the concern is with determining cause and effect. In both cases one needs to determine what is to be included and how it is to be measured.
- The *context* perspective recognizes the influence of politics and other organizational factors on the outcome of the evaluation. The business context, organizational culture, and management style all impact the final investment decision.

- The *process* perspective is concerned with the way in which the evaluation is carried out and the degree to which it is considered to be successful. Symons sees evaluation as having a learning, as well as a control, function. It provides people in organizations with an opportunity to adjust their mental model of IT and the business through bargaining and negotiating together to form a new consensus.

This model of evaluation will provide the basis of the discussion which follows.

6.1 Content

The preceding discussions have highlighted that there is not one "right" or "best" method for justifying IT investments. A series of case studies exploring organizations' experiences of evaluation revealed that organizations held widely differing attitudes towards effectiveness and evaluation and therefore had different requirements of a justification process (Simmons, 1993). However, a number of general conclusions could be drawn.

- Organizations required an evaluation method that provided an absolute rather than comparative measure of a project's value. It was accepted that value had a number of dimensions and therefore more than one measure was needed.
- Although projects that made a strategic contribution were identified and their strategic nature influenced the decision-making, organizations still wanted to use one justification approach for assessing all projects. Therefore the method must be flexible enough to cater for different types of project.
- The leading organizations who saw post-implementation reviews as providing an opportunity to ensure that the project objectives were achieved required performance measures from the justification process that could be used as benchmarks after implementation.

Few, if any, of the evaluations methods described in the literature satisfy these requirements. In practice, organizations generally use quantitative cost–benefit analysis supplemented by qualitative or quantitative descriptors of the less tangible, more strategic, benefits (Simmons, 1993; Willcocks and Lester, 1996).

Measurement is at the core of evaluation, and Farbey *et al.* (1993) suggested that the primary problems in this area revolve around technical measurement issues of estimation and measurement procedure. The issue of what is to be measured is influenced by the project objectives and the priorities of the organization's business strategy. The literature advises that project performance measures be derived from the organization's key result areas but this assumes that business planning does in fact take place and that procedures exist to link IT investment decisions to the business strategy. Hogbin and Thomas (1994) suggested that without a well-considered business strategy it is unlikely that the organization will obtain good value from IT investments.

One of the criticisms leveled against using cost–benefit analysis for project justification is that it is a deterministic technique and fails to acknowledge that the figures used are only estimates and hence subject to statistical variability. Remenyi *et al.* (1995) advised using simulations to explore the impact of variation in the estimated figures. A simpler approach to recognizing the inherent uncertainty in both costs and benefits is to consider the upper and lower limits—Hogbin and Thomas (1994) advocated using the upper estimates of costs and the lower estimates of benefits. I wonder how many projects have been justified using the reverse limits!

The issue of risk should be an integral part of any project evaluation. IT projects are concerned with innovation and organizational change, and hence inherently risky. Although the risks of not meeting the estimated costs and benefits can be included through the use of conservative estimates and overall risk can be factored into the investment decision by adjusting the required internal rate of return, risk needs to be acknowledged and managed explicitly. Risk management is a complete process which moves through the steps of identifying risks, quantifying risks, developing a risk management plan, and implementing the risk management activities (Charette, 1989). Risk assessment requires a high degree of judgment, based on experience and perception. Scores can be given that reflect the size of each risk and the chance of it occurring, allowing an overall risk rating to be aggregated. Information Economics is an evaluation technique which explicitly acknowledges risk in both the business and technical domains and incorporates it into the decision-making process (Parker and Benson, 1988). Identifying the risks of not achieving the project is the first step, and the most significant, in avoiding the risk. Taking action to minimize these risks may involve extra project costs. Charette contrasts this risk-oriented view of project management with the traditional approach that assumes success will result provided the proper processes are followed. Thus an assessment of the risks and the proposed management plan should be included in the project evaluation.

Another approach to handling risk and uncertainty uses Options theory. The Options Model shares a theoretical foundation with widely used models for assessing risk and making investment decisions in financial markets and derivative trading. Although the method can be extremely complex, Moad (1995) reported that it is particularly suited to infrastructure decisions where future flexibility is valued.

6.2 Context

The importance of the organizational, cultural, and political factors that surround decisions concerning IT investments cannot be underestimated. A project sponsor must recognize that decision-making is a political activity and understand who has to be persuaded and on what basis the project is likely to be approved (Hogbin and Thomas, 1994). The implications of context can be examined in terms of the business context, organizational culture and management style.

6.2.1 Business Context

The business environment of the organization influences the criteria used to evaluate proposals, attitudes towards measurement, and evaluation itself. The following examples are drawn from case studies reported in Simmons (1993). A public sector utility, shortly to be exposed to competition, was concerned only with the economic payback of projects and needed real cost savings to be realized within a short timeframe. In the banking organizations studied, IT was seen as a costly and strategic resource and measurement of the effectiveness of these investments was important. Increasing staff productivity and improving customer service were major objectives and these priorities were reflected in the criteria used to evaluate investment proposals. The strategic objectives of the organizations, framed in response to perceptions of threats and opportunities, thus strongly influenced their investment decisions.

Farbey *et al.* (1993) also raised the question of whether the system can be considered apart from the organizational background and other changes that are happening at the same time. In many cases, the IT system is part of a larger business initiative and it then makes little sense to attempt to evaluate the impact of the IT component in isolation.

6.2.2 Organizational Culture

The culture of the organization is reflected in both how the decision-making is performed and the nature of the decision (Hogbin and Thomas, 1994). The culture will determine whether to be creative or cautious, to be proactive or reactive, to consider ethical issues or not, and the emphasis placed on the human factors of change. The study described in Simmons (1993) found that the degree of organizational cohesion affected attitudes to evaluation. Two organizations in particular stood out as having a "unitary culture" (Legge, 1984); in both cases the organizations' objectives were well understood and all members were strongly committed to them. There was little emphasis on formal procedures and this was reflected in their approach to project justification and review.

Personal influence was likely to have a positive impact on a decision, as staff members placed the organization's objectives above their own. However, in some other organizations there was not the same feeling of common purpose. There was a concern that some business managers placed their own or departmental interests above those of the organization and influenced IT investment decisions so that the outcome would not necessarily provide the best value from an organizational perspective; such a culture was described by Legge as "pluralist." The risk was particularly high if the information systems department reported to another functional area, for example finance; in this case, IT investment was often biased towards financial systems which may not have been making optimal use of the organization's resources.

6.2.3 Management Style

It was found that organizations which had adopted value-based management and total quality management approaches were particularly concerned about measuring the effectiveness of IT investments as performance measurement is fundamental to these methods of management. Organizations which had developed Key Value Drivers and their Key Performance Indicators, complementing financial measures with operational measures that directly impact business objectives (Fisher, 1992), were able to use these operational measures to demonstrate how IT impacts business performance.

Information systems are only one kind of investment made by an organization. IT investments may need to be compared with other opportunities for investment and an organization which traditionally uses very formal methods for cost justification elsewhere might find it difficult to evaluate IT investment using a very different approach. Farbey *et al.* (1993) suggested that selection of an appropriate evaluation method needs to be sensitive to such a problem. One possible approach is to supplement the existing investment methods with a component that considers the strategic opportunities presented by the IT investment.

6.3 Process

The potential exists for evaluation to enhance the understanding and learning of the organization, but this is by no means inevitable. The very act of evaluation can add to mutual understanding and the development of a common language (Farbey *et al.*, 1993).

It cannot be assumed that all organizations actually undertake feasibility evaluations for all projects. However, a study conducted by Ballantine *et al.* (1996) revealed that 87% of their sample had evaluated their most recent project. Evaluation was found to be associated with organizations who had higher levels of turnover, and for larger projects, when measured relative to the total IS/IT budget.

One important issue is who should make the IT investment decision. There are dangers if either business management or IT management act alone, and Hogbin and Thomas (1994) recommended that an IT steering committee be established which consists of senior representatives from the business functions committing to deliver the benefits and the Chief Information Officer committing to deliver the system. Farbey *et al.* developed an internal stakeholder map, illustrating the spread of people or groups that had taken part in the decision process in the organizations covered by their survey. Management at board level, other general management, financial management, functional management, information systems people and users were all involved in some way. Thus there is a great opportunity for evaluation to enhance communication and understanding, although the gap that often exists between the IT department and other business functions, as indicated by different priorities and jargon, can easily lead to poor communication and lost opportunities to exploit IT for business advantage. The importance of including non-IS managers in the evaluation of IT investments is emphasized by Falconer and Hodgett (1996), who reported that successful projects (those that had met all or most of their pre-established performance criteria) had significantly higher involvement of non-IS managers participating in the approvals process.

Some of the solutions proposed in the literature to the problems involved in evaluating IT investments are very sophisticated and complex. Making business cases and decisions are team activities, demanding the understanding of a wide section of ordinary business managers. Thus the techniques and methods must be suited to their application and the people who will use them (Carlson and McNurlin, 1989).

Although post-implementation reviews are frequently included in project guidelines and methodologies, in practice they are often omitted. In the past, these reviews have tended to focus on the development process and, therefore, were not seen as worthwhile by the business managers (Kumar, 1990). A more proactive view treats such a review as an opportunity to ensure that the expected benefits were achieved. Feedback from the operational performance targets assists line managers to make the necessary organizational changes required to obtain the maximum benefit. Thus by changing its perception of the evaluation process, an organization can derive more value from both its IT investments and its evaluation process.

7. Managing the Benefits

Although the value that organizations obtain from their investment in IT has been of concern since the early 1970s, the focus of study and discussion has for the most part been on the problems and techniques for evaluating investments at the initial justification stage and, to a lesser extent, reviewing the project after implementation. An IT project has generally been viewed as a technical project, the objective of which was to install a system; procedures would be developed to accompany the new system, but beyond this little attention was paid to the organizational changes that would be required if the expected benefits were to eventuate. A more recent view perceives an IT system as one component of a business project, and rather than managing the implementation of the IT system, the focus is on the wider issue of the management of the successful implementation of large-scale change. This then leads to a different perception of IT evaluation. Instead of being seen as a "once-off" exercise, the evaluation of IT investments is seen as a process by which benefits from a potential investment are identified and appraised, realized in practice during a project and evaluated after implementation (Ward et al., 1996). The realization that IT does not on its own deliver benefits—benefits will only result from changes being made to the way business activities are performed or the way in which information is used— implies that the necessary organizational change must be actively managed. This overall process of evaluation and realization of IT benefits is termed *benefits management* and is defined by Ward et al. (1996, p. 214) as:

> The process of organizing and managing such that potential benefits arising from the use of IT are actually realized.

The importance of defining benefits and managing their achievement is emphasized by a survey on the views of senior managers as to the most common causes of project failure. The two most important issues were identified as (Norris, 1996, p. 204):

- Vague statement of benefits, leading to an uncertain allocation of responsibility for managing their delivery (95%).
- Underestimating the extent and scale of organizational change costs (95%).

The investment case is usually the joint responsibility of business and IT, with IT taking responsibility for the costs. Responsibility for achieving the benefits is often not as explicit, but when stated it is in the user domain. Thus IT benefits management is a central *business* management issue (Farbey et al., 1993). Norris pointed out that system development costs are rigorously monitored and controlled, but the achievement of the benefits is rarely monitored so closely.

Hogbin and Thomas (1994) suggested a number of reasons why so little attention has been paid to benefits management in the past.

- Thought and effort are required to determine a base position.

- Measurement procedures and disciplines are not established early in the project.
- The initial forecast and final assessment of tangible benefits involves an element of managerial judgment.
- When forecast benefits are not achieved, the result may be disguised or suppressed.

And perhaps most importantly,

- Responsibility for benefit achievement is not clearly expressed.

Post-implementation reviews are often part of an organization's development standards, but they are in general not carried out (Kumar, 1990), and the extent to which they support benefits management can be questioned. A survey reported by the Butler Cox Foundation (1990) found that the reasons given for their omission were as follows:

- *Too difficult*—to assess the benefits because of the multiple complex relationships between systems and business outcomes.
- *Not necessary*—some organizations took the view that if investment appraisal were undertaken correctly, the expected benefits would by definition accrue.
- *Too costly*—undertaking proper post-implementation reviews can be very costly. Some organizations felt resources could be better deployed on other initiatives.
- *Against our culture*—for IT departments that have worked to develop a partnership with a business area, it would not be helpful for IT to act as a watchdog over the achievement of business benefits.

The respondents to this survey perceived the post-implementation review as a single event, looking back at the development process and determining whether the benefits had been achieved. Although such a review can provide a number of useful results (see Norris, 1996), the focus is not on the proactive management and leverage of the benefits, so it can be seen, particularly by business management, to be of limited value.

Hogbin and Thomas (1994) saw effective benefit management as resting on three key activities:

- *Setting performance criteria*—in terms that reflect the business benefit and are measurable. That is, they should reflect the changes that are expected in key variables or performance indicators, for example credit days, cash balances (finance measures), stockouts, turnovers, inventory value (stock measures), satisfaction, and waiting time (measures of customer service). If higher level measures are used, for example cost reduction or revenue

increase, the connection with the IT project is less direct. The indicators and measures need to be explicitly stated as part of the project objectives.
- *Measuring the change*—generally through a process of post-implementation review, but not the once-off, backward looking, reactive review described above. Performance indicators need to be regularly monitored and the results available to the business managers responsible for achieving the benefit.
- *Delivering the change*—targets need to be agreed before implementation. They suggested that line management be responsible for their realization once the system is performing to specification, but this proviso could become a contentious point between IT and the line manager. If benefits management by line managers is to be effective, they suggested that the achievement of the benefits be built into their performance contracts and that operating budgets could include the benefits of projects expected to be completed in that period.

In addition to managing the realization of the benefits upon which the initial justification of the project was based, Hochstrasser and Griffiths (1991) stressed the importance of actively managing the *unexpected* changes that often result. They cited the following changes that have been observed when large-scale IT projects have been introduced:

- New patterns of work emerge as routine tasks are reduced and more information allows staff to consider broader implications and try alternative approaches.
- New team formations and working relationships are introduced as IT improves communication between staff and facilitates teams with members in different locations.
- New definitions of traditional functions and boundaries as IT offers the potential to overcome traditional splits between functions which were strictly demarcated as a result of vertical nature of work processes.
- New allocations of responsibilities as individuals experiment with innovative applications of technology to extend their current tasks.
- New distributions of internal power as managers who do not appreciate the opportunities offered by IT lose influence to those who understand and control the IT-enabled business opportunities.
- New organizational reporting structures as IT threatens the role of middle management by offering a more effective communication link between policy makers and line managers.

When an organization does not actively control these changes resulting from IT investments, changes will occur in an undirected and haphazard way.

This creates the opportunity for political forces of resistance or manipulation to undermine the intention of senior managers. Thus the introduction of IT alters the internal dynamics of an organization, and Hochstrasser and Griffiths suggest that these second-order effects require management also.

But a survey conducted by Ward *et al.* (1996) to establish a benchmark of the practice of benefits management found that although most respondents expressed confidence that their IT was delivering benefits to their organizations, an analysis of their responses revealed little ground for this confidence.

- Post-project reviews did not usually address delivery of the benefits.
- Few organizations allocated responsibility to managers for realizing benefits claimed in the justification.
- Although in 80% of the cases organizations had appointed a business project manager, the role was most often concerned with managing the interface between IT and the business, rather than being responsible for actively managing the project to deliver the business benefits.
- In the cases where managers were allocated responsibility for delivering the benefits, it was found in practice that although the line/department managers and users were held responsible, they would often not be in a position to engineer the necessary organizational change.

Thus it would seem that currently organizations are not effectively managing the benefits in order to derive the maximum value from their investment in IT; although they express concern about achieving expected benefits, they are doing little to actively manage them. This lack of focus on achieving the benefits is evidenced by the criteria used to define project success. Ward *et al.* found that project success was usually defined in terms of "working, on time, on budget" rather than directed towards achieving the business benefits.

However, Peters (1996) reported the experiences of some organizations that did take a positive attitude to managing benefits. These organizations set up project boards, led by a senior user, at an early stage of the project and followed the project through after implementation. In some cases members of the board took responsibility for delivering benefits for sub-components of the investment. Variables impacted by the investment were identified; all were measurable but not all in cost terms; for example, sales call per day, delivery schedules met, and customer throughput per hour. Project boards reviewed the benefits gained at regular intervals of up to three months, but they recognized the importance of the unplanned changes and were therefore also concerned with obtaining additional benefits that were not included in the original proposal. Peters was able to demonstrate the value of an active benefits management programme as he found "Projects which had clearly defined responsibilities with key variables *overperformed* their original appraisal." (Peters, 1996, p. 227)

Neiman (1992) provided an example of actively managing productivity gains in the maintenance team of an insurance company. The team achieved 25% productivity improvement in two and a half months, then set a new target of 40% improvement. He suggested that "The secret to producing the change was to *ask for it*." (p. 7)

A number of models of benefit management programmes are now emerging. Hains (1996) proposed a two-stage process which consists of a benefits development phase and a benefits realization phase.

- *Benefits development*—this entails identifying and qualifying key success measures. Key success measures are those that the sponsor agrees will justify the investment required to develop, operate, and maintain the solution. Key success measures are developed as each benefit objective, which may have more than one measure, is identified. The process of developing benefits is iterative and Hains suggested that this may best be tackled in a facilitated workshop with the sponsor. Identified benefit opportunities are captured in a Benefits Register which is the source of ongoing monitoring and reporting of benefit achievement.

- *Benefits realization*—monitoring and reporting of the Benefits Register occurs quarterly, with a management report for the sponsor highlighting variations to the original business case and progress towards achieving the target measure values. During the development and after implementation it is likely that some aspects of the business case will change, e.g. the scope may grow, the ongoing costs may become better understood, or organization restructuring may occur. For these reasons it is necessary to reassess the business case on a regular basis throughout the development and after implementation until the sponsor is satisfied that return on investment has been maximized.

Ward *et al.* (1996, pp. 216–217) have proposed a similar model, but expanded to five stages and based on the Deming quality management cycle of Plan, Do, Check, Act.

- *Identifying and structuring the benefits*—the proposed benefits are identified and, for each proposed benefit, suitable business measures are developed (both financial and non-financial). The benefits are structured in order to understand the linkages between technology effects, business changes, and overall business effects, e.g. business objectives. At this stage, it becomes possible to assess the overall business benefits. It is also possible to assess the current situation with the measures that have been developed.

- *Planning benefits realization*—for each benefit, specific responsibility for realizing the benefit is allocated within the business. The required business changes are also assessed and planned for, and a benefits realization plan is produced. At this stage, the full costs of both IT development and business changes can be assessed, in order to make a fully informed judgment as to the viability of the proposed project. Any intended benefit for which responsibility cannot be allocated and for which a delivery plan cannot be developed should be rejected at this stage.
- *Executing the benefits realization plan*—Alongside the implementation of the proposed IT application, the necessary business changes, as detailed in the benefits realization, are carried out.
- *Evaluating and reviewing results*—Following the full implementation of IT and business changes, the previously developed business measures are used to evaluate the effects of the project. Review of "before" and "after" measures provides an explicit mechanism for evaluating whether the proposed business benefits have actually been delivered.
- *Potential for further benefits*—As a result of the post-project review, it may become apparent that further benefits are now achievable which were not envisaged at the outset. This stage provides the opportunity to plan for, and realize, these further benefits. In a wider context, this stage also provides the opportunity to review and learn from the overall project process, thus facilitating the transfer of lessons learned to future projects.

Both models provide valuable assistance to organizations who are seeking to establish or improve a benefits management programme. The model proposed by Ward *et al.* offers a sound process, based on the well-established Total Quality Management cycle, and which includes an important stage which focuses on planning for the organizational changes that will have to take place if the benefits are to be achieved. Hains contributed two additional insights: that the viability of the business case should also be regularly reviewed and the very important concept of review being a regular, rather than a once-off, event. Thus a model of a benefits management process, based on a synthesis of the two described above but tailored to the specific needs and context of the organization, would provide a practical approach to increasing the business value obtained from IT investments.

8. Conclusion

Over the last 25 years, much has been written about the issues concerning the evaluation of IT investments. Much of the discussion has been concerned with the difficulty of measuring the less tangible benefits, the problems surrounding the application of the most commonly used method (cost–benefit analysis), and the search for a better approach. More recently, the importance of the organizational context has been more strongly recognized with an appreciation of how the business context, organizational culture, and management style can impact an organization's criteria for effectiveness and its attitude towards evaluation. The need for a flexible evaluation method that includes not only the financial but also the more strategic benefits, and that can be applied to the diversity of IT investment decisions, has been highlighted.

The most recent development in the area of IT evaluation is the recognition that benefits will not accrue automatically; the IT system provides the opportunity for changing business methods and processes, but it is these changes that will lead to the benefits, not the system itself. Thus the business changes and the delivery of the benefits need to be proactively managed; a model for managing this process has been proposed.

Over time, perceptions concerning the nature of IT investments have changed. An IT development used to be perceived as a technical system, with attention focused on the development process, after which it was handed over to the business users. An alternative view sees the IT system as part of a business project to change methods and processes, and managing the outcome to deliver the expected benefits is at least as important as managing the development of the IT component. The issue of demonstrating the value delivered by investments in IT used to be presented as a challenge to IT management, but the more recent view assigns responsibility for delivery of the benefits to the business management. Now, more than ever, there is a need for a strong partnership between IT and the rest of the business. This is facilitated in some organizations by a devolution of application development to individual business units, who take responsibility for their systems needs and the outcomes.

This chapter has also highlighted the changing focus of IT evaluation—from a "once-off" exercise, undertaken as a means of gaining approval for the investment, often with the knowledge that the claimed benefits can never be achieved—to seeing IT evaluation as part of a process which identifies the benefits, assigns responsibility for delivering them, plans for the organizational change which will be required, and regularly monitors the achievement.

Keen (1991, p. 160, quoting Franke) likened the use of IT in business to the introduction of Watt's coal-fired steam engine in 1775:

> There were no early increases in output and efficiency. Instead time seems to have been needed for technology diffusion and for human and organizational adjustment. It was not until the 1820s, about half a century later, that there began substantial increases of output, productivity and income.

Perhaps it is only now, when organizations have been using computers for more than 30 years, that we are at last beginning to understand how the real benefits of IT investments can be gained.

REFERENCES

Ahituv, N. (1989) Assessing the value of information: problems and approaches. *Proceedings of the 10th International Conference on Information Systems*. Boston MA.

Ballantine, J. A., Galliers, R. D., and Stray, S. J. (1996) Information systems/technology evaluation practices: evidence from UK organisations. *Journal of Information Technology* **11**, 129–141.

Banker, R., and Kauffman, R. (1988a) *A scientific approach to the measurement of IT business value, Part 1—A manager's guide to business value linkage impact analysis*. C.R.I.S., N.Y.U., Working Paper Series CRIS No.194, GBA No.89–96.

Banker, R., and Kauffman, R (1988b) *A scientific approach to the measurement of IT business value, Part 2—A case study of electronic banking operations at Meridian Bancorp*. C.R.I.S., N.Y.U., Working Paper Series CRIS No.195, GBA No.89–97.

Barua, A., Kriebel, C. H., and Mukhopadhayay, T. (1995) Information technology and business value: an empirical investigation. *Information Systems Research* **6**(1), 1–24.

Berger, P. (1988) Selecting enterprise level measures of IT value. *Measuring Business Value of IT*. ICIT Research Study Team No.2, ICIT Press.

Blackler, F., and Brown, C. (1988) Theory and practice in evaluation: the case of the new ITs. *Information System Assessment: Issues and Challenges* (eds N. Bjorn-Andersen and G. B. Davies. North-Holland, Amsterdam.

Broadbent, M., Lloyd, P., Hansell, P., and Dampney, C. N. G. (1992) Roles, responsibilities and requirements for managing IS in the 1990s. *International Journal of Information Management*, March.

Buss, M. D. J. (1983) How to rank computer projects. *Harvard Business Review* Jan–Feb.

Butler Cox Foundation (1990) Getting value from information technology. *Research Report 75*. Butler Cox Foundation, London.

Canada, J. R., and White, J. A. (1980) *Capital Investment Decision Analysis for Management and Engineering*. Prentice Hall, Englewood Cliffs NJ.

Carlson, W. M., and McNurlin, B. C. (1989) Measuring the value of IS. *IS Analyser Special Report*.

Charette, R. N. (1989) *Software Engineering Risk Analysis and Management*. Intertext Publications, McGraw-Hill Book Company, New York.

Chismar, W. G., and Kriebel, C. H. (1985) A method for assessing the economic impact of IS technology on organisations. *Proceedings of the 6th International Conference on IS*, Indianapolis.

Coleman, T., and Jamieson, M. (1994) Beyond return on investment: evaluating ALL the benefits of IT. *Information Management: The Evaluation of IS Investments* (ed. L. Willcocks), Chapman & Hall, London.

Copp, D. (1985) Morality, reason and management science: the rationale of cost benefit analysis. *Social Philosophy and Policy* **2**.

Cronk, M. and Fitzgerald, E. P. (1996) A conceptual approach to understanding IT business value. *Proc. 7th Australian Conference on IS*, Hobart.

Datamation (1991) *Datamation Spending Survey* 15 April.

DeLone, W. H. and McLean, E. R. (1992) Information systems success: the quest for the dependent variable. *Information Systems Research* **3**(1), 60–95.

Earl, M. (1989) *Management Strategies for Information Technology*. Prentice Hall, London.
Eason, K. (1988) *Information Technology and Organisational Change*. Taylor & Francis, London.
Edelman, F. (1981) Managers, computer systems and productivity. *Management Information Systems Quarterly*, September.
Falconer, D., and Hodgett, R. A. (1996) Participation in IS planning and development and the achievement of performance criteria in Australian companies. *Proc. 7th Australian Conference on IS*, Hobart.
Farbey, B., Land, F., and Targett, D. (1993) *How to Assess your IT Investment, A Study of Methods and Practice*. Butterworth-Heinemann, Oxford.
Fisher, J. (1992) Use of nonfinancial performance measures. *Cost Management* Spring.
Framel, J. E. (1993) Information value management. *Journal of Systems Management* December.
Hains, P. (1996) Measuring and managing to achieve business benefits. *Proc. 3rd Australian Conference on Software Metrics*, Melbourne.
Hirschheim, R. A., and Smithson, S. (1988) A critical analysis of IS evaluations. *Information Systems Assessment: Issues and Challenges* (eds N. Bjorn-Anderson and G. B. Davies). North Holland, Amsterdam.
Hitt, L. M., and Brynjolfsson, E. (1996) Productivity, business profitability and consumer surplus: three different measures of IT value. *Management Information Systems Quarterly* June, 121–142.
Hochstrasser, B., and Griffiths, C. (1991) *Controlling IT Investment: Strategy and Management*. Chapman & Hall, London.
Hogbin, G., and Thomas, D. V. (1994) *Investing in IT—The Decision-making Process* McGraw-Hill, London.
Ives, B., Olson, M., and Baroudi, J. J. (1983) Measuring user information satisfaction: a method and critique. *Communications of the ACM* **26**(10), 785–793.
Kaplan, R. S., and Norton, D. P. (1992) The balanced scorecard—measures that drive performance. *Harvard Business Review* Jan–Feb.
Kauffman, R. J., and Kriebel, C. H. (1988) Measuring and modelling the business value of IT. *Measuring Business Value of IT*. ICIT Research Study Team No.2, ICIT Press.
Kauffman, R. J. and Weill, P. (1989) *Methods for evaluating the performance effects of investments in IT*. Graduate School of Management, University of Melbourne, Working Paper No.13.
Keen, P. G. W. (1975) Computer based decision aids: the evaluation problem. *Sloan Management Review* Spring.
Keen, P. G. W. (1981) Value analysis: justifying DSS. *Management Information Systems Quarterly* March.
Keen, P. G. W. (1991) *Shaping the Future: Business Design Through IT*. Harvard Business School Press.
Knutsen, K. E., and Nolan, R. L. (1974) On cost/benefit of computer-based systems. *Managing the Data Resource Function* (ed. R. L. Nolan). West Publishing Co. pp. 277–292.
Kumar, K. (1990) Post implementation evaluation of computer based information systems—current practices. *Communications of the ACM* **33**(2).
Lay, P. M. (1985) Beware of the cost/benefit model for IS project evaluation. *Journal of Systems Management* June, 30–35.
Legge, K. (1984) *Evaluating Planned Organisational Change*. Harcourt Brace, Jovanovich, London.
Lincoln, T. (1988) Retrospective appraisal of IT using SESAME. *Information System Assessment: Issues and Challenges* (eds N. Bjorn-Andersen and G. B. Davies. North-Holland, Amsterdam.

Litecky, C. R. (1981) Intangibles in cost benefit analysis. *Journal of Systems Management* February, 15–17.

Loveman, G. W. (1988) *An assessment of the productivity impact of information technologies.* Working Paper, Management in the 1990s, Massachusetts Institute of Technology, Sloan School of Management.

Marchand, D. A., and Horton, F. W. Jr (1986) *Infotrends: Profiting from your Information Resource.* John Wiley & Sons, New York.

Marsden, J. R., and Pingrey, D. E. (1988) End user—IS design professional interaction—information exchange for firm profit or end user satisfaction? *Information and Management* 14.

Mayntz, R. (1984) Information systems and organisational effectiveness: the sociological perspective. *Beyond Productivity: IS Development for Organisational Effectiveness* (ed. Th. M. A. Bemelmans). Elsevier Science, North-Holland, Amsterdam.

Mirani, R., and Lederer, A. L. (1993) Making promises: the key benefits of proposed information systems. *Journal of Systems Management.* October, 16–20.

Moad, J. (1995) Time for a fresh approach to ROI. *Datamation* 15 February, 57–59.

Moody, D., and Walsh, P. (1996) Measuring the value of information: the key to evaluating IT investments. *Proc. 3rd Australian Conference on Software Metrics*, Melbourne.

Moreton, R. (1995) Transforming the organisation: the contribution of the information systems function. *Journal of Strategic IS* 4(2), 149–163.

Mukhopadhyay, T., Kekre, S., and Kalathur, S. (1995) Business value of IT: a study of electronic data interchange. *Management Information Systems Quarterly* June, 137–154.

Muralidhar, K., Santhanam, R., and Wilson, R. L. (1990) Using the analytic hierarchy process for information system project selection. *Information and Management* 18, 87–95.

Neiman, R. A. (1992) How IS groups can create more value: a financial services perspective. *Journal of Systems Management* May.

Norris, G. D. (1996) Post-investment appraisal. *Investing in Information Systems: Evaluation and Management* (ed. L. Willcocks). Chapman & Hall, London.

Orna, E. (1996) Valuing information: problems and opportunities. *The Fourth Resource: Information and its Management* (ed. D. P. Best). Aslib/Gower, Aldershot.

Parker, M. M., and Benson, R. J. (1988) *Information Economics: Linking Business Performance to Information Technology.* Prentice Hall, Englewood Cliffs NJ.

Peters, G. (1994) Evaluating your computer investment strategy. *Information Management: The Evaluation of IS Investments.* Chapman & Hall, London.

Peters, G. (1996) From strategy to implementation: identifying and managing benefits of IT investments. *Investing in Information Systems: Evaluation and Management* (ed. L. Willcocks). Chapman & Hall, London.

Remenyi, D., Money, A., and Twite, A. (1995) *Effective Measurement and Management of IT Costs and Benefits.* Butterworth-Heinemann, London.

Roach, S. S. (1988) Technology and the services sector: the hidden competitive challenge. *Technology Forecasting and Social Change* 34(4), 387–403.

Rotemberg, J. J., and Saloner, G. (1991) Interfirm competition and collaboration. *The Corporation of the 1990s* (ed. M. S. Scott Moreton). Oxford University Press, New York.

Sassone, P. G. (1988) Cost benefit analysis of information systems: a survey of methodologies. *Proceedings of the Conference on Office Information Systems*, Palo Alto CA.

Sassone, P. G., and Schaffer, W. A. (1978) *Cost Benefit Analysis: A Handbook.* Academic Press, New York.

Sassone, P. G., and Schwartz, A. P. (1986) Cost justifying office automation. *Datamation* 15 February.

Scott Morton, M. S. (1991) *The Corporation of the 1990s.* Oxford University Press, New York.

Simmons, P. M. (1993) Evaluating IT investments: an organisational perspective. *Proc. Fourth Australian Conference on Information Systems*, Australia.
Simmons, P. M. (1994) Measurement and evaluation of IT investments. *Proc. Software Metrics Symposium*, London.
Simmons, P. M. (1996) Quality outcomes: determining business value. *IEEE Software* January, 25–32.
Strassman, P. (1985) *Information Payoff: The Transformation of Work in the Electronic Age*. The Free Press, MacMillan Inc., New York.
Strassman, P. (1988) Management productivity as an IT measure. *Measuring Business Value of IT*. ICIT Research Study Team No.2, ICIT Press.
Strassman, P. (1990) *The Business Value of Computers*. The Information Economics Press, New Canaan CT.
Symons, V. (1990) Evaluation of information systems: IS development in the processing company. *Journal of Information Technology* **5**, 194–204.
Van Wegan, B., and De Hoog, R. (1996) Measuring the economic value of information systems. *Journal of Information Technology* **11**, 247–260.
Ward, J., Taylor, P., and Bond, P. (1996) Evaluation and realisation of IS/IT benefits: an empirical study of current practice. *European Journal of IS* **4**, 214–225.
Weill, P. (1989) *The relationship between investment in information technology and firm performance in the manufacturing sector*. Working Paper No. 18, University of Melbourne, Graduate School of Management.
Weill, P. (1990) *A study of information payoffs: implications for investment proposals*. Working Paper No. 13, University of Melbourne, Graduate School of Management.
Weill, P., and Broadbent, M. (1994) Infrastructure goes industry specific. *MIS* July, Australia.
Whiting, R., Davies, J., and Knul, M. (1996) Investment appraisal for IT systems. *Investing in Information Systems: Evaluation and Management* (ed. L. Willcocks). Chapman & Hall, London.
Willcocks, L. (1996) *Investing in Information Systems: Evaluation and Management*. Chapman & Hall, London.
Willcocks, L., and Lester, S. (1996) The evaluation and management of IS investments: from feasibility to routine operations. *Investing in Information Systems: Evaluation and Management*. (ed. L. Willcocks). Chapman & Hall, London.

Reliability Measurement, Analysis, and Improvement for Large Software Systems

JEFF TIAN

Department of Computer Science and Engineering
Southern Methodist University
Dallas, Texas 75275
USA

Abstract

This chapter surveys recent developments in software reliability engineering, and presents results in measuring test activities, analyzing product reliability, and identifying high risk areas for focused reliability improvement for large software systems. Environmental constraints and existing analysis techniques are carefully examined to select appropriate analysis techniques, models, implementation strategies, and support tools suitable for large software systems. The analysis and modeling activities include measure definition, data gathering, graphical test activity and defect tracking, overall quality assessment using software reliability growth models, and identification of problematic areas and risk management using tree-based reliability models. Various existing software tools have been adapted and integrated to support these analysis and modeling activities. This approach has been used in the testing phase of several large software products developed in the IBM Software Solutions Toronto Laboratory and was demonstrated to be effective and efficient. Various practical problems and solutions in implementing this strategy are also discussed.

1. Overview and Organization 160
2. Techniques and Models for Analyzing Software Reliability 162
   2.1 Software Quality, Reliability, and Analyses 162
   2.2 Testing Techniques and Operational Profiles 163
   2.3 Defining and Measuring Reliability in the Time Domain 165
   2.4 Input Domain Reliability Analysis 171
   2.5 General Assumptions and Their Implications 173
3. Analyzing Reliability for Large Software Systems 174
   3.1 Testing Process and Workload Characteristics 174
   3.2 Specifying Testing Environment, Measurements, and Constraints 176
   3.3 Reliability Analysis in Scenario-Based Testing 179
4. Usage Measurement and Reliability Analysis with SRGMs 181
   4.1 Test Workload Measurement and Reliability Growth Visualization 181

		4.2	Using Run Count and Execution Time Failure Data in SRGMs	187
		4.3	Using Homogeneous Test Runs for Reliability Modeling in Product D	192
		4.4	Transaction Measurement and Reliability Modeling for Product E	195
		4.5	Effective Use of SRGMs in Large Software Systems	197
5.	Tree-based Reliability Models (TBRMs)			198
		5.1	Integrated Analysis and Tree-based Modeling	199
		5.2	Reliability Analysis for Partitioned Subsets	201
		5.3	Analyses Integration and TBRM Applications	202
		5.4	Experience Using TBRM in Product D	205
		5.5	TBRM's Impact on Reliability Improvement: A Cross-Validation	207
		5.6	Findings and Future Development of TBRMs	209
6.	SRGM Based on Data Clusters (SRGM-DC)			210
		6.1	Data Partitioning for Individual Runs	211
		6.2	General Model Using Data Partitions	213
		6.3	Usage and Effectiveness of SRGM-DC and Its Dual Model	215
		6.4	Summary, Comparison, and Research Issues	218
7.	Integration, Implementation and Tool Support			219
		7.1	General Implementation and Process Linkage	219
		7.2	Tool Support for Data Collection, Analyses, and Presentation	221
		7.3	Integration and Future Development	227
8.	Conclusions and Perspectives			230
References				231

1. Overview and Organization

Reliability captures the likelihood of software failures for a given time period or a given set of input values under a specific environment, and can be used as the primary quality measure during software development, particularly in the testing phase. One fundamental assumption in reliability analysis and modeling is the in-feasibility of cost-effective prevention, detection, and elimination of *all* defects in software products [8, 34, 35, 40]. There is also a general trend of diminishing returns in quality improvement for resource spent on testing as more and more defects are removed from a software system [10, 40]. The need for the optimal combination of high quality and low cost requires us to collect appropriate measurement data, analyze them using various mathematical and statistical models to assess product quality, and make optimal resource allocation and product release decisions. These measurement and analysis activities can be integrated into the overall software process measurement and improvement framework [26] to help both developers and testers to detect and remove potential defects, to improve the development process to prevent injection of similar defects, and to manage risk better by planning early for product support and service.

This article examines the need for reliability analysis and improvement for large software systems in the component and system testing phases of the software development life cycle. Various models are used to track reliability growth and offer an overall assessment of product quality [60]. Other analyses include identification of specific problematic (or high-risk) areas and deriving remedial actions to solve or alleviate the problems identified [55]. To facilitate easy understanding and interpretation of data and results, visualization techniques and graphical representations are used to examine measurement data, track progress, and present modeling results. Software tools are used and integrated to support data collection, reliability analysis and modeling, and result presentation [64]. This approach has been demonstrated to be effective, efficient, and easily accepted by the development community [56]. So far, it has been used in several large commercial software products developed in the IBM Software Solutions Toronto Laboratory. Various practical problems and solutions in implementing and deploying this approach are also discussed.

Acronyms used throughout this chapter are listed in Table 1. Section 2 provides a survey of existing reliability analysis techniques and several commonly used software reliability models (SRMs), including both the time domain software reliability growth models (SRGMs) and the input domain reliability models (IDRMs), and discusses their common assumptions and applicability in general terms. Section 3 describes a testing environment for large software systems and the specific needs for quality assessment and improvement under such an environment. Section 4 examines test activities and workload measurements and presents some recent results applying various SRGMs in assessing and predicting reliability for large software systems. Section 5 outlines a tree-based reliability modeling (TBRM) technique and its usage in identifying high-risk (low-reliability) areas for focused reliability improvement. Section 6 presents SRGM-DC, a new type of SRGM based on data clustering analysis and its applications. Section 7 describes implementation and tool support for various reliability analyses described in this article. Section 8 summarizes the article and offers some future perspectives.

TABLE 1
ACRONYMS

SRE	software reliability engineering
SRM	software reliability model(s)
SRGM	software reliability growth model(s)
SRGM-DC	software reliability growth model(s) based on data clustering (partitioning)
IDRM	input domain reliability model(s)
TBM	tree-based modeling, or tree-based model(s)
TBRM	tree-based reliability model(s) that integrate SRGMs and IDRMs using TBM

2. Techniques and Models for Analyzing Software Reliability

Throughout the testing process, various measurement data need to be gathered and analyzed to track progress, assess product quality and reliability, manage resource allocation and product release, and optimize testing and development processes [26]. This section surveys existing reliability measurements and analysis techniques that are applicable to the testing process.

2.1 Software Quality, Reliability, and Analyses

Software quality can be defined and measured from various different views to reflect different concerns and aspects of "quality" [31]. In practice, it is generally defined either from a customer view based on external behavior of the software product or from a development view based on internal product attributes, and measured accordingly. According to Kan *et al.*, "Quality is conformance to customer's expectations and requirements" [29]. This definition emphasizes the central role of customers, who are the final arbiter of how "good" a software product is. These customer expectations and requirements are represented by the product specifications during product development. These specifications can be formally verified during specification and implementation processes using various formal verification techniques [75] or dynamically verified through different types of testing [8]. Various quality measures from the developer's perspective can be defined based on these specifications.

The keys to the conformance of customer's expectations and product specifications are the concepts of failure, fault, and error: A *failure* is a behavioral deviation from the user requirement or specification, a *fault* is the underlying cause within a software system that causes certain failure(s), while an *error* refers to human mistakes or misconceptions that result in faults being injected into software systems [1, 2]. Failure is a dynamic, behavioral definition, which is closer to the customer's view, while fault is a static, code-based definition, closer to the developer's view. Both failures and faults are often referred to as *defects* when the distinction between the cause (faults) and effect (failures) is not critical [34].

Various defect measures, such as defect count and defect density, are commonly used as direct quality measures in many software development organizations. However, such measures are defined from a developer's view, and it is hard to predict post-release defects based on observations of pre-release defects because of the differences in environments. Recently, the trend has been to move toward quality measures that are more meaningful to the customer. Software reliability and related measures, such as failure intensity or MTBF (mean time between failure), have gained wide acceptance [34, 40].

Generally speaking, a software system is said to be "reliable" if it performs its specified functions correctly over a long period of time or under a wide variety of usage environments and operations [24, 40, 54]. Reliability is a failure-centered quality measure that views the software system as a whole from a customer perspective. *Software reliability engineering* (SRE) is concerned with the assessment, prediction, and management of the reliability of software systems. SRE activities are generally concentrated on the system testing stage, because only by then are all the functions available to the customer available for testing.

One fundamental assumption in SRE is the existence of faults and the infeasibility of exhaustive testing that can be used to expose and remove all the faults in software systems. As a result, failure-free operations cannot be guaranteed, but only assured statistically based on past observations. A *software reliability model* (SRM) provides a systematic way of assessing and predicting software reliability. Based on different assumptions regarding the characteristics of the software systems and fault exposure, various reliability models have been proposed and used to analyze software reliability. There are two types of software reliability model:

- Time domain *software reliability growth models* (SRGMs): these models analyze time-indexed failure data to assess the software's ability to perform correctly over a specific time period under a given operational environment.
- *Input domain reliability models* (IDRMs): these models analyze input states and failure data to assess the software's ability to perform correctly for different input values.

These two approaches provide two different perspectives of reliability. The time domain approach stresses the assessment and prediction of the overall reliability. The input domain approach provides valuable information that can be used to test software products thoroughly due to the use of well-defined input states. However, they are generally used disjointly in practice. Recently, an integrated approach that combines some strengths of these two approaches was developed in [55] and [56] to provide analysis results that can be used to assess the reliability of software products as well as to guide reliability improvement.

2.2 Testing Techniques and Operational Profiles

Testing of small programs or small units of large programs (unit testing) is usually performed by the program developer with complete knowledge of the implementation details. Such testing is generally referred to as white-box (or structural) testing, which usually strives for complete coverage of all possible states, execution paths etc. [8]. There is no separation of duties between failure detection and quality assurance on the one side and problem tracking and fault removal on the other. However, for overall testing (or system testing) of large software systems, this approach becomes impractical because of the combinatorial explosion of possible states and execution paths. Professional testers are needed, black-box (or functional) testing techniques are often used, and automated testing tools become more of a necessity than a luxury [9]. To achieve effective failure detection and to provide statistically verifiable means of demonstrating the product's reliability, one must thoroughly test the software with a variety of inputs to cover important functions and relations. The concept of *operational profiles* (collections of functions and their usage frequencies by some target user group [38, 39]) has gained wide usage in system testing recently.

Operational profiles can be used to help testing teams to cover a maximal number of situations in which the program will be used by customers, within practical limits due to budget and/or schedule constraints. Most of the SRE activities also assume the availability and usage of operational profiles in testing, so that modeling results from this in-process reliability analysis can be extrapolated to predict in-field software reliability. Operational profiles define the usage environment, under which software reliability is defined and analyzed. The accuracy of the reliability analysis result is affected by the accuracy of operational profiles [17]. However, a recent study demonstrated that the predictive accuracy of reliability models is not heavily affected by errors in the estimate of the operational profiles [43], thus even rough operational profiles can provide valuable information for software testing and reliability analyses. Recently, new concepts in test selection and design for testability have also been developed by various researchers for use in conjunction with operational profiles for effective testing [39, 70].

There are several way to capture operational profiles, including: (1) actual measurement in customer settings, (2) user or customer surveys, and (3) usage information gathering in conjunction with software requirement information gathering [38]. The first method is the most accurate, but also the most costly, and may also be problematic because it has to deal with legal issues and problems concerning intellectual properties. The latter two are less costly, but the information captured may not be accurate or detailed enough for us to develop operational profiles directly. However, such surveys and information gatherings can be used as a general guide to the overall testing process to ensure that at least the high-level functions that are important to customers or frequently used by customers can be covered by testing [60]. A recent study also pointed out that a controlled laboratory environment, where customers are invited to product pre-release validations, may yield valuable data for the construction of operational profiles [33].

The results from measurements or surveys of customer usage can be organized into structured forms and used to derive test cases and generate test workloads. Commonly used models for organizing such information include (1) flat profiles which list end-to-end user operations and associated probabilities such as in [38]; and (2) individual units of operations and associated transition probabilities among the units that form a Markov chain [3, 73]. Test cases and test workload can be generated from this structured operational profile information according to various rules and criteria to cover important functions frequently used by target customers.

2.3 Defining and Measuring Reliability in the Time Domain

In the time domain approach, the reliability of a software system is defined to be the probability of its failure-free operations for a specific duration under a specific environment [1, 22, 40]. Reliability is usually characterized by hazard and reliability functions. The hazard function (or hazard rate) $z(t)$ is defined as:

$$z(t)\Delta t = P\{t < T < t + \Delta t | T > t\}$$

where T marks the failure time, P is the probability function, and $z(t)\Delta t$ gives the probability of failure in time interval $(t, t + \Delta t)$, given that the system has not failed before t. The reliability function $R(t)$ is defined as:

$$R(t) = \exp\left(-\int_0^t z(x)\,dx\right)$$

which gives the probability of failure free operations in the time interval $(0, t)$. MTBF (mean time between failure) is commonly used as a measure of reliability for its intuitiveness. MTBF can be calculated as:

$$\text{MTBF} = \int_0^\infty R(x)\,dx$$

In practical applications, comparing with other reliability measures, the measure MTBF is easy to interpret and directly meaningful to customers as well as software managers, developers, and testers.

Various measurement data are necessary for model fitting and usage. There are three key elements to time domain reliability measurement: failure, time, and usage environment. The key to failure measurement is consistency in failure definition and data interpretation. The environment is generally assumed to be similar to the actual customer usage environment, so that the analysis results can be directly extrapolated to the likelihood of in-field product failures [39]. For time measurement, there are various alternatives, falling into two categories:

- *Usage-independent time measurement*: only the failures are marked, either by the actual failure time or by failures loosely associated with a time period. Information about software usage is ignored. The commonly used calendar time and wall-clock time measurements fall into this category.
- *Usage-dependent time measurement*: only the time when software is used is counted, and the usage during testing is usually used to normalize the time measurement. For example, execution time measurement counts only the time when the software system is actually used [40]. Time can also be measured as some test activity count in a logical sequence, such as time-ordered test runs in [60] or transactions in [62].

If software usage is fairly constant, usage-independent time measurements are usable for reliability modeling. Otherwise, various test activity or workload measurements need to be taken for reliability modeling. Based on different time measurements and different assumptions about the underlying faults and the fault–failure linkages, different reliability growth models have been proposed and used [1, 22, 24, 40]. One underlying assumption common to all models is that the reliability grows as failure-causing faults are removed from the software, hence the name reliability *growth* models. Several SRGMs are listed in Table 2 and briefly described below.

TABLE 2
LABELS AND REFERENCES FOR SOME COMMONLY USED SRGMs

Label	Reference	Model
JM	[28]	Jelinski–Moranda de-eutrophication model
Sho	[51]	Shooman model
Geo	[36]	Moranda's geometric de-eutrophication model
GO	[25]	Goel–Okumoto NHPP model
S	[74]	Yamada–Ohba–Osaki S-shaped NHPP model
GP	[46]	Schafer *et al.* generalized Poisson model
SW	[47]	Schick–Wolverton model
BMB	[13]	Brooks–Motley model, binomial variation
BMP	[13]	Brooks–Motley model, Poisson variation
Musa	[37]	Musa's basic execution time model
MO	[41]	Musa–Okumoto logarithmic Poisson execution time model
Sch	[48]	Schneidewind model
LV	[32]	Littlewood–Varrel Bayesian model

2.3.1 De-eutrophication Models

De-eutrophication models link failure probability to the number of defects remaining in the current system in a functional form, thus capture reliability growth (or de-eutrophication) in testing as a result of defect observations and removals. In the Jelinski–Moranda model [28], one of the earliest and most widely used models, chance of failure for unit time is *proportional* to the number of defects remaining in the current system. That is, the hazard rate z_i for the ith failure is:

$$z_i = \phi(N - (i - 1))$$

where N is the total number of defects at the beginning of testing (i.e. before discovering the first failure), and ϕ a proportionality constant for the model. The hazard rate between successive failure observations remains constant, and the discovery and removal of each defect contribute the same to the hazard rate reduction. Therefore, the failure rates over successive failures form a step function of time, with uniform downward steps at corresponding failure observations.

The model proposed by Shooman [51] is essentially the same as the Jelinski–Moranda model above, but with different parameters, and uses period failure count data instead of time-between-failure data. Another similar de-eutrophication model is the geometric model by Moranda [36], with

$$z_i = z_0 \phi^{(i-1)}$$

where $\phi < 1$. The hazard function over the failure intervals forms a downward geometric sequence. The geometric model captures the slow-down effect in hazard rate reduction as more and more defects are discovered and fixed.

2.3.2 Generic NHPP Model and Variations

The failure arrivals can be viewed as a stochastic process and analyzed accordingly [30]. The most commonly used such process is the non-homogeneous Poisson process (NHPP), with the number of failures $X(t)$ for a given time interval $(0, t)$ prescribed by the probability $P[X(t) = n]$ as:

$$P[X(t) = n] = \frac{[m(t)]^n e^{-m(t)}}{n!}$$

where $m(t)$ is the *mean function*, and the failure rate $\lambda(t)$ (used in place of $z(t)$ in such situations) is the derivative of $m(t)$, i.e. $\lambda(t) = m'(t)$. Different choices of the mean function $m(t)$ can be used to model different failure arrival patterns. Two specific variations of the NHPP models used in this chapter are:

(1) The *Goel–Okumoto model* (also known as the exponential model) [25] is an NHPP model with

$$m(t) = N(1 - e^{-bt})$$

where N (estimated total defects) and b are constant. This model is the continuous equivalent of the discrete Jelinski–Moranda model.

(2) The *S-shaped reliability growth model* [74] is another NHPP model with

$$m(t) = N(1 - (1 + bt)e^{-bt})$$

where N (estimated total defects) and b are constant. This model better describes the commonly observed patterns of failure arrivals consisting of three phases: an initial slow start, a middle section characterized by numerous failure observations and fault removals, and finally a slow-down (saturation) of failure arrivals.

2.3.3 Generalized Poisson Model and Variations

The generalized Poisson model [46] is a generalization of Jelinski–Moranda model and several related models. In this model, the distribution of the number of failures f_i for the ith interval with test length t_i is a Poisson process, with the mean function $m_i(t_i) = E(f_i)$ specified as:

$$m_i(t_i) = \phi[N - M_{i-1}] \, g_i(t_1, t_2, \ldots, t_i)$$

where N is the estimated total defects, M_i the defects removed after ith period, and ϕ the Poisson constant. Three notable variations of this model are:

(1) *Jelinski–Moranda model* [28], with $f_i = 1$ and $g_i = t_i$.
(2) *Schick–Wolverton model* [47], with $f_i = 1$ and $g_i = t_i^2/2$. The hazard rate increases with time in this model, i.e. $\lambda_i = \phi \, [N - M_{i-1}] \, t_i$. Therefore the chance of failure observations increases more than linearly with time.
(3) Generalized Poisson model with estimated power term α, i.e. $g_i = (t_i)^\alpha$ [46]. This generalized model is data driven, and can fit to various different failure arrival patterns, from sub-linear ($\alpha < 1$), linear ($\alpha = 1$, i.e. the Jelinski–Moranda model), to super-linear ($\alpha > 1$, including the Schick–Wolverton model, with $\alpha = 2$, and others).

2.3.4 Brooks–Motley Model

The Brooks–Motley model [13] has two variations according to whether a Poisson or a binomial distribution of failure observations n_i over all possible $\{X\}$ for the ith period of length t_i is assumed:

$$P[X = n_i] = \begin{cases} \dfrac{(N_i\phi_i)^{n_i} e^{-N_i\phi_i}}{n_i!}, & \phi_i = 1-(1-\phi)^{t_i} \text{ (Poisson)} \\ \dbinom{N_i}{n_i} q_i^{n_i}(1-q_i)^{N_i-n_i}, & q_i = 1-(1-q)^{t_i} \text{ (binomial)} \end{cases}$$

where N_i is the estimated number of the defects at the beginning of the ith period; q and ϕ are the binomial and Poisson constants respectively. Unlike other models listed here that all assume that the full product is tested, the Brooks–Motley model allows for only a part of the product to be tested, making it the only choice under specific situations.

2.3.5 Execution Time SRGMs

The basic execution time model by Musa [37] is essentially the same as the Jelinski–Moranda model, but with the emphasis on using CPU execution time as the time measurement. This model also includes a predictive element, enabling the user of this model to estimate model parameters from the product and process characteristics, even before actual failures are observed. The Logarithmic execution time model by Musa and Okumoto [41] is a variation of the NHPP model with

$$m(\tau) = \frac{1}{\theta} \log(\lambda_0 \theta \tau + 1)$$

where τ measures CPU-execution time, λ_0 is the initial failure intensity, and θ is a model parameter. Both these models have been used successfully in various telecommunication systems [40], and are often used together to bound the reliability predictions from above (basic Musa) and below (Musa–Okumoto).

2.3.6 Schneidewind Model

In Schneidewind's model [48], the expected number of failures m_i in the ith period (all periods are of equal length) is given by

$$m_i = \frac{\alpha}{\beta} (e^{-\beta(i-1)} - e^{-\beta i})$$

with parameters α and β. This model is a special case of the generalized Poisson model which allows the analyzer to choose different weights for the past observations to reflect the closer linkage between reliability and the recent past than that between reliability and the distant past. Recently, Schneidewind has also proposed a method to optimally select data to use with this model [49].

2.3.7 Littlewood–Varrell Model

In the Bayesian model by Littlewood and Varrell [32], the ith inter-failure interval t_i follows the distribution:

$$f(t_i|\lambda_i) = \lambda_i e^{-\lambda_i t_i}$$

where the parameter λ_i follows a Γ distribution:

$$f(\lambda_i|\alpha, \psi(i)) = \frac{[\psi(i)]^\alpha \lambda_i^{\alpha-1} e^{-\psi(i)\lambda_i}}{\Gamma(\alpha)}$$

where $\psi(i)$ is an increasing function of i and α is a constant. Therefore this model adjusts the model parameter (λ_i) using the latest observations to analyze successive failure intervals (t_i). A wide variety of failure arrival patterns can be fitted to this model and analyzed accordingly.

2.3.8 Fitting and Using SRGMs

According to the specific types of data required for model fitting and usage, the SRGMs described above can be grouped into time between failure (TBF) models or period failure count (PFC) models [24]. TBF models require data for successive inter-failure intervals, i.e. $\{t_i, i = 1, 2, ..., n\}$, where t_i is the observed time duration, measured in different time units discussed above, between the $(i-1)$th failure and the ith failure. PFC models require data for successive period lengths (t_i for the duration of the ith period) and associated failure counts (f_i for the count of failures observed in the ith period), i.e. $\{\langle t_i, f_i \rangle, i = 1, 2, ..., n\}$. Different models can be fitted to such data collected during testing with the help of certain software tools (Section 7). These fitted SRGMs can be used for various purposes, including:

- *Assessing current reliability.* The current reliability of a software system can be estimated as the fitted model function ($z(t)$, $\lambda(t)$, $R(t)$, etc.) evaluated at the current time.
- *Assessing reliability growth.* The overall reliability growth since the start of testing is captured by the fitted curve for the model, such as in Fig. 8.

- *Predicting future reliability.* The reliability for any given time in the future can be predicted by extrapolating the fitted curves for corresponding models into the future.

- *Other predictions.* The time or resource needed to reach a given reliability target can also be estimated similarly by extrapolating the fitted curves and calculating related quantities.

- *Exit criterion.* The modeling result can also be used to serve as an exit criterion for product release, i.e. the product can only be released if its estimated current reliability meets a certain reliability target.

2.4 Input Domain Reliability Analysis

In input domain reliability analysis, the reliability of a software system is defined to be the probability of failure-free operation for specific input states. Besides failure measurement, the key to reliability measurement in input domain reliability modeling is input state measurement, which captures information on the precise input state for the software systems. This information can be related to testing results and used for reliability modeling.

Input domain reliability models (IDRMs) generally use data from repeated random sampling to analyze product reliability. Therefore they can be used directly for current reliability assessment and as an exit criterion for stop testing. Although IDRMs for a single set of data cannot be directly used to analyze reliability growth, IDRMs for successive data sets over time or for subsets of data associated with certain input states can be used for various other purposes in reliability analyses and improvement. These novel usages of IDRMs will be explored further in Section 5.

2.4.1 Nelson Model

In Nelson's input domain reliability model [42], an unbiased estimate of reliability is the ratio between input states that result in successful executions over the total sampled input states. The unbiased reliability estimate $\hat{R}$ in the Nelson model can be derived from observations of running the software for a sample of n inputs according to the following setup:

- The n inputs are randomly selected from the set $\{E_i : i = 1, 2, ..., N\}$, where each E_i is a set of data values needed to make a run.

- Sampling probability is according to the probability vector $\{P_i : i = 1, 2, ..., N\}$, where P_i is the probability that E_i is sampled. This probability vector defines the operational profile.

- If the number of failures is f, then the estimated reliability $\hat{R}$ is:

$$\hat{R} = 1 - \frac{f}{n} = \frac{n-f}{n}$$

That is, the estimated reliability $\hat{R}$ for a given input set equals the number of successes over the total number of runs.

Notice that in the Nelson model, the operational profile and sampling probability distribution are handled implicitly.

2.4.2 Brown–Lipow Model

In the model proposed by Brown and Lipow [14], the whole input domain is partitioned into subdomains; i.e. each E_i from input domain $\{E_i, i = 1, 2, ..., N\}$ represents a specific subdomain. The estimated reliability is:

$$\hat{R} = 1 - \sum_{j=1}^{N} \left(\frac{f_j}{n_j}\right) P(E_j)$$

where n_j is the number of runs sampled from subdomain E_j, f_j is the number of failures observed out of n_j runs, and $P(E_j)$ explicitly defines the probability that inputs in subdomain E_j are used in the actual customer's operational environment. This model adjusts for the different usage frequencies between the testing environment (as reflected by n_i as a proportion of all test runs) and the customer usage environment (as captured in $P(E_i)$); thus it is more widely applicable than the Nelson model. When there is an exact match between the two frequencies (i.e. $P(E_i) = n_i/\sum_{j=1}^{N} n_j$), the Brown–Lipow model reduces to the Nelson model.

2.4.3 IDRMs and Coverage Analysis

In both the Nelson model and the Brown–Lipow model, one common assumption is repeated random sampling without error fixing. However, in practical testing environments, whenever a failure is observed, appropriate actions are taken to identify, locate, and remove the underlying faults that have caused the failure. The reliability is changed due to defect removals. To assess the reliability at this point, another batch of runs needs to be executed, and the defect fixing problem arises again. A small subset of runs towards the end of testing can be used as a biased estimate of reliability. In general, the smaller the sampling window, the less bias there is. However, the confidence levels of the estimation are severely compromised because of the smaller sample size. This situation points to the need to use relevant time domain information to strengthen IDRMs, such as in the tree-based reliability models [55] using both time and input domain information, discussed in Section 5.

Realizing the impracticality of failure detection without fixing, many researchers focus instead on maximizing the product coverage of test suites. The implicit assumptions here are twofold: (1) all detected defects will be removed, and (2) higher coverage leads to higher reliability. Consequently, the focus of this approach is not on the reliability assessment, but rather on increasing the various coverage measures that can be defined and gathered, and maximizing testing effectiveness defined accordingly [68, 72]. An alternative way of using coverage information in reliability modeling is outlined in [16], where coverage analysis results for individual test runs were used to weight time intervals based on the assumption that only test runs that cover new territories are more likely to trigger failures.

2.5 General Assumptions and Their Implications

There are various assumptions about the testing process, defect characteristics, distribution, and handling assumed by the SRMs [24], including:

- *The software is used in an environment that resembles its actual usage by its target customers.* Operational profiles are commonly used to design, select, and guide the execution of test cases [39]. This assumption ensures the validity and appropriateness of reliability estimations and predictions.
- *Failure intervals are independent, which implies randomized testing.* This assumption restricts the usage of SRMs to late testing phases where randomized testing techniques are more likely to be used. For earlier phases of testing, white box testing techniques are often used together with structural coverage-based criteria for test process management [8].
- *The probability of failure in SRGMs is a function only of the number of faults existing in the software system, which implies a homogeneous distribution of faults.* Deviation from this assumption may lead to inaccuracies in the SRGM results. Defect distribution information reflected in the input domain data can be used in conjunction with time domain information for reliability analysis and modeling. The integrated model in [55] is an example of recent development in this direction.
- *Time is used as the basis to define failure rate in SRGMs, which implies equivalence of time units.* This assumption places a stringent requirement for proper time measurement, making usage-independent time measurements suitable only for systems with constant workload. For most software systems proper usage-dependent time measurements need to be selected to capture workload variations for reliability modeling.

Many general issues about model limitations due to these assumptions are discussed in [24], and some particular observations relevant to large commercial software systems are presented in [60]. In the next section, we characterize a typical software testing environment for large software systems, examine the validity of the above assumptions, and assess the applicability and effectiveness of different types of SRMs.

3. Analyzing Reliability for Large Software Systems

Various software measurements need to be collected during testing for effective progress tracking, reliability assessment, and improvement. However, before any such measurement and analysis devices are put into use in practical applications, a good understanding of the environment and the specific goals (or needs) of the measurement and analysis activities are necessary [5]. This section describes a typical testing environment, identifying specific needs and constraints for reliability analysis and improvement in large software systems.

3.1 Testing Process and Workload Characteristics

The products studied in this article are large software systems, where cost and time-to-market are some key concerns, competing with product quality goals. The product characteristics, market environment, and the software development and maintenance process all affect the suitability and effectiveness of various software technologies and analysis methods in project management and quality improvement.

Five large commercial software products, labeled A, B, C, D, and E, developed in the IBM Software Solutions Toronto Laboratory, were studied in a series of recent papers [33, 55, 56, 60–62, 64], and the results are summarized in this chapter. These products include relational database systems, language compilers, and computing environments. They range from several hundred thousand lines of code to several million lines of code, and have taken several years to develop, with system testing usually lasting several months to over a year. The development process for these products [27] roughly conforms to the so-called "waterfall" model [71], with separate phases for product requirement analysis and specification, design, coding, and testing, although significant overlap and rework over succeeding phases are common. Component and system testing generally follow after coding and unit testing (which are done by the development team) and are performed by a dedicated testing team. The code base for each product under component and system testing is under continuous change because of defect fixing and the addition of minor functions. However, no addition of major functions is allowed in this phase, to ensure the product being completed and delivered on schedule. Weekly status meetings are usually held to examine progress in terms of effort and quality improvement.

A commonly used testing strategy for such large software systems is to assure acceptable program behavior as defined by the product specifications through good coverage of all the major components and functionalities. High-level descriptions are used to describe test "scenarios." According to the different areas covered, these test scenarios can be grouped into different scenario types or classes. When testing is performed, a scenario description is used to construct an actual "test case," either manually or with the help of some test automation tools. Testing is also often divided among different testers and into several sub-phases, with a different focus for each one. This division allows the testing team to track progress on a smaller, more manageable, scale.

When a defect is discovered by the testing team, a report is created and handed over to the development team. The testing team usually suspends activities related to the testing scenarios that have triggered the defect and continues with others. This approach reduces the chance of repeatedly finding duplicate defects that provide little additional information for defect removal or quality improvement. When an integrated fix for the reported defect arrives from the development team, the failing scenario is rerun and the testing process continues. However, these repeated scenarios do not generally lead to the repetition of exactly the same test cases.

The test workload usually varies considerably during the testing process of large software products. Testing activities and efforts are affected by several factors, described below:

- *Shifting focuses*. Different testers usually concentrate on different functional areas and sub-phases. This division of testing activities forms some partial dependency sequences and causes the test workload to fluctuate: (1) there is a learning curve associated with this shift that affects how much testing can be done; (2) as different parts of the products may differ in quality, the overall failure curve is also affected by the shifting focuses, depending on which part is currently under intensive testing. In addition, the quality of sub-parts within a focused area is more likely to be affected by defect detection and removal in the same area than from more distant areas. Therefore, such shifts can bring many "mini-steps" to reliability growth.
- *Progression of test cases*. For test efficiency concerns, more complex test cases are rarely attempted until most simple test cases have already been successfully executed. Simple test cases can be easily used to

identify early (mostly easy to find) problems, while complex test cases can then be used to identify problems that have escaped earlier testing. Using complex test cases early in testing may be problematic because it may be difficult to identify the large number of possibilities that may have caused the failure in the test run. This progression of test cases also has a direct effect on the progression of test workload over time.

- *Testing strategy.* A commonly used testing strategy, "*Test until it breaks,*" also contributes to the uneven size of test runs and the progressively larger test runs. When this strategy is used, constant streams of user-oriented tasks are fed to the software system until it encounters a failure or until it reaches a predefined upper limit for test workload. This predefined upper limit is generally significantly higher than the "normal" workload for test cases. Therefore the use of such testing strategies also contributes to the uneven distribution of workload during testing.
- *Staffing level variations.* There is generally a gradual staffing-up process in system testing. This factor, combined with the increased familiarity with the product as testing progresses, contributes in general to more (complex) test cases run towards the later part of testing. It is also common for a group of similar products to share a common testing team, and to have more than one product undergoing testing simultaneously. Sometimes, "emergency" situations may arise in some projects that require immediate response and reallocation of resources, resulting in occasional wild fluctuations of staffing and workload levels for individual projects.
- *Code base stability.* Although major additions to the code base during component and system testing are not generally allowed, substantial change can be under way because of the detection of some major (high-severity or widespread) defects. This, in turn, affects the amount of testing that can be done and the number of potential defects (which may be masked or triggered by such changes) that can be detected.

Such workload variations need to be captured in the usage-dependent time measurements to provide a solid data basis for reliability analysis and modeling. Some quantitative results in examining the workload variations in several such large software systems are presented in Section 4.

3.2 Specifying Testing Environment, Measurements, and Constraints

A consistent view of the testing process and environment and a consistent interpretation of the collected data are important to ensure meaningful and appropriate analysis and modeling. To ensure such consistencies, we formally define the following terms:

Scenario   A testing *scenario* is a rough description of testing activities to be performed. It roughly corresponds to a collection of test cases. In contrast, the term *test case* in the literature usually refers to a more precise description of testing activities to be performed.

Scenario type Testing scenarios are grouped into scenario types or classes corresponding to the major functional areas they are designed to test. A scenario is usually identified by a name that consists of its scenario class name and a serial number within the class. Sometimes, multi-layered classifications are used to organized the large numbers of test scenarios for large software systems.

Run   An execution (also called an attempt) of a scenario is denoted as a *run*. For software systems that operate continuously, such as operating systems or telecommunication systems, a run is usually defined as a subdivision of the time period of program execution associated with user-oriented tasks [38]. Defect reporting is triggered by runs.

Failure   An unsuccessful run is treated as the arrival of a *failure*. An unsuccessful run is associated with the reporting of one or more valid defects.

Since a test scenario is only a high-level description of activities to be performed and components to be tested, and because the software under testing is continuously undergoing change because of defect discovery and fixing, each execution for the same test scenario will be different. A practical implication is that each run can be treated as an independent software usage operation.

All the activities for test tracking, analysis, and modeling require "good quality" (valid, consistent, and useful) data. Numerous data are routinely captured in many projects for test tracking and testing process management purposes [56]. These data, with possibly minor modifications, provide the input for progress tracking and reliability analyses. The information associated with test runs can generally be grouped into three categories:

- *Result* of test runs. This includes result information regarding individual runs, summary information for a group of runs, and possibly defect classification information for related defects collected using some systematic scheme, such as ODC (orthogonal defect classification [18]).

- *Timing*: this includes the specific time associated with each run, such as start time, normal termination time for successful runs, or failure time for failed runs, and possibly software usage information during test runs. Such information is generally used for time domain reliability growth modeling.
- *Input*: the descriptive information about each specific run generally specifies the input for the program and the testing environment. Specific information may include scenario classification, tester (and possibly other input state) identification, environmental setup, or specific input value.

In general, we can treat the data from testing as a multi-attribute data set with each data point corresponding to a specific run, and each data attribute corresponding to some specific information regarding the run. For input domain analysis, we need to analyze and establish relations between the input information and the test result. For time domain reliability modeling, we need to analyze the timing information and test result data.

To implement an effective strategy for test tracking and reliability analysis and to introduce process and quality improvements that can last, we have to overcome a number of obstacles within the constraints of the project environment. We have to work within the project schedule and minimize the risk of project delays and cost overruns because of the introduction of measurement and analysis activities. We also need to address various organizational issues to ensure effective and long-lasting improvements and process changes.

The uncertainty or risk associated with introducing a new technology and the unfamiliarity with the measurements and analysis methods can have a major effect on the success of such measurement and improvement programs. Adequate lead time should be allocated for planning, education, and training, to overcome inertia and dispel misunderstandings. An evolutionary approach needs to be adopted, to demonstrate the benefits step by step, eventually leading to a full implementation of a comprehensive measurement and analysis strategy. A gradual change is also more likely to be ingrained into the corporate culture and is more likely to last.

Some organizational issues also need to be addressed. In most large software development organizations, the product (or project) organizations, including software developers, testers, and project managers, are responsible for producing various software products to meet market needs; while a separate quality organization oversees the product quality and development process across all the different products. The product organizations are generally vertically integrated according to product lines and market segmentation. The quality organizations are generally structured horizontally, with each quality analyst or team covering a number of software technologies (such as design methods, code complexity analysis, or testing tools) or process areas (e.g. process definition and modeling, defect prevention). Involvement, buy-in, and commitment, and cooperation of the developers, testers, managers, and quality analysts, are essential to the success of any measurement and improvement initiative. A successful strategy for test tracking and analysis generally requires close collaboration between the product and quality organizations.

3.3 Reliability Analysis in Scenario-Based Testing

A quality measurement that is close to the customer view needs to be used to track and optimize testing activities. To satisfy this need, software reliability and related measures can be used to assess the overall quality of a software product by fitting various SRGMs to observed data. On the other hand, because product quality is generally uneven across different components or functions, there is a strong need to identify those parts with substantially more defects, so that the greatest improvement can be made with the least cost. Unfortunately, traditional SRGMs provide little such information. Analyses are needed to help in risk identification and management. In this way, various management decisions, such as resource allocation, test case selection and execution, can focus on those high-risk areas. Such information can also help us to plan for product service and for future update releases.

Overall, the mixture of structured (centered around the framework of scenario classes), clustered (focused on fault localization), and randomized testing, rather than purely randomized testing, dominates in large software system testing. The test workload also varies considerably, and defect distributions are non-uniform. All these seem to deviate from the common assumptions of various software reliability models (SRMs) summarized in Section 2.5. We next examine these issues to assess the applicability of existing SRMs and the need for new models and analysis methods.

- *Approximating scenario-based testing with random testing*. Despite the individual dependencies due to structured testing according to scenarios and scenario classes, testing is generally conducted by different testers in parallel, interleaving in some arbitrary fashion. As a result, the overall testing resembles random testing. The key to this approximation is parallelism and interleaving. If a substantial part of the test runs strictly follows some sequential order, such as stress testing following after other testing scenarios in [60], test runs and related data need to be divided into subsets (or sub-phases) with SRMs fitted to individual subsets. On the other hand, if fundamental differences exist among different scenario classes, they should be analyzed separately, such as in [55] for different sub-products.

- *Dealing with the defect fixing effect.* Each discovery of a defect generally triggers related test runs to locate the defect and additional test runs to verify the defect fix. However, in large software systems, usually hundreds or even thousands of defects are discovered and fixed during testing [55, 60]. When such large numbers of defects are discovered and fixed, the overall testing still resembles random testing, because of the lack of longer term dependencies among different testing periods, despite local dependencies. Therefore, when using SRMs, we have to make sure that adequate failure data exist for statistical modeling.
- *Selecting appropriate time measurement to capture test workload variations.* Because the test workload usually varies considerably, for large software systems, proper usage-dependent time measurements, including test run count, execution time, and transactions, need to be selected to capture workload variations for reliability analysis using SRGMs [60, 62].
- *Dealing with uneven distribution of faults.* Faults are generally distributed quite unevenly across components, with new and changed components and those with high complexity usually containing significantly more faults than the rest [66]. The uneven distribution of faults implies non-homogeneous chances of defect detections or failure arrivals when different components or subsets of operations are tested (only a portion of faults is at risk of being detected). This kind of uneven distribution can be characterized by various input domain reliability models with explicit usage of input states and testing results. Tree-based reliability models (TBRMs) can be used to handle input domain partitions systematically, and help identify high-risk areas (high likelihood for triggering failures) and guide focused remedial actions [55]. A general consequence of using such an approach is that the product quality across different components or functional areas will even out towards the end of testing. By then, SRGMs become more applicable because of the closer conformance to the assumption of homogeneous chances of fault detections.

To summarize, various SRMs are applicable under the scenario-based testing environment for large software systems. However, care must be taken to ensure that certain conditions are met for effective use of measurement data to track progress and SRGMs to assess and predict reliability. A new reliability model, TBRM [55], can be used to analyze both time and input domain information for risk identification and reliability improvement. All these analysis and modeling activities, together with their integration and tool support, will be discussed in the rest of the chapter.

4. Usage Measurement and Reliability Analysis with SRGMs

In this section, we examine two important data entities for large software systems in their system testing (testing activities and defects), and present reliability analysis results using time domain software reliability growth models (SRGMs) for several large software products. These results are presented in two ways:

- *Graphical* presentation to allow for visual inspection to detect trends and patterns between fitted models and actual observations. Either the cumulative data and models (e.g. the left graph in Fig. 8) or the rate data and models (e.g. the right graph in Fig. 8) can be used.
- *Tabular and textual* forms to present important model parameters and summary statistics, such as in Table 4 and related discussions. Sometimes this information can also be directly presented within graphs, such as in Fig. 9.

4.1 Test Workload Measurement and Reliability Growth Visualization

One common assumption in SRGMs is that elapsed time captures test workload and can be used as the basis to define failure rate and reliability (Section 2.5). This assumption implies equivalence of time units and places a stringent requirement on time measurement for reliability modeling. Usage-independent time can be measured by various physical measurements of time of different granularity, ranging from rough calendar dates to precise time stamps. All usage-dependent time measurements can be associated with test runs. Because the test cases are generally grouped into scenario classes according to customer usage information, each test run during testing represents a well-defined unit of software usage linked to some user-oriented operations. Consequently, various test workload measurements based on runs can serve as the basis of time measurement for reliability modeling:

- *Test run count*. The numbers of test runs associated with segments in the overall test execution sequence can be used as time measurements [60].
- *Execution time*. For runs falling into a given period, the time they actually spent in execution can be tallied for reliability modeling. This alternative was proposed by Musa [40], and has been successfully used in various software systems, particularly in telecommunication systems and some operating systems.
- *Transactions*. In this alternative, detailed task measurements for test runs, generically referred to as transactions, can be used as time measurements for reliability modeling [62].

Notice that in both execution time and transaction measurements, the measurement activities must be carried out dynamically because of the possibility of failures during test runs and the infeasibility of predicting actual execution time or transactions before execution. On the other hand, test runs can be measured more easily: we need only indicate whether a run takes place in the overall sequence of runs. The cost for data collection in above three alternatives also varies considerably: test runs can be captured easily and with minimal cost; execution time measurement involves the use of some independent monitor of system usage; and transaction measurement involves the use of specific tools that not only monitor system usage but also the specific types of usage to capture transactions. The collection of these measurements and related software tool support are discussed in Section 7. Each of the above time measurement alternatives as well as calendar time workload characterization, will be examined in detail below.

4.1.1 Tracking Workload and Failures over Calendar Time

To examine the workload progression and distribution, data from test activity logs were extracted for products A, B, and C [60] and plotted in Fig. 1. The sequences of bars from left to right represent the daily workload from the beginning to the end of system testing. Each bar indicates the number of testing runs for a particular day, with scales shown along the corresponding vertical axes.

It is immediately obvious from Fig. 1 that the daily workload distributions are quite uneven, with significantly more runs on certain clusters of days than others. We can also see a general trend of intensified testing effort as testing progresses, shown by the taller bars at the later part of testing (towards the right in each plot). Other products (D and E) we studied also demonstrate similar characteristics [55, 62]. These workload characteristics are affected by

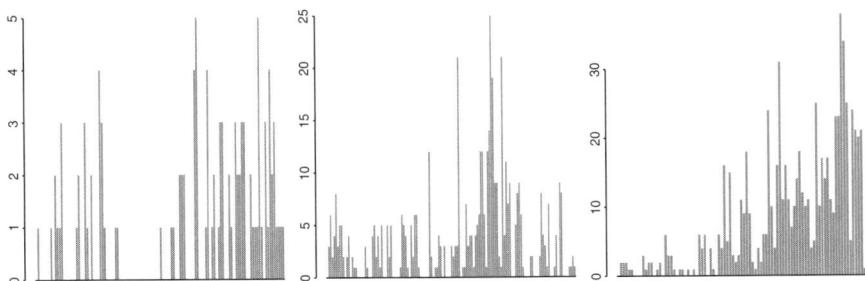

FIG. 1. Daily test runs for products A (left), B (middle), and C (right).

a number of factors discussed in Section 3.1. Figure 1 provides a quantitative characterization of their effect on workload characteristics.

Other entities, such as failure count and workload measured in execution time or transactions, can be measured and track in similar ways. However, to compare the overall progress and trend, cumulative plots, such as in Fig. 2, are often more informative because several entities can be presented side-by-side to allow for comparative examination. One major concern in such plots is the simplicity of the graphical representation. Therefore, for general tracking purposes, only essential information needs to be included, with the x-axis representing calendar time and the y-axis representing workload or defect count to plot (1) progression of workload (cumulative runs, execution time, and transactions) over time, and (2) progression of cumulative of failures over time. Summary information about total runs, failures, and defects to date can also be included for easy reference.

Figure 2 tracks the test effort and failure observations for product E studied in [62], with the summary statistics explicitly shown below the x-axis. The curves for cumulative runs and failures are shown to scale, while the curves for cumulative execution time and transactions are using different scales not explicitly shown (but can be deduced from the summary statistics shown below the x-axis). The information presented in graphs such as Fig. 2 can be used consistently over the whole testing process, helping product

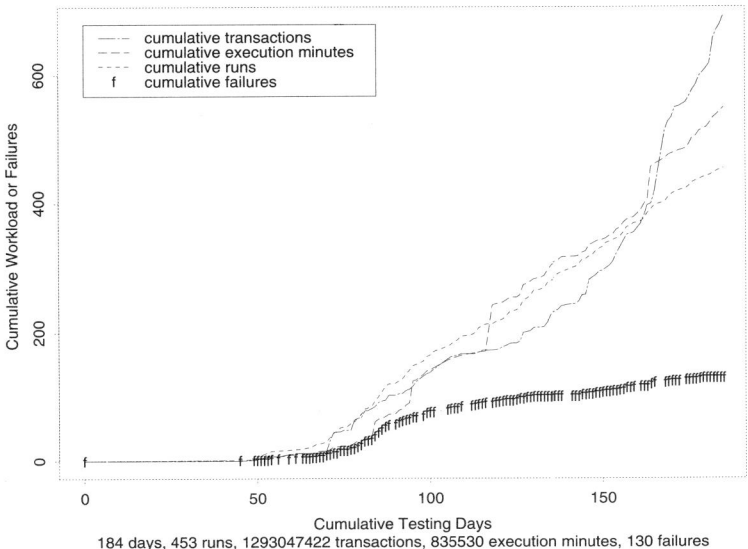

FIG. 2. Testing activity and defect tracking (product E).

organizations to visualize general effort and defect trends and variations, and manage project resources and schedules.

4.1.2 Visualizing Reliability Growth

Data visualization presents data in visual and graphical forms. It is a powerful tool that preserves much of the information and structure in the data, and provides a good way to examine the data for trends, distributions, and is particularly good for identifying anomalies [20]. As a result, graphical representation of data and analysis results is used throughout this article. In particular, failure arrivals over time can be visualized and examined for overall trends and patterns. Reliability growth over time can be characterized by the generally longer and longer between-failure intervals as time progresses. When the cumulative failures (vertical axis) are plotted against time (horizontal axis), such as in Fig. 2, the effect of reliability growth can be visualized by the leveling-off tails in the failure arrival curves, indicating gradually fewer failure arrivals towards the end. As seen from Fig. 2, there is no obvious trend of reliability growth over calendar time (see the cumulative failure curve) for product E, and no reliability growth models can be fitted to these data. The failure curve largely follows the general trend of workload (cumulative runs) curve. As expected, the number of runs in a given period has a strong influence on how many failures are expected for that period.

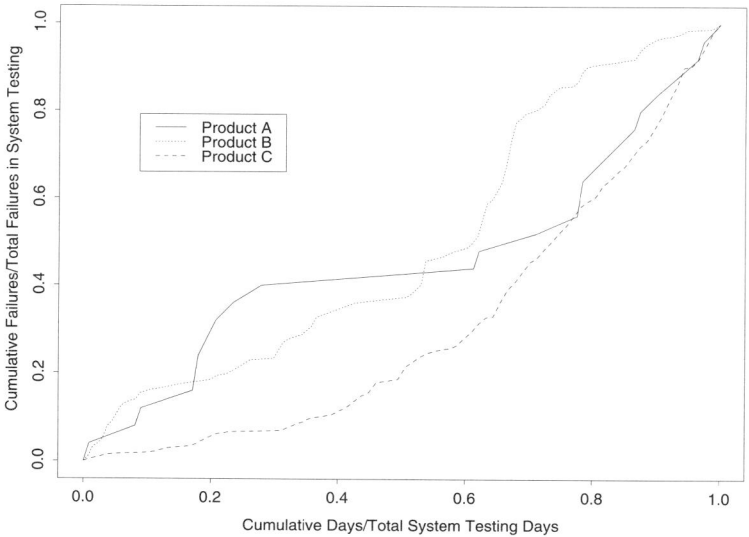

FIG. 3. Failure arrivals in calendar time for products A, B, and C.

Figure 3 shows the cumulative failure arrival curves, in calendar time, for the whole system testing phase for products A, B, and C. To better compare trends and patterns, normalized scales are used in Fig. 3. The horizontal axis is the ratio of cumulative testing days to total system test days, and the vertical axis is the ratio of cumulative failures to total failures observed in system testing. A quick inspection of the curves reveals no trend of reliability growth over calendar time exemplified by the leveling-off effect with time progression.

4.1.3 Usage Dependent Time Measurement

Test runs and execution time can be defined and measured independent of the specific product under study by counting the test runs and monitoring CPU or system usage (Section 7). However, transactions are product-specific workload measures and need to be defined and measured accordingly. Recently, transaction measurement and reliability modeling were performed for product E [62], a relational database management system (RDBMS) product, and is used below to illustrate the definition and measurement of transactions for reliability analysis.

A transaction in RDBMS products can be defined as an operation on a row in any table in the database manager. An operation in this context consists of the updating, selection, insertion, or deletion of a row. In effect, the transaction count for an application program or a test run is the sum of the number of rows updated, selected, inserted, or deleted by the application or corresponding test case when they are executed. This definition differs from the commonly used definition of a database transaction, which corresponds to a sequence of operations that transforms a database from one consistent state to another consistent state [21]. This conventional definition still covers transactions whose workload varies greatly, and thus it is not suitable as a detailed workload measure.

Figure 4 presents the transaction measurement result for product E [62]. The sequence of vertical lines represents the transactions for individual test runs presented in their execution sequence. The height of each vertical line represents the transactions for a particular run, with the scale shown by the vertical axis. The dotted line shows the cumulative transactions over the entire sequence of test runs, shown in a reduced 1 : 10 scale to highlight the effect of individual transactions on the cumulative transactions. As is clearly visible in Fig. 4, the distribution of transactions per run is quite uneven, and there is a general trend of intensified workload as testing progresses. This agrees with earlier observations comparing execution time to test runs [60]. This transaction measurement result gives us a quantitative characterization of the uneven workload distribution and the intensified workload as testing progresses.

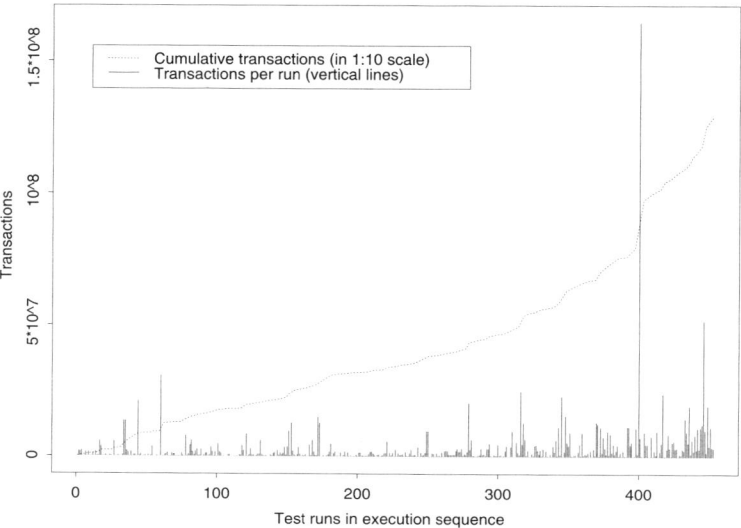

FIG. 4. Measured transactions (per run and cumulative; product E).

4.1.4 Comparing Reliability Growth in Different Time Measurements

Figure 5 plots the failure arrivals in product E against cumulative transactions, and contrasts it with failure arrivals indexed by cumulative test runs and days. To better compare the shapes and patterns, a common scale of 0 to 1 for the horizontal axis (time axis) is used, representing the ratios between the cumulative days, runs, or transactions to that of total days, runs, or transactions respectively used in the plot in Fig. 5. The general failure arrival patterns are examined below:

- *Failure arrivals in calendar time*: there is no pronounced reliability growth in calendar time because of the uneven workload distribution. In fact, the failure arrivals do not seem to follow any specific pattern except in the very beginning, where a slow start of failure detection is common.
- *Failure arrivals in test runs*: the pattern is more consistent than calendar time-indexed failure arrivals. For the initial portion lasting until approximately 60–70% of total test runs, a seemingly concave curve is visible with gradual flattening. However, after that, the failure arrivals seem to follow a steeper curve again. Figure 4 offers at least a partial explanation of this observed pattern: the cumulative test workload as measured in transactions follows a somewhat linear curve before a steep upturn at around 60–70% of test runs. Consequently, the intensified test runs as testing progresses induce a bias in the pattern of failure arrivals against test runs, particularly late in testing.

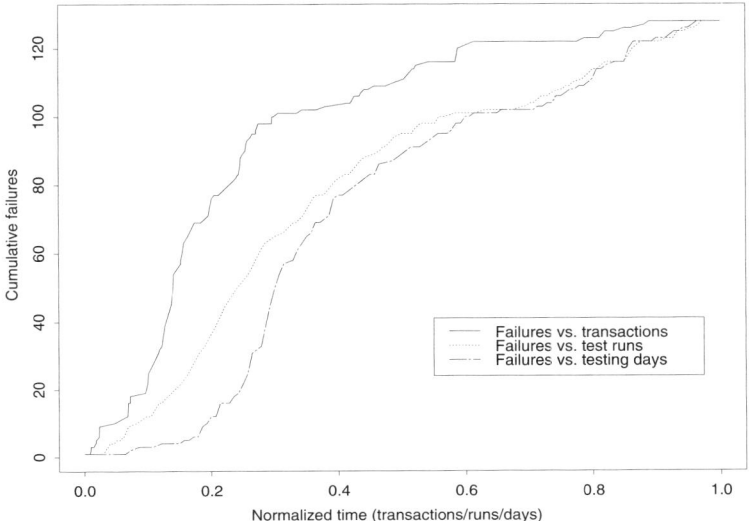

Fig. 5. Failure arrival patterns in different time.

- *Failure arrivals in transactions*: failure arrivals in transactions demonstrate considerable reliability growth, changing from a steep slope at the beginning to a flattened slope towards the end. This pattern also provides further evidence for the effectiveness of using an integrated analysis technique [55] for risk identification and reliability improvement early in testing (to be discussed in Section 5). It provides us with a better time measurement for reliability modeling.

4.2 Using Run Count and Execution Time Failure Data in SRGMs

As discussed in Section 3 and quantitatively examined above, test effort as measured by workload per time period varies considerably for large software systems in general. Therefore, calendar time-based measurement data are not suitable for reliability analysis using SRGMs. Consequently, in [60], an earlier study of products A, B, and C, only the test run count and execution time were used to index failures for reliability modeling.

4.2.1 Model Fitting and Overall Observations

Figure 6 plots the actual failure arrivals against runs and execution time for product B, and shows all the fitted models individually. Several of the SRGMs summarized in Table 2 were attempted, including BMB, BMP, GO, JM, LV, Geo, Musa, MO, and S. Notice that all the fitted models for each data

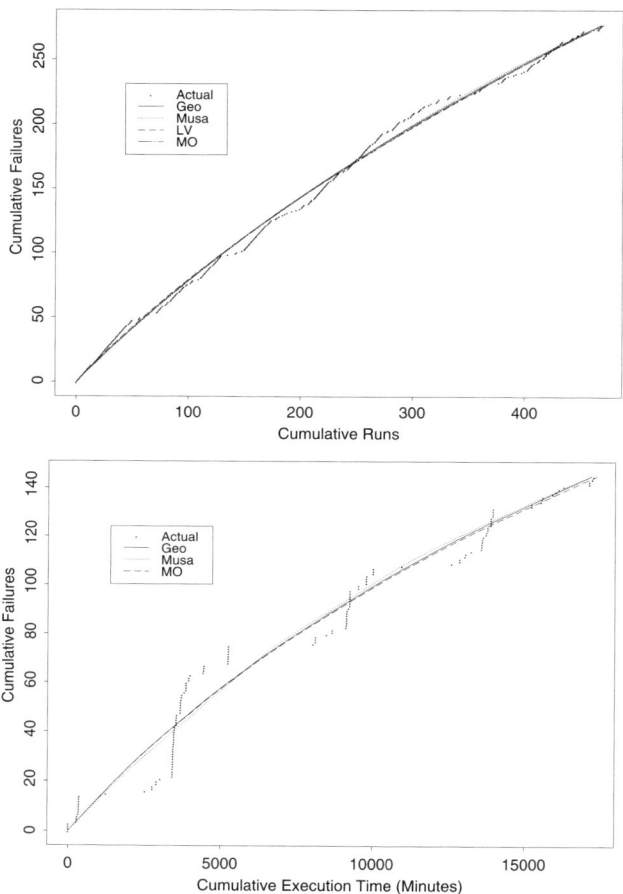

FIG. 6. SRGMs with run count (top) and execution time (bottom) data for product B.

set (failures against runs or execution time) give almost identical fitted curves, appearing to collapse into a single curve in Fig. 6. Similar patterns were also observed for products A and C [60], and similar conclusions for these products can be drawn from the subsequent discussions. Notice that the total number of failures plotted against execution time is less than that plotted against runs. The reason is that runs that consume no execution time were omitted in execution time normalization of the data. Most reliability models assume that no more than one failure can occur simultaneously. To be consistent with this assumption, all runs with zero execution time were omitted in execution time modeling.

Compared with failure arrivals in calendar time (Fig. 3), the normalization effect of runs and execution time is immediately visible in Fig. 6. A general trend of reliability growth over time is visible in all the failure arrivals against runs and execution time. Furthermore, the actual failure arrival patterns seem to conform to the fitted models fairly well, which is in sharp contrast to the seemingly random failure arrivals against calendar time in Fig. 3.

The curves of failure arrivals plotted against runs seem to be more stable both over time and across different products. This stability in failure arrival patterns leads to more consistent modeling results from different reliability growth models. SRGMs can also be fitted to these kinds of data fairly early in system testing, making these data and models good devices for test and reliability progress tracking. However, it is hard to assure the equivalence of runs in terms of to what degree each run exercises the software. As testing progresses, the test cases generally also become more complex and exercise the software more intensively. This fact causes biases in reliability estimations using such run-based models.

Although execution time seems to provide more information about test case executions and testing effort, it does not always provide a better picture of reliability growth. Because of the nature of the products A, B, and C, many complicated test scenarios involve little CPU execution time, thus making CPU execution time not always the preferred choice for time measurement used to normalize failure intervals. Setups and manual operations represent a major portion of many runs, but represent very little chance of encountering failures because they involve mostly the repeated usage of tested-and-proven operations. Such non-homogeneity of test scenarios has a strong effect on the probability of encountering a failure and therefore on the measured reliability.

Because of the problem with CPU execution time normalization, another variation, system execution time, was also tried. System execution time for each run is the difference in time-stamp values between start and termination of the run. In this case, the problem with setups and manual operations is magnified because the low CPU utilization in such cases is not accounted for, resulting in no improvement over the CPU execution time normalization. In fact, some deterioration in model fit was observed.

As seen in Fig. 6, sudden changes and clustering of failure intervals measured in execution time dominate the overall failure arrival patterns. SRGMs can only be fitted to failure interval data normalized by CPU execution time well past the 50th percentile of system testing. Furthermore, the arrival of new clusters and gaps can easily make predictions of earlier fitted models grossly inaccurate, and lead to quite different parameter estimations and reliability assessments. As a result, such models are highly unstable, and sensitive to the arrivals of new failure data. For system execution time normalization, this problem is even more severe than for CPU execution time normalization. The end result of all these is the inappropriateness of execution time-based models for reliability tracking for these products, especially in the early phases of system testing.

4.2.2 Modeling for Scenario Groups and Testing Sub-Phases

To track the reliability growth and assess product reliability with respect to certain groups of operations represented by different test scenario classes, separate reliability models can be constructed. Typical scenario classes used in testing product B are organized into 12 categories by the system test team. These 12 scenario classes can be collapsed into four related scenario groups. Of the runs falling into the four groups, group 2 has too few runs to warrant reliability growth modeling, and group 4 consists mostly of runs without CPU execution (zero CPU execution time). As a result, SRGMs were fitted to run-based failure interval data for groups 1, 3, and 4, and to execution time-based failure interval data for groups 1 and 3. This approach is similar to that in [45], where SRGMs were fitted to data associated with different types of defect.

Figure 7 shows the cumulative failure curves against cumulative runs for all test cases selected from groups 1, 3, and 4 respectively. The reliability growth models were fitted to failure interval data in runs for each group individually. Similar to the overall models above, all such run-based models fit well with

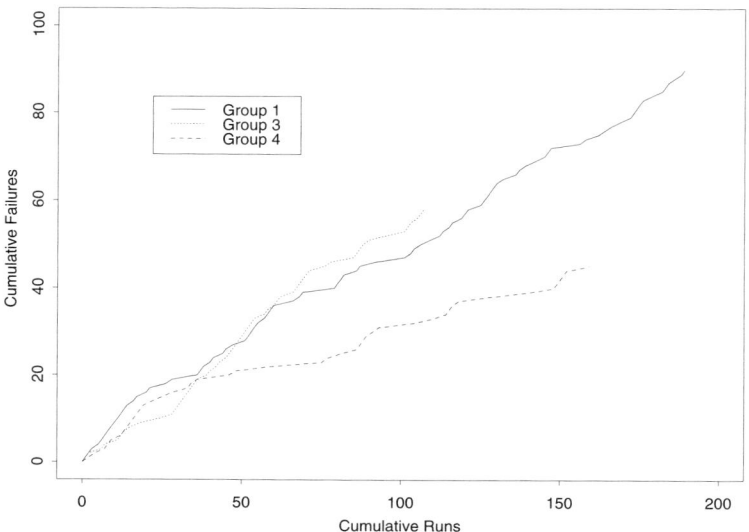

FIG. 7. Failure arrivals vs. runs for four scenario groups (product B).

actual observed failures. Reliability assessments from different models for a given set of data are almost identical. However, for group 4 considerably more reliability growth is realized than for the other two groups. This can be clearly visualized in the failure arrivals plotted against runs for the three groups in Fig. 7: After an initial period of similar failure arrival rates (failures per run), the failure arrival curve for group 4 levels off considerably more than the curves for the other groups. The current estimated reliabilities for these three groups are quite different, which points to the need for focused testing of certain features or functional areas,—a potential explored further in our tree-based reliability models (TBRMs) in Section 5.

Group 1 consists of mostly communication-related functions, where extensive and continuous usage is the norm. Execution time-based SRGMs for group 1 fit much better to actual failure observations, compared with the same models for overall data in Fig. 6. This result indicates the applicability of execution time-based models to communication-type operations. On the other hand, no model can be fitted to the execution time failure data for group 3, where I/O-related operations dominate.

4.2.3 Lessons Learned in Modeling Reliability for Products A, B, and C

Despite the problems of estimation biases, run-based models are robust across data sets and can always provide at least a rough estimate of the reliability of the products under testing. Therefore they should always be used as a starting point. If CPU execution time-based failure data reflects the main testing activities and operations, models could be fitted to such data to get more accurate results. In addition, inter-group differences between the run-based and execution time-based models seem to dominate intra-group variations for these products. As a consequence, the selection of data normalization (what time unit to use) should be the primary concern in practical applications. In many cases, multiple normalizations could be done to offer different but complementary views of reliability.

In general, the product characteristics and testing environment have a strong influence on the observed failures and measured reliability. As seen from the modeling results for the four scenario groups and individual testing sub-phases, information about restricted subsets of data could be used effectively to build SRGMs to better assess reliability. When CPU execution constitutes the dominant feature of operations, such as in communication-related scenarios and in the stress-testing sub-phase, execution time-based models should be selected to give better reliability assessment.

SRGM results for subsets of data can also be used to guide testing activities. For example, with Fig. 7 and related modeling results showing that product B is less likely to experience scenario group 4-related failures, the testing team can now shift their attention and focus their effort away from such scenarios. In general, testing can be focused on those "bottleneck" components or system functions which are more likely to experience failure than others. New test cases can be designed, enhanced, and executed with this focus in mind. In this way, the overall reliability target can be achieved at minimal cost.

The overall conclusion from studying the reliability of products A, B, and C [60] is that SRGMs are applicable to large software systems under scenario-based system testing, and can provide fairly accurate measurements and predictions of product reliability, provided that the time measurement reflects system usage or workload. This earlier study also identified various issues that were examined in followup studies [55, 62], including general guidelines for selecting proper time measurement, the need for alternative time measurement under specific situations, and the usage of data partitioning information for risk identification and reliability improvement.

4.3 Using Homogeneous Test Runs for Reliability Modeling in Product D

As demonstrated in the previous study [60] summarized above, the key to good modeling results using test run count as the time measurement is to ensure homogeneity of test runs. In product D, studied in [55], a large amount of such small, homogeneous test cases were used, making the test run count reflect the test workload and activities and therefore making it a good usage-dependent time measure.

Figure 8 plots the cumulative failure data (top graph) and the failure intensity data (or rate data, bottom graph) indexed by cumulative runs for product D, and two reliability growth models (GO and S) fitted to these data. Besides GO and S models, other models from Table 2 used to fit these data include JM, SW, GP, BMB, and BMP. JM, GP, BMB, and BMP models fit the observed data well, and follow curves very similar to that of GO; therefore, they are omitted in the plot to avoid overcrowding. Because all of these models essentially agree with each other on their estimations, an overall consistent quality assessment can be formed with a relatively high degree of confidence. The S-shaped model, which is relatively optimistic, is used to bound these estimations from above. On the other hand, the SW model is discarded because it does not fit the observed data well.

Table 3 summarizes some important information for all the fitted models for product D using the data of period failure count with period length measured by the number of runs. To examine the progression of models over testing process, models were fitted to four forward-inclusive sets of data identified as F_3, F_2, F_1 and F. Data set F corresponds to the entire system testing and the data

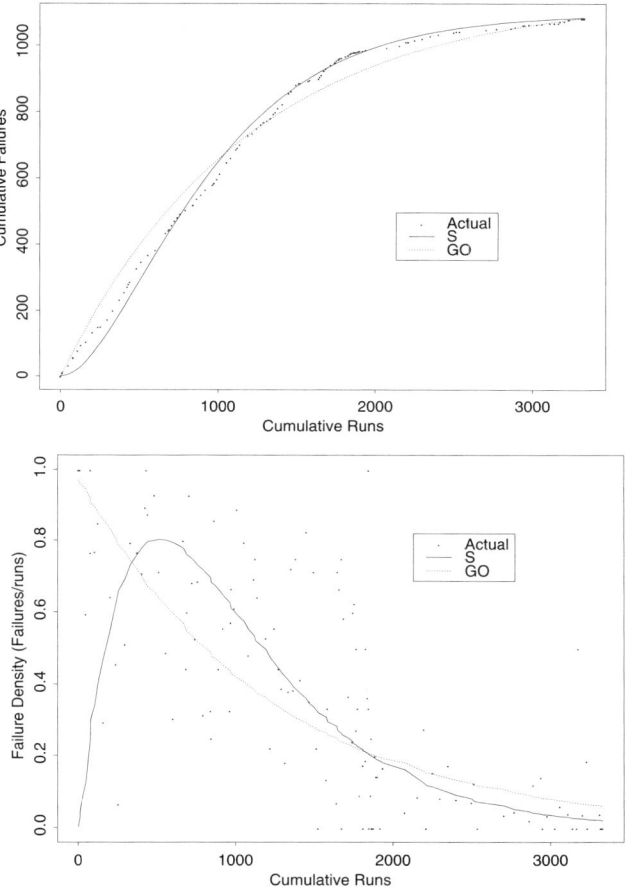

FIG. 8. Reliability modeling with SRGMs for product D.

used in Fig. 8. The cumulative data summary for each of these data sets is given in Table 4. The modeling results summarized in Table 3 include:

- Estimated mean time between failure (MTBF), which captures the overall product reliability in an easy-to-understand summary measure. Larger MTBF indicates higher reliability.
- Estimated total defects ($\hat{N}$) by different models. The difference between $\hat{N}$ and the current cumulative defects (number of failures observed so far) gives us an estimate of the number of defects still remaining in the system. This information can be used in practice to plan for product support and customer service after product release.

TABLE 3
RELIABILITY MODELING RESULTS (PRODUCT D)

Model	Data set F_3			Data set F_2			Data set F_1			Data set F		
	MTBF	$\hat{N}$	SSQ	MTBF	$\hat{N}$	SSQ	MTBF	$\hat{N}$	SSQ	MTBF	$\hat{N}$	SSQ
JM	2.86	1857	168	6.8	1230	263	11.2	1174	308	17.7	1152	323
SW	7.69	2902	669	23.1	1097	699	51.3	1077	825	60.2	1094	793
GP	1.89	1751	165	4.1	1240	240	6.4	1204	270	11.8	1167	323
GO	2.78	1881	168	6.6	1233	260	10.8	1178	294	16.9	1154	312
BMB	2.78	1870	167	6.7	1231	259	11.0	1176	303	17.2	1153	319
BMP	2.86	1847	167	6.7	1229	259	10.9	1177	302	17.2	1153	317
S	4.76	1112	412	14.7	1065	416	28.5	1083	444	52.8	1095	462

TABLE 4
DATA USED FOR RELIABILITY ANALYSIS
(PRODUCT D)

Data set	Cumulative		
	Days	Runs	Failures
F_3	126	1847	979
F_2	152	2444	1026
F_1	160	2898	1063
F	177	3331	1084

- Sum of squares for the residuals between model prediction and actual observations, SSQ. SSQ is a goodness-of-fit statistic, reflecting the degree of how satisfactorily the models fit actual observations. Smaller SSQ indicate better fit, and increased confidence in the assessments and predictions made by the models.

As we can see from Table 3, the modeling results from different models are converging, giving us stronger confidence in the modeling results as testing progresses towards the end. Future predictions can be easily derived from these models, picking specific points corresponding to management and scheduling concerns. For example, one major concern in project management is to predict the estimated reliability at the scheduled product release date. For product D, predictions of product reliability at product release (corresponding to data set F) made based on earlier data (data sets F_3, F_2, F_1) conform well with assessments made using the final data set F. These converging results and good predictions confirm the appropriateness of assessing reliability with the failure count data normalized by runs for this product. Therefore, SRGMs fitted to failure data indexed by test runs can provide accurate measurement and prediction of reliability and other quantities of concern (e.g. resource and schedule to reach a reliability goal) if homogeneity of test runs can be assured.

4.4 Transaction Measurement and Reliability Modeling for Product E

Intrinsically diverse test cases often need to be executed for some large commercial software systems, such as product E, a workstation-based RDBMS developed in the IBM Software Solutions Toronto Laboratory, with a large user population and diverse usage environments. Different users might want to use different features of the product in different environments. For example, some users might use product E as a standalone RDBMS, while others might use it as a server serving a large number of networked clients. To ensure correct operation under such diverse usage environments, test cases of different characteristics and vastly different complexity have to be constructed.

The usage of such diverse test cases makes it inappropriate to use raw test runs as the time-index for failure data in reliability modeling. In addition, it is often hard to break down the larger test cases into smaller ones because of the tight coupling among different subtasks and execution subsequences. Under such situations, neither can the homogeneity of individual test runs be assured nor can they be broken down to homogeneous sub-runs. Other alternative finer-grain measurements, such as transactions defined in Section 4.1, need to be gathered.

Figure 9 plots the failure arrivals against cumulative transactions and the fitted Goel–Okumoto model (GO) [25]. Various other models listed in

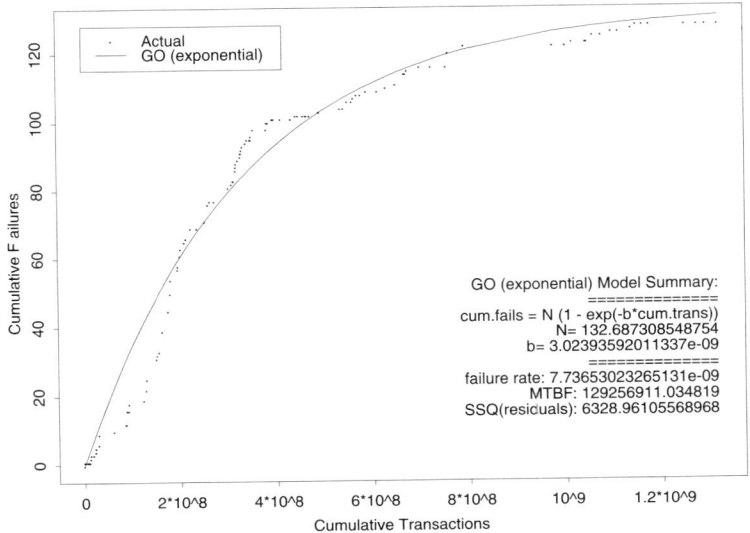

FIG. 9. Transaction-based modeling result (product E).

organized into different structures and executed in different sequences. Therefore, these early results can be extended to derive conditions for selecting proper test workload measurements:

- *Use of homogeneous runs and condition.* Because of the low cost and robustness, test runs can be used as a time-index to failures for reliability modeling, if homogeneity of test runs can be ensured or if larger test runs can be broken down to smaller homogeneous sub-runs. These conditions provide constructive information for future applications.
- *Use of transactions as detailed workload measurement.* When the above conditions (homogeneity and divisibility of runs) cannot be met, transaction measurement can be used to provide data that are not only usable for reliability modeling, but also meaningful to customers, so that modeling results can be easily used for project management to ensure quality from a customer perspective. Reliability modeling results using transaction-indexed failures confirm the appropriateness of transactions as the usage-dependent time measurement.

There are many research issues for more effective use of SRGMs in software reliability assessment and prediction: a small set of general rules can be developed to define appropriate transactions for different software systems, possibly with automated support for measurement capturing. Another way to correct for the estimation biases in the SRGMs using coarse grain test runs for time measurement is to calibrate data input or modeling output. This calibration is dependent on adequate historical data and a consistent trend in the measurement bias that can be quantitatively characterized. For example, if the test runs grow in size in a linear form as testing progresses, this linear relation could be used to weight the test runs so that the failure intervals measured in the weighted runs more accurately reflect software usage. The key to this result calibration is the existence of adequate measurement data. These data can also be used to establish functional relations between test case progression and biases in reliability modeling results to calibrate the modeling results.

5. Tree-based Reliability Models (TBRMs)

SRGMs offer overall reliability assessments and predictions for software products, but provide little information on how to improve reliability. However, there is strong empirical evidence that defect distribution is quite uneven in software products, and hence there is a strong need for risk identification and management [11, 50, 66]. Alternative analysis techniques and models are necessary in order to identify and correct problems for effective reliability improvement.

In an earlier study [60], summarized in Section 4.2, we observed that measuring and modeling reliability for different sub-groups of test scenarios or testing sub-phases provide valuable information about product reliability from a different perspective. Such input domain information can be used systematically in conjunction with the time domain and failure information traditionally used in SRGMs for problem identification and reliability improvement in a recently developed approach [55] using tree-based models. We next describe these tree-based reliability models (TBRMs) and discuss their applicability and effectiveness in reliability analysis and improvement.

5.1 Integrated Analysis and Tree-based Modeling

In input domain reliability analysis using IDRMs (Section 2.4), there is a precise definition of input states and usage of such information in reliability modeling. The reliability of a software system in IDRMs is defined as the probability of failure-free operation for a set of input states randomly sampled according to its operational profile [24, 54]. IDRMs can be easily extended to model reliability for data subsets. Each subset of data can be defined by some specific input state sub-domains from where the inputs are sampled or specific time periods when the inputs are sampled. This kind of approach could provide an up-to-date assessment of reliability if only proper subsets of recent runs are selected. Partitions based on the input states and the models built for these partitions can be used to analyze reliability variations across different functional areas or product components, and to identify problematic areas. Such problematic areas can be characterized by the low reliability for the partitioned subsets and the conditions for these partitions. However, there are a large number of possible partitions, which cannot be handled adequately by *ad hoc* partitions such as in [60]. Systematic ways of handling the partitions are needed.

As stated in Section 3.2, the information associated with test runs includes test results, input state and environmental information, and timing information. We can associate each run with a data point, and treat these individual pieces of information as individual data attributes. Among these attributes, some are numerical (timing and workload, failure count, etc.), while others are categorical (scenario classification, environmental identification, defect type, etc.). To integrate the analysis in a systematic way, we need the support of analysis techniques and tools that can handle this diverse information. Tree-based modeling techniques [19, 69] and related software tools (Section 7) are selected to support such integrated reliability analyses.

Tree-based modeling (TBM) is a statistical analysis technique that attempts to establish predictive relations through recursive partitioning. This technique originates from the social sciences, where the data often consist of both numerical and non-numerical components with complicated interactions, making classical statistical models inadequate [19]. Selby and Porter pioneered the use of this technique to analyze various software engineering data [44, 50]. We have also used this technique to analyze defects and metrics data for various software systems recently [57, 63, 66], and gained valuable experience in handling such data and interpreting analysis results for large software systems.

In tree-based models (TBMs), modeling results are represented in tree structures. Each node in a tree represents a set of data, which is recursively partitioned into smaller subsets. The data used in such models consist of multiple attributes, with one attribute identified as the *response* variable (or

TABLE 6
ALGORITHM FOR TREE-BASED MODEL (TBM) CONSTRUCTIONS

(0) *Initialization.* Create a list of data sets to be partitioned, referred to as **Slist**, and put the data set as the singleton element in **Slist**. Select the size and homogeneity thresholds T_s and T_h for the algorithm.

(1) *Overall control.* Remove a data set S from **Slist** and execute step 2. Repeat this step until **Slist** becomes empty.

(2) *Size test.* If $|S| < T_s$, stop; otherwise, execute steps 3 through 6. $|S|$ is the size (or the number of data points) of data set S.

(3) *Defining binary partitions.* A binary partition of S is a division of data into two subsets using a *split condition* defined on a specific predictor p by a comparison operator "<" and a cutoff value c. Data points with $p < c$ form one subset (S_1) and those with $p \geqslant c$ form another subset (S_2). If p is a categorical variable, then a unique binary grouping of its categories forms a binary partition.

(4) *Computing predicted responses and prediction deviances for S, S_1, and S_2.* The predicted value $v(S)$ for the response for a set S is the average over the set; i.e.

$$v(S) = \frac{1}{|S|} \sum_{i \in S} (v_i)$$

and the prediction deviance $D(S)$ is

$$D(S) = \sum_{i \in S} (v_i - v(S))^2$$

where v_i is the response value for data point i.

(5) *Selecting the optimal partition.* Among all the possible partitions (all predictors with all associated cutoffs or binary groupings), the one that minimizes the deviance of the partitioned subsets is selected; i.e. the partition with minimized $D(S_1) + D(S_2)$ is selected.

(6) *Homogeneity test*: Stop if this partitioning cannot improve prediction accuracy beyond a threshold T_h, i.e. stop if

$$\left(1 - \frac{D(S_1) + D(S_2)}{D(S)}\right) \leqslant T_h$$

Otherwise, append S_1 and S_2 to **Slist**

response) and several other attributes identified as *predictor* variables (or predictors). Recursive partitioning minimizes the difference between predicted response values and the observed response values. The process of recursive partitioning is computationally intensive; thus proper software tools are needed to support its implementation. A binary variant of recursive partitioning is used, with the specific tree construction algorithm summarized in Table 6. Tool support for TBM and other analyses is discussed in Section 7.

5.2 Reliability Analysis for Partitioned Subsets

With each run treated as a data point, Nelson's [42] estimate of reliability for any given subset of runs can be easily derived. Let n_i be the number of runs falling into a specific subset i, and f_i be the number of failures. The estimated reliability $\hat{R}_i$ for subset i according to the Nelson model is $\hat{R}_i = 1 - f_i/n_i$ (Section 2.4). Each subset can be defined by some partition conditions on input sub-domains which need to be satisfied by all the runs falling into it, with the specific partitions selected by the recursive partitioning algorithm (Table 6). Each input subdomain generally corresponds to some function areas or operations.

Figure 10 is a TBM that provides reliability estimates for different input sub-domains. Each subset of data associated with a node in the tree is uniquely described by the path from the root to that node, with each edge along the path representing a split condition. To label the nodes, we use an "l" to indicate a left branching, and an "r" to indicate a right branching, following

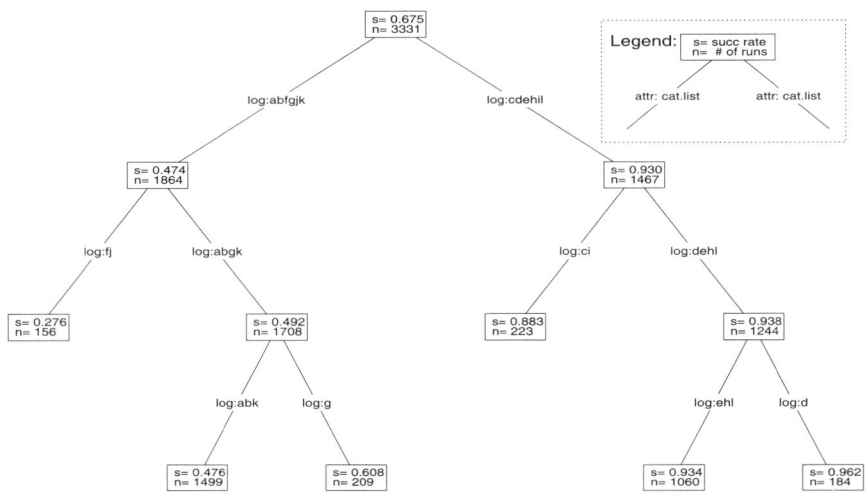

FIG. 10. Reliability across input sub-domains *log* (product D).

the sequence from the root to the specific nodes. For example, for the tree in Fig. 10, the third leaf node from left, with 209 runs and 0.608 success rate, is labeled "lrr."

The success rate s_i in Fig. 10 for the subset of runs associated with a tree node i is the Nelson reliability $\hat{R}_i$. The split conditions, written at the edge leading to each node, define the groupings of input sub-domains. In this example, each input subdomain is denoted by its test log (data attribute log) where the data is taken from. From the TBM in Fig. 10, we can see that the input sub-domains defined by runs from test logs f and j (156 runs associated with node "ll", with success rate of 0.276) have particularly lower reliability than other sub-domains, a signal of possible problems that need to be addressed.

For a subset of runs falling into a time period, the estimated failure rate and MTBF can be obtained from the Nelson model by viewing the serialized runs as equivalent repeated random sampling. This can be viewed as a special case of the above input domain reliability model based on partitions. When drawn graphically, such as in Fig. 14, this time partition-based model gives us a piecewise linear curve for the cumulative failures, maintaining constant failure arrival rate for each time segment. The interpretation and use of such piecewise linear SRGMs are discussed in Section 6.

5.3 Analyses Integration and TBRM Applications

For tree-based reliability models (TBRMs) that integrate both time and input domain analysis of reliability, the result indicator can be treated as the response variable, and the timing and input state information associated with each run are the predictor variables. The result indicator r_{ij} (the jth run from subset i) has value 1 for a successful run or 0 for a failed run. Let there be n_i runs with f_i failures for subset i. The predicted result s_i for subset i according to Step 4 of the algorithm in Table 6 is:

$$s_i = \frac{1}{n_i} \sum_{j=1}^{n_i} r_{ij} = \frac{n_i - f_i}{n_i} = \hat{R}_i$$

which is exactly the Nelson estimate of reliability $\hat{R}_i$. This result can also be easily mapped to the estimated failure rate $\hat{\lambda}_i$ or MTBF $\hat{T}_i$ in the time domain. As a result, the TBRM for the combined data gives us a systematic way of analyzing reliability for the partitioned subsets, providing reliability estimates that have valid interpretations in both the time domain and the input domain.

Figure 11 shows a TBRM that uses both the time domain attributes and the input domain attributes in reliability modeling. Among the multiple time and input domain attributes from Table 7 supplied as predictors, only a subset is

TABLE 7
DATA ATTRIBUTES (IN *ITALIC*) IN TBRMS FOR PRODUCT D

- Timing: calendar date (*year, month, day*), *tday* (cumulative testing days since the start of testing), and *rsn* (run sequence number, which uniquely identifies a run in the overall execution sequence).
- Input state: *SC* (scenario class), *SN* (scenario number), *log* (corresponding to a sub-product with a separate test log) and *tester*.
- Result: *result* indicator of the test run, with 1 indicating success and 0 indicating failure.

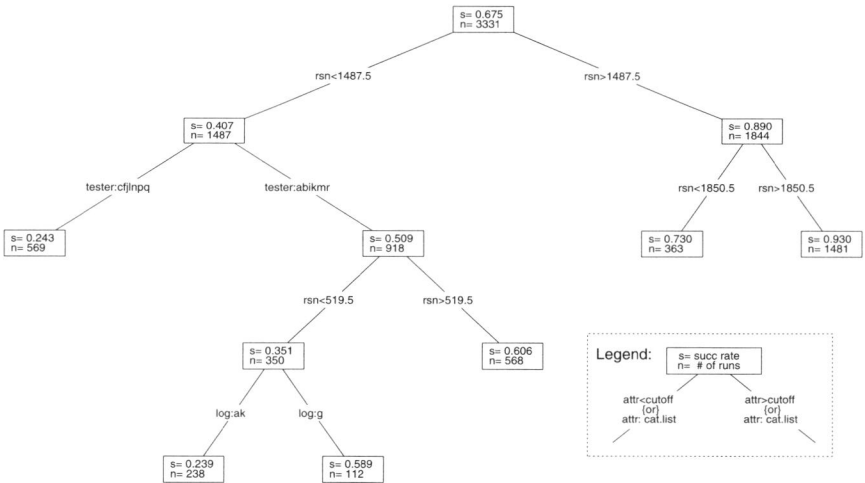

FIG. 11. Tree-based reliability model (TBRM) for product D.

selected by the tree construction algorithm (Table 6) to recursively partition the data. The selected partitions and associated split conditions are local optimums according to the selection criterion (Step 5 in the algorithm of Table 6) for TBM construction. Therefore the ordering of split conditions from the root to the leaves of the tree represents the progression from more general and important characteristics for the analyzed data to more specific ones. For example, for the tree in Fig. 11, *rsn* cutoff at 1487 represents the most significant turning point in reliability growth, which also dominates reliability variations across different input sub-domains. For a general understanding of important characteristics that differentiate data into different levels of reliability, only those few high-level partitions near the root need to be considered. These high-level partitions identify key factors linked to reliability.

For a set of data associated with an interior node of a tree, if a time predictor is selected by the algorithm in Table 6 to partition the data set we can interpret that reliability change over time is predominant. The binary partition distinguishes two clusters of runs, one of higher estimated reliability after (or before) a certain cutoff time and another of lower reliability before (or after) that cutoff. If an input state variable is selected as the predictor to partition the data set, the interpretation is that the product is more reliable in handling certain subsets of input states than others, and this input state partition is linked more closely to reliability differences than partitions by any other factors. What is more, the split condition characterizes the two partitioned subsets of the input states. This information can be used to guide further analysis to find out if indeed certain functional areas or components are of lower quality, and if so, appropriate remedial actions can be carried out.

The main uses of TBRMs include:

- *Assessing reliability and factors closely linked to reliability.* Each node in the tree gives the estimated reliability for a specific subset, and the series of split conditions from the tree root to individual tree nodes gives us a good picture of important factors linked to product reliability.

- *Assessing current reliability and predicting future reliability.* When timing variables are selected as predictors in tree-based models, the partition that corresponds to the latest time segment can be used to assess current reliability and to predict future reliability. This subject is examined further in Section 6.

- *Monitoring change in reliability over time and across different input states.* As testing progresses, new trees can be constructed to analyze the constant streams of new data. These progressing trees provide us with a picture of changing reliability and changing key factors linked to reliability. Consequently, such a series of trees help us track the progress in testing and reliability.

- *Identifying problematic areas for further analyses and remedial actions.* Subsets of runs with exceptionally low reliability can be easily identified in TBRMs and can be characterized by the split conditions leading to the nodes associated with those subsets. The low reliability indicates possible problems in some related functional areas or product components. Further analyses, such as root cause analysis, can be performed for these subsets to identify the problems and devise remedial actions. Since the weakest part of a product determines to a large degree the overall reliability, the identification of such problematic areas also represents great opportunities for cost-effective reliability improvements. The partitioning information, obtained from the path leading to those specific low reliability subsets of runs from the root of the tree, can be used to guide causal analysis and help devise remedial actions.

- *Enhancing existing exit criteria.* A product should exit from testing only if its latest TBRMs show no particularly low reliability subsets of runs that can be traced to specific functional areas or product components. These trees at the testing exit point can be typified by major partitions, particularly those associated with runs from later portions of testing, defined on timing variables, with subsets associated with later runs demonstrating higher reliability than earlier subsets. The TBRM in Fig. 11 is such an example.

To summarize, TBRM provides two key benefits: (1) a systematic way to analyze software reliability using both input domain and time domain data through data partitioning, and (2) information for problem identification and reliability improvement in addition to reliability assessment and prediction. These benefits and most of the above uses cannot be achieved individually by SRGMs or by IDRMs.

5.4 Experience Using TBRM in Product D

Tree-based reliability models (TBRMs) have been applied to several products developed in the IBM Software Solutions Toronto Laboratory, including products D and E studied in [55, 62]. The data attributes for product D used in the previous and subsequent sample TBRMs in this section are listed in Table 7. Among the nine data attributes, *SC* and *tester* are **categorical** variables and the rest are **numerical** variables. The result indicator, *result*, is used as the **response** variable; the rest are treated as **predictor** variables. The complete date information, or its equivalent *tday*, can be used to indicate the overall time passage. However, there might be some seasonal fluctuations that affect the measured reliability. To assess such seasonal effects, the individual date variables (*year*, *month*, *day*) were also included in the modeling.

The left tree in Fig. 12, covering data at approximately the halfway point of testing for a sub-product in product D, represents typical results in the earlier part of testing. Here, the most important factor linked to the estimated reliability is the test scenario information (*SC* and *SN*), which indicates that different parts or function groups are of different quality. Notice that scenario number *SN* also reflects test case characteristics because most obvious scenarios were usually constructed first (low *SN*) to cover major functions in the scenario class for product D, and then "odd" scenarios were constructed later (high *SN*) to complete the coverage. From this tree, we can see that the estimated reliability is 0.8 for runs selected from scenario classes *d* and *h* (node "r"), a significant difference from runs from other scenario classes (node "l"). We can also identify some subsets with very low success rates: nodes "llll" (the leftmost node) and "lr" (the center node with

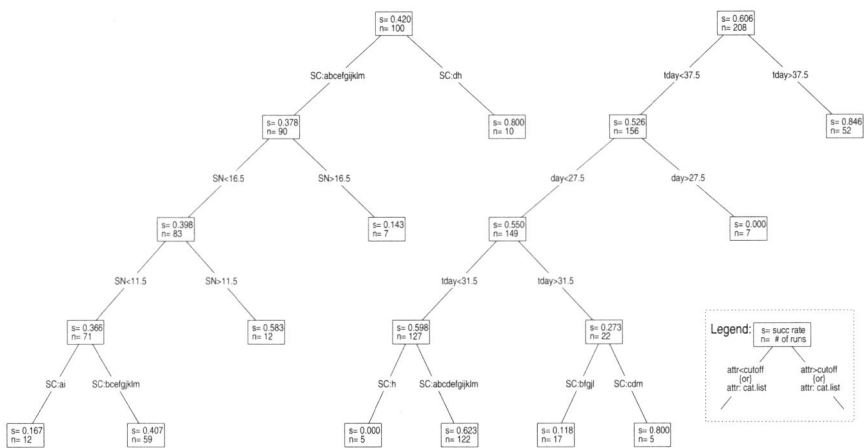

FIG. 12. Tree-based reliability modeling for a sub-product in product D.

$s = 0.143 \wedge n = 7$). With the help of further analysis that identified other characteristics of the runs associated with these nodes, appropriate remedial actions were taken to detect and remove related defects.

The right tree in Fig. 12, covering the whole testing phase for the same sub-product, represents typical results towards the end of each testing phase. The time information has become a major factor linked to success rate. Worth noting is the primary split at the root, with test runs in the later days ($tday > 37.5$) having a much higher success rate (0.846) than early ones (0.526 for $tday < 37.5$). Reliability growth over time dominates reliability variations across different functional areas or product components. All the subsets associated with particularly low success rates (nodes "llll", "llrl", and "lr") are associated with early runs. This kind of result can be interpreted as the product becoming more homogeneous in quality as time progresses, as reflected by a similar success rate across different test scenarios and major function groups for later runs.

For the products we studied, such progression is universal. The presence of this latter kind of tree was used as an exit criterion for product release. Throughout testing, a series of conscious decisions was made to focus on problematic areas, which led to a product exiting the testing with uniformly high quality. This is in sharp contrast to products A, B, and C, where tree-based models were only used as a post-mortem analysis [57]. In those earlier products, the quality of different parts was still quite uneven as they exited from testing.

The same kind of analyses as described above was carried out for each sub-product or sub-product group. When the sub-products were integrated for the bundled release, integration testing was performed. Figure 11 shows the TBRM built for the complete set of data for product D covering all the components and the whole testing. For this specific tree, the data set for node "ll" has much lower reliability than the rest of the tree and could be analyzed further. However, as we can see from Fig. 11, these are the runs executed early in testing ($rsn < 1487.5$), and further analysis showed that the problem has been corrected. Therefore, this product satisfied this exit criterion, and was fit for release to the market-place.

5.5 TBRM's Impact on Reliability Improvement: A Cross-Validation

TBRM analysis results were actively used by managers, developers, and testers to focus on problematic areas for reliability improvement, leading to products exiting testing with uniformly high quality. A shift of focus from reliability assessment to reliability improvement is evident, particularly in the early part of testing. This shift of focus also helps the closer collaboration between the testers who detect failures and the developers who fix defects, because more potentially useful information is presented in the tree structures. TBRM results are more likely to be used by the developers to fix discovered defects and to focus on highly problematic functional areas or product components.

TBRM's effectiveness in improving reliability can be examined visually by looking at its effect on failure arrival curves. Trends and patterns in the failure arrival data for product D can be visually examined and compared with three earlier products, A, B, and C studied in [60] and summarized in Section 4.2, where the TBRMs were not used. These products share many common characteristics that make them comparable: They are similar in size, and all were developed in the IBM Software Solutions Toronto Laboratory using similar development and testing processes. Figure 13 plots the failure arrivals against cumulative test run counts for products A, B, C, and D. Normalized scales (cumulative runs or failures as a proportion of the total number of runs or failures, respectively) are used to better compare the failure arrival patterns: Visibly more reliability growth was realized for product D than for the other products, as seen by the more concave curvature and much flatter tail. This is a good indication that TBRM helped improve the reliability for product D, particularly because early problematic areas were identified and effective remedial actions were carried out.

To compare the reliability growth quantitatively, the *purification level* ρ, as defined in [55], can be used. ρ captures overall reliability growth and testing effectiveness, and is defined to be the ratio between the failure rate reduction during testing and the initial failure rate at the beginning of testing. Notice that

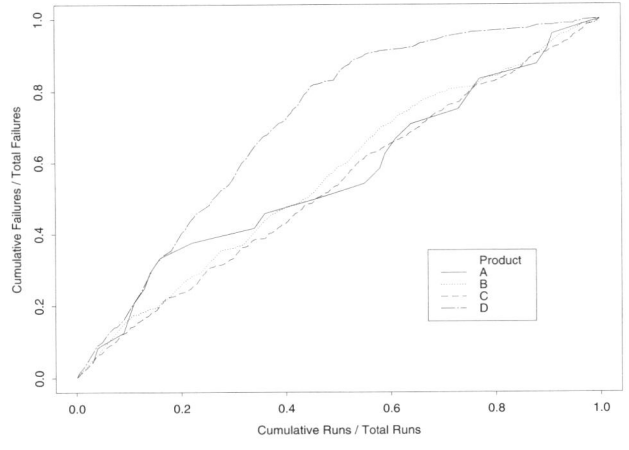

FIG. 13. Comparison of failure arrivals for products A, B, C, and D.

ρ is unitless and normalized to have a range from 0 to 1. This definition avoids the problems in comparing such measures as failure rate or MTBF, which may not be valid because the unit used (in this case *runs*) may not be equivalent across different products.

The table in Fig. 13 shows the purification levels estimated by different fitted SRGMs, with the maximum, minimum, and median estimates for ρ shown, for the four products. In product D, where TBRMs were actively used, there is a much stronger reliability growth, as captured in the purification level ρ, than in the earlier products. This quantitative comparison strongly support the effectiveness claim of TBRMs. In fact, both the TBRM and SRGM results were used to support the decision to release this product ahead of schedule. And preliminary in-field data also seemed to support this early release decision, with the observed in-field defects at or below the projected level.

5.6 Findings and Future Development of TBRMs

The tree-based reliability models (TBRMs), built on both time domain and input domain measurement data, combine some strengths of the existing SRGMs and IDRMs, and can help us improve the reliability of software products as well as assessing them. Initial results from applying this approach in several software products developed in the IBM Software Solutions Toronto Laboratory demonstrated its effectiveness and efficiency. Some key findings are summarized below:

- *Integration*: combining the ability to provide overall reliability assessment by the time domain reliability growth models and the ability to associate product reliability with subsets of input states in input domain reliability analysis, TBRM offers an integrated framework that provides both reliability assessment and guidance for reliability improvement.
- *Applications*: TBRM provides models that identify key predictors of the differences in measured reliability. Problematic areas can be easily identified and characterized, and remedial actions focused on those areas can be derived. The analysis results can also be used to manage the testing process and to enhance existing exit criteria by evaluating reliability levels and homogeneity across functional areas or product components.
- *Efficiency*: TBRM provides efficient utilization of the measurement data collected for general test tracking purposes, providing all the above benefits at little additional cost.
- *Cross-validation*: initial results comparing products where TBRM was used versus earlier products demonstrated the effectiveness of this approach in reliability improvement.

Future research includes alternative analysis techniques that also use other information collected during the software development process for process and quality improvement. Primary candidate data for these analyses include early measurement data, such as design and code metrics data for different products [15, 66], and detailed defect data collected under some systematic framework such as ODC (orthogonal defect classification [18]). The selection of appropriate measures to use in such expanded reliability analyses can be guided by formal models for measure evaluations and selection [65]. In terms of the analysis technique, alternative tree structures, other structured analyses, and synthesized analyses can be explored. For example, natural groupings and hierarchies of input states can be used directly to form multi-way partitions instead of binary partitions. Graph structured analysis methods, such as optimal set reduction [12], can also be used. For data associated with a tree node, SRGMs can be used instead of the Nelson model. This synthesis of tree-based models and reliability growth models would be very computationally intensive and requires the selection of appropriate algorithms and good software support.

The strategy described in this section tends to even out reliability variations across different subsets of data associated with different operations or components. However, operational reliability for the software in the field depends on the actual operational profile [39]. Consequently, such information can be used in TBRMs so that we can focus on the operational profile weighted reliability instead of raw reliability for different subsets. This way, we can identify areas that have the most impact on operational reliability and focus reliability improvement actions on them.

6. SRGM Based on Data Clusters (SRGM-DC)

In practical applications, it is common to have considerable data fluctuations, such as observed in Section 4.1 when we examined the test workload measurement results for several large software systems. Such fluctuations are usually caused by variations in product and process characteristics. As discussed in Section 3, in the scenario-based testing of large software systems there may exist dependencies among test runs within a short time window, but there are few long-term dependencies, and the overall testing process still resembles random testing at a coarse granularity. Different data clusters may have different failure rates, with little dependency between clusters. Properly grouped data, such as using clusters with similar failure rates, can generally reduce such fluctuations and produce models that conform more closely with the observations. Tree-based models (TBMs) can be used to derive a new type of software reliability growth model based on these clusters, and filter data for use in traditional SRGMs [61]. We next discuss this new modeling approach.

For a given time period, the average failure rate, referred to as the *period failure rate*, can be defined by the number of failures per unit time to approximate the instantaneous hazard function defined in Section 2.3. The generic computational procedure for this period failure rate is outlined in Table 8. The number of failures can be easily counted, and the time period length can be measured using different time measurements. As demonstrated in Section 4, because of the uneven workload in the testing of most large software systems, only usage-dependent time measurements are appropriate for reliability modeling. For subsequent discussions, time is measured either by test run count or transactions. Notice that the term *transaction* used here is the generic

TABLE 8
GENERIC PROCEDURE FOR PERIOD FAILURE RATE COMPUTATION

(1) Determine the period P.
(2) Identify each test run (run i) falling into the period ($i \in P$).
(3) Count the number of runs, n, and the number of failures, f, for the period P.
(4) Compute the transactions for the period, t, as the summation of the transactions for all the individual runs, t_i for the ith run, falling into the period. That is, $t = \sum_{i \in P} t_i$.
(5) Compute the failure rate, λ, as failures divided by either runs or transactions, i.e. $\lambda = f/n$ or $\lambda = f/t$.

workload measure, and execution time can be considered as a special case of transactions where workload per execution time unit is constant. A period can be marked by using either the sequential numbering of test runs or some external delimiters, as discussed in Sections 6.1 and 6.2, respectively.

6.1 Data Partitioning for Individual Runs

When the run sequence number (*rsn*) is available, each run corresponds to a data point that can be grouped into a time period for reliability modeling. The individual failure rate (or point failure rate) for a successful run is always 0. The individual failure rate for a failed run is 1 if time is measured by test runs, and the inverse of associated transactions (or 1/trans) if time is measured by transactions. These individual runs can be grouped according to homogeneity criteria into consecutive but disjoint time periods, forming a partition of the overall reliability data. A lower bound on the period length in the partitioned segments (measured by the number of runs) can be selected to reflect short-term dependencies. Usually these short-term dependencies last over several test runs, so the default lower bound is set at 10.

Although run dependency analysis can be used to determine the partitions of time segments, such analysis could be too costly because of the large amount of data and test cases. Automated data grouping is needed for practical applications. Based on the assumption of short-term dependency and long-term independence of consecutive test runs, we can cluster runs with homogeneous failure rates as a group to reflect short-term dependency and runs with different failure rates into separate time segments. This grouping can be carried out using a statistical analysis technique called tree-based modeling [19] used in Section 5 to build TBRMs. The partitions derived from tree-based models (TBMs) give us a series of segments in the table of Fig. 14, with data points within a segment having similar failure rates, while data points from different segments have different failure rates. We call these models SRGMs based on data clusters, or SRGM-DC for short.

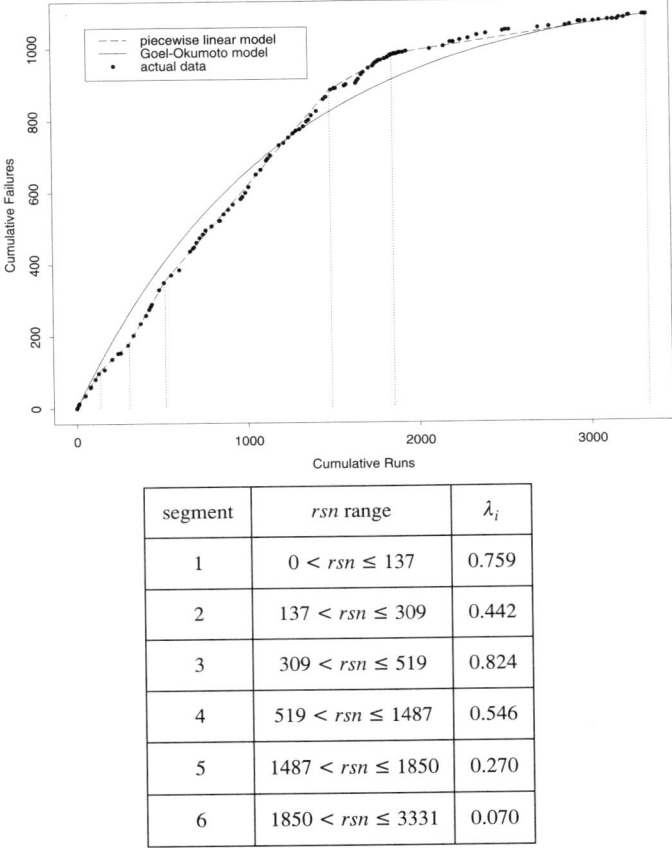

FIG. 14. Partition-based model for test runs (product D).

In using TBMs in SRGM-DC, f_{ij} indicates the presence ($f_{ij} = 1$) or absence ($f_{ij} = 0$) of failure for the jth run in the ith time segment with n_i runs and f_i failures. According to the tree construction algorithm in Table 6 (Section 5.1), the predicted period failure rate for data falling into a time segment is then:

$$\frac{\sum_{j=1}^{n_i} f_{ij}}{n_i} = \frac{f_i}{n_i} = \lambda_i$$

which is exactly the period failure rate defined in Table 8 applied to period i. Consequently, this TBM groups individual test runs into clusters of homogeneous failure rates by specifying the *rsn* range for the segments of runs.

When represented graphically, SRGM-DC gives us a piecewise linear curve for the cumulative failures, maintaining a constant failure arrival rate for each time segment. Figure 14 plots the cumulative failure arrivals against runs (the dots) and the SRGM-DC (the piecewise linear curve represented by the dashed lines), and contrasts it with the Goel–Okumoto model [25] (the fitted smooth curve). The period failure rate (λ_i) over the time segments is can be represented by discrete functions, such as in the table in Fig. 14, taking different values for different *rsn* ranges. The cutoff points for the partitions are determined by the TBM, shown in Fig. 15.

6.2 General Model Using Data Partitions

When exact sequencing information for individual runs is not available, external delimiters can be used to delineate the partitions. For example, for runs loosely associated with calendar date, the data associated with each individual date can be treated as one indivisible group, and the same rules can be followed to group these raw data groups into clusters of homogeneous failure rate. In general, when the time durations (measured by runs or transactions) are not the same for individual data points, the above simplistic use of TBMs must be modified. The failure rate for an individual data point cannot be indicated by a binary indicator (f_{ij}) as before, but rather by the number of failures over the measured time duration for the data point, following the definition in Table 8.

We next illustrate the general case of SRGM-DC using test transactions as the time measurement. The same technique can be applied to the case where a run is the time measurement for indivisible groups associated with a variable number of runs. The period failure rate computation in Table 8 is modified in

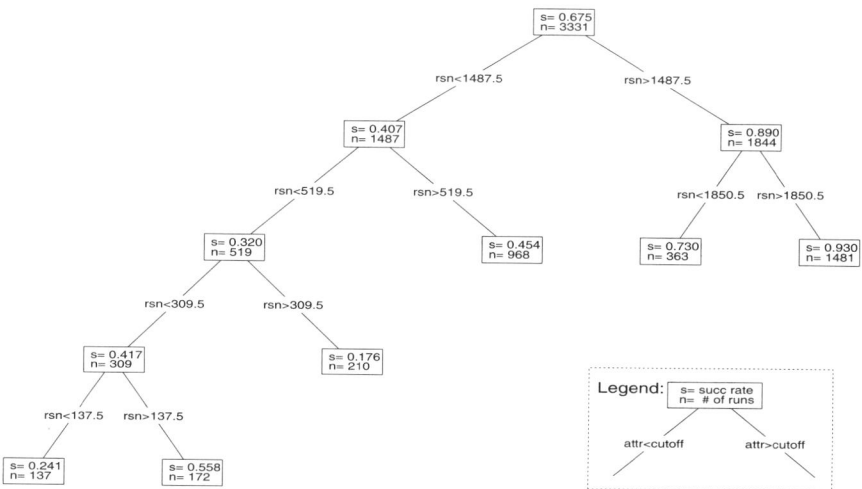

FIG. 15. Reliability over *rsn* (run numbering) cutoff points (product D).

TABLE 9
PERIOD FAILURE RATE (FAILURES/TRANSACTIONS) COMPUTATION

(1) Select the external delimiter d_j for data point j. Let l_i and u_i be the lower and upper bounds that delineate segment i, i.e. $l_i < d_j \leqslant u_i$.
(2) Compute the individual failure rate λ_j for a data point as $\lambda_j = f_j/t_j$, where f_j and t_j are the number of failures and transactions for data point j respectively.
(3) Compute the total transactions T_i for segment i as $T_i = \Sigma_{j, l_i < d_j \leqslant u_i} t_j$.
(4) Compute the total failures F_i for segment i as $F_i = \Sigma_{j, l_i < d_j \leqslant u_i} f_j$.
(5) Compute the period failure rate Λ_i for segment i as $\Lambda_i = F_i/T_i$.

Table 9 to compute the period failure rate, which can be implemented by using a TBM technique. When a TBM technique is used to determine the clusters, the arithmetic mean is no longer appropriate, because it gives the predicted period failure rate for segment i with N_i data points as:

$$\frac{\Sigma_{j, l_i < d_j \leqslant u_i} \lambda_j}{N_i} = \frac{\Sigma_{j, l_i < d_j \leqslant u_i} f_j/t_j}{N_i}$$

which is generally different from the desired Λ_i defined in Table 9 unless all the t_js are equal. Instead, a weighted average of the individual failure rates can be used, weighted by the corresponding individual transactions, i.e.

$$\frac{\Sigma_{j, l_i < d_j \leqslant u_i} t_j \lambda_j}{\Sigma_{j, l_i < d_j \leqslant u_i} t_j} = \frac{\Sigma_{j, l_i < d_j \leqslant u_i} f_j}{\Sigma_{j, l_i < d_j \leqslant u_i} t_j} = \frac{F_i}{T_i} = \mathbf{L}_i$$

This formula gives us a systematic way to compute the period failure rate, defined as the total number of failures divided by the cumulative transactions for a given cluster of runs (Table 9). This computation is also automatically supported by some software tools (Section 7), and therefore provides us with a systematic and automated means of analyzing the reliability for data clusters.

Figure 16 is an example of an SRGM-DC built for product E. The figure on the left is the cumulative failure plot and the figure on the right is the failure rate plot. Two representations of the same SRGM-DC are shown in its piecewise linear form for cumulative data (top) and as a step function for rate data (bottom). The partitions are listed in the table inside the top figure, with the left column specifying the upper bound for cumulative transactions for each consecutive segment, and the right column the average failure rate for the runs falling into the segment. The external time index, calendar date, was used to delimit the partitions. The fitted model in Fig. 16 follows essentially the same pattern as that in Fig. 14. It conforms well with the actual observations, clustering individual data points into groups of data with homogeneous failure rates.

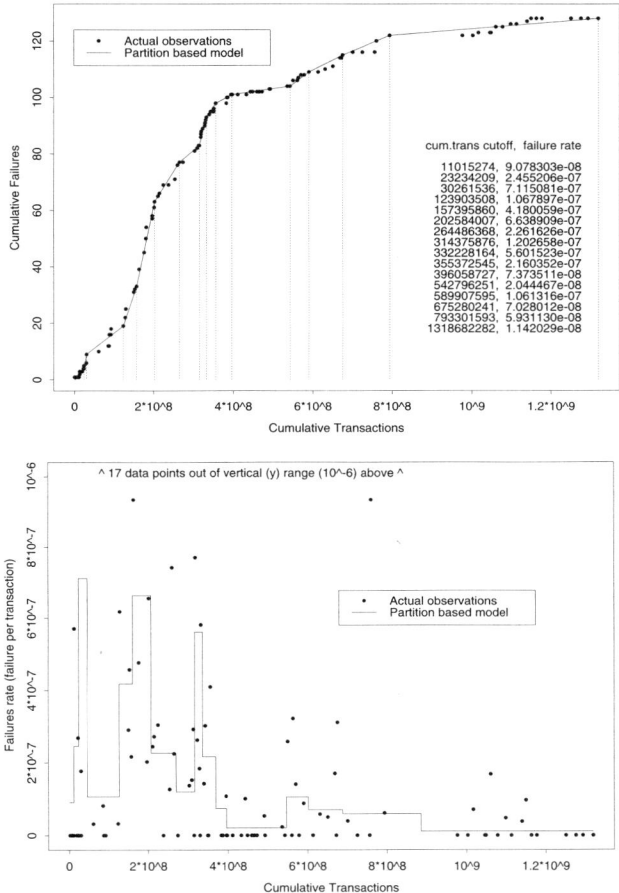

FIG. 16. Partition-based reliability model for period transaction failures.

6.3 Usage and Effectiveness of SRGM-DC and Its Dual Model

Reliability growth over the whole period covered by the measurement data can be represented by the gradual reduction of failure rates as we move from earlier segments to later ones. Local fluctuations in period failure rates are expected: occasionally later segments will have higher failure rates than earlier ones, such as in Fig. 16. However, if these kinds of "out-of-place" segments are a persistent phenomenon, it could well be an indication that there are problems in the product or in the testing process which need to be fixed. In addition, these SRGM-DCs can be readily integrated into TBRMs, focusing on problematic areas to ensure maximal reliability improvement.

When interpreted as piecewise reliability models, such as in Figs. 14 and 16, SRGM-DC fits observed data better than traditional SRGMs (such as the Goel–Okumoto model fitted to the same set of data in Fig. 14). A quick visual inspection of Figs. 14 and 16 confirms this observation. The piecewise model derived from data partitions generally follows the failure arrival trends closely. This comparison can be quantified by the various goodness-of-fit statistics, such as SSQ used in Section 4, computed for different fitted models. For example, in the SRGM-DC for product E, SSQ = 304.4, while $SSQ = 6329$ for the Goel–Okumoto model fitted to the same data.

The data partition that corresponds to the latest time segment can be used as the estimated current reliability. For example, the estimated reliability for product D associated with Fig. 14 at the product release (current time) can be characterized by its present failure rate of 0.070 per test run (for the latest segment $1850 < rsn \leqslant 3331$). For earlier periods, the reliability assessment is given by the corresponding predicted failure rate for the corresponding time segment from the model.

The data partition that corresponds to the latest time segment can also be directly extrapolated to predict future reliability. This extrapolation generally offers accurate short-term predictions, because data tends to cluster in short runs in practical applications. When future data is obtained, a weighted moving average can be used, with the weight proportional to the associated transactions for each additional data point to better utilize the latest information. For example, to predict failure rate for product E in Fig. 16 after an additional 500 000 000 transactions have been processed with two observed failures, these new data points can be weighted into the last segment (with 1 318 682 282 − 793 301 593 = 525 380 689 transactions and six failures; see Fig. 16) and calculate the predicted failure rate as,

$$\frac{6+2}{525\,380\,689 + 500\,000\,000} = 7.801\,98 \times 10^{-9}$$

In effect, the last time segment is expanded from 525 380 689 to 1 025 380 689 transactions to include the new runs, and the predicted failure rates recalculated. Alternatively, a new SRGM-DC can be built with the new observations rolled in.

The lack of assumed functional form between failure rates in different segments is both the strength and weakness of SRGM-DC: it leads to a robust model, being able to fit to almost any data; while the model lacks parameters that have meaningful global interpretations such as N, the total defects, in the Goel–Okumoto model [25] summarized in Section 2.3. Long-term predictions by SRGM-DC deteriorate because the data for the last segment become less relevant as time progresses. Traditional SRGMs may provide better long-term predictions because they capture the overall trend in the whole range covered by the data input. To compensate for this weakness, a dual model to SRGM-DC can be constructed, using the partitions as grouped data for use with selected failure count models. For example, the 16 segments in the SRGM-DC constructed for product E (Fig. 16) can be used as 16 data points to be fitted to some existing SRGMs. This treatment of data is similar to Schneidewind's approach, where data-sensitive groupings of the original data can be selected to produce a better fitted model [49].

Figure 17 shows such a fitted dual model, where the Goel–Okumoto model is fitted to the grouped data. With the availability of such dual models for SRGM-DC, the shortcomings of SRGM-DC can be alleviated. For example, SRGM-DC can still be used to perform the reliability analysis and problem identification functions identified before. But for long-term predictions and for practical and meaningful interpretations of model parameters, the dual failure count models fitted to the grouped data can be used.

Another advantage of using these dual models is their robustness, unparalleled in models fitted to individual data. Model parameters for the Goel–Okumoto model fitted to individual data and to grouped data are compared. For the last four sets of data (failure arrivals indexed by transactions) for product E studied in [62], the difference from the estimated N in the Goel–Okumoto model is 24.8% for models fitted to individual data, and 4.95% for models fitted to grouped data. Long-term prediction can be provided by a dual model that uses these grouped data as input fitted to some failure count variations of the traditional software reliability growth models.

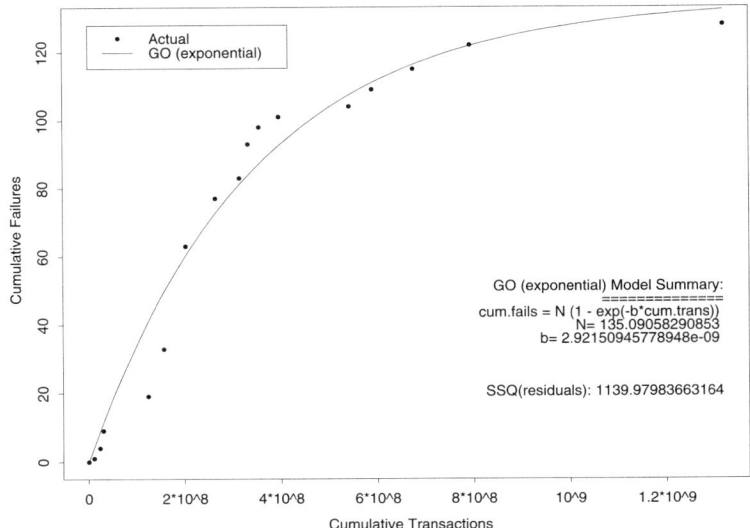

FIG. 17. Reliability model for grouped data (product E).

6.4 Summary, Comparison, and Research Issues

SRGMs based on data clusters (SRGM-DC) described in this section group failures and associated test execution time measured in runs or transactions into clusters of homogeneous failure rates. This model is based on several basic assumptions that can be justified and easily satisfied in large software system testing: (1) the testing environment roughly resembles the actual usage environment by the product's target customers; (2) there are no long-term dependencies in the testing process, although short-term dependencies are allowed; (3) proper usage measurements are used to normalize the time intervals in the reliability data; and (4) a constant failure rate is assumed for each cluster of test runs associated with a variable time window.

SRGM-DC can be directly used to assess the reliability of a software system for any given time segment covered by the input data. Therefore, such models can be used to evaluate the reliability growth throughout the overall testing process, to assess the current reliability, to predict future reliability, and to analyze general trends and patterns presented in the series of time segments so that anomalies can be easily identified. These models generally fit better than traditional SRGMs and provide modeling results that can help us evaluate the overall reliability and identify anomalies. Combined with its dual model using the grouped data as input fitted to traditional SRGMs, these models also provide good reliability predictions and meaningful interpretations of modeling results. Integration of this research with TBRMs described in Section 5 could lead to a more effective way to measure and improve reliability.

When a test run is used as the time measurement, the predicted failure rate λ for each segment from the SRGM-DC is the same as that from the Nelson model [42] summarized in Section 2.4. When a transaction is used as the unit of time measurement, SRGM-DC for each segment is essentially the same as the Brown–Lipow model [14] (Section 2.4). If we substitute data segment i for sub-domain i, measured transactions for n_i, and the ratio between the ith transactions over the total transactions ($n_i/\sum_i n_i$) for p_i, then the SRGM-DC for the segment is identical to the Brown–Lipow model.

Similar to the Jelinski–Moranda model [28] and Moranda's geometric model [36] (JM and Geo models) summarized in Section 2.3, where failure rate remains constant during inter-failure intervals, a constant failure rate is assumed in SRGM-DC for each time period within a data cluster identified by TBMs. When the failure rate plot is drawn, such as in the rate plot (right) in Fig. 16, the failure rates over segments form a step function similar to the JM and Geo models, but with different step sizes (both up and down) determined by the observations in the segment instead of down-steps of constant step-size (JM) or geometrically diminishing step-size (Geo). SRGM-DC does not assume a functional form for failure rates over different time segments associated with data clusters. SRGM-DC is data driven and data determined, depending on the exact clusters of data in the input. This is similar to the approach in the Littlewood–Verrall model [32], also summarized in Section 2.3, where the failure rate varies with latest observations.

There are many research issues: a pilot study applying this model in an integrated fashion with other reliability measurement and improvement initiatives is planned. A thorough study comparing different data grouping techniques could also help us to identify better rules for data grouping for specific applications. Progress in these research initiatives could yield a set of alternative modeling techniques to traditional SRGMs that can be more effectively used for reliability assessment as well as readily integrated with TBRMs for reliability improvement.

7. Integration, Implementation, and Tool Support

The analysis and modeling activities described in the previous sections share many common sub-activities, and need to be implemented under the environmental constraints and supported by selected software tools. We next summarize relevant research in this area [56, 64] and discuss issues about activity integration, practical implementation, and software tool support.

7.1 General Implementation and Process Linkage

When the analysis and modeling activities described in the previous sections are carried out in the testing process, they represents changes to the existing testing process, as illustrated in Fig. 18. These activities can be grouped into the following three categories in the modified testing process (shown within the dotted rectangle in Fig. 18):

- *Graphical tracking of testing efforts and defect trends.* Various data visualization techniques are used to examine the general trends and patterns of efforts and failure arrivals, and to visualize testing progress and reliability growth over time.
- *Reliability analysis and modeling.* Various existing SRGMs and SRGM based on data clusters (SRGM-DC) can be fitted to observed testing data to assess and predict product reliability and help make product release decisions.
- *Tree-based reliability modeling (TBRM) for problem identification and risk management.* This includes analyzing the complete set of project testing data by constructing TBRMs, identifying problematic areas, and guiding process adjustment and remedial actions.

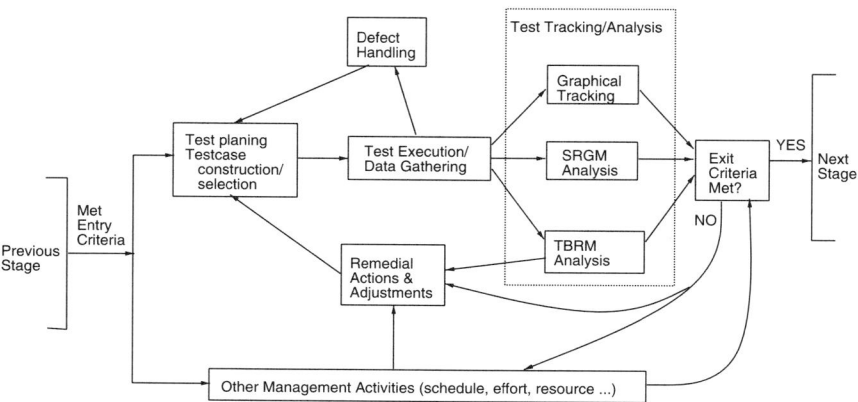

FIG. 18. Integrating tracking and analysis into the testing process.

This combination of analysis and modeling activities attempts to utilize the collected data to the fullest potential. SRGMs are mainly used to evaluate product "readiness," which serves as an exit criterion, while TBRMs are central to guiding remedial actions. Over time, these two analyses also complement one another nicely: early in testing, local data fluctuations tend to dominate the overall data pattern, and the trend of reliability growth is not expected to be very visible. The focus of analysis should be on using TBRMs to identify early problematic areas and guide improvement actions. Toward the end of testing, as a result of actions focused on problematic areas early on, there should not be any particularly weak part in the software system. The focus of analysis is now shifted to using SRGMs to assess overall product quality and to evaluate product "readiness" for release.

Analysis, modeling, and result presentation require good understanding of the models and analysis techniques and familiarity with various analysis and modeling tools. Thus they require the involvement of some dedicated quality analysts to work in cooperation with the product development organization, possibly over a long period of time for effective implementation and technology transfer. As mentioned in Section 3, in most large software development organizations the project organizations are usually organized around product groups, while the separate quality organizations are usually organized around software technology areas. Long-term collaboration between the two organizations is required for effective implementation and technology transfer.

- At the beginning of the engagement, the responsibility of the project organization is limited to ensuring accurate, timely, and consistent data collection, and using the analysis results provided by the quality analyst to manage their projects.

- As the engagement proceeds, the product organization will gain understanding and familiarity with the analyses and related tools, and could become more effective in implementing such analyses themselves because of their deep product and process specific knowledge. The longer term goal is to package the experience, much like in a mature experience factory [4, 6], and transfer the analysis methodology and make long-lasting process improvements.

The project organizations eventually take over implementation of the strategy for test tracking and analysis, performing most or all of the analyses themselves.

7.2 Tool Support for Data Collection, Analyses, and Presentation

The individual activities described above share many common elements: data must be collected and appropriate analysis and presentation techniques must be selected to handle the diverse information. Various software tools are needed to support these common activities.

(1) *Gathering testing measurements*. Defect information, as well as time and input domain testing measurements, need to be gathered using various tools to provide input for analyses.
(2) *Performing analyses on the collected data*. Failure intervals normalized by test activities can be fitted to SRGMs (Section 4) or analyzed by SRGM-DC (Section 6). Input domain and timing information for associated test runs can be analyzed using TBRMs (Section 5). Software tools are needed to support the data processing, analysis, and modeling.
(3) *Examining and presenting analysis results*. Analysis results need to be fed back to the software development teams so that appropriate actions can be taken to address the specific problems identified. Appropriate presentation tools need to be selected or constructed to make the interpretation of analysis results easy and to support exploration of alternatives.

Among the various tools that can be adapted and used to support test tracking and analysis activities, there is no single tool that satisfies all the needs for data collection, analysis, and presentation. One option is to construct a comprehensive tool to satisfy all these needs. However, this solution is impractical because of the significant effort required. It is also wasteful because many individual tools have already been used to support various other activities within the development life cycle. An alternative strategy is to use a collection of loosely integrated tools. Existing tools can be adapted to support some individual needs, and special-purpose tools can be constructed for specific applications where no appropriate tool exists. In general, the choice of tools depends on their internal characteristics and external constraints. Important issues include functionality, usability, automation, and flexibility. Since these tools need to work together toward the common goals, various issues regarding interoperability and integration also need to be addressed [76].

Central to many of the analyses described in the previous sections is tree-based modeling (TBM), a structured statistical analysis technique that attempts to establish predictive relationships among data attributes [19, 69]. The construction of tree-based models (TBMs) involves recursive partitioning of input data into smaller subsets of increasing homogeneity. The process of recursive partitioning is computationally intensive and needs to be supported by proper software tools. A binary variant of recursive partitioning prescribed in the algorithm in Table 6 (Section 5.1) is supported by a commercial software tool S-PLUS[1]. S-PLUS consists of the S[2] language, a high-level interpretive language [7], and extensive facilities for graphics, data analysis, and statistical modeling [53, 69]. It supports easy visualization of measurement data, regression analysis, and more importantly, TBM. It is the only commercial tool available for TBM. In addition, by using the underlying S language in S-PLUS, special-purpose utilities for data processing, reliability modeling, and result presentation can be easily developed. This flexibility can also be exploited to integrate the support tool suite. Consequently, S-PLUS was selected as the central tool to support our reliability analysis and improvement activities. Together with other tools for data collection, analysis, and presentation, this forms a comprehensive tool suite [64] discussed below.

7.2.1 Tool Support for Data Collection and Processing

For many large software development organizations, defect data are routinely collected during development using various tools to log defect information and track the resolution and integration of particular defects. In general, such defect tracking tools (or defect logs) record defect data in some underlying databases, from which defect and failure information can be extracted.

These defect logs are used for defect tracking, but are not designed to

---

[1] S-PLUS is a trade mark of Statistical Sciences, Inc.
[2] S is a trade mark of the American Telephone and Telegraph Company.

handle timing and input state information. Directly modifying them to record additional test data may interfere with their use in defect tracking, configuration management, and development process control. Consequently, other data gathering tools are generally needed to capture information associated with test execution and failure arrivals, with possible automated support for time-stamping, input state grouping, user prompting, and consistency checking. Our solution to test and reliability data collection is to use test logs: manual log files, spreadsheets, or semi-automated logging tools.

In addition to using test logging tools to collect general input and time domain information, other detailed workload information-capturing tools are generally needed if usage-dependent data other than simple run counts need to be used. Detailed workload information (e.g. transactions or execution time) during test runs can be captured with the help of such tools or by modifying the program source code. To induce minimal disruption to the testing process, system monitoring tools can be used to gather detailed workload information:

- For execution time measurement, CPU monitoring utilities that come with the operating system can be used to capture the measurements for individual test runs and export them to the test run logging tool.
- For transaction measurement, product- or content-sensitive monitors are needed. For example, transaction information capturing for product E, an RDBMS product initially studied in [62], is implemented using application program interfaces (APIs) provided with the product, which allow access to monitor information at the database level. This information is logged to disk at predetermined intervals by a background program which is started at the same time as the system test scenario.

The data captured in the data collection tools are the individual test runs and information associated with them, such as run result (success or failure), execution time or transactions extracted from detailed data capturing tools, and test case information for the runs. To use this information for reliability modeling, observed inter-failure intervals (for time between failure models, such as the Jelinski–Moranda model [28] or time periods associated with corresponding number of failures (for period failure count models, such as Goel–Okumoto model [25]) need to be computed (Section 2.3). The time periods are measured in terms of test runs, execution time, or transactions. Test runs and associated execution time, transactions, or failures can be tallied using utility programs in the S language implemented under S-PLUS to compute these normalized time periods and associated failure counts [64].

Individual testing days are commonly used to identify different periods. A testing day is a day where some testing activities occur, as signified by one or more test runs associated with that day. The number of test runs, transactions, and failures can be tallied for each day to use as the input data for reliability modeling. Another advantage of this is that such data indexing by testing days can be easily used for data grouping, because most of the test activities and management decisions can be associated with calendar days. Often they are *only* associated with calendar days. With this testing day-based period indexing, data grouped according to weeks, months, or numerous sub-phases for large projects can be easily derived for reliability modeling to provide modeling results that can be readily used to guide scheduling, product release, and other management decisions.

7.2.2 Tool Support for Data Analysis and Modeling

S-PLUS is used to support various key activities, including test tracking, reliability growth modeling, and tree-based reliability modeling:

- *Tracking* of test progress and failure arrivals. This activity includes the visual examination of various entities over time, primarily test runs, workloads, and failures. Utility programs written in the S language under S-PLUS were used to tally such entities and visualize their progress.
- *Reliability growth modeling.* Various reliability growth models can be easily implemented in S-PLUS. For example, the Goel–Okumoto model [25] fitted to observed failure data in Fig. 9 was produced by nonlinear models in S-PLUS to fit the mean function $m(t) = N(1 - e^{-bt})$, substituting cumulative failures, `cum.fails`, for $m(t)$, and cumulative transactions, `cum.trans`, for t. These data used for model fitting can be calculated from the raw data by using data processing utilities implemented in S under S-PLUS.
- *Tree-based reliability modeling* of reliability using all the time domain and input domain measurement information. S-PLUS is used to construct TBRMs (Section 5) and SRGM-DC (Section 6).

Although some software reliability growth models (SRGMs) can be easily fitted in S-PLUS, most SRGMs contain various options and can use different parameter estimation methods, and thus would require significant effort to implement them in S-PLUS. Fortunately, there are various existing tools for reliability growth modeling, including SMERFS (Statistical Modeling and Estimation of Reliability Functions for Software), SRMP (Software Reliability Modeling Program), GOEL (Goel–Okumoto modeling tool), ESTM (Economic Stop Testing Model), AT&T SRE ToolKit, SoRel (Software Reliability Program), and CASRE (Computer-Aided Software Reliability Estimation), discussed and compared in [52]. Some IBM internal tools for reliability analysis were also compared with some of the above mentioned tools in [59].

Among these reliability modeling tools, SMERFS provides a comprehensive collection of models, runs on multiple platforms, and is widely available to researchers and practitioners [23, 52]. Therefore it was selected as the centerpiece for reliability modeling for products studied in this article, which removes the need for implementing many models in S-PLUS. However, SMERFS places strict requirements on the input data format and lacks good graphical presentation of results. Therefore new facilities were developed to make SMERFS more accessible and usable [58]. Much of the data processing, visualization, and result presentation were automated under S-PLUS. Utility programs written in AWK, S, and C were used to extract the raw data and convert it into a format acceptable to SMERFS.

7.2.3 Tool Support for Result Presentation and Exploration

The measurement data and modeling results can be examined using various visualization techniques supported by S-PLUS. For example, we can visually examine the trends in the observed failure data, plotting cumulative failure arrivals against the normalized time intervals, as well as fitted models, such as in Section 4. SRGMs fitted by S-PLUS or SMERFS can be easily represented in graphical forms in S-PLUS using the automated support program we developed in S. The fitted model objects in S-PLUS contain all the parameters for the models. Alternatively, model parameters can be imported from SMERFS. The modeling results presented in graphical forms, such as in Section 4, can be examined visually, and extrapolation of the fitted curve can be used for predictions into the future.

Complete information for the constructed TBMs (TBRMs or SRGM-DC) is stored internally in S-PLUS and can be extracted using built-in and customized utilities. The built-in graphical display of trees draws dendrograms that show only a little information for the models: (1) for an interior node, only the split condition is shown; and (2) for a leaf node, only the predicted response value is shown. Such dendrograms were presented to the developers and testers, sometimes with augmented information handwritten on the dendrograms, but a lot of explanations were still needed. Automated support for tree drawing is necessary to produce trees that are easily understandable and visually appealing. The key information that needs to be presented in such trees includes:

- *Node information*: key information for each node associated with a set of data includes the size of the data set, the predicted response variable value, and the distribution summary.
- *Branching information*: each branch represents a binary partition according to some split condition. The essential information needed here is the

split condition, which takes two forms: (1) a cutoff value for a selected numerical predictor, or (2) a binary grouping for a selected categorical predictor.

The tree drawings in Section 5 are drawn by the new utility programs we implemented in S. Each set of data associated with a tree node is summarized by its predicted success rate (s) and the number of runs (n) in the set. Notice that the response distribution summary is omitted, because the response variable is a binary variable (1 for success and 0 for failure) and the response distribution can be deduced from the set size and predicted response. The split conditions were clearly marked by the edge leading to each partitioned subset. From this kind of tree drawing, we can easily identify nodes with exceptionally low success rates and characterize them by the series of split conditions leading to them from the tree root. Such representations are easy to interpret and useful to the development teams.

Other information can also be extracted and examined from TBM results in connection with the original input data. For example, we may want to examine the data and distribution of other variables, and examine the linkage between the response variable and other predictor variables. However, presenting such information in a static tree drawing like in Fig. 11 would be impractical, because too much information will simply ruin the simplicity and direct appeal of such graphs. Some interactive exploration facilities for TBMs need to be considered.

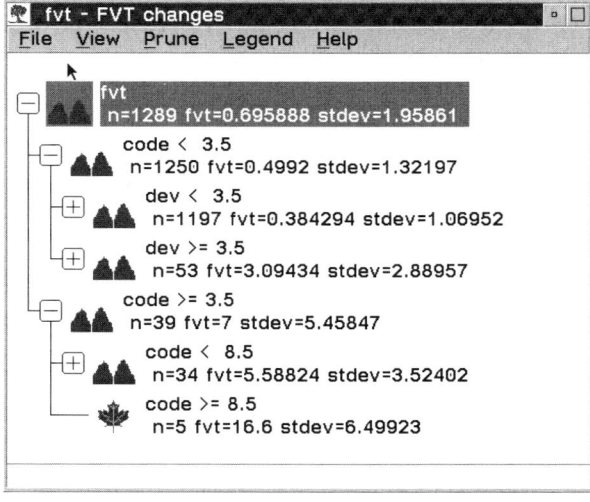

FIG. 19. TBM exploration in TreeBrowser.

To make tree exploration easy for developers to use, we recently built a tool called TreeBrowser [67]. The TBMs produced by S-PLUS and the original measurement data are exported to TreeBrowser. TreeBrowser shows the imported models in a hierarchical display. Each tree can be displayed by double clicking on its icon, and its interior nodes can be interactively expanded (by clicking the "+" icon) or pruned (by clicking the "−" icon). Displayed at each tree node is a statistical summary of the subset of data associated with the node and a node type indicator, with a maple leaf icon to indicate a leaf node and an icon with a split in the middle (signaling that it can be further split) to indicate an interior node. This data subset can be displayed in tabular form by double clicking on the tree node. Figure 19 is an example of an interactive display of a TBM in TreeBrowser.

7.3 Integration and Future Development

The tools used for data gathering, analysis, and presentation need to work together to support test tracking and reliability analyses. Figure 20 illustrates the individual tools discussed above and shows their interconnections. Each tool is shown graphically as a rectangle, with the name of the tool identified in boldtext and the main functions listed under the name. The tools are grouped into three classes: data capturing tools, analysis tools, and presentation tools. The sources for the data capturing tools and the reports produced by the presentation tools are shown in ovals. The interconnections (directed links) show the information flow among the different tools, with the result of one tool used as input to another tool.

As is clearly visible from Fig. 20, S-PLUS (and its associated S programs) plays a very important role in this tool suite. All the other tools are connected to this block, either as an information consumer (TreeBrowser uses TBM results from S-PLUS, and SMERFS imports formatted data from S-PLUS) or as information providers (SMERFS provides analysis results for presentation, and all other data gathering tools provide raw data for analyses). Consequently, S-PLUS and associated S programs can be used to integrate the tool suite.

In general, tool integration can be achieved primarily through three means:

- *External rules adopted for data contents and formats to ensure interoperability of tools.* In general, before any data collection, analysis, or presentation activity is carried out, all the parties involved have to agree on the data contents and formats. The selection of data contents is primarily determined by the goals of the activities and is prescribed for individual analyses. The format of the data is usually determined by the application environment and the capability of the tools. In general, it is

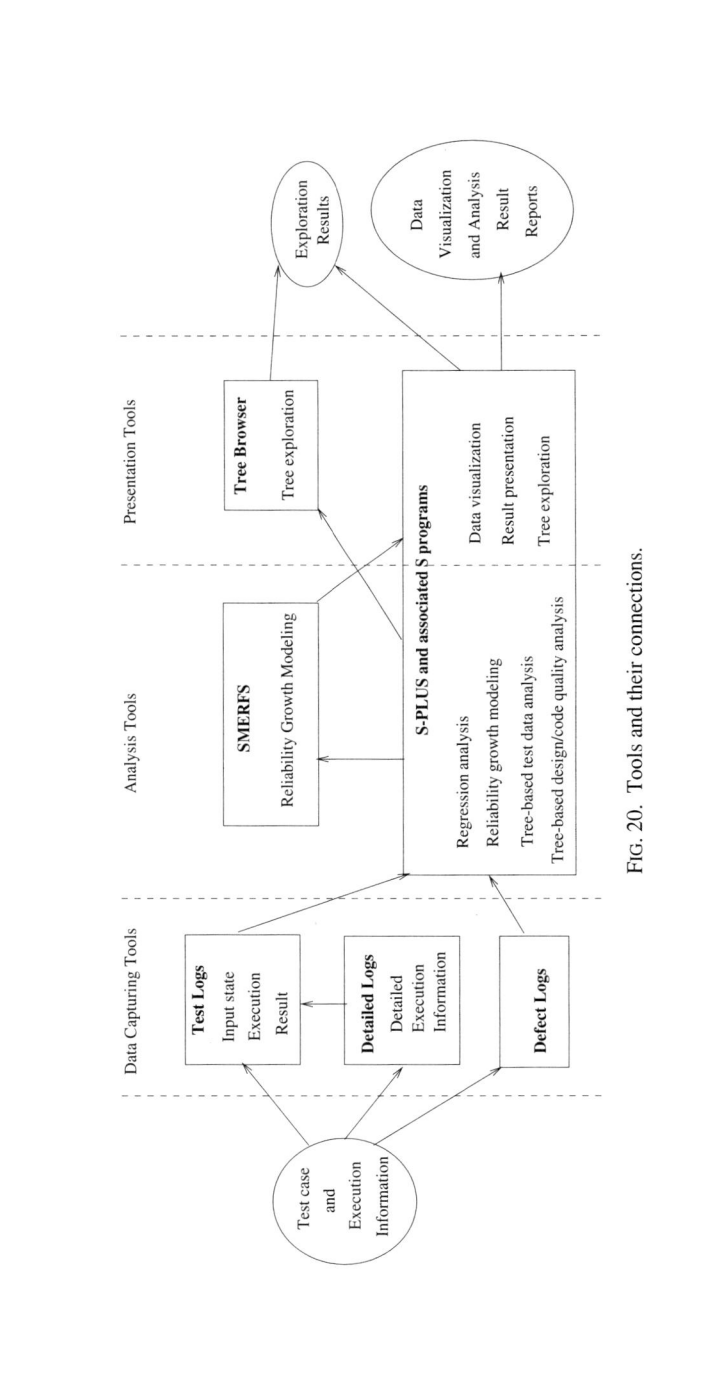

FIG. 20. Tools and their connections.

easier to deal with data of different formats in the tools that have greater flexibility. Therefore the data format is generally selected so that it is easy to handle by the less flexible tools.

- *Using common tools for multiple purposes.* For example, S-PLUS, together with the customized S programs, serves multiple purposes and occupies a central place in the tool suite. S-PLUS can be used for some reliability growth modeling instead of SMERFS. In addition, as shown in Fig. 20, S-PLUS is connected to all the other tools. It could potentially become the sole integration device, with the user dealing only with S-PLUS while hiding all the other tools in the background. However, this approach would require significant effort and can only be achieved gradually, by incremental additions to utility programs written in S language.

- *Other utility programs that convert data for interoperability of tools.* For example, various AWK and PERL scripts can be used to extract data for analysis and check for data consistency, which is generally easier to implement than directly processing the raw data in S-PLUS. Some C programs were used to convert failure internal data to the format required by SMERFS for reliability modeling. This collection of small utility programs can be used with integration utilities in S-PLUS to ensure that the tools work together.

To summarize, an integrated implementation and support strategy for various software measurement, analysis, and quality improvement activities has many benefits: collected data, analyses, and presentation facilities can be shared among different activities to reduce cost, and integrated analyses can yield results that cannot be obtained by individual analyses alone. Careful planning for the implementations that minimize disruption to existing development and testing processes also helps the reception of this integrated strategy in the short-term and the technology transfer in the long-term, where development organization takes over all the responsibilities for quality and process optimization in addition to product development.

Appropriate tool support is essential to these activities. To accommodate the diverse software measurement environments and data sources, and to support different analyses and uses of the analysis results, a comprehensive suite of tools can be used. The tools can be integrated to work together by observing common data content and format rules, using common tools for multiple purposes, and using utility programs specifically constructed for tool integration. This approach has been used successfully in supporting software measurement and quality improvement for several large commercial software products developed in the IBM Software Solutions Toronto Laboratory.

There is still much potential waiting to be explored, particularly in the integration of tools so that a unified and easy-to-use environment can emerge. The current users of the tool suite described in this section have to work with several tools and environments. A simplified tool suite where related functionalities are consolidated into fewer tools and most of the standard usage sequences are automated could produce a more homogeneous and easy-to-use tool suite to better support initiatives in software measurement, analysis, and quality improvement.

8. Conclusions and Perspectives

This chapter has presented some recent developments and advances in reliability analysis and improvement for large software systems. Existing analysis techniques were surveyed and discussed. Particular attention was paid to recent developments that not only provide a realistic assessment of product reliability but also help identify problematic areas for focused reliability improvement in a series of studies for large software systems reported in [55, 56, 60–62, 64]. This chapter summarizes the results from these previous research initiatives, and provides a systematic framework to integrate and share these results. Key observations and findings in this chapter are summarized below:

- A key ingredient of a successful measurement program is to maximize the utilization of measurement data while minimizing incremental cost and disruption to the existing process. One way to maximize the data utility is to perform an integrated suite of analyses, not only to assess the product quality but also to provide guidance for quality improvement. Visualization techniques and graphical representations can be used to make it easy to interpret and use these analyses results.

- Software reliability growth models (SRGMs) provide an overall quality assessment for products under testing when proper data and measurement information are captured. Run-based reliability modeling seems to provide the maximal utility with minimal cost, provided that homogeneous runs are used or runs can be broken down to homogeneous sub-runs. Otherwise, time measurement that captures detailed usage information, such as transactions, can be used for reliability analysis with SRGMs.

- Tree-based reliability modeling (TBRM) is a practical technique that can help improve the software development process and product quality. Because of the non-homogeneity of defect distribution within the software products and varied degrees of defect detection effectiveness by

different testing scenarios, the identification of specific subsets for remedial actions provides a cost-effective way to improve quality.
- SRGMs based on data clusters (SRGM-DC) are a viable alternative to traditional SRGMs. SRGM-DC generally provides better assessment of current reliability and short-term predictions than traditional SRGMs. Long-term predictions can be made using the same data clusters as grouped data fitted to traditions SRGMs.
- Integration of various analysis methods provides much more benefit than individual analyses alone. TBRMs and SRGMs complement one another, with the former used *early* in testing to guide actions that lead to improved quality, and the latter used *late* in testing to assess overall quality and to serve as an exit criterion.
- Proper tool support is a key ingredient of a successful implementation of software measurement, analysis, and improvement strategies. Sharing and integration of software tools can reduce the cost and provide better support for data collection, analysis and modeling, and results presentation.

Future development of this integrated strategy of reliability measurement and improvement using multiple models and analysis techniques includes many of the specific research issues, developments, and directions discussed at the end of previous sections. All these individual developments could help us form a more comprehensive strategy to build effective models for quality, reliability, and process improvement and optimization in the testing and development of large software systems.

Acknowledgments

We would like to express our sincere gratitude to Ian Burrows, Mark Changfoot, George Dadoun, John Henshaw, Ron Holt, Larry Keeling, Peng Lu, Michael Ng, Joe Palma, David Shier, Joel Troster, Joe Wigglesworth, Paul Yee, and members and managers of several testing teams within the IBM Software Solutions Toronto Laboratory. Their support, participation, and feedback are invaluable to our study, particularly to the implementation and deployment of the related software reliability measurement, analysis, and improvement activities described in this chapter. We also thank the editor, Dr. Marvin V. Zelkowitz, for his numerous suggestions which led to a much improved chapter.

References

1. ANSI/AIAA (1992) *American National Standard: Recommended Practice for Software Reliability*. Number ANSI/AIAA R-013-1992. American Institute of Aeronautics and Astronautics.
2. ANSI/IEEE (1991) *Standard Glossary of Software Engineering Terminology*. Number STD-729-1991. ANSI/IEEE.

3. Avritzer, A., and Weyuker, E. J. (1995) The automatic generation of load test suites and the assessment of the resulting software. *IEEE Trans. Software Engineering* **21**(9), 705–716.
4. Basili, V. R., Caldiera, G., and Cantone, G. (1992) A reference architecture for the component factory. *ACM Trans. Software Engineering and Methodology* **1**(1), 53–80.
5. Basili, V. R., and Rombach, H. D. (1988) The TAME project: towards improvement-oriented software environments. *IEEE Trans. Software Engineering* **14**(6), 758–773.
6. Basili, V. R., Zelkowitz, M. V., McGarry, F. E., Page, J., Waligora, S., and Pajerski, R. (1995) SEL's software process-improvement program. *IEEE Software* **12**(6), 83–87.
7. Becker, R. A., Chambers, J. M., and Wilks, A. R. (1988) *The New S Language: A Programming Environment for Data Analysis and Graphics*. Wadsworth & Brooks/Cole, Pacific Grove CA.
8. Beizer, B. (1990) *Software Testing Techniques*, 2nd edn. International Thomson Computer Press, London.
9. Beizer, B. (1995) *Black-Box Testing: Techniques for Functional Testing of Software and Systems*. John Wiley & Son, New York.
10. Boehm, B. W. (1981) *Software Engineering Economics*. Prentice Hall, Englewood Cliffs NJ.
11. Boehm, B. W. (1991) Software risk management: principles and practices. *IEEE Software* **8**(1), 32–41.
12. Briand, L. C., Basili, V. R., and Hetmanski, C. J. (1993) Developing interpretable models with optimal set reduction for identifying high-risk software components. *IEEE Trans. Software Engineering* **19**(11), 1028–1044.
13. Brooks W. D., and Motley, R. W. (1980) Analysis of discrete software reliability models. *Technical Report RADC-TR-80-84*, Rome Air Development Center.
14. Brown, J. R., and Lipow, M. (1975) Testing for software reliability. *Proc. Int. Conf. Reliable Software*, Los Angeles. pp. 518–527.
15. Card, D. N., and Glass, R. L. (1990) *Measuring Software Design Quality*. Prentice Hall, Englewood Cliffs NJ.
16. Chen, M. H., Lyu, M. R., and Wong, W. E. (1996) An empirical study of the correlation between code coverage and reliability estimation. *Proc. 3rd International Software Metrics Symp.*, Berlin. pp. 133–141.
17. Chen, M. H., Mathur, A. P., and Rego, V. J. (1994) A case study to investigate sensitivity of reliability estimates to errors in operational profile. *Proceedings of Fifth International Symposium on Software Reliability Engineering*.
18. Chillarege, R., Bhandari, I., Chaar, J., Halliday, M., Moebus, D., Ray, B., and Wong, M.-Y. (1992) Orthogonal defect classification—a concept for in-process measurements. *IEEE Trans. Software Engineering* **18**(11), 943–956.
19. Clark, L. A., and Pregibon, D. (1992) Tree based models. *Statistical Models in S* (eds J. M. Chambers and T. J. Hastie). Wadsworth & Brooks/Cole, Pacific Grove CA. pp. 377–419.
20. Cleveland, W. S., (1993) *Visualizing Data*. Hobart Press, Summit NJ.
21. Date, C. J., (1990) *An Introduction to Database Systems*, Vol. 1. Addison-Wesley, Reading MA.
22. Farr, W. J., (1995) Software reliability modeling survey. *Handbook of Software Reliability Engineering* (ed. M. R. Lyn). McGraw-Hill, New York.
23. Farr, W. J., and Smith, O. D. (1991) Statistical modeling and estimation of reliability functions for software (SMERFS) users guide. *Technical Report NSWC TR 84-373*, Revision 2. Naval Surface Warfare Center.
24. Goel, A. L. (1985) Software reliability models: assumptions, limitations, and applicability. *IEEE Trans. Software Engineering* **11**(12), 1411–1423.
25. Goel, A. L., and Okumoto, K. A time dependent error detection rate model for software reliability and other performance measures. *IEEE Trans. Reliability* **28**(3), 206–211.

26. Humphrey, W. (1989) *Managing the Software Process*. Addison-Wesley, Reading MA.
27. IBM (1991) *Programming Process Architecture*, Version 2.1. IBM.
28. Jelinski, Z., and Moranda, P. L. (1972) Software reliability research. *Statistical Computer Performance Evaluation* (ed. W. Freiberger). Academic Press, New York. pp. 365–484.
29. Kan, S. H., Basili, V. R., and Shapiro, L. N. (1994) Software quality: an overview from the perspective of total quality management. *IBM Systems Journal* **33**(1), 4–19.
30. Karlin, S., and Taylor, H. M. (1975) *A First Course in Stochastic Processes*, 2nd edn. Academic Press, New York.
31. Kitchenham, B., and Pfleeger, S. L. (1996) Software quality: the elusive target. *IEEE Software* **13**(1), 12–21.
32. Littlewood, B., and Verrall, J. L. (1973) A Bayesian reliability growth model for computer software. *Applied Statistics* **22**, 332–346.
33. Lu, P., and Tian, J. Applying software reliability engineering in large-scale software development. *Proc. 3rd Int. Conf. on Software Quality*, Lake Tahoe, Nevada. pp. 323–330.
34. Lyu, M. R. (ed.) (1995) *Handbook of Software Reliability Engineering*. McGraw-Hill, New York.
35. DeMillo, R. A., McCracken, W. M., Martin, R. J., and Passafiume, J. F. (1987) *Software Testing and Evaluation*. Benjamin/Cummings, Menlo Park CA.
36. Moranda, P. B. (1975) Prediction of software reliability during debugging. *Annual Reliability and Maintainability Symp.*, Washington DC. pp. 327–332.
37. Musa, J. D. (1971) A theory of software reliability and its application. *IEEE Trans. Software Engineering* **1**, 312–327.
38. Musa, J. D. (1993) Operational profiles in software reliability engineering. *IEEE Software* **10**(2), 14–32.
39. Musa, J. D., and Ehrlich, W. (1996) Advances in software reliability engineering. *Advances in Computers*, Vol. 42 (ed. M. V. Zelkowitz). Academic Press, New York. pp. 77–117.
40. Musa, J. D., Iannino, A., and Okumoto, K. (1987) *Software Reliability: Measurement, Prediction, Application*. McGraw-Hill, New York.
41. Musa, J. D. and Okumoto, K. (1984) A logarithmic Poisson execution time model for software reliability measurement. *Proc. 7th Int. Conf. on Software Engineering*. pp. 230–238.
42. Nelson, E. (1978) Estimating software reliability from test data. *Microelectronics Reliability* **17** 67–74.
43. Pasquini, A., Crespo, A., and Matrella, P. (1996) Sensitivity of reliability-growth models to operational profile errors vs. testing accuracy. *IEEE Trans. Reliability* **45**(4), 531–540.
44. Porter, A. A., and Selby, R. W. (1990) Empirically guided software development using metric-based classification trees. *IEEE Software* **7**(2), 46–54.
45. Ray, B., Bhandari, I., and Chillarege, R. (1991) Reliability growth for typed defects. *Proc. IEEE Reliability and Maintainability Symp.*
46. Schafer, R. E., Alter, J. F., Angus, J. E., and Emoto, S. E. (1979) Validation of software reliability models. *Technical Report RADC-TR-79-147*. Rome Air Development Center.
47. Schick, G. J., and Wolverton, R. W. (1978) An analysis of competing software reliability models. *IEEE Trans. Software Engineering* **4**(2), 104–120.
48. Schneidewind, N. F. (1975) Analysis of error processes in computer software. *Proc. Int. Conf. Reliable Software*, Los Angeles. pp. 337–346.
49. Schneidewind, N. F. (1993) Software reliability model with optimal selection of failure data. *IEEE Trans. Software Engineering* **19**(11), 1095–1104.
50. Selby, R. W., and Porter, A. A. (1988) Learning from examples: generation and evaluation of decision trees for software resource analysis. *IEEE Trans. Software Engineering* **14**(12), 1743–1757.

51. Shooman, M. L. (1972) Probabilistic models for software reliability prediction. *Statistical Computer Performance Evaluation* (ed. W. Freidberger). Academic Press, New York. pp. 485–502.
52. Stark, G. Software reliability tools. *Handbook of Software Reliability Engineering* (ed. M. R. Lyu). McGraw-Hill, New York. pp. 729–745.
53. StatSci (1993) *S-PLUS Reference Manual*, Version 3.2. StatSci, A Division of MathSoft, Inc., Seattle WA.
54. Thayer, R., Lipow, M., and Nelson, E. (1978) *Software Reliability*. North-Holland, Amsterdam.
55. Tian, J. (1995) Integrating time domain and input domain analyses of software reliability using tree-based models. *IEEE Trans. Software Engineering* **21**(12), 945–958.
56. Tian, J. (1996) An integrated approach to test tracking and analysis. *Journal of Systems and Software* **35**(2), 127–140.
57. Tian, J., and Henshaw, J. (1994) Tree-based defect analysis in testing. *Proc. 4th Int. Conf. on Software Quality*, McLean VA.
58. Tian, J., and Lu, P. (1993) An integrated environment for software reliability modeling. *Proc. 17th Int. Computer Software and Applications Conf.* pages 395–401.
59. Tian, J., and Lu, P. (1993) Measuring and modeling software reliability: data, models, tools, and a support environment. *Technical Report TR-74.117*, IBM PRGS Toronto Laboratory.
60. Tian, J., Lu, P., and Palma, J. (1995) Test execution based reliability measurement and modeling for large commercial software. *IEEE Trans. Software Engineering* **21**(5), 405–414.
61. Tian, J., and Palma, J. (1996) Data partition based reliability modeling. *Proc. 7th Int. Symp. on Software Reliability Engineering*. pp. 354–363.
62. Tian, J., and Palma, J. (1997) Test workload measurement and reliability analysis for large commercial software systems. *Annals of Software Engineering* **4**, 201–222.
63. Tian, J., Porter, A. A., and Zelkowitz, M. V. (1992) An improved classification tree analysis of high cost modules based upon an axiomatic definition of complexity. *Proc. 3rd Int. Symp. on Software Reliability Engineering*. pp. 164–172.
64. Tian, J., Troster, J., and Palma, J. (1997) Tool support for software measurement, analysis, and improvement. *Journal of Systems and Software* **39**(2), 165–178.
65. Tian, J., and Zelkowitz, M. V. (1995) Complexity measure evaluation and selection. *IEEE Trans. Software Engineering* **21**(8), 641–650.
66. Troster, J., and Tian, J. (1995) Measurement and defect modeling for a legacy software system. *Annals of Software Engineering* **1**, 95–118.
67. Troster, J., and Tian, J. (1996) Exploratory analysis tools for tree-based models in software measurement and analysis. *Proc. 4th Int. Symp. on Assessment of Software Tools*, Toronto. pp. 7–17.
68. Tsoukalas, M. Z., Duran, J. W., and Ntafos, S. C. (1993) On some reliability estimation problems in random and partition testing. *IEEE Trans. on Software Engineering* **19**(7), 687–697.
69. Venables, W. N., and Ripley, B. D. (1994) *Modern Applied Statistics with S-Plus*. Springer-Verlag, Berlin.
70. Voas, J. M., and Miller, K. W. (1995) Software testability: the new verification. *IEEE Software*. **12**(3), 17–28.
71. von Mayrhauser, A. (1990) *Software Engineering: Methods and Management*. Academic Press, New York.
72. Weyuker, E. J., and Jeng, B. (1991) Analyzing partition test strategies. *IEEE Trans. Software Engineering* **17**(7), 703–711.
73. Whittaker, J. A., and Poore, J. H. (1993) Markov analysis of software specifications. *ACM Trans. Software Engineering and Methodology* **2**(1), 93–106.

74. Yamada, S., Ohba, M., and Osaki, S. (1983) S-shaped reliability growth modeling for software error detection. *IEEE Trans. Reliability* **32**(5), 475–478.
75. Zelkowitz, M. V. (1993) Role of verification in the software specification process. *Advances in Computers*, Vol. 36 (ed. M. C. Yovits). Academic Press, New York. pp. 43–109.
76. Zelkowitz, M. V. (1996) Modeling software engineering environment capabilities. *Journal of Systems and Software* **35**(1), 3–14.

Role-based Access Control[1]

RAVI S. SANDHU[2]

Laboratory for Information Security Technology
Information and Software Engineering Department, MS 4A4
George Mason University
Fairfax, VA 22030
USA

Abstract

The basic concept of role-based access control (RBAC) is that permissions are associated with roles, and users are made members of appropriate roles, thereby acquiring the roles' permissions. This idea has been around since the advent of multi-user computing. Until recently, however, RBAC has received little attention from the research community. This chapter describes the motivations, results, and open issues in recent RBAC research.

The chapter focuses on four areas. First, RBAC is a multidimensional concept that can range from very simple at one extreme to quite complex and sophisticated at the other. This presents problems in coming up with a definitive model of RBAC. We see how this impasse is resolved by having a family of models which can accommodate all these variations. Second, we discuss how RBAC can be used to manage itself. Recent models developed for this purpose are presented. Third, the flexibility of RBAC can be demonstrated in many ways. Here we show how RBAC can be configured to enforce different variations of classical lattice-based mandatory access controls. Fourth, we describe a conceptual three-tier architecture for specification and enforcement of RBAC. The chapter concludes with a discussion of open issues in RBAC.

1. Introduction 238
   1.1 Motivation and Background 239
   1.2 RBAC Limitations 241
   1.3 What is a Role? 241
   1.4 Roles versus Groups 242
2. The RBAC96 Models 243
   2.1 Base Model: $RBAC_0$ 243
   2.2 Role Hierarchies: $RBAC_1$ 247

---

[1] Portions of this chapter have been published earlier in Sandhu *et al*. (1996), Sandhu (1996), Sandhu and Bhamidipati (1997), Sandhu *et al*. (1997) and Sandhu and Feinstein (1994).

[2] Ravi Sandhu is also affiliated with SETA Corporation, 6862 Elm Street, McLean, VA 22101, USA.

	2.3	Constraints: $RBAC_2$	251
	2.4	Consolidated Model: $RBAC_3$	254
	2.5	Discussion	254
3.	The ARBAC97 Administrative Models		257
	3.1	URA97 for User–Role Assignment	261
	3.2	PRA97 for Permission–Role Assignment	264
	3.3	RRA97 for Role–Role Assignment	266
	3.4	Discussion	269
4.	Roles and Lattices		270
	4.1	Lattice-Based Access Controls	271
	4.2	Basic Lattices	273
	4.3	Composite Confidentiality and Integrity Roles	275
	4.4	Discussion	277
5.	Three-Tier Architecture		278
	5.1	The Three Tiers	280
	5.2	The Central Tier	281
	5.3	Harmonizing the Top Two Tiers	281
	5.4	Harmonizing the Bottom Two Tiers	283
	5.5	Discussion	284
6.	Conclusion		284
References			285

1. Introduction

The concept of role-based access control (RBAC) began with multi-user and multi-application online systems pioneered in the early 1970s. The central notion of RBAC is that permissions are associated with roles, and users are assigned to appropriate roles. Roles are created for the various job functions in an organization and users are assigned roles based on their responsibilities and qualifications. Users can be easily reassigned from one role to another. Roles can be granted new permissions as new applications and systems are incorporated, and permissions can be revoked from roles as needed.

This basic idea has been around in one form or another for a long time, yet it has received surprisingly little attention from the research community until recently. This chapter describes the motivations, results, and open issues in recent RBAC research.

This section introduces RBAC and discusses general issues related to it. In Section 2 we show that RBAC is a multidimensional concept, ranging from very simple at one end to quite sophisticated at the other. This makes it difficult to construct a single definitive model of RBAC. Instead we describe a family of models which can accommodate all these variations. In Section 3 we discuss how RBAC can be used to manage itself. In Section 4 we demonstrate the flexibility and power of RBAC by showing how it can be configured to enforce different variations of classical lattice-based mandatory access controls. Section 5 describes a conceptual three-tier architecture for specification and enforcement of RBAC. Section 6 concludes the chapter with a brief discussion of open issues in RBAC.

1.1. Motivation and Background

A recent study by the US National Institute of Standards and Technology (NIST) (Ferraiolo *et al.*, 1993) demonstrated that RBAC addresses many needs of the commercial and government sectors. In this study of 28 organizations, access control requirements were found to be driven by a variety of concerns, including customer, stockholder, and insurer confidence, privacy of personal information, preventing unauthorized distribution of financial assets, preventing unauthorized usage of long-distance telephone circuits, and adherence to professional standards. The study found that many organizations based access control decisions on "the roles that individual users take on as part of the organization." Many organizations preferred to control and maintain access rights centrally, not so much at the system administrator's personal discretion but more in accordance with the organization's protection guidelines. The study also found that organizations typically viewed their access control needs as unique and felt that available products lacked adequate flexibility.

Other evidence of strong interest in RBAC comes from the standards arena. Roles are being considered as part of the emerging SQL3 standard for database management systems, based on their implementation in Oracle 7. Roles have also been incorporated in the commercial security profile of the Common Criteria (Common Criteria Editorial Board, 1996). There are ongoing efforts by NIST to provide standards and guidance for RBAC.

RBAC is also well matched to prevailing technology and business trends. A number of products support some form of RBAC directly, and others support closely related concepts, such as user groups, that can be utilized to implement roles.

Many commercially successful access control systems for mainframes implement roles for security administration. For example, an operator role can access all resources but not change access permissions; a security officer role can change permissions but have no access to resources; and an auditor role can access audit trails. This administrative use of roles is also found in modern network operating systems, e.g. Novell's NetWare and Microsoft Windows NT.

Recent resurgence of interest in RBAC has focused on general support of RBAC at the application level. Specific applications have been, and are being, built with RBAC encoded within the application itself. Existing operating systems and environments provide little support for application-level use of

RBAC. Such support is beginning to emerge in some products. The challenge is to identify application-independent facilities that are sufficiently flexible, yet simple to implement and use, to support a wide range of applications with minimal customization.

Sophisticated variations of RBAC include the capability to establish relations between roles as well as between permissions and roles and between users and roles. For example, two roles can be established as mutually exclusive, so the same user is not allowed to take on both roles. Roles can also take on inheritance relations, whereby one role inherits permissions assigned to a different role. These role–role relations can be used to enforce security policies that include separation of duties and delegation of authority. Heretofore, these relations would have to be encoded into application software; with RBAC, they can be specified once for a security domain.

With RBAC it is possible to predefine role–permission relationships, which makes it simple to assign users to the predefined roles. The NIST study cited above indicates that permissions assigned to roles tend to change relatively slowly compared with changes in user membership of roles. The study also found it desirable to allow administrators to confer on and revoke membership of users in existing roles without giving these administrators authority to create new roles or change role–permission assignments. Assignment of users to roles will typically require less technical skill than assignment of permissions to roles. It can also be difficult, without RBAC, to determine what permissions have been authorized to what users.

Access control policy is embodied in various components of RBAC, such as role–permission, user–role, and role–role relationships. These components collectively determine whether a particular user will be allowed to access a particular resource or piece of data. RBAC components may be configured directly by the system owner or indirectly by appropriate administrative roles, as delegated by the system owner. The policy enforced is the net result of the precise configuration of various RBAC components as directed by the system owner. Moreover, the access control policy will evolve incrementally over the system life cycle. The ability to modify policy to meet the changing needs of an organization is an important benefit of RBAC.

Although RBAC is policy neutral, it directly supports three well-known security principles: *least privilege*, *separation of duties*, and *data abstraction*. Least privilege is supported because RBAC can be configured so that only those permissions required for the tasks conducted by members of the role are assigned to the role. Separation of duties is achieved by ensuring that mutually exclusive roles must be invoked to complete a sensitive task, such as requiring an accounting clerk and account manager to participate in issuing a check. Data abstraction is supported by means of abstract permissions, such as credit and debit for an account object, rather than the read, write, execute permissions typically provided by the operating system. However, RBAC cannot enforce application of these principles. The security officer can configure RBAC so that it violates these principles. Also, the degree to which data abstraction is supported will be determined by the implementation details.

1.2 RBAC Limitations

As a cautionary note it is important to emphasize that RBAC is not a panacea for all access control issues. More sophisticated forms of access control are required to deal with situations where sequences of operations need to be controlled. For example, a purchase requisition requires various steps before it can lead to issuance of a purchase order. RBAC does not attempt to directly control the permissions for such a sequence of events. Other forms of access control can be layered on top of RBAC for this purpose. Mohammed and Dilts (1994), Sandhu (1988, 1991) and Thomas and Sandhu (1994, 1997) discuss some of these issues. We view control of sequences of operations to be outside the direct scope of RBAC, although RBAC can be a foundation on which to build such controls.

1.3 What is a Role?

A role is properly viewed as a semantic construct around which access control policy is formulated. The particular collection of users and permissions brought together by a role is transitory. The role is more stable because an organization's activities or functions usually change less frequently.

There can be several distinct motivations for constructing a role, including the following. A role can represent competency to do specific tasks, such as a physician or a pharmacist. A role can embody authority and responsibility, e.g. project supervisor. Authority and responsibility are distinct from competency; Alice may be competent to head several departments, but is assigned to head one of them. Roles can reflect specific duty assignments that are rotated through multiple users, e.g. a duty physician or shift manager. RBAC models and implementations should be able to conveniently accommodate all of these manifestations of the role concept.

The concept of a role originated in organizational theory long before the advent of computerized information systems. Even in the context of modern information systems roles have significance beyond their application in security and access control. From the perspective of RBAC it is therefore important to distinguish the concept and scope of a role for access control purposes as opposed to the more general organizational context in which roles arise. Roles have greater significance than access control, but we should not be tempted to expand the access control arena as a consequence. Instead, we should focus on aspects of roles that are relevant from the access control perspective. This question does impact activities such as the design of roles, which may need to take the bigger picture into account even though the immediate focus is on roles for access control purposes.

1.4 Roles versus Groups

A frequently asked question is "What is the difference between roles and groups?" Groups of users as the unit of access control are commonly provided in many access control systems. A major difference between most implementations of groups and the concept of roles is that groups are typically treated as a collection of users and not as a collection of permissions. A role is both a collection of users on one side and a collection of permissions on the other. The role serves as an intermediary to bring these two collections together.[3]

Consider the Unix operating system. Group membership in Unix is defined in two files, /etc/passwd and /etc/group. It is thus easy to determine the groups to which a particular user belongs or all the members of a specific group. Permissions are granted to groups on the basis of permission bits associated with individual files and directories. To determine what permissions a particular group has will generally require a traversal of the entire file system tree. It is thus much easier to determine the membership of a group than to determine the permissions of the group. Moreover, the assignment of permissions to groups is highly decentralized. Essentially, the owner of any sub-tree of the Unix file system can assign permissions for that sub-tree to a group. (The precise degree to which this can be done depends on the particular variant of Unix in question.) However, Unix groups can be used to implement roles in certain situations, even though groups are not the same as our concept of roles.

To illustrate the qualitative nature of the group versus role distinction, consider a hypothetical system in which it takes twice as long to determine group membership as to determine group permissions. Assume that group permissions and membership can only be changed by the system security officer. In this case, the group mechanism would be very close to our concept of a role.

The preceding discussion suggests two characteristics of a role: it should be approximately equally easy to determine role membership and role

---

[3] It should be mentioned that sometimes a role is defined to be a collection of permissions (Baldwin, 1990; Guiri, 1995; Notargiacomo, 1997). We will see in Section 3 that, for administrative purposes, it is actually beneficial to distinguish three kinds of roles respectively containing only users, only permissions, and both users and permissions.

permissions, and control of role membership and role permissions should be relatively centralized in a few users. Many mechanisms that are claimed to be role-based fail one or both of these requirements.

Groups are also an established concept with a generally well-understood meaning, much like other well-known concepts such as a directory. Although groups can be extended to provide the same features as roles, it is better to coin a new term to avoid confusion with the existing concept of a group. Moreover, groups are a useful concept without being extended to roles. It is therefore better to keep these two concepts separated.

2. The RBAC96 Models

Notwithstanding the recognized usefulness of the RBAC concept, there has been little agreement on what RBAC means. As a result, RBAC is an amorphous concept interpreted in different ways, ranging from simple to elaborate and sophisticated.

To understand the various dimensions of RBAC we define a family of four conceptual models. $RBAC_0$, the base model, specifies the minimum requirement for any system that fully supports RBAC. $RBAC_1$ and $RBAC_2$ both include $RBAC_0$, but add independent features to it. They are called advanced models. $RBAC_1$ adds the concept of role hierarchies (situations where roles can inherit permissions from other roles). $RBAC_2$ adds constraints (which impose restrictions on acceptable configurations of the different components of RBAC). $RBAC_1$ and $RBAC_2$ are incomparable to one another. The consolidated model, $RBAC_3$, includes $RBAC_1$ and $RBAC_2$ and, by transitivity, $RBAC_0$. We refer to this family of models as RBAC96 (for RBAC '96). The relationship between the four models of RBAC96 is shown in Fig. 1(a) and the consolidated model $RBAC_3$ is portrayed in Fig. 1(b).

These models provide a guideline for development of products and their evaluation by prospective customers. For the moment, we assume that there is a single security officer who is the only one authorized to configure the various sets and relations of these models. We will introduce a more sophisticated management model in Section 3.

2.1 Base Model: $RBAC_0$

$RBAC_0$ consists of that part of Fig. 1(b) not identified with one of the three advanced models; that is, it omits the role hierarchy and constraints. There are three sets of entities, called users (U), roles (R), and permissions (P). The diagram also shows a collection of sessions (S).

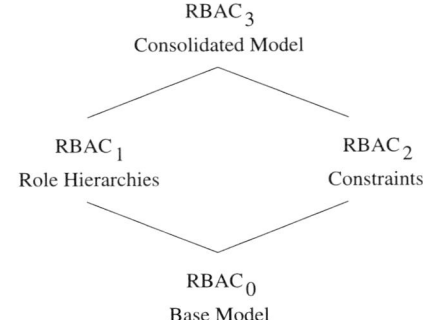

(a) Relationship among RBAC96 models.

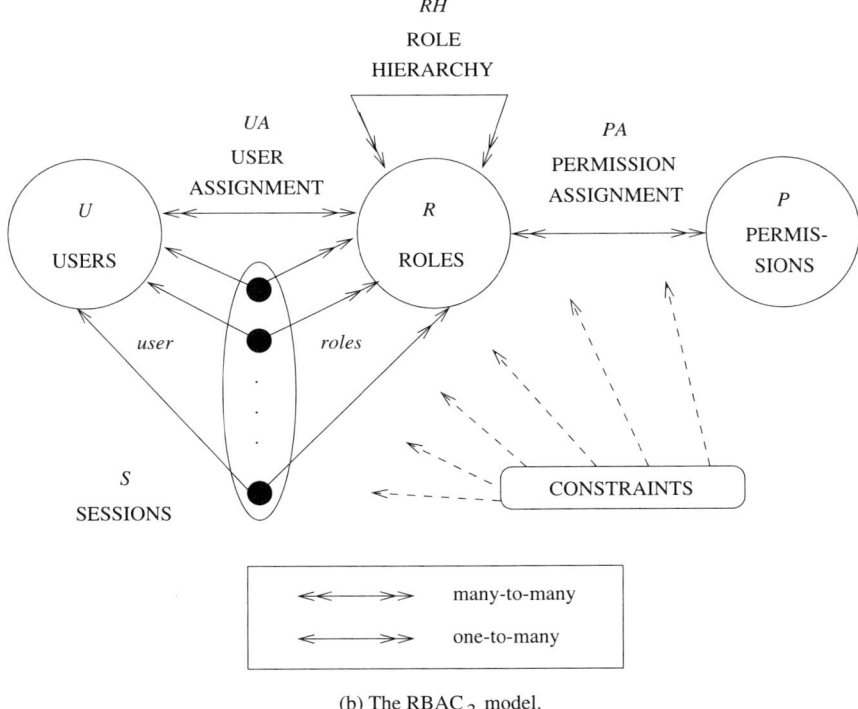

(b) The $RBAC_3$ model.

FIG. 1. The RBAC96 family of models.

A *user* in this model is a human being. The concept of a user can be generalized to include intelligent autonomous agents such as robots, software agents, immobile computers, or even networks of computers. For simplicity, we focus on a user as a human being. A *role* is a job function or job title within the organization with some associated semantics regarding the authority and responsibility conferred on a member of the role.

A *permission* is an approval of a particular mode of access to one or more objects in the system. The terms authorization, access right, and privilege are also used in the literature to denote a permission. Permissions are always positive and confer the ability on the holder of the permission to perform some action(s) in the system. Objects are data objects as well as resource objects represented by data within the computer system. Our conceptual model permits a variety of interpretations for permissions, from very coarse grain (e.g. where access is permitted to an entire subnetwork) to very fine grain (e.g. where the unit of access is a particular field of a particular record). Some access control literature talks about "negative permissions" which deny, rather than confer, access. In our framework denial of access is modeled as a constraint rather than a negative permission.

The nature of a permission depends on the implementation details of a system and the kind of system that it is. A general model for access control must therefore treat permissions as uninterpreted symbols to some extent. Each system protects objects of the abstraction it implements. Thus an operating system protects such entities as files, directories, devices, and ports with operations such as read, write, and execute. A relational database management system protects relations, tuples, attributes, and views with operations such as SELECT, UPDATE, DELETE, and INSERT. An accounting application protects accounts and ledgers with operations such as debit, credit, transfer, create-account, and delete-account. It should be possible to assign the credit operation to a role without being compelled also to assign the debit operation to that role. Note that both operations require read and write access to the operating system file that stores the account balance.

Permissions can apply to single objects or to many. For example, a permission can be as specific as read access to a particular file or as generic as read access to all files belonging to a particular department. The manner in which individual permissions are combined into a generic permission so that they can be assigned as a single unit is highly implementation-dependent.

Figure 1(b) shows *user assignment* (*UA*) and *permission assignment* (*PA*) relations. Both are many-to-many relations. A user can be a member of many roles, and a role can have many users. Similarly, a role can have many permissions, and the same permission can be assigned to many roles. The key to RBAC lies in these two relations. Ultimately, it is a user who exercises permissions. The placement of a role as an intermediary to enable a user to exercise a permission provides much greater control over access configuration and review than does directly relating users to permissions.

Each *session* is a mapping of one user to possibly many roles, i.e. a user establishes a session during which the user activates some subset of roles that he or she is a member of. The double-headed arrow from the session to R in Fig. 1(b) indicates that multiple roles are simultaneously activated. The permissions available to the user are the union of permissions from all roles activated in that session. Each session is associated with a single user, as indicated by the single-headed arrow from the session to U in Fig. 1(b). This association remains constant for the life of a session.

A user may have multiple sessions open at the same time, each in a different window on the workstation screen, for instance. Each session may have a different combination of active roles. This feature of $RBAC_0$ supports the principle of least privilege. A user who is a member of several roles can invoke any subset of these that is suitable for the tasks to be accomplished in that session. Thus, a user who is a member of a powerful role can normally keep this role deactivated and explicitly activate it when needed. We defer consideration of all kinds of constraints, including constraints on role activation, to $RBAC_2$. So in $RBAC_0$ it is entirely up to the user's discretion as to which roles are activated in a given session. $RBAC_0$ also permits roles to be dynamically activated and deactivated during the life of a session. The concept of a session equates to the traditional notion of a *subject* in the access control literature. A subject (or session) is a unit of access control, and a user may have multiple subjects (or sessions) with different permissions active at the same time.

The following definition formalizes the above discussion.

Definition 1 The $RBAC_0$ model has the following components:

- U, R, P, and S (users, roles, permissions, and sessions respectively)
- $PA \subseteq P \times R$, a many-to-many permission to role assignment relation
- $UA \subseteq U \times R$, a many-to-many user to role assignment relation
- *user*: $S \to U$, a function mapping each session s_i to the single user $user(s_i)$ (constant for the session's lifetime)
- *roles*: $S \to 2^R$, a function mapping each session s_i to a set of roles $roles(s_i) \subseteq \{r \mid (user(s_i), r) \in UA\}$ (which can change with time) and session s_i has the permissions $\cup_{r \, roles(s_i)} \{p \mid (p, r) \in PA\}$. □

We expect each permission and user to be assigned to at least one role.

It is possible for two roles to be assigned exactly the same permissions but still be separate roles. Likewise for users. A role is properly viewed as a semantic construct around which access control policy is formulated. The particular collection of users and permissions brought together by a role is transitory. For example, when a role is created it may have no users or permissions assigned to it. At any instant there may be several such roles that have been created. This situation may persist for days. Nevertheless, the roles should not be viewed as identical.

As noted earlier, $RBAC_0$ treats permissions as uninterpreted symbols because the precise nature of a permission is implementation- and system-dependent. We do require that permissions apply to data and resource objects and not to the components of RBAC itself. Permissions to modify the sets U, R, and P and relations PA and UA are called *administrative permissions*. These will be discussed later in the management model for RBAC. For now we assume that only a single security officer can change these components.

Sessions are under the control of individual users. As far the model is concerned, a user can create a session and choose to activate some subset of the user's roles. Roles active in a session can be changed at the user's discretion. The session terminates at the user's initiative. (Some systems will terminate a session if it is inactive for too long. Strictly speaking, this is a constraint and properly belongs in $RBAC_2$.)

$RBAC_0$ does not have a notion of one session creating another session. Sessions are created directly by the user. For simplicity we have omitted this aspect, but we recognize that there are situations where an existing session will need to create another session, possibly with different roles.

Some authors include duties (Jonscher, 1993), in addition to permissions, as an attribute of roles. A duty is an obligation on a user's part to perform one or more tasks, which are generally essential for the smooth functioning of an organization. In our view duties are an advanced concept which do not belong in $RBAC_0$. We have also chosen not to incorporate duties in our advanced models. One approach is to treat them as similar to permissions. Other approaches could be based on new access control paradigms such as task-based authorization (Sandhu, 1988, 1991; Thomas and Sandhu, 1994, 1997).

2.2 Role Hierarchies: $RBAC_1$

$RBAC_1$ introduces role hierarchies (RH). Role hierarchies are almost inevitably included whenever roles are discussed in the literature (Ferraiolo and Kuhn, 1992; Hu *et al.*, 1995; Nyanchama and Osborn, 1995; von Solms and van der Merwe, 1994). They are also commonly implemented in systems that provide roles.

Role hierarchies are a natural means of structuring roles to reflect an organization's lines of authority and responsibility. Examples of role hierarchies are shown in Fig. 2. By convention more powerful (or senior) roles are shown toward the top of these diagrams, and less powerful (or junior) roles toward the bottom. In Fig. 2(a) the junior-most role is health-care provider. The

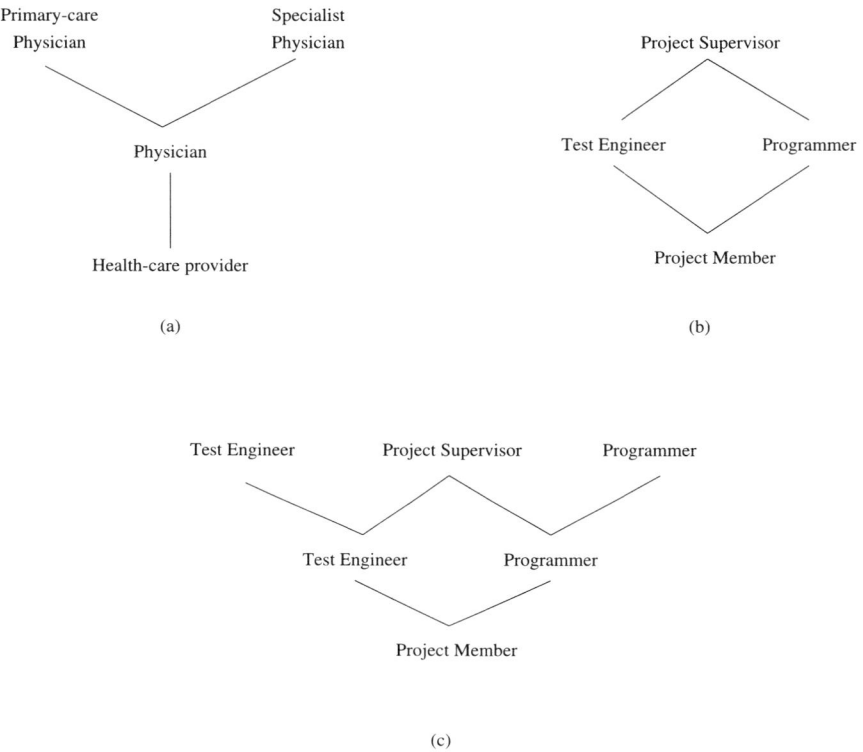

FIG. 2. Examples of role hierarchies.

physician role is senior to health-care provider and thereby inherits all permissions from health-care provider. The physician role can have permissions in addition to those inherited from the health-care provider role. Inheritance of permissions is transitive so, for example, in Fig. 2(a), the primary-care physician role inherits permissions from the physician and health-care provider roles. Primary-care physician and specialist physician both inherit permissions from the physician role, but each one of these will have different permissions directly assigned to it. Figure 2(b) illustrates multiple inheritance of permissions, where the project supervisor role inherits from both test engineer and programmer roles.

Mathematically, these hierarchies are partial orders. A partial order is a reflexive, transitive and antisymmetric relation. Inheritance is reflexive because a role inherits its own permissions, transitivity is a natural requirement in this context, and antisymmetry rules out roles that inherit from one another and would therefore be redundant.

The formal definition of $RBAC_1$ is given below.

Definition 2 The $RBAC_1$ model has the following components:

- U, R, P, S, PA, UA, and *user* are unchanged from $RBAC_0$
- $RH \subseteq R \times R$ is a partial order on R called the role hierarchy or role dominance relation, also written as $\geq$ in infix notation
- *roles*: $S \rightarrow 2^R$ is modified from $RBAC_0$ to require $roles(s_i) \subseteq \{r \mid (\exists r' \geq r)[(user(s_i), r') \in UA]\}$ (which can change with time) and session s_i has the permissions $\cup_{r \in roles(s_i)} \{p \mid [(\exists r'' \leq r)[p, r''] \in PA]\}$. □

We also write $x > y$ to mean $x \geq y$ and $x \neq y$.

Note that a user is allowed to establish a session with any combination of roles junior to those the user is a member of. Also, the permissions in a session are those directly assigned to the active roles of the session as well as those assigned to roles junior to these.

It is sometimes useful in hierarchies to limit the scope of inheritance. Consider the hierarchy of Fig. 2(b), where the project supervisor role is senior to both the test engineer and programmer roles. Now suppose test engineers wish to keep some permissions private to their role and prevent their inheritance in the hierarchy to project supervisors. This situation can exist for legitimate reasons; for example, access to incomplete work in progress may not be appropriate for the senior role, while RBAC can be useful for enabling such access to test engineers. This situation can be accommodated by defining a new role called test engineer' and relating it to test engineer as shown in Fig. 2(c). The private permissions of test engineers are assigned to role test engineer'. Test engineers are assigned to role test engineer' and inherit permissions from the test engineer role, which are also inherited upward in the hierarchy by the project supervisor role. Permissions of test engineer' are, however, not inherited by the project supervisor role. We call roles such as test engineer' as *private roles*. Figure 2(c) also shows a private role programmer'. In some systems the effect of private roles is achieved by blocking inheritance of certain permissions. In this case the hierarchy does not depict the distribution of permission accurately. It is preferable to introduce private roles and keep the meaning of the hierarchical relationship among roles intact.

Figure 3 shows, more generally, how a private subhierarchy of roles can be constructed. The hierarchy of Fig. 3(a) has four task roles, $T1, T2, T3$, and $T4$, all of which inherit permissions from the common project-wide role P. Role S at the top of the hierarchy is intended for project supervisors. Tasks $T3$ and $T4$ are a subproject with $P3$ as the subproject-wide role, and $S3$ as the subproject supervisory role. Role $T1'$ in Fig. 3(c) is a private role for members of task $T1$. Suppose the subproject of Fig. 3(a) comprising roles $S3, T3, T4$, and $P3$, requires a private subhierarchy within which private permissions of the

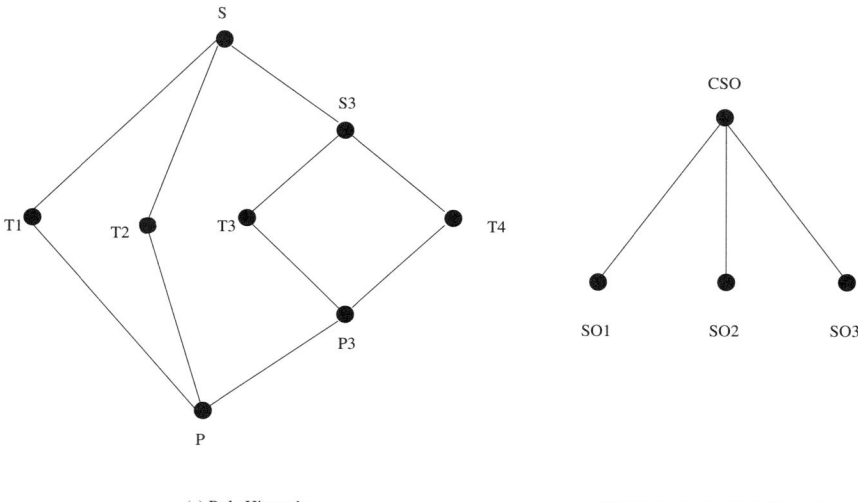

(a) Role Hierarchy

(b) Administrative Role Hierarchy

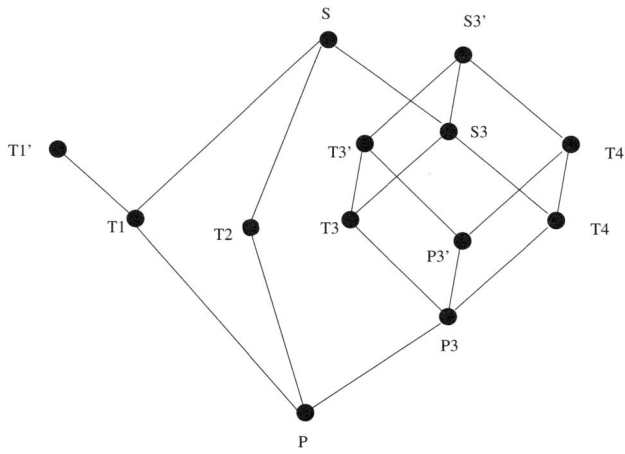

(c) Private and Scoped Roles

FIG. 3. Role hierarchies for a project.

project can be shared without inheritance by S. The entire subhierarchy is replicated in the manner shown in Fig. 3(c). The permissions inheritable by S can be assigned to $S3$, $T3$, $T4$, and $P3$, as appropriate whereas the private ones can be assigned to $S3'$, $T3'$, $T4'$, and $P3'$, allowing their inheritance within the subproject only. As before, members of the subproject team are directly assigned to $S3'$, $T3'$, $T4'$, or $P3'$. Figure 3(c) makes it clear as to which private roles exist in the system and assists in access review to determine what the nature of the private permissions is.

2.3 Constraints: $RBAC_2$

$RBAC_2$ introduces the concept of constraints. Constraints apply to all aspects of RBAC, as indicated in Fig. 1(b). Although we have called our models $RBAC_1$ and $RBAC_2$, there isn't really an implied progression. Either constraints or role hierarchies can be introduced first. Hence the incomparable relation between $RBAC_1$ and $RBAC_2$ in Fig. 1(a).

Constraints are an important aspect of RBAC and are sometimes argued to be the principal motivation for RBAC. A common example is that of mutually disjoint roles, such as purchasing manager and accounts payable manager. In most organizations the same individual will not be permitted to be a member of both roles, because this creates a possibility for committing fraud. This is a well-known and time-honored principle called separation of duties.

Constraints are a powerful mechanism for enforcing higher-level organizational policy. Once certain roles are declared to be mutually exclusive, there need not be so much concern about the assignment of individual users to roles. The latter activity can be delegated and decentralized without fear of compromising the overall policy objectives of the organization. So long as the management of RBAC is entirely centralized in a single security officer, constraints are a useful convenience; but the same effect can largely be achieved by judicious care on the part of the security officer. However, if management of RBAC is decentralized (as will be discussed later), constraints become a mechanism by which senior security officers can restrict the ability of users who exercise administrative privileges. This enables the chief security officer to lay out the broad scope of what is acceptable and impose this as a mandatory requirement on other security officers and users who participate in RBAC management.

With respect to $RBAC_0$, constraints can apply to the *UA* and *PA* relations and the *user* and *roles* functions for various sessions. Constraints are predicates which, applied to these relations and functions, return a value of "acceptable" or "not acceptable." Constraints can also be viewed as sentences in some appropriate formal language. Intuitively, constraints are better viewed according to their kind and nature. We discuss constraints informally rather than stating them in a formal notation. Hence the following definition.

Definition 3 $RBAC_2$ is unchanged from $RBAC_0$ except for requiring that there be a collection of constraints that determine whether or not values of various components of R_0 are acceptable. Only acceptable values will be permitted. □

Implementation considerations generally call for simple constraints that can be efficiently checked and enforced. Fortunately, in RBAC simple constraints can go a long way. We now discuss some constraints that we feel are reasonable to implement. Most, if not all, constraints applied to the user assignment relation have a counterpart that applies to the permission assignment relation and vice versa. We therefore discuss constraints on these two components in parallel.

The most frequently mentioned constraint in the context of RBAC is *mutually exclusive* roles. The same user can be assigned to at most one role in a mutually exclusive set. This supports separation of duties. Provision of this constraint requires little motivation. The dual constraint on permission assignment receives hardly any mention in the literature. Actually, a mutual exclusion constraint on permission assignment can provide additional assurance for separation of duties. This dual constraint requires that the same permission can be assigned to at most one role in a mutually exclusive set. Consider two mutually exclusive roles, accounts-manager and purchasing-manager. Mutual exclusion in terms of *UA* specifies that one individual cannot be a member of both roles. Mutual exclusion in terms of *PA* specifies that the same permission cannot be assigned to both roles. For example, the permission to issue checks should not be assigned to both roles. Normally such a permission would be assigned to the accounts-manager role. The mutual exclusion constraint on *PA* would prevent the permission from being inadvertently, or maliciously, assigned to the purchasing-manager role. More directly, exclusion constraints on *PA* are a useful means of limiting the distribution of powerful permissions. For example, it may not matter whether role *A* or role *B* gets signature authority for a particular account, but we may require that only one of the two roles gets this permission.

More generally, membership by users in various combinations of roles can be deemed to be acceptable or not. Thus it may be acceptable for a user to be a member of a programmer role and a tester role in different projects, but unacceptable to take on both roles within the same project. Similarly for permission assignment.

Another example of a user assignment constraint is that a role can have a maximum number of members. For instance, there is only one person in the role of chairman of a department. Similarly, the number of roles to which an individual user can belong could also be limited. We call these *cardinality constraints*. Correspondingly, the number of roles to which a permission can be assigned can have cardinality constraints to control the distribution of powerful permissions. It should be noted that minimum cardinality constraints may be difficult to implement. For example if there is a minimum number of occupants of a role, what can the system do if one of them disappears? How will the system know this has happened?

The concept of *prerequisite roles* is based on competency and appropriateness, whereby a user can be assigned to role A only if the user is already a member of role B. For example, only those users who are already members of the project role can be assigned to the testing task role within that project. In this example the prerequisite role is junior to the new role being assumed. Prerequisites between incomparable roles can also occur in practice. A similar constraint on permission assignment can arise in the following way. It could be useful, for consistency, to require that permission p can be assigned to a role only if that role already possesses permission q. For instance, in many systems permission to read a file requires permission to read the directory in which the file is located. Assigning the former permission without the latter would be incomplete. More generally we can have *prerequisite conditions* whereby a user can be assigned to role A only if the user is already a member or not a member of specified roles, and similarly for permissions. This idea is used in the administrative models of Section 3.

User assignment constraints are effective only if suitable external discipline is maintained in assigning user identifiers to human beings. If the same individual is assigned two or more user identifiers, separation and cardinality controls break down. There must be a one-to-one correspondence between user identifiers and human beings. A similar argument applies to permission constraints. If the same operation is sanctioned by two different permissions, the RBAC system cannot effectively enforce cardinality and separation constraints.

Constraints can also apply to sessions, and the *user* and *roles* functions associated with a session. It may be acceptable for a user to be a member of two roles but the user cannot be active in both roles at the same time. Other constraints on sessions can limit the number of sessions that a user can have active at the same time. Correspondingly, the number of sessions to which a permission is assigned can be limited.

A role hierarchy can be considered as a constraint. The constraint is that a permission assigned to a junior role must also be assigned to all senior roles. Or equivalently, the constraint is that a user assigned to a senior role must also be assigned to all junior roles. So in some sense, $RBAC_1$ is redundant and is subsumed by $RBAC_2$. However, we feel it is appropriate to recognize the existence of role hierarchies in their own right. They are reduced to constraints only by introducing redundancy of permission assignment or user assignment. It is preferable to support hierarchies directly rather than indirectly by means of redundant assignment.

2.4 Consolidated Model: RBAC$_3$

RBAC$_3$ combines RBAC$_1$ and RBAC$_2$ to provide both role hierarchies and constraints. There are several issues that arise by bringing these two concepts together.

Constraints can apply to the role hierarchy itself. The role hierarchy is required to be a partial order. This constraint is intrinsic to the model. Additional constraints can limit the number of senior (or junior) roles that a given role may have. Two or more roles can also be constrained to have no common senior (or junior) role. These kinds of constraints are useful in situations where the authority to change the role hierarchy has been decentralized, but the chief security officer desires to restrict the overall manner in which such changes can be made.

Subtle interactions arise between constraints and hierarchies. Suppose that test engineer and programmer roles are declared to be mutually exclusive in the context of Fig. 2(b). The project supervisor role violates this mutual exclusion. In some cases such a violation of a mutual exclusion constraint by a senior role may be acceptable, while in other cases it may not. We feel that the model should not rule out one or the other possibility. A similar situation arises with cardinality constraints. Suppose that a user can be assigned to at most one role. Does an assignment to the test engineer role in Fig. 2(b) violate this constraint? In other words, do cardinality constraints apply only to direct membership, or do they also carry on to inherited membership?

The hierarchy of Fig. 2(c) illustrates how constraints are useful in the presence of private roles. In this case the test engineer', programmer', and project supervisor roles can be declared to be mutually exclusive. Because these have no common senior for these roles, there is no conflict. In general private roles will not have common seniors with any other roles because they are maximal elements in the hierarchy. So mutual exclusion of private roles can be specified without conflict. The shared counterpart of the private roles can be declared to have a maximum cardinality constraint of zero members. In this way test engineers must be assigned to the test engineer' role. The test engineer role serves as a means for sharing permissions with the project supervisor role.

2.5 Discussion

We have presented the RBAC96 family of models that systematically spans the spectrum from simple to complex. RBAC96 provides a common frame of reference. $RBAC_0$ is simple and free of built-in constraints so as to provide a foundation for the more advanced models. $RBAC_2$ allows us to accommodate existing systems and models that have built-in constraints, such as "only one role can be used at any time." $RBAC_1$ models the commonly occurring case of hierarchical roles, and $RBAC_3$ consolidates all of these. We conclude this section by discussing some salient aspects of RBAC96.

2.5.1 Users and Sessions

The distinction between a user and a session is a fundamental aspect of RBAC and consequently arises in $RBAC_0$. A user is a human being, or other intelligent agent, capable of autonomous activity in the system. To support the principle of least privilege a user should be allowed to login to a system with only those roles appropriate for a given occasion.

Many systems will turn on all permissions of a user irrespective of what the user wishes to accomplish in a particular session. Thus, a user who has powerful permissions (or roles) that are used only rarely when needed finds that these permissions are turned on all the time. It is possible to set up separate accounts, one in which the usual permissions are turned on and another in which the powerful permissions are turned on. Assigning multiple accounts to the same user introduces problems with respect to auditing, accountability, and constraints such as separation of duties. It is not a desirable general-purpose solution but can be employed in the short term to simulate RBAC on existing platforms.

In $RBAC_0$ the distinction between users and sessions is useful only if users exercise discipline regarding the roles they normally invoke. With constraints it may not be possible for a user to activate all their roles simultaneously. Consider a constraint that stipulates two roles which can be assigned to the same user but cannot be simultaneously activated in a session. For instance, a user may be qualified to be a pilot and a navigator but at any time can activate at most one of these roles. In the presence of such constraints a user cannot establish a single session with all the user's roles activated.

An important property of a session is that the user associated with a session cannot change. In many applications there are long-lived sessions where one user hands over to another without a logout and login. This preserves the integrity of the computing activity being performed in the session. We feel that this problem is an artifact of existing system architectures. Continuity of activity across multiple security sessions should be possible in properly engineered systems. Also our models are conceptual models seeking to capture what needs to be achieved. In implementations on specific platforms we will need to simulate the requirements with the mechanisms available.

The RBAC96 models do not address the issues of idle session termination and lockout. In practice this is an important issue. In our conceptual framework termination and lockout is most easily modeled as a constraint and belongs in $RBAC_1$. As a practical matter it would be hard to do $RBAC_0$ effectively without bringing in at least a small number of constraints of this nature.

Changing the roles activated in a session is a security-sensitive act and should be acknowledged to the security system via a so-called trusted path which guarantees that the user is making the request rather than some program acting on the user's behalf. Such changes can be regulated by constraints in $RBAC_1$. For instance, certain roles may not be dynamically added but can only be acquired when a session is created. $RBAC_0$ allows dynamic changing of roles in a session for two reasons. From a conceptual viewpoint constraints belong in $RBAC_1$ and higher, and should not be present in $RBAC_0$. We could still define $RBAC_0$ to disallow all changes in a session's roles. We felt that this is impractical and too restrictive for a base model.

RBAC96 does not address how one session might create another session. This issue is discussed in Thomson (1991). RBAC96 takes the view that a user creates a session, and in the absence of other constraints can change the roles of this session as the user pleases. However, it is possible for one session to create another session with different roles under program control rather than under direct user control. Thomsen uses a domain transition table to authorize this. This issue needs further work in RBAC96.

2.5.2 Permissions

It is difficult to identify the nature of permissions precisely in an abstract general purpose model such as RBAC96. Permissions tend to be implementation-dependent. In lattice-based access control models (Sandhu, 1993) it is possible to abstract the essential operations into read and write. This is because these models are focused on one-directional information flow in a lattice of security labels.

RBAC models are policy-neutral. Hence the nature of permissions has to be open ended. In applying RBAC to a particular system the interpretation of permissions is among the most important steps to be performed.

We deliberately decided to exclude so-called negative permissions from RBAC96. Negative permissions deny rather than confer access. They are used in some discretionary access control models to disallow a user from obtaining a permission from some alternate source. The use of constraints in RBAC is a much more useful mechanism to achieve the same result. The literature on negative permissions is fraught with problems concerning their interaction and relative strength with respect to positive permissions. In the presence of role hierarchies this could become very complicated and arcane. We would be very reluctant to add negative permissions into a complex model such as RBAC96.

The scope of RBAC is also consciously limited to classical permissions. Sequencing or temporal dependencies between permissions are important in emerging applications such as workflow (Sandhu, 1988, 1991; Thomas and Sandhu, 1994, 1997) We decided to limit the scope of RBAC to exclude these for two reasons. First, these are not yet well understood and much further basic research is required for this purpose. Second, RBAC must have a well-delineated scope otherwise it will be an amorphous concept which can be taken to include all kinds of security and authorization issues.

2.5.3 Model Conformance

What does it mean for a system to conform to RBAC96? RBAC96 is best viewed as a family of reference models which play a dual role. On one hand RBAC96 provides a framework for analyzing the capabilities of existing systems to assess how well and how extensively they can support RBAC. RBAC96 also provides guidance to vendors and developers regarding access controls to be implemented in future systems.

It is not necessary for a system to conform completely to $RBAC_0$ before it includes features of $RBAC_1$ or $RBAC_2$. Many existing systems do not distinguish between users and sessions. We would say that these systems have aspects of $RBAC_0$, $RBAC_1$, and $RBAC_2$, but are also missing other aspects of $RBAC_0$. These systems essentially have built-in constraints that all roles must be turned on in a session and none can be dropped. Other systems have hard-wired constraints, such as "a session can only have one role at a time." Such systems cannot accommodate $RBAC_0$, because they do too much without any choice in the matter. But we can still place them within the RBAC96 family.

3. The ARBAC97 Administrative Models

So far we have assumed that all components of RBAC are under the direct control of a single security officer. In large systems the number of roles can be in the hundreds or thousands. Managing these roles and their interrelationships is a formidable task that is often highly centralized and delegated to a small team of security administrators. Because the main advantage of RBAC is to facilitate administration of permissions, it is natural to ask how RBAC can be used to manage RBAC itself. We believe that the use of RBAC for managing RBAC will be an important factor in the success of RBAC. Decentralizing the details of RBAC administration without losing central control over broad policy is a challenging goal for system designers and architects.

We mention some approaches to access control management that have been discussed in the literature. ISO has developed a number of security management related standards and documents. These can be approached via the top-level System Management Overview document (ISO, 10040). The ISO model is object-oriented and includes a hierarchy based on containment (a directory contains files and a file contains records). Roles could be integrated into the ISO approach.

There is a long tradition of models for propagation of access rights, where the right to propagate rights is controlled by special control rights. Among the most recent and most developed of these is Sandhu's typed access matrix model (Sandhu, 1992). While it is often difficult to analyze the consequences of even fairly simple rules for propagation of rights, these models indicate that simple primitives can be composed to yield very flexible and expressive systems.

One example of work on managing RBAC is by Moffet and Sloman (1991) who define a fairly elaborate model based on role domains, owners, managers, and security administrators. In their work authority is not controlled or delegated from a single central point, but rather is negotiated between independent managers who have only a limited trust in each other.

Our management model for RBAC is illustrated in Fig. 4. The top half of this figure is essentially the same as Fig. 1(b). The constraints in Fig. 4 apply to all components. The bottom half of Fig. 4 is a mirror image of the top half for administrative roles and administrative permissions. It is intended that administrative roles AR and administrative permissions AP be respectively disjoint from the regular roles R and permissions P. The model shows that permissions can only be assigned to roles, and administrative permissions can only be assigned to administrative roles. This is a built-in constraint, stated formally as follows.

Definition 4 Administrative permissions AP authorize changes to the various components that comprise $RBAC_0$, $RBAC_1$, $RBAC_2$, or $RBAC_3$, whereas regular permissions P do not. Administrative permissions are disjoint from regular permissions, i.e. $AP \cap P = \varnothing$. Administrative permissions and regular permissions can only be assigned to administrative roles AR and regular roles R respectively. Administrative roles are disjoint from regular roles, i.e. $AP \cap R = \varnothing$. □

The top half of Fig. 4 can range in sophistication across $RBAC_0$, $RBAC_1$, $RBAC_2$, and $RBAC_3$. The bottom half can similarly range in sophistication across $ARBAC_0$, $ARBAC_1$, $ARBAC_2$, and $ARBAC_3$, where the A denotes administrative. In general we would expect the administrative model to be

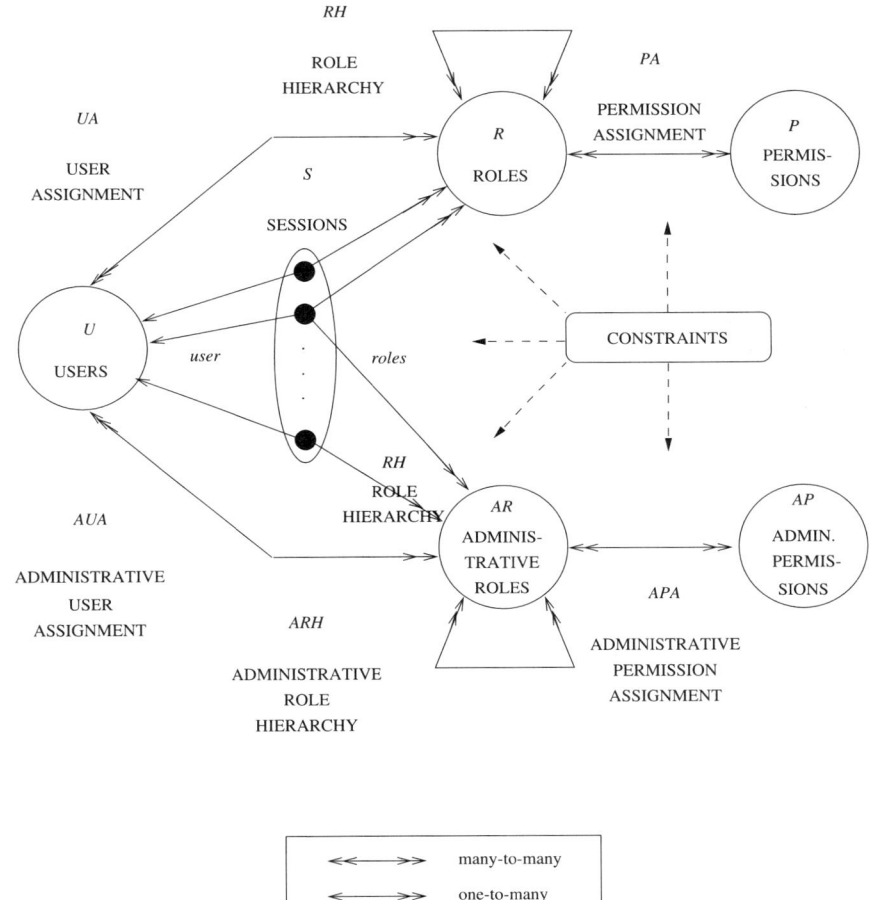

FIG. 4. RBAC administrative model.

simpler than the RBAC model itself. Thus $ARBAC_0$ can be used to manage $RBAC_3$, but there seems to be no point in using $ARBAC_3$ to manage $RBAC_0$.

It is also important to recognize that constraints can cut across both top and bottom halves of Fig. 4. We have already asserted a built-in constraint that permissions can only be assigned to roles and administrative permissions can only be assigned to administrative roles. If administrative roles are mutually exclusive with respect to regular roles, we will have a situation where security administrators can manage RBAC but not use any of the privileges themselves.

How about management of the administrative hierarchy? In principle one could construct a second level administrative hierarchy to manage the first level one and so on. We feel that even a second level of administrative hierarchy is unnecessary. Hence the administration of the administrative hierarchy is left to a single chief security officer. This is reasonable for a single organization or a single administrative unit within an organization. The issue of how these units interact is not directly addressed in our model. More generally, administrative roles could themselves manage administrative roles.

One of the main issues in a management model is how to scope the administrative authority vested in administrative roles. To illustrate this, consider the hierarchies shown in Fig. 3(a). The administrative hierarchy of Fig. 3(b) shows a single chief security officer role (CSO), which is senior to the three security officer roles SO1, SO2, and SO3. The scoping issue concerns which roles of Fig. 3(a) can be managed by which roles of Fig. 3(b). Let us say the CSO role can manage all roles of Fig. 3(a). Suppose SO1 manages task T1. In general we do not want SO1 to automatically inherit the ability to manage the junior role P also. So the scope of SO1 can be limited exclusively to T1. Similarly, the scope of SO2 can be limited to T2. Assume SO3 can manage the entire subproject consisting of S3, T3, T4, and P3. The scope of SO3 is then bounded by S3 at the top and P3 at the bottom.

In general, each administrative role will be mapped to some subset of the role hierarchy it is responsible for managing. There are other aspects of management that need to be scoped. For example, SO1 may only be able to add users to the T1 role, but their removal requires the CSO to act. More generally, we need to scope not only the roles an administrative role manages, but also the permissions and users which that role manages. It is also important to control changes in the role hierarchy itself. For example, because SO3 manages the subhierarchy between S3 and P3, SO3 could be authorized to add additional tasks to that subproject.

As we have seen there are many components to RBAC. RBAC administration is therefore multi-faceted. In particular we can separate the issues of assigning users to roles, assigning permissions to roles, and assigning roles to roles to define a role hierarchy. These activities are all required to bring users and permissions together. However, in many cases, they are best done by different administrators or administrative roles. Assigning permissions to roles is typically the province of application administrators. Thus a banking application can be implemented so that credit and debit operations are assigned to a teller role, whereas approval of a loan is assigned to a managerial role. Assignment of actual individuals to the teller and managerial roles is a personnel management function. Assigning roles to roles has aspects of user–role assignment and role–permission assignment. Role–role relationships establish broad policy. Control of these relationships would typically be relatively centralized in the hands of a few security administrators.

In this section we describe a model for role-based administration of RBAC. Our model is called ARBAC97 (administrative RBAC '97). It has three components as follows.

(1) The *user–role assignment* component of ARBAC97 is called URA97 (user–role assignment 1997).
(2) The *permission–role assignment* component of ARBAC97 is a dual[4] of URA97 and is called PRA97 (permission–role assignment 1997).
(3) The *role–role assignment* 2 component of ARBAC97 itself has several components which are determined by the kind of roles that are involved. We defer discussion of the role-role assignment model until Section 3.3.

3.1 URA97 for User–Role Assignment

The URA97 model was originally defined by Sandhu and Bhamidipati (1997), who also developed an Oracle implementation of this model. We use the hierarchies of Figs 5(a) and 5(b) in our running example through this section. Figure 5(a) shows the regular roles in an engineering department. There is a junior-most role E to which all employees belong. The engineering department has a junior-most role ED and senior-most role DIR. In between there are roles for two projects within the department, project 1 on the left and project 2 on the right. Each project has a senior-most project lead role (PL1 and PL2), a junior-most engineer role (E1 and E2), and in between two incomparable roles, production engineer (PE1 and PE2) and quality engineer (QE1 and QE2). Figure 5(b) shows the administrative role hierarchy, with the senior security officer (SSO) role at the top, and two project security officer roles (PSO1 and PSO2) and a department security officer (DSO) role.

URA97 is concerned with administration of the user-assignment relation *UA* which relates users to roles. Authorization to modify this relation is controlled by administrative roles. Thus members of the administrative roles in Fig. 5(b) are authorized to modify membership in the roles of Fig. 5(a). Assignment of users to administrative roles is outside the scope of URA97 and is assumed to be done by the chief security officer.

There are two aspects to decentralization of user–role assignment. We need to specify the roles whose membership can be modified by an administrative

---

[4] In our work we have often observed a duality between user–role and permission-role relationships. For example, every constraint on user–role relationships has a dual counterpart with respect to permission–role relationships, and vice versa. We see this duality exhibited here too.

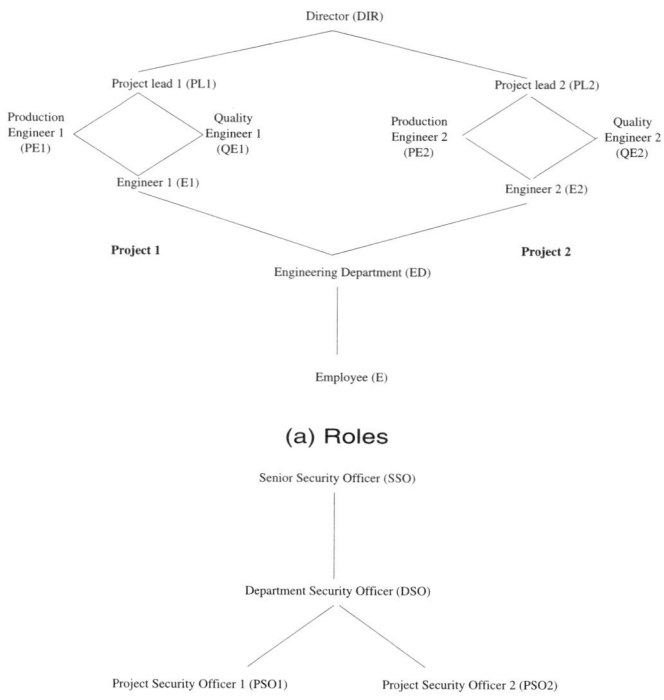

FIG. 5. Example role and administrative role hierarchies.

role. We also need to specify a population of users eligible for membership. For example, URA97 will let us specify that the administrative role PSO1 can assign users to the roles PE1, QE1, and E1, but these users must previously be members of the role ED. The idea is that PSO1 has freedom to assign users to roles in project 1 (excepting the senior-most role PL1), but these users must already be members of the engineering department. This is an example of a prerequisite role. More generally, URA97 allows for a prerequisite condition as follows.

Definition 5 A prerequisite condition is a boolean expression using the usual $\wedge$ and $\vee$ operators on terms of the form x and $\bar{x}$, where x is a regular role (i.e. $x \in R$). For a given set of roles R let CR denotes all possible prerequisite conditions that can be formed using the roles in R. A prerequisite condition is evaluated for a user u by interpreting x to be true if $(\exists x' \geq x)(u, x') \in UA$ and $\bar{x}$ to be true if $(\forall x' \geq x)(u, x') \notin UA$. □

Definition 6 User–role assignment and revocation are respectively authorized in URA97 by the following relations, $\text{can-assign} \subseteq AR \times CR \times 2^R$ and $\text{can-revoke} \subseteq AR \times 2^R$. □

The meaning of $\text{can-assign}(x, y, Z)$ is that a member of the administrative role x (or a member of an administrative role that is senior to x) can assign a user whose current membership, or non-membership, in regular roles satisfies the prerequisite condition y to be a member of regular roles in range Z.[5] The meaning of $\text{can-revoke}(x, Y)$ is that a member of the administrative role x (or a member of an administrative role that is senior to x) can revoke membership of a user from any regular role $y \in Y$.

Figure 6 illustrates these relations. Role sets are specified in URA97 by the following *range notation*.

$$[x, y] = \{r \in R \mid x \geqslant r \land r \geqslant y\} \qquad [x, y) = \{r \in R \mid x \geqslant r \lor r > y\}$$
$$(x, y] = \{r \in R \mid x > r \land r \geqslant y\} \qquad (x, y) = \{r \in R \mid x > r \lor r > y\}$$

By Fig. 6(a), PSO1 can assign users in ED to the roles E1, PE1, and QE1, and similarly for PSO2 with respect to E2, PE2, and QE2. DSO can assign a user in ED to PL1 provided that user is not already in PL2, and similarly for PL2 with respect to PL1.

Administrative Role	Prerequisite Condition	Role Range
PSO1	ED	[E1, PL1)
PSO2	ED	[E2, PL2)
DSO	ED ∧ $\overline{\text{PL1}}$	[PL2, PL2]
DSO	ED ∧ $\overline{\text{PL2}}$	[PL1, PL1]

(a) can-assign

Administrative Role	Role Range
PSO1	[E1, PL1)
PSO2	[E2, PL2)
DSO	(ED, DIR)

(b) can-revoke

FIG. 6. Example of *can-assign* and *can-revoke*.

---

[5] User–role assignment is subject to additional constraints, such as mutually exclusive roles or maximum cardinality, that may be imposed. The assignment will succeed if and only if it is authorized by *can-assign* and it satisfies all relevant constraints.

A notable aspect of revocation in URA97 is that revocation is independent of assignment. If Alice, by means of some administrative role, can revoke Bob's membership in a regular role the revocation takes effect independent of how Bob came to be a member of that regular role. This is consistent with the RBAC philosophy, where granting and revoking of membership is done for organizational reasons and not merely at the discretion of individual administrators.

3.1.1 Weak and Strong Revocation

The revocation operation in URA97 is said to be weak because it applies only to the role that is directly revoked. Suppose Bob is a member of PE1 and E1. If Alice revokes Bob's membership from E1, he continues to be a member of the senior role PE1 and therefore can use the permissions of E1. Various forms of strong revocation can be considered as embellishments to URA97. Strong revocation cascades upwards in the role hierarchy. If Alice has administrative role PSO1 and she strongly revokes Bob's membership from E1 as per Fig. 6, his membership in PE1 is also revoked. However, if Charles is a member of E1 and PL1, and Alice strongly revokes Charles' membership in E1 the cascaded revoke is outside of Alice's range and is disallowed. The question remains whether or not Charles' membership in E1 and PE1 should be revoked even though the cascaded revoke from PL1 failed. It seems appropriate to allow both options depending upon Alice's choice. In general, URA97 treats strong revocation as a series of weak revocations each of which must be individually authorized by *can-revoke*. In this way we keep the basic URA97 model simple while allowing for more complex revocation operations to be defined in terms of weak revocation. At the same time we feel it is important to support strong revocation.

3.2 PRA97 for Permission–Role Assignment

PRA97 is concerned with permission–role assignment and revocation. From the perspective of a role, users, and permissions have a similar character. They are essentially entities that are brought together by a role. Hence, we propose PRA97 to be a dual of URA97. The notion of a prerequisite condition is identical to that in URA97, except the boolean expression is now evaluated for membership and non-membership of a permission in specified roles.

Definition 7 Permission–role assignment and revocation are respectively authorized by the following relations, *can-assignp* $\subseteq AR \times CR \times 2^R$ and *can-revokep* $\subseteq AR \times 2^R$. □

The meaning of *can-assignp*(*x*, *y*, *Z*) is that a member of the administrative role *x* (or a member of an administrative role that is senior to *x*) can assign a permission whose current membership, or non-membership, in regular roles satisfies the prerequisite condition *y* to regular roles in range *Z*.[6] The meaning of *can-revokep*(*x*, *Y*) is that a member of the administrative role *x* (or a member of an administrative role that is senior to *x*) can revoke membership of a permission from any regular role $y \in Y$.

Figure 7 shows examples of these relations. The DSO is authorized to take any permission assigned to the DIR role and make it available to PL1 or PL2. Thus a permission can be delegated downward in the hierarchy. PSO1 can assign permissions from PL1 to either PE1 or QE1, but not to both. The remaining rows in Fig. 7(a) are similarly interpreted.

Figure 7(b) authorizes DSO to revoke permissions from any role between ED and DIR. PSO1 can revoke permissions from PE1 and QE2, and similarly for PSO2.

Administrative Role	Prerequisite Condition	Role Range
DSO	DIR	[PL1, PL1]
DSO	DIR	[PL2, PL2]
PSO1	PL1 ∧ $\overline{QE1}$	[PE1, PE1]
PSO1	PL1 ∧ $\overline{PE1}$	[QE1, QE1]
PSO2	PL2 ∧ $\overline{QE2}$	[PE2, PE2]
PSO2	PL2 ∧ $\overline{PE2}$	[QE2, QE2]

(a) can-assignp

Administrative Role	Role Range
DSO	(ED, DIR)
PSO1	[QE1, QE1]
PSO1	[PE1, PE1]
PSO2	[QE2, QE2]
PSO2	[PE2, PE1]

(b) can-revokep

FIG. 7. Example of *can-assignp* and *can-revokep*.

---

[6] Permission–role assignment may be subject to additional constraints. In other words *can-assignp*(*x*, *y*, *Z*) is a necessary but not sufficient condition.

Revocation in PRA97 is weak, so permissions may still be inherited after revocation. Strong revocation can be defined in terms of weak revocation as in URA97. Strong revocation of a permissions cascades down the role hierarchy, in contrast to cascading up of revocation of user membership.

3.3 RRA97 for Role–Role Assignment

Finally, we consider the issue of role–role assignment. Our treatment is informal and preliminary at this point because the model is still evolving. Our focus is on the general direction and intuition.

For role–role assignment we distinguish three kinds of role, roughly speaking as follows.

(1) **Abilities** are roles that can only have permissions and other abilities as members.
(2) **Groups** are roles that can only have users and other groups as members.
(3) **UP-Roles** are roles that have no restriction on membership, i.e. their membership can include users, permissions, groups, abilities, and other UP-roles.

The term UP-roles signifies user and permission roles. We use the term "role" to mean all three kinds of role or to mean UP-roles only, as determined by context. The three kinds of role are mutually disjoint and are identified respectively as *A, G*, and *UPR*.

The main reason to distinguish these three kinds of role is that different administrative models apply to establishing relationships between them. The distinction was motivated in the first place by abilities. An ability is a collection of permissions that should be assigned as a single unit to a role. For example, the ability to open an account in a banking application will encompass many different individual permissions. It does not make sense to assign only some of these permissions to a role because the entire set is needed to do the task properly. The idea is that application developers package permissions into collections called abilities, which must be assigned together as a unit to a role. The function of an ability is to collect permissions together so that administrators can treat these as a single unit. Assigning abilities to roles is therefore very much like assigning permissions to roles. For convenience it is useful to organize abilities into a hierarchy (i.e. partial order). Hence the PRA97 model can be adapted to produce the very similar ARA97 model for ability–role assignment.

Once the notion of notion of abilities is introduced, by duality there should be a similar concept on the user side. A group is a collection of users who are assigned as a single unit to a role. Such a group can be viewed as a team which is a unit even though its membership may change over time. Groups can also be organized in a hierarchy. For group–role assignment we adapt the URA97 model to produce the GRA97 model for group–role assignment.

This leads to the following models.

Definition 8 Ability–role assignment and revocation are respectively authorized in ARA97 by *can-assigna* $\subseteq AR \times CR \times 2^{UPR}$ and *can-revokea* $\subseteq AR \times 2^{UPR}$. □

Definition 9 Group–role assignment and revocation are respectively authorized in GRA97 by *can-assigng* $\subseteq AR \times CR \times 2^{UPR}$ and *can-revokeg* $\subseteq AR \times 2^{UPR}$. □

For these models the prerequisite conditions are interpreted with respect to abilities and groups respectively. Membership of an ability in a UP-role is true if the UP-role dominates the ability and false otherwise. Conversely, membership of a group in a UP-role is true if the UP-role is dominated by the group and false otherwise.

Assigning an ability to an UP-role is mathematically equivalent to making the UP-role an immediate senior of the ability in the role–role hierarchy. Abilities can only have UP-roles or abilities as immediate seniors and can only have abilities as immediate juniors. In a dual manner, assigning a group to an UP-role is mathematically equivalent to making the UP-role an immediate junior of the group in the role–role hierarchy. Groups can only have UP-roles or groups as immediate juniors and can only have groups as immediate seniors. With these constraints the ARA97 and GRA97 models are essentially identical to the PRA97 and URA97 models respectively.

This leaves us with the problem of managing relationships between UP-roles.[7] Consider Fig. 5(a) again. We would like the DSO to configure and change the hierarchy between DIR and ED. Similarly, we would like PSO1 to manage the hierarchy between PL1 and E1, and likewise for PSO2 with respect to PL2 and E2. The idea is that each department and each project has autonomy in constructing its internal role structure.

Definition 10 Role creation, role deletion, role–role edge insertion, and role–role edge deletion are all authorized in UP-RRA97 by *can-modify*: $AR \rightarrow 2^{UPR}$. □

The meaning of *can-modify*(x, Y) is that a member of the administrative role x (or a member of an administrative role that is senior to x) can create and

---

[7] Strictly speaking we also have to deal with administration of group–group and ability–ability relationships. These can be handled in the same way as relationships between UP-roles to give us analogously the G-RRA97 and A-RRA97 models.

Administrative Role	UP-Role Range
PSO1	(E1, PL1)
DSO	(ED, DIR)

FIG. 8. Example of *can-modify*.

delete roles in the range Y, except for the endpoints of Y, and can modify relationships between roles in the range Y. This authority is, however, tempered by constraints that we discuss below.

Figure 8 illustrates an example of *can-modify* relative to the hierarchies of Fig. 5. By convention the UP-role ranges are shown as open intervals since the endpoints are not included. DSO can create, delete, and alter relationships between all roles in the engineering department (except the endpoints ED and DIR). When a DSO creates a new role it will be senior to ED and junior to DIR, and will remain so (unless some more senior administrator changes this relationship). PSO1 has similar authority with respect to roles in project 1.

3.3.1 Restrictions on can-modify

The authority conferred by *can-modify* is constrained by global consistency requirements. It is not possible to change pieces of the role hierarchy in arbitrary ways without impacting larger relationships. Here we identify two conflicts that arise and explain how RRA97 deals with them.

Suppose DSO is given the authority to create and delete edges and roles in the hierarchy between DIR and ED. If PL1 gets deleted, Figs. 6 and 7 will be left with dangling references to a non-existent role. To avoid this situation we require that roles that are referenced in any *can-assign* or *can-revoke* relation cannot be deleted. In this way the DSO's power to delete roles is restricted to maintain global consistency of the authorizations.

The second problem arises if the DSO introduces roles X and Y, as shown in Fig. 9. Now suppose PSO1 has authority to create and delete edges and roles in the hierarchy between PL1 and E1. If PSO1 makes PE1 junior to QE1 the effect is indirectly to make Y junior to X. Now PSO1 was given authority in the range (PL1,E1), but has effectively introduced a relationship between X and Y. There are several approaches to resolving this issue. We can prevent the DSO from introducing X and Y as shown, because this violates the range integrity of (PL1,E1) with respect to PSO1. We can allow Fig. 9 to happen and prevent PSO1 from later making PE1 junior to QE1. Or we can tolerate the possibility of PSO1 affecting UP-role to UP-role relationships that are outside the authorized range of (E1, PL1). RRA97 allows all three possibilities.

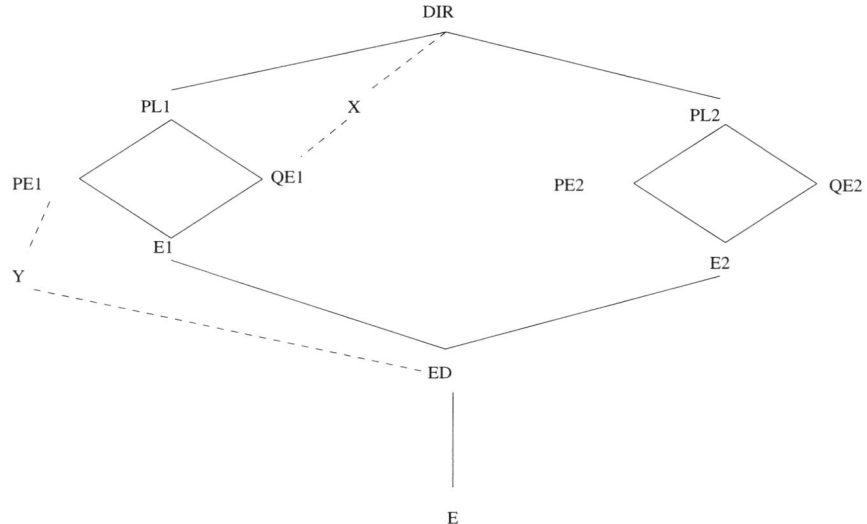

FIG. 9. Out of range impact.

There may be other issues that will arise as we evolve this model. Our general principle for decentralized administration of role–role relationships is a sound one. We wish to give administrative roles autonomy within a range but only so far as the global consequences of the resulting actions are acceptable. To do so we need to disallow some operations authorized by the range, thereby tempering the administrative role's authority.

3.4 Discussion

In this section we have described the motivation, intuition and outline of a new model for RBAC administration called ARBAC97 (administrative RBAC 1997). ARBAC97 has three components: URA97 (user–role assignment 1997), PRA97 (permission–role assignment 1997), and RRA97 (role–role assignment 1997). URA97 was recently defined by Sandhu and Bhamidipati (1997). ARBAC97 incorporates URA97, builds upon it to define PRA97 and some components of RRA97, and introduces additional concepts in developing RRA97.

RRA97 itself consists of three components. ARA97 and GRA97 deal with ability–role assignment and group–role assignment respectively, and are very similar to PRA97 and URA97 respectively. The component dealing with role–role assignment is still evolving but we have identified the basic intuition and important issues that need to be dealt with.

An interesting property of ARBAC97 is that it allows multiple user membership in a chain of senior to junior roles. Thus Alice can be a member of PE1, ED and E simultaneously in Fig. 5(a), that is, (Alice,PE1)∈UA, (Alice,ED)∈UA and (Alice,E)∈UA. There are models in the literature that prohibit this, so we could only have (Alice,PE1)∈UA. The net effect regarding the permissions of Alice is identical in both cases. However, there is a substantial difference when we look at the administrative model. In ARBAC97 Alice's membership in PE1, ED and E could be achieved by different administrators and could be revoked independently of one another. In fact, prior membership in a prerequisite role could lead to later membership in more senior roles. We feel this is a more flexible model. Insisting that Alice can only be in a single role in a senior to junior chain of roles has a dramatic impact on revocation and decentralized user–role assignment. Similar comments apply to permission–role assignment.

ARBAC97 does not address all issues of RBAC administration. For example, it does not talk about creation and deletion of users and permissions. It also does not address the management of constraints. Another issue omitted in ARBAC97 is delegation of roles, whereby one user can authorize another to represent the former in the capacity of one or more roles. Delegation of roles to automated agents acting on behalf of a user is also outside the scope of ARBAC97. Clearly there are many interesting issues in the management of RBAC that remain to be investigated.

4. Roles and Lattices

An important characteristic of RBAC is that it is policy-neutral. RBAC provides a means for articulating policy rather than embodying a particular security policy. The policy enforced in a particular system is the net result of the precise configuration and interactions of various RBAC components as directed by the system owner. Moreover, the access control policy can evolve incrementally over the system life cycle. In large systems it is almost certain to do so. The ability to modify policy incrementally to meet the changing needs of an organization is an important benefit of RBAC.

Classic lattice-based access control (LBAC) models (Sandhu, 1993), on the other hand, are specifically constructed to incorporate the policy of one-directional information flow in a lattice. There is nonetheless a strong similarity between the concept of a security label and a role. In particular, the same user cleared to, say, Secret can on different occasions login to a system at Secret and Unclassified levels. In a sense the user determines what role (Secret or Unclassified) should be activated in a particular session.

This leads us naturally to ask whether or not LBAC can be simulated using RBAC. If RBAC is policy-neutral and has adequate generality it should indeed be able to do so, particularly because the notion of a role and the level of a login session are so similar. This question is theoretically significant because a positive answer would establish that LBAC is just one instance of RBAC, thereby relating two distinct access control models that have been developed with different motivations. A positive answer is also practically significant, because it implies that the same system can be configured to enforce RBAC in general and LBAC in particular. This addresses the long held desire of multi-level security practitioners that technology which meets needs of the larger commercial market-place be applicable to LBAC. The classical approach to fulfilling this desire has been to argue that LBAC has applications in the commercial sector. So far this argument has not been terribly productive. RBAC, on the other hand, is specifically motivated by the needs of the commercial sector. Its customization to LBAC might be a more productive approach to dual-use technology.

In this section we show how several variations of LBAC are easily accommodated in RBAC by configuring a few RBAC components.[8] Our constructions show that the concepts of role hierarchies and constraints are critical to achieving this result. Changes in the role hierarchy and constraints lead to different variations of LBAC.

4.1 Lattice-Based Access Controls

Lattice-based access control (LBAC) enforces one-directional information flow in a lattice of security labels. LBAC is also known as mandatory access control (MAC) or multilevel security.[9] LBAC can be applied for confidentiality, integrity, confidentiality and integrity together, or for aggregation policies such as Chinese Walls (Sandhu, 1993). The mandatory access control policy is expressed in terms of security labels attached to subjects and objects. A label on an object is called a *security classification*, while a label on a user is called a *security clearance*. It is important to understand that a Secret user may run the same program, such as a text editor, as a Secret subject or as an Unclassified subject. Even though both subjects run the same program on behalf of the same user, they obtain different privileges due to their security labels. It is usually assumed that the security labels on subjects and objects, once assigned, do not change.

---

[8] It should be noted that RBAC will only prevent overt flows of information. This is true of any access control model, including LBAC. Information flow contrary to the one-directional requirement in a lattice by means of so-called covert channels is outside the purview of access control *per se*. Neither LBAC nor RBAC addresses the covert channel issue directly. Techniques used to deal with covert channels in LBAC can be used for the same purpose in RBAC.

[9] LBAC is typically applied in addition to classical discretionary access controls (DAC) (Sandhu and Samarati, 1994), but for our purpose we will focus only on the MAC component.

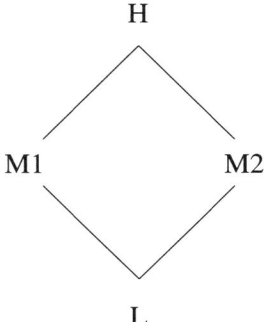

FIG. 10. A partially ordered lattice.

An example of a security lattice is shown in Fig. 10. Information is only permitted to flow upward in the lattice. In this example, H and L respectively denote high and low, and M1 and M2 are two incomparable labels intermediate to H and L. This is a typical confidentiality lattice where information can flow from low to high but not vice versa. The labels in the lattice are partially ordered by the dominance relation written $\geqslant$, for example, H $\geqslant$ L in our example. Lattices also have a least upper bound operator. Our constructions apply to partially ordered security labels in general, so this operator is not relevant.

The specific mandatory access rules usually specified for a lattice are as follows, where λ signifies the security label of the indicated subject or object.

- (**Simple Security**) Subject s can read object o only if $\lambda(s) \geqslant \lambda(o)$
- (**Liberal ★-property**) Subject s can write object o only if $\lambda(s) \leqslant \lambda(o)$

The ★-property is pronounced as the star-property. For integrity reasons sometimes a stricter form of the ★-property is stipulated. The liberal ★-property allows a low subject to write a high object. This means that high data may be maliciously destroyed or damaged by low subjects. To avoid this possibility we can employ the strict ★-property given below.

- (**Strict ★-property**) Subject s can write object o only if $\lambda(s) = \lambda(o)$

The liberal ★-property is also referred to as write-up and the strict ★-property as non-write-up or write-equal. There are also variations of LBAC where the one-directional information flow is partly relaxed to achieve selective downgrading of information or for integrity applications (Bell, 1987; Lee, 1988; Schockley, 1988).

We now show how these two variations of LBAC can be simulated in RBAC. It turns out that we can achieve this by suitably changing the role hierarchy and defining appropriate constraints. This confirms that role hierarchies and constraints are central to defining policy in RBAC.

4.2 Basic Lattices

Consider the example lattice of Fig. 10 with the liberal ⋆-property. Subjects with labels higher up in the lattice have more power with respect to read operations but have less power with respect to write operations. Thus this lattice has a dual character. In role hierarchies subjects (sessions) with roles higher in the hierarchy always have more power than those with roles lower in the hierarchy. To accommodate the dual character of a lattice for LBAC we will use two dual hierarchies in RBAC, one for read and one for write. These two role hierarchies for the lattice of Fig. 10 are shown in Fig. 11(a). Each

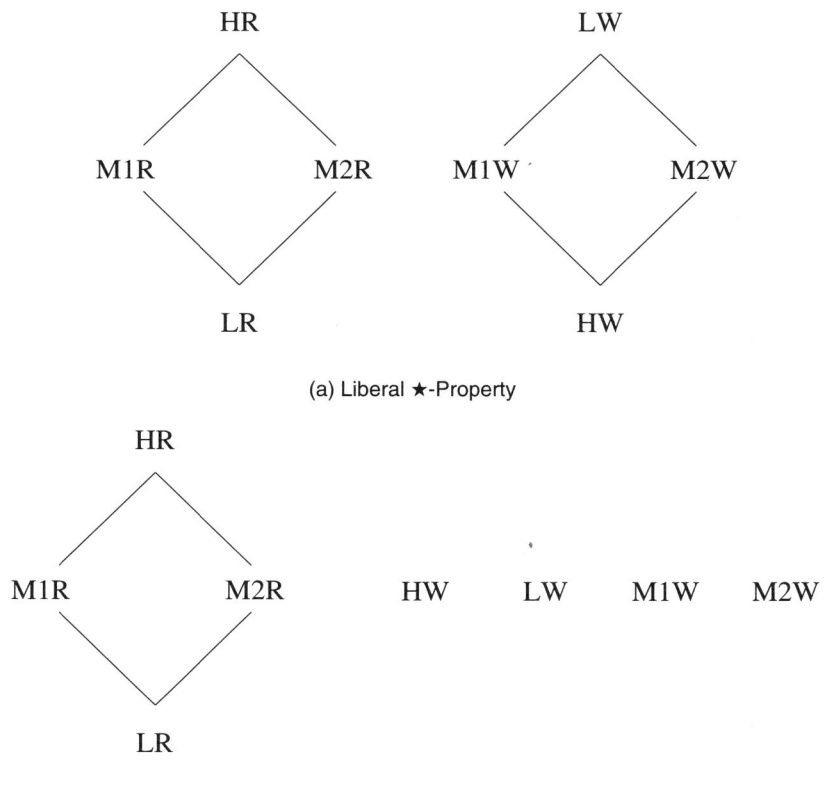

FIG. 11. Role hierarchies for the lattice of Fig. 10.

lattice label x is modeled as two roles xR and xW for read and write at label x respectively. The relationship among the four read roles and the four write roles is respectively shown on the left- and right-hand sides of Fig. 11(a). The duality between the left and right lattices is obvious from the diagrams.

To complete the construction we need to enforce appropriate constraints to reflect the labels on subjects in LBAC. Each user in LBAC has a unique security clearance. This is enforced by requiring that each user in RBAC is assigned to exactly one role xR determined by the user's clearance x. Each user is also assigned to *all* the maximal write roles. In this case there is one maximal write role LW. An LBAC user can login at any label dominated by the user's clearance. This requirement is captured in RBAC by requiring that each session has exactly two matching roles yR and yW. The condition that $x \geq y$, that is the user's clearance dominates the label of any login session established by the user, is not explicitly required because it is directly imposed by the RBAC model anyway.

LBAC is enforced in terms of read and write operations. In RBAC this means our permissions are read and writes on individual objects written as (o,r) and (o,w) respectively. An LBAC object has a single sensitivity label associated with it. This is expressed in RBAC by requiring that each pair of permissions (o,r) and (o,w) be assigned to exactly one matching pair of xR and xW roles respectively. By assigning permissions (o,r) and (o,w) to roles xR and xW respectively, we are implicitly setting the sensitivity label of object o to x.

The above construction is formalized below.

Example 1 (*Liberal ⋆-Property*)

- $R = \{\text{HR, M1R, M2R, LR, HW, M1W, M2W, LW}\}$
- *RH* as shown in Fig. 11(a)
- $P = \{(o,r), (o,w) \mid o \text{ is an object in the system}\}$
- Constraint on *UA*: Each user is assigned to exactly one role xR and to all maximal write roles (in this case being the single role LW)
- Constraint on sessions: Each session has exactly two roles yR and yW
- Constraints on *PA*:
  — (o,r) is assigned to xR iff (o,w) is assigned to xW
  — (o,r) is assigned to exactly one role xR   □

The set of permissions *P* remains the same in all our examples, so we will omit its explicit definition in subsequent examples.

Variations in LBAC can be accommodated by modifying this basic construction in different ways. In particular, the strict ⋆-property retains the hierarchy on read roles but treats write roles as incomparable to each other, as shown in Fig. 11(b).

Example 2 (*Strict ⋆-Property*) Identical to Example 1 except

- RH is as shown in Fig. 11(b)
- Each user is assigned in UA to all roles of form yW (since all of these are now maximal roles) ☐

Now the permission (o,w) is no longer inherited by other roles as is the case in Example 1. Extensions of this construction to lattices with trusted write range are given in Sandhu (1996).

4.3 Composite Confidentiality and Integrity Roles

LBAC was first formulated for confidentiality purposes. It was subsequently observed that if high integrity is at the top of the lattice and low integrity at the bottom then information flow should be downward rather than upward (as in confidentiality lattices). In Sandhu (1993) it is argued that it is simpler to fix the direction of information flow and put high integrity at the bottom and low integrity at the top in integrity lattices. Because the confidentiality models were developed earlier we might as well stay with lattices in which information flow is always upwards.

Figure 12(a) shows two independent lattices. The one on the left has HS (high secrecy) on the top and LS (low secrecy) on the bottom. The one on the right has LI (low integrity) on the top and HI (high integrity) on the bottom. In both lattices information flow is upward. The two lattices can be combined into the single composite lattice shown in Fig. 12(b).[10]

One complication in combining confidentiality and integrity lattices (or multiple lattices in general) is that these lattices may be using different versions of the ⋆-property. We have discussed earlier that the strict ⋆-property is often used in confidentiality lattices due to integrity considerations. In integrity lattices there is no similar need to use the strict ⋆-property, and one would expect to see the liberal ⋆-property instead.

Consider the composite lattice of Fig. 12(b).[11] The RBAC realization of three combinations of liberal or strict ⋆-properties is shown in Fig. 13.[12] Since the simple-security property does not change we have a similar role hierarchy for the read roles shown on the left-hand side of the three role hierarchies of Figs. 13(a), (b), and (c). In each case the hierarchy for the write roles needs to be adjusted as shown on the right-hand side of each of these figures. The constructions are formally described below.

---

[10] It is always possible to combine multiple lattices mathematically into a single lattice.

[11] Similar constructions for the distinct lattices of Fig. 12(a) are given in Sandhu (1996).

[12] The fourth combination of liberal confidentiality and strict integrity could be easily constructed but is rather unlikely to be used in practice so is omitted.

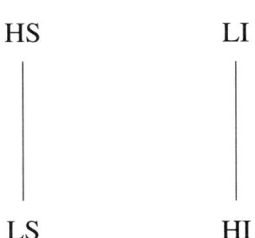

(a) Two Independent Lattices

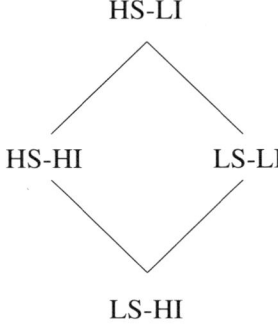

(b) One Composite Lattice

FIG. 12. Confidentiality and integrity lattices.

Example 3 (*Liberal Confidentiality and Liberal Integrity ⋆-Property*)

- R = {HSR-LIR, HSR-HIR, LSR-LIR, LSR-HIR, HSW-LIW, HSW-HIW, LSW-LIW, LSW-HIW}
- *RH* as shown in Fig. 13(a)
- Constraint on *UA*: Each user is assigned to exactly one role xSR-yIR and all maximal write roles
- Constraint on sessions: Each session has exactly two roles uSR-vIR and uSW-vIW
- Constraints on *PA*:
  — (o,r) is assigned to xSR-yIR iff (o,w) is assigned to xSW-yIW
  — (o,r) is assigned to exactly one role xSR-yIR   □

Example 4 (*Strict Confidentiality and Liberal Integrity ⋆-Property*)
Identical to Example 3 except that *RH* is as shown in Fig. 13(b).   □

Example 5 (*Strict Confidentiality and Strict Integrity ⋆-Property*)
Identical to Example 3 except that *RH* is as shown in Fig. 13(c).   □

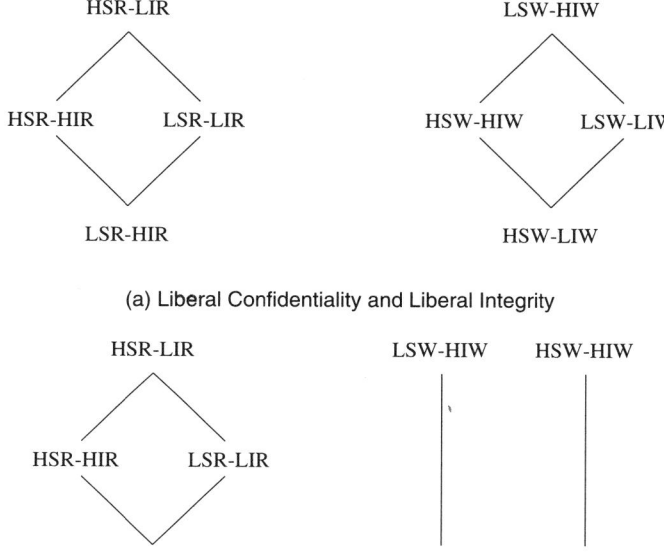

(a) Liberal Confidentiality and Liberal Integrity

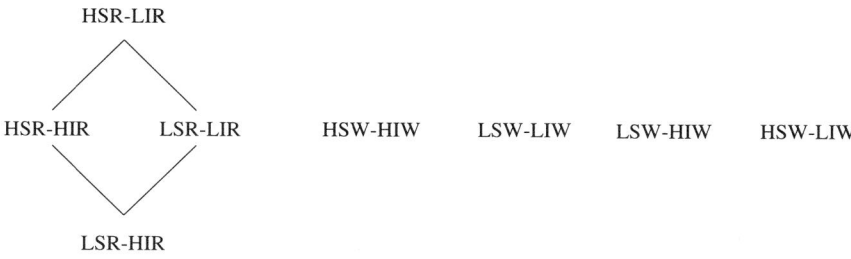

(b) Strict Confidentiality and Liberal Integrity

(c) Strict Confidentiality and Strict Integrity

FIG. 13. Composite confidentiality and integrity roles.

The constructions indicate how a single pair of roles can accommodate lattices with different variations of the $\star$-property. The construction can clearly be generalized to more than two lattices.

4.4 Discussion

In this section we have shown how different variations of lattice-based access controls (LBAC) can be simulated in role-based access control

(RBAC). RBAC is itself policy-neutral but can be easily configured to specify a variety of policies as we have shown. The main components of RBAC that need to be adjusted for different LBAC variations are the role hierarchy and constraints. This attests to the flexibility and power of RBAC.

A practical consequence of our results is that it might be better to develop systems that support general RBAC and specialize these to LBAC. RBAC has much broader applicability than LBAC, especially in the commercial sector. LBAC can be realized as a particular instance of RBAC. This approach provides the added benefit of greater flexibility for LBAC, for which we have seen there are a number of variations of practical interest. In LBAC systems these variations so far require the rules to be adjusted in the implementation. RBAC provides for adjustment by configuration of role hierarchies and constraints instead.

5. Three-tier Architecture

In this section we present a conceptual framework, or reference architecture, for specifying and enforcing RBAC. Our framework has three tiers, by loose analogy with the well-known ANSI/SPARC architecture for database systems (Tsichritizis and Klug, 1978), illustrated in Fig. 14. Although we take

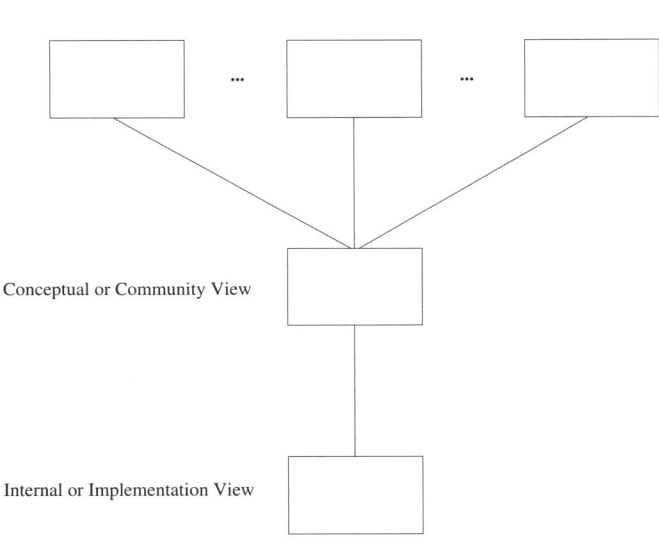

FIG. 14. ANSI/SPARC database architecture.

our inspiration from the database domain, we emphasize that our proposed RBAC architecture is germane to applications and systems in general and is not limited to databases *per se*.

Our reference architecture is motivated by two main considerations. First, a number of RBAC features have been incorporated in commercial products, and more such products can be expected to appear in future. Vendors tend to integrate RBAC facilities in products in different ways, because of the economics of integrating such features into existing product lines. Over time the emergence of standards may impose some order in this arena, but the near term is likely to display a divergence of approaches. Even as standards emerge, we can expect a diversity of support for RBAC due to the longevity of legacy systems.

Second, in large organizations there will be a large number of roles and complex relationships between the roles and permissions authorized by them. In most contexts it would be appropriate to take a simplified view appropriate for the task at hand. For example, in some situations all members of a particular department can be treated as belonging to a single role; whereas in other situations more refined roles, such as managers, technical staff, and administrative staff need to be distinguished.

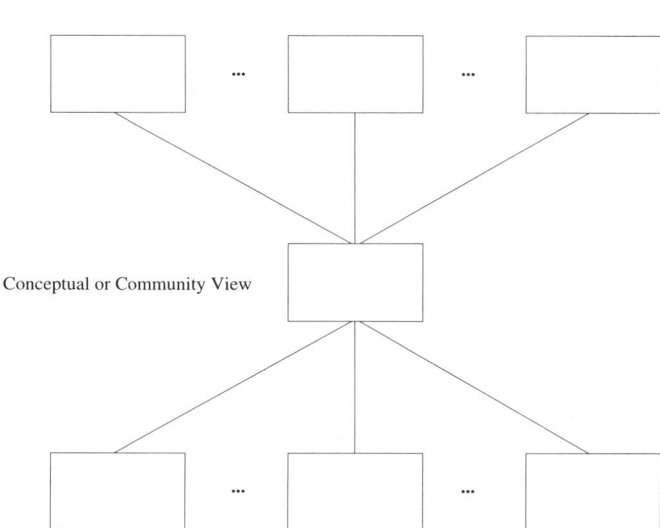

FIG. 15. A three-tier architecture for RBAC.

The central tier of our architecture resides in a single community view of RBAC as it applies to the entire organization in question. This community view will typically be large and complex, reflecting the reality of modern organizations. The specialized context-specific views of RBAC tailored to particular applications and situations are accommodated in multiple user views that reside above the central tier. The views of RBAC embodied in different products are embodied in multiple implementation views residing below the implementation tier. Figure 15 illustrates these three tiers. The central tier serves as the focal point for mapping the external user views to the internal implementation views.

5.1 The Three Tiers

The ANSI/SPARC report (Tsichritizis and Klug, 1978) described a three-tier architecture for a database, consisting of:

(1) the external or user view which is concerned with the way data is viewed by end users,
(2) the conceptual or community view which amalgamates diverse external views into a consistent and unified composite, and
(3) the internal or implementation view which is concerned with the way that data is actually stored.

This database architecture is shown in Fig. 14.

Note that there are multiple external views, but only a single conceptual and a single internal view. This three-tier approach to database systems has stood the test of time, and is remarkably independent of the particular data model being used.

We believe a similar approach is suitable for developing a common framework or reference architecture for RBAC. RBAC is concerned with the meaning and control of access control data (i.e. data used to control access to the actual data of the organization). In other words we are concerned with a special-purpose database system. It is therefore sensible to adapt the approach used for general purpose database systems. However, there is one significant difference. In database systems, it is intended that the implementation will eventually be on a particular database management platform. Consequently, the internal or implementation view is closely tied to the particular platform that is selected. With RBAC we do not have the luxury of assuming a homogeneous implementation environment. Instead we must confront the reality of heterogeneous implementations up-front. This leads us to modify the three-tier ANSI/SPARC architecture by introducing multiple internal views, corresponding to different platforms on which the implementation is done. This RBAC reference architecture is shown in Fig. 15.

Our three-tiered approach to RBAC therefore consists of multiple external views, a single conceptual view, and multiple implementation views.

Next, let us consider the appropriate model for each of these tiers. We again turn to the ANSI/SPARC architecture for inspiration. There is a conspicuous difference between the models used at the implementation and conceptual tiers. We expect a similar difference in our RBAC reference architecture. Why is this so? We expect the model used at the conceptual level to have richer constructs and primitives, because it is intended to express a composite system-wide view of RBAC. Practical considerations will inevitably dictate that not all these features can be directly supported in an implementation. Hence the implementation models will be simpler and less user-friendly. Moreover, we expect a range of sophistication from rather primitive mechanisms (say on a vanilla Unix platform) at one end to very elaborate ones (say on an object-oriented database management system) at the other. Note that this viewpoint lets us accommodate legacy systems co-existing with newer ones. It should also be clear that the effort required to translate a conceptual view will be less or greater depending upon the sophistication of the implementation platform being targeted. In some cases, a translation may not even be feasible (or practical) without enhancement of the target platform.

The difference between the conceptual and external tiers is less marked. Whether or not there should be any difference is open to debate. For relational databases, both tiers are often identical and directly based on the relational data model. However, sometimes a richer model, such as the entity-relationship model, is used for the external view while a relational model is used at the conceptual view. We anticipate a similar situation in the RBAC reference architecture. Based on historical experience with the ANSI/SPARC architecture, it might well happen that initially the same RBAC model is used at both tiers, but over time richer models are developed for the external view.

5.2 The Central Tier

The central tier of our reference architecture consists of a single community view of RBAC applicable to the entire information system and its myriad applications. This community view is the essential conceptual vehicle for effective deployment of enterprise-wide RBAC. The RBAC96 family of models provides us with a flexible and general framework for this tier.

5.3 Harmonizing the Top Two Tiers

Let us now consider the relationship between the top two tiers of the reference architecture, reproduced in Fig. 16. Each external view gives one perspective on the common community view, relevant to the particular

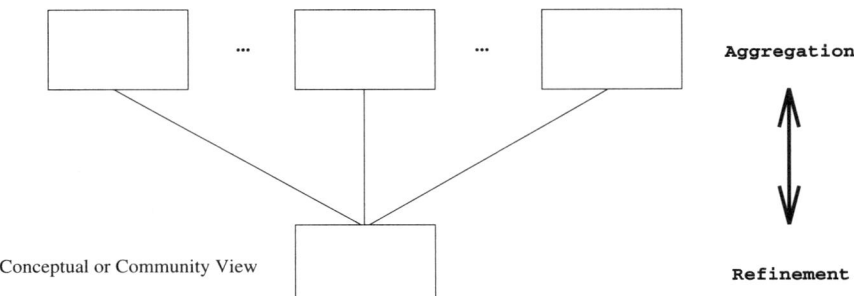

FIG. 16. Harmonizing the top two tiers.

context at hand. The relationship between the top two tiers is one of aggregation and refinement, as indicated in the figure.

Aggregation is a process by which several distinct roles are combined into a single role, because the distinction is not relevant in the given context. For example, the community view might have distinct roles for, say, Undergraduate Students, Master's Students, and Doctoral Students. In an application where are all students are treated alike, these roles could be collapsed (i.e. aggregated) into a single Student role. In other applications, which confer different privileges on the various student roles, this distinction is significant. Refinement is simply the opposite operation to aggregation.

Different external views will aggregate different collections of roles from the community view. Some external views may aggregate the student roles into a single one. Others may keep the distinction between student roles but aggregate distinct faculty roles into one. Still others may aggregate both or none of the student and faculty roles. Our expectation is that a relatively small portion of the overall role set from the community view will be needed more or less intact in a particular external view. Most of the roles will, however, be aggregated. In other words, each external view will see only a small part of the roles set in all its detail.

So long as entire roles are being aggregated or refined, the mapping between the top two tiers is relatively simple. There may be situations where the role relevant to the external view does not come about so cleanly by aggregation. For example, suppose the community view has roles A and B, whereas the external view requires a role which has some (but not all) members of A and some (but not all) members of B. We identify below some techniques for accommodating such an external view.

- One could modify the community view to create a new role C and

explicitly assign those members of A and B who should belong to this role. This treats A, B, and C as unrelated roles.
- One could modify the community view to partition A into A_1 and A_2 (with $A_1 \cap A_2 = \varnothing$), and B into B_1 and B_2 (with $B_1 \cap B_2 = \varnothing$) so that the aggregate role $C = A_1 \cup B_1$ can be defined in the desired external view. This would require external views which use A to now treat A as an aggregate of A_1 and A_2, instead of being a role from the community view, and similarly for external views which use role B.
- We could allow aggregation which can select the appropriate subsets of A and B, based on some condition for identifying members who should belong to the aggregated role C. This will complicate the aggregation operation and might dilute the central role of the conceptual view.

This list is not intended to be exhaustive. The point is that various alternatives are available as the community and external views adapt to the ever-changing demands of the applications. One needs a systematic methodology for dealing with such changes.

5.4 Harmonizing the Bottom Two Tiers

Now consider harmonization of the bottom two tiers, shown in Fig. 17. Each of the implementation views will aggregate roles from the community view. The aggregation done here will constrain which external views can be hosted on which implementation views. An implementation view that aggregates distinct student roles into a single role obviously cannot support an external view that requires this distinction to be maintained. In an ideal situation the implementation view may do no aggregation, in which case it could support all the external views. In practice, however, one would expect considerable aggregation to occur; if only because of legacy systems which have directly built in the external view without consideration of the common community view. Performance considerations may also require such aggregation to occur. Note that in both Figs. 16 and 17 aggregation is in the direction away from the central community view, and refinement is directed towards this view.

The second mapping shown in Fig. 17 is between implicit and explicit mechanisms. This mapping recognizes that the implementation platform may not support all the features of RBAC in the community view. For example, role hierarchies may not be supported. Suppose there are two roles, Faculty and Staff, such that every member of the Faculty role is automatically a member of the Staff role (but not vice versa). Thus a new faculty member need only be enrolled in the Faculty role, and will automatically be enrolled in the Staff role. Support for such role inheritance in the community view is

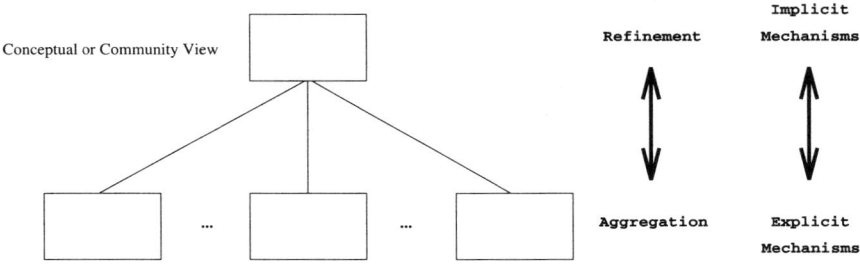

FIG. 17. Harmonizing the bottom two tiers.

highly desirable, but such support will not be available on every implementation platform. To continue our example, at the community view it suffices to enrol a new faculty member into the Faculty role. However, in the implementation view the new faculty member will need to be enrolled in both Faculty and Staff roles. Similarly, a departing faculty member needs to be removed from the Faculty role in the community view; but in the implementation view requires removal from both Faculty and Staff roles.

5.5 Discussion

In this section we have described a three-tiered reference architecture for role-based access control (RBAC), and have identified some of the issues that need to be addressed in making this framework a reality. We note that the appeal of RBAC is in the simplification of the management of authorizations. For example, maintaining cognizance of the permission set of an individual and the consequence of assigning particular role sets to a user is vital. It is also important for a security administrator to know exactly what authorization is implied by a role. This is particularly so when roles can be composed of other roles. Moreover, as new roles and transactions are introduced the security administrator needs tools to assist in their integration into the existing system. Future work in RBAC should identify useful tools for security administration and point the way toward designing these. We feel that the central role of the community view in our reference architecture will greatly assist in this objective.

6. Conclusion

This article has described the motivations, results, and open issues in recent RBAC research, focusing on the RBAC96 family of models, the ARBAC97 administrative models, the flexibility and power of RBAC in simulating variations of classical lattice-based control, and a three-tier conceptual architecture for enforcing RBAC in large heterogeneous environments. Although the basic ideas of role-based access control are very simple, we hope to have convinced the reader that there are a number of interesting technical challenges and much further research to be done.

In conclusion we would like to note two major areas that need considerable work to fully realize the potential of RBAC. The first area is that of *role engineering*, that is the discipline and methodology for configuring RBAC in an organization, and most importantly designing the role hierarchy. The second area is *role transition* meaning the means for moving towards RBAC in coexistence with legacy modes of access control.

ACKNOWLEDGMENTS

This work was funded in part by contracts 50-DKNA-4-00122 and 50-DKNB-5-00188 from the National Institute of Standards and Technology through SETA Corporation, and by grant CCR-9503560 from the National Science Foundation through George Mason University. The author acknowledges the assistance of the following people in conducting this research: Venkata Bhamidipati, Edward Coyne, Hal Feinstein, Srinivas Ganta, Qamar Munawer and Charles Youman. The author also acknowledges the following people for useful discussions on these topics: John Barkley, David Ferraiolo, Serban Gavrila, and Roshan Thomas.

REFERENCES

Baldwin, R. W. (1990) Naming and grouping privileges to simplify security management in large database. *Proceedings of IEEE Symposium on Research in Security and Privacy*, Oakland CA, pp. 61–70.

Bell, D. E. (1987) Secure computer systems: a network interpretation. *Proceedings of 3rd Annual Computer Security Application Conference*. pp. 32–39.

Common Criteria Editorial Board (1996) *Common Criteria for Information Technology Security*, Version 1.0.

Ferraiolo, D. F., and Kuhn, R. (1992) Role-based access controls. *Proceedings of 15th NIST-NCSC National Computer Security Conference*, Baltimore MD. pp. 554–563.

Ferraiolo, D. F., Gilbert, D. M., and Lynch, N. (1993) An examination of federal and commercial access control policy needs. *Proceedings of NIST-NCSC National Computer Security Conference*, Baltimore MD. pp. 107–116.

Guiri, L. (1995) A new model for role-based access control. *Proceedings of 11th Annual Computer Security Application Conference*, New Orleans LA. pp. 249–255.

Hu, M.-Y., Demurjian, S. A., and Ting, T. C. (1995) User-role based security in the ADAM object-oriented design and analyses environment. *Database Security VIII: Status and Prospects* (eds J. Biskup, M. Morgernstern, and C. Landwehr. North-Holland, Amsterdam.

ISO (1992) *ISO/IEC 10040: Information Technology—Open Systems Interconnection—Systems Management Overview*. International Organization for Standardization, Geneva.

Jonscher, D. (1993) Extending access controls with duties—realized by active mechanisms. *Database Security VI: Status and Prospects* (eds B. Thuraisingham and C. E. Landwehr). North-Holland, Amsterdam. pp. 91–111.

Lee, T. M. P. (1988) Using mandatory integrity to enforce "commercial" security. *Proceedings of IEEE Symposium on Security and Privacy*, Oakland CA, pp. 140–146.

Mohammed, I., and Dilts, D. M. (1994) Design for dynamic user-role-based security. *Computers & Security* **13**(8), 661–671.
Moffett, J. D., and Sloman, M. S. (1991) Delegation of authority. *Integrated Network Management II* (eds I. Krishnan and W. Zimmer). Elsevier Science Publishers, Amsterdam. pp. 595–606.
Notargiacomo, L. (1997) Role-based access control in ORACLE7 and Trusted ORACLE7. *Proceedings of the 1st ACM Workshop on Role-Based Access Control.* ACM. Gaithersburg, MD.
Nyanchama, M., and Osborn, S. (1995) Access rights administration in role-based security systems. *Database Security VIII: Status and Prospects* (eds J. Biskup, M. Morgernstern, and C. Landwehr). North-Holland, Amsterdam.
Sandhu, R. S. (1988) Transaction control expressions for separation of duties. *Proceedings of 4th Annual Computer Security Application Conference*, Orlando FL. pp. 282–286.
Sandhu, R. S. (1991) Separation of duties in computerized information systems. *Database Security IV: Status and Prospects* (eds S. Jajodia and C. E. Landwehr). North-Holland, Amsterdam. pp. 179–189.
Sandhu, R. S. (1992) The typed access matrix model. *Proceedings of IEEE Symposium on Research in Security and Privacy*, Oakland CA. pp. 122–136.
Sandhu, R. S. (1993) Lattice-based access control models. *IEEE Computer* **26**(11), 9–19.
Sandhu, R. S. (1996) Role hierarchies and constraints for lattice-based access controls. *Proc. Fourth European Symposium on Research in Computer Security* (ed. E. Bertino). Springer-Verlag, Rome. Published as *Lecture Notes in Computer Science, Computer Security— ESORICS96.*
Sandhu, R., and Bhamidipati, V. (1997) The URA97 model for role-based user-role assignments. *Database Security XI: Status and Prospects* (eds T. Y. Lin and X. Qian). North-Holland, Amsterdam.
Sandhu, R. S., and Feinstein, H. L. (1994) A three tier architecture for role-based access control. *Proceedings of 17th NIST-NCSC National Computer Security Conference*, Baltimore MD. pp. 34–46.
Sandhu, R., and Samarati, P. (1994) Access control: principles and practice. *IEEE Communications* **32**(9), 40–48.
Sandhu, R. S., Coyne, E. J. Feinstein, H. L., and Youman, C. E. (1996) Role-based access control models. *IEEE Computer* **29**(2), 38–47.
Sandhu, R., Bhamidipati, V., Coyne, E., Ganta, S., and Youman, C. (1997) The ARBAC97 model for role-based administration of roles: preliminary description and outline. *Proceedings of the 2nd ACM Workshop on Role-Based Access Control.* ACM. Fairfax, VA.
Schockley, W. R. (1988) Implementing the Clark/Wilson integrity policy using current technology. *Proceedings of NIST-NCSC National Computer Security Conference.* pp. 29–37.
Thomas, R., and Sandhu, R. S. (1994) Conceptual foundations for a model of task-based authorizations. *Proceedings of IEEE Computer Security Foundations Workshop 7*, Franconia NH. pp. 66–79.
Thomas, R. and Sandhu, R. (1997) Task-based authorization controls (TBAC): models for active and enterprise-oriented authorization management. *Database Security XI: Status and Prospects* (eds T. Y. Lin and X. Qian). North-Holland, Amsterdam.
Thomsen, D. J. (1991) Role-based application design and enforcement. *Database Security IV: Status and Prospects* (eds S. Jajodia and C. E. Landwehr). North-Holland, Amsterdam. pp. 151–168.
Tsichritizis, D. C., and Klug, A. (eds) (1978) The ANSI/X3/SPARC DBMS framework: Report of the study group on data base management system, *American National Standards Institute*.
von Solms, S. H., and van der Merwe, I. (1994) The management of computer security profiles using a role-oriented approach. *Computers & Security* **13**(8), 673–680.

Multithreaded Systems

KRISHNA M. KAVI

Department of Electrical and Computer Engineering
The University of Alabama in Huntsville.
Huntsville, Alabama 35899, USA

BEN LEE

Electrical and Computer Engineering Department
Oregon State University
Corvallis, OR 97331
USA

ALI R. HIRSON

Computer Science and Engineering Department
The Pennsylvania State University
University Park, PA 16802
USA

Abstract

Recent studies have shown that the single-threaded paradigm used by conventional programming languages and run-time systems can utilize less than 50% of the processor capabilities. Yet advances in VLSI technology have led to faster clocks and processor designs that can issue multiple instructions per cycle with more on-chip cache memories. In order to garner the potential performance gains from these technological advances, it is necessary to change the programming paradigm. Multithreading has emerged as one of the most promising and exciting avenues for exploiting the technological advances. Multithreading can be applied to achieve concurrency using multiple processing resources (e.g. SMP and NOWs), where individual threads can be executed on different processors with appropriate coordination among the threads. Multithreading can also be used to hide long latency operations such as slower memory accesses. The memory latency is further compounded in high-end workstations that use multiple levels of cache memory and multiprocessor configurations involving remote memory accesses.

The idea of multithreading is not new. Fine-grained multithreading was implicit in the dataflow model of computation. Multiple hardware contexts (i.e. register files, PSWs) to aid switching between threads were implemented in systems such as Dorado and HEP. These systems were not successful, owing to a lack of innovations in programming languages, run-time systems, and operating system kernels. There is, however, a renewed interest in multithreading primarily due to a confluence of several independent research directions which have united over a common set of issues and techniques. A number of research projects are under way for designing multithreaded systems, including new architectures, new programming languages, new compiling techniques, more efficient interprocessor communication, and customized microkernels. Some of these projects have produced substantial improvements over single-threaded abstractions. The success of multithreading as a viable computational model depends on the integration of these efforts. In this chapter, we introduce the concept of multithreading, illustrate how multithreaded programs can be written in various programming languages, compare different thread packages and kernel-level threads, and describe how multithreaded architectures can be implemented.

1. Introduction 288
2. Programming Models 290
   2.1 Threaded abstract Machine (TAM) 295
   2.2 Cilk 299
   2.3 Cid 300
3. Execution Models 302
   3.1 Design Issues 302
4. Architectural Support for Multithreading 307
5. Example Multithreaded Systems 308
   5.1 Tera MTA 308
   5.2 StarT 310
   5.3 EM-X 312
   5.4 Alewife 314
   5.5 M-Machine 316
   5.6 Simultaneous Multithreading 317
6. Performance Models 319
7. Conclusions and Prognostication 323
Glossary 324
References 325

1. Introduction

The past couple of decades have seen tremendous progress in the technology of computing devices, both in terms of functionality and performance. It is predicted that over the next five years, it will be possible to fabricate processors containing billions of transistor circuits operating at gigahertz speeds [21]. While there has been continuing growth in the density of DRAM memory chips, improvements in the access times and I/O bandwidth of memory parts have not kept pace with processor clock rates. This has widened the relative performance of processors and memory. The memory latency problem is further compounded by complex memory hierarchies which need to be traversed between processors and main memory. In symmetric multiprocessors (SMPs), which have become dominant in commercial and scientific computing environments, contention due to the shared-bus located between the processor's L2 cache and the shared main memory subsystem adds additional delay to the memory latency. The delays becomes even more severe for scalable Distributed Shared Memory (DSM) systems that span the spectrum from systems with physically distributed memory and hardware support for cache coherency to Networks of Workstations (NOWs) interconnected by a LAN or WAN and software support for shared-memory abstraction. In either case, a miss on the local memory requires a request to be issued to the remote memory, and a reply to be sent back to the requesting processor. Stalls due to the round-trip communication latency are and will continue to be an aggravating factor that limits the performance of scalable DSM systems.

Memory latency, while growing, is not a new phenomenon. There have been varied efforts to resolve the memory latency problem. The most obvious approach is to reduce the physical latencies in the system. This involves making the pathway between the processor requesting the data and the remote memory that contains the data as efficient as possible, e.g. reducing the software overhead of sending and receiving messages and improving the connectivity of networks. The second approach is to reduce the frequency of long latency operations by keeping data local to the processor that needs it. When data locality cannot be exploited, prefetching or block transferring (as opposed to cache-line transfers) of data can be used. Caches are the most prevalent solution to the problem of memory latency. Unfortunately, they do not perform well if an application's memory access patterns do not conform to hard-wired policies. Furthermore, increasing cache capacities, while consuming increasingly large silicon areas on processor chips, will only result in diminishing returns.

Although the aforementioned approaches reduce latency, they do not eliminate it. *Multithreading* has emerged as a promising and exciting avenue to tolerate the latency that cannot be eliminated. A multithreaded system contains multiple "loci of control" (or threads) within a single program; the processor is shared by these multiple threads, leading to higher utilization. The processor may switch between the threads, not only to hide memory latency but also to hide other long latency operations, such as I/O latency; or it may interleave instructions on a cycle-by-cycle basis from multiple threads to minimize pipeline breaks due to dependencies among instructions within a single thread. Multithreading has also been used strictly as a programming paradigm on general purpose hardware to exploit thread parallelism on SMPs and to increase applications' throughput and responsiveness. However, lately there has been increasing interest in providing hardware support for multithreading. Without adequate hardware support, such as multiple hardware contexts, fast context-switch, non-blocking caches, out-of-order instruction issue and completion, and register renaming, we will not be able to take full advantage of the multithreading model of computation. As the feature size of logic devices reduces, we feel that the silicon area can be put to better use by providing support for multithreading.

The idea of multithreading is not new. Fine-grained multithreading was implicit in the dataflow model of computation [34]. Multiple hardware contexts (i.e. register files, PSWs) to speed up switching between threads were implemented in systems such as Dorado [38], HEP [42], and Tera [4]. Some of these systems were not successful due to a lack of innovations in programming languages, run-time systems, and operating system kernels. There is, however, a renewed interest in multithreading, primarily due to a confluence of several independent research directions which have united over a common set of issues and techniques. A number of research projects are under-way for designing multithreaded systems that include new architectures, new programming languages, new compiling techniques, more efficient inter-processor communication, and customized microkernels. Some of these projects have produced substantial improvements over single-threaded abstractions. The success of multithreading as a viable computational model depends on the integration of these efforts.

This chapter is organized as follows. Section 2 discusses multithreading in terms of user-level programming models, such as TAM [19], Cilk [13], and Cid [37]. Section 3 reviews the execution models and run-time support of multithreading. Thread libraries and kernel-level thread support will be the main focus of this section. Section 4 discusses the architectural support for multithreading, with the emphasis on reducing the cost of context switching. Section 5 provides an overview of various multithreaded architectures along with their key features. The survey includes Tera MTA, StarT, EM-X, Alewife, M-Machine, and Simultaneous Multithreading. Section 6 presents analytical models for studying the performance of multithreading. Finally, Section 7 concludes the chapter with a brief discussion of future developments and challenges in multithreading.

2. Programming Models

Multithreading has become increasingly popular with programming language designers, operating system designers, and computer architects as a way to support applications. In this section we will concentrate on multi-threaded models as seen from a programmer perspective. Concurrency can be supported by programming languages in many ways. It can be achieved by providing user-level thread libraries to C and C++ programmers, whereby the programmer can insert appropriate calls to these libraries to create, invoke, and control threads. A variety of such libraries have been available to programmers, including C-threads, Pthreads, and Solaris Threads. We will discuss these libraries in the next section.

Some programming languages provide concurrency constructs as an integral part of the language. Ada-95 permits users to create and control concurrent programming units known as tasks [31]. Synchronization among tasks can be achieved using either shared-memory (protected objects) or message-passing (rendezvous using select and accept statements). Consider the following function which forks (recursively) threads to compute Fibonacci numbers:

```
Function Fibonacci (N : In Integer) Return Integer Is

Task Type Fib Is
--- This is the task specification (prototype).
--- Task type is declared here with two entry points.
--- Tasks can rendezvous at these entry points.
    Entry Get_Input (N: In Integer);
    Entry Return_Result (Result : Out Integer);
End Fib;

Type Fib_Ptr Is Access Fib;
        --- A pointer to the task type is defined here.

Function Create_Fib_Task Return Fib_Ptr Is
Begin
--- This function is used to create and spawn new tasks
---          of type Fib by allocating the pointer type.
--- The function is needed to eliminate recursive
---              definition inside the task body below.
    Return New Fib;  --- The construct New allocates
                                        --- the task
End Create_Fib_Task;

Task Body Fib Is
--- This is the task body for the task Fib.

Input, Result_N, Result_N_1, Result_N_2 : Integer;
Fib_N_1, Fib_N_2 : Fib_Ptr;
```

```
Begin
    Accept Get_Input (N : In Integer) Do
    --- This entry point is used to receive the argument.
        Input := N;
    End Get_Input;

    If (Input <= 2) Then
        Result_N := Input;
    Else
        Fib_N_1 := Create_Fib_Task;  --- Create a new
                        --- thread to compute Fib (N-1).
        Fib_N_2 := Create_Fib_Task;  --- Create a new
                        --- thread to compute Fib (N-2).
        Fib_N_1.Get_Input (Input-1);  --- The spawned
            --- task Fib(N-1) receives the argument n-1
        Fib_N_2.Get_Input (Input-2);  -- The spawned
            --- task Fib(N-2) receives the argument n-2

        Fib_N_1.Return_Result (Result_N_1);  -- Receive
                    --- the result from task Fib(N-1)
        Fib_N_2.Return_Result (Result_N_2);  -- Receive
                    --- the result from task Fib(N-2)
        Result_N := Result_N_1 + Result_N_2;

        Accept Return_Result (Result : Out Integer) Do
        ---
        --- This entry point is used to return the
        ---                     result to the parent

            Result := Result_N;
        End Return_Result;
      End If;
End Fib;

--- This is the main procedure that contains the task Fib
---                                         declaration.
Result : Integer;
Fib_N := Fib_Ptr;

Begin
    Fib_N := Create_Fib_Task;
    Fib_N.Get_Input (N);
    Fib_N.Return_Result (Result);
    Return Result;
End Fibbonnacci;
```

Forking of tasks is accomplished by allocating a pointer type that points to a task type. Each new task spawns two additional tasks to compute Fib(N-1) and Fib(N-2), and waits for the results from the spawned tasks. In most implementations, individual Ada-95 tasks of a program are bound to threads provided by the system (either kernel-level or user-level threads). Ada-95 facilitates various means for creating, initiating, and managing synchronization among tasks. Single tasks are scheduled as soon as the block in which they are defined is entered. Variables of task types are enabled for execution as soon as the body containing the variable declarations is entered. Access (pointer type) variable to task types become enabled when allocated. Tasks cease to exist when they complete execution, and only when all their child tasks complete execution. Tasks can also be explicitly aborted. The primary synchronization in Ada is the rendezvous mechanism using select and accept statements. Entry points can be guarded. In Ada-95, the concept of protected objects is introduced to implement monitors and conditional waiting inside a monitor.

Java programming language supports multithreading by defining classes for creation and synchronization of threads [9]. Consider the following Java implementation of Fibonacci numbers.

```
public class Fibonacci extends Thread
{       int fib;
        Fibonacci(int n)
        {       fib=n;
        }
        public void run()
        {       if (fib == 0 || fib == 1)
                {       fib=1;
                }
                else
                {       Fibonacci thread1= new Fibonacci(fib-1);
                                // create a child thread for N-1
                        Fibonacci thread2= new Fibonacci(fib-2);
                                // create a child thread for N-2
                        thread1. start (); // execution of created
                                           // thread starts here.
                        thread2. start (); // execution of created
                                           // thread starts here.
                        try
                        {       thread1. join (); // wait for child
                                                  // threads
                                thread2. join (); // wait for child
                                                  // threads
                                fib=thread1.getFib()+thread2.getFib();
                        }
```

```
                            catch ( InterruptedException e)
                                  // Java requires this section to
                                  // handle exceptions
                                  {       e.printStackTrace();
                                  }
                    }
          } // end of run()
          public final int getFib()
          {       return fib;
          }
          public static void main(String arg[])   // this is the
                                                  // main program
          {       Fibonacci fib;
                  int n=new Integer(arg[0]).intValue();
                  fib=new Fibonacci(n);
                  fib. start ();
                  try
                  {       fib. join ();
                          System.out.println("The Fibonacci for
                                  "+ n+" is: "+ fib.getFib());
                  }
                  catch (InterruptedException e)
                  {       e.printStackTrace();
                  }
          }
}
```

As in the Ada-95, Java threads are blocking (and coarse-grained). The parent thread that created and started two new threads to compute Fibonacci(N-1) and Fibonacci(N-2) must wait for the threads to complete using a barrier synchronization "Join." Java is based on C++. In the above example, a class Fibonacci is defined as thread class. In the body of the class, two new threads for computing Fibonacci of N-1 and N-2 are created recursively. The parent will wait for (using Join) the two child threads complete execution; and the values returned by the child threads are added. Some of the characteristic of Java threads are listed in the next section.

Programming languages with support for multithreading normally permit coarse-grained and blocking threads. The blocking nature requires synchronization among the threads using such common techniques as mutual exclusion using semaphores or mutexes, condition variables, events, rendezvous, guards, and monitors. They provide for thread scheduling constructs such as yield, suspend, detach, abort, or terminate. Some functional programming languages, such as Multilisp [27] and Id90 [35] have proposed a different attack on multithreading, often supporting fine-grained threads. In such languages, actions that traditionally block or are synchronous are made non-blocking and asynchronous. For example, in traditional von Neumann languages, function calls are synchronous: when a function is invoked, the thread of control is transferred to the called function (blocking the execution of the caller) and the control is returned to the caller upon its completion. In Multilisp, function calls (called *futures*) are non-blocking so that several futures can be invoked without waiting for their completion. Likewise, languages can be designed with other asynchronous or non-blocking actions. In general, a multithreaded programming language may permit programs where even conditional statements can be made asynchronous. Languages based on a data-driven model of synchronization support fine-grained and non-blocking threads. In such systems, a thread is not ready for execution until all its synchronization requirements are satisfied; and once initiated, the thread executes to completion with no further synchronization requirements. In the remainder of this section, we will introduce three such languages.

2.1 Threaded Abstract Machine (TAM)

TAM [19] has its roots in the dataflow model of execution, but can be understood independently of dataflow. A language called Threaded Machine Language, TL0, was designed to permit programming using the TAM model. TAM recognizes three major storage resources—code-blocks, frames, and structures—and the existence of critical processor resources, such as registers. A program is represented by a collection of re-entrant code-blocks, corresponding roughly to individual functions or loop bodies in the high-level program text. A code-block comprises a collection of threads and inlets. Invoking a code-block involves allocating a frame—much like a conventional call frame—depositing argument values into locations within the frame, and enabling threads within the code-block for execution. Instructions may refer to registers and to slots in the current frame: the compiler statically determines the frame size for each code-block and is responsible for correctly using slots and registers under all possible dynamic thread orderings. The compiler also reserves a portion of the frame as a continuation vector, used at run-time to hold pointers to enabled threads. The global scheduling pool is the set of frames that contain enabled threads.

Executing a code-block may fork several frames concurrently, since the caller is not suspended as in a conventional language. Therefore the set of frames in existence at any time form a tree (the activation tree) rather than a stack, reflecting the dynamic call structure. This is shown in Fig. 1. To allow greater parallelism and to support languages with non-strict function call semantics, the arguments to a code-block may be delivered

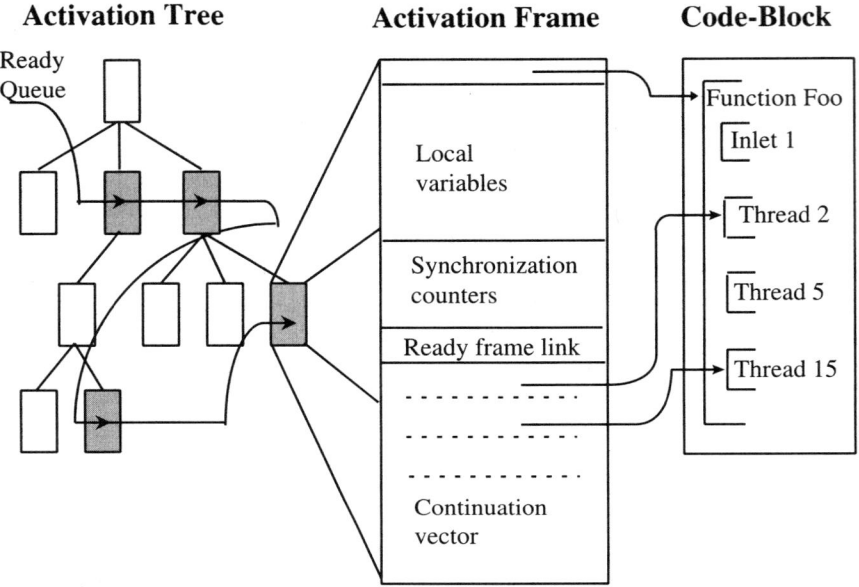

FIG. 1. TAM activation tree.

asynchronously. An activation is enabled if its frame contains any enabled threads. At any time, a subset of enabled activations may be resident on processors.

Threads come in two forms, synchronizing and non-synchronizing. A synchronizing thread specifies a frame slot containing the entry count for the thread. Each *fork* to a synchronizing thread causes the entry count (synchronization count) to be decremented, but the thread executes only when the count reaches zero, indicating that all synchronization requirements were met. A non-synchronizing thread is ready for executing immediately. Synchronization occurs only at the start of a thread: once successfully initiated, a thread executes to completion. Fork operations may occur anywhere in a thread, causing additional threads to be enabled for execution. An enabled thread is identified by a continuation—its instruction pointer and frame pointer. A thread ends with an explicit *stop* instruction, which causes another enabled thread to be scheduled. Conditional flow of execution is supported by *switch*, which forks one of two threads based on a boolean input value. The compiler is responsible for establishing correct entry counts for synchronizing threads. This is facilitated by allowing a distinguished initialization thread in each code-block, which is the first thread executed in an activation of the code-block. Long latency operations, such as I-Fetch or

Send, implicitly fork a thread that resumes when the request completes. This allows the processor to continue with useful work while the remote access is outstanding.

The storage hierarchy is explicit in TAM. In addition, scheduling is explicit and reflects the storage hierarchy. In order to execute threads from an activation, the activation must be made resident. When an activation is made resident on a processor, it has access to processor registers. Furthermore, it remains resident and executing until no enabled threads for the activation exist. The set of threads executed during a single residency is called a quantum.

The following is an implementation of the Fibonacci program in TL0:

```
FRAME_BODY RCV = 3             -- defines a frame with 3 arguments
   islot1.i, islot1.i, islot2.i -- one argument and two results
   pfslot1.pf, pfslot2.pf      -- frame pointers for recursive calls
   sslot0.s                    -- synchronization variable for
                               -- thread 6
   pfsloto.pf, jsloto.j        -- parent's frame pointer and inlet
REGISTER                       -- Registers used
   breg0.b, ireg0.i            -- boolean and integer temps.
INLET 0                        -- recv parent fr. ptr, return inlet
                               -- and argument
   RECEIVE pfslot0.pf, jslot0.j, isloto.i
   FINIT                       -- initialize frame
   SET_ENTER 7, t              -- set enter-activation thread
   SET_LEAVE 8, t              -- set leave-activation thread
   POST 0.t
   STOP
INLET 1                        -- receive frame pointer of first
                               -- recursive call

   RECEIVE pfslot1.pf
   POST 3.t
   STOP
INLET 2                        -- receive result from first
                               -- recursive call

   RECEIVE islot1.i
   POST 5.t
   STOP
INLET 3                        -- receive frame pointer of second
                               -- recursive call

   RECEIVE pfslot2.pf
   POST 4.t
   STOP
INLET 4                        -- receive result from second
                               -- recursive call

   RECEIVE islot2.i
   POST 5.t
   STOP
```

```
THREAD 0                            -- test argument against 2
  LT brego.b = islot0.i 2 i
  SWITCH breg0.b 1.t 2.t
  STOP
THREAD 1                            -- if argument <2, return argument
  MOVE ireg0.i = 1.i
  FORK 6.t                          -- thread 6 returns this value
  STOP
THREAD 2                            -- allocate frames for recursive
                                    -- calls
  MOVE sslot0.s = 2.s               -- set synchronization counter
  FALLOC 1.j = FIB.pc
  FALLOC 3.j = FIB.pc
  STOP
THREAD 3                            -- send n-1 to first recursive call
  SUB ireg0.1 = islot0.1 1. i
  SEND pfslot1.pf[0.i] <-fp.pf 2.j ireg0.i
  STOP
THREAD 4                            -- send n-2 to second recursive call
  SUB ireg0.1 = islot0.1 2. i
  SEND pfslot2.pf[0.i] <-fp.pf 4.j ireg0.i
  STOP
THREAD 5                            -- waits for results from both calls
  SYNC sslot0.s
  ADD ireg0.i = islot1.1 islot2.i-- add the two results
  FORK 6.t
  STOP
THREAD 6                            -- send result to parent
  SEND pfslot0.pf[jslot0.j] <- ireg0.i
  FREE fp.pf
  SWAP                              -- swap to next activation
  STOP
THREAD 7                            -- enter point for this activation
  STOP
THREAD 8                            -- leave this activation
  SWAP
  STOP
```

Here, Thread 0 checks if the argument received is less than 2. If the value is greater than 2, two new Fibonacci activations are allocated (corresponding to the recursive calls). The allocation of frames is performed by Thread 2. It is possible to indicate that the activations be executed on either a local or a remote processor. The arguments n-1 and n-2 for the two recursive calls are computed and sent by Thread 3 and Thread 4, respectively. Thread 5 waits for two results from the spawned activation frames (indicated by the synchronization counter value of 2). The two received values are added, and the result is sent to the parent by Thread 6. If the argument is less than 2, Thread 1 calculates the base value (=1), and Thread 6 returns this value to the parent.

There are four Inlets, two to receive the frame pointers for the recursive calls, and two to receive results from the spawned frames. The synchronization counter of a thread is decremented when either a thread or an inlet "posts" to that thread.

2.2 Cilk

The Cilk [13] language is an extension of C, providing an abstraction of threads in explicit continuation passing[1] style. The Cilk run-time supports "work stealing" for scheduling threads and achieves load balancing across a distributed processing environment. A Cilk program consists of a collection of procedures, each in turn consisting of threads. These threads of a Cilk program can be viewed as the nodes of a directed acyclic graph, as shown in Fig. 2. Each horizontal edge represents the creation of a successor thread, a downward vertical edge represents the creation of child thread, and the curved upward edges represents data dependencies.

Like TAM threads, Cilk threads are non-blocking. This requires the creation of successor threads which receive results from child threads. The successor thread is blocked until the necessary synchronization events (or release conditions) arrive. Cilk threads can spawn child threads to execute a new procedure. The child threads normally return values or synchronize with the successor threads created by their parent thread.

The run-time system keeps track of the active threads and threads awaiting initiation. The data structure used for thread management is called a

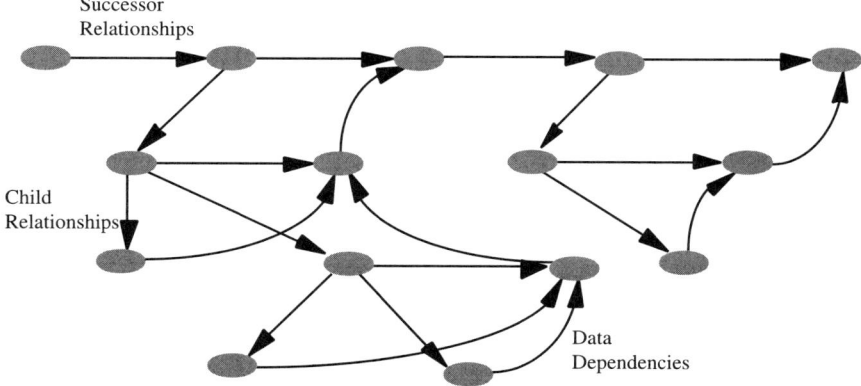

FIG. 2. An example of a Cilk program.

[1] More recent implementations of Cilk (e.g. Cilk 5) have deviated from Continuation Passing style, and chose shared memory for passing arguments.

"Closure." A closure consists of a pointer to the code of the thread, a slot for each of the input parameters for the thread, and a join counter indicating the number of missing values (or synchronization events). The closure (hence the thread) becomes ready to execute when the join counter becomes zero; otherwise the closure is known as waiting. The missing values are provided by other threads using "continuation passing" which identifies the thread closure and the argument position in the thread closure. The following shows a Cilk program segment for computing the Fibonacci numbers.

```
thread fib (cont int k, int n)
{
    if (n<2)
        send_argument (k, n)
    else{
        cont int x, y;
        spawn_next sum (k, ?x, ?y);    /* create a successor thread
        spawn fib (x, n-1);            /* fork a child thread
        spawn fib (y, n-2);            /* fork a child thread
        }
    thread sum (cont int k, int x, int y)
    send_argument (k, x+y);            /* return results to parent's
                                       /* successor
}
```

The program consists of two threads, fib and its successor sum (which waits for the recursive fib calls to complete and provide the necessary values to sum). The fib thread tests the input argument n, and if it is greater than 2 it spawns the successor thread sum by passing the continuation k and the indication that sum requires two inputs x and y before becoming enabled. It also spawns two (recursive) child threads with n-1 and n-2 as their arguments, as well as the slot where they should send their results (specified by the cont parameter). The statement send_argument sends the results to the appropriate continuation. The closures for the above Fibonacci program are shown in Fig. 3. The similarities between the Cilk run-time system and the continuation passing methods used in dynamic dataflow systems should be clear to the reader.

The Cilk run-time system uses an innovative approach to load distribution known as "work stealing." In short, an idle worker randomly selects a heavily loaded processor and steals a portion of its work. Note that only ready to execute threads are stolen, to avoid the complications that could result in locating the continuation slots of the stolen threads.

2.3 Cid

Unlike TAM and Cilk, Cid threads can block waiting for synchronization [37]. Each Cid thread can be viewed as a C function with an appropriate

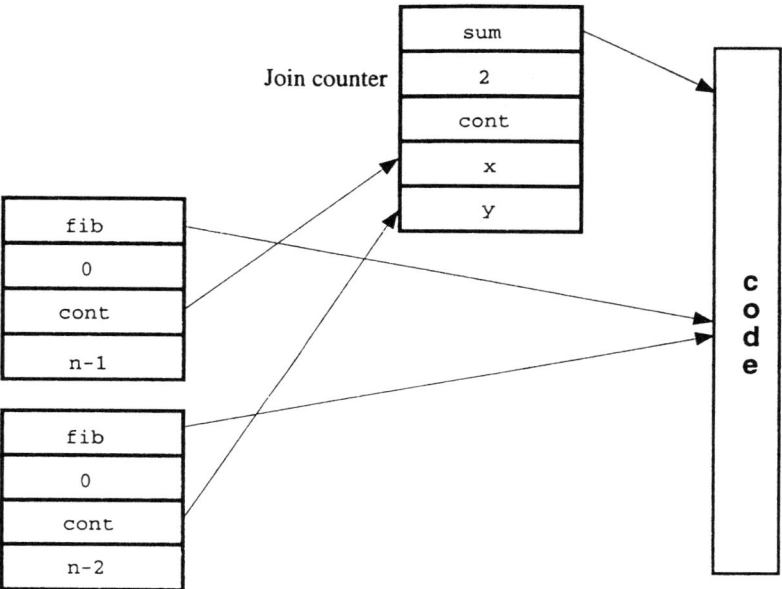

FIG. 3. The closures for the Fibonacci program.

mechanism to specify synchronization. The simplest type of synchronization is based on Join (and join variables). Consider the following Cid implementation of the Fibonacci function.

```
int fib(int n)
{   int fibN1, fibN2;
    cid_initialized_jvar(joinvariable);
        if (N<2) return n
        else
        {   cid_fork(joinvariable;) fibN1=fib(n-1);
                                    fibN2=fib(n-2);
            cid_jwait(&joinvariable);
            return fibN1+fibN2; } }
```

When the value of N is greater than 2, two new threads are forked using cid_fork to compute fib(n-1) and fib(n-2). The cid_fork also indicates that these computations synchronize using join on the joinvariable specified. The parent thread will wait for the completion of the child threads and then returns the sum of fib(n-1) and fib(n-2) and signals appropriate joinvariable. Note that the Cid system is responsible for initializing joinvariable (as indicated by cid_initialized_ jvar).

As can be seen from the description of the various programming models shown above, concurrency using multithreading is becoming prevalent in modern programming languages. Traditional imperative languages support coarse-grained threads, where the thread synchronization is based on locks, rendezvous, or monitors (protected object of Ada-95). Functional and data-driven languages often permit fine-grained and non-blocking threads, using continuation passing and synchronization counters. Thread libraries can be used with languages such as C and C++ to interleave different sections of the program, mimicking concurrency. We feel that the popularity of Java will only increase the interest in multithreading at programming level, and more programming languages will introduce constructs for the creation and management of multithreaded programs.

3. Execution Models

In this section we describe how the underlying system can support multiples threads. We will only concentrate on operating system level or run-time support for threads. Section 4 will discuss architectural level support for multithreading. The notion of threads evolved from a need for an execution model that supports cooperating activities within a process. A thread can be viewed as a unit of execution that is active within a process, sharing certain resources such as files and address space with other threads in the process space. However, each thread is associated with its own execution status. This notion of threads or lightweight processes was originally supported in Mach [15]. The main advantage of such a threaded model is to permit programming applications using "virtual processes," such that a process can continue execution even when one or more of its threads is blocked. Figure 4 illustrates the concept of threads as related to conventional Unix-like processes.

The multithreaded programming model is becoming very common, since most modern operating systems (including DEC Unix, Solaris, Windows 95, Windows NT, and Rhapsody) support threads. In addition, standardized user-level libraries are being provided by numerous vendors. Such packages permit users to create and manage threads. It should be noted that OS threads and user-level thread packages normally support coarse-grained threads that are blocking.

3.1 Design Issues

The execution models for multithreading can be distinguished from several viewpoints: implementation (user-level vs. kernel-level), scheduling (pre-emptive vs. non-preemptive, binding of threads to processors and LWPs) and

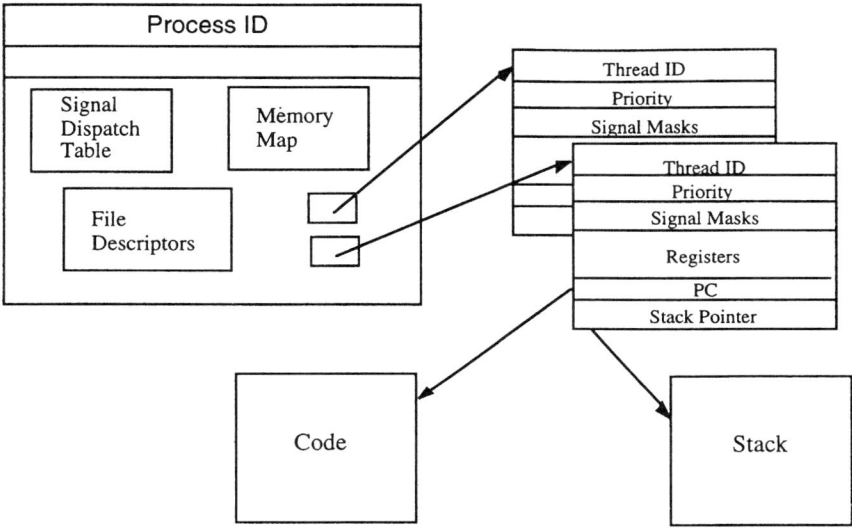

FIG. 4. Processes and threads.

thread management functions (mutual exclusion, barriers, etc.). Threads can be implemented at either the kernel-level or user-level (see Fig. 5). *User-level threads* [11, 23, 26, 44] are created and managed entirely at the user-level, and the kernel has no knowledge of the existence of these threads. Such packages can be implemented on top of any operating system, with or without kernel-level threads. The run-time system will intercept any calls made by user-level threads that could potentially block. The run-time system will not make the system call, but will suspend the thread and schedule a new user thread. The required call is made if it results in no blocking or when there are no runnable user threads. The major advantage of such threads is efficiency

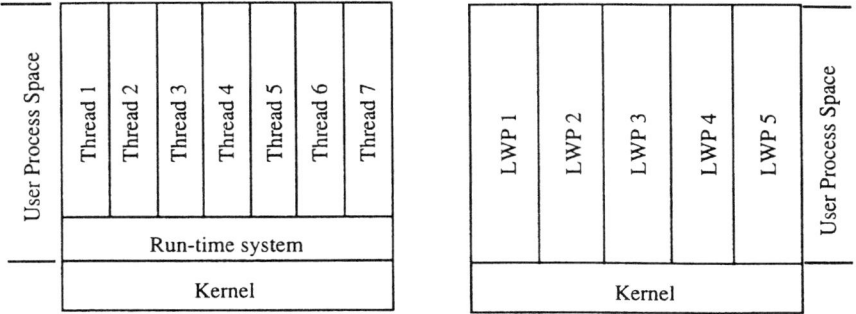

FIG. 5. User-level and kernel-level threads.

in implementing thread functionality. It has been found that user-level thread management functions are as much as two orders of magnitude faster than kernel-level thread management functions. This in turn permits each user-level process to have a larger number of threads, leading to more user-level concurrency. However, since the kernel is unaware of the existence of such threads, when one user-level thread is blocked in the kernel the entire process is blocked, thus nullifying the benefits of multithreading. Other disadvantages include a lack of control for preempting threads, or the ability to directly notify a thread of kernel events.

Kernel-level threads are essentially lightweight processes (LWP) which have the same address space as the "parent" process (see Fig. 4). Hence it is less expensive to create threads than processes, and less expensive to switch between threads than between processes. However, kernel-level thread management functions are more expensive than those for user-level threads. Moreover, since each thread requires some kernel resources, the number of threads that can be supported within a process space is limited. These factors dictate that only coarse-grained concurrency be used to exploit multithreading using kernel-level threads.

More recently, thread packages are becoming available that multiplex several user-level threads onto one or more kernel-level threads (or LWPs), resulting in *hybrid threads*. Each user process can have multiple LWPs, and the run-time system can bind user-level threads to these LWPs. In such systems, scheduling occurs at two levels. The multiplexing of user-level threads onto LWPs is under the control of the run-time system, while the scheduling of LWPs onto physical processors is under the control of the kernel. The hybrid model was originally implemented in Scheduler Activations [5]. When a user-level thread (scheduled on a LWP) is blocked, the kernel notifies (*upcall*) the run-time system and provides sufficient information about the event that caused the block. The run-time system will then schedule another user-level thread (possibly on another LWP). When the blocking event is cleared, the kernel notifies the run-time system, which either schedules the blocked thread or starts a new thread.

Thread implementations can also be distinguished based on the scheduling control given to the user:

- *Non-preemptive scheduling*. In such systems, a thread runs until it is blocked on a resource request or completes its execution, before releasing the processing resources. In some recent implementations, it is possible for a thread to "yield" the processing resources voluntarily. Such non-preemptive scheduling is possible only for user-level thread packages, since the kernel cannot permit runaway threads that do not relinquish their resources. For well-behaved programs this model is very efficient, since very little run-time scheduling is involved. Another advantage of this model is that it reduces the reliance on locks for synchronizing threads, since the running thread knows when it is giving up control of the processor. The reduced use of locks will reduce the overhead due to thread synchronization functions. The major drawback of this model is that, for some CPU-intensive applications, very little performance gain can be obtained using multithreading.

- *Preemptive scheduling.* When threads can be preempted, we can consider various scheduling approaches to dynamically schedule runnable threads, including priority scheduling and time-sliced (round-robin) scheduling. The priority-based scheduling can also be used with the non-preemptive model, where the selection of a new thread to run occurs when the running thread blocks or yields. In most systems, the thread priority is fixed and assigned statically. When time-slicing is used, the running thread is preempted when its time-slice expires, and it awaits its turn in the round-robin queue. Kernel-level threads often permit preemption of running threads on interrupts or when a higher priority thread becomes runnable. In most systems, the kernel attempts to prevent the starvation of lower priority threads by periodically increasing their priority.

Thread packages also differ in how user-level threads can be bound to processing resources. In a many-to-one model, all user-level threads are bound to a single processing resource (or kernel-level LWP). This is the only model feasible when the kernel does not support threads. In a one-to-one model, each user-level thread is bound to a different kernel-level LWP. The many-to-many model is the most flexible, since it allows a different number of user-level threads to be bound to each kernel LWP. Solaris systems support all of the above models, while DEC Unix 3.0 and Win32 threads support a one-to-one model.

In addition to the differences in the design decisions described above, thread implementations differ in the thread management and synchronization functions they provide. Table 1 summarizes the thread functions supported by Pthreads, Win32, and Solaris threads. Java threads are included for completeness sake, even though Java threads are a language feature, and they are either supported using threads provided by the underlying run-time and/or kernel threads, or simulated with interleaved execution of threads.

The multithreaded model of execution is becoming popular with programmers, since user-level thread packages and kernel threads are becoming readily available, along with debugging and analysis tools [16, 31]. A majority of the systems provide reasonable control over the creation and management of threads. They differ in the flexibility of synchronization primitives, control

TABLE 1
COMPARISON OF THREAD IMPLEMENTATIONS

Features	Java	POSIX	Solaris	Win32
User or Kernel level	K	N/A	K and U	K
Cancellation	No	Yes	No	No
Priority scheduling	Yes	Yes	Yes	Yes
Priority inversion	?	Yes	Yes	Yes
Mutex attributes	No	Yes	Yes	No
Shared and private mutexes	Yes	Yes	Yes	No
Thread attributes	No	Yes	Yes	No
Synchronization	Yes	Yes	Yes	Yes
Stack size control	No	Yes	Yes	Yes
Base address control	No	Yes	Yes	No
Detached threads	Yes	Yes	Yes	No
Joinable threads	Yes	Yes	Yes	No
Condition variables	Yes	Yes	Yes	?
Semaphores	Yes	Yes	Yes	Yes
Thread ID comparison	Yes	Yes	Yes	No
Call-once functions	Yes	Yes	Yes	No
Thread suspension	Yes	No	Yes	Yes
Specify concurrency	?	No	Yes	Yes
Reader/writer locking	Yes	No	Yes	No
Processor-specific thread allocation	No	No	No	Yes
Fork all threads	Yes	No	Yes	No
Fork calling thread only	Yes	Yes	Yes	No

K = Kernel-level; U = User-level

Base address control: allows identification of where the thread will reside in physical memory.

Call-once-functions: an ability to limit execution of a particular function/routine only once. Subsequent call will return without execution and error.

Cancellation: killing threads from within the program.

Condition variables: these are similar to mutex variables. A thread waits until another thread signals a condition.

Detached threads do not permit join.

Fork all threads: a flag which forces all thread-creation calls to be forks with shared memory.

Fork calling thread: some systems activate only the thread that is specified in a call.

Joinable threads: the ability to merge threads into a single execution context.

Kernel-level threads: threads that are handled/scheduled by the kernel.

Mutex: mutex exclusion. A mutex can lock a specific section of memory using access flags.

Mutex attributes: allow the user to specify if a mutex can be shared by threads belonging to different processes, and if a mutex holder can inherit the priority of a thread waiting for the mutex.

Priority inversion: high priority threads are forced to wait on low priority threads.

Priority scheduling: programmatically identifying the order of, priority of, or next threads to execute.

Processor-specific thread allocation: the ability to designate a specific thread to a specific processor. Useful for processors that handle special things like interrupts or exclusions.

Reader/writer locking: in Solaris, threads can have one writer and several readers at the same time.

Semaphores: a pair of functions that lock data sets, p() and v() (lock and unlock).

Shared and private mutexes: having separate spaces for mutexes.

Specify concurrency: the ability to identify which threads will be multiprocessed.

Stack size control: the ability to limit, resize or check the thread's stack usage.

Synchronization: ensures that multiple threads coordinate their activities.

Thread: the smallest context of execution.

Thread attributes: allow users to select stack size, scheduling priority, what signals to accept.

Thread ID comparison: some systems permit the comparison of thread IDs so that specific actions can be directed to specific threads.

Thread suspension: temporarily halting execution of a thread.

User-level threads: threads that are handled/scheduled within a single task by special libraries.

over a thread's priority, stack size for a thread, and ability to share the kernel resources across multiple processing units. There are experimental systems currently being developed that permit even greater control over threads. Such systems will allow the microkernel functionality to be customized for a specific application by specifying the actions to be performed in response any thread function. Such systems (e.g. SPIN [12] and Exo Kernel [22]) are beyond the scope of this chapter.

4. Architectural Support for Multithreading

The previous sections discussed multithreading support from a purely software point of view. This section presents the hardware mechanisms used to support multithreading. The hardware support needed for multithreading varies depending on whether thread execution blocks on long latency operation (i.e. blocked scheme) or is interleaved on a cycle-by-cycle basis (interleaved scheme). Both schemes, however, require support for multiple hardware contexts (i.e. states) and context switching, but their implementations differ.

In the blocked scheme, the simplest way to support multiple contexts is to provide a register file with each context. This will reduce the cost of context-switching. However, these register partitions are fixed and inflexible, making them difficult to utilize effectively when the number of registers required per thread varies dynamically. This problem can be alleviated by allowing the contexts to share a large register file, but this is likely to increase the register file access time.

Once multiple threads exist in the processor, it must decide when to context-switch. A context-switch can occur when there is a cache miss. This will require additional logic to signal cache misses. A processor will probably not context-switch on an L1 cache miss, since the latency to fetch the cache line from L2 cache is small. Whether to context-switch on an L2 cache will depend on the cost of context-switching, the thread run-length, and the latency of an L2 cache miss. The context-switching cost depends on how much support is provided in the hardware, while thread run-length depends on the miss rate. Latency of L2 cache misses depends on the organization of a node. A single processor node will have lower latency than a node in an SMP. Finally, context-switching will be necessary for misses on local memory that require requests to be sent to a remote node.

Once the need to context-switch is detected, a number of possibilities exist for scheduling the next available thread. A simple technique that can be used is to select the next thread using round-robin scheduling. This can be implemented by a bit vector with warp-around indicating which threads are ready to be scheduled. Having selected the next thread to schedule, a context-switch is performed by saving the PC of the first uncompleted instruction from the current thread, squashing all the incomplete instructions from the pipeline, saving the control/status registers from the current thread, switching the control to the register file for the new context, restoring the control/status registers from the new thread, and starting execution of instructions from the PC of the new thread.

5. Example Multithreaded Systems

Multithreading is desired when the performance of a parallel machine suffers from the latencies involved in the communication and synchronization. Multithreaded architectures provide various software and hardware features in order to support multithreading, including lightweight synchronization, fast context-switching mechanisms, effective and intelligent management of threads, efficient communication mechanisms, and a shared-memory model for ease of programming. This section provides an overview of various multithreaded architectures and discusses some of the software and hardware features that represent the past and the current research efforts in the multithreading community. The architectures included in the discussion are Tera [4], MIT's StarT project [6, 18, 36], Electrotechnical Lab's EM-X [32, 39], MIT's Alewife [3], M-Machine [25], and Simultaneous Multithreading [48, 49].

5.1 Tera MTA

The Tera MTA (MultiThreaded Architecture) computer is a multistream MIMD system developed by Tera Computer Company [4]. It is the only commercially available multithreaded architecture available in 1997. The designers of the system tried to achieve the following three goals: (1) provide a high-speed, highly-scalable architecture, (2) be applicable to a wide variety of problems, including numeric and non-numeric problems, and (3) ease the compiler implementation.

The interconnection network of Tera is composed of pipelined packet-switching nodes in a three-dimensional mesh with a wrap-around. Each link is capable of transmitting a packet containing source and destination addresses, an operation, and 64-bit data in both directions simultaneously on every clock cycle. For example, a 256 processor system consists of 4096 switching nodes arranged in $16 \times 16 \times 16$ toroidal mesh, among which 1280 nodes are attached to 256 processors, 512 data memory units, 256 I/O cache units, and 256 I/O processors as shown in Fig. 6. In general, the number of

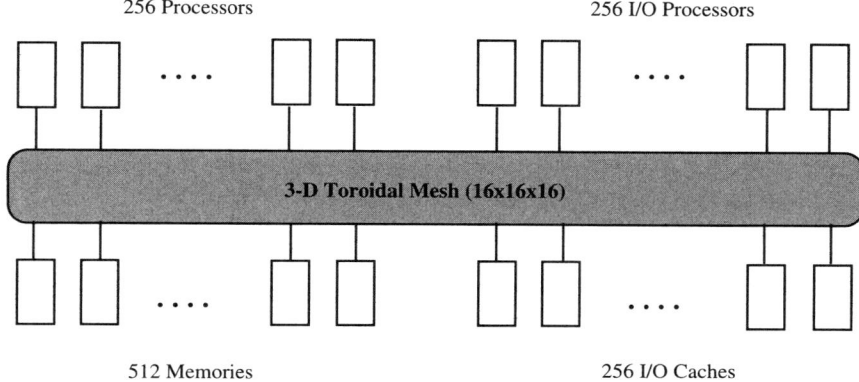

FIG. 6. The organization of Tera MTA.

network nodes grows as a function of $p^{3/2}$, where p is the number of processors in the system.

Each processor in Tera can simultaneously execute multiple instruction streams from one to as many as 128 active program counters. On every clock cycle, the processor logic selects an instruction stream that is ready to execute and a new instruction from a different stream may be issued in each cycle without interfering with the previous instruction. Each instruction stream maintains the following information: one 64-bit Stream Status Word (SSW), 32 64-bit General Purpose Registers (R0-R31), and eight 64-bit Target Registers (T0-T7). Thus, each processor maintains 128 SSWs, 4096 General Purpose Registers, and 1024 Target Registers, facilitating context-switching on every clock cycle. Program addresses are 32 bits long, and the program counter is located in the lower half of the SSW. The upper half is used to specify the various modes (e.g. floating-point rounding), a trap mask, and four recently generated condition statuses. Target Registers are used for branch targets, and the computation of a branch address and the prediction of a branch are separated, allowing the prefetching of target instructions. A Tera instruction typically specifies three operations: a memory reference operation, an arithmetic operation, and a control operation. The control operation can also be another arithmetic operation. Thus, if the third operation specifies an arithmetic operation, it will perform a memory and two arithmetic operations per cycle.

Each processor needs to execute on average about 70 instructions to maintain peak performance by hiding remote latencies (i.e. the average latency for remote access is about 70 cycles). However, if each instruction stream can execute some of its instructions in parallel (e.g. two successive loads), fewer than 70 streams are required to achieve peak performance. To reduce the required number of streams, the Tera architecture introduced a new technique called *explicit-dependence lookahead* to utilize instruction-level parallelism. The idea is that each instruction contains a three-bit lookahead field that explicitly specifies how many instructions from this stream will be issued before encountering an instruction that depends on the current instruction. Since seven is the maximum possible lookahead value with three bits, at most eight instructions can be executed concurrently from each stream. Thus, in the best case only nine streams are needed to hide 72 clock cycles of latency, compared with 70 different streams required for the worst case.

A full-size Tera system contains 512 128-Mbyte data memory units. Memory is 64-bit wide and byte-addressable. Associated with each word are four additional *access state bits* consisting of two data trap bits, a forward bit, and a full/empty bit. The trap bit allows application-specific use of data breakpoints, demand-driven evaluation, run-time exception handling, implementation of active memory objects, stack limit checking, etc. The forward bit implements invisible indirect addressing, where the value found in the location is interpreted as a pointer to the target of the memory reference rather than as the target itself. The full/empty bit is used for lightweight synchronization. Load and store operations use the full/empty bit to define three different synchronization modes along with the access control bits defined in the memory word. The values for access control for each operation are shown in Table 2.

For example, if the value of the access control field is 2, LOAD and STORE operations wait until the memory location is full (i.e. written) before proceeding. When a memory access fails, it is placed in a retry queue and the memory unit retries the operation several times before the stream that issued the memory operation results in a trap. Retry requests are interleaved with new memory requests to avoid the saturation of the communication links with the requests that recently failed.

5.2 StarT

The StarT project attempts to develop general-purpose scalable parallel systems while using commodity components. StarT-NG (Next Generation) is

TABLE 2

Value	Load	Store
0	Read regardless	Write regardless and set full
1	Not used	Not used
2	Wait until full and then read	Wait until full and then write
3	Read only when full and then set empty	Write only when empty and then set full

the first effort at developing such a system [6]. Based on a commercial PowerPC 620, a 64-bit, 4-way superscalar processor with a dedicated 128-bit wide L2 cache interface and a 128-bit wide L3 path to memory, StarT-NG is a SMP system that supports user-level messaging and globally-shared cache coherent memory.

StarT-NG has four processor card slots, where one to four slots are filled with Network-Endpoint-Subsystem (NES) cards. Each NES contains a single PowerPC 620 processor with 4 Mbyte of L2 cache and a Network Interface Unit (NIU), as depicted in Fig. 7. Each site has an Address Capture Device (ACD) on the NES board, which is responsible for bus transactions. When an access to global shared-memory is necessary, one of the processors is dedicated to servicing the ACD and is called a service processor (sP). On the other hand, when a processor is used for running an application, the processor is called an application processor (aP).

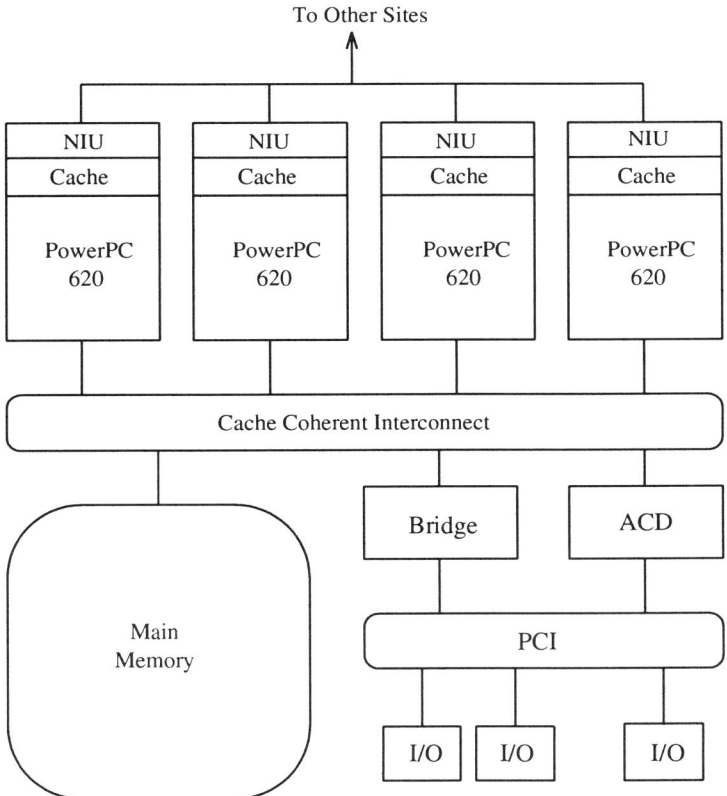

FIG. 7. A site structure of StarT-NG.

StarT-NG is built on a *fat-tree* network using MIT's Arctic routers connected to NIU [14]. The NIU's packet buffers are memory-mapped into an application's address space enabling users to send and receive messages without kernel intervention. The arrival of a message can be signaled either by polling or interrupt. Generally, PowerPC 620 polls the NIU by reading a specified location of the packet buffer, resulting in lower overhead. An interrupt mechanism can also be used either for a kernel message or a user message when the frequency of the message arrival is estimated to be low, to minimize the overhead of polling. The dual-ported buffer space of NIU is divided into four regions, allowing receiving and transmitting of messages with both high- and low-level priorities.

Cache-coherent distributed shared-memory in StarT-NG is implemented in software by programming the ACD and sP. This allows the designers of StarT-NG to experiment with various cache-coherence protocols, such as cache-only memory architecture.

Influenced by its predecessor *T [36], multithreading in StarT-NG relies heavily on software support. The instruction `fork` creates a thread by pushing a continuation specified in registers onto a continuation stack. For thread switching, the compiler is required to generate `switch` (branch) instructions in the instruction stream. Also, the compiler needs to generate the necessary save/restore instructions to swap the relevant register values from the continuation stack, resulting in a large context-switching cost. StarT-NG examines how the multithreaded codes can run on a stock processor and emphasizes the importance of cache-coherent global shared-memory supported by efficient message-passing.

StarT-Voyager, which replaces StarT-NG, is based on dual-PowerPC 604 SMP system [7]. Each SMP uses a typical PC/workstation class motherboard with two processor cards, but one of the processor cards is replaced with an NES card. Each NES card is then attached to the Arctic network to facilitate a scalable architecture. The NES has been programmed to support S-COMA coherent shared memory that allows local DRAM to act as a cache for global data. A two-node StarT-Jr system [29], consisting of Pentium Pro processors connected by a network interface attached to their PCI buses, was demonstrated at Fall Comdex95 in Las Vegas. StarT-Jr provides much of the same functionality of StarT-Voyager at a lower development cost and lower performance. A four-node StarT-Voyager system is expected to be completed in 1998.

5.3 EM-X

The EM-X parallel computer, which is a successor to the EM-4 architecture [40], is being built at Electrotechnical Laboratory in Japan [32, 39]. The

EM-X architecture is based on the dataflow model, which integrates the communication pipeline into the execution pipeline by using small and simple packets. Sending and receiving of packets do not interfere with the thread execution. Threads are invoked by the arrival of the packets from the network or by matching two packets. When a thread suspends, a packet on the input queue initiates the next thread. EM-X also supports direct matching for synchronization of threads, and the matching is performed prior to the buffering of the matching packets. Therefore, one clock cycle is needed for pre-matching of two packets, but the overhead is hidden by executing other threads simultaneously.

The EM-X consist of EMC-Y nodes interconnected by a circular Omega Network with a virtual cut through routing scheme. The structure of its single-chip processor EMC-Y is depicted in Fig. 8. The Switching Unit is a 3-by-3 crossbar connecting the input and output of the network and the processor. Packets arriving at a processor are received in the Input Buffer Unit (IBU). The IBU has an on-chip packet buffer which holds a maximum of eight packets. When the on-chip buffer overflows, packets are stored in data memory, and brought back to on-chip buffers when space becomes available.

EM-X implements a flexible packet scheduling by maintaining two separate priority buffers. Packets in the high-priority buffer are transferred to the Matching Unit (MU), and the low-priority packets are transferred to MU

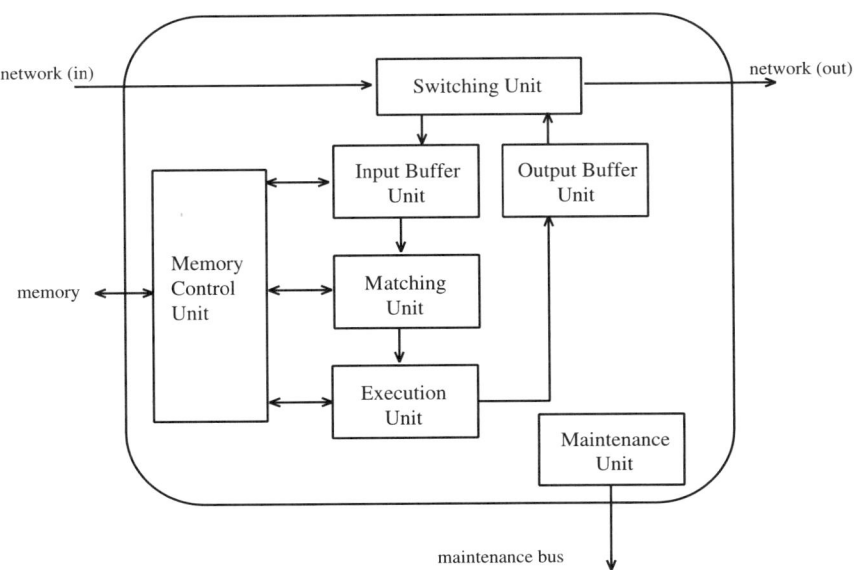

FIG. 8. The structure of EMC-Y.

only when the high-priority buffer is empty. The MU prepares the invocation of a thread by using the direct matching scheme [32]. This is done by first extracting the base address of the operand segment from the incoming packet. The operand segment is basically an activation frame which is shared among threads in a function and holds the matching memory and local variables. Next, the partner data is loaded from the matching memory specified in the packet address, and the corresponding presence flag is cleared. Then, a template (i.e. a code frame) is fetched from the top of the operand segment, and the first instruction of the enabled thread is executed on the Execution Unit (EXU). The EXU is a RISC-based thread execution unit with 32 registers. The EXU provides four SEND instructions for invoking a thread, accessing remote memory, returning the result after the thread execution, and implementing variable size operand segments or a block access of remote memory [32].

EM-X performs remote memory access by invoking packet handlers at the destination processor, and the packets are entirely serviced by hardware which does not disrupt the thread execution in the execution pipeline. The round trip distances of the Omega Network in EM-X are 0, 5, 10, and 15 hops for request/reply sequences, with an average of 10.13 hops requiring less than 1 μs on an unloaded network. On a loaded network, the latency is 2.5 μs on average, with random communication of 100 Mpackets/s.

5.4 Alewife

MIT's Alewife machine improves scalability and programmability of modern parallel systems by providing software-extended coherent cache, global memory space, integrated message-passing, and support for fine-grained computation. Underneath Alewife's abstraction of globally shared memory, each PE has a physically distributed memory managed by a Communication and Memory Management Unit (CMMU). This memory hardware manages the locality by caching both private and shared data on each node. A scalable software-extended scheme called LimitLESS maintains the cache coherence [17]. The LimitLESS scheme implements a full-map directory protocol which can support up to five read requests per memory line directly in hardware and by trapping into software for more widely-shared data.

Some of the ideas on cache coherency based on directory protocol have their roots in Stanford DASH and FLASH systems [38, 33].

Each Alewife node, shown in Fig. 9, consists of a Sparcle processor, 64 Kbyte of direct-mapped cache, 4 Mbyte of data and 2 Mbyte of directory, 2 Mbyte of private unshared memory, a floating-point unit, and a mesh routing chip. The nodes communicate via a two-dimensional mesh network using a wormhole routing technique.

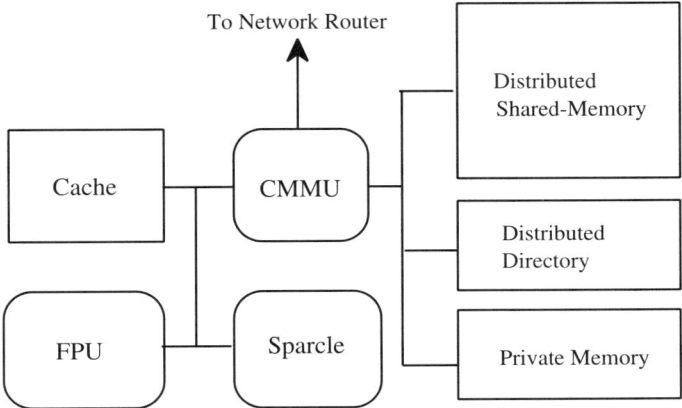

FIG. 9. The organization of an Alewife node.

Sparcle is a modified SPARC processor that facilitates block multithreading, fine-grained synchronization, and rapid messaging. The register windows of SPARC are modified to represent four independent contexts in Sparcle: one for trap handlers and the other three for user threads. A context-switch is initiated when the CMMU detects a remote memory access and causes a synchronous memory fault to Sparcle. The context-switching is implemented by a short trap handler that saves the old program counter and status register, switches to a new thread by restoring a new program counter and status register, then returns from the trap to begin execution in the new context. Currently the context-switching takes 14 clock cycles, but it is expected to be reduced to four clock cycles.

Sparcle also provides new instructions that manipulates the full/empty bits in memory for data-level synchronization [2]. For example, `ldt` (read location if full, else trap) and `stt` (write location if empty, else trap) instructions can be used to synchronize on an element-by-element basis. When a trap occurs due to a synchronization failure, the trap handler software decides what must be done next.

Fast message handling is implemented via special instructions and a memory-mapped interface to the interconnection network. To send messages, Sparcle first writes a message to the interconnection network queue using the `stio` instruction, and then the `ipilaunch` instruction is used to launch the message into the network. A message contains the message opcode, the destination node address, and data values (e.g. content of a register or address and a length pair which invokes DMA on blocks from memory). The arrival of a message invokes a trap handler that loads the incoming message into registers using an **ldio** instruction or initiates a DMA sequence to store the message into memory.

5.5 M-Machine

The M-Machine is an experimental multicomputer being developed by MIT. The M-Machine efficiently exploits increased circuit density by devoting more chip area to the processor. It is claimed that a 32-node M-Machine system with 256 Mbyte of memory has 128 times the peak performance of a uniprocessor with the same memory capacity at 1.5 times the area, an 85-fold improvement in peak performance/area [25]. The M-Machine consists of a collection of computing nodes interconnected by a bidirectional 3D mesh network. Each node consists of a multi-ALU processor (MAP) and 8 Mbyte of synchronous DRAM. A MAP contains four execution clusters, four cache banks, a network interface, and a router. Each of the four MAP clusters is a 64-bit, three-way issue, pipelined processor consisting of a Memory Unit, an Integer Unit, and a Floating-Point Unit as shown in Fig. 10. The Memory Unit is used for interfacing to the memory and the cluster switch (C-Switch). The cache is organized as four word-interleaved 32-kbyte banks to permit four

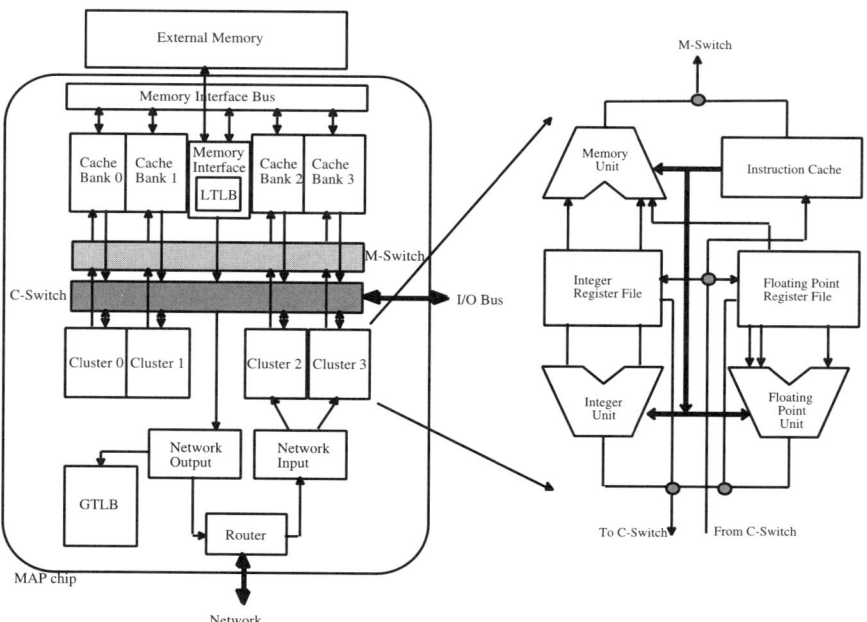

FIG. 10. The MAP architecture and its four clusters.

consecutive accesses. Each word has a synchronization bit which is manipulated by special load and store operations for atomic read–modify–write operations.

The M-Machine supports a single global virtual address space through a global translation lookaside buffer (GTLB). GTLB is used to translate a virtual address into a physical node identifier in the message. Messages are composed in the general registers of a cluster and launched automatically using user-level send instructions. Arriving messages are queued in a register-mapped FIFO, and a system-level message handler performs the requested operations specified in the message.

Each MAP instruction contains one to three operations and may execute out-of-order. The M-Machine exploits instruction-level parallelism by running up to 12 parallel instruction sequences (called H-Threads) concurrently. In addition, MAP interleaves the 12-wide instruction streams (called V-Threads) from different threads of computation to exploit thread-level parallelism and to mask various latencies that occur in the pipeline (i.e. during memory accesses and communication). Six V-Threads are resident in a cluster, and each V-Thread consists of four H-Threads. Each V-Thread consists of a sequence of 3-wide instructions containing an integer, a memory, and a floating-point operation. Within an H-Thread, instructions are issued in order but may complete out of order. Synchronization and communication among H-Threads in the same V-Thread are done using a scoreboard bit associated with each register. However, H-Threads in different V-Threads may only communicate and synchronize through memory and messages.

5.6 Simultaneous Multithreading

Simultaneous multithreading (SMT) is a technique that allows multiple independent threads from different programs to issue multiple instructions to a superscalar processor's functional units. Therefore, SMT combines the multiple instruction-issue features of modern superscalar processors with the latency-hiding ability of multithreaded architectures, alleviating the problems of long latencies and limited per-thread parallelism. This means that the SMT model can be realized without extensive changes to a conventional superscalar processor architecture [45, 46, 48, 49].

Figure 11 shows the hardware organization of an 8-thread simultaneous multithreading machine proposed in [48, 49]. The processor execution stage is composed of three Floating-Point Units and six Integer Units. Therefore the peak instruction bandwidth is nine. However, the throughput of the machine is bounded to eight instructions per cycle owing to the bandwidth of the Fetch and Decode Units. Each Integer and Floating-Point Instruction Queue (IQ) holds 32 entries, and the caches are multiported and interleaved. In addition,

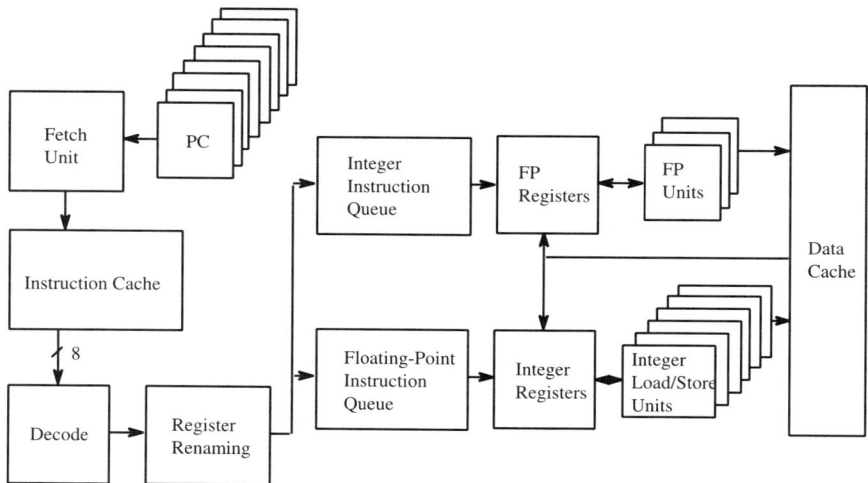

FIG. 11. A basic simultaneous multithreading hardware architecture.

an 8-thread SMT machine has 256 physical registers (i.e. 32 registers per thread) and 100 additional registers for register renaming.

The throughput of the basic SMT system is 2% less than a superscalar with similar hardware resources when running on a single thread, because of the need for longer pipelines to accommodate a large register file. However, its estimated peak throughput with multiple threads is 84% higher than that of a superscalar processor. Also, the system throughput peaks at four instructions per cycle, even with eight threads. This early saturation is caused by three factors: (1) small IQ size, (2) limited fetch throughput (only 4.2 useful instructions are fetched per cycle), and (3) lack of instruction-level parallelism. However, the performance of simultaneous multithreading hardware can be improved by modifying the Fetch Unit and Instruction Queues. The fetch throughput can be improved by optimizing fetch efficiency (i.e. partitioning the Fetch Unit among threads), fetch effectiveness (i.e. selective instruction fetch or fetch policies), and fetch availability (i.e. eliminating conditions that block the fetch unit).

It has been shown that the best performance is obtained when the Fetch Unit is partitioned in such a way that eight instructions are fetched from two threads, and the priority is given to the threads with the smaller number of instructions in the decode stage [49]. Fetch misses can be reduced by examining the I-cache tag one cycle earlier, and then selecting only threads that cause no cache miss. However, this scheme requires extra ports on the I-cache tags and increases misfetch penalties, owing to an additional pipeline stage needed for early tag lookup. The resulting performance shows a factor of 2.5

throughput gain over a conventional superscalar architecture when running at 8 threads, yielding 5.4 instructions per cycle. These experiments lead to the following observations:

- Techniques such as dynamic scheduling and speculative execution in a superscalar processor are not sufficient to take full advantage of a wide-issue processor without simultaneous multithreading.
- Instruction scheduling in SMT is no more complex than that of a dynamically scheduled superscalar processor.
- Register file data paths in SMT are no more complex than those in a superscalar processor, and the performance implication for the register file and its longer pipeline is small.
- The required instruction fetch throughput is attainable, without increasing the fetch bandwidth, by partitioning the Fetch Unit and intelligent instruction selection to fetch.

6. Performance Models

Whether we deal with finely multithreaded or coarsely multithreaded architectures, there are limitations to the improvements in processor utilization that can be achieved. The most important limitation is that applications running on a multithreaded system may not exhibit sufficiently large degrees of parallelism to permit the identification and scheduling of multiple threads on each processor. Even if sufficient parallelism exists, the cost of multithreading should be traded off against any loss of performance due to active threads sharing the cache and processor cycles wasted during context switches. In this section we will outline analytical models that can be used to describe these competing aspects of multithreaded systems.

In the simplest case, we assume that the processor switches between threads only on long latency operations, such as remote memory accesses. Let L denote a fixed latency for such operations. Let R be the average amount of time that each thread executes before encountering a long latency operation. Let C be the (fixed) overhead in switching between threads. Consider the case when there is only one thread. The processor utilization can be described by

$$U_1 = \frac{R}{R+L} \qquad (1)$$

The utilization is limited by the frequency of long latency operations, $\rho = 1/R$, and the average time required to service the long latency operation L.

If L is much larger than C, the time to switch between threads, then useful work can be performed during the latency operations. In addition, if the number of threads is sufficiently large, long latency operations can be completely hidden. In such a case, the processor utilization can be described as

$$U_{N_{SAT}} = \frac{R}{R+C} \qquad (2)$$

where N_{SAT} is the number of threads required to totally mask L. Note that increasing the number of threads beyond N_{SAT} will not increase the processor utilization. We will denote this as the saturation number of threads, which satisfies:

$$N_{SAT} \geq \frac{R+L}{R+C} \qquad (3)$$

If there is an insufficient number of threads to totally mask the latency L, the processor utilization can be described by

$$U_N = \frac{NR}{R+L} \qquad (4)$$

Note that the overhead of switching among thread does not appear in the above equation since this time would have been idle (or wasted) in a single-threaded system.

Using the above equations, the speedup that can be achieved is given by

$$S_N = \frac{U_N}{U_1} = \begin{cases} N & \text{if } N < N_{SAT} \\ \dfrac{R+L}{R+C} & \text{otherwise} \end{cases} \qquad (5)$$

As shown in (5), the minimum number of threads needed to achieve maximum utilization, $N_{SAT} \geq (R+L)/(R+C)$, depends on time between thread switches (R), the time to service long latency operation (L), and the thread-switching overhead (C). For example, a fine-grained multithreaded system, $R = 1$, with negligible thread-switching overhead (e.g. using multiple hardware contexts) requires at least $(1 + L)$ threads to achieve optimum utilization. When C is not negligible, R should be much larger (i.e. coarser-grain multithreading) to achieve useful performance gains using multithreaded systems.

The above model ignores the performance impact due to higher cache miss rates in a multithreaded system and higher demands on the network placed by higher processor utilization. In addition, the above model assumed fixed latencies, and fixed frequency of long latency operations in threads. If we assume that a thread switch occurs on every cache miss, then we can equate cache miss rate m with the frequency of long latency operations, $\rho = 1/R$.

Realistically, a thread switch occurs only on non-local cache misses. The speedup of a multithreaded system can be rewritten as

$$S_N = \frac{U_N}{U_1} = \begin{cases} N & \text{if } N < N_{SAT} \\ \dfrac{1+mL}{1+mC} & \text{otherwise} \end{cases} \quad (6)$$

The cache miss penalty is the primary contributor to L. Note that we assume a constant cache miss rate and miss penalty in the above equation. The effect of thread-switching on other long latency operations such as synchronization delays can also be added to the above equation.

In deriving (6), we have assumed that the cache miss rate and miss penalties are not affected by multithreading. However, the cache miss rate is negatively affected by increasing the degree of multithreading. Likewise, the miss penalty increases with the number of threads, owing to higher network utilization (leading to longer delays in accessing remote memory modules).

Let us consider the impact of multiple threads on network delays (or miss penalties). The average rate of network requests by a single thread is equal to the miss rate $m = 1/R$. As the number of threads is increased, the rate of requests is increased proportionately to mN, until N becomes equal to N_{SAT}. Using a simple M/M/1 model for network delays, we can compute the average response time from the network as $T = (\mu - \lambda_N)^{-1}$, where μ is the service time and λ_N is the rate of arrivals. Assuming a Poisson distribution for the cache misses, we obtain $T = (\mu - mN)^{-1}$.

Note that the above derivation must be modified to account for the non-Poisson process that underlies cache misses. Network service time must reflect the topology, bandwidth, and routing algorithms of specific networks. For example, in [1] the miss penalties due to multiple threads assuming a k-ary n-dimensional cube network was computed. This analysis shows that network delays increase almost linearly with the number of threads, which is given as

$$T = \frac{T_0}{2} + \frac{BNk}{6} - \frac{1}{2m} + \frac{1}{2}\left[\left(T_0 - \frac{BNk}{3} + \frac{1}{m}\right)^2 + 8NB^2 n \frac{k}{3}\left(1 - \frac{3}{k}\right)\right]^{1/2} \quad (7)$$

where N represents the memory access time, B is the message size, n is the network dimension, k is the radix of the network radix, and T_0 represents the network delay without contention, i.e. $T_0 = 2nk_d + N + B - 1$, where k_d represents the average number of hops that a message travels in each dimension.

In order to compute the impact of multiple threads on cache miss rates, let us review the behavior of cache memories. It has been shown that the components of cache misses can be classified as *nonstationary, intrinsic-interference, multiprogramming-related,* and *coherency-related invalidations*. Nonstationary misses, m_{ns}, are due to "cold start" misses that bring blocks into the cache for the first time. Intrinsic-interference misses, m_{intr}, result from misses caused by conflicts among cache blocks of a working set that compete for the same cache set. Multiprogramming-related misses account for the cases when one thread displaces the cache blocks of another thread. Coherency related invalidation, m_{inv}, occurs in multiprocessor systems where the changes made in one processor may require invalidation of other processor cache entries.

Increasing the degree of multithreading will affect both the intrinsic-interference and multiprogramming components of cache misses. When more threads occupy the cache, we can assume that each thread is allocated a smaller working set, and this in turn leads to higher intrinsic conflicts. Likewise, as the number of threads is increased, the multiprogramming-related component also increases, since there is a higher probability that the cache blocks of active threads will displace those of inactive threads. The miss rate in the presence of N threads is derived by Agarwal [1], which is given as.

$$m(N) \approx m_{fixed} + m_{intr} + m_{intr}(N-1)\left(1 + \frac{1}{c}\right) \qquad (8)$$

where c represents the collision rate and m_{intr} is a function of c, working set u, the time interval used to measure the working set τ, and the number of cache sets S, i.e.

$$m_{intr} \approx \frac{c\ u^2}{\tau\ S}$$

It is interesting to note that, with sufficiently large cache memories, the multiprogramming-related component of the cache miss rate is not affected by the number of threads. This is because the cache memory is large enough to hold the working sets of all resident threads. The number of threads proportionately increases the intrinsic-interference component of cache misses. Set associativity is another issue that significantly affects the performance of cache memories for multithreaded systems; higher associativities can compensate for the increased intrinsic interference in a multithreaded system. The collision rate parameter used in deriving cache miss rates by Agarwal [1] must be described as a function of set associativity. Alternatively, set associativity can be modeled by treating the cache memory as several smaller direct-mapped caches, each allocated to a different thread. This is the case when instructions from different threads are interleaved to achieve higher pipeline utilizations.

7. Conclusions and Prognostication

The past couple of decades have seen tremendous progress in the technology of computing devices, both in terms of functionality and performance. It is predicted that over the next five years, it will be possible to fabricate processors containing billions of transistor circuits operating at gigahertz speeds [21]. While there has been continuing growth in the density of DRAM memory chips, improvements in the access times and I/O bandwidth of memory parts have not kept pace with processor clock rates. This has widened the relative performance of processors and memory. The memory latency problem is further compounded by the complex memory hierarchies which need to be traversed between processors and main memory. Multithreading is becoming increasingly popular as a technique for tolerating memory latency. It requires concurrency and complicated processors. However, it offers the advantage of being able to exploit MIMD concurrency as well as interleaving multiple users so as to maximize system throughput.

In this chapter we have introduced the multithreaded paradigm as supported in programming languages, run-time systems, OS kernels, and processor architectures. We have also presented simple analytical models that can be used to investigate the limits of multithreaded systems. Without adequate hardware support, such as multiple hardware contexts, fast context-switching, non-blocking caches, out-of-order instruction issue and completion, and register renaming, we will not be able to take full advantage of the multithreading model of computation. As the feature size of logic devices reduces, we feel that the silicon area can be put to better use by providing support for multithreading. The addition of more cache memory (or more levels of cache) will result in only insignificant and diminishing performance improvements. The addition of more pipelines (as in superscalar) will only prove effective with multithreading model of execution.

Hardware support alone is not sufficient to exploit the benefits of multithreading. We believe that the performance benefits of multithreading can only be realized when the paradigm is applied across all levels: from applications programming to hardware implementations. Fortunately, a number of research projects are under way for designing multithreaded systems that include new architectures, new programming languages, new compiling techniques, more efficient interprocessor communication, and customized microkernels.

New programming languages supporting both fine-grained and coarse-grained multithreaded concurrency are becoming available. Unless applications are programmed using these languages, the exploitable parallelism (in single-threaded applications) will be very limited. New compile-time analysis and optimization approaches must be discovered to map user-level concurrency onto processor-level threads. For example, it may be necessary to rethink register usages: it may be worthwhile loading multiple registers (belonging to different threads) with the same value, thus eliminating unnecessary data dependencies. It may be necessary to use speculative execution aggressively, and to mix instructions from unrelated threads to increase thread run-lengths.

While some of the research projects described in this paper have produced improvements over single-threaded abstractions, in a majority of cases they have shown only small or incremental improvements in performance. One of the issues often ignored by multithreaded systems is the performance degradation of single-threaded applications due to increased hardware data paths. Recently, numerous alternative approaches to tolerating memory latencies have been proposed, including datascalar [10], multiscalar [43], and preload/prefetch techniques [8, 20, 24]. There has been a proposal for moving the processor onto DRAM chips to reduce the latency [41]. It is our belief that the multithreaded model of execution should be combined with some of these approaches proposed for sequential (single-threaded) execution systems. For example, preloading can be adapted to multithreaded systems. The success of multithreading as a viable computational model depends on the integration of these efforts.

ACKNOWLEDGMENTS

This research was supported in part by grants from NSF, MIP-9622593 and MIP-9622836.

GLOSSARY

Barrier: synchronizes concurrent threads (or processes) residing on different processors. Threads are not allowed to proceed beyond the barrier until the synchronization process is completed. A barrier can be implemented by mutual exclusion that keeps track of the number of processes reaching the barrier.

Cache coherency: refers to the state in a multiprocessor system in which all copies of common data within the caches are the same. Multiprocessors implement protocols to ensure cache coherency.

Context: the state of the processor during execution of a thread, which is represented by a register file, a condition register, and a stack pointer.

Context switching: involves switching from the currently running context (i.e. a thread) to another. In software, this process requires saving the state of the current thread, scheduling a new thread, restoring the state of the new thread, and starting instruction execution from the new thread. In hardware, the process simply involves switching to the next ready register bank and executing instructions from the new hardware context.

Distributed shared memory (DSM) systems: unlike SMPs, DSM systems have physically distributed main memory. The processors in a DSM systems are interconnected by a network, such as a mesh or a hypercube, and shared-memory abstraction is provided by software. Due to the structure of their interconnect, DSM systems are scalable.

L1 and L2 caches: modern microprocessors have an on-chip L1 cache and an off-chip L2 cache. Misses on the L2 cache require access to the main memory subsystem.

Memory latency: the number of processor clock cycles required to access memory. Memory latency increases as the gap between processor cycle time and memory access time becomes wider.

Multiple contexts: can be implemented in software or hardware. Software implementation involves keeping a Thread Descriptor (TD) with each thread. Each TD contains the state of the processor and signal handling information. Hardware implementation usually involves keeping multiple register banks, each register bank assigned to a thread.

Mutual exclusion: allows only one thread (or process) to enter a section of a code, called the critical section, which modifies a shared variable. Mutually exclusive access to shared variables can be accomplished by using locks, semaphores, monitors, etc.

Symmetric multiprocessors (SMPs): refers to a system where multiple processors are interconnected by a shared-bus. The shared-bus is located between the processor's private caches and the shared main memory subsystem. Due to contention for the shared-bus, SMPs are not scalable.

REFERENCES

1. Agarwal, A. (1992) Performance tradeoffs in multithreaded processors. *IEEE Transactions on Parallel and Distributed Systems* **3**, 525–539.
2. Agarwal, A., Kubiatowicz, J., Kranz, D., Lim, B.-H., Yeung, D., D'Souza, G., and Parkin, M. (1993) Sparcle: an evolutionary processor design for large-scale multiprocessors. *IEEE Micro* June, pp. 48–61.
3. Agarwal, A., Bianchini, R., Chaiken, D., Johnson, K. L., Kranz, D., Kubiatowicz, J., Lim, B.-H., Mackenzie, K., and Yeung, D. (1995) The MIT Alewife machine: architecture and performance. *Proc. of the 22nd International Symposium on Computer Architecture*. Sanata Margherita Ligure, Italy. pp. 2–13.
4. Alverson, R., Callahan, D., Cummings, D., Koblenz, B., Porterfield, A., and Smith, B. (1990) The Tera computer system. *International Conference on Supercomputing*. Amsterdam, The Netherlands. pp. 1–6.
5. Anderson, T. E., Bershad, B. N., Lazowska, E. D., and Levy, H. M. (1992) Schedular activations: effective kernel support for the user-level management of parallelism. *ACM Transactions on Computer Systems*. Feb., pp. 53–79.
6. Ang, B. S., Arvind, and Chiou, D. (1992) StartT the Next Generation: integrating global caches and dataflow architecture. *Proc. of the 19th International Symposium on Computer Architecture*. Gold Coast, Australia. Dataflow workshop.

7. Ang, B. S., Chiou, D., Rudolph, L., and Arvind (1996) *Message Passing Support in StarT-Voyager*. MIT Laboratory for Computer Science, CSG Memo 387, July.
8. Baer, J.-L., and Chen, T. (1991) An effective on-chip preloading scheme to reduce data access penalty. *Proc. of Supercomputing '91* pp. 178–186.
9. Berg, D. J. (1995) *Java Threads*. White Paper, Sun Microsystems.
10. Berger, D. Kaxiras, S., and Goodman, J. (1997) Datascalar architecture. *Proc. of the 24th International Symposium on Computer Architecture*.
11. Bershad, B. N., Anderson, T. E., Lazowska, E. D., and Levy, H. M. (1990) Lightweight remote procedure call. *ACM Transactions on Computer Systems*. Feb., pp. 37–55.
12. Bershad, B. N., Chambers, C., Eggers, S., Maeda, C., McNee, D., Pardyak, P., Savage, S., and Sirer, E. G. (1994) *SPIN — An Extensible Microkernel for Application-Specific Operating System Services. Technical Report.* 94–03–03. Department of Computer Science, University of Washington.
13. Blumofe, R. D., Joerg, C. F., Kuszmaul, B., Leiserson, C. E., Randall, K. H., and Zhou, Y. (1995) Cilk: an efficient multithreaded runtime system. *Proc. of the 5th ACM Symposium on Principles and Practice of Parallel Programming (PPoP)*. Santa Barbara CA. pp. 207–216.
14. Boughton, G. A. (1994) Arctic routing chip. *Proc. of the 1st International Workshop, PCRCW*. Lecture Notes in Computer Science 853. Springer-Verlag, Berlin. pp. 310–317.
15. Boykin, J., Kirschen, D., Langerman, A., and Lo Verso, S. (1993) *Programming Under Mach*. Addison-Wesley, Reading MA.
16. Catanzaro, B. (1994) *Multiprocessor System Architecture*. Prentice Hall, Englewood Cliffs NJ.
17. Chaiken, D., Kubiatowics, J., and Agarwal, A. (1991) LimitLESS directories: a scalable cache coherence scheme. *The 4th International Conference on Architectural Support for Programming Languages and Operating Systems*. Santa Clara CA. pp. 224–234.
18. Chiou, D., Ang, B. S., Greiner, R., Arvind, Hoe, J. C., Beckerle, M. J., Hicks, J. E. and Boughton, A. (1995) StatT-NG: delivering seamless parallel computing. *Proc. of EURO-PAR*, Stockholm. pp. 101–116.
19. Culler, D. E, Goldstein, S. C., Schauser, K. E., and von Eicken, T. (1993) TAM-A compiler controlled threaded abstract machine. *Journal of Parallel and Distributed Computing*. **18**, 347–370.
20. Dahlgren, F., Dubois, M., and Stenstrom, P. (1993) Fixed and adaptive sequential prefetching in shared memory uniprocessors. *Proc. of the International Conference on Parallel Processing*.
21. DARPA (1997) *Multithreaded and Other Experimental Computer Architectures*. BAA 97-03.
22. Engler, D. R., Kaashoek, F. M., and O'Toole, J. (1995) Exokernel: an operating system architecture for application-level resource management. *Proc. of the 15th Symposium on Operating Systems Principles*.
23. Eykholt, J. R., Kleiman, S. R., Barton, S., Faulkner, S., Shvalingiah, A., Smith, M., Stein, J., Voll, M., Weeks, M., and Williams, D. (1992) Beyond multiprocessing—multithreading the Sun OS kernel. *1992 Summer USENIX Conference Proceedings*. San Antonio TX. pp. 11–18.
24. Farkas, K., Jouppi, N., and Chow, P. (1995) How useful are non-blocking loads, stream buffers and speculative execution in multiple issue processors? *Proc. of the First HPCA*. Raleigh NC. pp. 78–79.
25. Fillo, M., Keckler, S. W., Dally, W., Carter, N. P., Chang, A., Gurevich, Y., and Lee, W. S. (1995) The M-Machine multicomputer. *Proc. of MICRO-28*. (Also available as MIT AI Lab Memo 1532.)
26. Feeley, M. J., Chase, J. S., Lazowska, E. D. (1993) *User Level Threads and Interprocess Communication. Technical Report*. 92-02-03. Department of Computer Science, University of Washington.

27. Halstead, R. (1985) Multilisp: a language for concurrent symbolic computation. *ACM Transactions on Prog. Lang. and Syst.* Oct., pp. 501–538.
28. Heinrich, M., Kuskin, J., Ofelt, D., Heinlein, J., Baxter, J., Singh, J. P., Simoni, R., Gharachorloo, K., Nakahira, D., Horowitz, M., Gupta, A., Rosenblum, M., and Hennessy, J. (1994) Integration of message passing and shared memory in the Stanford FLASH multiprocessor. *Proc. of the 6th International Conference on Architectural Support for Programming Languages and Operating Systems.* San Jose CA. pp. 274–285.
29. Hoe, J. C., and Ehrlich, M. (1996) StarT-Jr: a parallel system from commodity technology. *Proc. of the 7th Transputer/Occam International Conference*, Tokyo. (Also available as MIT Computer Structure Group Memo 384.)
30. ISO (1995) *Annotated Ada Reference Manual: Version 6.0.* ISO/IEC 8652:1995 (E). International Organization for Standardization, Geneva.
31. Kleiman, S., Shah, D., and Smaalders, B. (1996) *Programming with Threads.* Prentice Hall, Englewood Cliffs NJ.
32. Kodama, Y., Sakane, H., Sato, M., Yamana, H., Sakai, S., and Yamaguchi, Y. (1995) The EM-X parallel computer: architecture and basic performance. *Proc. of the 22nd International Symposium on Computer Architecture.* Santa Margherita Ligure, Italy. pp. 14–23.
33. Kuskin J., Ofelt, D., Heinrich, M., Heinlein, J., Simoni, R., Gharachorloo, K., Chapin, J., Nkahira, D., Baxter, J., Horowitz, M., Gupta, A., Rosenblum, M., and Hennessy, J. (1994) The Stanford FLASH multiprocessor. *Proc. of the 21st International Symposium on Computer Architecture*, Chicago IL. pp. 302–313.
34. Lee, B., and Hurson, A. R. (1994) Dataflow architectures and multithreading. *IEEE Computer* August, pp. 27–39.
35. Nikhil, R. (1991) *Id (Version 90.1) Reference Manual. Technical Report.* CSG Memo 284-2, MIT Laboratory for Computer Science.
36. Nikhil, R. S., Papadopoulos, G. M., and Arvind (1992) *T: a multithreaded massively parallel architecture. *Proc. of the 19th International Symposium on Computer Architecture.* Gold Coast, Australia. pp. 156–167.
37. Nikhil, R. S. (1994) Cid: a parallel shared-memory C for distributed memory machines. *Proc. of 7th International Workshop on Languages and Compilers for Parallel Computing*, Ithaca Springer-Verlag, Berlin. pp. 377–390.
38. Pier, K. A. (1983) A retrospective on the Dorado. A high performance personal computer. *Proc. of the 10th International Symposium on Computer Architecture*, Stockholm, Sweden. pp. 252–269.
39. Sakane, H., Sato, M., Kodama, Y., Yamana, H., Sakai, S., and Yamaguchi, Y. (1995) Dynamic characteristics of multithreaded execution in the EM-X multiprocessor. *Proc. of 1995 International Workshop on Computer Performance Measurement and Analysis (PERMEAN '95)*, Beppu Ohita, Japan. pp. 14–22.
40. Sato, M., Kodama, Y., Sakai, S., Yamaguchi, Y., and Koumura, Y. (1992) Thread-based programming for EM4 hybrid dataflow machine. *Proc. of the 19th International Symposium on Computer Architecture.* Gold Coast, Australia. pp. 146–155
41. Saulsbury, A., Pong, F., and Nowatzyk, A. (1996) Missing the memory wall: a case for processor/memory integration. *Proc. of the 23rd International Symposium on Computer Architecture*, Philadelphia PA. pp. 90–101.
42. Smith, B. (1985) The architecture of HEP. *Parallel MIMD Computation: HEP Supercomputer and Applications.* (ed. J. S. Kowalik). MIT Press, Cambridge MA.
43. Sohi, G., Breach, S., and Vijaykumar, T. (1995) Multiscalar processors. *Proc. of the 22nd International Symposium on Computer Architecture*, Santa Margherita Ligure, Italy. pp. 414–424.

44. Stein, D., and Shaw, D. (1997) Implementing lightweight threads. *Proc. of the 1992 Summer USENIX Conference*, San Antonio TX. pp. 1–9.
45. Thekkath, R., and Eggers, S. J. (1994) The effectiveness of multiple hardware contexts. *Proc. of the 6th International Conference on Architectural Support for Programming Languages and Operating Systems*, San Jose CA. pp. 328–337.
46. Thekkath, R., and Eggers, S. J. (1994) Impact of sharing-based thread placement on multi-threaded architectures. *Proc. of the 21st International Symposium on Computer Architecture*, Chicago IL. pp. 176–186.
47. Theobald, K. B. (1993) *Panel Session of the 1991 Workshop on Multithreaded Computers. ACAPS Technical Memo* 30, McGill University.
48. Tullsen, D. M., Eggers, S. J., and Levy, H. M. (1995) Simultaneous multithreading: maximizing on-chip parallelism. *Proc. of the 22nd International Symposium on Computer Architecture*, Santa Margherita Ligure, Italy. pp. 392–403.
49. Tullsen, D. M., Eggers, S. J., Emer, J. S., Levy, H. M., Lo, J. L. and Stamm, R. L. (1996) Exploiting choice: instruction fetch and issue on an implementable simultaneous multi-threading processor. *Proc. of the 23rd International Symposium on Computer Architecture*, Philadelphia PA. pp. 191–202.

Coordination Models and Languages

GEORGE A. PAPADOPOULOS

Department of Computer Science
University of Cyprus
Nicosia
Cyprus

FARHAD ARBAB

Department of Software Engineering
CWI
Amsterdam
The Netherlands

Abstract

A new class of models, formalisms, and mechanisms has recently evolved for describing concurrent and distributed computations based on the concept of "coordination." The purpose of a coordination model and associated language is to provide a means of integrating a number of possibly heterogeneous components by interfacing with each component in such a way that the collective set forms a single application that can execute on and take advantage of parallel and distributed systems. In this chapter we initially define and present in sufficient detail the fundamental concepts of what constitutes a coordination model or language. We then go on to classify these models and languages as either "data-driven" or "control-driven" (also called "process-" or "task-oriented"). In the process, the main existing coordination models and languages are described in sufficient detail to let the reader appreciate their features and put them into perspective with respect to each other. The chapter ends with a discussion comparing the various models and some conclusions.

1.	Introduction	330
	1.1 Background and Motivation	330
	1.2 Organization of the Chapter	331
2.	From Multilingual and Heterogeneous Systems to Coordination Models	331
	2.1 Need for Multilinguality and Heterogeneity	331
	2.2 The Coordination Paradigm	332
3.	Coordination Models and Languages	334
	3.1 Data- vs. Control-driven Coordination	334

	3.2	Data-driven Coordination Models	336
	3.3	Control-driven (Process-oriented) Coordination Models	367
4.	Comparison		391
5.	Conclusions		394
	References		396

1. Introduction

1.1 Background and Motivation

Massively parallel and distributed systems open new horizons for large applications and present new challenges for software technology. Many applications already take advantage of the increased raw computational power provided by such parallel systems to yield significantly shorter turn-around times. However, the availability of so many processors to work on a single application presents a new challenge to software technology: coordination of the cooperation of large numbers of concurrent active entities. Classical views of concurrency in programming languages that are based on extensions of the sequential programming paradigm are ill-suited to meet the challenge.

Exploiting the full potential of massively parallel systems requires programming models that explicitly deal with the concurrency of cooperation among very large numbers of active entities that comprise a single application. This has led to the design and implementation of a number of coordination models and their associated programming languages. Almost all of these models share the same intent, namely to provide a framework which enhances modularity, reuse of existing (sequential or even parallel) components, portability, and language interoperability. However, they also differ in how they precisely define the notion of coordination, what exactly is being coordinated, how coordination is achieved, and what the relevant metaphors are that must be used.

The purpose of this survey chapter is twofold: (1) to present a thorough view of the contemporary state-of-the-art research in the area of coordination models and languages, and (2) to provide enough information about their historical evolution, design, implementation, and application to give the reader an appropriate understanding of this important and rapidly evolving research area in computer science to appreciate its potential.

In the process, we argue that these coordination models and languages can be classified into two main categories: those that are "data-driven," where the evolution of computation is driven by the types and properties of data involved in the coordination activities, and those that are "control-driven" (or process-oriented) where changes in the coordination processes are triggered by events signifying (among other things) changes in the states of their coordinated processes.

1.2 Organization of the Chapter

The rest of this chapter is organized as follows: Section 2 provides a historical perspective on coordination programming and explains how and why it has evolved into its current form. Section 3 describes in detail the most important coordination models and languages using the above mentioned classification. Section 4 presents a general comparison and classification of the models described in the previous section and Section 5 ends the chapter with some conclusions.

2. From Multilingual and Heterogeneous Systems to Coordination Models

2.1 Need for Multilinguality and Heterogeneity

With the evolution of distributed and parallel systems, new programming paradigms were developed to make use of the available parallelism and the often massive number of processors comprising a system. These languages were able to exploit parallelism and perform communication but also be fault tolerant. They differed in the granularity or unit of parallelism they offered (e.g. sequential process, object, parallel statements) and the communication mechanism employed (e.g. message-passing models such as rendezvous or remote procedure calls, data sharing models such as distributed data structures or shared variables). The increased availability of massively parallel and open distributed systems led to the design and implementation of complex and large applications, such as vehicle navigation, air traffic control, intelligent information retrieval and multimedia-based environments, to name but a few. Gradually, it became apparent that no unique programming language or machine architecture was able to deal in a satisfactory way with all the facets of developing a complex and multifunctional application. Furthermore, issues such as reusability, compositionality, and extensibility became of paramount importance.

Thus, in order to deal with all these requirements of programming-in-the-large applications, the notions of multilinguality and heterogeneity came into play. *Multilingual* or *multiparadigm* programming [73] is able to support a number of diverse paradigms and provide interoperation of these paradigms while at the same time isolating unwanted interactions between them. Furthermore, a multilingual or multiparadigm programming environment aims at accommodating the diverse execution models and mechanisms of the various paradigms, managing the resources required for implementing them, and offering intuitive ways for combining code written in a mixture of paradigms, while at the same time providing orthogonal programming interfaces to the involved paradigms. There are basically two ways to produce multilingual or multiparadigm languages: either design a new superlanguage that offers the facilities of all paradigms intended to be used, or provide an interface between existing languages. The first approach has the advantage of usually providing a more coherent combination of different paradigms. However, it also has the disadvantages of introducing yet another programming language that a programmer must learn, plus the fact that such a single language cannot possibly support all the functionality of the languages it aims to replace. The second approach can in fact be realized with different degrees of integration ranging from using the operating system's communication primitives for intercomponent collaboration to providing concrete integration of the various languages involved, as in the case of, say, Module Interconnection Languages [63]. Multilinguality is closely related to *heterogeneity* [70], since heterogeneous systems (whether metacomputers or mixed-mode computers) demand that a programming language used must be able to express many useful models of computation. It is, however, usually impossible to find a single language able to deal satisfactorily with an extensive variety of such models; a mixture of language models may have to be employed.

Over the years, a number of models and metaphors were devised, their purpose being (partially) to abstract away and encapsulate the details of communication and cooperation between a number of entities forming some computation from the actual computational activities performed by these entities. A typical example is the *blackboard* model [53], developed for the needs of Distributed Artificial Intelligence, where a blackboard is a common forum used by a number of autonomous agents forming a multi-agent system to solve a problem in a cooperative manner. Another typical example is the *actor* model [1], based on the principles of concurrent object-oriented programming, where actors represent self-contained computational entities, using only message-passing (and not direct manipulation of each other's internal data structures) to coordinate their activities towards finding the solution for some problem. All these examples are concerned primarily with the development of parallel or distributed systems. For (mostly) sequential systems, one can mention the various component interconnection mechanisms that have been developed [52], with MILs (mentioned before) being an instance of the general model.

2.2 The Coordination Paradigm

The coordination paradigm offers a promising way of alleviating the problems and addressing some of the issues related to the development of complex distributed and parallel computer systems as outlined above.

Programming a distributed or parallel system can be seen as the combination of two distinct activities: the actual *computing* part, comprising a number of processes involved in manipulating data, and a *coordination* part responsible for the communication and cooperation between the processes. Thus, coordination can be used to distinguish the computational concerns of some distributed or parallel application from the communication ones, allowing the separate development but also the eventual amalgamation of these two major development phases.

The concept of coordination is closely related to those of multilinguality and heterogeneity. Since the coordination component is separate from the computational one, the former views the processes comprising the latter as black boxes; hence the actual programming languages used to write computational code play no important role in setting up the coordination apparatus. Furthermore, since the coordination component offers a homogeneous way for interprocess communication and abstracts away the machine-dependent details, coordination encourages the use of heterogeneous ensembles of architectures.

The concept of coordination is by no means limited to computer science. In a seminal paper [49], Malone and Crowston characterize coordination as an emerging research area with an interdisciplinary focus, playing a key issue in many diverse disciplines such as economics and operational research, organization theory, and biology. Consequently, there are many definitions of what coordination is, ranging from simple ones such as:

> Coordination is managing dependencies between activities.

to rather elaborate ones such as:

> Coordination is the additional information processing performed when multiple, connected actors pursue goals that a single author pursuing the same goals would not perform.

In the area of programming languages, probably the most widely accepted definition is given by Carriero and Gelernter [21]:

> Coordination is the process of building programs by gluing together active pieces.

Consequently:

> A coordination model is the glue that binds separate activities into an ensemble.

A *coordination model* can be viewed as a triple (**E**, **L**, **M**), where **E** represents the entities being coordinated, **L** the media used to coordinate the entities, and **M** the semantic framework the model adheres to [27, 71]. Furthermore, a *coordination language* is the linguistic embodiment of a coordination model, offering facilities for controlling synchronization, communication, creation, and termination of computational activities.

Closely related to the concept of coordination is that of *configuration* and *architectural description*. Configuration and architectural description languages share the same principles with coordination languages. They view a system as comprising *components* and *interconnections*, and aim at separating the structural description of components from component behavior. Furthermore, they support the formation of complex components as compositions of more elementary components. Finally, they understand changing the state of some system as an activity performed at the level of interconnecting components rather than within the internal purely computational functionality of some component.

Thus, if one adopts a slightly liberal view of what coordination is, one can also include configuration and architectural description languages in the category of coordination languages. Conversely, one can also view coordination as dealing with architectures (i.e. configuration of computational entities). In the following, we present a number of coordination models and languages, where by "coordination" we also mean "configuration" or "architectural description." (However, we will not cover those cases where ordinary languages are used for coordination, such as the framework described in [57].) Other collections of work on coordination models and languages are [4, 28, 29], and [27] is a survey article where the focus is on the first family of models and languages according to the classification presented below.

3. Coordination Models and Languages

3.1 Data- vs. Control-driven Coordination

The purpose of this section is to present the most important coordination models and languages. There are a number of dimensions in which one can classify these models and languages, such as the kind of entities that are being coordinated, the underlying architectures assumed by the models, the semantics a model adheres to, issues of scalability and openness [27, 71]. Although we do provide a classification and a summary comparison of the models and languages in Section 4, here we argue that these models fall into one of two major categories of coordination programming, namely either *data-driven* or *control-driven* (or task- or process-oriented).

The main characteristic of the data-driven coordination models and languages is the fact that the state of the computation at any moment in time is defined in terms of both the values of the data being received or sent and the actual configuration of the coordinated components. In other words, a coordinator or coordinated process is responsible for both examining and manipulating data as well as for coordinating either itself and/or other processes by invoking the coordination mechanism that each language provides. This does not necessarily mean that there does not exist a useful clear separation between the coordination functionality and the purely computational functionality of some process. But it usually does mean that, at least stylistically and linguistically, there exists a mixture of coordination and computation code within a process definition. A data-driven coordination language typically offers some coordination primitives (coupled with a coordination metaphor) which are mixed within the purely computational part of the code. These primitives do encapsulate in a useful way the communication and configurational aspects of some computation, but must be used in conjunction with the purely computational manipulation of data associated with some process. This means that processes cannot easily be distinguished as either coordination or computational processes. It is usually up to the programmer to design his program in such a way that the coordination and the computational concerns are clearly separated and are made the responsibility of different processes; however, most of the time such a clear separation is not enforced at the syntactic level by the coordination model.

The main difference between the models of the data-driven category and those of the control-driven category is that in the latter case we have an almost complete separation of coordination from computational concerns. The state of the computation at any moment in time is defined only in terms of the coordinated patterns that the processes involved in some computation adhere to. The actual values of the data being manipulated by the processes are almost never involved. Stylistically, this means that the coordination component is almost completely separated from the computational component; this is usually achieved by defining a brand new coordination language where the computational parts are treated as black boxes with clearly defined input/output interfaces. Consequently, whereas in the case of the data-driven category the coordination component is usually a set of primitives with predefined functionality which is used in connection with some "host" computational language, in the control-driven category the coordination component is usually a fully fledged language. This also means that it is easier in the second case (in fact, it is usually being enforced by the model) to syntactically separate the processes (or at least program modules) into two distinct groups, namely purely computational ones and purely coordination ones.

Aside from the stylistic differences between the two categories which affect the degree of separation between computational and coordination concerns, each category also seems to be suitable for a different type of application domain. The data-driven category tends to be used mostly for parallelizing computational problems. The control-driven category tends to be used primarily for modeling systems. This may be attributed to the fact that from within a configuration component a programmer has more control over the manipulated data in the case of data-driven coordination languages than in the case of control-driven ones. Thus the former category tends to coordinate data, whereas the latter tends to coordinate entities (which, in addition to ordinary computational processes, can also be devices, system components, etc.).

We should stress the point here that the data- vs. control-driven separation is by no means a clear-cut one. For instance, regarding application domains, the data-driven coordination language LAURA is used for distributed systems whereas the control-driven coordination languages MANIFOLD and ConCoord are also used for parallelizing data-intensive programs. Furthermore, regarding the degree of syntactic decoupling between the computational and the coordination components, Ariadne does have a concrete and separate coordination component, although it belongs to the data-driven category. However, the main difference between these two general categories does hold: i.e. in the data-driven category the coordination component "sees" the manipulated data, whereas in the control-driven category the actual structure and content of the data is of little or no importance. In the following, we describe in more detail the major members of each one of these two main categories of coordination models and languages.

3.2 Data-driven Coordination Models

Almost all coordination models belonging to this category have evolved around the notion of a *shared dataspace*. A shared dataspace [64] is a common, content-addressable data structure. All processes involved in some computation can communicate among themselves only indirectly via this medium. In particular, they can post or broadcast information into the medium and they can also retrieve information from the medium either by actually removing this information from the shared medium or merely by taking a copy of it. Since interprocess communication is done only via the shared dataspace and the medium's contents are independent of the life history of the processes involved, this metaphor achieves decoupling of processes in both space and time. Some processes can send their data into the medium and then carry on doing other things or even terminate execution while other processes asynchronously retrieve this data; a producer need not know the identity of a consumer (and vice versa) or, indeed, whether the data it has posted into the medium has been retrieved or read by anyone. Figure 1 illustrates the general scenario advocated by most of the coordination languages in this category.

Round objects represent processes, whereas square ones represent data. Empty square boxes are templates and are used by processes to somehow

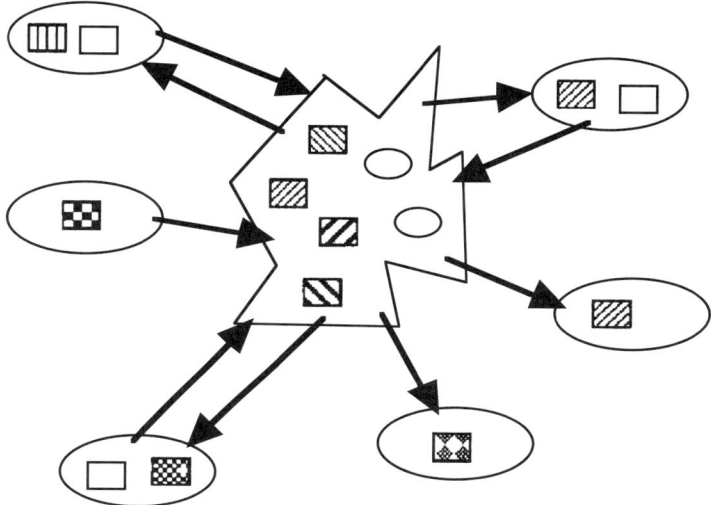

FIG. 1. Data-driven Coordination via a Shared Medium

specify what sort of data should be retrieved (by removal or copying) from the shared medium. Filled square boxes represent various kinds of data structures. Finally, small round objects represent "*active*" data structures; these are effectively processes which, once their execution terminates, turn into passive ordinary data. A process may be a pure producer or a pure consumer or both.

The various models in this category are different with respect to a number of parameters. For instance, one parameter is the actual structure of the data; in some cases they are flat tuples or records and in other cases nested tuples and records are also supported. Another parameter is the actual mechanism employed to retrieve data. Some models are based on various forms of pattern matching, whereas others use more sophisticated techniques that view the shared medium as something more than a flat unstructured space (e.g. they view it as a multiset). Yet another distinction is related to issues such as locality of reference within the shared medium, security, and efficiency.

Strictly speaking, not all coordination models in this category follow the above pattern of coordination (although even for the cases of using, say, shared variables, one could treat these variables as a restricted version of a shared dataspace). For instance, synchronizers (Section 3.1.13) use a message-passing (rather than a shared dataspace) based mechanism. However, all models are data-driven in the sense defined in Section 3.1.

3.2.1 Linda

Linda [2, 20] is historically the first genuine member of the family of coordination languages. It provides a simple and elegant way of separating computation from communication concerns. Linda is based on the so-called *generative communication* paradigm: if two processes wish to exchange some data, then the sender generates a new data object (referred to as a *tuple*) and places it in some shared dataspace (known as a *tuple space*) from which the receiver can retrieve it. This paradigm decouples processes in both space and time: no process need know the identity of other processes, nor is it required of all processes involved in some computation to be alive at the same time. In addition to passive tuples containing data, the tuple space can also contain active tuples representing processes which, after the completion of their execution, turn into ordinary passive tuples.

Linda is in fact not a fully fledged coordination language but a set of some simple coordination primitives. In particular, out(t) is used to put a passive tuple t in the tuple space, in(t) retrieves a passive tuple t from the tuple space, rd(t) retrieves a copy of t from the tuple space (i.e. t is still there), and eval(p) puts an active tuple p (i.e. a process) in the tuple space. The primitives rd and in are blocking primitives and will suspend execution until the desired tuple has been found. The primitives out and eval are non-blocking primitives. A process that executes eval(p) will carry on executing in parallel with p, which will turn into a passive tuple when it completes execution. Over the years, a number of additional primitives have been introduced into the basic model; for instance rdp(t) and inp(t) are non-blocking variants of rd(t) and in(t), respectively, which when the desired tuple is not found in the tuple space will return FALSE.

Tuples are actually sequences of typed fields. They are retrieved from the tuple space by means of *associative pattern matching*. More to the point, the parameter t of the primitives in, inp, rd, and rdp is actually a *tuple schemata* containing formal parameters; pattern matching of t with an actual tuple ta in the tuple space will succeed provided that the number, position, and types of t's fields match those of ta.

The Linda primitives are indeed completely independent of the host language; thus, it is possible to derive natural Linda variants of almost any programming language or paradigm (imperative, logic, functional, object-oriented, etc.). Linda's "friends" are C, Modula, Pascal, Ada, Prolog, Lisp, Eiffel, and Java, to name but a few [2, 17, 20, 61]. The following example is an implementation of the Dining Philosophers in C-Linda. In the Dining Philosophers problem, a number (typically 5) of philosophers are seated around a table, with a plate of food (typically spaghetti) in front of each one of them, and a fork between each plate. To eat, they must use both forks adjacent to them. But if all act independently, then each may pick up the left fork first and all enter a "deadlocked" state waiting forever for the right fork to become available. This is a standard problem for developing coordination solutions among independently executing processes.

```
#define NUM 5

philosopher(int i)                  main()
{                                   {
  while (1)                           int i;
  {                                   for (i=0, i<=NUM, i++)
    think();                          {
    in("room ticket");                  out("fork",i);
    in("fork",i);                       eval(philosopher(i));
    in("fork",(i+1)%NUM);               if (i<(NUM-1))
    eat();                                out("room ticket");

    out("fork",i);                    }
    out("fork",(i+1)%NUM);          }
    out("room ticket");
  }
}
```

Although the Linda model is appealing, it is also deceptively simple when it comes to implementing it, especially if distributed (as it is usually the case) environments are to be considered. There are a number of issues that a Linda implementor must address, such as where precisely the tuples are stored and how are they retrieved, how load balancing is achieved, and choices in implementing the `eval` primitive. Furthermore, since programmers usually adhere to specific communication and coordination patterns, often-used protocols should be optimized. There are a number of different approaches in implementing Linda [35, 72]. Piranha [41] for example is an execution model for Linda, particularly suited to networks of workstations. Piranha features *adaptive parallelism*, where processor assignment to executed processes changes dynamically. A typical Piranha program is usually a variant of the master–slave paradigm. In particular, there exists a *feeder* process responsible for distributing computations and selecting results and a number of *piranhas* which perform computations. Piranhas are statically distributed over the available nodes in a network (i.e. they do not migrate at run-time). They remain *dormant* as long as the node they reside on is *unavailable*; when the node becomes *available* they get activated. If the node is claimed back by the system and is removed from the list of available nodes then the piranha residing on it must *retreat*. Work on the current task is stopped and the retreating piranha posts to the tuple space enough information to allow some other piranha to take up the rest of the work. Typical applications suitable for the Piranha paradigm are Monte Carlo simulations and LU decompositions. The general structure of a Piranha program is as follows.

```
#define DONE -999
int index;

feeder()                                piranha()
{                                       {
  int count;                              struct Result result;
  struct Result result;
                                          while (1)
  /* put out the tasks */                 {
  for (count=0; count<TASKS;                in("task",?index);
    count++)out("task",count);              if (index==DONE)
                                            {
  /* help compute results */                  /* all tasks are done */
  piranha();                                  out("task",index);
                                            }
  /* collect results */                     else
  for (count=0; count<TASKS;                {
    count++)in("result",count,
    ?result_data);                            /* do the task */
}                                             do_work(index,&result);
                                              out("result",index,
                                                          result);
retreat()                                     in("tasks done",?index);
{                                             out("tasks done",i+1);
  /* replace current task */                  if ((i+1)==TASKS)
  out("task",index);                            out("task",DONE);
}                                           }
                                          }
                                        }
```

Linda has inspired the creation of many other similar languages—some are direct extensions to the basic Linda model, but others differ significantly from it. These derivatives aim to improve and extend the basic model with multiple tuple spaces, enforcement of security and protection of the data posted to the tuple space, etc. Some of these proposals will be described below.

3.2.2 Bauhaus Linda

Bauhaus Linda [22] is a direct extension of the "vanilla" Linda model featuring multiple tuple spaces implemented in the form of *multisets* (msets).

Bauhaus Linda does not differentiate between tuples and tuple spaces, tuples and anti-tuples (i.e. tuple templates), and active and passive tuples. Instead of adding tuples to and reading or removing tuples from a single flat tuple space, Bauhaus Linda's `out`, `rd` and `in` operations add multisets to and read or remove multisets from another multiset. Consequently, Linda's *ordered* and position dependent associative pattern matching on tuples is replaced by *unordered* set inclusion.

Assuming the existence of the multiset `{a b b {x y Q} {{z}} P}` where elements in capital letters denote processes and the rest denote ordinary tuples, then if P executes `out {x->R}` the multiset will become `{a b b {x y Q R} {{z}} P}`. If the multiset has the form `{a b b {x y} {{z}} P}` and P executes `mset m := rd {x}` then m will get assigned the structure `{x y}`. Finally, if the multiset has the form `{a b b {x y Q} {R {z}} P}` and P executes `mset m := in {x}`, then m is assigned the structure `{x y Q}` (and thus it becomes a live mset due to the presence of the element Q).

Furthermore, the language introduces the new primitive `move` which allows tuples to move up and down the levels of a multiset. For instance, if the multiset has the form `{a b b {x y Q} {w {z}} P}` and P executes `move {w}` then the result is `{a b b {x y Q} {w {z} P}}`. There also exist two other variants of `move`: `up`, which causes the issuing process to go one level up the structure, and `down m` (equivalent to `move -> {m}` where m is a multiset) which causes the issuing process to go down to a sibling node that contains m.

It is thus possible to organize data into useful hierarchies, such as:
```
{"world"
   {"africa" ...}
   {"antarctica" ...}
   ...
   {"north america"
      {"usa" ...
         {"ct" ...
            {"new haven" ...
               {"yale" ...
                  {"cs" ...}
               ...}
            ...}
         ...}
      ...}
   ...}
}
```
and assuming that the vector of strings `Path[]` represents a traveling course, we can move around by means of commands such as:
```
for (i=0; Path[i]; i++) down {Path[i]};
```

3.2.3 Bonita

Bonita [65] is a collection of new Linda-like primitives aiming at enhancing the functionality of the basic model as well as improving its performance. The first goal is achieved by providing the functionality for multiple tuple spaces and aggregate tuple manipulation. The second goal is achieved by providing a finer grain notion of tuple retrieval, where a request by some process for finding a tuple in the tuple space is treated separately from checking whether it has actually been delivered to the requesting process; thus, these activities can be done in parallel and consequently the related overhead is minimized.

In particular, Bonita supports (among others) the following coordination primitives:

- `rquid=dispatch(ts, tuple)`
  Non-blocking; puts `tuple` in `ts` and returns a tuple id to be used by other processes which may want to retrieve the tuple.
- `rquid=dispatch(ts, template, d|p)`
  Non-blocking; retrieves a tuple from `ts` matching `template`, either removing it (if d is specified) or getting a copy of it (if p is specified), and returns a request id as before.
- `rquid=dispatch_bulk(ts1, ts2, template, d|p)`
  Non-blocking; moves (d) or copies (p) from `ts1` to `ts2` all tuples matching `template`.
- `arrived(rquid)`
  Non-blocking; tests *locally* in the environment of the issuing process whether the tuple with the indicated id has arrived, and returns true or false accordingly.
- `obtain(rquid)`
  Blocking; suspends until the tuple with the indicated id is available.

The rather subtle differences between the basic Linda model and Bonita can be understood by considering the retrieval of three tuples from a single tuple space (in general, more than one tuple space may be involved):

```
Linda                      Bonita

                           int rqid1, rqid2, rqid3;

in("ONE");                 rqid1=dispatch(ts,"ONE",d);
in("TWO");                 rqid2=dispatch(ts,"TWO",d);
in("THREE");               rqid3=dispatch(ts,"THREE",d);

                           get(rqid1);
                           get(rqid2);
                           get(rqid3);
```

Whereas, in Linda, the first **in** operation must complete execution before the second one commences, Bonita follows a finer grain scenario: the three requests for the sought tuples are dispatched and the underlying system starts executing them in parallel. Thus, the time taken to retrieve one tuple can be overlapped with the time taken to retrieve the other tuples. In Bonita, it is also possible to express more efficiently (than in the basic Linda model) a non-deterministic selection construct:

Linda

```
while(1)
{
  if (inp("ONE"))
    { do_first(); break; }
  if (inp("TWO"))
    { do_second(); break; }
}
```

Bonita

```
int rqid1, rqid2;

rqid1=dispatch(ts,"ONE",d);
rqid2=dispatch(ts,"TWO",d);

while(1)
{
  if (arrived(rqid1))
    { do_first(rqid1); break; }
  if (arrived(rqid2))
    { do_second(rqid2); break; }
}
```

The Linda version repeatedly polls the global tuple space in order to check whether the requested tuples have appeared; furthermore, execution of the two inp operations is serialized. The Bonita version dispatches the two requests, which the underlying system is now able to serve in parallel, and then keeps checking locally in the environment of the process whether the requested tuples have arrived. The literature on Bonita shows that in many cases the finer grain notion of tuple handling that this model has introduced produces substantial gains in performance.

3.2.4 Law-Governed Linda

Whereas both Bauhaus Linda and Bonita extend the basic language by actually modifying the model and its underlying implementation, Law-Governed Linda [51] superimposes a set of "laws" which all processes wishing to participate in some exchange of data via the tuple space must adhere to. In particular, there exists a *controller* for every process in the system, and all controllers have a copy of the law. A controller is responsible for intercepting any attempted communication between the process it controls and the rest of the world. The attempted communication is allowed to complete only if it adheres to the law.

A Law-Governed Linda system is understood as a 5-tuple <C,P,CS,L,E> where C is the tuple space, P is a set of processes, CS is a set of control states (one associated with each process), L is the law which governs the system, and E is the set of controllers that enforce the law. Although the law can be formulated in any language (and a natural choice would be the host language that a Linda system is using), the designers of Law-Governed Linda have chosen a restricted subset of Prolog enhanced with the following primitives: complete actually carries out the operation being invoked; complete (arg') does the same, but the original argument of the operation is replaced with arg'; return is used in conjunction with the Linda primitives rd and in and its effect is actually to deliver the requested tuple to the issuing process; return(t') does the same but t' is delivered instead of the matched (from a previous rd or in operation) tuple t; out(t) is the conventional Linda primitive; and remove removes the issuing process from the system. Furthermore, tuple terms may contain the following attributes: self(i), where i is the unique id of the process; clock(t), where t is the current local time of the process; and op(t), where t is the argument of the latest Linda operation invoked by the issuing process. In addition, do(p) adds p (a sequence of one or more primitive operations) to a *ruling list* R which is executed after the ruling of the law is complete, and +t and −t add and remove respectively a term t from the control state of a process. Finally, every process is in a certain *state*, represented by the global variable CS and examined by means of the operator "@".

A user may now enhance the basic Linda functionality by formulating a suitable law. For instance, the following Prolog clauses implement secure message passing, where a message is a tuple of the form [msg,from(s), to(t),contents] where msg is a tag identifying the tuple as a message, s is the sender process, t is the receiver process, and contents represents the actual contents of the message.

```
R1. out([msg,from(Self),to(_)|_]) :- do(complete).
R2. in([msg,from(...),to(Self)|_]) :- do(complete)
                                   :: do(return).
R3. out([X|_]) :- not(X=msg), do(complete).
R4. in/rd([X|_]) :- not(X=msg), do(complete)
                                   :: do(return).
```

R1 allows a process to out messages only with its own id in the sender field (thus a message cannot be forged). R2 allows a process to remove a tuple from the tuple space only when its own id is in the receiver field. R3 and R4 simply send to or read/retrieve from the tuple space, respectively, any other tuple which need not adhere to the above law.

It is also possible in Law-Governed Linda to establish multiple tuple spaces by means of laws like the following:

```
R1. out([subspace(S)|_]) :- hasAccess(S)@CS,
                                            do(complete).
R2. in/rd([subspace(S)|_]) :-actual(S), hasAccess(S)@CS,
                                   do(complete) :: do(return).
```

where initially every process has any number of `hasAccess(s)` terms in its control state, identifying the subspaces it can access. R1 allows a process to `out` a tuple to the subspace `s` provided the term `hasAccess(s)` is in its control state. R2 uses the primitive `actual` to make sure that the variable representing the name of a subspace is actually instantiated to some ground value (a process cannot attempt to query multiple subspaces at once) before proceeding to retrieve or read a tuple from the subspace.

3.2.5 Objective Linda

Objective Linda [45] is another direct variant of the basic Linda model, influenced by Bauhaus Linda and particularly suited to modelling open systems. Objective Linda introduces an *object model* suitable for open systems and independent of the host programming language (objects in Objective Linda are described in the *Object Interchange Language* (OIL)—a language-independent notation). Objects make use of the object space by means of suitably defined object-space operations which address the requirements of openness. Furthermore, the language supports hierarchies of multiple object spaces and the ability for objects to communicate via several object spaces. Object spaces are accessible through *logicals* (i.e. object space references passed around between objects); logicals can be `outed` by some object to the tuple space and then retrieved by another space via a special `attach` operation.

In particular, Objective Linda supports, among others, the following operations which are variants of Linda's basic coordination primitives:

- `bool out(MULTISET *m, double timeout)`
  Tries to move the objects contained in `m` into the object space. Returns true if the attempted operation is successful and false if the operation could not be completed within timeout seconds.
- `bool eval(MULTISET *m, double timeout)`
  Similar to the previous operation, but now the moved objects are also activated for execution.
- `MULTISET *in(OIL_OBJECT *o, int min, int max, double timeout)`

Tries to remove multiple objects $o'_1 \ldots o'_n$ matching the template object o from the object space and returns a multiset containing them if at least `min` matching objects could be found within `timeout` seconds. In this case, the multiset contains at most `max` objects, even if the object space contained more. If `min` objects could not be found within `timeout` seconds, `NULL` is returned instead.

- `MULTISET *rd(OIL_OBJECT *o, int min, int max, double timeout)`
  Similar to the previous operation, but now clones of multiple objects $o'_1 \ldots o'_n$ are returned.
- `int infinite_matches`
  Constant value interpreted as infinite number of matching objects when provided as a `min` or `max` parameter.
- `double infinite_time`
  Constant value interpreted as infinite delay when provided as a `timeout` parameter.

The following C++ example models a collision avoidance scenario for cars driving in a cyclic grid.

```
class Position: public OIL_OBJECT
{
 private: bool match_position;  // switching the matching mode
 public: int x, y;              // the grid position
         int car;               // the car s id
   bool match( OIL_OBJECT * obj)
   {
    if (match_position)
      return ( (((Position*)obj)->x == y) && (((Position*)
                                              obj)->y==y) );
    else return ((Position*)obj)->car==car;
   };
   set_match_position() { match_position=true; }
   set_match_car()      { match_position=false; }
};

class Car: public OIL_OBJECT
{
 private: int x, y;          // the grid position
          int car;            // the car's id
          direction dir;      // the direction to move
   void wait(){};  // wait for an arbitrary interval
```

```
void evaluate()
{
 MULTISET m = new MULTISET ;
 Position *p; int nx, ny, px, py;
 while(true)
{
 m->put(new Position(id,x,y));
 (void)context->out(m,context->infinite_time);
 wait();
 // store next position to move to in nx and ny
 nx = ... ; ny = ... ;
 p = new Position(id,nx,ny); p->set_match_position();
 m = context-> rd (p,1,1,0);
 if (m) // there is a car in front of us
    { delete m; delete p; }
 else { delete p;
       // store position with priority in px and py
       px = ... ; py = ... ;
       p = new Position(id,px,py); p->set_match_position();
       m = context-> rd (p,1,1,0);
       if (m) // there is a car with priority
          { delete m; delete p; }
       else { x = nx; y = ny// move
             delete p;
            }
      }
 }
 p = new Position; p->car = id; p->set_match_car();
 m = context-> in (p,1,1,context->infinite->time);
 p = m->get(); delete p;
 }
}
}
```

Agents responsible for steering cars communicate via the object space. Every agent puts an object of type `Position` into the object space which carries the agent's id as well as its position and grid. When changing its position, an agent consumes (`ins`) the `Positio`object with its own id and replaces it by a new one with the updated position. Before an agent changes position, it checks whether it can `rd` a `Position` object directly in front of it, in which case it will wait. Also, it checks whether some other car is approaching from another direction, in which case again it waits. This functionality is modelled by `Car`.

3.2.6 LAURA

LAURA [69] is another approach to deriving a Linda-like coordination model suitable for open distributed systems. In a LAURA system, *agents* offer *services* according to their functions. Agents communicate via a *service-space* shared by all agents and by means of exchanging forms. A *form* can contain a description of a *service-offer*, a *service-request* with arguments, or a *service-result* with results. Suitable primitives are provided by the language with the intention to put and retrieve offer-, request- and result-forms to and from the service-space. More to the point, SERVE is used by clients to ask for service, SERVICE is used by servers to offer service, and RESULT is used by servers to produce a result-form. Identification of services is not done by means of naming schemes but rather by describing an interface signature consisting of a set of operation signatures. Operation signatures consist of a name and the types of arguments and parameters. As in the case of Objective Linda, a host language-independent *interface description language* (STL for Service Type Language) is used for this purpose. Furthermore, the service-space is monolithic and fault tolerant.

The following code models the activities of a travel ticket purchase system.

```
SERVE large-agency operation
  (getflightticket : cc * <day,month,year> * dest ->
                    ack * <dollar,cent>;
    getbusticket   : cc * <thedate.day,thedate.month,
                                             thedate.year>
                    * dest -> ack * <dollar,cent> * line;
   gettrainticket  : cc * <day,month,year> * dest ->
                    ack * <dollar,cent>).
SERVE


RESULT large-agency operation
  (getflightticket : cc * <day,month,year> * dest ->
                    ack * <dollar,cent>;
    getbusticket   : cc * <thedate.day,thedate.month,
                                             thedate.year>
                    * dest -> ack * <dollar,cent> * line;
   gettrainticket  : cc * <day,month,year> * dest ->
                    ack * <dollar,cent>).
RESULT


SERVICE small-agency
  (getflightticket : cc * <thedate.day,thedate.month,
                                             thedate.year>
                    * dest -> ack * <dollar,cent>).
SERVICE
```

A service with the interface large-agency is offered and the code for the selected operation should be bound to operation. Depending on which one of the three services offered by large-agency is requested, the respective program variables (cc, day, etc.) will be bound with the arguments offered by the service-user. When SERVE executes, a serve-form is built from the arguments, the service-space is scanned for a service-request form whose service-type matches the offered type, and the code of the requested operation and the provided arguments are copied to the serve-form and bound to the program variables according to the binding list. After performing the requested service, the service-provider uses RESULT to deliver a result-form to the service-space. Finally, another agent with interface small-agency which wishes to invoke the service getflightticket executes SERVICE; program variables are then bound accordingly in order for small-agency to provide large-agency with needed information (such as cc and dest) and also let large-agency pass back to small-agency the results of the service (such as ack).

3.2.7 Ariadne/HOPLa

Ariadne and its modelling language HOPLa [36] are an attempt to use Linda-like coordination to manage hybrid collaborative processes. As in all the Linda-like models, Ariadne uses a shared workspace, which, however, holds tree-shaped data and is self-descriptive, in the sense that in addition to the actual data it also holds constraints (i.e. type definitions) that govern its structure. Both highly structured data (e.g. forms consisting of typed fields) and semi-structured data (e.g. email messages) can be handled. The processes comprising an Ariadne system are defined in the Hybrid Office Process Language (HOPLa) and use the concept of *flexible records* enhanced with constructors such as Set for collections (aggregate operations) and constraints. Tasks are defined by means of Action terms and use the following coordination operators: Serie for sequential execution, Parl for parallel execution, and Unord for execution in random order. The following example models an electronic discussion between a group of people:

```
Discussion<Process(
    group -> Set+Action(type -> Actor; value -> PS: set)
    discuss -> Thread<Data+Serie(
        message -> String+Action(actor -> {p | p in PS)};
        replies -> Set+Parl(type -> Thread)))
```

First, the set of actors participating in the discussion is defined by setting the feature group. After the group has been established, a string for the message feature must be provided by one of the actors in the group. After that, replies can be added in parallel by other members of the group, each one spawning a different thread of execution.

3.2.8 Sonia

Sonia [10] is another approach to using Linda-like coordination languages to model activities in information systems. In fact, Sonia is not so much an extension of Linda with extra functionality but rather an adaptation of the latter for coordinating human and other activities in organizations. The basic Linda functionality is expressed by higher level metaphors which should be understandable by everyone, including non-computer specialists.

Thus, in Sonia, there exists an *agora* (the equivalent of a tuple space) and a number of *actors* communicating by means of posting to and extracting messages from it. An agora [50] is a first-class citizen and many (nested) agoras can be defined. Messages are written as tuples of named values, e.g. `Tuple(:shape "square" :color "red")`. Nested and typed tuples are also supported. The traditional Linda primitives `out`, `in`, and `rd` are replaced by the more intuitively named primitives `post`, `pick` and `peek`, respectively. A new primitive, `cancel`, is also introduced intended to abort an outstanding `pick` or `peek` request. Templates can be enhanced with timeout functionality and rules: the template `Template(:shape any :color Rule("value='red' or :[value='blue']"))` would match a tuple with any shape as long as its color is either red or blue.

3.2.9 Linda and the World Wide Web

Recently, the concept of coordination has been introduced into the development of middleware web-based environments. The Shared Dataspace paradigm of Linda is particularly attractive for orchestrating distributed web-based applications and a number of extensions have been proposed to the basic Linda model suitable for developing interactive WWW environments. The basic advantage of introducing a coordination formalism into a web application is that it then becomes easier to separate I/O from processing concerns. CGI scripts deal only with I/O (e.g. getting data by means of electronic forms and/or displaying them), whereas the coordination formalism becomes responsible for the sending/receiving of data via the tuple space. The system is also enhanced with the two major features of a coordination formalism: heterogeneous execution of applications and multilinguality [31].

Jada [30] is a combination of Java with Linda, able to express mobile object coordination and multithreading, and is suited for open systems. Suitable classes such as `TupleServer` and `TupleClient` have been defined for providing remote access to a tuple space and communication is done by means of sockets. A `TupleClient` needs to know the host and port id of `TupleServer` and the language provides appropriate constructs for specifying this information. Jada can be used both as a coordination language *per se* and as a kernel language for designing more complex coordination languages for the WWW. The following Jada program implements a symmetric ping-pong.

```
//--PING--
import jada.tuple.*;
import java.client.*;

public class Ping
{
  static final String ts_host="foo.bar";

  public void run()
  {
    // a tuple client interacts with remote server
    TupleClient ts = new TupleClient(ts_host);
    // do ping-pong
    while (true)
     {
       ts.out(new Tuple("ping"));
       Tuple tuple = ts.in(new Tuple("pong"));
     }
  }

  public static void main(String args[])
  {
   Ping ping=new Ping();
   ping.run();
  }
}

//--PONG--
import jada.tuple.*;
import java.client.*;

public class Pong
{
  static final String ts_host = "foo.bar";
```

```
public void run()
{
  // a tuple client interacts with a remote server
  TupleClient ts = new TupleClient(ts_host);
  // do ping-pong
  while (true)
    {
      ts.out(new Tuple("pong"));
      Tuple tuple = ts.in(new Tuple("ping"));
    }
}

public static void main(String args[])
{
  Pong pong = new Pong();
  pong.run();
}
}
```

SHADE [24] is a higher level object-oriented coordination language for the Web. In SHADE the coordinated entities are Java objects. However, whereas Jada is based on singleton tuple transactions, SHADE is based on multiset rewriting. Each object in SHADE has a name, a class, and a state. The name is the pattern used to deliver messages. The type defines the object behavior. The state is the contents of the multiset associated with the object. The above ping-pong program can be defined in SHADE as follows.

```
class ping_class =              class pong_class =
{                               {
  in do_ping;                     in do_pong;
  send pong, do_pong              send ping, do_ping
  #                               #
  in done;                        in done;
  terminate                       terminate
}                               }
```

Each class comprises two methods (separated by "#"). The first method is activated when one of the items ping or pong appear in the proper object's multiset. When the method is activated in the object ping (say), a message (do_pong) is sent to the object pong (and vice versa). When the message is delivered to an object, it is put in the object's multiset and triggers the activation of the first method of that object, and so on. The second method is triggered by the item done and causes the termination of the object.

3.2.10 GAMMA

The GAMMA (General Abstract Model for Multiset mAnipulation) model [9] is a coordination framework based on *multiset rewriting*. The basic data structure in GAMMA is a *multiset* (or *bag*), which can be seen as a chemical solution and, unlike an ordinary set, can contain multiple occurrences of the same element. A simple program is a pair (Reaction Condition, Action), and its execution involves replacing those elements in a multiset satisfying the reaction condition by the products of the action. The result is obtained when no more such reactions can take place, and thus the system becomes stable.

There is a unique control structure associated with multisets, namely the Γ operator, whose definition is as follows.

```
Γ((R1,A1), ...,(Rm,Am)) (M) =
   if   ∀ i ∈ [1,m] ∀ x1, ...,xn ∈ M,]Ri(x1, ,xn)
   then M
   else let x1, ...,xn ∈ M, let i ∈ [1,m] such that ]Ri(x1, ...,xn) in
   Γ((R1,A1),...,(Rm,Am)) ((M-{x1,...,xn})+Ai(x1,...,xn))
```

where `{...}` represents multisets and `(Ri,Ai)` are pairs of closed functions specifying reactions. The effect of `(Ri,Ai)` on a multiset `M` is to replace in `M` a subset of elements `{x1,...,xn}` such that `Ri(x1,...,xn)` is true for the elements of `Ai(x1,...,xn)`. GAMMA enjoys a powerful *locality property* in that `Ri` and `Ai` are pure functions operating on their arguments. Thus, if the reaction condition holds for several disjoint subsets, the reactions can be carried out in parallel. The following code implements a prime number generator.

```
prime_numbers(N) = Γ((R,A))
                   ({2, ...,N}) where
                   R(x,y) = multiple(x,y)
                   A(x,y) = {y}
```

The solution consists of removing multiple elements from the multiset `{2,...,N}`. The remaining multiset contains exactly the prime numbers less than `N`.

Although the operational behavior of the model is strictly implicit (the programmer does not specify any order of execution and the latter is by default completely parallel), practical use of it reveals that a number of program schemes can be identified which are the ones most often used by programs. These schemes, referred to as *tropes*, are: `Transmuter(C,f)`, which applies the same operation `f` to all the elements of the multiset until no element satisfies the condition `C`; `Reducer(C,f)`, which reduces the size of the multiset by applying the operation `f` to pairs of elements satisfying `C`;

Optimiser(<,f1,f2,S), which optimizes the multiset according to some criterion expressed through the ordering < between the functions f1 and f2, while preserving the structure S of the multiset; Expander(C,f1,f2), which decomposes the elements of a multiset into a collection of basic values according to the condition C and by applying f1 and f2 to each element; and S(C), which removes from the multiset all those elements satisfying C. Tropes can be combined to form complex programs; the following combination of tropes (as opposed to using the fundamental Γ operator) implements the functionality of a Fibonacci function:

```
fib(n) = add(zero(dec({n})))
dec    = E(C,f1,f2) where C(x)=x>1, f1(x)=x-1, f2(x)=x-2
zero   = T(C,f)     where C(x)=(x=0), f(x)=1
add    = R(C,f)     where C(x,y)=true, f(x,y)=x+y
```

The vanilla GAMMA model has been enriched with sequential and parallel operators, higher-order functionality and types. Furthermore, in order to express structure, a variant of the basic model has been proposed, namely Structured GAMMA, featuring *structured multisets*. These can be seen as a set of addresses satisfying specific relations and associated with a value. A type is defined in terms of rewrite rules and a structured multiset belongs to a type T if its underlying set of addresses satisfies the invariant expressed by the rewrite system defining T. In Structured GAMMA reactions test and/or modify the relations on addresses and/or the values associated with those addresses. Structured GAMMA is particularly suited to the concept of coordination, since addresses can be interpreted as individual entities to be coordinated. Their associated value defines their behavior (in a given programming language which is independent of the coordination one) and the relations correspond to communications links. Also, a structuring type provides a description of the shape of the overall configuration. Structured GAMMA has been used for modelling software architectures, a particular type of coordination usually modelled by the coordination languages of the control-driven family. For instance, the following Structured GAMMA code models a client–server architecture:

```
CS  = N n
N n = cr c n, ca n c, N n
N n = sr n s, sa s n, N n
N n = m n
```

where cr c n and ca n c denote respectively a communication link from a client c to a manager n and the dual link from n to c. A new client can now be added by means of the rewrite rule

```
m n => m n, cr c n, ca n c
```

3.2.11 LO and COOLL

Linear Objects (LO [3, 5, 15]) is an object-oriented language based on the Interaction Abstract Machines computational model. The concept of "interaction" is closely related to the principles underpinning the theory of Linear Logic, and in fact LO amalgamates linearity with multiset rewriting (as in GAMMA) and asynchronous, actor-like communication by means of broadcasting. LO views the computation as a system of communicating agents whose state is represented as a multiset. Agents evolve in terms of transitions which are transformations from one state to another; in addition, agents can be created or terminated. Inter-agent communication is achieved by means of broadcasting.

An LO program is a set of (effectively multi-headed) rewrite rules taking the general form

```
<multiset> <broadcast> <built-ins> o— <goal>

multiset = a1 @ ... @ an
broadcast = ^a | ^a @ broadcast
goal = a1 @ ... @ an | goal1 & ... & goaln | #t | #b
```

where the symbols "@" ("par"), "&" ("with"), "o—" (implication), #t ("top") and #b ("bottom") are taken from Linear Logic. The following example implements Multiminds, a multiplayer version of Mastermind.

```
coder(S) @ current(I) @ ^go(I) o— coder(S)
/* coder calls the player ("go(I)") */

coder(S) @ try(I,G) @ players(N) @ ^result(I,G,B,C) @
  { answer(S,G,B,C), C=\=0, next_player(N,I,I1) } o—
    coder(S) @ current(I1) @ players(N).
/* coder sends to the player I the answer (bulls B and
cows C) to the guess G. */

coder(S) @ try(I,G) @ ^victory(I,G) @
  { answer(S,G,B,C), C=:=0 } o— #t.
/* player I has guessed the secret code with G - coder
informs players before ending */

decoder @ alp_l([A|List]) @ n_decod(N) @
                            { nextplayer(N,N1) } o—
    decoder @ alp_l(List) @ n_decod(N1) &
    decoder(N) @ db([]) @ alph(A).
/* creation of players */
```

```
decoder(I) @ go(I) @ db(L) @ alph(A) @ ^try(I,G) @
                                    { compute(A,L,G) } o—
    decoder(I) @ db(L) @ alph(A).
/* after receiving the message "go(I)", player I computes
a guess G, sends it to the coder ("try(...)"), and waits
for an answer */

decoder(I) @ result(I,G,B,C) @ db(L) o—
    decoder(I) @ db([tried(G-[B,C])|L]).
/* player I stores the answer to the guess G
                                    ("result(...)") */
```

Note that the purely computational procedures `answer` and `compute` would normally be implemented in some ordinary programming language, with Prolog or one of its variants being the most natural choice. A initial query to the program above could be the following:

```
coder([h,a,l,l,o]) @ players(2) @ current(0) &
decoder @ n_decod(0) @ alp_l([[l,o,l,h,a],[h,l,a,o,l]])
```

COOLL [23] extends the basic LO model with modularity and a new form of broadcast-like communication, namely *group* (multicast) communication. A COOLL program is a set of theories, each theory having the following structure:

```
theory theory_name o—
        method1
        #
        .
        .
        .
        #
        methodN
```

Communication can be either broadcast or group communication, the latter directed to specific theories:

```
Communications = ^A | !(dest,msg) | Communications @
                                    Communications
```

where `dest` is the name of a theory which will receive `msg`.

Methods have the general form:

```
Conditions => Communications => Body
```

where `Conditions` specify when methods will be triggered, `Communications` specifies broadcast and/or group communication, and

Body defines a transition to a new configuration. The previous LO program can be written in COOLL as follows.

```
theory coder o—
   current(I) => !(decoder,go(I)) => #b
 #
   try(I,G) a{ code(S) @ players(N) } @
             { { answer(S,G,B,C),C=\=0,
                               next_player(N,I,I1) } }
              => !(decoder,result(I,G,B,C)) => current(I1)
 #
   try(I,G) a{ code(S) } @
             { { answer(S,G,B,C), C=:=0 } }
              => ^victory(I,G) => #t.

theory decoder o—
   alpl([L|List]) @ n_decod(N) @ { next_player(N,N1) }
         => => alp_l(List) @ n_decod(N1) & id(N) @ db([])
                                              @ alph(L)
 #
   go(I) a{ id(I) @ alph(A) @ db(L) } @
             { { compute(A,L,G) } } => !(coder,try(I,G)) => #b
 #
   result(G,B,C) @ db(L) => => db([tried(G-[B,C])|L])
 #
   victory(X,G) => => #t
```

The program is structured naturally into two theories; furthermore, through employing group communication, the decoder refrains from receiving guesses from other decoders. The previous query now takes the following form:

```
*coder @ code([h,a,l,l,o]) @ players(2) @ current(0) &
*decoder @ n_decod(0) @ alp_l([[l,o,l,h,a],[h,l,a,o,l]])
```

where "*" denotes the name of a theory.

3.2.12 MESSENGERS

MESSENGERS [40] is a coordination paradigm for distributed systems, particularly suited to mobile computing. MESSENGERS is based on the concept of *Messengers*, which are autonomous messages. A Messenger, instead of carrying just data (as is the case for ordinary passive messages), contains a process, i.e. a program together with its current status information (program counter, local variables, etc.). Each node visited by the Messenger resumes the interpretation of the Messenger's program until a navigational command is encountered that causes it to leave the current node. A distributed application is thus viewed as a collection of functions whose coordination is managed by a group of Messengers navigating freely and autonomously through the network. In addition to navigational autonomy, MESSENGERS supports both inter- and intra-object coordination.

As is the case for the Linda-like paradigms, MESSENGERS also supports the concept of a structured global state space. However, MESSENGERS explicitly partitions it by means of the navigational features it supports. The following example models a manager–worker scenario.

```
manager_worker()
{
 create(ALL);
 hop(ll = $last);
 while ((task = next_task()) != NULL)
   {
     hop(ll = $last);
     res = compute(task);
     hop(ll = $last);
     deposit(res);
   }
}
```

The above Messenger script is injected into the *init* node of some daemon. It first creates logical nodes connected to the current node on every neighboring daemon. It also causes a replica of the Messenger to be created on each node and start executing. Each of the Messengers hops back to the original node by following the most recently traversed logical link, which is obtained by accessing the system variable $last. It then attempts to get a new task to work on. If successful, it hops back to its logical node, computes the result, and carries it back to the central node to deposit it there. This activity is repeated until no further work is left to do, in which case it ceases to exist. The primary role in the Messenger functionality is played by the hop statement, which is defined as follows:

```
hop(ln=n;ll=l;ldir=d)
```

where ln represents a logical node, ll represents a logical link and ldir represents the link's direction. The triple (n, l, d) is a destination specification in the network; n can be an address, a variable, or a constant (including the special node init); l can be a variable, a constant, or a virtual link (corresponding to a direct jump to the designated node); finally, d can be one of the symbols "+," "-," or "*" denoting "forward," "backward," or "either" respectively, with the latter also playing the role of being the default value. The wild card "*" applies also to n and l with obvious meanings.

As another example consider the matrix multiplication.

```
distribute_A(s)
{
  M_sched_time_abs((j-i) mod s);
  msgr_A = copy_block(resid_A);
  hop(ll = "row");
  new_resid_A = copy_block(msgr_A);
}

rotate_B(m)
{
  msgr_B = copy_block(resid_B);
  for (k=0; k<m; k++)
    {
      M_sched_time_dlt(.5);              /* synchronisation */
      resid_C = block_multiply(msgr_B,resid_A,resid_C);
                                         /* Cij = Aij*Bij */
      hol(ll = "column"; ldir = -);
                                         /* rotate B to column i-1 */
{ }
```

The code comprises two Messengers. distribute_A implements the movement of the array A using *temporal coordination*, which is also supported by the model (each of the distribute_A Messengers schedules itself to wake up at the time corresponding to its position in the logical network). rotate_B is the embodiment of one of the blocks of the matrix B, which it copies from the node resid_B to its private area msgr_B. It then enters a loop during which it keeps moving the block it is responsible for along its respective column. Temporal coordination is also used here, and in fact the two Messengers always alternate between their respective executions. Each time rotate_B wakes up, it performs a block multiplication using its own block of B and the currently resident block of A, adds it to the resident block of C, and hops to its northern neighbor.

3.2.13 Synchronizers

Synchronizers [38, 39, 62] are based on the Actor model of computation and are a set of tools able to express coordination patterns within a multi-object language framework based on specifying and enforcing constraints that restrict invocation of a set of objects. Constraints are defined in terms of the interface of objects being invoked rather than their internal representation. Constraints can enforce access restrictions either temporarily or permanently. These constraints are typically used to express certain properties fundamental to concurrent object-oriented languages, such as temporal ordering or atomicity of method invocation.

Synchronizers are expressed in an abstract format which is independent of both the syntax of the particular host languages as well as the underlying protocols used to enforce the required object properties. Thus, the programmer specifies multi-object constraints in an abstract and high-level manner which is independent of the details involved in explicit message-passing. Furthermore, the implementation of synchronizers can involve direct communication between the constrained objects or indirect communication with a central coordinator process. Synchronizers are not accessed directly by message-passing but indirectly through pattern matching. The following code defines a synchronizer that enforces a collective bound on allocated resources.

```
AllocationPolicy(adm1,adm2,max)
{
  init prev:=0;

  prev >= max disables (adm1.request or adm2.request),
  (adm1.request or adm2.request) updates prev:=prev+1,
  (adm1.release or adm2.release) updates prev:=prev-1
}
```

The above synchronizer has a local constraint (`prev >= max`) that prevents (by means of using the keyword `disable`) allocation of more resources than the system provides (by disabling the invocation of the `request` method). Furthermore, upon encountering an invocation pattern, the local variable `prev` is updated accordingly. The next example shows how the coordination code for the five philosophers can be encapsulated into a synchronizer.

```
PickUpConstraint(c1,c2,phil)
{
   atomic ( (c1.pick(sender) where sender=phil),
            (c2.pick(sender) where sender=phil) ),
   (c1.pick where sender=phil) stops
}
```

The synchronizer is parameterized with the two chopsticks (`c1` and `c2`) and the philosopher who accesses the chopsticks (`phil`). Furthermore, the synchronizer applies only to `pick` messages sent by `phil`. We assume the existence of an `eat` method which invokes concurrently `pick` on each of the needed chopsticks. The synchronizer enforces atomic access to the two chopsticks; when `phil` has successfully acquired both chopsticks, the constraint is terminated.

3.2.14 Compositional Programming

The concept of *compositionality* [25], an important design principle for task parallel programs, shares the same goals with coordination, namely reusability of sequential code, generality, heterogeneity, and portability; as such it can be seen as a coordination model. A compositional programming system is one in which properties of program components are preserved when those components are composed in parallel with other program components. Thus, it is possible to define in a compositional way recurring patterns of parallel computation, whether configuration ones (such as mapping techniques) or communication ones (such as streamers and mergers), as building blocks and combine them together to form bigger programs. If desired, the compositional assembly preserves the deterministic behavior of its constituent parts, thus simplifying program development by allowing program components to be constructed and tested in isolation from the rest of their environment.

There are basically two approaches to deriving compositional programs. The first approach is based on *concurrent logic programming* and is exemplified by languages such as Strand, the Program Composition Notation (PCN), Fortran-M, and Compositional C++ [37]. Concurrent logic programming offers a powerful computational model for parallel computing, and over the years a number of techniques have been developed for expressing useful coordination patterns. In the case of Strand, the language is used to express the coordination aspects of some parallel program, whereas the actual computation code is written in some other more suitable language, typically C or Fortran. The following code implements a genetic sequence alignment algorithm.

```
align_chunk(Sequences,Alignment) :-
    pins(Chunks,BestPin),
    divide(Sequences,BestPin,Alignment).

pins(Chunk,CpList) :-
    cps(Chunk,CpList),
    c_form_pins(CpList,PinList),
    best_pin(Chunk,PinList,BestPin).

cps([Seq|Sequences],CpList) :-
    CpList := [CPs|CpList1],
    c_critical_points(Seq,CPs),
    cps(Sequences,CpList1).
```

```
cps([],CpList) :- CpList := [].
divide(Seqs,Pin,Alignment) :-
    Pin =\= [] | split(Seqs,Pin,Left,Right,Rest),
                 align_chunk(Left,LAlign) @ random,
                 align_chunk(Right,RAlign) @ random,
                 align_chunk(Rest,RestAlign) @ random,
                 combine(LAlign,RAlign,RestAlign,
                                              Alignment).
divide(Seqs,[],Alignment) :-
    c_basic_align(Seqs,Alignment).
```

In the above program, the coordination/communication component is quite separate from the computational one. The first component is expressed in Strand itself; in fact, the actual details are taken care of by the underlying concurrent logic model using standard techniques such as shared single assignment variables, dependent AND-parallelism, list composition and, where appropriate, guarded clauses. The second component, the three procedures with the c_ prefix, is written in C. Note that different mapping techniques can be explored using the @ notation (in this case random specifies that the indicated procedure calls will be executed on randomly selected processors).

Whereas Strand is a concrete language (and thus it needs a dedicated WAM-based implementation to run), the Program Composition Notation (PCN) is more like a set of notations adhering to the concurrent logic paradigm (and thus PCN can be implemented as an extension of the host language(s) to be used). The above program can be written in PCN as follows.

```
align_chunk(sequences,alignment)
{ ||
    pins(chunks,bestpin),
    divide(sequences,bestpin,Alignment)
}
pins(chunk,cplist)
{ ||
    cps(chunk,cplist),
    c_form_pins(cplist,pinlist),
    best_pin(chunk,pinlist,bestpin)
}
cps(sequences,cplist)
{ ? sequences ?= [seq|sequences1] ->
    { ||
        cplist = [cps|cplist1],
        c_critical_points(seq,cps),
        cps(sequences1,cplist1)
    },
    sequences ?= [] -> cplist=[]
}
```

```
divide(seqs,pin,alignment)
{ ? pin != [] ->
    { ||
        split(seqs,pin,left,right,rest),
        align_chunk(left,lalign) @ node(random),
        align_chunk(right,ralign) @ node(random),
        align_chunk(rest,restalign) @ node(random),
        combine(lalign,ralign,restalign,alignment)
    },
    pin == [] -> c_basic_align(seqs,alignment)
}
```

The reader may recall the use of logic programming in expressing coordination laws in Law-Governed Linda (Section 3.2.4). There, logic programming is interfaced to some other coordination formalism (namely the tuple space). Here, however (concurrent) logic programming is itself the coordination formalism used.

The second approach to deriving compositional programs originates from *functional programming* and is expressed in the form of *skeletons*. Skeletons [32, 67] are higher-order functional forms with built-in parallel behavior. They can be used to abstract away from all aspects of a program's behavior, such as data partitioning, placement, and communication. Skeletons are naturally data parallel and inherit all the desirable properties of the functional paradigm, such as abstraction, modularity, and transformation. The latter capability allows a skeletons-based program to be transformed to another, more efficient one, while at the same time preserving the properties of the original version. Thus, all analysis and optimization can be confined to the functional coordination level which is more suitable for this purpose. Furthermore, one is able to reason about the correctness of the programs produced or derived after transformations. Skeletons can be both *configuration* and *computational* ones and, being independent of the host computational language, they can be combined with C, Fortran, etc. The following is a configuration skeleton.

```
distribution (f,p) (g,q) A B = align (p ° partition f A)
                                     (q ° partition g B)
```

`distribution` takes two function pairs; f and g specify the required partitioning strategy of A and B, respectively, and p and q specify any initial data rearrangement that may be required. `partition` divides a sequential array into a parallel array composed of sequential subarrays. `align` pairs corresponding subarrays in two distributed arrays together, to form a new configuration which is an array of tuples. A specialized `partition` for a $1 \times m$ two-dimensional array using `row_block` can be defined as follows.

```
partition (row_block p) A = << ii := B | ii <- [1..p] >>
   where B = SeqArray (1:1/p,1:n)
          [ (i,j) := A (i+(ii-1)*1/p,j) | i <- [1..l/p],
                                          j <- [1..n] ]
```

A computational skeleton for a matrix addition performed in parallel using the configuration skeleton above can be defined as follows:

```
matrixAdd A B = (gather ° map ° SEQ_ADD)
                                (distribution fl dl)
   where C = SeqArray ((1..SIZE(A,1)), (1:SIZE(A,2)))
         fl = [((row_block p),id), ((row_block p),id),
                                   ((row_block p),id)]
         dl = [A,B,C]
```

Note that SEQ_ADD is defined in some other computational language. There is no unique set of skeletons and a number of them have been designed with some special purpose in mind [14, 18, 33, 34].

3.2.15 CoLa

CoLa [44] is particularly suited for distributed artificial intelligence applications implemented using massive parallelism. It is effectively a set of primitives (quite independent of the host programming language) that introduce and enforce a number of desired properties such as high-level communication abstraction (*correspondents*), virtual communication topologies, and a *local view* of computation for each process. In particular, associated with each process is a *Range of Vision* which defines the set of correspondents the process can locally communicate with, plus a *Point of View* which indicates a specific communication topology the process is involved in. The following program models bidirectional communication in a tree topology.

```
with csTopoVision            -- CoLa base topology class
class csTreeVision is        -- Define Point of View
   father(csCor, const csCor);
                             -- father node in Point of View
   son(csCor, const csCor);  -- son node in Point of View
end class;

implementation csTreeVision is
                -- Implementation of the Point of Views
   son is rule son(X,Y) :- csTopoVision.isLinked(X,Y).
   father is rule father(X,Y) :- son(Y,X).
                             -- Prolog like clauses
```

```
end implementation;
procedure p(T: in csTreeVision) is
  F: csSet := {X in T | father(X,self)};
                              -- Compute correspondence
  S: csSet := {X in T | son(X,self)};
  myMsgDep := csMsgSendAssDep (highest_prio(S),T,csREAD);
  myMsgId:= csMsgAss (myMsgBody,myMsgDep,csFIFO);
  csMsgSend (myMsgId);         -- Send in the tree topology
  M := {};                                   -- Enter loop
  csLoop do                           -- Read all messages
    myMsgDep:= csMsgRecvAssDep (C in S, T);
    myMsgRecvId := csMsgAss (myMsgBody,myMsgDep,
                                              csIMMEDIATE);
    csMsgRecv (myMsgRecvId);
    M := union (M,{C});
    exit if csIsSmallSubset(M,S);
  end csLoop
  myMsgDep := csMsgSendAssDep (F,T,csREAD);
                                       -- Build depiction
  myMsgId:= csMsgAss (myMsgBody,myMsgDep,csCAUSAL);
  csMsgSend (myMsgId);
                   -- Send results upward to father node
end procedure
```

A process sends information to a set of other processes (computed by the relation son and the filter highest_prio) and expects a reply from some, but not necessarily all of its addressed processes. It then sends some computed results upwards to its father. The program uses a predefined topology (csTopoVision) whose specification and implementation are also given. On setup of the procedure p, it first computes its father and children correspondents, using the appropriate Points of View supplied as parameters. It then constructs the message Depiction for the destination processes and finally sends a message to all its children selected by the filter highest_prio. To receive an answer, the program enters a loop and specifies from whom in the topology it is ready to process a message, and then forwards the results to the father node. Note the declarative Prolog-like style for implementing Points of View. Note also the use of predefined communication view primitives (such as csMsgSendAssDep) throughout the code.

3.2.16 Opus

Opus [19] is effectively a coordination superlanguage on top of High Performance Fortran (HPF), for which it was designed, for the purpose of coordinating concurrent execution of several data-parallel components. Interaction between concurrently executing tasks is achieved via the *ShareD Abstraction* (SDA), a Linda-like common forum. An SDA is in fact an abstract data type containing a set of data structures that define its state and a set of methods for manipulating this state. SDAs can be used either as traditional ADTs that act as data servers between concurrently executing tasks or as computation servers driven by a main, controlling task. In that respect, Opus combines data- and task-parallelism.

Execution of an Opus program begins with a single coordinating task that establishes all the participating computation and data servers. The coordinating task drives the computation by invoking the proper methods within the computation SDAs. Communication and synchronization between the concurrently executing tasks is managed by the data SDAs. The following code implements a data server for a FIFO bounded buffer.

```
SDA TYPE buffer_type(size)
   INTEGER               ::size
   REAL, PRIVATE         ::fifo(0:size-1) ! FIFO buffer
   INTEGER, READ ONLY    ::count=0        ! number of full
                                            elements in fifo
   INTEGER, PRIVATE      ::px=0           ! producer index
   INTEGER, PRIVATE      ::cx=0           ! consumer index
   ...
   CONTAINS
     SUBROUTINE put(x) WHEN (count .LT. size)
        REAL, INTENT(IN) ::x
        fifo(px)=x ! put x into first empty buffer element
        px=MOD(px+1,size)
        count=count+1
     END
     SUBROUTINE get(x) WHEN (count .GT. 0)
        REAL, INTENT(OUT) ::x
        x=fifo(cx)       ! get next element from full buffer
        cx=MOD(cx+1,size)
        count=count-1
     END
     ...
END buffer_type
```

SDAs of the above type are created and activated as follows:

```
PROCESSORS R(128)

SDA (buffer_type)::buffer1, buffer2
...
CALL buffer1%CREATE(256) on PROCESSORS R(1)
CALL buffer2%CREATE(000000,STAT=create_status)
                                            ON PROCESSORS R
```

The first CREATE statement generates an SDA with buffer size 256 and allocates it on processor R(1) with the variable buffer1 playing the role of a handle. The second CREATE statement allocates a much bigger buffer size across the rest of the processors with buffer2 as the handle.

Opus is in fact one of the few languages in the data-driven category which separates quite clearly the coordination component from the HPF computational component. However, we choose to include the model in this category rather than the one on control-driven coordination languages because of the SDA mechanism it employs, which is quite reminiscent of the shared dataspace one.

3.3 Control-Driven (Process-Oriented) Coordination Models

In control-driven or process-oriented coordination languages, the coordinated framework evolves by means of observing state changes in processes and, possibly, broadcast of events. Contrary to the case of the data-driven family, where coordinators directly handle and examine data values, here processes (whether coordination or computational ones) are treated as black boxes; data handled within a process is of no concern to the environment of the process. Processes communicate with their environment by means of clearly defined interfaces, usually referred to as *input* or *output ports*. Producer–consumer relationships are formed by means of setting up *stream* or *channel* connections between output ports of producers and input ports of consumers. By nature, these connections are *point-to-point*, although *limited broadcasting* functionality is usually allowed by forming $1-n$ relationships between a producer and n consumers, and vice versa. Certainly though, this scheme contrasts with the shared dataspace approach usually advocated by the coordination languages of the previous family. In addition to using ports, processes often send out to their environment *control messages* or *events* with the purpose of letting other interested processes know in which *state* they are or informing them of any *state changes*. Figure 2 depicts these concepts.

In particular, the figure shows a configuration involving one producer with one input and two output ports and two consumers, one with a single input port and a single output port and the other with two input ports and one output port. Stream connections have been established between the output ports of the producer and the input ports of the consumers, sometimes with more than one stream entering an input port or leaving an output port. Furthermore, the producer and one of the consumers either raises and/or observes the presence of some events. Most of the coordination languages to be described in this section realize in one way or another the above CSP- or occam-like formalism. However, they differ in the exact functionality of the involved concepts. For instance, in some languages events can be parametric with types and data

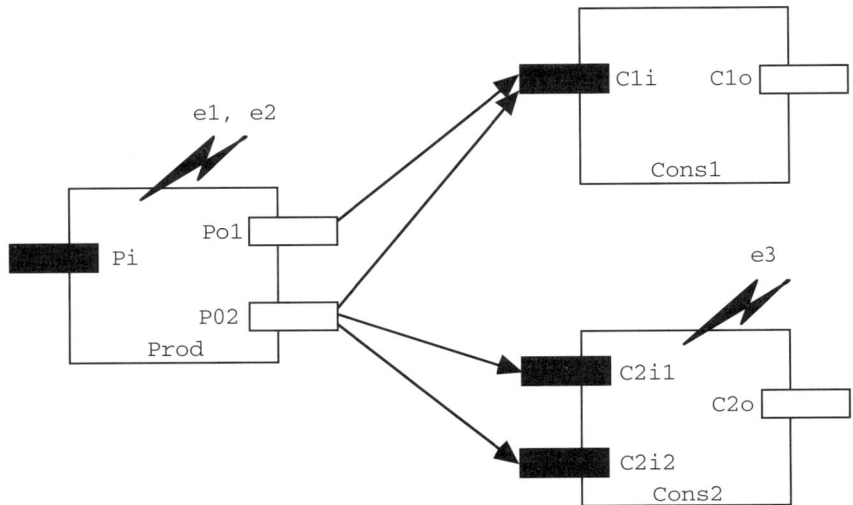

FIG. 2. Control-Driven Coordination via Point-to-Point Communication

values (effectively another mechanism for interprocess communication) whereas in other languages events are strictly simple units signifying state changes. Furthermore, in some languages events are broadcast by means of mechanisms different from stream connections, whereas in other languages events actually travel through streams. Stream connections themselves can be realized in a number of ways; for instance, they may or may not support synchronous communication. In some cases streams are interfaced to some common medium (such as a "data bus") rather than being point-to-point connections between ports; even in this latter case, however, the medium is not used for unrestricted broadcasting. Also, some languages support dynamic creation of ports and exporting of their id for use by other processes, whereas others limit such functionality.

The ability to visualize the evolution of computation in this family of coordination models using metaphors similar to the ones shown in Fig. 2 is not irrelevant to the fact that for many of these coordination languages graphical programming environments exist [16].

3.3.1 PCL (Proteus Configuration Language)

PCL [68] is a language designed to model architectures of multiple versions of computer-based systems. Furthermore, it has been used to model static as well as dynamic configurations. Coordination in PCL is understood as a *configuration*; the unit of configuration is a family entity, representing one or more versions of a logical component or system. A family entity may be related to other family entities through inheritance, composition, and relationship participation. A family entity has various kinds of associated information, namely a composition structure, a classification (specifying its type), a list of attributes, a parts section specifying the composition of the entity in terms of other entities, and a number of version descriptors.

In the configuration paradigm, an application is presented as a cooperating set of components. A component *encapsulates* state and may provide and require services, to and from other components. There exist *single* and *composite* components, the latter merely providing abstraction mechanisms, since at run-time the system unfolds to one comprising only simple components realized as processes. Simple components may be classified as *active* (that provide services to other components, but are also able to execute in the absence of external stimuli) and *passive* (acting only when some external stimulus requests a service from them). Another major element of the configuration paradigm is the *ports* which are used to represent either provided or required service. A component may have a number of required and/or provided ports. Inter-component communication is facilitated indirectly by transmitting messages through bindings, where a *binding* is used to connect two ports. Communication can either be synchronous or asynchronous.

The following example models a scenario involving a log component, a controller component, and three sensor components. log provides two services: an add service allowing a sensor component to register a value and a readings service allowing the controller component to read the last n sensor readings registered. Only the code for log is shown below.

```
family log inherits component
   class
      type => active
   end
   attributes
      persistentState=true
   end
   interface
      provides => (add,readings)
   end
   structure
      portBindLeastOnce => add, (sensor)
      portBindExactlyOnce => readings, (controller)
   end
   behavior
      intraAtomicOperation => (writeToDisk)
   end
end
```

log is defined as an active component which periodically writes data to the disk; meanwhile, this component may not be substituted with another one. Furthermore, log supports persistent state in the sense that, during dynamic reconfiguration, persistent information should survive.

The above-mentioned framework inherently supports a clear distinction between the configuration component (namely PCL) and what is being configured (i.e. computational components written in any conventional programming language). Furthermore, components are context-independent, since inter-component interaction and communication is achieved only by means of indirect interfaces comprising ports connected by means of bindings. Thus, a separation is achieved between the functional description of individual component behaviors and a global view of the formed system as a set of processes with interconnections. In addition, port connections are effectively unlimited buffers. If component replacement is to take place, any outstanding messages not yet delivered to a to-be-replaced component are retained by the run-time system and eventually forwarded to the component's replacement.

Finally, note that PCL is object-oriented and polymorphic. Thus, inheritance can be exploited to build hierarchies of family entities (in the example above, for instance, log inherits the basic functionality of a component). In addition, it is easy to create reusable descriptions of configuration scenarios.

3.3.2 Conic

Conic [47] is another language where coordination is viewed as configuration. In fact, Conic is two languages: a programming language (which is a variant of Pascal enhanced with message passing primitives) and a configuration language, similar in nature to PCL, featuring logical nodes that are configured together by means of links established among their input/output ports. A *logical node* is a system configuration unit comprising sets of tasks which execute concurrently within a shared address space. Configured systems are constructed as sets of interconnected logical nodes; these sets are referred to as *groups*.

The programming subcomponent of Conic is based on the notion of *task module types*, which are self-contained, sequential tasks; these are used at runtime by the Conic system to generate respective module instances, which exchange messages and perform various activities. The modules' interface is defined in terms of strongly typed ports. An *exitport* denotes the interface at which message transactions can be initiated and provides a local name and type holder in place of the source name and type. An *entryport* denotes the interface at which message transactions can be received and provides a local name and typeholder in place of the source name and type. A link between an exitport and an entryport is realized by means of invoking the message-passing facilities of the programming subcomponent. The system supports both unidirectional asynchronous and bidirectional synchronous communication. Since all references are to local objects, there is no direct naming of other modules or communication entities. Thus each programming module is oblivious to its environment, which renders it highly reusable, simplifies reconfiguration, and clearly separates the activities related to the latter from purely programming concerns.

The following example illustrates the syntax of the configuration subcomponent of Conic; it is part of a typical (regarding configuration languages) example describing a patient-monitoring system comprising nurses and patients.

```
group module patient;
  use monmsg: bedtype, alarmstype;
  exitport alarm: alarmstype;
  entryport bed: signaltype reply bedtype;
  << code >>
end.

group module nurse;
  use monmsg: bedtype, alarmstype;
  entryport alarm[1..maxbed]: alarmstype;
  exitport bed[1..maxbed]: signaltype reply bedtype;
  << code >>
end.
```

The first module models the monitoring device of a patient. The device periodically reads sensors attached to the patient. If any readings are detected which are outside their established ranges, suitable alarm messages are sent to the exitport. Also, a request message received in the entryport returns the current readings. The second module displays alarms received at the entryports and can request the display of the readings associated with a patient from its exitports. Note that a nurse may be monitoring more than one patient (hence the use of arrays of ports).

The following configuration code creates instances of the above modules (at specified machine locations in the system) and establishes the required communication links.

```
system ward;
  create
    bed1: patient at machine1;
    nurse: nurse at machine2;
  link
    bed1:alarm to nurse.alarm[1];
    nurse.bed[1] to bed[1].bed;
  end.
```

Conic supports a limited form of *dynamic reconfiguration*. First of all, the set of task and group types from which a logical node type is constructed is fixed at node compile time. Furthermore, the number of task and group instances within a node is fixed at the time a node is created. Dynamic changes to link setups can be achieved through the unlink command. The following example shows how the above system can evolve at run-time to one where the nurse module instance changes behavior and starts monitoring the readings of another patient (such a scenario would make sense if the nurse already monitors the maximum number of patients it can handle).

```
manage ward;
  create
    bed2: patient at machine1;
  unlink
    bed1:alarm from nurse.alarm[1];
    nurse.bed[1] from bed[1].bed;
  link
    bed2:alarm to nurse.alarm[1];
    nurse.bed[1] to bed[2].bed;
end.
```

Another limitation of the dynamic reconfiguration functionality of Conic is related to the very nature of the links that are being established between entryports and exitports. In particular, these links are not viewed as (unbounded) buffer areas. Thus, when some link is severed between a pair or set of ports, the module instances involved in communication must have stopped exchanging messages, otherwise information may be lost and inconsistent states may result. The Conic developers have designed a system reconfiguration model whereby links may be severed only between nodes which enjoy a *quiescence* property. More to the point, a node is quiescent if: (i) it is not currently involved in a transaction that it initiated, (ii) it will not initiate new transactions, (iii) it is not currently engaged in servicing a transaction, and (iv) no transactions have been or will be initiated by other nodes which require service from this node. Finally, one cannot underestimate the fact that in Conic a user is constrained by using a single programming language (the Pascal-like Conic programming subcomponent).

3.3.3 Darwin/Regis

The Regis system and the associated configuration language Darwin [48] are effectively an evolution of the above-mentioned Conic model. Darwin generalizes Conic by being largely independent of the language used to program processes (although the Regis system actually uses a specific language, namely C++). Furthermore, Darwin realizes a stronger notion of dynamic reconfiguration: it supports (lazy) component instantiation and (direct) dynamic component instantiation (in contrast, Conic supports only static configuration patterns which can be changed at run-time only by explicitly invoking a configuration manager). Furthermore, it allows components to interact through user-defined communication primitives (whereas Conic offers only a predefined set of such primitives). Finally, there is a clear separation of communication from computation (in Conic, the computation code is intermixed with the communication code).

As in Conic, a Darwin configuration comprises a set of *components* with clearly defined interfaces which are realized as *ports*, the latter being queues of typed messages. Ports are of two types: those used by a process to receive data (effectively input ports) are understood as being *provided* to the environment of the process for the benefit of other processes to post the messages, and those used to send data (effectively output ports) are understood as *requiring* a port reference to some remote port in order to post there the involved data. In fact, ports in Darwin/Regis are viewed as the more general concept of *services* (either provided or required); combined with port references, this allows the realization of rather liberal notions of port connections. In addition to the provided/required ports included in a process definition, processes may at run-time realize various communication and configuration patterns by exchanging port references and then using them to send/receive messages.

The following example calculates in a distributed fashion the number π. It consists of three groups of processes: a set of worker processes dividing among themselves the computational work to be done, a supervisor process which combines the results, and a top-level coordinator process which sets up the whole apparatus. First we show the configuration component of the example written in Darwin.

```
component supervisor (int w)
{
 provide
    result <port,double>;
 require
    labour <component,int,int,int>;
}
component worker (int id, int nw, int intervals)
{
 require
    result <port,double>;
}
```

```
component calcpi2(int nw)
{
 inst
   S:supervisor(nw);
 bind
   worker.result -- S.result;
   S.labour -- dyn worker;
}
```

The `supervisor` process is responsible for dynamically spawning new `worker` processes. Note that the **require** part of `supervisor` specifies as the required type of service a component rather than merely a port. The coordinator process `calcpi2` generates an instance of `supervisor`; furthermore, it dynamically generates instances of `labour` (by means of the **dyn** primitive which in this case creates instances of `worker` when invoked) and sets up the port connections accordingly.

The criteria that dictate precisely when new `worker` processes are spawned, as well as the actual computation code from the Regis C++ based computation subcomponent, are shown below.

```
worker::worker(int id, int nw, int intervals)
{
 double area=0.0;
 double width=1.0/intervals;
 for (int i=id; i<intervals; i+=nw)
   {
     double x=(i+0.5)*width;
     area+=width*(4.0/(1.0+x*x));
   }
 result.send(area);
 exit();
}

supervisor::supervisor(int nw)
{
 const int intervals=400000;
 double area=0.0;
 for (int i=0; i<nw; i++)
   {
     labour.at(i);
     labour.inst(i,nw,intervals);
   }
  for (int i=0; i<nw; i++)
   {
     double tmp;
     result.in(tmp);
     area+=tmp;
   }
 printf("Approx pi %20.15lf\n",area);
}
```

Note the use of the communication primitives send and in, which are used to post and retrieve, respectively, a message to/from a port. Furthermore, note the expression labour.inst(i,nw,intervals) which actually invokes a new worker process (the at primitive in the previous command line is used to specify on which processor the new process should run).

3.3.4 Durra

Durra [11, 12] is yet another architecture configuration language. A Durra application consists of a set of *components* and a set of *configurations* specifying how the components are interrelated. Components consist of application *tasks*, which feature *input/output ports*, and communication *channels*. At runtime, tasks create *processes* and channels create *links*; composite process configurations are achieved by using links to connect input/output ports between different processes.

Durra's main concern is how to coordinate resources, i.e. load and execute programs at different locations (thus supporting heterogeneous processing), route data, reconfigure the application, etc. As all the other members in this family of coordination languages, it makes a clear distinction between application structure and behavior. Tasks implement the functionality of the application, whereas channels implement communication facilities. Thus, it is possible to support different kinds of communication; furthermore, reusability of components is enhanced.

The following example shows how one can realize a producer–consumer scenario in Durra. In particular, it presents the definitions for a producer task, a consumer task, and a FIFO channel.

```
task producer                           task consumer
  ports                                   ports
    output: out message;                    input: in message;
  attributes                              attributes
    processor="sun4";                       processor="sun4";
    procedure_name="producer";              procedure_name="consumer";
    library="/usr/durra/srclib";            library="/usr/durra/srclib";
  end producer;                           end consumer;

channel fifo(msg_type:identifier, buffer_size:integer)
  ports
    input: in msg_type;
    output: out msg_type;
  attributes
    processor="sun4";
    bound=buffer_size;
    package_name="fifo_channel";
    library="/usr/durra/channels";
  end fifo;
```

The above piece of code defines a producer task with an output port of type message. Furthermore, the Durra code specifies that task instances of producer should run on the indicated machine, and that the task's implementation code can be found in the procedure producer in the directory /usr/durra/srclib. Similar things can be said about the task consumer and the channel fifo (the description of the latter also generically specifies, through parameters, the types of message its two ports can receive and other relevant information, such as the size of the channel). The actual implementation of the above tasks and channel are not shown here; they can be written in any conventional programming language.

The following Durra code uses the above-defined entities to generate a compound task description featuring dynamic reconfiguration.

```
task dynamic_producer_consumer
  components
    p: task producer;
    c[1..2]: task consumer;
    buffer: channel fifo(message,10);
  structures
    L1: begin
          baseline p, c[1], buffer;
          buffer: p.output >> c[1].input;
        end L1;
    L2: begin
          baseline p, c[2], buffer;
          buffer: p.output >> c[2].input;
        end L2;
  reconfigurations
    enter => L1;
    L1 => L2 when signal(c[1],1);
  clusters
    cl1: p, buffer;
    cl2: c[1], c[2];
end dynamic_producer_consumer;
```

The scenario involves one producer, two consumers, and a FIFO channel of buffer size 10. Two different configuration scenarios are possible: L1, involving the producer, the first consumer, and the channel, and L2, of similar in nature to L1, where the second consumer is used instead. In either case, the producer sends data via its output port to the input port of the first or the second consumer through the channel. Initially, the configuration L1 is active; transition to L2 is done when some particular signal is raised by the first consumer.

Durra is tailored more to support rapid prototyping of distributed heterogeneous applications and test different configuration strategies, rather than as a means to actually implement these applications. Its task emulator supports a number of useful features, including timing constraints (thus rendering the language suitable for real-time applications), but its implementation is centralized. Furthermore, although in principle any implementation language can be used, the Durra system is tailored towards the use of Ada. Finally, unrestricted dynamic creation of task instances is not possible; for instance, the above code restricts the involved entities at run-time to be one producer, two consumers, and a channel.

3.3.5 CSDL

CSDL (Cooperative Systems Design Language [58, 59]) is a specification and design language that supports the definition of the coordination aspects and the definition of the logical architecture of a cooperative system. A CSDL configuration comprises users, applications, and *coordinators*, where the latter define the cooperation policies and control the data flowing between users and shared applications. A coordinator is composed of three parts: a *specification* that defines *groups* and cooperation policies in terms of *requests* exported selectively to members of different groups; a *body* that defines the *access rights* associated with the groups in terms of communication system control; and a *context* that defines coordinator dependencies in terms of groups mapping. The following CSDL code defines the specification and body of an X-Window coordinator.

```
coordinator XWindow
{
  group ConnectedUsers;
  group Output
    nestedIn ConnectedUsers;
  group Input
    nestedIn Output;
  invariant #Input <= 1;
  requests
  {
  exportedTo extern
  {
    join Output other
    {
     actions: insert ConnectedUsers other;
              insert Output other;
    }
    join Input other
    {
      requires: other in Output and #Input = 0;
```

```
      actions: insert Input other;
    }
  }
  leave Output other
  {
    actions: extract Output other;
            extract ConnectedUsers other;
  }
  leave Input other
  {
    actions: extract Input other;
  }
  }
}

coordinator body XWindow
{
  S: switcher inOut XSwitcher;
  group ConnectedUsers
  { connected; inOff; outOff; }
  group Output
  { outOn; }
  group Input
  { inOn; }
}
```

The specification includes declaration of group identifiers that may involve the definition of a *type* and of a *nesting*. It also includes an invariant stating some constraints on group cardinality and membership through logical expressions, and a set of requests (such as `join` or `leave`) exported selectively to members of groups according to a desired policy. For instance, `exportedTo extern` refers to any sender not belonging to the group of the coordinator. Exchange of information between components is done by means of *virtual switches*, defined within the body of a coordinator, that model multiplexing and demultiplexing of data streams. Declaration of switches is accompanied by kinds and modes of access; in the example above, members of the `ConnectedUsers` group can be connected but cannot send and/or receive data, since they have both their input and their output channels disabled.

3.3.6 POLYLITH

POLYLITH [26, 60] is a software interconnection system, effectively a MIL enhanced with functionality (such as input/output ports and, more recently, events) found usually in coordination languages. POLYLITH clearly separates functional requirements from interfacing requirements, thus enhancing decoupling and reuse of software components. A component is treated as a *module*; modules have interfaces for each communication channel upon which the running instances of a module (i.e. processes) will send or receive messages. An abstract decoupling agent, called the *software bus*, is used as a means for process communication; message-passing routines provided by the system allow processes to get "plugged" to or "unplugged" from the bus.

The program code for a module is written separately from the rest of the code describing how it interfaces with the rest of the system and, in fact, the language supports the mixed language approach. Furthermore, the software bus actually encapsulates separately the interfacing decisions of the involved modules. Thus it is possible to use the same set of modules with different buses, say, one for distributed systems based on the TCP/IP paradigm, another one tailored to use shared memory, etc.

The following code shows the outline of the implementation and the specification of two modules.

```
main(argc,argv)                         main(argc,argv)
/* a.c (exec in a.out) */               /* b.c (exec in b.out) */
{                                       {
 char str[80];                           char str[80];
 ...                                     ...
 mh_write("out", ...,"msg1");            mh_read("in", ...,str);
 ...                                     ...
 mh_read("in", ...,str);                 mh_write("out", ...,
                                                           "msg2");
 ...                                     ...
}                                       }

service "A":                            orchestrate "example":
{                                       {
 implementation: {binary: "a.out"}       tool "foo": "A"
 source "out": {string}                  tool "bar": "B"
 sink "in": {string}                     tool "bartoo": "B"
}                                        bind "foo out" "bar in"
                                         bind "bar out" "bartoo in"
service "B":                             bind "bartoo out" "foo in"
{                                       }
 implementation: {binary: "b.out"}
 source "out": {string}
 sink "in": {string}
}
```

In the implementation part and using the primitives `mh_read` and `mh_write`, each of the two modules sends to its output channel `out` the messages `msg1` and `msg2`, respectively, and receives a message of type `string` from its own input channel `in` into its local variable `msg`. In the specification part, two services A and B are defined of type `a.out` and `b.out`, respectively, and furthermore, it is specified that each of them has an outgoing interface out and an incoming interface in, both of type string. The application definition example (effectively the "coordinator" process) actually creates a specific scenario involving one instance of a.out and two instances of b.out and properly connects their respective input/output channels.

Recently, the model has been enhanced with *events* allowing event-based interaction: modules register their interest in observing the raising of an event, at which point they invoke a procedure associated with the event. Furthermore, "event coordinators" are used to match together events of the same functionality but with different names among a number of modules realizing a composite interaction. The following code illustrates some of these points.

```
module "A":                              module "B":
{                                        {
  declare Sig1 {integer,string};           declare Sig2 {integer};
  generate Sig1;                           generate Sig2;
  when Sig2 => Proc1;                      when Sig1 => Proc2;
}                                        }

main()                                   main()
{                                        {
  char *event_type, *event;                char *event_type, *event;

  /* initialisation */                     /* initialisation */
  Init(argc,argv,NULL,NULL);               Init(argc,argv,NULL,NULL);
  Init(argc,argv,NULL,NULL);

  /* events declaration */                 /* events declaration */
  DeclareEvent("IS","Sig1");               DeclareEvent("I","Sig2");

  /* register interest */                  /* register interest */
  RegisterEvent("Sig2");                   RegisterEvent("Sig1");

  while (true)                             while (true)
  {                                        {
    /* get next event */                     /* get next event */
    GetNextEvent(event_type,event);          GetNextEvent
                                                 (event_type,event);

    /* invoke corresp proc */                /* invoke corresp proc */
    if (strcmp("Sig2",event_type)==0         if (strcmp
                                                 ("Sig1",event_type)==0)
       Proc1(event);                            Proc2(event);
  }                                        }
}                                        }
```

Each module declares an event and registers its interest in observing the raising of some other event. Upon detecting the presence of the specified event, the module calls some procedure. The first part of the code specifies the intended interaction, while the second part presents the outline of the implementation using C. Note that events are actually parameterized with data, so in fact they substitute the use of input/output channels in the previous version of POLYLITH.

3.3.7 The Programmer's Playground

The Programmer's Playground [42] shares many of the aims of languages such as Conic, Darwin, and Durra, in that it is a software library and runtime system supporting dynamic reconfiguration of distributed components. Furthermore, the model supports a uniform treatment of discrete and continuous data types and, as in the case of the other models in this family, a clear separation of communication from computation concerns.

The Programmer's Playground is based on the notion of *I/O abstraction*. I/O abstraction is a model of interprocess communication in which each *module* in the system has a presentation that consists of data structures that may be externally observed and/or manipulated. An *application* consists of a collection of independent modules and a *configuration of logical connections* among the data structures in the module presentations. Whenever published data structures are updated, communication occurs implicitly according to the logical connections.

I/O abstraction uses *declarative* communication (as opposed to *imperative* communication) in the sense that the user declares high-level logical connections among state components of modules (rather than expressing direct communication within the control flow of the program). Declarative communication enhances the separation of communication from computation, is less error-prone, and facilitates the automatic updating of the modules' states in cases where changes in the state of one module should be reflected in some other module. This last functionality is achieved by means of *connections*: if an item x in a module A is connected to an item y in another module B, then any change in x's value will cause an appropriate update in the value of y. Such connections can be *simple* (point-to-point) or *element-to-aggregate* (one-to-many); furthermore, the former can be *unidirectional* or *bidirectional*.

The following producer–consumer apparatus illustrates some of the above points.

```
#include "PG.hh"

PGint next=0;
```

```
PGstring mess;
send_next(PGstring mess, static int i)
{
  if (strcmp(mess,"ok")==0)
     next=i++;
}

main()
{
  PGinitialise("producer");
  PGpublish(next,"next_int",READ_WORLD);
  PGpublish(mess,"ok",WRITE_WORLD);

  while (1)
  {
   PGreact(mess,send_next);
  }
  PGterminate();
}

#include "PG.hh"

PGint next=0;
PGstring mess;

void consume_int(PGint i)
{ /* consumes list of integers */ }

main()
{
 PGinitialise("consumer");
 PGpublish(mess,"ok",READ_WORLD);
 PGpublish(next,"next_int",WRITE_WORLD);

 while (1)
 {
  PGreact(next,consume_int);
  mess="ok";
 }
 PGterminate();
}
```

The above program consists of two modules forming a producer–consumer pair communicating synchronously to exchange an infinite list of integers.

Both modules use an integer variable used to send/receive the integers and a string variable used by the consumer to declare that it is ready to receive the next integer. These variables are published by the two modules with an external name and a protection flag (read/write). The procedure `PGreact` is used to suspend execution of the module until the variable indicated in its first argument has been updated. The logical connection between the two variables in the respective modules is assumed to have already been established (in the Programmer's Playground this is achieved graphically: modules are shown as boxes, published variables as input/output "ports," and logical connections as lines drawn between their respective ports).

The Programmer's Playground is based on the C/C++ language formalism and has been implemented on Sun Solaris. Although it claims to clearly separate communication from computation concerns, at least stylistically the two different types of code are intermixed within a module. The model was developed primarily for developing distributed multimedia applications and in fact it places emphasis on supporting uniform treatment of discrete and continuous data, where differences in communication requirements are handled implicitly by the run-time system. Since the nature of the data being handled is here of more importance than in most of the other coordination models comprising the control-driven category, the Programmer's Playground could also be included in the data-driven category. We chose to place it here though, because of the well-defined input/output connections that each process possesses as well as for sharing the same application domains with configuration languages.

3.3.8 RAPIDE

RAPIDE [66] is an architecture definition language and in that respect shares many of the aims of languages such as Conic and Durra. It supports both component and communication abstractions as well as a separation between these two formalisms. An *architecture* in RAPIDE is an executable specification of a class of systems. It consists of *interfaces, connections,* and *constraints*. The interfaces specify the behavior of components of the system, the connections define the communication between the components using only those features specified by the components' *interfaces*, and the constraints restrict the behavior of the interfaces and connections. RAPIDE is *event-driven*; components generate (independently from one another) and observe events. Events can be parameterized with data and types. Asynchronous communication is modelled by connections that react to events generated by components and then generate events at other components. Synchronous communication can be modelled by connections between function calls. The result of executing a RAPIDE architecture (i.e. a set of interfaces and connections) is a *poset* showing the dependencies and independencies between events.

The following producer–consumer example illustrates some of the above points.

```
type Producer(Max: Positive) is interface
  action out Send(N: Integer);
  action in Reply(N: Integer);
behavior
  Start => Send(0);
  (?X in Integer) Reply(?X) where ?X < Max => Send(?X+1);
end Producer;

type Consumer is interface
  action in Receive(N: Integer);
  action out Ack(N: Integer);
behavior
  (?X in Integer) Receive(?X) => Ack(?X);
end Consumer;

architecture ProdCons() return SomeType is
  Prod: Producer(100);
  Cons: Consumer;
connect
  (?n in Integer)
  Prod.Send(?n) => Cons.Receive(?n);
  Cons.Ack(?n) => Prod.Reply(?n);
end architecture ProdCons;
```

The above code initially declares two types of component. Producer is designed to accept events of type Reply and broadcast events of type Send, both parameterized with an integer value. Upon commencing execution, Producer broadcasts the event Send(0) and upon receiving an event Reply(X) it will reply with the event Send(X+1) provided that X is less than a certain value. Consumer has similar functionality. The "coordinator" ProdCons() creates two process instances for Producer and Consumer, and furthermore it associates the output event of the former with the input event of the latter and vice versa. Note that the above code specifies how the two components interact with each other but the actual details of their implementation are left unspecified.

3.3.9 ConCoord

ConCoord [43] is a typical member of this family of control-driven coordination languages. A ConCoord program is a dynamic collection of computation processes and coordination processes. A computation process executes a sequential algorithm and can be written in any conventional programming language augmented with some communication primitives.

Coordination processes are written in CCL, ConCoord's Coordination Language. Communication between processes is done in the usual way of sending data to output ports they own and receiving data from input ports they also own, thus effectively achieving complete decoupling of producers from consumers. Processes raise or broadcast their state which is, in fact, an event or signal parameterized with data. States are communicated by message-passing. The following example shows a dynamically evolving pipeline of generic processes.

```
coordinator <t_node, t_data> gen_dyn_pipeline
{
  inport <t_data> in;
  outport <t_data> out;
  states error(), done();

  create t_node n bind in -- n.left, n.out -- out;
  loop
  {
    choose
    {
      sel(t_node n | n.new and not n.right--)
        => create t_node new_n
           bind n.right -- new_n.left, new_n.out -- out;
      sel(t_node n | n.new and n.right--)
        => error();
    }
  }
}
```

`gen_dyn_pipeline` is a coordinator parameterized with the types of both the computation processes forming the pipeline (`t_node`) and the data being communicated (`t_data`). The pipeline of nodes communicates with the outside world by means of the `in` and `out` ports of `gen_dyn_pipeline`; namely, the first process will get data via `in` and all processes will output data via `out`. Initially, one process is created and its own ports `left` and `out` are bound to `gen_dyn_pipeline`'s `in` and `out` respectively. Then, each time a process at the end of the pipeline raises the state `new`, a new process is created and inserted in the pipeline. Whether a process raising the state `new` is actually the last one in the pipeline is determined by means of examining whether its port `right` is linked to some other port (in this particular configuration to the port `left` of some other process). If that is indeed the case, then instead of creating a new process `gen_dyn_pipeline` raises the state `error`.

The language features nested hierarchies of coordination domains and synchronous or asynchronous communication between components. In particular, a computational process raising a state blocks until this is treated by the coordinator process in charge of it; thus, communication appears to be synchronous from the process's point of view and asynchronous from the point of view of the coordinator process. Coordinator processes and their groups of coordinated processes are configured in a hierarchical manner, with the top level of the configuration being a coordinator. Furthermore, the language enforces and encourages the building of structured programs by treating each pair of coordinator–coordinated processes as a separate domain. The coordinator of some domain is unaware of any nested subdomains and treats homogeneously computational and coordination processes within the latter. Furthermore, state change notification by some process is only visible in the domain of its supervisor coordinator process.

3.3.10 TOOLBUS

The TOOLBUS coordination architecture [13] is reminiscent of models such as POLYLITH, featuring a component interconnection metaphor (the toolbus) on which tools can be "plugged in". The toolbus itself consists of a number of processes which manage the tools forming the system. Although the number of tools comprising a system is static, the number of processes changes dynamically according to the intended functionality of the system. Thus, in addition to the straightforward one-to-one correspondence between tools and processes, it is also possible to have a tool controlled by a number of processes or groups of tools controlled by one process. Tools communicate implicitly via the toolbus; no direct tool-to-tool communication is allowed. A number of primitives are offered by the system, realizing both synchronous and asynchronous communication among the processes and between processes and tools. The TOOLBUS architecture recognizes a common format for the interchanged data; thus, each tool must use an *adapter* which changes data formats accordingly. Furthermore, the intended behavior of the system is specified by means of *T-scripts* which contain a number of definitions for processes and tools followed by a configuration statement. The following example shows how compiler–editor cooperation can be modelled in TOOLBUS.

```
define COMPILER =
  (rec-msg(compile,Name) . snd-eval(compiler,Name) .
    (rec-value(compiler,error(Err),loc(Loc)) .
      snd-note(compile-error,Name,error(Err),loc(Loc))
    ) * rec-value(compiler,Name,Res) . snd-msg(compile,Name,Res)
  ) * delta
define EDITOR =
  subscribe(compile-error) .
  ( rec-note(compile-error,Name,error(Err),loc(Loc)) .
      snd-do(editor,store-error(Name,error(Err),loc(Loc))
    + rec-event(editor,next-error(Name)) .
```

```
           snd-do(editor,visit-next(Name)) . snd-ack-event(editor)
) * delta

define UI =
  ( rec-event(ui,button,(compile,Name)) .
      snd-msg(compile,Name) . rec-msg(compile,Name,Res)
                             . snd-ack-event(ui)
) * delta
```

COMPILER receives a compilation request (from UI), starts the compilation, broadcasts any errors it encounters and finally sends the result back to the process that invoked it. EDITOR either receives a message with a compilation error and stores the compiled program and the error location for future reference or receives a next-error event from the editor and goes to a previously stored error location. Finally, UI is a user interface with a compile button which when pushed causes a compile message to be sent and waits for a reply.

The following TOOLBUS primitives are used in the above program: snd-msg is used by a process to send a message synchronously to another process, which the latter will receive by invoking rec-msg; snd-note is used by a process to broadcast messages asynchronously to other processes, which the latter receive by invoking rec-note, and subscribe is used by a process to declare its interest in receiving certain asynchronous broadcasts from other processes. Furthermore, rec-event and rec-value are used by a process to receive, respectively, an event and the evaluation result from some tool, and snd-do is used by a process to request the evaluation of some term by a tool. Finally, "+" and "·" are the selection and sequential operators, respectively, and delta signifies process termination.

Using the above definitions, a number of configurations are possible to set up, namely:

    toolbus(COMPILER,EDITOR,UI)   toolbus(COMPILER,UI)

where in the latter case a simpler system is configured without the ability to refer back to error locations.

The TOOLBUS enjoys formal semantics (the T-scripts can be formally analysed in terms of process algebras) and recently it has been extended with the notion of discrete time. A prototype interpreter C-based implementation exists and has been used to test the model's effectiveness in a number of applications.

3.3.11 MANIFOLD

MANIFOLD [8] is one of the latest developments in the evolution of control-driven or process-oriented coordination languages. As is the case in most of the other members of this family, MANIFOLD coordinators are clearly distinguished from computational processes, which can be written in any conventional programming language augmented with some communication primitives. Manifolds (as MANIFOLD coordinators are called) communicate by means of *input/output ports*, connected between themselves by means of *streams*. Evolution of a MANIFOLD coordination topology is *event-driven* based on *state transitions*. More to the point, a MANIFOLD coordinator process is at any moment in time in a certain state, where typically it has set up a network of coordinated processes communicating by sending and/or receiving data via stream connections established between respective input/output ports. Upon observing the *raising* of some event, the process in question breaks off the stream connections and evolves to some other predefined state where a different network of coordinated processes is set up. Note that, unlike the case with other coordination languages featuring events, MANIFOLD events are not parameterized and cannot be used to carry data—they are used purely for triggering state changes and causing the evolution of the coordinated apparatus. The following example is a bucket sorter written in MANIFOLD.

```
export manifold Sorter()
{
 event filled, flushed, finished.
 process atomsort is AtomicSorter(filled).
 stream reconnect KB input -> *.
 priority filled < finished.
 begin:
    ( activate(atomsort), input -> atomsort,
         guard(input,a_everdisconnected!empty,finished)
    ).
 finished:
    { ignore filled.
      begin: atomsort -> output
    }.
 filled:
    { process merge<a,b | output> is AtomicIntMerger.
      stream KK * -> (merge.a, merge.b).
      stream KK merge -> output.
      begin:
         ( activate(merge),
           input -> Sorter -> merge.a,
           atomsort -> merge.b,
           merge -> output
         ).
      end | finished: .
    }.
 end:
```

```
    { begin:
        ( guard(output,a_disconnected,flushed),
          terminated(void)
        ).
      flushed: halt.
    }.
}
```

The apparatus created by the above program functions more or less as follows: Sorter initially activates a computation process performing the actual sorting (AtomicSorter). This latter process, which is capable of performing very fast sorting of a bucket of numbers of size k, will raise the event filled once it receives the maximum number k of numbers to sort. Upon detecting the raising of filled, Sorter will activate a new sorting computation process as well as a merger process which is responsible for merging the output of both sorting processes into one stream. Depending on the bucket size k and the number of units to be sorted, an arbitrary number of sorting and merger processes may be created and linked together at run-time. Note that every process has by default an input and an output port; additionally, it may have other named ports too. The triggering process, which, in fact, is also responsible for passing the units to be sorted to Sorter and printing out the output, is shown below.

```
manifold Main
{
  auto process read is ReadFile("unsorted").
  auto process sort is Sorter.
  auto process print is printunits.
  begin: read -> sort -> print.
}
```

Although many of the concepts found in MANIFOLD have been used in other control-oriented coordination languages, MANIFOLD generalizes them into abstract linguistic constructs, with well-defined semantics that extend their use. For instance, the concept of a port as a first-class linguistic construct representing a "hole" with two distinct sides is a powerful abstraction for anonymous communication: normally, only the process q that owns a port p has access to the "private side" of p, while any third-party coordinator process that knows about p can establish a communication between q and some other process by connecting a stream to the "public side" of p. Arbitrary connections (from the departure sides to the arrival sides) of arbitrary ports, with multiple incoming and multiple outgoing connections, are all possible and have well-defined semantics. Also, the fact that computation and coordinator processes are absolutely indistinguishable from the point of view of other processes, means that coordinator processes can, recursively, manage the communication of other coordinator processes, just as if they were computation processes. This means that any coordinator can also be used as a higher-level or meta-coordinator to build a sophisticated hierarchy of coordination protocols. Such higher-level coordinators are not possible in most other coordination languages and models.

MANIFOLD advocates a liberal view of dynamic reconfiguration and system consistency. Consistency in MANIFOLD involves the integrity of the topology of the communication links among the processes in an application, and is independent of the states of the processes themselves. Other languages (such as Conic) limit the dynamic reconfiguration capability of the system by allowing evolution to take place only when the processes involved have reached some sort of a safe state (e.g. quiescence). MANIFOLD does not impose such constraints; rather, by means of a plethora of suitable primitives, it provides programmers with the tools to establish their own safety criteria to avoid reaching logically inconsistent states. For example, in the above program the stream connected to the input port of Sorter has been declared of type KB (keep-break) meaning that even if it is disconnected from its *arrival side* (the part actually connected to Sorter) it will still remain connected at the *departure side* (the part connected to the process which sends data down the stream—in our case read). Hence, when read must break connection with a filled sorter and forward the rest of the data to be sorted to a new sorting process, the data already in the stream will not be lost. Furthermore, *guards* are installed in the input and output ports of Sorter to make sure that all units to be sorted have either been received by Sorter or got printed successfully. These primitives, e.g. *guards*, inherently encourage programmers to express their criteria in terms of the externally observable (i.e. input/output) behavior of (computation as well as coordination) processes. In contrast to this extensive repertoire of coordination constructs, MANIFOLD does not support ordinary computational entities such as data structures, variables, or conditional or loop statements, although syntactically sugared versions of them do exist for a programmer's convenience.

Although not shown here, manifolds can actually be parameterized; these highly reusable generic manifolds are called *manners*. MANIFOLD has been successfully ported to a number of platforms including IBM SP1/SP2, Solaris 5.2, SGI 5.3/6.3, and Linux. Furthermore, it has been used with many conventional programming languages including C, C++, and Fortran [7]. Recently it has been extended with real-time capabilities [54]. Its underlying coordination model IWIM [6], which is in fact independent of the actual language, has been shown to be applicable to other coordination models and frameworks [55, 56].

4. Comparison

In the previous section we described in some detail the most important members of the two major families of coordination models and languages, namely the data-driven and the control-driven ones. In this section we present in a tabular form a comparison between these formalisms along some major dimensions that characterize a coordination formalism.

These dimensions are the following: (i) the entities being coordinated; (ii) the mechanism of coordination; (iii) the coordination medium or architecture; (iv) the semantics, rules or protocols of coordination employed; (v) whether a model supports a different (from the computational component) coordination language or involves the use of "add-on" primitives; (vi) whether a model supports and encourages the use of many computational languages; (vii) what is the most relevant application domain for each model and (viii) what is the implementation status of the proposed framework.

These are by no means the only issues that differentiate one model from another. For instance, regarding the category of control-driven coordination models, an issue worth comparing is the exact nature of the port-to-port connections via streams each model employees (where this is indeed the case) and whether and how any dynamic reconfigurations are realized. For example, some models only support static configurations or restrict access to ports to their owners, whereas other models support dynamic (re)configurations and exporting of ports identifiers. Although such a rather low-level comparison is useful, we felt that it would run the danger of obscuring the main differences between all the models involved across both main categories. In any case, we have outlined differences of this nature in the respective sections for each model.

5. Conclusions

The purpose of this chapter was to provide a comprehensive survey of those models and languages forming the family of coordination formalisms. In the process, we have classified the members of the coordination family into two broad categories, namely the data-driven and control-driven ones. Furthermore, we have described in some depth the most prominent members in each family, highlighting their features and presenting typical examples of their use.

Most members of the first family have evolved around the notion of a Shared Dataspace which plays the dual role of being both a global data repository and an interprocess communication medium. Processes forming a computation post and/or retrieve data from this medium. The most prominent member of this family (and, indeed, historically the first genuine coordination model) is Linda, where the common medium is a tuple space and processes use it to send to or retrieve from it tuples. Linda has been used extensively and over the years a number of other similar models evolved, their main purpose being to address some of the deficiencies, weaknesses, and inefficiencies of the basic vanilla model, such as issues of security, locality of reference, hierarchy of global data, and optimization in tuple access. A

TABLE 1a

Coordination Language	Entities being Coordinated	Mechanism of Coordination	Medium of Coordination	Semantics/Rules Protocols
Linda	active tuples	tuple exchange	Shared tuple space	associative pattern matching
Bauhaus Linda	active tuples	multisets	hierachies of tuple spaces	set inclusion
Bonita	processes	single or group tuple handling	multiple tuple spaces	associative pattern matching
Law-Governed Linda	processes supervised by 'law enforcers'	tuples enhanced with control info	logically structured tuple space	laws defining acceptable tuple access
Objective Linda	objects	ADTs and logicals (object refs)	multiset, hierachies of object spaces	type interfaces
LAURA	servers and clients	exchange of type forms	shared service space	typed interface description of services
Ariadane/HOPLa	hybrid processes	matching of (semi-) structured data	tree-shaped tuple space	flexible records
Sonia	actors (people, s/w tools)	possibly nested tuples	agora (shared tuple space)	typed template associative matching
Jada/SHADE	mobile agents	exchange of Java applets	Internet as multiple tuple space	Java/HTML
GAMMA	distributed data structures	chamical reactions via fixpoint op	possibly structured multiset (bag)	CHAM
LO/COOLL	agents as linear multiset objects	interagent broadcast group broadcast	multiset, Forum	Linear Logic
MESSENGERS	mobile processes	autonomously executable messages	explicitly partitioned distributed shared mem	intra/inter-object invocation
Synchronizers	objects	constraints on accessing objects	message passing	actor model
PCN/Strand	concurrent processes	commited-choice rule selection	shared declarative variables	concurrent logic programming
Functional Skeletons	sequential functions	function application and composition	distributed graph structures	string/graph reduction
CoLa	sequential processes	correspondents	hierachically formed points/ranges of view	message passing

number of other shared dataspace-based coordination models have been proposed, where the emphasis is on providing even more implicit (than Linda's associative pattern matching) semantics of tuple handling such as multiset rewriting. However, not all members of this family are adhering to the shared dataspace concept; there are a few which use the message-passing metaphor or a limited form of shared dataspace in the form of common buffer areas

TABLE 1a *continued*

Degree of Decoupling	Range of Comp Languages	Application Domain	Implementation Status
coordination primitives	wide range of comput. models	data parallel programs	different robust implementations
coordination primitives	wide range of comput. models	groupware	Unix-based prototype
coordination primitives	wide range of comput. models	data 'batch parallel' programs	PVM-based using the Linda-kernel
coordination rules written in Prolog	many shared-dataspace models	open and secured (distributed) systems	needs h/w support to enforce the laws
coordination primitives	object-orientated languages	modeling open distributed systems	PVM-based prototype
separate service description notation	potentially wide	modeling information systems	prototype-based on the ISIS toolkit
separate coordination component	potentially wide	collaborative environments	prototype
coordination primitives	Smalltalk-oriented	office automation	prototype
primitives coupled with Java code	Java	WWW, intranet open systems	prototype
parametric coord. patterns (tropes)	potentially wide	modelling s/w achitectures	Connection Machine iPSC2
rule based coord. component	logic programming oriented	parallel symbolic computing, DAI	shared memory prototype
coordination primitives	potentially wide	mobile computing	Sun-based implementation
constraints specified separately	potentially many OOP languages	object-oriented systems	not known
separate coordination component	many message passing languages	scientific computing	distributed implem. on many platforms
separate skeleton templates	potentially wide	data parallel programs	various families of skeletons
separate coordination components	potentially wide	distributed A.I.	PVM-based implementation

or global synchronization variables being manipulated concurrently by a number of processes.

Whereas the first family has been influenced by the concept of a shared medium, the second family has evolved around the Occam notion of distinct entities communicating with the outside world by means of clearly marked interfaces, namely input/output ports, connected together in some appropriate

TABLE 1b

Coordination Language	Entities being Coordinated	Mechanism of Coordination	Medium of Coordination	Semantics/Rules Protocols
Opus	sequential tasks	method invocation	Shared abstraction	data parallelism
PCL	tools forming family entities	exchanging services via ports	hierarchies of tool family entities	dynamic configuration
Conic	system components	exchanging data via ports	hierarchies of logical nodes	state transitions based on quiescence
Darwin/Regis	mostly sequential processes	exchanging data via ports	dynamically evolving component graphs	dynamically evolving state transitions
Durra	components and resources	events and channel connections	statically defined component graphs	event driven state transitions
CSDL	tools	coordinators specifying access rights	group connections	CSCW metaphors
POLYLITH	software components	event-based triggering	software bus	MILs metaphors
Programmer's playground	devices	implicit communication	discrete/continuous data streams	I/O abstraction
RAPIDE	system components	observing/reaching to events	connections between well-defined interf's	poset model
ConCoord	sequential processes	satisfying conditions on domain states	hierarchical config. of event/state domains	pairs of condition-action
TOOLBUS	software components	exchange of messages and notes	software bus	process-oriented T-scripts
MANIFOLD	sequential processes	events and streams	configuration of process networks	event-driven state transitions

fashion by means of streams or channels. In fact, the coordination paradigm offered by this second family is sometimes characterized as being *channel-based* as opposed to the *medium-based* notion of coordination supported by the first family. Traditionally, languages of this family where initially proposed for configuring systems and modelling software architectures. However, recently a number of proposals have been put forward where control-driven languages are designed with more conventional coordination application areas in mind. Most members of this family share the concept of a separate coordination language (as opposed to the case of the data-driven models where a set of coordination primitives are used in conjunction with a host language) which is used to define pure coordination modules featuring ports, streams or channels and possibly event broadcasting. They differ though in issues such as whether the id of ports can become public or not, whether the communication is asynchronous or synchronous (or both), or whether events carry values.

TABLE 1b *continued*

Degree of Decoupling	Range of comp Languages	Application Domain	Implementation Status
separate coordination component	potentially wide but FORTRAN-oriented	scientific computing	prototype on top of Chant
separate coordination component (PCL)	potentially wide	modeling system architectures	prototype
semi-separate coord component	PASCAL	configuring distributed systems	Unix/VMS with graphical interface
separate fully fledged coord component	C++ oriented	configuring distributed programs	Unix-based implementation
separate fully fledged coord component	Ada	rapid prototyping of distributed programs	prototype
separate fully fledged coord component	potentially wide	cooperative systems	prototype
MIL-like-specification syntax	potentially wide	transparent transportation of s/w systems	distributed implementation
data exchange primitives	potentially wide	distributed multi-media systems	distributed C++-based implementation
separate coord component	not applicable	prototyping system architectures	prototype
separate coordinations language (CCL)	potentially wide	distributed/concurrent process oriented algs	prototype on top of Regis
separate coordination component	potentially wide	system integration	prototype
separate coordination lang (MANIFOLD)	potentially wide	scientific computing s/w architectures	fully implemented on many platforms

An interesting and quite fruitful "confrontation" between the data- and control-driven coordination approaches is with respect to whether and to what extent a program need be structured and locality of communication be supported. The shared dataspace vanilla models, such as Linda and GAMMA, encourage a flat unstructured communication medium employing global broadcasting. However, some of their variants, such as Bauhaus Linda and Structured GAMMA, provide hierarchical levels of their communication medium which are able to express locality of communication and support structure. On the other hand, control-driven coordination languages, such as MANIFOLD, support multiple port-to-port stream connections which employ limited forms of broadcasting. Furthermore, these streams are first-class citizens, able to hold data within themselves while stream connections break off and get reconnected between different coordinated processes, thus providing to a certain extent the functionality of a shared communication medium. It is the authors' belief that a number of novel coordination models and languages will be proposed which will further converge these two approaches towards the formation of communication media which will provide the desired (ideal?) degree of shared or point-to-point communication as well as support naturally the structuring of programs.

The issue of coordination is rather broad [46, 49] and in this chapter we have only concentrated on the "programming languages" aspect; furthermore, we have advocated a practical flavor. Thus, aspects of coordination related to, say, workflow management, cooperative work, and software composition (to name but a few) have not been addressed. Neither did we delve into theoretical issues such as semantics, formal specification, and reasoning. Coordination models and languages have evolved rapidly over the past few years and the concept of coordination is now being introduced in many aspects of contemporary computer science, including middleware domains such as the web and CORBA-like platforms, modelling activities in information systems, and "coordination-in-the-large" application areas such as software engineering and open distributed systems. Thus, we expect a proliferation of many more models and languages over the years to come, addressing these issues and possibly also offering unified solutions for a number of different application domains.

ACKNOWLEDGMENTS

A number of people have provided useful feedback in improving the presentation of the survey and its contents. Special thanks are due to Anne-Alexandra Holzbacher Jensen and Andrea Omicini for detailed comments on earlier drafts of this chapter.

This work has been partially supported by the INCO-DC KIT (Keep-in-Touch) program 962144 "Developing Software Engineering Environments for Distributed Information Systems," financed also by the Commission of the European Union.

REFERENCES

1. Agha, G. (1986) *Actors: A Model of Concurrent Computation in Distributed Systems*. MIT Press Cambridge MA.
2. Ahuja, S., Carriero, N., and Gelernter, D. (1986) Linda and friends. *IEEE Computer* **19**(8), 26–34.
3. Andreoli, J.-M., Gallaire, H., and Pareschi, R. (1996) Rule-based object coordination. *First International Conference on Coordination Models, Languages and Applications (Coordination '96)*, Cesena, Italy. Lecture Notes in Computer Science 1061. Springer-Verlag, Berlin. pp. 1–13.
4. Andreoli, J-M., Hankin, C., and Le Métayer, D. (1996) *Coordination Programming: Mechanisms, Models and Semantics*. World Scientific, Singapore.
5. Andreoli, J.-M., and Pareschi, R. (1991) Linear objects: logical processes with built-in inheritance. *New Generation Computing* **9**(3–4), 445–473.
6. Arbab, F. (1996) The IWIM model for coordination of concurrent activities *First*

International Conference on Coordination Models, Languages and Applications (Coordination '96), Cesena, Italy. Lecture Notes in Computer Science 1061. Springer-Verlag, Berlin. pp. 34–56.
7. Arbab, F., Blom, C. L., Burger, F. J., and Everaars, C. T. H. (1996) Reusable coordinator modules for massively concurrent applications. *Europar'96*, Lyon. Lecture Notes in Computer Science 1123. Springer-Verlag, Berlin. pp. 664–677.
8. Arbab, F., Herman, I., and Spilling, P. (1993) An overview of Manifold and its implementation. *Concurrency: Practice and Experience* **5**(1), 23–70.
9. Banâtre, J.-P., and Le Métayer, D. (1996) GAMMA and the chemical reaction model: ten years after. *Coordination Programming: Mechanisms, Models and Semantics* (eds J.-M. Andreoli, H. Gallaire, and D. Le Métayer). World Scientific, Singapore. pp. 1–39.
10. Banville, M. (1996) Sonia: an adaptation of Linda for coordination of activities in organizations. *First International Conference on Coordination Models, Languages and Applications (Coordination '96)*, Cesena, Italy. Lecture Notes in Computer Science 1061. Springer-Verlag, Berlin. pp. 57–74.
11. Barbacci, M. R., Weinstock, C. B., Doubleday, D. L., Gardner, M. J., and Lichota, R. W. (1996) Durra: a structure description language for developing distributed applications. *IEE Software Engineering Journal* March, pp. 83–94.
12. Barbacci, M. R., and Wing, J. M. (1990) A language for distributed applications. *International Conference on Computer Languages (ICCL '90)*, New Orleans LA. IEEE Press. pp. 59–68.
13. Bergstra, J. A., and Klint, P. (1996) The TOOLBUS coordination architecture. *First International Conference on Coordination Models, Languages and Applications (Coordination '96)*, Cesena, Italy. Lecture Notes in Computer Science 1061. Springer-Verlag, Berlin. pp. 75–88.
14. Botorog, G. H., and Kuchen, H. (1996) Skil: an imperative language with algorithmic skeletons for efficient distributed programming. *Fifth IEEE International Symposium on High Performance Distributed Computing (HPDC-5)*, New York. IEEE Press. pp. 243–252.
15. Bourgois, M., Andreoli, J.-M., and Parechi, R. (1993) Concurrency and communication: choices in implementing the coordination language LO. *Object-Based Distributed Programming ECOOP'93 Workshop*, Kaiserslautern, Germany. Lecture Notes in Computer Science 791. Springer-Verlag, Berlin. pp. 73–92.
16. Bouvry, P., and Arbab, F. (1996) Visifold: a visual environment for a coordination language. *First International Conference on Coordination Models, Languages and Applications (Coordination '96)*, Cesena, Italy. Lecture Notes in Computer Science 1061. Springer-Verlag, Berlin. pp. 403–406.
17. Brogi, A., and Ciancarini, P. (1991) The concurrent language shared-Prolog. *ACM Transactions on Programming Languages and Systems* **13**(1), 99–123.
18. Burkhart, H., Frank, R., and Hächler, G. (1996) ALWAN: a skeleton programming language. *First International Conference on Coordination Models, Languages and Applications (Coordination '96)*, Cesena, Italy. Lecture Notes in Computer Science 1061. Springer-Verlag, Berlin. pp. 407–410.
19. Chapman, B., Haines, M., Mehrotra, P., Rosendale, J. V., and Zima, H. (1997) Opus: a coordination language for multidisciplinary applications. *Scientific Programming* **6**(2).
20. Carriero, N., and Gelernter, D. (1989) Linda in context. *Communications of the ACM* **32**(4), 444–458.
21. Carriero, N., and Gelernter, D. (1992) Coordination languages and their significance. *Communications of the ACM* **35**(2), 97–107.
22. Carriero, N., Gelernter, D., and Zuck, L. (1994) Bauhaus Linda. *Object-Based Models and*

Languages for Concurrent Systems, Bologna, Italy. Lecture Notes in Computer Science 924. Springer-Verlag, Berlin. pp. 66–76.
23. Castellani, S., and Ciancarini, P. (1996) Enhancing coordination and modularity mechanisms for a language with objects-as-multisets. *First International Conference on Coordination Models, Languages and Applications (Coordination '96)*, Cesena, Italy. Lecture Notes in Computer Science 1061. Springer-Verlag, Berlin. pp. 89–106.
24. Castellani, S., Ciancarini, P., and Rossi, D. (1996) *The ShaPE of ShaDE: a Coordination System*. Technical Report UBLCS 96–5, Dipartimento di Scienze dell'Informazione, Università di Bologna, Italy.
25. Chandy, K. M., and Misra, J. (1989) *Parallel Program Design: A Foundation*. Addison-Wesley, Reading MA.
26. Chen, C., and Purtilo, J. M. (1994) Configuration-level programming of distributed applications using implicit invocation. *IEEE TENCON '94*, Singapore. IEEE Press.
27. Ciancarini, P. (1997) *Coordination Models, Languages, Architectures and Applications: a Personal Perspective*. University of Leuven. http://www.cs.unibo.it/~cianca/coord_ToC.html.
28. Ciancarini, P., and Hankin, C. (eds) (1996) *First International Conference on Coordination Models, Languages and Applications (Coordination '96)*, Cesena, Italy. Lecture Notes in Computer Science 1061. Springer-Verlag, Berlin. pp. 43–49.
29. Ciancarini, P., Nierstrasz, O., and Yonezawa, A. (eds) (1994) *Object-Based Models and Languages for Concurrent Systems*, Bologna, Italy. Lecture Notes in Computer Science 924. Springer-Verlag, Berlin.
30. Ciancarini, P., and Rossi, D. (1996) Jada: coordination and communication for Java agents. *Second International Workshop on Mobile Object Systems: Towards the Programmable Internet (MOS '96)*, Linz, Austria. Lecture Notes in Computer Science 1222, Springer-Verlag, Berlin. pp. 213–228.
31. Ciancarini, P., Tolksdorf, R., and Vitali, F. (1996) Weaving the web using coordination. *First International Conference on Coordination Models, Languages and Applications (Coordination '96)*, Cesena, Italy. Lecture Notes in Computer Science 1061. Springer-Verlag, Berlin. pp. 411–415.
32. Cole, M. (1989) *Algorithmic Skeletons: Structured Management of Parallel Computation*. Pitman/MIT Press, Cambridge MA.
33. Danelutto, M., Di Meglio, R., Orlando, S., Pelagatti, S., and Vanneschi, M. (1994) A methodology for the development and the support of massively parallel programs. *Programming Languages for Parallel Processing*. IEEE Press. pp. 319–334.
34. Darlington, J., Guo, Y., To, H. W., and Yang, J. (1995) Functional skeletons for parallel coordination. *EUROPAR'95*, Stockholm. Lecture Notes in Computer Science 966. Springer-Verlag, Berlin. pp. 55–68.
35. Feng, M. D., Gao, Y. Q., and Yuen, C. K. (1994) Distributed Linda tuplespace algorithms and implementations. *Parallel Processing: CONPAR '94-VAPP VI*, Linz, Austria. Lecture Notes in Computer Science 854. Springer-Verlag, Berlin. pp. 581–592.
36. Florijn, G., Bessamusca, T., and Greefhorst, D. (1996) Ariadne and HOPLa: flexible coordination of collaborative processes. *First International Conference on Coordination Models, Languages and Applications (Coordination '96)*, Cesena, Italy. Lecture Notes in Computer Science 1061. Springer-Verlag, Berlin. pp. 197–214.
37. Foster, I. (1996) Compositional parallel programming languages. *ACM Transactions on Programming Languages and Systems* **18**(4), 454–476.
38. Frølund, S., and Agha, G. (1994) A language framework for multi-object coordination. *Object-Based Models and Languages for Concurrent Systems*, Bologna, Italy. Lecture Notes in Computer Science 924. Springer-Verlag, Berlin. pp. 107–125.

39. Frølund, S. and Agha, G. (1993) Abstracting interactions based on message sets. *Seventh European Conference on Object-Oriented Programming (ECOOP '93)*, Kaiserslautern, Germany. Lecture Notes in Computer Science 707. Springer-Verlag, Berlin. pp. 346–360.
40. Fukuda, M., Bic, L. F., Dillencourt, M. B., and Merchant, F. (1996) Intra- and inter-object coordination with MESSENGERS. *First International Conference on Coordination Models, Languages and Applications (Coordination '96)*, Cesena, Italy. Lecture Notes in Computer Science 1061. Springer-Verlag, Berlin. pp. 179–196.
41. Gelernter, D., and Kaminsky, D. (1992) Supercomputing out of recycled garbage: preliminary experience with Piranha. *Sixth ACM International Conference on Supercomputing*, Washington DC. ACM Press. pp. 417–427.
42. Goldman, K. J., Swaminathan, B., McCartney, T. P., Anderson, M. D., and Sethuraman, R. (1995) The Programmer's Playground: I/O abstractions for user-configurable distributed applications. *IEEE Transactions on Software Engineering* **21**(9), 735–746.
43. Holzbacher, A. A., (1996) A software environment for concurrent coordinated programming. *First International Conference on Coordination Models, Languages and Applications (Coordination '96)*, Cesena, Italy. Lecture Notes in Computer Science 1061. Springer-Verlag, Berlin. pp. 249–266.
44. Hirsbrunner, B., Aguilar, M., and Krone, O. (1994) CoLa: a coordination language for massive parallelism. *ACM Symposium on Principles of Distributed Computing (PODC '94)*, Los Angeles CA. p. 384.
45. Kielmann, T. (1996) Designing a coordination model for open systems. *First International Conference on Coordination Models, Languages and Applications (Coordination '96)*, Cesena, Italy. Lecture Notes in Computer Science 1061. Springer-Verlag, Berlin. pp. 267–284.
46. Klein, M. (1996) Challenges and directions for coordination science. *Second International Conference on the Design of Cooperative Systems*, Juan-les-Pins, France. pp. 705–722.
47. Kramer, J., Magee, J., and Finkelstein, A. (1990) A constructive approach to the design of distributed systems. *Tenth International Conference on Distributed Computing Systems (ICDCS '90)*, Paris. IEEE Press. pp. 580–587.
48. Magee, J., Dulay, N., and Kramer, J. (1996) Structured parallel and distributed programs. *IEE Software Engineering Journal* March, pp. 73–82.
49. Malone, T. W., and Crowston, K. (1994) The interdisciplinary study of coordination. *ACM Computing Surveys* **26**, 87–119.
50. Marchini, M., and Melgarejo, M. (1994) Agora: groupware metaphors in OO concurrent programming. *Object-Based Models and Languages for Concurrent Systems*, Bologna, Italy. Lecture Notes in Computer Science 924. Springer-Verlag, Berlin.
51. Minsky, N. H., and Leichter, J. (1994) Law-Governed Linda as a coordination model. *Object-Based Models and Languages for Concurrent Systems*, Bologna, Italy. Lecture Notes in Computer Science 924. Springer-Verlag, Berlin. pp. 125–145.
52. Motschnig-Pitrik, R., and Mittermeid, R. T. (1996) Language features for the interconnection of software components. *Advances in Computers* **43**, 51–139.
53. Nii, H. P., (1989) Blackboard systems. *The Handbook of Artificial Intelligence* Vol. 4. Addison Wesley, Reading MA. pp. 1–82.
54. Papadopoulos, G. A., and Arbab, F. (1996) Coordination of systems with real-time properties in Manifold *Twentieth Annual International Computer Software and Applications Conference (COMPSAC'96)*, Seoul, Korea. IEEE Press. pp. 50–55.
55. Papadopoulos, G. A., and Arbab, F. (1997) Control-based coordination of human and other activities in cooperative information systems. *Second International Conference on Coordination Models, Languages and Applications (Coordination'97)*, Berlin. Lecture Notes in Computer Science 1282. Springer-Verlag, Berlin. pp. 422–425.
56. Papadopoulos, G. A., and Arbab, F. (1997) Control-driven coordination programming in

shared dataspace. *Fourth International Conference on Parallel Computing Technologies (PaCT-97)*, Yaroslavl, Russia. Lecture Notes in Computer Science 1277. Springer-Verlag, Berlin. pp. 247–261.
57. Papathomas, M., Blair, G. S., and Coulson, G. (1994) A model for active object coordination and its use for distributed multimedia applications. *Object-Based Models and Languages for Concurrent Systems*, Bologna, Italy. Lecture Notes in Computer Science 924. Springer-Verlag, Berlin. pp. 162–175.
58. DePaoli, F., and Tisato, F. (1993) Development of a collaborative application in CSDL. *Thirteenth International Conference on Distributed Computing Systems*, Pittsburgh PA. IEEE Press. pp. 210–217.
59. DePaoli, F., and Tisato, F. (1994) Cooperative systems configuration in CSDL. *Fourteenth International Conference on Distributed Computing Systems*, Poznan, Poland. IEEE Press. pp. 304–311.
60. Purtilo, J. M. (1994) The POLYLITH software bus. *ACM Transactions on Programming Languages and Systems* **16**(1), 151–174.
61. Rem, M. (1981) Associons: a program notation with tuples instead of variables. *ACM Transactions on Programming Languages and Systems* **3**(3), 251–262.
62. Ren, S., and Agha, G. A. (1995) RTsynchronizer: language support for real-time specifications in distributed systems. *ACM SIGPLAN Workshop on Languages, Compilers and Tools for Real-Time Systems*, La Jolla CA. pp. 50–59.
63. Rice, M. D., and Seidman, S. B. (1994) A formal model for module interconnection languages. *IEEE Transactions on Software Engineering* **20**, 88–101.
64. Roman, G.-C., and Cunningham, H. C. (1990) Mixed programming metaphors in a shared dataspace model of concurrency. *IEEE Transactions on Software Engineering* **16**(12), 1361–1373.
65. Rowstron, A., and Wood, A. (1997) BONITA: a set of tuple space primitives for distributed coordination. *30th Hawaii International Conference on Systems Sciences (HICSS-30)*, Maui, Hawaii. IEEE Press. Vol. 1, pp. 379–388.
66. Shaw, M., DeLine, R., Klein, D. V., Ross, T. L., Young, D. M., and Zelesnik, G. (1995) Abstractions for software architecture and tools to support them. *IEEE Transactions on Software Engineering* **21**(4), 314–335.
67. Skillicorn, D. B. (1995) Towards a higher level of abstraction in parallel programming. *Programming Models for Massively Parallel Computers (MPPM '95)*, Berlin. IEEE Press. pp. 78–85.
68. Sommerville, I., and Dean, G. (1996) PCL: a language for modelling evolving system architectures. *Software Engineering Journal* March, pp. 111–121.
69. Tolksdorf, R. (1996) Coordinating services in open distributed systems with LAURA. *First International Conference on Coordination Models, Languages and Applications (Coordination '96)*, Cesena, Italy. Lecture Notes in Computer Science 1061. Springer-Verlag, Berlin. pp. 386–402.
70. Weems, C. C., Weaver, G. E., and Dropsho, S. G. (1994) Linguistic support for heterogeneous parallel processing: a survey and an approach. *Third Heterogeneous Computing Workshop*, Canceen, Mexico. pp. 81–88.
71. Wegner, P. (1996) Coordination as constrained interaction. *First International Conference on Coordination Models, Languages and Applications (Coordination '96)*, Cesena, Italy. Lecture Notes in Computer Science 1061. Springer-Verlag, Berlin. pp. 28–33.
72. Wilson, G. (1991) (ed.) *Linda-Like Systems and Their Implementation*. Edinburgh Parallel Computing Centre, TR-91-13.
73. Zave, P. (1989) A compositional approach to multiparadigm programming. *IEEE Software*. September, pp. 15–25.

Multidisciplinary Problem-Solving Environments for Computational Science

ELIAS N. HOUSTIS, JOHN R. RICE,
NAREN RAMAKRISHNAN

Department of Computer Sciences, Purdue University
West Lafayette, IN 47907-1398
USA

TZVETAN DRASHANSKY

Juno Online Services, L.P.
120 West 45th Street
New York, NY 10036
USA

SANJIVA WEERAWARANA

IBM T.J. Watson Research Center
Hawthorne, NY 10532
USA

ANUPAM JOSHI

Department of Computer Engineering & Computer Science
University of Missouri,
Columbia, MO 65211
USA

C. E. HOUSTIS

Department of Computer Science
University of Crete
Crete, Greece

Abstract

The process of prototyping is part of every scientific inquiry, product design, and learning activity. Economic realities require fast, accurate prototyping using knowledge and computational models from multiple disciplines in science and engineering [1, 3, 15, 47, 49]. Thus rapid multidisciplinary problem solving or prototyping is a new grand challenge for computational science and engineering (CS&E) [11, 14, 48]. In this prototyping scenario it is safe to assume that the network (the *Net*) is the computer [29] consisting of geographically distributed computational units, ranging from workstations to massively parallel machines and physical instruments, and software resources (i.e. libraries and problem-solving environments (PSEs)). Moreover, the *Web* and its technologies can be viewed as an object-oriented operating system kernel that allows the development of an MPSE as a distributed application utilizing resources and services from many sources. The realization of this vision will require the formulation and development of new mathematical and software frameworks for PSEs [27] and multidisciplinary PSEs (MPSEs), including the tools, enabling technologies, and underlying theories needed to support physical prototyping in the classroom, laboratory, desk, and factory. MPSEs will be network-based, adaptable, and intelligent with respect to end-users and hardware platforms, and will use collaborating software systems and agent-based techniques. They will allow wholesale reuse of scientific software and provide a natural approach to parallel and distributed problem solving. In this chapter, we describe the research that is needed to realize the MPSE concept and present a software architecture of an MPSE framework based on the *agent* approach supported by domain-specific knowledge bases in a networked computing setting. The viability of such a framework is demonstrated for partial differential equation applications.

1. Introduction 402
2. Domain-specific PSEs 404
3. MPSEs for Prototyping of Physical Systems 405
4. Agent-based Computing Paradigm for MPSEs 408
5. The Resource Selection Paradigm for MPSEs 409
6. SciAgents System 412
   6.1   Coordination of the Solution Process 416
   6.2   Software Reuse and Evolution 418
7. PYTHIA System 418
8. Case Studies 421
   8.1   Solving Composite PDE Problems 421
   8.2   Intelligent PDE Computing with PYTHIA 427
   8.3   Learning and Adaptation in Multi-agent Systems 430
9. Conclusions 435
References 435

1. Introduction

It is predicted that, by the beginning of the next century, the available computational power will enable anyone with access to a computer to find an answer to any question that has a known or effectively computable answer. In [9] we have made several research recommendations for the development of *problem-solving environment* (PSE) technologies. We believe that PSE technologies will contribute to the realization of this prediction for physical modeling in order to provide students, scientists, and engineers with environments that allow them to spend more time doing science and engineering, and less time struggling with the details of the underlying computation.

The predicted growth of computational power and network bandwidth suggests that computational modeling and experimentation will be one of the main tools in *big* and *small* science. In this scenario, computational modeling will shift from the current single physical component design to the design of a whole physical system with a large number of components that have different shapes, obey different physical laws and manufacturing constraints, and interact with each other through geometric and physical interfaces. For example, the analysis of an engine involves the domains of *thermodynamics* (gives the heat flows throughout the engines), *reactive fluid dynamics* (gives the behavior of the gases in the piston–cylinder assemblies), *mechanics* (gives the kinematic and dynamic behaviors of pistons, links, cranks, etc.), *structures* (gives the stresses and strains on the parts), and *geometry* (gives the shape of the components and the structural constraints). The design of the engine requires that these different domain-specific analyses interact in order to find the final solution. The different domains share common parameters and interfaces but each has its own parameters and constraints. We refer to these multi-component-based physical systems as *multidisciplinary applications* (MAs) and their PSEs as *multidisciplinary problem-solving environments* (MPSEs). In the following, we will specifically concentrate on such environments for physical systems modeled by partial differential equations (PDEs) and ordinary differential equations (ODEs).

The realization of the above scenario, which is expected to have significant impact in industry, education, and training, will require (i) the development of new algorithmic strategies and software for managing the complexity and harvesting the power of the expected high-performance computing and communication (HPCC) resources, (ii) PSE technology to support programming-in-the-large and reduce the overhead of HPCC computing, (iii) an *active programming* paradigm capable of realizing the interactions between the physical and software components in a reusable mode, and (iv) the selection of computational/hardware resources and the determination of their parameters for the specified simulations. Some of the objectives of this chapter include review of the research issues involved in the development of MPSEs, identification of a framework for the numerical simulation of multidisciplinary applications, and the specification of some enabling theories and technologies needed to support and realize this framework in targeted applications. The MPSE is the software implementation of this framework. It is assumed that its elements are discipline-specific problem-solving environments (PSEs) and libraries. The MPSE design objective is to allow the natural specification of multidisciplinary applications and their simulation with interacting PSEs through mathematical and software interfaces across networks of heterogeneous computational resources.

Another safe prediction is that the future global information infrastructure (GII) will impact many aspects of life, including the way we learn and do science, access information, work, and collaborate. It will allow computing everywhere [17]. Learning and training simulators will be part of every classroom and laboratory. The concept of the classroom, the laboratory, and the student/scientist/engineer desk environments will evolve to some virtual form based on an array of multimedia devices. These virtual environments, sometimes called *collaboratories*, can be implemented naturally using the MPSE technology. The discipline-specific PSEs will be used to build learning and training simulators in some areas of computational science and engineering.

For the scope of this discussion, the network (the *Net*) is assumed to be the host for multidisciplinary problem solving. We assume existing network software infrastructure to support distributed applications, PSEs, libraries of solvers, and distance learning and collaboratory services over the Net. We envisage that all these resources and services will take the form of special servers in the network which are constantly updated by their creators. The problem-solving power of math/engineering libraries will be encapsulated into PSEs that users will access over the Net as a routine part of science and engineering. We have already developed such servers to experiment with web-based dissemination and use of PDE software and PSEs [27, 51].

This chapter is organized as follows. We start by defining the terms of PSEs and MPSEs and discuss the research issues involved in Sections 2 and 3. Then in Sections 3 and 4 we present an agent-based approach for designing and building MPSEs together with the problems of resource and solution methodology selection. We then introduce, in Section 6, the *SciAgents* system, which provides the solver and mediator agents for PDE-based application MPSEs. In Section 7, we describe PYTHIA, a multiagent advisory system that uses a distributed knowledge corpus. We show how these various agents can interact with each other to automate the process of solving multi-physics problems. Finally, in Section 8 we consider in detail two case studies using current prototypes that show the applicability and the potential of the MPSE concept and that demonstrate our approach for its implementation.

2. Domain-specific PSEs

Even in the early 1960s, scientists had begun to envision problem-solving computing environments not only powerful enough to solve complex problems, but also able to interact with users on human terms. The rationale of the PSE research is that the dream of the 1960s will be the reality of the 21st century: high-performance computers combined with better algorithms and better understanding of computational science have put PSEs well within our reach.

What are PSEs? A PSE is a computer system that provides all the computational facilities needed to solve a target class of problems. These facilities include advanced solution methods, automatic selection of appropriate methods, use of the applications language, selection of appropriate hardware and powerful graphics, symbolic and geometry-based code generation for parallel machines, and programming-in-the-large. The scope of a PSE is the extent of the problem set it addresses. This scope can be very narrow, making the PSE construction very simple, but even what appears to be a modest scope can be a serious scientific challenge. For example, we have created a PSE for bioseparation analysis [13] which has a narrow scope, but is still a complex challenge as we incorporate both a computational model and an experimental process supported by physical laboratory instruments. We are also creating a PSE called PDELab [52] for partial differential equations (PDEs). This is a far more difficult area than bioseparation and the resulting PSE will be less powerful (less able to solve all the problems posed to it), less reliable (less able to guarantee the correctness of results), but more generic (more able to attempt to solve a broad class of PDE problems). Nevertheless, PDELab will provide a quantum jump in the PDE solving power delivered into the hands of the working scientist and engineer. What are the PSE-related research issues to be addressed? A substantive research effort is needed to lay the foundations for building PSEs. This effort should be directed towards (i) a PSE kernel for building scientific PSEs, (ii) a knowledge-based framework to address computational intelligence issues for PDE based PSEs, (iii) infrastructure for solving PDEs, and (iv) parallel PDE methodologies and virtual computational environments.

3. MPSEs for Prototyping of Physical Systems

If PSEs are so powerful, what then is an MPSE? In simple terms, an MPSE is a framework and software kernel for combining PSEs for tailored, flexible multidisciplinary applications. A physical system in the real world normally consists of a large number of components where the physical behavior of each component is modeled by a PDE or ODE system with various formulations for the geometry, PDE, ODE, interface/boundary/linkage, and constraint conditions in many different geometric regions. One needs a mathematical/software framework which, first, is applicable to a wide variety of practical problems; second, allows for software reuse in order to achieve lower costs and high quality; and, finally, is suitable for some reasonably fast numerical methods. Most physical systems can be modeled as a mathematical network whose nodes represent the physical components in a system or artifact. Each node has a mathematical model of the physics of the component it represents and a solver agent for its analysis. The relationship between a physical phenomenon and the mathematical network is illustrated in Fig. 1. Individual components are chosen so that each node corresponds to a simple PDE or ODE problem defined on a regular geometry.

What are the mathematical network methodologies required? What are the research issues? There exist many standard, reliable PDE/ODE solvers that can be applied to these local node problems. In addition there are nodes that correspond to interfaces (e.g. ODEs, objective functions, relations, common parameters and their constraints) that model the collaborating parts in the global model. To solve the global problem, we let these local solvers collaborate with each other to relax (i.e. resolve) the interface conditions. An interface controller or mediator agent collects boundary values, dynamic/shape coordinates, and parameters/constraints from neighboring subdomains and adjusts boundary values and dynamic/shape coordinates to better satisfy the interface conditions. Therefore the network abstraction of a physical system or artifact allows us to build a software system which is a network of collaborating well defined numerical objects through a set of interfaces. Some of the theoretical issues of this methodology are addressed in [5, 39] for the case of collaborating PDE models. The results obtained so far verify the feasibility and potential of network-based prototyping.

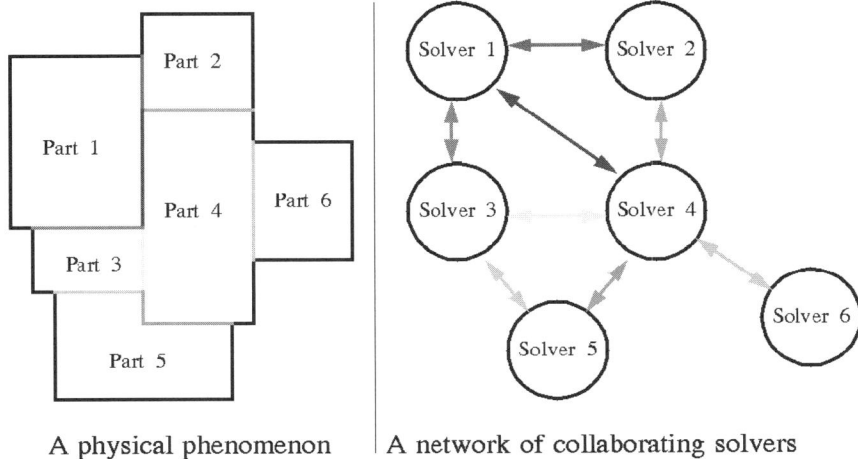

FIG. 1. The representation of a physical phenomenon (left) by a mathematical network (right) of solvers (circles) and interface conditions (arrows).

What are the software methodologies for implementing the mathematical network? What are the research issues? A successful architecture for PSEs requires heavy reuse of existing software within a modular, object-oriented framework consisting of layers of objects. The kernel layer integrates those components common to most PSEs or MPSEs for physical systems. We observe that this architecture can be combined with an agent-oriented paradigm and collaborating solvers [5] to create an MPSE as a powerful prototyping tool using a variety of infrastructure tools. The designs for MPSEs must be application- and user-driven. We should not restrict our design just to use the current technology of high-performance computers, powerful graphics, modular software engineering, and advanced algorithms. We should see an MPSE as delivering problem solving services over the Net. This viewpoint leads naturally to collaborating agent-based methodologies. This, in turn, leads to very substantial advantages in both software development and quality of service, as follows. We envision that users of MPSE will receive at their location only the user interface. Thus, the MPSE server will export to the user's machine an agent that provides an interactive user interface while the bulk of the software and computing is done at the server's site using software tailored to a known and controlled environment. The server site can, in turn, request services from specialized resources it knows, e.g. a commercial PDE solver, a proprietary optimization package, a 1000 node supercomputer, an *ad hoc* collection of 122 workstations, or a database of physical properties of materials. Each of these resources is contacted by an agent from the MPSE and all of this can be managed without involving the user, without moving software to arbitrary platforms, and without revealing source codes.

What are the design objectives of an MPSE for physical system design? What are the research issues? These mathematical networks can be very big for major applications. For a realistic vehicle simulation, there are perhaps 100 million variables and many different time-scales. This problem has very complex geometry and is very non-homogeneous. The answer is 20 gigabytes in size and requires about 10 teraflops to compute. An answer is a data set that allows one to display an accurate approximate solution at any point. This data set is much smaller than the computed numerical solution. The mathematical network has about 10 000 subdomains and 35 000 interfaces. A software network for this simulation is a natural mapping of a physical system and simulates how the real world evolves. This allows software reuse for easy software update and evolution, things that are extremely important in practice. The real world is so complicated and diverse that we believe it is impractical to build monolithic universal solvers for such problems. In this application each physical component can be viewed both as a physical object and as a software object. In addition, this mathematical network approach is naturally suitable for parallel computing as it exploits the parallelism in physical systems. One can handle issues like data partition, assignment, and load balancing on the physics level using the structure of a given physical system. Synchronization and communication are controlled by the mathematical network specifications and are restricted to interfaces of subdomains, which results in a coarse-grained computational problem.

4. Agent-based Computing Paradigm for MPSEs

We envisage an MPSE as a mathematical network whose nodes represent the physical components in a system or artifact. Each node has a mathematical model of the physics of the component it represents and a solver agent for its analysis. We propose to use the *multi-agent computing framework* to provide run-time support for MPSEs where we replace the multiphysics problem by a set of simple(r) simulation problems on simple geometries which must be solved simultaneously while satisfying a set of interface conditions. These simpler problems may reflect the underlying structure/geometry/physics of the system to be simulated, or may be artificially created by techniques such as domain decomposition. Given a collection of *solver agents* for these smaller problems on simple geometries, we create a network of collaborating solvers by introducing *mediator agents* between them. Each solver deals with one of the subproblems defined earlier. The original multiphysics problem is solved when one has all the equations satisfied on the individual components and these solutions "match properly" on the interfaces between the components. This latter part is the responsibility of the mediator agents which facilitate the collaboration between solver agent pairs. The term "match properly" is defined by the physics if the interface is where the physics changes. For heat flow, for example, this means that temperature is the same on both sides of the interface and that the amount of heat flowing into one component is the same as the amount flowing out of the other. If the interface is artificial (introduced to make the geometry simple or the work smaller) then "match properly" is defined mathematically and means that the solutions join smoothly (have continuous values and derivatives).

Many agent-based systems have been developed [12, 42, 43, 46, 55] which demonstrate the power of the agent-oriented paradigm. It provides modularity and flexibility, so it is easy to dynamically add or remove agents, to move agents around the computing network, and to organize the user interface. An agent-based architecture provides a natural method of decomposing large tasks into self-contained modules, or conversely, of building a system to solve complex problems by a collection of agents, each of which is responsible for a small part of the task. Agent-based systems can minimize centralized control.

The agent-based paradigm is useful in scientific computing to handle complex mathematical models in a natural and direct way. It allows *distributed problem solving* [32] which is distinct from merely using distributed computing. The expected behavior of the simple problem solvers, computing locally and interacting with the neighboring solvers, naturally take on the behavior of a *local problem solver* agent. The task of mediating interface conditions between adjacent subproblems is given to *mediator* agents and their ability to pursue their goals autonomously can resolve the problems during the solution process without user intervention and converge to the global solution.

Several researchers have addressed the issue of coordinating multi-agent systems. For instance Smith and Davis [44] propose two forms of multi-agent cooperation: task sharing and result sharing. Task sharing essentially involves creating subtasks, and then farming them off to other agents. Result sharing is more data-directed. Different agents are solving different tasks, and keep on exchanging partial results to cooperate. They also proposed using "contract nets" to distribute tasks. Wesson *et al.*, showed [54] how many intelligent sensor devices could pool their knowledge to obtain an accurate overall assessment of a situation. The specific task presented in their work involves detecting moving entities, where each "sensor agent" sees only a part of the environment. They reported results using both a hierarchical organization and an "anarchic committee" organization, and found that the latter was as good as, and sometimes better than, the former. Cammarata *et al.* [4] present strategies for cooperation by groups of agents involved in distributed problem solving, and infer a set of requirements on information distribution and organizational policies. They point out that different agents may have different capabilities and limited knowledge and resources, and thus differing appropriateness in solving the problem at hand. Lesser *et al.* [26] describes the FA/C (functionally accurate, cooperative) architecture in which agents exchange partial and tentative results in order to converge to a solution. Joshi [16] presents a learning technique which enhances the effectiveness of such coordination. It combines neuro-fuzzy techniques [45] with an epistemic utility criterion.

5. The Resource Selection Paradigm for MPSEs

In this paradigm for a networked MPSE environment, the solver and mediator agents form a potentially large pool of computational objects spread across the Net. Moreover, there are many possible choices for their instantiation. For example, the past few decades has seen a huge amount of sophisticated code being developed to solve specific homogeneous problems.

Mediators today are almost nonexistent and a large number will have to be created to allow disparate solvers to interact. Clearly, expecting the user to be aware of all the potentially useful solvers on the Net is not realistic. Nor is a user likely to know all the hardware choices available to solve the problem. This problem is an obvious generalization of the *algorithm selection* problem formulated by Rice [40]; we call it the *resource selection* problem in the context of MPSEs. We propose the use of *advisory agents* that accept a problem definition and some performance/success criteria from the user, and that then suggest software components and hardware resources that can be deployed to solve this problem. This is very similar to the idea of *recommender systems* that is being proposed for harnessing distributed information resources. While the recommender problem has been identified for networked information resources and initial research done [38], the resource selection problem remains largely ignored for harnessing networked computational resources. Note that the problem is different from invoking a known method remotely on some object, a problem where many distributed object-oriented techniques are being developed and proposed. To appreciate the need for advisory agents, consider the present-day approximation to "networked" scientific computing. Several software libraries for scientific computing are available, such as Netlib and Lapack/ScaLapack. There are even some attempts to make such systems accessible over the web, such as Web //ELLPACK (from Purdue, http://pellpack.cs.purdue.edu/) and NetSolve (from UTK/ORNL, http://www.cs.utk.edu/netsolve/). The GAMS [2] system helps users to identify and locate the right class of software for their problem. However, the user has to select the specific routine most appropriate for the given problem, download the software (along with its installation and use instructions), install the software, compile (and possibly port) it, and then learn how to invoke it appropriately. Clearly this is a non-trivial task even for a single piece of software, and it can be enormously complex when multiple software components need to be used. Using networked resources today can be viewed as the modern-day equivalent of programming ENIAC, which required direct manipulation of connecting wires. Systems are needed to abstract away the detail of the underlying networked system from the user and allow interaction with this system in the application domain. This is where MPSEs with inherent "intelligence" come in. We posit that multi-agent systems, consisting of a broad class of solver, mediator, and advisory agents, can be used to create MPSEs with the desired characteristics.

As mentioned earlier, our prototype software to validate these ideas is being created for PDE-based systems. The numerical solution of PDEs depends on many factors, including the nature of the operator, the mathematical behavior of its coefficients and its exact solution, the type of boundary and initial conditions, and the geometry of the space domains of definition. Most numerical solvers for PDEs normally require a number of parameters (mesh sizes, iteration parameters, sparse matrix representations) from the user in order to obtain a solution within a specified error level while satisfying certain resource (e.g. memory and time) constraints. The problem of selecting a solver and its parameters for a given PDE problem to satisfy the user's computational objectives is difficult and of great importance. The user must also select a machine from among the many available on the network, including parallel machines. Depending on the mathematical characteristics of the PDEs, there are "thousands" of numerical methods to apply, since very often there are several choices of parameters or methods at each of the several phases of the solution. It is unrealistic to expect that engineers and scientists will or should have the deep expertise to make "intelligent" combinations of selections of methods, their parameters, and computational resources that will satisfy their objectives.

The PYTHIA [53] project at Purdue has focused on creating a knowledge based system that selects scientific algorithms to achieve desired tasks in computing. It determines a near-optimal strategy (i.e. a solution method and its parameters) for solving a given problem within user specified resource (i.e. limits on execution time and memory usage) and accuracy requirements (i.e. level of error). While the ideas behind PYTHIA are quite general, our current implementations operate in conjunction with systems that solve (elliptic) partial differential equations (PDEs), such as the ELLPACK and //ELLPACK PSEs developed at Purdue. The methodology of PYTHIA is to gather performance information about PDE solvers on standardized test problems and use this data plus feature information about PDE problems to determine good algorithms to solve the PDEs. The efficacy of this approach is dependent on the breadth and diversity of the method and problem sets used to create the performance evaluation information.

We now briefly describe some attempts at developing intelligent systems for assisting in various aspects of the PDE solution process. In [41], Rice describes an abstract model for the algorithm selection problem, which is the problem of determining a selection (or mapping) from the problem feature space to the algorithm space. Using this abstract model Rice describes an experimental methodology for applying this abstract model in the performance evaluation of numerical software. In [30], Moore *et al.* describe a strategy for the automatic solution of PDEs at a different level. They are concerned with the problem of determining (automatically) a geometry discretization that leads to a solution guaranteed to be within a prescribed accuracy. In [6, 7], Dyksen and Gritter describe a rule-based expert system for selecting solution methods for elliptic PDE problems based on problem characteristics. This work differs significantly from our approach, which uses only performance data as the basis of the algorithm selection methodology. While these rules help some, we argue that using problem characteristics solely is not sufficient because the performance of a solver depends on quantities which cannot be measured symbolically and *a priori*. Further, software performance depends not only on the algorithms used, but on their implementations as well. In [23], Kamel *et al.* describe the expert system ODEXPERT for selecting numerical solvers for initial-value ordinary differential equation (ODE) systems. ODEXPERT uses textual parsing to determine some properties of the ODEs and performs some automatic tests (e.g. a stiffness test) to determine others. Once all the properties are known, it uses its knowledge base information about available ODE solution methods (represented as a set of rules) to recommend a certain method. After a method has been determined, it selects a particular implementation of that method based on other criteria and then generates source code (Fortran) for the user. If necessary, symbolic differentiation is used to generate code for the Jacobian as well. Leake has recently begun some work in the area of using traditional case-based reasoning systems to select appropriate methods for solving sparse linear systems [24]. Our group has also been actively involved in using several techniques, such as neural nets, neuro-fuzzy systems, and Bayesian nets [19–22, 35, 53]) to address related issues of classifying PDE problems based on their performance characteristics, and then using this classification to predict an appropriate solution method for new problems. We have also formulated the algorithm selection problem as conducting knowledge discovery in domains of computational science [36, 37]. This work shows that such data mining approaches can be used to form relational descriptions of PDE objects which lead to more powerful schemas for resource selection (in terms of both representation and prediction).

6. SciAgents System

In this section, we describe in detail the *SciAgents* software architecture, and explain how to use it for complex PDE-based models from MPSEs. As an application of our MPSE approach, SciAgents employs two major types of computing agent—*solvers* and *mediators*. It interacts with the *recommender* agents as described later. Each solver agent is considered a "black box" by the other agents and it interacts with them using an inter-agent language for the specific problem. This feature allows all computational decisions for solving one individual subproblem to be taken independently from the decisions in any other subproblem—a major difference from the traditional approaches to multidisciplinary simulations. Each mediator agent is responsible for adjusting an interface between two neighboring subproblems. Since the interface between any two subproblems might be complex in itself, there may be more than one mediator assigned to adjust it, each of them operating on separate piece of the whole interface. Thus the mediators control the data exchange between the solvers working on neighboring subproblems by applying mediating formulas and algorithms to the data coming from and going to the solvers. Different mediators may apply different mediating formulas and algorithms depending on the physical nature of their interfaces. The mediators are also responsible for enforcing global solution strategies and for recognizing (locally) that some goal (like "end of computations") has been achieved.

The solvers and mediators form a network of agents to solve the given global problem. A schematic view of the functional architecture of a SciAgents MPSE containing an example network is given in Fig. 2. The computations (and the major data exchange) are concentrated in the network of solver (PSE) and mediator agents. The solver agents communicate with the recommender agents (as consultants) through queries to obtain "advice" on

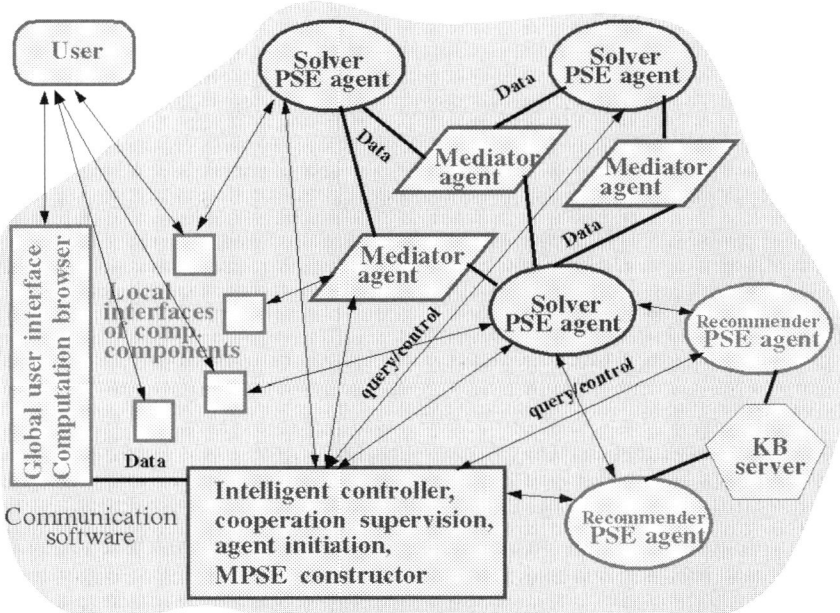

FIG. 2. Functional architecture of a SciAgents solver for an MPSE. The computations (and the major data exchange) are concentrated in the network of solver (PSE) and mediator agents. The solver agents communicate with the recommender ones through queries to obtain "advice" on computational parameters. The user interacts with the system through the global and local user interfaces, which send queries and receive replies from the various agents.

computation parameters. The user interacts with the system through the global and local user interfaces, which send queries and receive replies from the various agents. The intelligent controller and the MPSE constructor can be integrated into a single "agent" which controls the global state of the computations and instantiates, queries, and manages (if necessary) the other agents.

We now describe how the user builds ("programs") this network. The agent framework provides a natural abstraction to the user in the problem domain and hides the details of the actual algorithms and software involved in the problem solving. The user first breaks down the geometry of the composite domain into simple subdomains with simple models to define the subproblems for each subdomain. Then the physical conditions along each interface between the subdomains are identified. All this is done in the terms of the user's problem domain. The user is provided with an *MPSE constructor* (*agent instantiator*)—a process which displays information about the templates and creates active agents of both kinds, capable of computing. Initially, only *templates of agents*—structures that contain information about solver and mediator agents and how to *instantiate* them, are available. Then the user constructs the proper network of computing agents by simply *instantiating* various agents. The user selects solvers that are capable of solving the corresponding subproblems and mediators that are capable of mediating the physical conditions along the specific interfaces, and assigns subproblems and interfaces, respectively, to each of them. The user interacts with the system using a visual programming approach which has proved useful in allowing non-experts to "program" by manipulating images and objects from their problem domain. In our case, a visual environment is useful for the MPSE constructor, or when the user wants to request some action or data.

Once an agent is instantiated, it takes over the communication with the user and with its environment (the other agents) and tries to acquire all necessary information for its task. Each PSE (solver agent) retains its own interface and can interact with the user. It is convenient to think of the user as another agent in these interactions. The user defines each subproblem independently, interacting with the corresponding solver agent through its user interface and similarly interacting with the mediators to specify the physical conditions holding along the various interfaces.

The agents *actively* exchange partial solutions and data with other agents without outside control and management. In other words, each solver agent can request the necessary domain- and problem-related data from the user and decide what to do with it (should it, for instance, start the computations or should it wait for other agents to contact it?). After each mediator agent has been supplied with the connectivity and mediating data by the user, it contacts the corresponding solver agents and requests the information it needs. This information includes the geometry of the interface, the functional capabilities of the solvers with respect to providing the necessary data for adjusting the interface, visualization capabilities, etc. All this is done without user involvement. By instantiating the individual agents (concentrating on the individual subdomains and interfaces) the user builds the highly interconnected and interoperable network that is tailored to solve the particular multiphysics problem, by *cooperation* between individual agents.

The user's high-level view of the MPSE architecture is shown in Fig. 3. The global communication medium used by all entities in the MPSE is called a *software bus* [50]. The MPSE constructor communicates with the user through the user interface builder and uses the software bus to communicate with the templates in order to instantiate various agents. Agents communicate with each other through the software bus and have their own local user interfaces to interact with the user. The order of instantiating the agents is not important. If a solver agent is instantiated and it does not have all the data it needs to compute a local solution (i.e. a mediator agent is missing), then it suspends the computations and waits for some relaxer agent to contact it and to provide the missing values (this is also a way to "naturally" control the

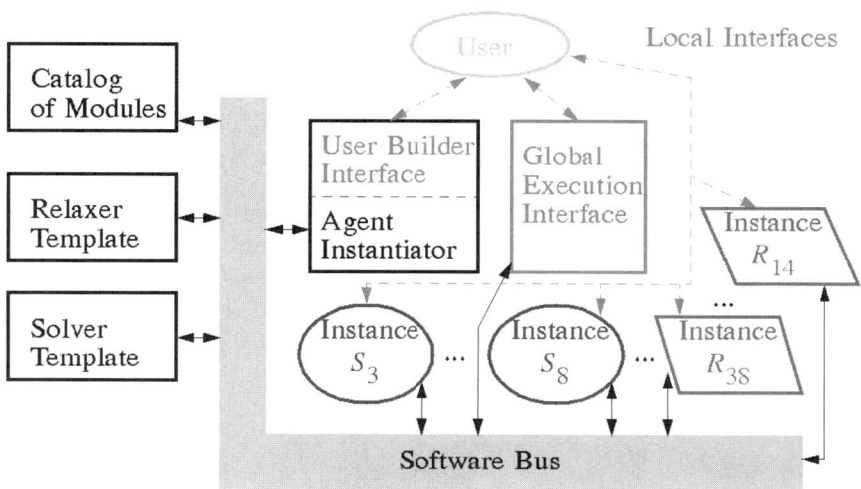

FIG. 3. Software architecture of an MPSE: the user's abstraction. The user initially interacts with the User Interface Builder to define the global composite problem. Later the interaction is with the Global Execution Interface to monitor and control the solution of the problem. Direct interaction with individual solvers and mediators is also possible. The agents communicate with each other using the *software bus*.

solution process). If a mediator agent is instantiated and a solver agent on either side of its interface is missing, then it suspends its computations and waits for the solver agents with the necessary characteristics (the right subdomain assigned) to appear. This built-in synchronization is, we believe, an important advantage of the SciAgents architecture. It results from each agent adapting to its environment. We go into more detail about inter agent communication later.

Since agent instantiation happens one agent at a time, the data which the user has to provide (domain, interface, problem definition, etc.) is strictly local, and the agents collaborate in building the computing network. The user actually does not even need to know the global model. We can easily imagine a situation when the global problem is very large. Different specialists may only model parts of it. In such a situation, a user may instantiate a few agents and leave the instantiating of the rest of the cooperating agents to colleagues. Naturally, some care must be taken in order to instantiate all necessary agents for the global solution and not to define contradictory interface conditions or mediation schemes along the "borders" between different users.

The collection of agent interfaces that a user interacts with is the only software the user actually needs to run locally in order to solve a problem. Therefore this architecture abstracts successfully from the user the location of the main computations (the location of the solvers and the mediators) and allows for great flexibility in this direction, including running the MPSE over the Internet and distributing the agents over the Net.

This user view of the SciAgents architecture is too abstract for an actual implementation where one has to design the internal architecture of each agent and the detailed communication among the agents. We refer the reader to [5] for these important details. We only mention here that the agent architecture utilizes the locality of the communication patterns described before and the fact that whenever a mediator is active (computing), the corresponding solvers are idle and vice versa. Also, the asynchronicity of the communication and the need of implementing the "pro-active" feature of the agents prompt us to employ many active threads in a single agent (multithreading).

6.1 Coordination of the Solution Process

We discuss now some important aspects of the cooperation between the agents during the solution process. There are well-defined global mathematical conditions for terminating the computations; for example, reaching a specified accuracy, or the impossibility of achieving convergence. In most cases, these global conditions can be "localized" either explicitly or implicitly. For instance, the user may require different accuracy for different subdomains and the computations may be suspended locally if local convergence is achieved. Note that local convergence can be achieved and then later lost due to changes from other agents.

The local computations are governed by the mediators (the solvers simply solve the PDE problems). The mediator agents collect the errors after each iteration and, when the desired accuracy is obtained, *locally* suspend the computations and report the fact to the intelligent controller. The suspension is done by issuing an instruction to the solvers on both sides of this interface to use the boundary conditions for the interface from the previous iteration in any successive iterations they may perform (the other interfaces of the two subdomains might still not have converged). The solvers continue to report the required data to the submediators and the submediators continue to check whether the local interface conditions are satisfied with the required accuracy. If a solver receives instructions to use the old iteration boundary conditions for all its interfaces, then it stops the iterations. The iterations may be restarted if the interface conditions handled by a given mediator agent are no longer accurately satisfied (even though they once were). In this case, the mediator issues instructions to the two solvers on both sides of its interface to resume solving with new boundary conditions. If the maximum number of iterations is reached, the mediator reports failure to the intelligent controller and suspends the computations. The only global control exercised by the intelligent controller is to terminate all agents in case all mediators report local convergence or one of them reports a failure. The messages used in the interagent communication are given in full detail in [18]; we provide a small example in the next section.

The above scheme provides a robust mechanism for cooperation among the computing agents. Using *only* local knowledge, they perform only local computations and communicate only with "neighboring" agents. They *cooperate* in solving a global, complex problem, and none of them exercises centralized control over the computations. The global solution "emerges" in a well-defined mathematical way from the local computations as a result of intelligent decision-making done locally and independently by the mediator agents. The agents may change their goals dynamically according to the local status of the solution process—switching between observing results and computing new data.

Other global control policies can be imposed by the user if desired—the system architecture allows this to be done easily by distributing the control policy to all agents involved. Such global policies include continuing the iterations until all the interface conditions are satisfied, and recomputing the solutions for all subdomains if the user changes something (conditions, method, etc.) for any domain.

6.2 Software Reuse and Evolution

One of the major goals of this MPSE approach is to design a system that allows for low-cost and less time-consuming methods of building the software to simulate a complex mathematical model of physical processes. This goal cannot be accomplished if the existing rich variety of problem-solving software for scientific computing is not used. More precisely, there are many well-tested, powerful, and popular PSEs for solving problems very similar or identical to the subproblems that appear when breaking the global model into "simple" subproblems defined on a single subdomain. These PSEs could easily and accurately solve such a "simple" subproblem. It is, therefore, natural to reuse such PSEs as solver agents. However, our architecture requires the solvers to behave like agents (e.g. understand agent languages, use them to communicate data to other agents), something the existing PSEs in scientific computing do not do.

Our solution to this problem is to provide an *agent wrapper* for PSEs and other software modules, which takes care of the interaction with the other agents and with the other aspects of emulating agent behavior. The wrapper encapsulates the original PSE and is responsible for running it and for the necessary interpretation of parameters and results. This is not simply a "preprocessor" that prepares the PSE's input and a "postprocessor" that interprets the results, since the mediation between subproblems may require communicating intermediate results to the mediators and/or accepting some additional data from them. Designing the wrapper is sometimes complicated by the "closed" nature of extant PSEs—their original design is not flexible or "open" enough to allow access to various parts of the code and the processed data. However, it is our opinion that the PSE developers can design and build such a wrapper for a very small fraction of the time and the cost of designing and building entire new PSE or custom software for every new problem. The wrapper, once written, will enable the reuse of this PSE as a solver agent in different MPSEs, thus amortizing the cost further. As part of the specifications of the wrapper the developers have to consider the mediation schemes involving submodels within the power of the PSE. An additional task is to evaluate the PSE's user interface—since the user defines the local submodel through it, it is important that the interface facilitates the problem definition in user's terms well enough. Our experience with //ELLPACK was that building a wrapper for a substantial (more than a million lines of code), diverse, and non-homogeneous PDE solver could be done efficiently, it required about a thousand lines of code.

7. PYTHIA System

We see that the role played by the recommender agents is paramount for the effectiveness of *SciAgents*. When queried by the solver agents, they provide consulting advice on a suitable scheme (and associated computation parameters) to solve a given problem so as to achieve desired performance criteria. An example PDE problem is given in Fig. 4. A prescribed solution strategy could be *"Use the 5-point star algorithm with a* 200×200 *grid on an nCube/2 with 16 processors. Confidence: 0.90."* (Notice that a recommender agent provides a level of confidence in the selected strategy). In essence, the recommender agents serve as knowledge engines that provide domain-specific inference for PDE problems. If any particular recommender agent lacks the expertise to provide this recommendation, it will collaborate with other recommender agents and select the best answer. These agents can also be made to interact directly with the user, via the agent instantiator. Thus PYTHIA is a collaborative, multi-agent system [33] that uses collective knowledge to prescribe a strategy to solve a given problem in scientific computation. The agents themselves are referred to as PYTHIA agents and are implemented by a combination of C language routines, shell scripts, and systems such as CLIPS (the C Language Integrated Production System) [10]. The agents communicate using the Knowledge Query and Manipulation Language (KQML) [8], using protocol-defined performatives. All PYTHIA agents understand and utilize a private language (PYTHIA-Talk) that describes the meaning (content) of the KQML performatives. This design allows the seamless integration of the recommender agents into the MPSE architecture.

A PYTHIA agent relies heavily on the problem set used in its performance evaluation knowledge base so the effectiveness of a recommender agent

Problem #28	$(\omega u_x)_x + (\omega u_y)_y = 1$, where $\omega = \begin{cases} \alpha, \text{ if } 0 \leq x,y \leq 1 \\ 1, \text{ otherwise.} \end{cases}$
Domain	$[-1, 1] \times [-1, 1]$
BC	$u = 0$
True	unknown
Operator	Self-adjoint, discontinuous coefficients
Right side	Constant
Boundary conditions	Dirichlet, homogeneous
Solution	Approximate solutions given for $\alpha = 1, 10, 100$. Strong wave fronts for $\alpha \geq 1$.
Parameter	α adjusts size of discontinuity in operator coefficients which introduces large, sharp jumps in solution.

FIG. 4. A problem from the PDE population.

depends on its "experience." For example, one agent's expertise might come from its test base of computational fluid dynamics PDE solvers and problems while a second agent's expertise might be based on heat conduction problems. Our mulit-agent methodology recognizes that there are many, many different kinds of PDE problems and any single recommender agent is likely to be limited by its knowledge base. Thus, the approach taken is to create several different PYTHIA agents, each of which has information about some class(es) of PDE problems and can predict an appropriate solver for a given PDE of those classes. If a PYTHIA agent discovers that it does not have enough confidence in the prediction it is making, it could query all other PYTHIA agents, obtain answers from all of them and use this information to decide which one is "most reasonable." This could entail a huge amount of network traffic and inordinate delays. A better approach is to use the information obtained by the initial broadcast type of queries to infer the most experienced PYTHIA agent for the problem at hand. This naturally raises the following issues:

(1) Given more than one applicable agent, how does one determine the best agent(s) for a given PDE problem? In other words, what is the mapping from a given problem to the best PYTHIA agent?
(2) Can the notion of best agent be inferred automatically or does it require user input?
(3) How does one learn and adapt to the changing dynamics of the scenario? Agents may come into existence, some may go extinct, their knowledge corpus may change dynamically, etc. How do we learn the mapping in this case and update it suitably?

We use a quantitative measure of reasonableness [16, 34], to automatically generate exemplars to learn the mapping from PDE problems to PYTHIA agents. This is needed because the computational scientist cannot be expected to have such information in this dynamic scenario. For example, in response to a query from the user about a particular PDE problem, each PYTHIA agent might suggest a different method with varying levels of confidence in the recommended strategy. Moreover, each of these agents might have different levels of expertise (such as the kind of PDEs it knows about) and different "training" history. The user, thus, cannot be expected to know which one of them is most suitable for the problem if all these responses are supplied. Our measure of reasonableness allows the automatic "ranking" of the PYTHIA agents for a particular problem (class). This measure combines two factors, the probability of an agent's prediction q being true, and the predictor's utility. Specifically, the reasonableness of a proposition is defined as follows [25]:

$$r(q) = p(q)U_t(q) + p(\sim q)U_f(q)$$

where $U_t(q)$ denotes the positive utility of accepting q if it is true, $U_f(q)$

denotes the negative utility of accepting q if it is false and $p(q)$ be the probability that q is true.

In the case of PYTHIA, each agent produces a number denoting confidence in its recommendation being correct, so $p(q)$ is trivially available, and $p(\sim q)$ is simply $1 - p(q)$. For the utility, we use the following definition:

$$U_t(q) = -U_f(q) = f(N_e)$$

where f is some squashing function mapping the domain of $(0, \infty)$ to a range of $(0, 1)$, and N_e is the number of exemplars of a given type (that of the problem being considered) that the agent has seen. We chose $f(x) = [2/(1 + e^{-x})] - 1$ because it reflects the number ($x = N_e$) of problems of the present type that it has seen.

Having defined our notion of reasonableness, we still need a way to learn a mapping from a PDE problem to the most reasonable PYTHIA agent. We have evaluated standard statistical methods, gradient descent methods, machine learning techniques, and other classes of algorithms [22], but it has been our experience that specialized techniques developed for this domain perform better than conventional off-the-shelf approaches [20]. In particular, we have designed a neuro-fuzzy technique that infers efficient mappings, caters to mutually non-exclusive classes (as the PDE problem classes naturally are), and learns the classifications in an on-line manner [22]. For the purposes of this chapter, it is sufficient to understand that this scheme provides a mapping from a PDE problem to the best available recommender agent and that the mappings can be learnt in an incremental fashion using this reasonableness measure. While this mapping could be done by any of the PYTHIA agents by "housing" a copy of the learned classification in each of them, we chose to create a central agent, PYTHIA-C, whose main task is to perform this mapping. This just serves to demonstrate the learning aspect of the agents as distinct from their other capabilities.

8. Case Studies

8.1 Solving Composite PDE Problems

The main issue is what mediation schemes can be applied to a composite PDE problem—in other words, how to obtain a global solution out of the local solutions produced by the single-domain solvers. To do this, SciAgents uses interface relaxation [5, 28]. Important mathematical questions of the convergence of the method, the behavior of the solution in special cases, etc. are addressed in [31]. Typically, for second-order PDEs, there are two physical or mathematical interface conditions involving values and normal derivatives of the solutions on the neighboring subdomains. The interface relaxation technique is as follows.

Step 1. Make initial guesses as boundary conditions to determine the subproblem solutions.

Step 2. Solve the subproblem in each subdomain and obtain a local solution.

Step 3. Use the solution values on the interfaces to evaluate how well the interface conditions are satisfied. Use a *relaxation formula* to compute new values of the boundary conditions.

Step 4. Iterate steps 2 and 3 until convergence.

We now describe the solution of a composite PDE problem using four solvers and five mediators. It models the heat distribution in the walls of a chemical or a nuclear reactor and in the surrounding isolating and cooling structures; see Fig. 5. The subdomains are shown, with the solver agents S_i, $i = 0, \ldots, 3$, simulating the local process in each subdomain and the mediators M_j, $j = 0, \ldots, 4$, mediating the interface piece they are written on. The unknown function is T and the exterior boundary conditions are shown next to

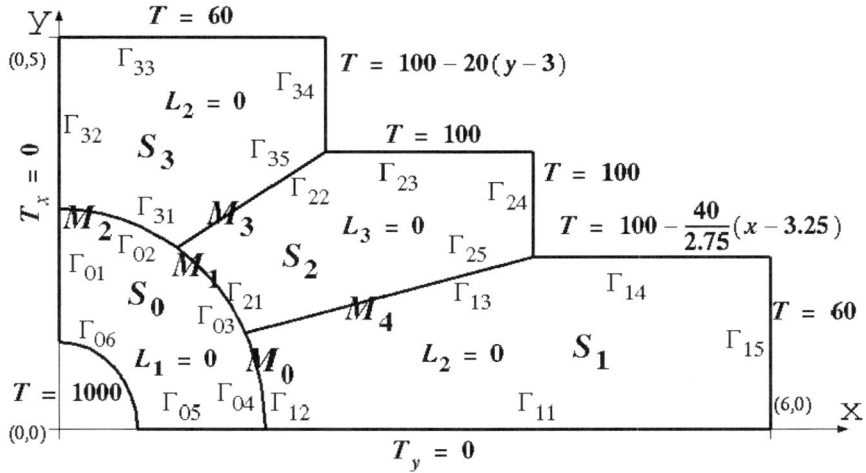

FIG. 5. A sketch of a composite PDE problem modeling the heat distribution in the walls of a chemical or nuclear reactor and in the surrounding isolating and cooling structures. The subdomains are shown, with the solver agents S_i, $i = 0, \ldots, 3$, simulating the local process in each subdomain and the mediators M_j, $j = 0, \ldots, 4$ mediating the interface piece they are written on. The unknown function is T and the exterior boundary conditions are shown next to the corresponding boundaries. We denote by Γ_{ik} the kth boundary piece of the ith subdomain.

the corresponding boundary pieces. The reactor keeps the inside temperature of its wall at 1000 degrees and the outside walls of the cooling structures are kept at, more or less, room temperature. The boundary conditions along the x- and y-axes reflect the symmetry of the construction. We denote by Γ_{ik} the k-th boundary piece of the i-th subdomain. The differential operators L_i, $i = 1, 2, 3$, are

$$L_1: T_{xx} + T_{yy} + \alpha_1 T = \beta_2(x^2 + y^2 - 2)$$
$$L_2: T_{xx} + T_{yy} + \alpha_2 T = 0 \qquad (1)$$
$$L_3: T_{xx} + T_{yy} - \gamma_3(T_x + T_y) + \alpha_3 T = 0$$

The parameters are: $\alpha_1 = 0.2$, $\alpha_2 = 0.4$, $\alpha_3 = 0.3$, $\beta_2 = -60$, $\gamma_3 = 10$. We denote by Ω_i the subdomain associated with S_i, $i = 0, \ldots, 3$. We use as interface conditions the continuity of temperature and heat flow across the subdomain interfaces. Note that even though the interface between Ω_0 and Ω_1, Ω_2, and Ω_3 looks like a single curve from the point of view of Ω_0, it is divided into three pieces Γ_{02}, Γ_{03} and Γ_{04}, so that the mediators M_0, M_1, and M_2 can each be assigned a single piece to mediate. The time we spent from writing down the problem on paper to getting a contour plot of the solution on the screen was five hours (this includes some manual calculations and adjusting the relaxation formulas for better convergence).

A user begins solving this problem by drawing Fig. 5. The sketch identifies the subdomains (the solvers), the mediators, each boundary piece in every subdomain, and the endpoints of the interfaces. The sketch is necessary since the currently implemented version of SciAgents requires input as a script file. However, we believe that (with the possible exception of the boundary piece identifiers) such a sketch will be necessary even with the best imaginable graphical user interface. We only expect the user to annotate this initial sketch.

After making the sketch the user constructs the SciAgents input file and starts SciAgents. This starts the global controller (containing the agent instantiator) and it instantiates the agents on the appropriate machines and builds the network of four solvers and five mediators that is to solve the problem. After that, the "computing" thread of the global controller starts a shell-like interface with two major commands: pause and tolerance for control and steering the computations. The pause prompts the controller to issue messages to all agents to save their current state and to exit. The tolerance command changes dynamically the tolerance of a given mediator or of all mediators.

After the initial exchange of data to check that all agents are ready, the user sees four copies of the //ELLPACK user interface (see Fig. 6). All four subproblems are defined (see Fig. 7 for a snapshot during this process) and

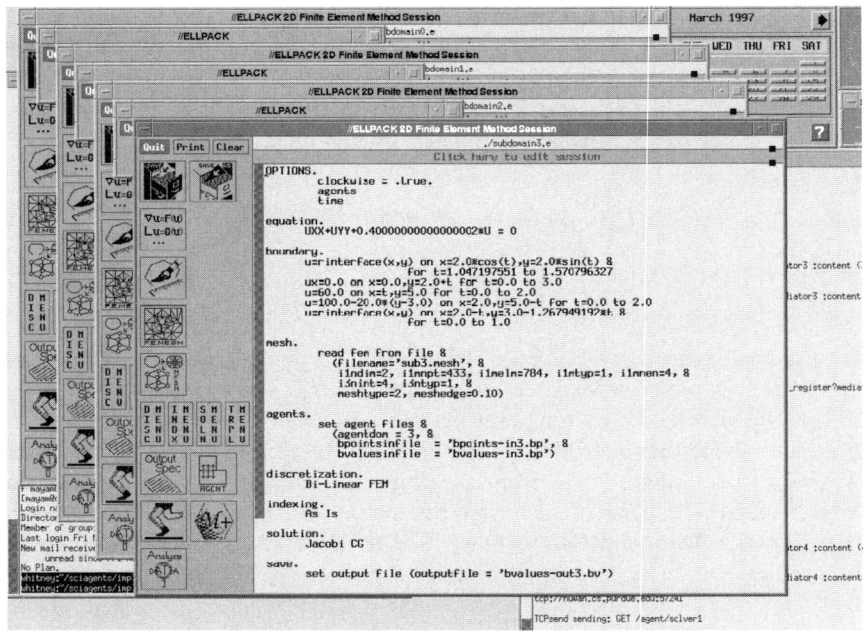

FIG. 6. Four copies of the //ELLPACK interface are presented to the user for defining the four PDE subproblems.

selecting a discretizer, linear solver, etc., in one subdomain does not lead to any requirement or necessity about selections in the neighboring subdomains. If a subdomain is huge, one may choose to use a 32-node Intel Paragon for it, while the neighboring tiny subdomain may be simulated on the same host where the wrapper is running. There are only two requirements for global synchronization of the local definitions: each subdomain geometry has to be input in terms of the global coordinate system (hence the need of the coordinates of the boundary pieces in the sketch), and for each interface piece, the right-hand side of the boundary conditions has to be the function r interface(x,y). It is the user's responsibility to make sure that the relaxation formulas used for each interface piece correspond to the left-hand sides of the boundary conditions entered in the two solvers' user interfaces. For the example, the boundary condition used at all interfaces is T = rinterface(x,y) and the relaxation formula is (U is the solution on the "left" side, V is the solution on the "right" side; U_n is the normal derivative; f is a factor given below; the formula is always applied pointwise for each point from any solver's grid/mesh on the interface):

$$U^{\text{new}} = V^{\text{new}} = (\tfrac{1}{2}\,(U^{\text{old}} + V^{\text{old}}) - f \times (U_n^{\text{old}} - V_n^{\text{old}}) \qquad (2)$$

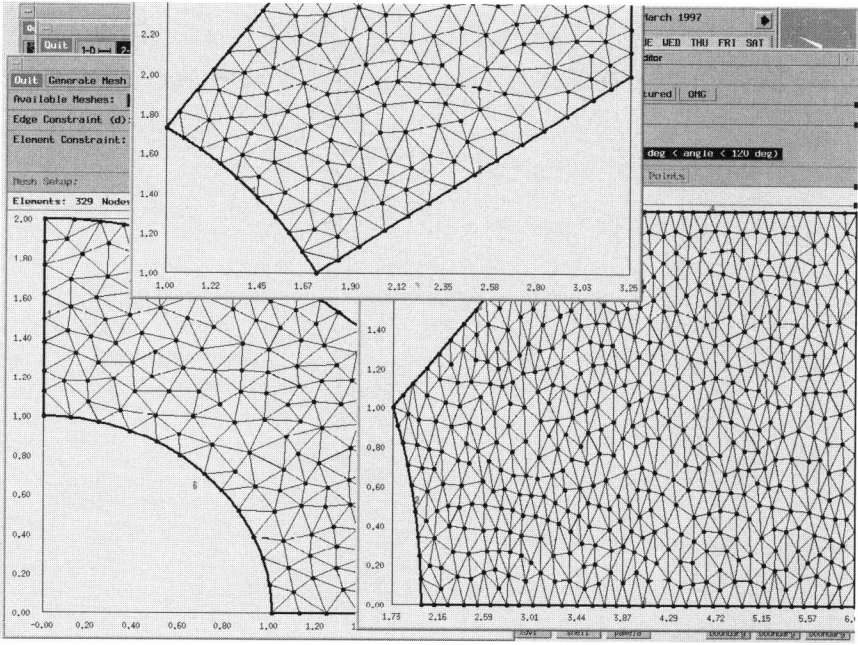

FIG. 7. A snapshot of the display during the subproblem definition process. Parts of three //ELLPACK domain tools containing three of the subdomain geometries and finite element meshes are visible. The user can discretize each subdomain completely independently from the others. For example, the densities of the above meshes are different.

The form of the factor f is

$$f = \frac{|U^{\text{old}}| + |V^{\text{old}}|}{(|U_n^{\text{old}}| + |V_n^{\text{old}}|)f_0}$$

which scales the relaxation properly (and avoids dependencies on the choice of the coordinate system) and regulates the rate of change of the boundary conditions along the interface from iteration to iteration by changing f_0. It is sometimes hard to predict the "optimal," or even the acceptable, values of f_0.

The user input results in writing the script for the actual future runs. The user exits the //ELLPACK interface, which prompts the wrapper to collect the initial data and to send them to the mediators. They compute initial right-hand sides of the boundary conditions. After the mediators provide all necessary boundary conditions, the wrapper runs the script which, in turn, runs the executable(s). When the iteration is completed the wrapper takes over again and extracts all required data from the computed solution and sends it to the mediators, waiting for the new boundary conditions from them. Thus, at the next iteration, no new compilation and user actions are necessary, since the same script (and executable(s)) is run by the wrapper.

For this example, we had to change the factor f_0 twice before the process began to converge, especially for mediators M_3 and M_4. This seems to be due to the natural singularity that occurs at the reentrant corners of the global domain which affects the stability of the convergence.

When a mediator observes convergence (the change of the boundary conditions for the next iteration is smaller than the tolerance), it reports this to the global controller, and after all mediators report convergence, the global controller issues a message to all agents to stop. In this case we had convergence after 53 iterations. Figure 8 shows a combined picture of all four subdomain solutions. Note that all contour lines match when crossing from one subdomain to another, there are even a few which go through three subdomains,

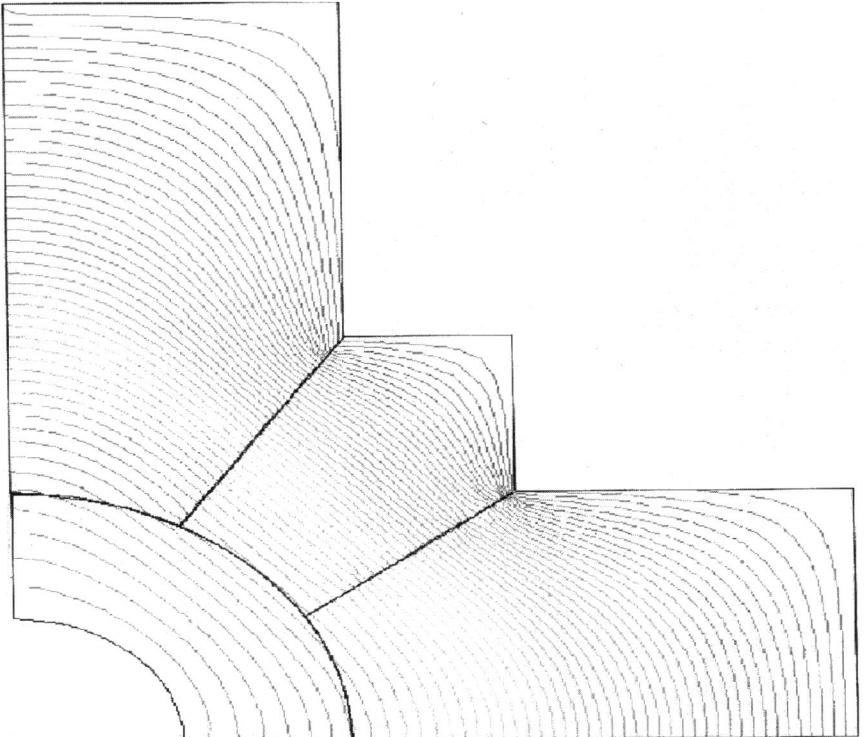

FIG. 8. A combined picture of all subdomain solutions of the example problem in Equation (1). The global solution corresponds to the physical intuition about the behavior of the modeled real-world system. All contour lines match when crossing from one subdomain to another; there are even a few which go through three subdomains and one going through all four subdomains.

and one going through all four subdomains. This is solid evidence that the interface relaxation technique works in this problem.

To experiment with the applicability of SciAgents to more difficult problems we solved several variations of the above example, replacing $L_1, L_2,$ and L_3 with nonlinear operators (exhibiting different nonlinearity for different L_i). Since //ELLPACK uses a Newton iterative procedure to solve a nonlinear problem, the global solution process becomes a multi-level iteration where one SciAgents step involves a complete Newton iteration in it. Also, while one can plausibly handle the linear example above by considering a single PDE with discontinuous coefficients on a single domain, this approach is not feasible for nonlinear problems. Using SciAgents we were able to solve the following sets of PDEs (the increased complexity is reflected in a two- to three-fold increase of the number of iterations necessary for the convergence to the global solution).

—Set 1

—L_1: $TT_{xx} + (1 + T)T_{yy} + aT(1 + T) = b(x^2 + y^2 - 2)$

—L_2: $T_{xx}/(1 + (x - y)^2) + T_{yy}/(1 + (4x - 5y)^2) + cT/(101 + t) = 0$

—L_3: $T_{xx} + T_{yy} - d(T_x + T_y) + cT = 0$

—Set 2

—L_1: $T_{xx} + T_{yy} + ae^{x+y+T/500} = b(x^2 + y^2 - 2)$

—L_2: $TT_{xx} + TT_{yy} + (T_x + 20)T_y + 2(T_x - 20)T_x = 0$

—L_3: $T_{xx} + T_{yy} - b(T_x + T_y) + aT = 0$

—Set 3

—L_1: $T_{xx} + T_{yy} + \alpha_1 T(1 + T/1000) = \beta_2(x^2 + y^2 - 2)$

—L_2: $T_{xx} + T_{yy} \alpha_2 T = 0$

—L_3: $T_{xx} + (1 + T/1000)T_{yy} + (T_x/500 + 3)T_x + \alpha_3 T = 0$

8.2 Intelligent PDE Computing with PYTHIA

In this section, we describe how PYTHIA can be used to determine reasonable strategies for PDE problem solving. In our prototype implementation, our PYTHIA agents' expertise stems from the following classes of PDEs (we also list the number of samples in each class from our study that involves about 167 PDE problems):

(1) SINGULAR: PDE problems whose solutions have at least one singularity (6 exemplars).

(2) ANALYTIC: PDE problems whose solutions are analytic (35 exemplars).
(3) OSCILLATORY: PDE problems whose solutions oscillate (34 exemplars).
(4) BOUNDARY-LAYER: Problems with a boundary layer in their solutions (32 exemplars).
(5) BOUNDARY-CONDITIONS-MIXED: Problems that have mixed boundary conditions in their solutions (74 exemplars).
(6) SPECIAL: Problems that do not belong to the above classes (10 examplars).

Note that these classes are not mutually-exclusive, so their total membership is 191 problems. In other words, there are different PYTHIA agents, each of which can recommend a solver for a PDE belonging to its representative class(es) of problems. Also, a problem can belong to more than one class simultaneously (a given PDE can *both be* analytic *and have* mixed boundary conditions). Detecting the presence of such mutually non-exclusive classes is critical to selecting a good solver for the PDE.

To test our ideas, we made five experiments, with 2, 3, 4, 5 and 6 PYTHIA agents respectively. In each experiment, each PYTHIA agent knows about a certain class(es) of PDE problems. For example, with 6 PYTHIA agents, each agent knows about one of the above classes of PDEs. In the "3-agent" experiment, agent 1 knows about problem classes 1 and 2, agent 2 knows about classes 3 and 4 and the third agent knows about classes 5 and 6. The population of 167 PDE problems was split into two parts: a large set of 111 problems and a smaller set of 56 problems. We conducted two sets of experiments: In each scenario, we first trained our technique on the larger set of {problem, agent} pairs (using the notion of reasonableness defined earlier) and tested our learning on the smaller set of 56 exemplars. In the second experiment, the roles of these two sets were reversed. We also compared our technique with two very popular gradient descent techniques for training feedforward neural networks, namely, Vanilla (Plain) Backpropagation (BProp) and Resilient Propagation (RProp). Figure 9 summarizes the results.

It can be easily seen that our method consistently outperforms BProp and RProp on learning the mapping from problems to agents. Also, performance on the larger training set was expectedly better than that on the smaller training set. Moreover, our algorithm operates in an on-line mode; new data do not require retraining on the old. Our technique was also tested for this ability; for the larger training set, we incrementally trained our algorithm on the 111 PDEs and the accuracy figures on the test set were found to rise steadily to the figures shown in Fig. 9. In the collaborative networked scenario of an MPSE, where the resources change dynamically, this feature of our

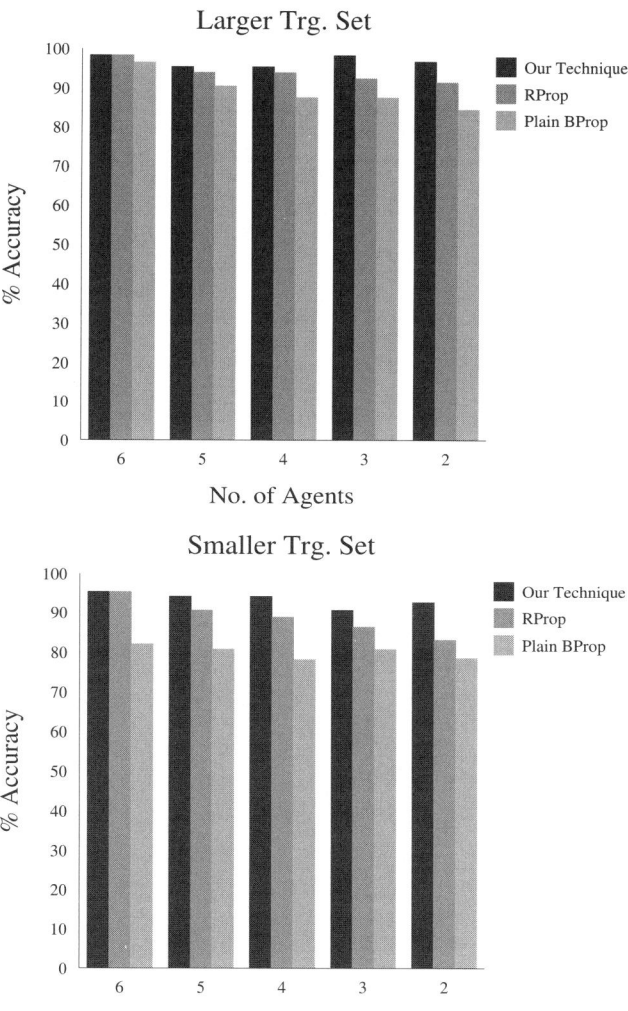

FIG. 9. Performance of learning algorithms. The graph on the left depicts the results with the larger training set and the one on the right shows the results with the smaller training set. In each case, recommendation accuracy figures for the five experiments (with 2, 3, 4, 5, and 6) agents are presented for all the three learning algorithms considered in this chapter.

neuro-fuzzy system enables us to automatically infer the capabilities of multiple PYTHIA agents. If the capabilities of agent 1 were to change, for example, in the 6-agent scenario, then our network could infer the new mappings without losing the information already learnt. This feature is absent in most other methods of classification, such as BProp and RProp, in which the dimensionality of the network is fixed and it is imperative that the old data be kept around if these networks are to update their learning with new data.

The PYTHIA project web pages at http://www.cs.purdue.edu/research/cse/pythia provide information about this collaborative PYTHIA methodology and facilities to invoke it remotely. At the outset, there is a facility to provide feature information about a PDE problem. In particular, there are forms that guide the user in providing information about the operator, function, domain geometry and boundary conditions. Once these details are given, the information is submitted to the central PYTHIA agent, PYTHIA-C, that performs further processing. As mentioned before, it first classifies the given PDE problem into categories of problems as described above. Having classified the problem into one or more of these classes, the PDE is taken to an appropriate PYTHIA agent for this class of problems, which in turn predicts an optimal strategy and reports back to the user.

8.3 Learning and Adaptation in Multi-Agent Systems

The above experiment can be visualized as an example where the central agent PYTHIA-C is in a *learning mode*, cycles through the training set, and learns mappings from the given PDEs to appropriate agents. From this point on PYTHIA-C is in the *stable mode*. It will only ask the best agent to answer a particular question. If PYTHIA-C finds a PYTHIA agent's recommendation unacceptable, it will ask the next best agent, until all agents are exhausted. This is facilitated by our neuro-fuzzy learning algorithm. By varying an acceptance threshold in the algorithm, we can get an enumeration of "not so good" agents for a problem type. If PYTHIA-C determines no plausible solution exists among its agents or itself, then PYTHIA-C gives the answer that "is best." When giving such an answer, the user is notified of PYTHIA-C's lack of confidence.

While this scheme serves most purposes, an issue still pending is the mode of switching between the learning and stable modes. PYTHIA-C switches from learning to stable mode after an *a priori* fixed number of problems (this was 111 in our first set of experiments, for example). The timing of the reverse switch back to learning is a more interesting problem; we report on three different methods.

Time based: This simple approach is where PYTHIA-C reverts to learning after a fixed time period. At such points, PYTHIA-C cycles through its training set, queries other agents, gets back answers, determines reasonableness values and finally learns new mappings for the PDE problems. Figure 10 depicts the results with the six-agent case and the time-based approach using the larger training set. Initially, each agent starts up with approximately $1/3$ of

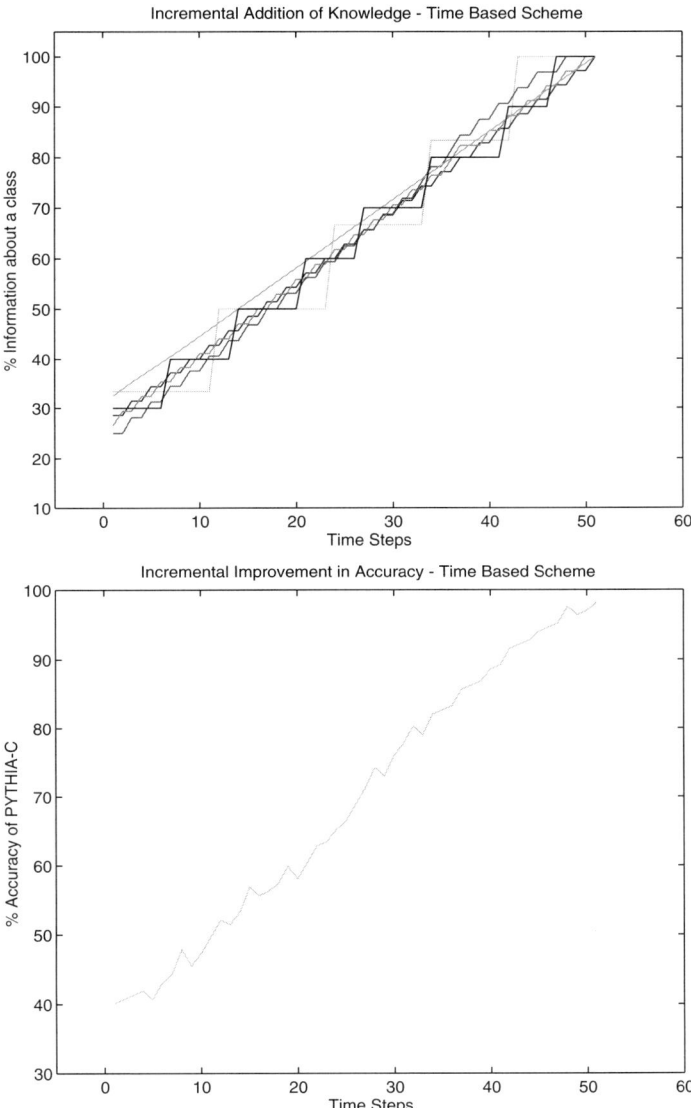

FIG. 10. Results with the time-based scheme for six agents using the larger training set. The top graphs show the systematic increase in the abilities for each of the agents individually, and the bottom one shows the corresponding improvement in accuracy of the central agent, PYTHIA-C.

their total knowledge base and this knowledge steadily increases with time. At periodic time intervals, PYTHIA-C switches to learning mode and cycles through the larger training set with each of the agents in the experiment. The performance is then measured with the smaller training set. As can be seen, the accuracy figure steadily improves for each of the six individual agents to the accuracy observed in the previous static experiment. PYTHIA-C's accuracy improves from 40.85% to 98.20% in this experiment.

We conducted another experiment with this method, one more realistic for multi-agent systems. We begin the experiment with no "known" agents, i.e. PYTHIA-C initially does not know about the existence of any agents or their capabilities. Then, each agent is introduced into the experiment with a small initial knowledge base and then their knowledge bases are slowly increased. For example, Agent 1 comes into the setup with a small knowledge base and announces its existence to PYTHIA-C, which creates a class for Agent 1. It then reverts to learning mode (though wasteful) and learns mappings from PDE problems to agents (in this case, there is only one agent). After some time, Agent 3 comes into the experiment and this process is repeated. This is repeated until all six agents are introduced. While the addition of new agents and associated classes is taking place, the abilities of existing agents (like Agent 1) also increase simultaneously. Thus, these events happen in parallel; i.e. addition of new agents and additions to the knowledge base of existing agents. Because our neuro-fuzzy scheme has the ability to introduce new classes on the fly, PYTHIA-C can handle this situation well. The accuracy figures converge to the values previously obtained.

Reactive: In this method, a PYTHIA agent notifies PYTHIA-C whenever its confidence for some class of problems has changed significantly. PYTHIA-C reverts to learning when it next receives a query about this class of problems. Each agent started with the same initial knowledge base as before and this is slowly increased. As the agents indicate the resulting increase in confidence to PYTHIA-C, it reverts to learning mode from time to time. The accuracy figures for PYTHIA-C approach the same values as before; they follow a monotonic pattern, but a more slowly increasing pattern, see Fig. 11.

Time-based reactive: This is a combination of the two methods above where PYTHIA-C sends out a "has anyone's abilities changed significantly" message at fixed time intervals, and switches to learning if it receives a positive response. Each agent, starts with the same knowledge base and this is slowly increased. Figure 12 shows that the accuracy figures for PYTHIA-C are again monotonic increasing and rising slightly faster than for the reactive method.

Our experiments with the three methods show that they enable the central agent PYTHIA-C to keep track of the dynamic capabilities (in our case, the knowledge base) of other agents. These methods also enable PYTHIA-C to handle situations where agents appear and disappear over time.

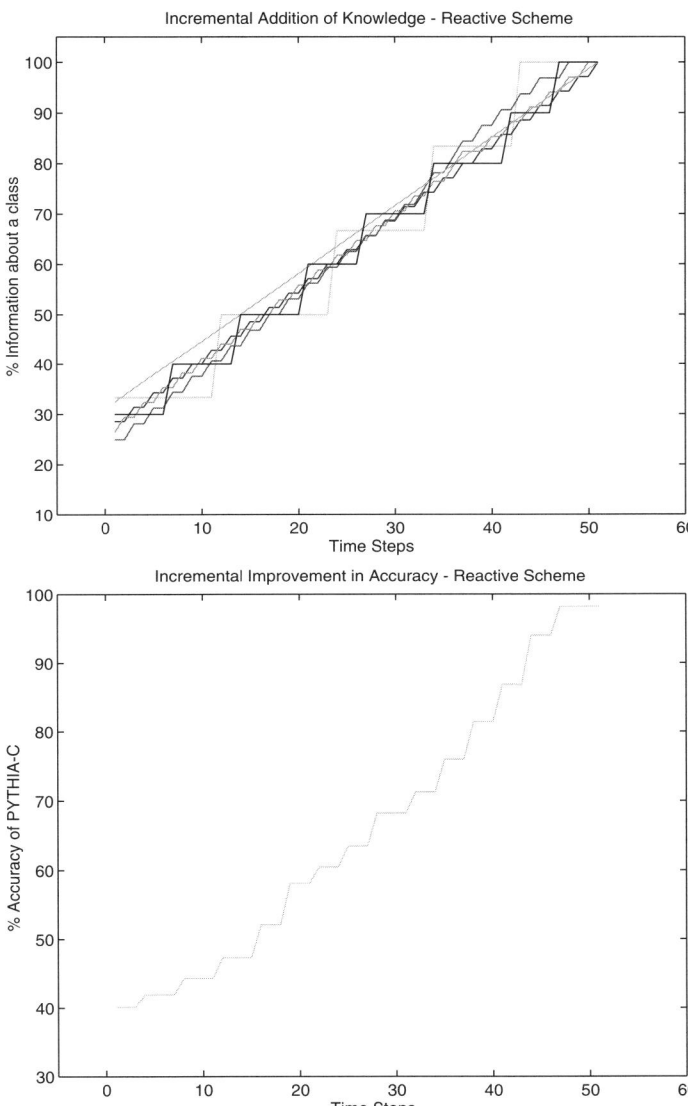

FIG. 11. Results with the reactive method for six agents using the larger training set. The top graphs show the systematic increase in the abilities of each of the agents and the bottom one shows the corresponding improvement in accuracy of PYTHIA-C.

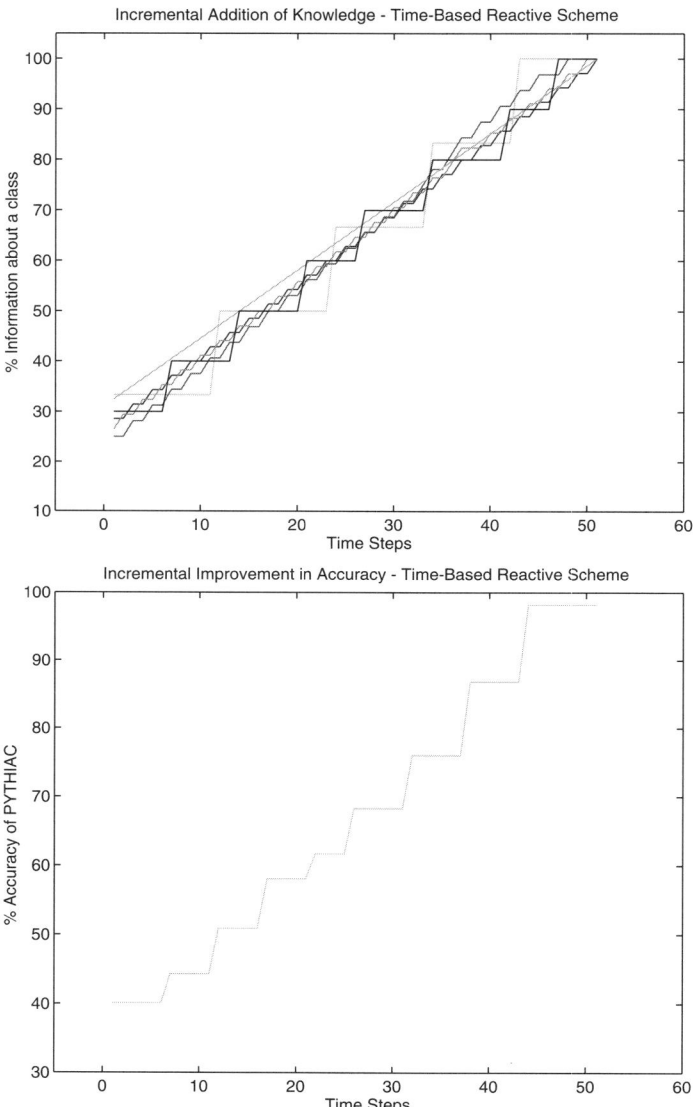

FIG. 12. Results with the time-based reactive method for six agents using the larger training set. The top graphs show the systematic increase in the abilities of each of the PYTHIA agents and the bottom one shows the corresponding improvement in accuracy of PYTHIA-C.

9. Conclusions

In this chapter, we have described an agent-oriented architecture for MPSEs, consisting of solver, mediator, and recommender agents. This architecture enables us to combine existing PSEs and libraries into MPSEs. The SciAgents [5] and PYTHIA [33] systems provide the solver, mediator, and recommender agents required to realize multidisciplinary problem solving environments. Our ongoing research focuses on many more aspects of these problems. We are extending the functionality of the SciAgents system to address more complex problem domains and are also investigating strategies to choose interface relaxation schemes. In the PYTHIA system, we are working on enhancing the knowledge bases to provide more flexible resource selection schemes. In the PDE domain, for instance, PYTHIA can be used to select partitioning strategies (for parallel PDE solving), mesh refinement techniques and selecting solvers for linear systems that arise from the discretization of PDEs. We are also interfacing the PYTHIA system with the GAMS system for mathematical software to facilitate software delivery. Together, the systems presented here address rapid multidisciplinary prototyping—one of the most important grand challenge problems in computational science and engineering.

ACKNOWLEDGMENTS

Work supported in part by NSF awards ASC 9404859 and CCR 9202536, ARPA ARO award DAAH04-94-G-0010DARPA, Intel Corporation and Purdue Research Foundation.

REFERENCES

1. Bernard, K. C. (1992) Ordering chaos: supercomputing at the edge. *Technology 2001: The Future of Computing and Communications* (ed. D. Leebaert). MIT Press, Cambridge MA.
2. Boisvert, R. F., Howe, S. E., and Kahaner, D. K. (1991) The guide to available mathematical software problem classification system. *Commun. Stat. Simul. Comp.* **20**(4), 811–842.
3. Burkart, R. E. (1994) *Reducing the R&D Cycle Time.* Technical Report, Research Technology Management.
4. Cammarata, S. *et al.* (1988) Strategies of cooperation in distributed problem solving. *Readings in Distributed Artificial Intelligence.* Morgan Kaufmann, San Francisco. pp. 102–105.
5. Drashansky, T. T. (1996) An agent-based approach to building multidisciplinary problem solving environments. *Ph.D. thesis*, Department of Computer Science, Purdue University.
6. Dyksen, W. R., and Gritter, C. R. (1989) Elliptic expert: an expert system for elliptic partial differential equations. *Mathematics and Computers in Simulation* **31**, 333–343.
7. Dyksen, W. R., and Gritter, C. R. (1992) Scientific computing and the algorithm selection problem. *Expert Systems for Scientific Computing* (eds E. N. Houstis, J. R. Rice, and R. Vichnevetsky. North-Holland, Amsterdam. pp. 19–31.
8. Fritzson, R. (1994) KQML—A language and protocol for knowledge and information exchange. *Proc. 13th Intl. Distributed Artificial Intelligence Workshop.* Springer-Verlag, Berlin. pp. 134–143.

9. Gallopoulos, E., Houstis, E. N., and Rice, J. R. (1994) Computer as thinker/doer: problem-solving environments for computational science. *IEEE Computational Science and Engineering* **1**(2), 11–23.
10. Giarratano, J. C. (1991) *CLIPS User's Guide*, Version 5.1. NASA Lyndon B. Johnson Space Center.
11. Grimajl, S. S. (1995) *The First ICASE/LARC Industry Roundtable: Session Proceedings.* Technical Report ICASE Interim Report 26, ICASE. NASA Langley Research Center, Hampton VA.
12. Hayes-Roth, B., *et al.* (1992) Guardian. A prototype intelligent agent for intensive-care monitoring. *Artif. Intell. Med* **4**(2), 165–185.
13. Hoffmann, C. M., Houstis, E. N., Rice, J. R., Catlin, A. C., Gaitatzes, M., Weerawarana, S., Wang, N.-H., Takoudis, C., and Taylor, D. (1994) SoftLab—a virtual laboratory for computational science. *Math. Comp. in Simulation* **36**, 479–491.
14. Houstis, E. N., Joshi, A., Rice, J. R., and Weerawarana, S. (1996) *MPSEs: Multidisciplinary Problem Solving Environments.* White paper presented at the *America in the Age of Information: A forum*. Committee on Information and Communications, National Science and Technology Council.
15. Industrial Research Institute (1992) *Proceedings: Roundtable Meeting on Reducing R&D Cycle Time.* Technical Report, Industrial Research Institute, Washington DC.
16. Joshi, A. (1996) To learn or not to learn ... *Adaptation and Learning in Multiagent Systems* (eds G. Weiss and S. Sen), Lecture Notes in Artificial Intelligence 1042. Springer-Verlag, Berlin. pp. 127–139.
17. Drashansky, T., Joshi, A., Houstis, E., and Weerawarana, S. (1996) SciencePad: Intelligent electronic notepad for ubiquitous scientific computing. Scientific Computing in a Ubiquitous Environment, Microcomputer Applications, Special Issue-Intelligent Information Systems, **15**(3), 85–92.
18. Joshi, A., Drashansky, T. T., Rice, J. R., Weerawarana, S., and Houstis, E. N. (1995) *On Learning and Adaptation in Multiagent Systems: A Scientific Computing Perspective.* Technical Report TR-95-040. Department of Computing Sciences, Purdue University.
19. Joshi, A., Ramakrishnan, N., Rice, J. R., and Houstis, E. (1996) A neuro-fuzzy approach to agglomorative clustering. *Proc. IEEE Intl. Conf. on Neural Networks*, Vol. 2. IEEE Press. pp. 1028–1033.
20. Joshi, A., Ramakrishnan, N., Rice, J. R., and Houstis, E. (1996) On neurobiological, neuro-fuzzy, machine learning and statistical pattern recognition techniques. *IEEE Trans. Neural Networks* **8**(1), 18–31.
21. Joshi, A., Weerawarana, S., and Houstis, E. N. (1994) The use of neural networks to support "intelligent" scientific computing. *Proceedings Int. Conf. Neural Networks, World Congress on Computational Intelligence*, Vol. IV. pp. 411–416.
22. Joshi, A., Weerawarana, S., Ramakrishnan, N., Houstis, E. N., and Rice, J. R. (1996) Neuro-fuzzy support for PSEs: a step towards the automated solution of PDEs. *IEEE Computer & IEEE Computational Science and Engineering* **3**(1), 44–56.
23. Kamel, M. S., Ma, K. S., and Enright, W. H. (1993) ODEXPERT: an expert system to select numerical solvers for initial value ODE systems. *ACM Trans. Math. Software* **19**, 44–62.
24. Leake, D. (1996) Case-based selection of problem solving methods for scientific computation. http//www.cs.indiana.edu/hyplan/leake/cbmatrix.html.
25. Lehrer, K. (1990) *Theory of Knowledge*. Westview Press, Boulder CO.
26. Lesser, V. R. (1991) A retrospective view of FA/C distributed problem solving. *IEEE Transactions on Systems, Man, and Cybernetics* **21**(6), 1347–1363.
27. Markus, S., Weerawarana, S., Houstis, E. N., and Rice, J. R. (1997) *Scientific Computing*

via the World Wide Web: The Net//ELLPACK PSE Server. Technical Report CSD TR-97-022. Department of Computer Sciences, Purdue University.
28. McFaddin, S., and Rice, J. (1992) Collaborating PDE solvers. *Appl. Num. Math* **10**, 279–295.
29. Sun Microsystems (1996) *The Network is the Computer.* Trademark.
30. Moore, P. K., Ozturan, C., and Flaherty, J. E. (1990) Towards the automatic numerical solution of partial differential equations. *Intelligent Mathematical Software Systems* (eds E. N. Houstis, J. R. Rice, and R. Vichnevetsky). North-Holland, Amsterdam. pp. 15–22.
31. Mu, M., and Rice, J. R. (1995) Modeling with collaborating PDE solvers—theory and practice. *Computing Systems in Engineering* **6**, 87–95.
32. Oates, T. *et al.* (1994) *Cooperative Information Gathering: A Distributed Problem Solving Approach.* Technical Report TR-94-66. Computer Science, University of Massachusetts, Amherst.
33. Ramakrishnan, N. (1997) Recommender systems for problem solving environments. *Ph.D. thesis*, Department of Computer Sciences, Purdue University.
34. Ramakrishnan, N., Joshi, A., Houstis, E. N., and Rice, J. R. (1997) Neuro-fuzzy approaches to collaborative scientific computing. *Proceedings of the IEEE International Conference on Neural Networks*, Vol. I. IEEE Press. pp. 473–478.
35. Ramakrishnan, N., Joshi, A., Weerawarana, S., Houstis, E. N., and Rice, J. R. (1995) Neuro-fuzzy systems for intelligent scientific computing. *Proc. Artificial Neural Networks in Engineering ANNIE '95.* pp. 279–284.
36. Ramakrishnan, N., and Rice, J. R. (1996) *GAUSS: An Automatic Algorithm Selection System for Quadrature.* Technical Report TR-96-048. Department of Computer Sciences, Purdue University.
37. Ramakrishnan, N., Rice, J. R., and Houstis, E. N. (1996) *Knowledge Discovery in Computational Science: A Case Study in Algorithm Selection.* Technical Report TR-96-081. Department of Computer Sciences, Purdue University.
38. Resnick, P., and Varian, H. (1997) Recommender Systems. *Comm. ACM* **40**(3), 56–58.
39. Rice, J. R. (1994) *Processing PDE Interface Conditions.* Technical Report TR-94-041. Department of Computer Sciences, Purdue University.
40. Rice, J. R. (1976) The algorithm selection problem. *Advances in Computers* **15**, 65–118.
41. Rice, J. R. (1979) Methodology for the algorithm selection problem. *Performance Evaluation of Numerical Software* (ed. L. Fosdick). North-Holland, Amsterdam. pp. 301–307.
42. Schlimmer, J. C., and Hermens, L. A. (1993) Software agents: completing patterns and constructing user interfaces. *Journal of Artificial Intelligence Research* **1**, 61–89.
43. Shoham, Y. (1993) Agent-oriented programming. *Artificial Intelligence* **60**(1), 51–92.
44. Smith, R. G., and Davis, R. (1988) Frameworks for cooperation in distributed problem solving. *Readings in Distributed Artificial Intelligence.* Morgan Kaufmann, San Francisco. pp. 61–70.
45. Tsoukalas, L. H., and Uhrig, R. E. (1997) *Fuzzy and Neural Approaches in Engineering.* John Wiley & Sons, New York.
46. Varga, L. Z. *et al.*, (1994) Integrating intelligent systems into a cooperating community for electricity distribution management. *Intl. J. Expert Systems with Applications* **7**(4), 42–49.
47. Vessey, J. T. (1991) *Speed-to-Market Distinguishes the New Competitors.* Technical report, Research Technology Management.
48. Voigt, R. G. (1989) *Requirements for Multidisciplinary Design of Aerospace Vehicles on High Performance Computers.* Technical Report ICASE Report No. 89–70. ICASE, NASA Langley Research Center, Hampton VA.
49. Johnson, W. R. Jr (1992) Anything, anytime, anywhere: the future of networking. *Technology 2001: the Future of Computing and Communications* (ed. D. Leebaert). MIT Press, Cambridge MA.

50. Weerawarana, S. (1994) Problem solving environments for partial differential equation based systems. *Ph.D. Thesis*, Department of Computer Sciences, Purdue University.
51. Weerawarana, S., Houstis, E., Rice, J., Gaitatzes, M., Markus, S., and Joshi, A. (1996) *Web//ELLPACK: A Networked Computing Service on the World Wide Web*. Technical Report TR 96-011. Department of Computer Sciences, Purdue University.
52. Weerawarana, S., Houstis, E. N., Rice, J. R., Catlin, A. C., Crabill, C. L., Chui, C. C., and Markus, S. (1994) PDELab: an object-oriented framework for building problem solving environments for PDE based applications. *Proc. Second Annual Object-Oriented Numerics Conference*. Rogue-Wave Software, Corvallis OR. pp. 79–92.
53. Weerawarana, S., Houstis, E. N., Rice, J. R., Joshi, A., and Houstis, C. E. (1996) PYTHIA: a knowledge based system to select scientific algorithms. *ACM Trans. Math. Software* **22**(4), 447–468.
54. Wesson, R. *et al.* (1988) Network structures for distributed assessment. *Readings in Distributed Artificial Intelligence*. Morgan Kaufmann, San Francisco. pp. 71–89.
55. Wooldridge, M., and Jennings, N. (1998) Intelligent agents: theory and practice (in press).

Author Index

Numbers in italics indicate the pages on which complete references are given.

A

Abdel-Hamid, T.K., 61, *101*
Agarwal, A., 308, 315, 321, 322, *325*
Agha, G., 332, 359, *396*, *399*
Agha, G.A., *400*
Aguilar, M., 364, *399*
Ahituv, N., 118, *154*
Ahuja, S., 338, *396*
Alter, J.F., 166, 168, *233*
Alverson, R., 290, 308, *325*
Anderson, M.D., 381, *399*
Anderson, T.E., 304, *325*
Andreoli, J.-M., 334, 355, *396*
Ang, B.S., 308, 311, 312, *325*
Angus, J.E., 166, 168, *233*
Anonymous, 46, 53, 73, *101*
ANSI/AIAA, 162, 165, 166, *231*
ANSI/IEEE, 162, *231*
Arbab, F., 368, 388, 390, *396*, *397*, *399*
Armenise, P., 40, 77, 82, 92, *101*
Armitage, J.W., 41, 43, 72, *101*, *102*
Arnold, P., 46, *105*
Arvind,, 308, 311, 312, 325, *327*
Avritzer, A., 165, *232*
Awad, M., 75, 95, *102*

B

Babel, P., 28, *30*
Bach, J., 14, *30*
Baer, J.-L., 324, *325*
Baldwin, R.W., 242, *285*
Ballantine, J.A., 145, *154*
Banâtre, J.-P., 353, *397*
Bandinelli, S.C., 41, 77, *102*
Banker, R., 130, *154*
Banville, M., 350, *397*
Barbacci, M.R., 375, *397*
Baresi, L., 41, 77, *102*
Barghouti, N.S., 55, *105*
Barker, H., 17, *30*
Baroudi, J.J., 135, *155*
Barua, A., 115, *154*
Basili, V.R., 39, 42, 46, 50, 55, 65, 72, 73, 75, 77, 85, 86, 92, 98, *102*, *106*, 162, 174, 210, 221, *232*, *233*
Bate, R.R., 9, 15, *30*, 72, 77, *104*
BCS, 4, *30*
Bean, T., 50, *102*
Becker, R.A., 222, *232*
Beizer, B., 160, 162, 164, 173, *232*
Bell Canada, 28, *30*
Bell, D.E., 272, *285*
Bels, F., 39, 55, *103*
Benington, H.D., 38, *102*
Benson, R.J., 118, 127, 133, 143, *156*
Berg, D.J., 293, *325*
Berger, D., 324, *326*
Berger, P., 119, *154*
Bergstra, J.A., 386, *397*
Bernard, K., 401, 419, *435*
Bershad, B., 303, 307, *326*
Bessamusca, T., 349, *398*
Besselman, J.J., 3, 14, *30*
Bhamidipati, V., 237, 261, 269, *286*
Bhandari, I., 177, 190, 209, *232* , *233*
Bic, L.F., 357, *399*
Blackler, F., 126, 131, *154*
Blaha, M., 75, 95, *107*
Blair, G.S., 334, *400*
Blom, C.L., 390, *397*
Blumofe, R.D., 290, 299, *326*
Boehm, B.W., 38, 39, 46, 55, *102*, *103*, 160, 198, 232

Boeing, 14, *30*
Boisvert, R.F., 410, *435*
Bollinger, T., 14, *30*
Bond, P., 111, 112, 129, 138, 147, 150, 151, *157*
Bothwell, C., 13, *32*
Botorog, G.H., 364, *397*
Botsdorf, J.E., 40, 41, 42, 43, 55, *104*
Boughton, G.A., 312, *326*
Bourgois, M., 355, *397*
Bouvry, P., 368, *397*
Boykin,, 302, *326*
Brandl, D., 55, 77, *103*
Breach, S., 324, *327*
Briand, L.C., 41, 43, 72, *102*, 210, *232*
Broadbent, M., 110, 117, *154*, *157*
Brogi, A., 338, *397*
Brooks, W.D., 166, 169, *232*
Brown, C., 126, 131, *154*
Brown, J.R., 172, 218, *232*
Brown, N., 29, *30*
Bruckhaus, T.F., 41, 42, *104*, *106*
Brynjolfsson, E., 114, 115, 117, *155*
Buetow, R.C., 8, 30 , 54, *103*
Burger, F.J., 390, *397*
Burkart, R.E., 401, *435*
Burkhart, H., 364, *397*
Burrel, G., 73, *103*
Bush, M., 44, 66, *107*
Buss, M.D.J., 134, *154*
Butler Cox Foundation, 148, *154*
Byrnes, P., 3, 14, *30*

C

Caldiera, G., 40, 41, 42, 43, 50, 55, 65, 72, 73, 77, 92, *102*, *104*, 221, *232*
Cammarata, S., 409, *435*
Canada, J.R., 134, *154*
Cantone, G., 72, 73, 77, *102*, 221, *232*
Card, D.N., 209, *232*
Carlson, W.M., 119, 124, 146, *154*
Carriero, N., 333, 338, 340, *396*, *397*
Castellani, S., 352, 356, *398*
Catanzaro, B., 305, *326*
Catlin, A.C., 405, *436*, *438*
Chaar, J., 177, 209, *232*
Chaiken, D., 314, *326*
Chambers, J.M., 222, *232*

Champy, J., 44, 45, *103*, *104*
Chandy, K.M., 361, *398*
Chapman, B., 365, *397*
Charette, R.N., 143, *154*
Chen, C., 378, *398*
Chen, M.H., 164, 173, *232*
Chen, T., 324, *325*
Chichakly, K.J., 61, *103*
Chillarege, R., 177, 190, 209, *232*, *233*
Chiou, D., 308, 311, 312, *325*, *326*
Chismar, W.G., 129, 135, *154*
Chow, P., 324, *326*
Chrissis, M.B., 9, 12, 15, 16, *31*, *32*, 44, 53, 58, 66, *106*, *107*
Christerson, M., 95, *105*
Christie, A.M., 55, 82, *103*
Chui, C.C., 403, *436*
Ciancarini, P., 333, 334, 338, 350, 352, 356, *398*
Cianfrani, C., 8, *32*
Ciarfella, W.A., 46, 55, *107*
Clark, L.A., 199, 200, 211, 222, *232*
Cleveland, W.S., 184, *232*
Cole, M., 363, *398*
Coleman, T., 138, *154*
Common Criteria Editorial Board, 239, *285*
Conradi, R., 41, 46, 50, 77, *103*, *105*
Cook, J.E., 41, *103*
Cooper, J., 9, 15, *30*
Copp, D., 128, *154*
Coulson, G., 334, *400*
Coyne, E.J., 237, *286*
Crabill, C.L., 405, *438*
Crespo, A., 164, *233*
Cronk, M., 118, *154*
Crowley, J., 72, 77, *103*, *104*
Crowston, K., 333, 396, *399*
Culler, D.E., 290, 295, *326*
Culver-Lozo, K., 41, *103*
Cunningham, H.C., 336, *400*
Curran, E., 7, 32
Curtis, B., 39, 40, 41, 42, 43, 46, 53, 55, 58, 66, 72, 76, 77, 82, *103*, *106*
Curtis, W., 9, 12, 15, *30*, *31*, *32*

D

Dahlgren, F., 324, *326*
Dampney, C.N.G., 110, *154*

Danelutto, M., 364, *398*
Darlington, J., 339, 364, *398*
DARPA, 288, 323, *326*
Daskalantonakis, M.K., 65, *103*
Datamation, 110, *154*
Date, C.J., 185, *232*
Davies, J., 116, 124, *157*
Davis, R., 409, *437*
Dean, G., 368, *400*
Decrinis, P., 28, *31*, 58, *104*
De Hoog, R., 118, *157*
DeLine, R., 383, *400*
DeLone, W.H., 124, *154*
DeMarco, T., 2, *30*
DeMillo, R.A., 160, *233*
Deming, W.E., 60, *103*
Demurjian, S.A., 247, *285*
DePaoli, F., 377, *400*
Dillencourt, M.B., 357, *399*
Dilts, D.M., 241, *286*
Di Meglio, R., 364, *398*
Di Nitto, E., 41, *102*
Dorling, A., 3, 17, *30*, 40, *103*
Doubleday, D.L., 375, *397*
Dowson, M., 40, 46, 55, 77, *104*
Drashansky, T.T., 404, 406, 407, 416, 417, 421, *435, 436*
Dropsho, S.G., 332, *400*
DTI, 4, *30*
Dubois, M., 324, *326*
Dulay, N., 372, *399*
Dunaway, D.K., 14, *30*
Duran, J.W., 173, *234*
Dutton, J.E., 41, 55, *104*
Dyksen, W.R., 409, *435*

E

Earl, M., 111, *155*
Eason, K., 111, 119, *155*
Edelman, F., *155*
Eggers, S.J., 317, *327*
Ehrlich, M., 312, 314, *326*
Ehrlich, W., 164, 173, 210, *233*
Emam, K.E., 27, *30*
Emoto, S.E., 166, 168, *233*
Engler, D.R., 307, *326*
Enright, W.H., 410, *436*
Ericsson, M., 45, 50, *105*

Ett, W.H., 46, *105*
Everaars, C.T.H., 390, *397*
Eykholt, J.R., 303, *326*

F

Falconer, D., 146, *155*
Farbey, B., 111, 114, 116, 117, 120, 123, 126, 131, 139, 142, 144, 145, 146, 147, *155*
Farkas, K., 324, *326*
Farr, W.J., 165, 166, 225, *232*
Feeley, M.J., 303, *326*
Feiler, P.H., 46, 72, 77, 79, 89, *104*
Feinstein, H.L., 237, *286*
Feng, M.D., *398*
Ferguson, J., 9, 15, 16, *30, 31*
Fernstrom, C., 40, 41, 46, 50, 59, 77, 82, *103, 104*
Ferraiolo, D.F., 239, 247, *285*
Fillo, M., 308, 316, *326*
Finkelstein, A., 40, *104*, 370, *399*
Fisher, J., 145, *155*
Fitzgerald, E.P., 118, *154*
Flaherty, J.E., 411, *437*
Florijn, G., 349, *398*
Foster, I., 361, *398*
Frailey, D.J., 72, 77, *104*
Framel, J.E., 112, 113, *155*
Frank, R., 364, *397*
Fritzson, R., 419, *435*
Frølund, S., 359, *398, 399*
Fuggetta, A., 39, 41, 46, 50, 59, 77, *102, 103, 104*
Fukuda, M., 357, *399*

G

Gaitatzes, M., 404, 405, *436, 438*
Gallaire, H., 355, *396*
Galliers, R.D., 145, *154*
Gallopoulos, E., 402, *436*
Ganta, S., 237, *286*
Gao, Y.Q., *398*
Garcia, S.M., 15, 16, *31, 32*, 44, 66, *107*
Gardner, M.J., 375, *397*
Garg, P.K., 40, *104*
Gelernter, D., 333, 338, 339, 340, *396, 397, 399*

Gelman, S., 41, *103*, *104*
Ghezzi, C., 40, 41, 77, 82, 92, *101*, *102*
Giarratano, J.C., 419, *436*
Gibbs, W.W., 2, *31*
Gilbert, D.M., 239, *285*
Glass, R.L., 209, *232*
Goel, A.L., 163, 166, 168, 170, 173, 174, 195, 199, 213, 216, 223, 224, *232*
Goldenson, D.R., 27, *30*
Goldman, K.J., 381, *399*
Goldstein, S.C., 290, 295, *326*
Goodman, J., 324, *326*
Graydon, A.W., 26, *31*
Greefhorst, D., 349, *398*
Green, S., 98, *102*
Griffiths, C., 110, 112, 116, 120, 123, 138, 140, 149, *155*
Grimajl, S.S., 402, *436*
Gritter, C.R., 411, *435*
Gros, J.G., 50, *102*
Guiri, L., 242, *285*
Guo, Y., 339, 364, *398*

H

Haase, V., 28, *31*, 58, *104*
Hächler, G., 364, *397*
Haines, M., 365, *397*
Hains, P., 151, *155*
Halliday, M., 177, 209, *232*
Halstead, R., 294, *326*
Hamel, G., 44, *107*
Hammer, M., 44, 45, *104*
Hankin, C., 334, *396*, *398*
Hansell, P., 110, *154*
Hansen, G.A., 40, 42, 43, *105*
Harauz, J., 8, *31*
Harel, D., 42, 75, 82, 95, *104*
Harrington, H.J., 52, *104*
Hayes-Roth, B., 408, *436*
Hefley, B., 15, 16, *31*
Hefley, W.E., 9, 15, *30*
Heineman, G.T., 40, 41, 42, 43, 55, *104*
Heinlein, J., 314, *326*
Henshaw, J., 200, 206, *234*
Herman, I., 388, *397*
Hermens, L.A., 408, *437*
Herzwurm, G., 3, 8, *32*
Hetmanski, C.J., 210, *232*

Hills, S., 72, 77, *104*
Hirsbrunner, B., 364, *399*
Hirschheim, R., 73, *104*
Hirschheim, R.A., 126, *155*
Hitt, L.M., 114, 115, 117, *155*
Hochstrasser, B., 110, 112, 116, 120, 123, 138, 140, 149, *155*
Hodgett, R.A., 146, *155*
Hoe, J.C., 312, 314, *326*
Hoffman, C.M., 405, *436*
Hogbin, G., 114, 116, 122, 123, 125, 134, 141, 143, 144, 146, 147, 148, *155*
Holtje, D., 41, 42, *104*, *106*
Holzbacher, A.A., 384, *399*
Hong, W., 41, 42, *104*, *106*
Horton, F.W. Jr., 118, *156*
Houstis, C.E., 411, 412, *438*
Houstis, E.N., 402, 404, 405, 411, 412, 417, 420, 421, *436*, *437*, *438*
Howe, S.E., 410, *435*
Hu, M.-Y., 247, *285*
Hull, R., 95, *104*
Humphrey, W.S., 3, 15, *31* , 40, 41, 42, 43, 46, 52, 55, 72, 77, 79, 89, *104*, 160, 162, *233*
Hunter, R., 26, *33*
Hurson, A.R., 290, *327*
Huseth, S., 40, 77, *104*

I

Iannino, A., 160, 163, 165, 166, 169, 181, *233*
IBM, 174, *233*
IEEE Computer, 4, *31*
Industrial Research Institute, 401, *436*
Iscoe, N., 39, 40, 42, 46, 55, *103*
ISO, 3, 7, 8, 9, 17, 20, 21, 26, *31*, 52, 53, 58, *104*, *105*, *285*, 314, *326*
Ives, B., 135, *155*

J

Jaccheri, M.L., 41, *105*
Jackson, M.A., 38, *106*
Jacobson, A., 45, 50, *105*
Jacobson, I., 45, 50, 95, *105*
Jamieson, M., 138, *154*
Jazayeri, M., 40, *104*

Jelinski, Z., 166, 167, 168, 218, 223, *233*
Jeng, B., 173, *234*
Jennings, N., 408, *438*
Johnson, W.R. Jr., 401, *437*
Jones, C., 14, 29, *31*
Jonscher, D., 247, *285*
Jonsson, P., 95, *105*
Joshi, A., 402, 404, 409, 411, 412, 417, 420, 421, *436*, *437*, *438*
Jouppi, N., 324, *326*
Judd, C.M., 98, *105*

K

Kaashoek, F.M., 307, *326*
Kahaner, D.K., 410, *435*
Kaiser, G.E., 40, 41, 42, 43, 55, *104*, *105*
Kalathur, S., 113, *156*
Kamel, M.S., 412, *436*
Kaminsky, D., 339, *399*
Kan, S.H., 162, *233*
Kaplan, R.B., 44, *105*
Kaplan, R.S., 122, 124, 125, *155*
Karlin, S., 167, *233*
Katayama, T.A., 72, *105*
Kauffman, R.J., 110, 114, 125, 130, *154*, *155*
Kaxiras, S., 324, *326*
Keen, P.G.W., 110, 113, 117, 129, 153, *155*
Kekre, S., 113, *156*
Kellner, M.I., 39, 40, 41, 42, 43, 46, 55, 61, 72, 76, 77, 80, 82, 92, *101*, *102*, *103*, *104*, *105*
Kidder, L.H., 98, *105*
Kielmann, T., 345, *399*
King, R., 95, *104*
Kitchenham, B., 162, *233*
Kitson, D.H., 15, 16, 27, *31*, 66, *105*
Kleiman, S., 291, 305, 314, *326*
Klein, D.V., 383, *400*
Klein, H.K., 73, *104*
Klein, M., 396, *399*
Klint, P., 386, *397*
Klug, A., 278, 280, *286*
Knul, M., 116, 124, *157*
Knutsen, K.E., 113, 119, 128, *155*
Koch, G.R., 28, *31*, 40, 58, 66, *104*, *105*
Kodama, Y., 308, 312, 314, *326*, *327*
Konrad, M., 15, 16, *31*
Konrad, M.D., 16, 26, *31*, *32*

Kontio, J., 41, 55, 61, 66, 73, 82, 84, 89, 92, *105*
Kramer, J., 40, *104*, 370, 372, *399*
Krasner, H., 39, 40, 42, 46, 55, *103*, *105*
Kriebel, C.H., 115, 125, 129, 130, 135, *154*, *155*
Krone, O., 364, *399*
Kuchen, H., 364, *397*
Kugler, H.J., 28, *31*, 58, *104*
Kuhn, T.S., 73, *105*
Kuhn, R., 247, *285*
Kumar, K., 44, *105*, 112, 146, 148, *155*
Kuskin, J., 314, *327*
Kuusela, J., 75, 95, *102*
Kuvaja, P., 28, *31*
Kuzara, R., 14, *32*, 50, *107*

L

Lachover, H., 42, 82, *104*
Lai, R.C.T., 46, *106*
Laitenberger, O., 98, *102*
Land, F., 111, 114, 116, 117, 120, 123, 126, 131, 139, 142, 144, 145, 146, 147, *155*
Lanubile, F., 98, *102*
Lavazza, L., 41, 77, *102*
Lay, P.M., 129, *155*
Leake, D., 412, *436*
Lederer, A.L., 2, *31*, 123, *156*
Lee, B., 290, *327*
Lee, T.M.P., 272, *286*
Legge, K., 144, *155*
Lehman, M.M., 40, 46, *106*
Lehrer, K., 420, *436*
Leichter, J., 343, *399*
Le Métayer, D., 334, 353, *396*
Lesser, V.R., 409, *436*
Lester, S., 110, 138, 139, 142, *157*
Lichota, T.W., 375, *397*
Lin, C.J., 3, 14, *30*
Lincoln, T., 132, *155*
Linehan, A., 46, *105*
Lipow, M., 163, 172, 199, 218, *232*, *234*
Litecky, C.R., 132, *156*
Littlewood, B., 166, 170, 219, *233*
Lloyd, P., 110, *154*
Lloyd's Register, 4, *32*
Longchamp, J., 46, 47, 50, 78, 79, *106*

Lorensen, W., 75, 95, *107*
Lott, C.M., 65, *106*
Loveman, G.W., 110, *156*
Lu, P., 161, 164, 165, 166, 174, 179, 180, 181, 182, 185, 187, 188, 192, 196, 197, 199, 207, 224, 225, 230, 233, *234*
Lynch, N., 239, *285*
Lyu, M.R., 160, 162, 163, 173, *232*, *233*

M

Ma, K.S., 412, *436*
McCartney, T.P., 381, *399*
McConnell, S., 29, *32*
McCracken, D.D., 38, *106*
McCracken, W.M., 160, *233*
McFaddin, S., 421, *437*
McFeeley, R., 12, *32*
McGarry, F.E., 40, 47, 50, 65, 72, *102*, *106*, *107*, 221, *232*
McGowan, C.L., 14, 30, 82, 92, 96, *106*
Mackenzie, R.A., 49, *106*
Mackie, C.H., *32*
McLean, E.R., 124, *154*
Maclennan, F., 27, *32*
McNurlin, B.C., 119, 124, 146, *154*
Madhavji, N.H., 40, 41, 42, 43, 50, 55, *104*, *106*
Madnick, S.E., 61, *101*
Magee, J., 370, 372, *399*
Maguire, S., 29, *32*
Malone, T.W., 333, 396, *399*
Marca, D.A., 82, 92, 96, *106*
Marchad, D.A., 118, *156*
Marchini, M., 350, *399*
Markus, S., 402, 404, 405, *436*, *438*
Marquardt, D., 8, *32*
Marsden, J.R., 135, *156*
Marshall, P., 27, *32*
Martin, R.J., 160, *233*
Masters, S.M., 13, 14, *30*, *32*, 66, *105*
Mathews, J., 45, *106*
Mathur, A.P., 164, *232*
Matrella, P., 164, *233*
Matsubara, T., 8, *32*
Mayntz, R., 141, *156*
Mehrotra, P., 365, *399*
Melgarejo, M., 350, *399*
Mellis, W., 3, 8, *32*

Mellor, S., 95, *107*
Merchant, F., 357, *399*
Messnarz, R., 58, *104*
Miller, K.W., 164, *234*
Miller, S., 9, 15, *30*
Minsky, N.H., 343, *399*
Mirani, R., 123, *156*
Misra, J., 361, *399*
Mittermeid, R.T., 332, *399*
Moad, J., *156*
Moebus, D., 177, 209, *232*
Moffett, J.D., 258, *286*
Mohammed, I., 241, *286*
Money, A., 117, 122, 125, 127, 139, 143, *156*
Moody, D., 118, *156*
Moore, P.K., 411, *437*
Moranda, P.B., 166, 167, 218, *233*
Moranda, P.L., 166, 167, 168, 218, 223, *233*
Moreton, R., 112, 114, 115, *156*
Morgan, G., 73, *103*
Morzenti, A., 40, 77, 82, 92, *101*
Motley, R.W., 166, 169, *232*
Motschnig-Pitrik, R., 332, *399*
Mu, M., 421, *437*
Mukhopadhayay, T., 115, *154*
Mukhopadhyay, T., 113, *156*
Muralidhar, K., 135, *156*
Murata, T., 59, 82, 92, *106*
Murdock, L., 44, *105*
Musa, J.D., 160, 163, 164, 165, 166, 169, 173, 177, 181, 210, *233*

N

Naamad, A., 42, 82, *104*
Neiman, R.A., 151, *156*
Nejmeh, B.A., 77, *104*
Nelson, E., 163, 171, 199, 201, 218, *233*, *234*
Nierstrasz, O., 334, *398*
Nii, H.P., 332, *397*
Nikhil, R.S., 290, 294, 300, 308, 312, *327*
Nolan, R.L., 113, 119, 128, *155*
Norris, G.D., 147, 148, *156*
Norton, D.P., 122, 124, 125, *155*
Notargiacomo, L., 242, *286*
Notkin, D., 39, *106*
Nowatzyk, A., 324, *327*
Ntafos, S.C., 173, *234*

AUTHOR INDEX

Nuseibeh, B., 40, *104*
Nyanchama, M., 247, *286*

O

Oates, T., 409, *437*
Ochimizu, K., 40, *106*
O'Hara, A.C., 46, 55, *107*
Ohba, M., 166, 168, *235*
Okumoto, K., 160, 163, 165, 166, 168, 169, 181, 195, 213, 216, 223, 224, *232*, *233*
Olson, M., 135, *155*
Olson, T., 44, *106*
Orlando, S., 364, *398*
Orna, E., 118, *156*
Osaki, S., 166, 168, *235*
Osborn,, 247, *286*
Osterweil, L.J., 39, 40, 46, 47, 55, *106*
O'Toole, J., 307, *326*
Ould, M.A., 82, 97, *106*
Over, J., 39, 40, 41, 42, 43, 46, 55, 72, 76, 77, 82, *102*, *103*
Over, J.W., 41, 43, 44, 72, *102*, *106*
Overgaard, G., 95, *105*
Ozturan, C., 411, *437*

P

Page, G., 50, 72, *102*, *106*
Page, J., 221, *232*
Pajerski, R., 50, 72, *102*, *106*, 221, *232*
Palma, J., 161, 164, 166, 174, 179, 180, 181, 182, 183, 185, 187, 188, 192, 196, 197, 199, 205, 207, 210, 217, 219, 222, 223, 230, *234*
Papadopoulos, G.A., 390, *399*
Papadopoulos, G.M., 308, 312, *327*
Papathomas, M., 334, *400*
Pareschi, R., 355, *396*
Parker, M.M., 118, 127, 133, 143, *156*
Pasquini, A., 164, *233*
Passafiume, J.F., 160, *233*
Paulk, M.C., 3, 9, 12, 14, 15, 16, 26, 27, *30*, *31*, *32*, 44, 53, 58, 66, *103*, *106*, *107*
Pearlstein, S., 45, *107*
Pelagatti, S., 364, *398*
Penedo, M.H., 41, *107*

Peters, G., 120, 123, 140, 150, 151, *156*
Pfleeger, S.L., 65, *107*, 162, *233*
Phillips, M., 3, 14, *30*
Phillips, R.W., 41, 43, 72, *102*
Pier, K.A., 290, *327*
Pingrey, D.E., 135, *156*
Pneuli, A., 42, 82, *104*
Politi, M., 42, 82, *104*
Pong, F., 324, *327*
Poore, J.H., 165, *234*
Porter, A.A., 198, 200, *233*, *234*
Pralahad, C.K., 44, *107*
Prasad, J., 2, *31*
Pregibon, D., 199, 200, 211, 222, *232*
Premerlani, W., 75, 95, *107*
Puranik, R., 3, 14, *30*
Purtilo, J.M., 378, *398*, *400*

R

Radice, R.A., 46, 55, *107*
Ramakrishnan, N., 412, 419, 420, 421, 435, *436*, *437*
Ray, B., 177, 190, 209, *232*, *233*
Rego, V.J., 164, *232*
Rein, G.L., 46, 82, 97, *107*
Reizer, N., 44, *106*
Rem, M., 338, *400*
Remenyi, D., 117, 122, 125, 127, 139, 143, *156*
Ren, S., 359, *400*
Resnick, P., 410, *437*
Rice, J.R., 402, 404, 405, 406, 410, 411, 412, 417, 420, 421, *436*, *437*, *438*
Rice, M.D., 332, *400*
Riddle, W.E., 55, 77, *104*, *107*
Rigby, P.G., *32*
Ripley, B.D., 199, 222, *234*
Roach, S.S., 110, *156*
Roberts, C., 82, 97, *106*
Roman, G.-C., 336, *400*
Rombach, H.D., 39, 40, 42, 50, 55, 65, 77, 80, 82, 92, *102*, *105*, *106*, *107*, 174, *232*
Rosendale, J.V., 365, *397*
Ross, T.L., 383, *400*
Rossi, D., 350, 352, *398*
Rossi, S., 44, 93, *107*
Rotemberg, J.J., 111, *156*
Roth, N.K., 46, 55, *107*

Rowstron, A., 342, *400*
Royce, W.W., 38, *107*
Rudolph, L., 312, *325*
Rumbaugh, J., 75, 95, *107*

S

Saiedian, H., 50, *107*
Saiedian, S., 14, *32*
Sakai, S., 308, 312, 314, *326*, *327*
Sakane, H., 308, 312, 314, *326*, *327*
Saloner, G., 111, *156*
Samarati, P., 271, *286*
Sanders, J., 7, *32*
Sandhu, R.S., 237, 241, 247, 256, 257, 258, 261, 269, 270, 271, 275, *286*
Santhanam, R., 135, *156*
Sassone, P.G., 128, 130, 131, *156*
Sato, M., 308, 312, 314, *326*, *327*
Saulsbury, A., 324, *327*
Schafer, R.E., 166, 168, *233*
Schäfer, W., 41, *106*
Schaffer, W.A., 128, *156*
Schauser, K.E., 290, 295, *326*
Schick, G.J., 166, 168, *233*
Schlimmer, J.C., 408, *437*
Schneidewind, N.F., 166, 169, 170, 217, *233*
Schockley, W.R., 272, *286*
Schwartz, A.P., 131, *156*
Scott Morton, M.S., 111, *156*
Seidman, S.B., 332, *400*
Selby, R.W., 198, 200, *233*
Sethuraman, R., 381, *399*
Shah, D., 291, 305, 314, *326*
Shapiro, L.N., 162, *233*
Shaughnessy, R.N., 7, *32*
Shaw, D., 303, *327*
Shaw, M., 2, 32, 383, *400*
Shen, V., 39, 40, 46, 55, *103*
Sherman, R., 42, 82, *104*
Shoham, Y., 408, *437*
Shooman, M.L., 166, 167, *234*
Shtul-Trauring, A., 42, 82, *104*
Shu, C., 41, *107*
Shull, F., 98, *102*
Sillander, T., 44, 93, *107*
Silverthorn, M., 77, *103*
Simila, J., 28, *31*

Simmons, P.M., 112, 116, 123, 124, 129, 138, 139, 140, 142, 144, *157*
Simms, P., 17, *30*
Simon, J.L., 98, *107*
Singh, B., 46, 82, 97, *107*
Skillicorn, D.B., 363, *400*
Sloman, M.S., 258, *286*
Smaalders, B., 291, 305, 314, *326*
Smith, B., 290, *327*
Smith, E.R., 98, *105*
Smith, O.D., 225, *232*
Smith, R.G., 407, *435*
Smithson, S., 126, *155*
Snowdon, R., 46, *103*
Sohi, G., 324, *327*
Sokolsky, M., 55, *105*
Sommerville, I., 368, *400*
Sorumgard, S., 98, *102*
Spilling, P., 388, *397*
Stalk, G. Jr., 53, *107*
Stark, G., 224, 225, *234*
StatSci, 222, *234*
Stein, D., 303, *327*
Stelzer, D., 3, 8, *32*
Stenstrom, P., 324, *326*
Strassman, P., 118, 124, 131, *157*
Stray, S.J., 145, *154*
Sun Microsystems, 402, *437*
Swaminathan, B., 381, *399*
Sweet, W.L., 3, *31*
Symons, V., 141, *157*

T

Taivalsaari, A., 98, *107*
Takoudis, C., 405, *436*
Targett, D., 111, 114, 116, 117, 120, 123, 126, 131, 139, 142, 144, 145, 146, 147, *155*
Taylor, D., 405, *436*
Taylor, H.M., 167, *233*
Taylor, P., 111, 112, 129, 138, 147, 150, 151, *157*
Terrel, J., 46, *105*
Thayer, R.H., 49, *107*, 163, 199, *234*
Thekkath, R., 317, *327*
Theobald, K.B., 317, *327*
Thomas, D.V., 114, 116, 122, 123, 125, 134, 141, 143, 144, 146, 147, 148, *155*

AUTHOR INDEX

Thomas, M., 40, 47, 65, *107*
Thomas, R., 241, 247, 257, *286*
Thomsen, D.J., 256, *286*
Tian, J., 161, 163, 164, 165, 166, 173, 174, 177, 179, 180, 181, 182, 183, 185, 187, 188, 192, 196, 197, 198, 199, 200, 205, 206, 207, 209, 210, 217, 219, 222, 223, 224, 225, 227, 230, *233*, *234*
Ting, T.C., 247, *285*
Tisato, F., 377, *400*
To, H.W., 339, 364, *398*
Tobin, M., 27, *32*
Tolksdorf, R., 348, 350, *395*, *400*
Troster, J., 161, 174, 180, 198, 200, 209, 219, 222, 223, 227, 230, *234*
Tsiakals, J., 8, *32*
Tsichritizis, D.C., 278, 280, *286*
Tsoukalas, L.H., 409, *437*
Tsoukalas, M.Z., 173, *234*
Tullsen, D.M., 308, 318, *327*
Turner, A., 39, 46, *102*
Twite, A., 117, 122, 125, 127, 139, 143, *156*

U

Uhrig, R.E., 409, *437*
US Air Force, 28, 32, *33*

V

Vaaraniemi, S., 98, *107*
van der Merwe, I., 247, *286*
Vanneschi, M., 364, *398*
Van Wegan, B., 118, *157*
Varga, L.Z., 408, *437*
Varian, H., 410, *437*
Venables, W.N., 199, 222, *234*
Verlage, M., 82, *107*
Verrall, J.L., 166, 170, 219, *233*
Vessey, J.T., 401, *437*
Vijaykumar, T., 324, *327*
Vines, D., 40, 77, *104*
Vitali, F., 350, *395*
Voas, J.M., 164, *234*
Voigt, R.G., 402, *437*
von Eicken, T., 290, 295, *326*

von Mayrhauser, A., 174, *234*
von Solms, S.H., 247, *286*

W

Waligora, S., 50, 72, *102*, *106*, 221, *232*
Walsh, P., 118, *156*
Wang, N.-H., 405, *436*
Ward, J., 111, 112, 129, 138, 147, 150, 151, *157*
Ward, P., 95, *107*
Weaver, G.E., 332, *400*
Weber, C.V., 9, 12, *32*, 44, 53, 58, 66, *106*, *107*
Weems, C.C., 332, *400*
Weerawarana, S., 402, 404, 405, 411, 412, 415, 417, 421, *436*, *437*, *438*
Wegner, P.N., 333, 334, *400*
Weill, P., 110, 114, 116, 117, 133, 139, *155*, *157*
Weinstock, C.B., 375, *397*
Welke, R.J., 44, *105*
Wesson, R., 409, *438*
Weyuker, E.J., 165, 173, *232*, *234*
White, J.A., 134, *154*
Whiting, R., 116, 124, *157*
Whittaker, J.A., 165, *234*
Wilks, A.R., 222, *232*
Willcocks, L., 110, 116, 117, 138, 139, 142, *157*
Wilson, G., 339, *398*
Wilson, R.L., 135, *156*
Wing, J.M., 375, *397*
Wolf, A.L., 41, *103*
Wolverton, R.W., 166, 168, *233*
Wong, M.-Y., 177, 209, *232*
Wong, W.E., 173, *232*
Wood, A., 342, *400*
Woodman, I., 26, *33*
Wooldridge, M., 408, *438*
Worley, J.H., 55, *103*

Y

Yamada, S., 166, 168, *235*
Yamaguchi, T., 40, *106*
Yamaguchi, Y., 308, 312, 314, *326*, *327*
Yamana, H., 308, 312, 314, *326*, *327*
Yang, J., 339, 364, *398*
Yin, R.K., 98, *107*
Yonezawa, A., 334, *398*
Youman, C.E., 237, *286*

Young, D.M., 383, *398*
Yourdon, E., 96, 97, *107*
Yuen, C.K., *396*

Z

Zave, P., 331, *398*
Zelesnik, G., 383, *398*

Zelkowitz, M.V., 72, 98, *102*, *106*, 162, 200, 209, 221, 222, *232*, *234*, *235*
Ziegler, J., 75, 95, *102*
Zima, H., 365, *395*
Zuck, L., 340, *395*

Subject Index

A

Access control, role-based. *See* Role-based access control (RBAC)
Access state bits, 310
Actor model, 332
Ada-95, 293
Adaptive parallelism, 339
Address Capture Device (ACD), 311
Administrative roles, 262
Advisory agents, 410
Agent-based computing paradigm for MPSEs, 408–9
Alewife, 314–16
Algorithm selection problem, 410
Analytic hierarchy process, 134–5, 136
ANSI/SPARC architecture, 278, 280–1
ARA97 (ability–role assignment) model, 266–7
$ARBAC_0$, 258
$ARBAC_1$, 258
$ARBAC_2$, 258
$ARBAC_3$, 258
ARBAC97 administrative models, 257–70
ARBAC97 model, components, 261
Architectural description, 334
Ariadne/HOPLa, 349–50
Associative pattern matching, 338
AT&T SRE ToolKit, 224
Automatic teller machines (ATM), 130
Automation, 59, 60
  process execution, 65

B

Bauhaus Linda, 340–1, 395
Behavioral specification, 76, 97–8
Benchmarking, 50, 60
Benefits management, 112
Blackboard model, 332
Bonita, 342–3
Bootstrap, 28
Branching information, 225–6

Brooks–Motley model, 169
Brown–Lipow model, 172, 218
Business process re-engineering (BPR), 44–6
Business value analysis, 133–4
Business value linkage impact analysis, 130, 136

C

Capability Maturity Model for Software (CMM or SW–CMM). *See* CMM
Cardinality constraints, 253
CASE tool, 96
CASRE, 224
Cid, 300–2
Cilk, 299–300
CMM, 3, 9–33, 66–7
  future, 16–17
  in context, 12–13
  Level 1, 9
  Level 2, 9
  Level 3, 10
  Level 4, 11
  Level 5, 12
  maturity levels, 10
  overview, 9–12
  phases, 12–13
  strengths and weaknesses, 14–16
CMM-based appraisal (CBA), 13–14
CMM-based Appraisal for Internal Process Improvement (CBA IPI), 14
Code base stability, 176
CoLa, 364–5
Collaboratories, 404
Communication and Memory Management Unit (CMMU), 314–15
Competitor analysis, 50
Compositional programming, 361–4
Concepts and terminology, 75
Conceptual analysis, 93–5
ConCoord program, 336, 384–6
Concurrent logic programming, 361
Configuration, 334, 368–70

Conic, 370–2
    configuration subcomponent, 371
    dynamic reconfiguration, 372
Control of projects, 58–9
Control-driven coordination models, 367–91
Control-driven coordination programming, 334–6
COOLL program, 356–7
Coordination, concept, 333
Coordination languages, 329–400
    definition, 333–4
Coordination models, 329–400
    background and motivation, 330
    control-driven, 367–91
    data-driven, 336–67
    definition, 333
Coordination paradigm, 332–4
Coordination programming
    control-driven, 334–6
    data-driven, 334
    historical perspective, 331–4
CORBA, 396
Cost–benefit analysis (CBA), 127–9, 132, 136, 138
Coverage analysis, 172–3
CPU execution time, 189–91
CSDL (Cooperative Systems Design Language), 377–8
Current reliability, 170

D

Darwin, 372–5
Data collection, analyses and presentation, tool support for, 221–7
Data-driven coordination languages, 336
Data-driven coordination models, 336–67
Data-driven coordination programming, 334
Data envelopment analysis (DEA), 130
DCF value analysis, 133
Declarative communication, 381
De-eutrophication models, 167
Defect fixing effect, 180
Defect tracking, 183
Defects, 162
Distributed Artificial Intelligence, 332
Distributed problem solving, 409
Distributed Shared Memory (DSM) systems, 289

Domain-specific PSEs, 404–5
Durra, 375–7

E

Elicit method, 41–2
ELLPACK, 411, 423, 425, 427
EMC-Y, 313
EM-X parallel computer, 312–14
Enactable process definition, 76
Enacting processes, 76
ENIAC, 410
Entryport, 370
EPDP method, 132
Error, 162
ESTM, 224
Excess tangible cost method, 132–3
Execution time failure data, SRGMs, 187–92
Execution time models, limited applicability, 197
Execution time SRGMs, 169
Exit criteria, 171, 205
Exitport, 370
Experience capture, 98
Explicit-dependence lookahead, 310

F

Failure, 162, 177
    definition, 165
    measurement, 165
    probability, 167
Failure arrivals
    in calendar time, 184–6
    in test runs, 186
    vs. runs, 190
Failures tracking over calendar time, 182–4
Fat-tree network, 312
Fault, 162
Fault distribution, 180
Fibonacci numbers, 291, 293
Fibonacci program, 287–8
Future reliability, 171, 204

G

GAMMA model, 353–4, 395
Generalized Poisson model, 168

SUBJECT INDEX 451

Generic process definition, 75, 96
Global information infrastructure (GII), 404
Global translation lookaside buffer (GTLB), 317
GOEL, 224
Goel–Okumoto model, 168, 196, 216, 217, 223
GRA97 (group–role assignment) model, 267
Groups, 370
    versus roles, 242–3

H

Heterogeneous systems, 331–4
High performance computing and communication (HPCC) resources, 403
High Performance Fortran (HPF), 365
Hybrid Office Process Language (HOPLa), 349–50
Hybrid threads, 304

I

IDRM, 161, 163, 171
    and coverage analysis, 172–3
Information economics, 133–4
Information technology (IT), 109–57
    and business performance, 114–15
    and management style, 145
    and organizational culture, 144–5
    benefits, 119–23
        classifying and measuring, 123–5
        development, 151
        management, 146–52
        realization, 151, 152
    business context, 144
    capabilities, 111
    changing role, 113–14
    content perspective, 141–3
    context perspective, 141, 144
    contribution to organizations' business performance, 110
    cost–benefit analysis, 127–9, 132, 136, 138
    delivering change, 149
    evaluation, 112, 153
    evaluation frameworks, 138–41
    evaluation methods, 126–38
    evaluation of investments, 116–17
    evaluation problem, 113–17

    expenditure, 113–14
    functionality, 124
    identifying and structuring benefits, 151
    investment decision, 141–6, 146
    management return, 131
    organizational change, 111
    performance criteria, 148
    post-implementation review, 149
    process perspective, 142, 145–6
    project evaluation methods, 137
    transformation, 111
    unexpected changes, 149
    user information satisfaction, 135
    value measurement, 117–25
Input domain reliability model. *See* IDRM
Integrated analysis, 199–201
    and TBRM applications, 202–5
Interface description language, 348
International Federation for Information Processing (IFIP), 111
I/O abstraction, 381
ISO 15504, 3, 17–27, 29
    DTR draft, 19
    future, 26, 27
    overview, 18–20
    process assessment, 19–20
    requirements, 17–18
    strengths and weaknesses, 23–7
ISO 15504-2 DTR, 21–3
ISO 15504-2 reference model, overview, 20–3
ISO 15504-5 PDTR, 24–5
ISO 9000, 3–9, 29
    certification, 7
    future, 8–9
    strengths and weaknesses, 7–8
ISO 9000, 3, 4, 9
ISO 9001, 3, 4, 29, 53
    certification, 8
    clauses, 5–6
    fundamental premise, 4
    in context, 7
    overview, 4–7
Iterative enhancement model, 46

J

Jada program, 350–1
Java programming language, 293
Jelinski–Moranda model, 167, 168, 218, 223

K

Kellnerts' process perspectives, 44
Kernel-level threads, 304

L

Lattice-based access control model. *See* LBAC
Lattices, 270–8
LAURA system, 336, 348–9
Law-Governed Linda, 343–5, 363
LBAC, 270–8
    composite confidentiality, 275–7
    integrity roles, 275–7
Learning algorithms, 428–9
Level of granularity, 89
Life cycle, 46
Life cycle model, 38, 46
Lightweight processes (LWP), 304
Linda, 338–40, 395
    and World Wide Web, 350–2
Linear Objects (LO) program, 355–6
Littlewood–Varrell model, 170
Local problem solver, 409
Local view, 364
Logical node, 370

M

Management information system (MIS), 54
Management return of information technology, 131
MANIFOLD, 336, 388–91, 395
Manners, 391
Mathematical network methodologies, 404–5
Mean time between failures (MTBF), 193
Mediator agents, 408
MESSENGERS, 357–9
Method and tool definition, 96
M-Machine, 316–17
Module Interconnection Languages (MILs), 332
MPSE, 401
    agent-based computing paradigm for, 408–9
    architecture, 415
    case studies, 421–32
    prototyping of physical systems, 405–8
    resource selection paradigm for, 409–12
    with inherent 'intelligence', 410

MTBF (mean time between failure), 163, 165, 197
Multi-agent computing framework, 408
Multi-agent systems, learning and adaptation, 430–32
Multi-ALU processor (MAP), 316–17
Multidisciplinary applications (MAs), 403
Multidisciplinary problem-solving environment. *See* MPSE
Multilingual programming, 331
Multilingual systems, 331–4
Multiparadigm programming, 331
Multithreading systems, 287–327
    architectural support, 307–8
    components of cache misses, 322
    concept, 290
    concurrency constructs, 291
    examples, 308–19
    execution models, 302–7
        design issues, 302–7
    fine-grained, 290
    forking of tasks, 293
    glossary of terms, 324–5
    latency tolerance, 289–90
    performance models, 319–22
    processor utilization, 319
    programming models, 290–302
    scheduling control, 304–5
    speedup, 321
    thread functions, 305
    thread implementations, 306
Mutually exclusive roles, 252

N

Nelson input domain reliability model, 171–2
Network-based prototyping, 408
Network–Endpoint–Subsystem (NES), 311
Networks of Workstations (NOWs), 289
New capabilities, 54
Node information, 225
Non-homogeneous Poisson process (NHPP), 167–8, 196

O

Object Interchange Language (OIL), 345
Objective Linda, 345–7

ODEXPERT, 412
Operational profiles, 163–5
Operations research, 130–1
Options model, 143
Options theory, 143
Opus, 365–7
Ordinary differential equations (ODEs), 403, 405, 406, 412

P

Paradigm definition, 73, 93
Partial differential equations (PDEs), 403, 405, 406, 411
 intelligent computing, 427–30
 solving composite problems, 421–27
Partitioned subsets, reliability analysis, 201–2
PCL (Proteus Configuration Language), 368–70
Perceived business value, 53
Period failure count (PFC), 170
Petri Nets, 92
Physical system design objectives, 407–8
Piranha, 339–40
Plan process modeling, 92–3
Point of View, 364–5
POLYLITH, 378–81
PRA97 (permission-role assignment) model, 264–6
Predictability and consistency improvement, 70
Predictor variables, 201
Prerequisite roles, 253
PRISM, 41
Problem-solving environment (PSE)
 definition, 405
 domain-specific, 404–5
 technologies, 402
Problematic areas, identifying, 204
Process activities, 77
Process agents, 79
Process appraisal and improvement, 1–33
Process architecture, 72
Process artifacts, 77
Process assessment, 19, 20
Process asset management, 50
 criteria, 62–3
Process behavior, 77
Process capture, 40
Process certification, 53, 58

Process classes, 47, 48, 52
Process concept definition, 95
Process consistency and predictability, 53
Process cycle time, 53
Process definition, 48, 52
Process development process (PDP), 43
Process development scenario, 69, 70
Process elicitation and representation activity, 93–8
Process enactment, 48
Process engineering, 50
 background, 38–52
 objectives, 54–5
Process engineering framework, 35–107
 practical experiences, 98–100
Process execution, 48, 59
 automation, 65
Process improvement, 49, 61, 85
 goals, 67–71
 objectives, 52–5, 68
Process information content, 80–2
Process information flow, 80
Process infrastructure, 79
Process instance, 47
Process management, 49, 52–71
 improving, 54, 61
 process, 84–100
Process manager, 52
Process Model Focus Grid, 89–91
Process model information entities, 77–80
Process model utilization profile assessment, 88
Process modeling, 38–44, 48, 58, 60, 61
 architectural framework, 74
 formalisms, 59
 methodology, 41
 reference architecture, 71–7
Process modeling objectives, 55–68, 80–2
 analysis, 63
 comprehensive list, 56
 dependencies, 61–7
 goals, 67–71
 taxonomy, 55–61
Process modeling process, 86–98
 characterization, 88
 organizational scope, 89
 set goals, 91–2
Process monitoring, 50, 59, 66
Process owner, 50–2
Process performance, 48

Process perspectives, 82–4
Process productivity improvement, 53, 70
Process reference architecture, 71–84
    levels, 72
Process representation, 40
Process resources, 79
Process reuse, 60, 66
Process simulation and analysis, 60–1, 66
Process terminology, 46–52
Product quality improvement, 52, 69
Production frontier analysis, 129–30, 136
Program Composition Notation (PCN), 362
Programmer's Playground, 381–3
Project characterization statement, 88
Project management artifacts, 77
Project planning support, 58–9
Purpose and scope definition, 75
PYTHIA, 411, 418–21, 435
    intelligent PDE computing, 427–30
PYTHIA-C, 430–32

Q

Quality Improvement Paradigm, 42, 75, 86
Quiescence property, 372

R

Random testing, 179
Range of Vision, 364
RAPIDE, 383–4
    architecture, 383
RBAC, 237–86
    administration, 257–70
    administrative permissions, 247, 258–61
    concept of, 238
    limitations, 241
    motivation and background, 239–41
    permissions, 245, 256–7
    sessions, 246, 255–6
    three-tier architecture, 278–84
    user assignment, 245
    users, 245, 255–6
    variations, 240
$RBAC_0$ model, 243–7, 258
    components, 246
    constraints, 251
$RBAC_1$ model, 243, 247–51, 258
    components, 249

$RBAC_2$ model, 243, 251–4, 258
$RBAC_3$ model, 243, 254, 258
RBAC96 models, 243–57
    model conformance, 257
Regis system, 372–5
Relational database management system (RDBMS), 185
Reliability analysis, 162–74
    large software systems, 174–80
    partitioned subsets, 201–2
    scenario-based testing, 179–80
    SRGMs, 181–98
Reliability assessment, 204
Reliability change monitoring, 204
Reliability engineering, 159–235
Reliability function, 165
Reliability growth, 170
    comparison in different time measurements, 186–7
    modeling, 166, 224
    purification level, 207–8
    visualization, 184–5
Reliability improvement, TBRM, 207–9
Reliability modeling, 161
    grouped data, 217
    homogeneous test runs, 192–4
    lessons learned, 191–2
    transaction measurement, 195–7
Resource selection paradigm for MPSEs, 409–12
Responsibility definition, 97
Role-based access control. See RBAC
Role hierarchies, 247–51, 253, 262, 273
Roles, 241–2, 262, 270–8
    versus groups, 242–3
RRA97 (role-role assignment) model, 266–9
    restrictions on can-modify, 268–9
Run, 177
Run count, SRGMs, 187–92

S

SADT, 92
Scenario-based testing, reliability analysis, 179–80
Scenario group modeling, 190–1
Schick–Wolverton model, 168
Schneidewind model, 169–70
SciAgents, 412–18, 435
    architecture, 416

coordination of solution process, 416–17
functional architecture, 413
software reuse and evolution, 418
Security classification, 271
Security clearance, 271
SESAME method, 132, 136
Set goals, 91–2
SHADE, 352
ShareD Abstraction (SDA), 366–7
Simultaneous multithreading (SMT), 317–19
SMERFS, 224, 225, 227, 229
Software bus, 415
Software capability evaluation (SCE), 14
Software CMM. See CMM
Software Development Capability/Capacity Review (SDCCR), 28
Software Development Capability Evaluation (SDCE), 28
Software development process, 47
Software Engineering Institute (SEI), 41–3
process perspectives, 43
Software process. See Process
Software quality, 162
Software reliability engineering (SRE). See Reliability engineering
Software reliability growth model. See SRGM
Software reliability model (SRM), 161, 163
Sonia, 350
SoRel, 224
SPARC processor, 315
SPICE, 3, 24–6
Spiral life cycle model, 46
S-PLUS, 224, 225, 227, 229
SPR (Software Productivity Research), 28–9
SRGM, 161, 163, 166, 179, 180, 190, 192, 196, 198, 230–1
based on data clusters. See SRGM–DC
effective use in large software systems, 197–8
execution time, 169
execution time failure data, 187–92
failure rate, 173
fitting and using, 170–1
model fitting and overall observations, 187–90
probability of failure, 173
reliability analysis, 181–98
run count, 187–92
usage measurement, 181–98
SRGM-DC, 161, 210–19, 231
data partitioning for individual runs, 211–13

dual model, 217
general model using data partitions, 213–14
research issues, 218–19
usage and effectiveness, 215–17
SRM, 179, 180
general assumptions and their implications, 173–4
SRMP, 224
S-shaped reliability growth model, 168
SSQ, 197
Staffing level variations, 176
StarT project, 310–12
StarT-Jr system, 312
StarT-NG, 311–12
StarT-Voyager system, 312
STL (Service Type Language), 348
Sub-phase testing, 190–1
Support harmonization and standardization, 58, 65, 67
Support planning, 58–9
and control of projects, 65
Support process execution, 65
Support process monitoring, 65
Support understanding and communication, 58, 65, 67
Symmetric multiprocessor (SMP), 289
Synchronizers, 359–60

T

Task module types, 370
TBRM, 161, 180, 191, 198–210, 230–1
applications, 209
cross validation, 209
efficiency, 209
findings and future development, 209–10
integrated analysis, 202–5
integration, 209
key benefits, 205
main uses, 204
practical experience using, 205–7
reliability improvement, 207–9
TCP/IP paradigm, 379
Technology assessment models, 50
Technology monitoring, 50
Telecom Design Environment (TDE), 98–100
Temporal coordination, 359
Tera MTA (MultiThreaded Architecture) computer, 308–10
Testing environment, 176–9

Testing processes, 174–6
Testing scenario, 177
Testing strategy, 176
Testing techniques, 163–5
Threaded Abstract Machine (TAM), 295–9
  activation tree, 296
  storage hierarchy, 297
TickIT, 4
Time between failure (TBF), 170
Time-domain, reliability in, 165
Time measurement, 180
  robustness of run count as, 197
  usage-dependent, 166, 185
  usage-independent, 166
Time to market, 53
Tool support, 219–30
  for data analysis and modeling, 224–5
  for data collection, analyses and presentation, 221–7
  for result presentation and exploration, 225–7
  integration and future development, 227–30
TOOLBUS, 386–7
Total Quality Management (TQM), 3
Tree-based model (TBM), 199–201, 210–14, 222
Tree-based reliability model. *See* TBRM
TreeBrowser, 226, 227
Trillium, 28
Tuple schemata, 338

U

Unfair Contract Terms Act (1977), 4
UP-RRA97 model, 267–8

URA97, 261–4
  prerequisite condition, 262
  range notation, 263
  strong revocation, 264
  user–role assignment and revocation, 263–4
  weak revocation, 264
Usage-dependent time measurement, 166, 185
Usage-independent time measurement, 166
Usage measurement SRGM, 181–98
User information satisfaction in information technology, 135
User-level threads, 303

V

Value acceleration, 133
Value linking, 133
Value restructuring, 133

W

Waterfall model, 38, 46, 174
White-box (or structural) testing, 164
Work Value Model, 130–1
Workload
  characteristics, 174–6
  measurement, 181–7
  tracking over calendar time, 182–4
World Wide Web, 99, 350–2

X

X-Window coordinator, 377

Contents of Volumes in This Series

Volume 21

The Web of Computing: Computer Technology as Social Organization
  ROB KLING AND WALT SCACCHI
Computer Design and Description Languages
  SUBRATA DASGUPTA
Microcomputers: Applications, Problems, and Promise
  ROBERT C. GAMMILL
Query Optimization in Distributed Data-base Systems
  GIOVANNI MARIA SACCO AND S. BING YAO
Computers in the World of Chemistry
  PETER LYKOS
Library Automation Systems and Networks
  JAMES E. RUSH

Volume 22

Legal Protection of Software: A Survey
  MICHAEL C. GEMIGNANI
Algorithms for Public Key Cryptosystems: Theory and Applications
  S. LAKSHMIVARAHAN
Software Engineering Environments
  ANTHONY I. WASSERMAN
Principles of Rule-Based Expert Systems
  BRUCE G. BUCHANAN AND RICHARD O. DUDA
Conceptual Representation of Medical Knowledge for Diagnosis by Computer: MDX and Related Systems
  B. CHANDRASEKARAN AND SANJAY MITTAL
Specification and Implementation of Abstract Data Types
  ALFS T. BERZTISS AND SATISH THATTE

Volume 23

Supercomputers and VLSI: The Effect of Large-scale Integration on Computer Architecture
  LAWRENCE SNYDER
Information and Computation
  J. F. TRAUB AND H. WOZNIAKOWSKI
The Mass Impact of Videogame Technology
  THOMAS A. DEFANTI
Developments in Decision Support Systems
  ROBERT H. BONCZEK, CLYDE W. HOLSAPPLE, AND ANDREW B. WHINSTON
Digital Control Systems
  PETER DORATO AND DANIEL PETERSEN

International Developments in Information Privacy
   G. K. Gupta
Parallel Sorting Algorithms
   S. Lakshmivarahan, Sudarshan K. Dhall, and Leslie L. Miller

Volume 24

Software Effort Estimation and Productivity
   S. D. Conte, H. E. Dunsmore, and V. Y. Shen
Theoretical Issues Concerning Protection in Operating Systems
   Michael A. Harrison
Developments in Firmware Engineering
   Subrata Dasgupta and Bruce D. Shriver
The Logic of Learning: A Basis for Pattern Recognition and for Improvement of Performance
   Ranan B. Banerji
The Current State of Language Data Processing
   Paul L. Garvin
Advances in Information Retrieval: Where Is That /#*&@¢ Record?
   Donald H. Kraft
The Development of Computer Science Education
   William F. Atchison

Volume 25

Accessing Knowledge through Natural Language
   Nick Cercone and Gordon McCalla
Design Analysis and Performance Evaluation Methodologies for Database Computers
   Steven A. Demurjian, David K. Hsiao, and Paula R. Strawser
Partitioning of Massive/Real-Time Programs for Parallel Processing
   I. Lee, N. Prywes, and B. Szymanski
Computers in High-Energy Physics
   Michael Metcalf
Social Dimensions of Office Automation
   Abbe Mowshowitz

Volume 26

The Explicit Support of Human Reasoning in Decision Support Systems
   Amitava Dutta
Unary Processing
   W. J. Poppelbaum, A. Dollas, J. B. Glickman, and C. O'Toole
Parallel Algorithms for Some Computational Problems
   Abha Moitra and S. Sitharama Iyengar
Multistage Interconnection Networks for Multiprocessor Systems
   S. C. Kothari
Fault-Tolerant Computing
   Wing N. Toy
Techniques and Issues in Testing and Validation of VLSI Systems
   H. K. Reghbati

Software Testing and Verification
  LEE J. WHITE
Issues in the Development of Large, Distributed, and Reliable Software
  C. V. RAMAMOORTHY, ATUL PRAKASH, VIJAY GARG, TSUNEO YAMAURA, AND ANUPAM BHIDE

Volume 27

Military Information Processing
  JAMES STARK DRAPER
Multidimensional Data Structures: Review and Outlook
  S. SITHARAMA IYENGAR, R. L. KASHYAP, V. K. VAISHNAVI, AND N. S. V. RAO
Distributed Data Allocation Strategies
  ALAN R. HEVNER AND ARUNA RAO
A Reference Model for Mass Storage Systems
  STEPHEN W. MILLER
Computers in the Health Sciences
  KEVIN C. O'KANE
Computer Vision
  AZRIEL ROSENFELD
Supercomputer Performance: The Theory, Practice, and Results
  OLAF M. LUBECK
Computer Science and Information Technology in the People's Republic of China:
The Emergence of Connectivity
  JOHN H. MAIER

Volume 28

The Structure of Design Processes
  SUBRATA DASGUPTA
Fuzzy Sets and Their Applications to Artificial Intelligence
  ABRAHAM KANDEL AND MORDECHAY SCHNEIDER
Parallel Architecture for Database Systems
  A. R. HURSON, L. L. MILLER, S. H. PAKZAD, M. H. EICH, AND B. SHIRAZI
Optical and Optoelectronic Computing
  MIR MOJTABA MIRSALEHI, MUSTAFA A. G. ABUSHAGUR, AND H. JOHN CAULFIELD
Management Intelligence Systems
  MANFRED KOCHEN

Volume 29

Models of Multilevel Computer Security
  JONATHAN K. MILLEN
Evaluation, Description, and Invention: Paradigms for Human–Computer Interaction
  JOHN M. CARROLL
Protocol Engineering
  MING T. LIU
Computer Chess: Ten Years of Significant Progress
  MONROE NEWBORN
Soviet Computing in the 1980s
  RICHARD W. JUDY AND ROBERT W. CLOUGH

Volume 30

Specialized Parallel Architectures for Textual Databases
    A. R. Hurson, L. L. Miller, S. H. Pakzad, and Jia-Bing Cheng
Database Design and Performance
    Mark L. Gillenson
Software Reliability
    Anthony Iannino and John D. Musa
Cryptography Based Data Security
    George J. Davida and Yvo Desmedt
Soviet Computing in the 1980s: A Survey of the Software and its Applications
    Richard W. Judy and Robert W. Clough

Volume 31

Command and Control Information Systems Engineering: Progress and Prospects
    Stephen J. Andriole
Perceptual Models for Automatic Speech Recognition Systems
    Renato DeMori, Mathew J. Palakal, and Piero Cosi
Availability and Reliability Modeling for Computer Systems
    David I. Heimann, Nitin Mittal, and Kishor S. Trivedi
Molecular Computing
    Michael Conrad
Foundations of Information Science
    Anthony Debons

Volume 32

Computer-Aided Logic Synthesis for VLSI Chips
    Saburo Muroga
Sensor-Driven Intelligent Robotics
    Mohan M. Trivedi and Chuxin Chen
Multidatabase Systems: An Advanced Concept in Handling Distributed Data
    A. R. Hurson and M. W. Bright
Models of the Mind and Machine: Information Flow and Control between Humans and Computers
    Kent L. Norman
Computerized Voting
    Roy G. Saltman

Volume 33

Reusable Software Components
    Bruce W. Weide, William E. Ogden, and Stuart H. Zweben
Object-Oriented Modeling and Discrete-Event Simulation
    Bernard P. Ziegler
Human-Factors Issues in Dialog Design
    Thiagarajan Palanivel and Martin Helander
Neurocomputing Formalisms for Computational Learning and Machine Intelligence
    S. Gulati, J. Barhen, and S. S. Iyengar

Visualization in Scientific Computing
  THOMAS A. DEFANTI AND MAXINE D. BROWN

Volume 34

An Assessment and Analysis of Software Reuse
  TED J. BIGGERSTAFF
Multisensory Computer Vision
  N. NANDHAKUMAR AND J. K. AGGARWAL
Parallel Computer Architectures
  RALPH DUNCAN
Content-Addressable and Associative Memory
  LAWRENCE CHISVIN AND R. JAMES DUCKWORTH
Image Database Management
  WILLIAM I. GROSKY AND RAJIV MEHROTRA
Paradigmatic Influences on Information Systems Development Methodologies: Evolution and Conceptual Advances
  RUDY HIRSCHHEIM AND HEINZ K. KLEIN

Volume 35

Conceptual and Logical Design of Relational Databases
  S. B. NAVATHE AND G. PERNUL
Computational Approaches for Tactile Information Processing and Analysis
  HRISHIKESH P. GADAGKAR AND MOHAN M. TRIVEDI
Object-Oriented System Development Methods
  ALAN R. HEVNER
Reverse Engineering
  JAMES H. CROSS II, ELLIOT J. CHIKOFSKY AND CHARLES H. MAY, JR.
Multiprocessing
  CHARLES J. FLECKENSTEIN, D. H. GILL, DAVID HEMMENDINGER, C. L. MCCREARY,
  JOHN D. MCGREGOR, ROY P. PARGAS, ARTHUR M. RIEHL AND VIRGIL WALLENTINE
The Landscape of International Computing
  EDWARD M. ROCHE, SEYMOUR E. GOODMAN, AND HSINCHUN CHEN

Volume 36

Zero Defect Software: Cleanroom Engineering
  HARLAN D. MILLS
Role of Verification in the Software Specification Process
  MARVIN V. ZELKOWITZ
Computer Applications in Music Composition and Research
  GARY E. WITTLICH, ERIC J. ISAACSON, AND JEFFREY E. HASS
Artificial Neural Networks in Control Applications
  V. VEMURI
Developments in Uncertainty-based Information
  GEORGE J. KLIR
Human Factors in Human–Computer System Design
  MARY CAROL DAY AND SUSAN J. BOYCE

Volume 37

Approaches to Automatic Programming
    CHARLES RICH AND RICHARD C. WATERS
Digital Signal Processing
    STEPHEN A. DYER AND BRIAN K. HARMS
Neural Networks for Pattern Recognition
    S. C. KOTHARI AND HEEKUCK OH
Experiments in Computational Heuristics and Their Lessons for Software and
Knowledge Engineering
    JURG NIEVERGELT
High-Level Synthesis of Digital Circuits
    GIOVANNI DE MICHELI
Issues in Dataflow Computing
    BEN LEE AND A. R. HURSON
A Sociological History of the Neural Network Controversy
    MIKEL OLAZARAN

Volume 38

Database Security
    GÜNTHER PERNUL
Functional Representation and Causal Processes
    B. CHANDRASEKARAN
Computer-Based Medical Systems
    JOHN M. LONG
Algorithm-Specific Parallel Processing with Linear Processor Arrays
    JOSE A. B. FORTES, BENJAMIN W. WAH, WEIJA SHANG, AND KUMAR N. GANAPATHY
Information as a Commodity: Assessment of Market Value
    ABBE MOWSHOWITZ

Volume 39

Maintenance and Evolution of Software Products
    ANNELIESE VON MAYRHAUSER
Software Measurement: A Decision-Process Approach
    WARREN HARRISON
Active Databases: Concepts and Design Support
    THOMAS A. MUECK
Operating Systems Enhancements for Distributed Shared Memory
    VIRGINIA LO
The Social Design of Worklife with Computers and Networks: A Natural Systems Perspective
    ROB KLING AND TOM JEWETT

Volume 40

Program Understanding: Models and Experiments
    A. VON MAYRHAUSER AND A. M. VANS
Software Prototyping
    ALAN M. DAVIS

Rapid Prototyping of Microelectronic Systems
    APOSTOLOS DOLLAS AND J. D. STERLING BABCOCK
Cache Coherence in Multiprocessors: A Survey
    MAZIN S. YOUSIF, M. J. THAZHUTHAVEETIL, AND C. R. DAS
The Adequacy of Office Models
    CHANDRA S. AMARAVADI, JOEY F. GEORGE, OLIVIA R. LIU SHENG, AND JAY F. NUNAMAKER

Volume 41

Directions in Software Process Research
    H. DIETER ROMBACH AND MARTIN VERLAGE
The Experience Factory and Its Relationship to Other Quality Approaches
    VICTOR R. BASILI
CASE Adoption: A Process, Not an Event
    JOCK A. RADER
On the Necessary Conditions for the Composition of Integrated Software
Engineering Environments
    DAVID J. CARNEY AND ALAN W. BROWN
Software Quality, Software Process, and Software Testing
    DICK HAMLET
Advances in Benchmarking Techniques: New Standards and Quantitative Metrics
    THOMAS CONTE AND WEN-MEI W. HWU
An Evolutionary Path for Transaction Processing Systems
    CARLTON PU, AVRAHAM LEFF, AND SHU-WEI, F. CHEN

Volume 42

Nonfunctional Requirements of Real-Time Systems
    TEREZA G. KIRNER AND ALAN M. DAVIS
A Review of Software Inspections
    ADAM PORTER, HARVEY SIY, AND LAWRENCE VOTTA
Advances in Software Reliability Engineering
    JOHN D. MUSA AND WILLA EHRLICH
Network Interconnection and Protocol Conversion
    MING T. LIU
A Universal Model of Legged Locomotion Gaits
    S. T. VENKATARAMAN

Volume 43

Program Slicing
    DAVID W. BINKLEY AND KEITH BRIAN GALLAGHER
Language Features for the Interconnection of Software Components
    RENATE MOTSCHNIG-PITRIK AND ROLAND T. MITTERMEIR
Using Model Checking to Analyze Requirements and Designs
    JOANNE ATLEE, MARSHA CHECHIK, AND JOHN GANNON
Information Technology and Productivity: A Review of the Literature
    ERIK BRYNJOLFSSON AND SHINKYU YANG
The Complexity of Problems
    WILLIAM GASARCH

3-D Computer Vision Using Structured Light: Design, Calibration, and Implementation Issues
    FRED W. DEPIERO AND MOHAN M. TRIVEDI

Volume 44

Managing the Risks in Information Systems and Technology (IT)
    ROBERT N. CHARETTE
Software Cost Estimation: A Review of Models, Process and Practice
    FIONA WALKERDEN AND ROSS JEFFERY
Experimentation in Software Engineering
    SHARI LAWRENCE PFLEEGER
Parallel Computer Construction Outside the United States
    RALPH DUNCAN
Control of Information Distribution and Access
    RALF HAUSER
Asynchronous Transfer Mode: An Engineering Network Standard for High Speed Communications
    RONALD J. VETTER
Communication Complexity
    EYAL KUSHILEVITZ

Volume 45

Control in Multi-threaded Information Systems
    PABLO A. STRAUB AND CARLOS A. HURTADO
Parallelization of DOALL and DOACROSS Loops—a Survey
    A. R. HURSON, JOFORD T. LIM, KRISHNA M. KAVI AND BEN LEE
Programming Irregular Applications: Runtime Support, Compilation and Tools
    JOEL SALTZ, GAGAN AGRAWAL, CHIALIN CHANG, RAJA DAS, GUY EDJLALI, PAUL HAVLAK, YUAN-SHIN HWANG, BONGKI MOON, RAVI PONNUSAMY, SHAMIK SHARMA, ALAN SUSSMAN AND MUSTAFA UYSAL
Optimization Via Evolutionary Processes
    SRILATA RAMAN AND L. M. PATNAIK
Software Reliability and Readiness Assessment Based on the Non-homogeneous Poisson Process
    AMRIT L. GOEL AND KUNE-ZANG YANG
Computer-Supported Cooperative Work and Groupware
    JONATHAN GRUDIN AND STEVEN E. POLTROCK
Technology and Schools
    GLEN L. BULL

Volume 46

Software Process Appraisal and Improvement: Models and Standards
    MARK C. PAULK
A Software Process Engineering Framework
    JYRKI KONTIO
Gaining Business Value from IT Investments
    PAMELA SIMMONS
Reliability Measurement, Analysis, and Improvement for Large Software Systems
    JEFF TIAN

Role-based Access Control
    RAVI SANDHU
Multithrended Systems
    KRISHRA M. KAVI, BEN LEE AND ALI R. HURSON
Coordination Models and Languages
    GEORGE A. PAPADOPOULOS AND FARHAD ARBAB
Multidisciplinary Problem-solving Environments for Computational Science
    ELIAS N. HOUSTIS, JOHN R. RICE, NAREN RAMAKRISHNAN, TZVETAN DRASHANSKY,
    SANJIVA WEERAWARANA, ANUPAM JOSHI AND C. E. HOUSTIS

ISBN 0-12-012146-8